EMILY CARR

THE UNTOLD STORY

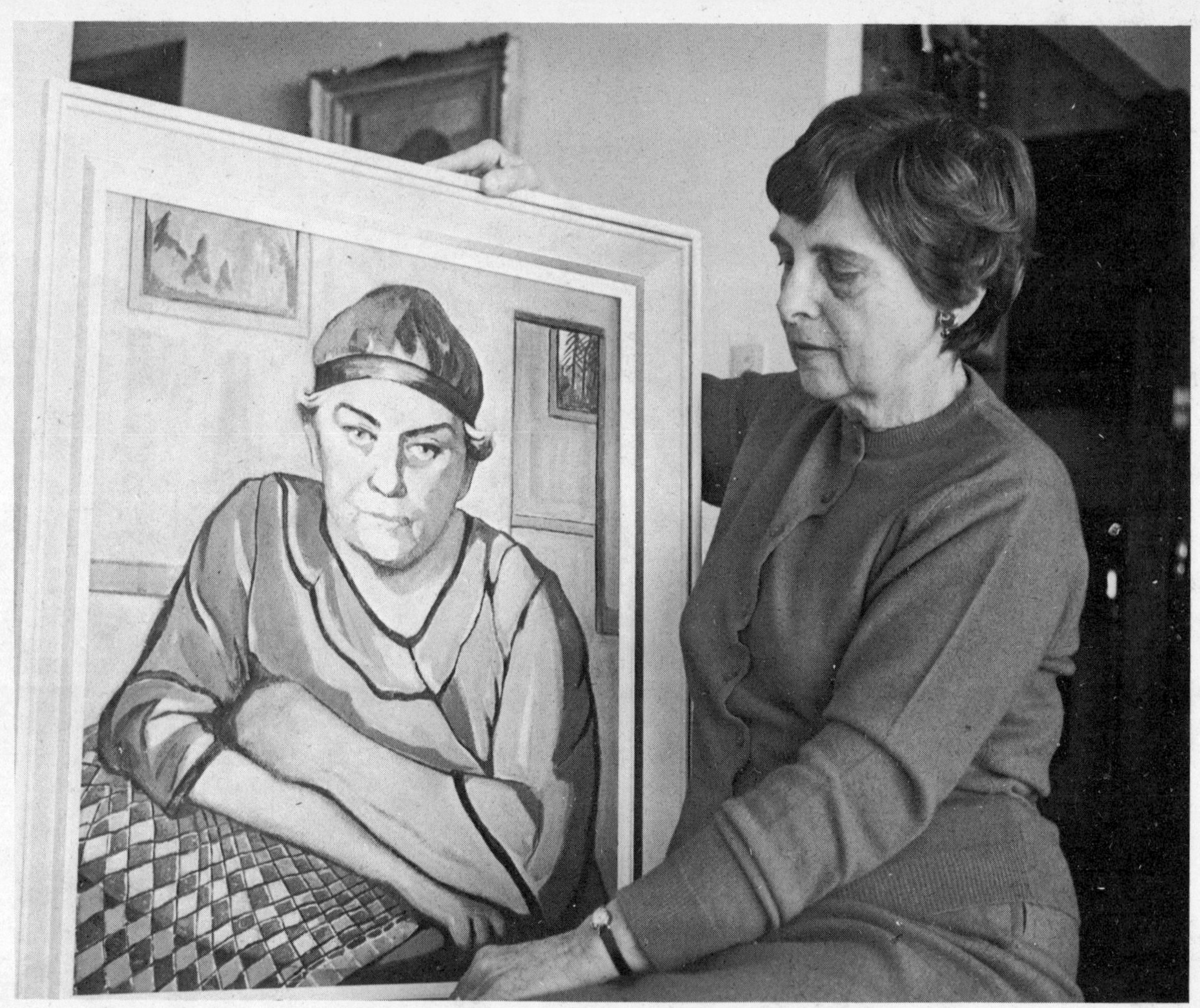

The author with one of several portraits she painted of Emily Carr.

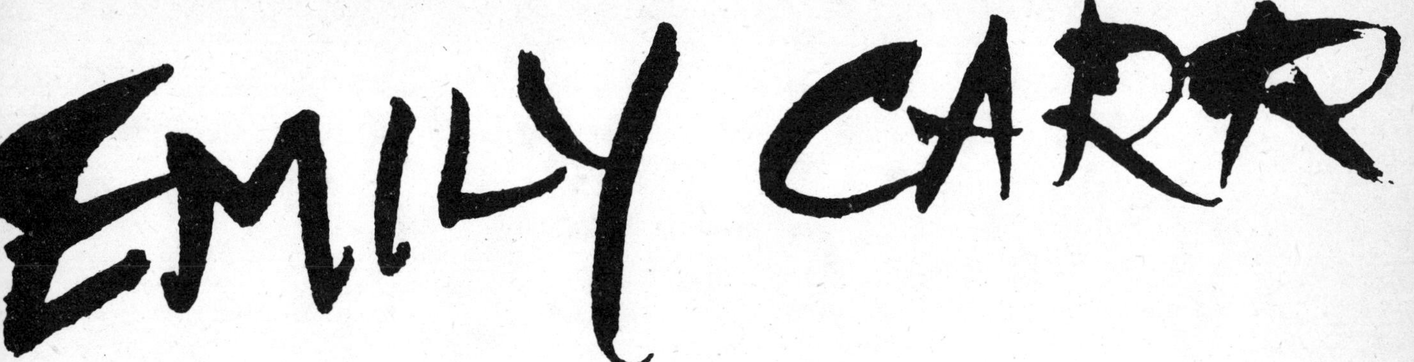

THE UNTOLD STORY

by Edythe Hembroff-Schleicher

"Her Only Sketching Partner"

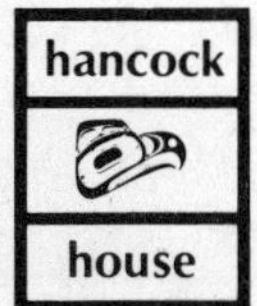

ISBN 0-88839-003-3

Schleicher, Edythe Hembroff.
Emily Carr

Bibliography: p.
Includes index.
ISBN 0-88839-003-3

1. Carr, Emily, 1871-1945. 2. Artists—British Columbia—Biography.
ND249.C3S34 759.11 C78-002096-0

Designed by NICHOLAS NEWBECK DESIGN

Published simultaneously in Canada and the United States by:

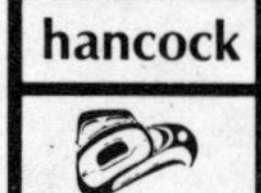

HANCOCK HOUSE PUBLISHERS LTD.
3215 Island View Road SAANICHTON, B.C. V0S 1M0

HANCOCK HOUSE PUBLISHERS INC.
12008 1st Avenue South SEATTLE, WA. 98168

Contents

Emily Carr's sketches, scattered throughout this book, and never published before, are in the collection of the Public Archives of Canada, and are reproduced here with their cooperation.

In Loving Memory of My Parents
Walter C. and Olive May Hembroff

Acknowledgements

During the preparation of this book, I have been greatly assisted by old friends, new friends, and numerous other patient people who have put up with my pestering in the interest of "the cause"—Emily Carr. Many are also Emily's old friends, from the days when we clustered around her. Others I met in the fascinating world of books and files in libraries, art galleries and museums across the country. To all I owe a debt of gratitude. Special thanks go to:

My childhood friends of Cordova Bay, Phylis Dilworth (Mrs. W.W. Inglis) and Edna Dilworth (Mrs. J.E.A. Parnall) and the latter's husband Jack Parnall, who grew up in my neighborhood in Victoria and is now Registrar of the University of British Columbia. Phylis Inglis and Jack Parnall have unreservedly placed at my disposal all Carr material for which they hold the copyright—a bountiful favor. In addition, Jack Parnall, as former trustee of the Emily Carr Trust, has given me helpful information.

Alistair Bell, Vancouver, also former trustee of the Trust has likewise given me helpful information in that capacity.

Lawren P. Harris, Ottawa, and Margaret Harris Knox, Vancouver, son and daughter of Lawren S. Harris, have given me their valued permission to quote from their father's letters.

Humphrey Toms, my reliable emergency investigator in Vancouver who, more objective than I, has given good advice.

Emily's close friends, Flora Hamilton Burns, Nan Lawson Cheney and Margaret Clay for their memories and permission to use certain private, unpublished letters; Frederick J. Brand, Max Maynard and Ruth Humphrey for editing portions of the manuscript; Myfanwy Spencer Pavelic for permission to quote from her unpublished Carr letters and my taped interview; and Madge Wolfenden Hamilton for drawings, photographs and information concerning Emily's early life.

I am also indebted to D.J. Lawson, Q.C., Victoria, for his willingness to make available to me a copy of the Emily Carr Trust document and his précis of it; to Dr. W. Kaye Lamb, Vancouver, Colin Graham of the Art Gallery of Greater Victoria, and Dr. Max Stern, Montreal, for background information; and to Wylie W. Thom for guidance given in his unpublished historical survey, *The Fine Arts in Vancouver, 1886-1930*.

I am equally indebted to the Canadian Embassy and the Canadian Cultural Centre in Paris for supplying two photographs and to the staff of many art galleries, libraries and archives in other provinces and countries. A big slice of my thanks should go to Evelyn McMann of the Vancouver Public Library and Charles C. Hill of the National Gallery of Canada, both of whom were tireless in tracking my leads. I also gratefully acknowledge assistance from A.R. Turner, British Columbia Provincial Archivist; Jerry Mossop, Curator: Paintings, Drawings and Prints; and Geoffrey Castle, Archivist, Map Collection, both of the Provincial Archives of British Columbia, as well as from Dr. Barbara S. Efrat, Curator of Linguistics; Robert Levine of the same division; Peter Macnair, Curator of Ethnology, and Dan Savard, Photographic Technician, all of the British Columbia Provincial Museum. In Alberta I was aided by Ms. L.E. Bartz of the Glenbow-Alberta Institute, Calgary; in Ontario by Ms. Jacqueline Hunter, Deputy Librarian at the National Gallery of Canada, and Ms. Sybille Pantazzi, Librarian at the Art Gallery of Ontario, Toronto; in Quebec by Ms. Juanita Toupin, Librarian at the Montreal Museum of Fine Arts; and in Seattle by Ms. Pauline DeHaart Adams, Registrar, Seattle Art Museum. The cooperation of Wylie W. Thom and Jean Martin, Registrar and Librarian respectively of the Vancouver Art Gallery is particularly appreciated as I may have placed them in a difficult situation.

My research was greatly facilitated by generous grants from the Canada Council and the British Columbia Cultural Fund; and when prospects for publication looked gloomy indeed, the Provincial Secretary of the Province of British Columbia kindly added a special editorial grant.

Finally, my husband, Julius F. Schleicher, also deserves credit. His eagle eye for error has been invaluable in proofreading the formidable columns of dates.

May I add that none of the above friends and helpers has more than scant knowledge of my text, nor have associated themselves with any of the opinions expressed or conclusions drawn. Responsibility for both is mine alone.

Introduction

Who was this woman who is generally recognized as one of Canada's foremost painters and who also achieved an enviable reputation as a writer? She is thought of by some as a cranky odd-ball who wore outlandish clothes, had innumerable pets, and painted strange pictures of Indian totem poles and towering trees. She is thought of by others as a lonely, misunderstood genius who struggled against misfortune, poverty and the tide of opinion in an effort to express, through her painting and her writings, the powerful thoughts and feelings that possessed her.

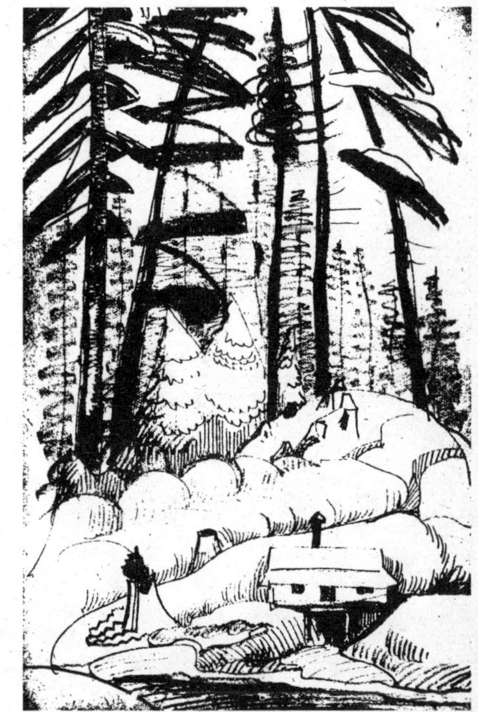

In some respects Emily Carr fits both of these images; in others she fits neither. She was not the sort of person who could be categorized easily. Many shallow observers thought her plain crazy. She was, in fact, many things to many people, but it is possible, I think, by examining the known facts of her life, and her own writings, to arrive at a clearer understanding of her complex personality.

Emily was born in Victoria, British Columbia, of English parents, in 1871. I have tried to examine all phases of her remarkable career almost from the date of her birth, but this has not always been easy as, with time, certain myths have grown up around her which have obscured the true facts and perspective.

Even before her death in March, 1945, tales of her colorful, difficult life circulated farther and farther afield as her fame grew. They gathered bizarre embellishments along the way and soon her reputation as an eccentric rivaled her reputation as an artist of the deeper imagination and she became a legend. Few friends were allowed even a glimpse into the depths of Emily's heart and innermost thoughts and she took the paradoxes of her personality and her secrets to the grave with her. But the legend is a false structure; it is a fabrication that her few surviving close friends must try to identify and expose.

Emily did not willingly suffer the wits, the tamperers, the fools, the know-it-alls but, until age and sickness soured her spirit, she was an easy and loyal friend to a handful of people. It is true that she usually felt the need to dominate a relationship, particularly one involving a younger friend like myself. But she relied on each and every one of us for help—help with writing, help with exhibitions and, despite her pride, occasional financial help.

Emily ticked a little faster than most people, and the pendulum of her moods swung in a narrow arc. She could be bouncy with *joie de vivre* in the morning and in black despair in the afternoon. She had her prickly side too. At times she reminded me of a plump little porcupine who, in sudden irritation or anger, could toss its quills indiscriminately at tenant, tradesman or even friend. But her fury usually collapsed of its own weight and spluttered out with a last unconvincing "idiot"—like the final defiant yap of one of her peppery little griffons. An unusual woman—yes. But eccentric—no, not to us. If others found her so it was because they did not understand her. There was nothing confused or inharmonious in her behavior. She acted always according to temperament and character. She was volatile, strongly individualistic. But genuine. She did not strike us as odd.

There are two main clues to Emily's personality: The comments of friends and her own writings. Unfortunately, neither is truly revealing. Most of the friends, all elderly now, merely tend to reaffirm opinions formed long ago from Emily's own dramatized accounts of her hard life. All too often this only nourishes the legend. As we shall see, her writings, too, can be misleading since they are unreliable about certain facts and dates. Some of the passages that are based on error are highly successful visual descriptions, but readers seeking information must beware.

Emily was never capable of a consciously dishonest thought or statement, and everything she painted or wrote germinated in a solid, authentic core. But as her picture, or story, "grew" (Emily's own word), they often assumed unfamiliar and twisted patterns. This is particularly true of her autobiographical writings, in which she left us a deeply subjective self-portrait—a triptych of her three personalities: Her everyday self (the Emily we knew best); "Small," her childhood self, and "t'other Emily," her inner self.

Even a friend like myself, who lived with Emily in close proximity for weeks on end and questioned her about her early life and attitudes, cannot hope to uncover the root of her artistic insight, nor explain the elusive source of her triple personality. Such a friend can, however, suggest that Emily, a sensitive, wilful child, developed a feeling of deep anxiety when very young, despite the strong emotional security of her parents' affection and an ordered family life. Her early rejection of her father and almost obsessive love for her mother were perhaps the first signs of "Small's" troubled mind; and after her mother's lingering illness and premature death, she felt emotionally on even more unsure ground. She sought refuge from the hurts of her environment in a private dream world to which she retreated for solace and inspiration throughout her life. There her imagination thrived. She saw herself in heroic proportions—the abused child, the misunderstood adolescent, the rejected painter, the suffering martyr, the champion of the Indians. She lived these parts with such intensity that they sometimes became more real than reality. Fact and imagination were often blurred. In a sense she fictionalized her own life.

Thus, after reflecting on all that Emily has said and written, she still remains, for me at least, a fascinating enigma. Frederick Brand, who remembers her with affection, has delved more deeply into her psyche and religion than any other old friend has (or could); and during our discussions about her, he expressed an interesting opinion that, basically, coincides with my own:

> It's not, I think, that she was more skilled in, and more elated by, showmanship than we thought, but that the exigencies—or temptation perhaps—of story-telling led her on—took over, shall we say, as they have a way of doing. What is important to me is there in her that her experience was genuine, and it is there in her work for us to explore. The heightened coloring, the embellishments that give emphasis in her writings, here and there occasionally, are of minor consequence. I am more impressed by her powers to reveal realities than by any variations of statement and failure of proportion in respect of details. There are correctable errors of fact but the whole corpus of her writing in root and spirit issue from the heart of her being. She has described her life as it was lived in its variety and extraordinary intensity.

As a person, what an amazing human being Emily was. I sensed this from the first and never lost sight of it during our long friendship that lasted until her death.

She was fifty-eight, I twenty-three, when we met, yet I never thought of her as an elderly woman. The disparity in our ages melted away in the fun and stimulation of her company. The thirties, when we were together so much, were her best, her most vital years. Despite continuing grave financial worries, two heart attacks and periods of depression, she was, on the whole, active and optimistic. She had reason to be. At long last she was beginning to win the recognition and acclaim that had eluded her so long.

Our relationship proved how unanticipated consequences can arise from inconsequential events, since the prospect of becoming acquainted with Emily Carr early in 1930 seemed very unimportant to me indeed. I had never heard of her before leaving home; we lived in different worlds. But during my six years absence from Victoria, she had become a local celebrity—not so much as a painter as "that cranky old landlady in James Bay." "She paints the most frightful daubs," my snobbish friends told me. "Can't draw a straight line. Besides, she's crazy. She shrieks at her tenants, pushes a pram full of animals when she goes shopping, walks with a monkey on her shoulder and wears such ridiculous clothes that she is the laughing stock of the neighborhood. Poor as a churchmouse too."

Thus, when Emily phoned me (she took the initiative), I was less than elated. "I have just seen your picture in the paper," she said, "and find that your art training in San Francisco and Europe exactly parallels mine. Do come over for tea and we will compare experiences and reminisce." I accepted, but with bad grace.

How could I suspect, as I drove down to James Bay on that fateful day in mid-May, that I was about to visit the studio of a great artist of the very near future? Nothing in her reputation suggested this to me at the time.

When Emily opened her front door (at the back of the house at the top of a steep flight of stairs), a pack of excited Belgian griffons burst forth like shot from a cannon. They jumped on my new Paris frock, snapped at my ankles, and I was so busy warding them off that I scarcely noticed Emily.

"Down, down," I heard a melodious, rather English voice half-heartedly scolding her "creatures." Only then, when quiet had been partially restored, I looked up and saw the woman who was to radically change my way of life for years to come. My first glance brought surprise. Where was the termagant? The Bohemian? The eccentric and crank? What I saw was a round, solid little person, conservatively dressed. The somberness of her clothing and the wisps of grey hair escaping over each ear from a black restraining band were offset by an almost radiant, rather pretty, round, wrinkle-free face accented by dark, finely-arched eyebrows over merry, blue-grey slanted eyes. "A really motherly type," I said to myself, startled as Emily smiled at me benignly and led me through a narrow hall into a spacious, well-lit studio. And she *was* motherly—to me, at least. In fact it was her determination to play the role of a mother in my life, and her resentment of my own mother, that led to our one and only serious quarrel.

But this was far in the future. Our first meeting, our first afternoon together in Emily's studio, was an unqualified success. All my false ideas about her were quickly dispelled. She was friendly, sincere, relaxed and modest. And the studio itself was a pleasant place to sit and chat. The walls were tapestried with paintings—new and old; with dusty plaster casts—mementos of her teaching years; family photographs and rugs—some Indian, some she had hooked herself from Indian designs. On the mantel were old and battered pewter jugs, steins and plates, Indian baskets and other memorabilia. Two sturdy homemade easels faced one another in a niche by the big north window, the canvasses they supported covered with dust sheets to hide them from prying eyes. A large clock, hung high above the door to the hall, ticked soothingly as we sipped our tea. The dogs dozed and snored before the fire and Woo, the monkey, with a piece of red flannel in her delicate, black hands, concentrated on her "sewing." The chipmunks whirred around on their little ferris wheel on the big work table, and pink-nosed little Susie, the white rat, wandered around Emily's neck and shoulders at will before snuggling for warmth and a nap between her well-developed breasts.

Everything was so peaceful, Emily so "normal." A natural story-teller, she related one tale after another as we compared notes and laughed about our exploits in various art schools. A foundation for a fond friendship was soon laid, partly, no doubt, because Emily, at that time, was starved for art companionship and art conversation. Because of her isolation from art centers she had very few painter friends during her lifetime. Not long before she died, she wrote that she had only had two: "Edythe and Nan[Cheney]." But she did have another, in the forties: Myfanwy Spencer Pavelic and, of course, Lawren Harris. But his influence was so strong, all-embracing and obvious that she no doubt felt it redundant to mention him at all.

After successful exhibitions in both east and west, Emily was calmer in the thirties than she had been in the tough twenties when, as rumor has it, she bristled easily and tongue-lashed her tenants. On occasion, these encounters even ended in physical violence: She plopped a zinc pail over the head of a screeching widow; she was struck across the cheek by the heavy fist of a "brutal" man who had complained about a frozen tap—and ended up in the coal bin. She turned the water hose on another fractious tenant, and to the great shame of her two prim sisters, was taken to court. But what sorely-tried landlady would not have been driven to desperation during the First World War and early post-war years? Rentals fell steadily, Emily's flats were often vacant and she was forced to accept any rowdy or slut who could meet the first month's reduced payment.

The story about Emily promenading her pets in a baby buggy is so firmly anchored in her legend that it would be well-nigh impossible to dislodge—even should it prove to be untrue. It has captured the imagination of readers and television viewers from coast to coast and is regarded as a classic example of her eccentricity. Perhaps she wheeled her animals around James Bay in a pram a few times (once would be enough to start tongues wagging) but, if so, it was for a solid practical reason. It was also long before I met her. None of her older friends I have talked to witnessed such outings, and certainly there was no sign of an old buggy anywhere in her house, in either attic or cellar, after 1930. Actually Emily walked very little. When she did, it was to exercise her dogs—not to pamper them. Woo, too, was made to walk. She was not in a buggy, not on Emily's shoulder, but chained to her waist.

Emily and I began sketching together soon after our first afternoon tea party, but our trips were short, mere outings of a few hours duration, with sketch sacks and animals, to nearby beaches and park. Because she hated "having people messing about" while painting, and because she had worked alone for so long, I think she was testing me as a sketching companion before inviting me to accompany her on a full-scale camping expedition.

Then, one day, unexpectedly, the invitation came. We were hooking rugs contentedly in the studio when Emily suddenly said, "Let's go out and paint a tree." I recognized this as propaganda (I did not identify with trees as she did, preferring to paint nudes and portraits), but agreed. We gathered up our sketching paraphernalia, wandered across Beacon Hill Park and set up our miniature easels before a small stand of dark firs, just at the bend of a shaded road which curved out to the sea. An old gnarled veteran stood like a sentinel at the corner spreading its branches before the background glade. "Draw *him,*" commanded Emily. "I will watch and play the teacher for a while."

"It's a good tree," she said when I had finished, "but it's only the portrait of that one tree. It does not express any universal feeling for *all* trees. It does not live among the other trees. It must breathe, have spirit! But it's a good start. You will learn more when we go into the woods together. There you will see only trees, think only trees and feel only trees. Can you go with me in May? The woods are then pulsating with the joy of new growth and it is the best time for work."

My heart skipped a beat with pleasure. The invitation meant that Emily had accepted me as a "worker," not just a painter. She always made a sharp distinction between the two.

Thus, early May 1931 we set out for the woods of Cordova Bay, and we made two further lengthy painting excursions together to other wooded areas in the environs of Victoria before Emily purchased her caravan trailer, the "Elephant," which radically changed her sketching habits. There was barely space enough in the dark, cumbersome van for Emily and her pets, none for a partner. She was again working alone.*

* *See chapter "Sketching Trips."*

These sketching trips were a memorable experience for me. A few bad moments were inevitable, living as I did in cramped primitive quarters with a hardy, domineering pioneer and her sometimes smelly animals. But these moments I scarcely remember today since harmony and humor usually prevailed. It is the hard work that comes to mind, Emily's ingenuity in making a rough camp run smoothly, the capers of Woo, the gamboling of our dogs, the isolation and silence of the woods and, most of all, my contentment in the deepening friendship with a truly remarkable woman.

There was so little friction in our relationship that the quarrel, when it came, shook me to the core. It is a sad, unpleasant story which I have never told before because I believed the telling might re-open the wound and perhaps be a reflection on Emily, or even on myself.

But she told her version of the story first—a slanderous version hidden away for twenty-four years after her death in private letters to Nan Cheney. But since 1969, when Nan's collection was purchased by the University of British Columbia Library, Special Collections, all have been able to read how Emily exploded in a furious and completely unjustified attack on my family.

The cleavage in Emily's personality became more pronounced as she grew older.* Towards the end, when she was absorbed in her autobiographical writing, she lived more and more in the past and "Small" sometimes took over completely. In her world of fantasy, she used this cleavage as a convenient mechanism to blame "Small" for the misdeeds of Emily and this salved her conscience. Under the weight of her painful illnesses

* *Emily entrusted her secret feelings about religion to only a half dozen people. Flora Burns' mother and F.B. Housser may have been among them. Certainly the author and Frederick Brand were confidants, but none as importantly as Lawren Harris and Ira Dilworth. Ira also used the word "cleavage"*

in his revealing comments about Emily ("Portrait in Memory—Emily Carr"): "This strange genius was a two-fold character. There was within her the Emily Carr who became the great painter.... The other person was a child.... This cleavage she met every day ... with all the conflict within her ..."

of the forties, the contradictions in her character became more evident, her moral fibre at times wore very thin and she said and did things that were unworthy of her great spirit.

Feeling depressed, lonely and neglected, she often flung her frustrations angrily at other people and, in the summer of 1940, after her first stroke, she began to inveigh against my mother and sister Helen. The dark, demonic side of her nature was finally exposed; the reservoirs of resentment gushed forth unchecked, the scenes she made adding to my worry and unhappiness at home. For my mother was desperately and terminally ill. Emily's own words, in one of these outbursts, seem highly irrational:

> Don't see much of Edythe. Ma keeps her to heel pretty tight. Ma always resented Edythe coming to or being fond of me and now of course had a good excuse and is one of those invalids who will not be left alone for one *minute.* Someone has to hold her hand while she sleeps. Oh Lor! PS: Edythe came today. . . . Ma still in hospital. Two daughters, *two special nurses,* one husband *all* holding her hand *all* day. The sister I call "Hussy" is here. Been married one week in the East. She is tripe.*

* *UBC Library, Emily to Nan Cheney, September 20, 1940.*

My sister came home one week after her marriage because my mother was dying. Emily knew that. And how could she have forgotten Helen's ready willingness to run errands for her, and their pleasant teas together when I was out of town? Or my mother's many kindnesses?

Deeply offended and hurt by her behavior, I said a lean farewell on the telephone when I left Victoria instead of an affectionate, tearful one in the studio. I brooded for a long time on the break in our friendship but, after a few months, in a flash of understanding, I realized that one must find special excuses for special people like Emily. She was old and sick, I young and healthy. It was up to me to pocket my pride. She, too, wanted to forget the unhappy interlude and we were soon corresponding again. Not with quite the same warmth as before, but regularly.

Then late 1944, when my father, too, was dying, I took leave of absence from my work in German censorship in Ottawa and stayed in Victoria for three months—until shortly before Emily's death. I saw her almost every day. She had two bosom friends by then, both men, but she still found room in her heart for me and at least spared me the criticism she heaped on so many old friends in her last letters.

I knew when I left Victoria I would never see Emily again

and, during my last visit, I searched for words to express my gratitude and affection. They were clumsy when they came, but the quarrel had been forgotten.

Now that I, too, am old and understand Emily better, I often feel remorse, remorse that she found me wanting in sympathy and patience when she needed me most.

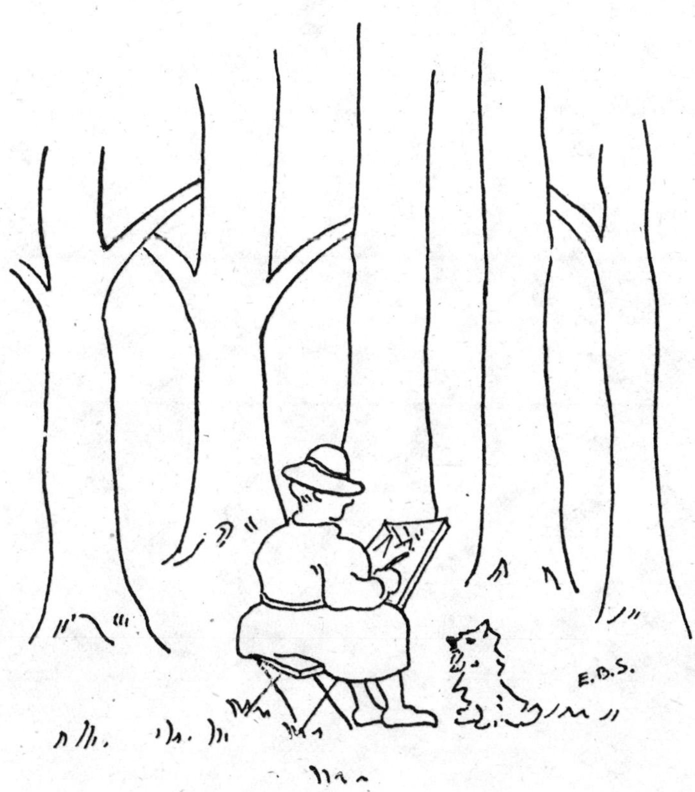

1931 Emily sketching in Cedar Grove (Flats), Goldstream Park. *Edythe Hembroff-Schleicher*

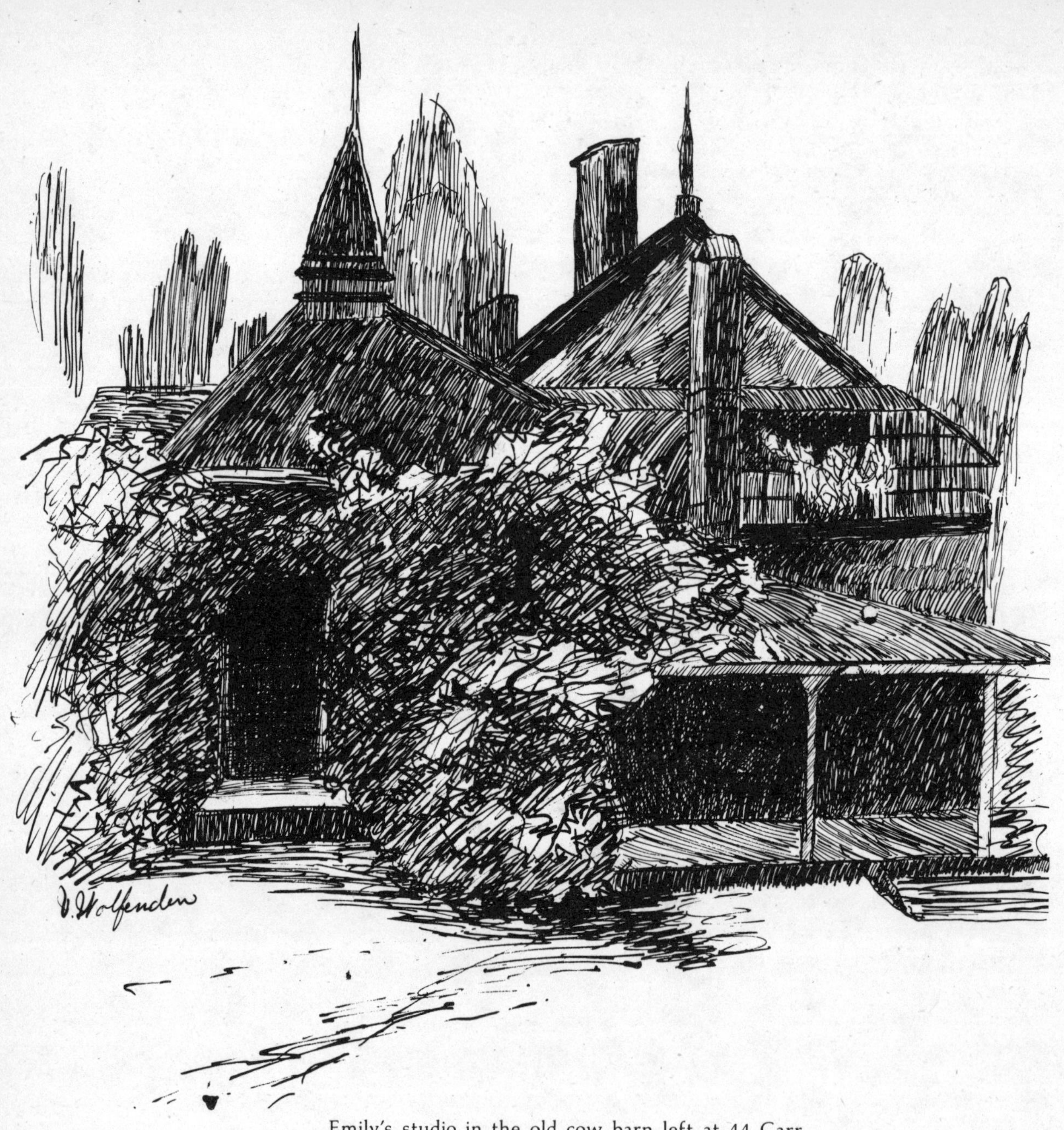

Emily's studio in the old cow barn left at 44 Carr Street. Sketch by Victor Wolfenden at age 14, in 1897 when he was a student of Emily's.

A Tribute

Edythe to Emily

Emily was bigger than life-size. She was a giant in talent and a giant in character. Forceful. Pithy. Solid as a rock. Sometimes under pressure the rock splintered and chips of anger flew off into space, hitting friend or foe indiscriminately. There were "ructions" for a few moments, but then Emily's temper cooled and her good humor was restored. It was only the suddenness of her explosions that made them upsetting, since they often seemed unprovoked. And yet, those of us who understood Emily well and knew of her hard life of incessant toil, bitterness and sacrifice realized that pressures inevitably built up and sought release in outbursts. Some were meaningless—snappy, indignant replies to tenants, tradesmen or the over-curious. But others were sometimes unjust and hurtful attacks on well-meaning friends. These she usually regretted later, and was at least objective and fair enough to admit that they were largely her own fault. She could even laugh at her tantrums and took a curious delight in labeling herself a "spit-cat," admitting spontaneously that she was often "un-nice." Her spirited, fascinating letters, reporting on work, friends and animals in her own inimitable style, were sometimes gaily gossipy, but at other times made devastating use of pungent adjectives to demolish the victim of the moment. It was only after 1940 that humor began to desert her and she occasionally dipped her pen into pure venom. It is regrettable that such later letters were not destroyed as they do an injustice to others but an even greater injustice to Emily herself. Not everybody will understand, as her friends do, that her long, shattering illness completely distorted her sense of values. Her physical strength was gone. Her judgment failed. Self-pity and tears often took over. And yet she clung to life with exemplary tenacity, and a courage that few of us could emulate. A dogged determination to complete her writing goals sustained her to the end. Whatever her faults, her virtues far outweighed them. She was superbly honest, straightforward, steadfast, indomitable and invincible. Her integrity was unshakable. These qualities made it easy for her friends to make many allowances.

I must therefore make it crystal clear that nothing I say

about Emily should be construed as harsh criticism, as criticism never goes more than skin deep. In a sense she was influential and powerful enough to be allowed her own code of behavior. My own feelings for her, despite our one tragic quarrel, were tunnel-deep, the roots lost in the darkness. She contributed so much to my life, and to a new way of "seeing" both life and art that I cannot imagine how it would have been without her. Her faults and blemishes are mentioned here only because they cannot be overlooked in any honest evaluation of her as a person.

In truth, Emily did nothing for effect. Because she was poor, she had to be purposeful and because she had much of the pioneer spirit inherited from her father, she found a way of making, fixing or simplifying almost everything. Appearance was never a concern. If a thing worked, it was satisfactory and no one's business but her own. She was therefore unconcerned about stares and suppressed giggles when people were confronted with her various contrivances. The chairs dangling a little precariously from the high studio ceiling were one striking example of her ingenuity. In the good old days when more visitors sometimes came to see her than she could accommodate, she hit on the idea of "movable seats" and skyed a few chairs by means of ropes and pulleys which she could lower to the floor as demand dictated. This was a perfect solution to her problem and a splendid conversation piece as well since no guest could remain stiff or solemn as he watched his chair descending.

Never flamboyant, Emily did not dress to *épater le bourgeois,* as most artists do today. Her garments—dresses, slips, nightgowns—all innocent of ruffles, yokes, gores, pleats or even buttons, were made quickly from the same pattern and enveloped her like a gunny sack. She scorned the usual artist's smock, but sometimes wore a kind of carpenter's apron—splashed with all the colors of the rainbow—and always the same sturdy, ugly shoes. Her one concern was to clothe herself sensibly, comfortably and cheaply because she was usually up to her elbows in dirty housework, dirty garden work or dirty painting. But when she went out, or had visitors, she dressed conservatively and correctly, and she rarely left the house, even to sketch in the woods, without a hat.

There are many examples of this blend of orthodox and unorthodox in her make-up. She was a woman of contrasts. Surprisingly, she was also a woman of unexpected physical beauty if one observed her closely. She scrubbed herself all over each morning with a hard, dry brush which seemed to make her skin glow. But there was also a glow from within Emily's private thoughts, when undisturbed by disruptive outside influences, were also beautiful, as some of her friends realized. Indians noticed this also. One aptly said that she had an "inner light." How perceptive he was.

It was a privilege to know Emily intimately and to be allowed to work with, and sometimes for, her. I have never met anyone who made such an enduring impression on me, partly because I myself admire most of the qualities she exemplified. She believed that a spartan life develops character, is good for body and soul, and brings its own rewards. She faced poverty at home and hardship in the rough country of northern British Columbia with fortitude and endurance. She faced illness and suffering with courage and forbearance. She had barely won the battle of poverty before she died, and she fought the battle of illness most of her life until she succumbed to it, still working, on March 2, 1945, aged 74.

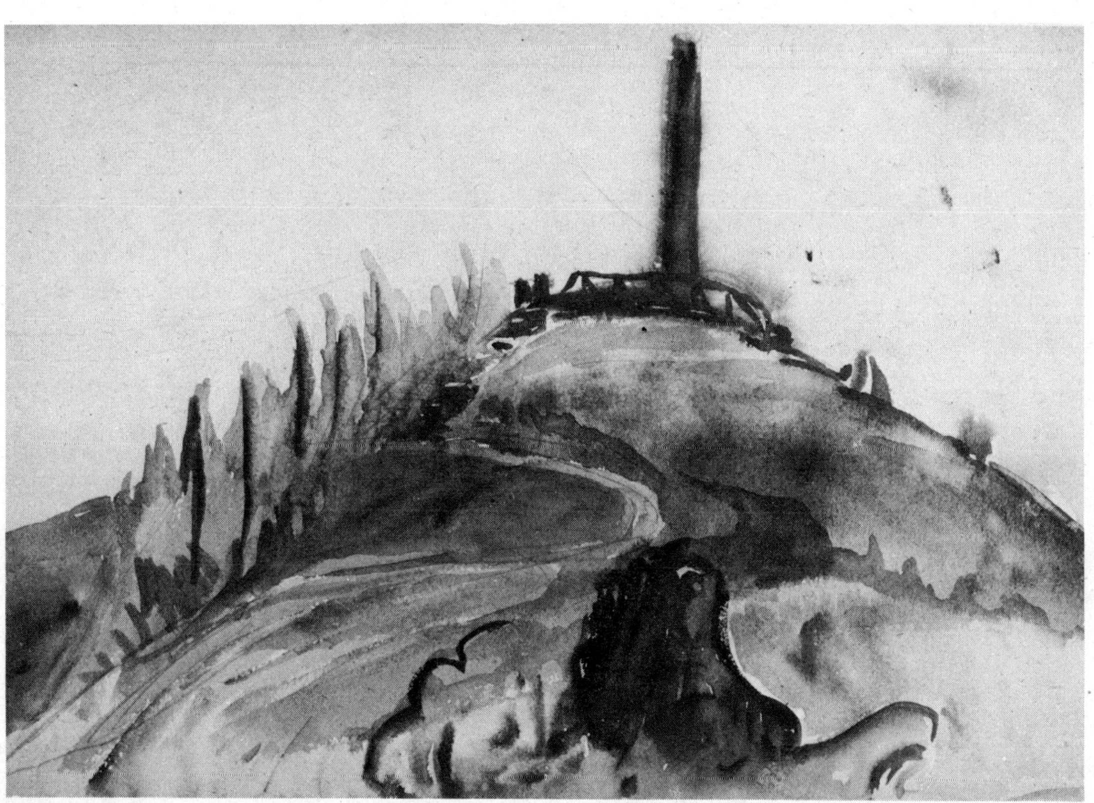

Abbreviations

AAM	Art Association of Montreal. Became Montreal Museum of Fine Arts in 1948.
AGGV	Art Gallery of Greater Victoria, Victoria
AGO	Art Gallery of Ontario, Toronto
AGT	Art Gallery of Toronto. Became the Art Gallery of Ontario in 1966
BCPM	British Columbia Provincial Museum, Victoria
BCSFA	British Columbia Society of Fine Arts, Vancouver
CGP	Canadian Group of Painters. An outgrowth of the Group of Seven
CNE	Canadian National Exhibition, Toronto. Annual summer exhibitions held in the Fine Arts Pavilion
CSPWC	Canadian Society of Painters in Water Color. Annual exhibitions held at the Art Gallery of Toronto
G of 7	Group of Seven, Toronto-based
IA&CS	Island Arts & Crafts Society, Victoria
MMFA	Montreal Museum of Fine Arts
NGC	National Gallery of Canada, Ottawa
OSA	Ontario Society of Artists. Annual exhibitions held at AGT
P&CC	Palette and Chisel Club, Vancouver
PABC	Provincial Archives of British Columbia, Victoria
PAC	Public Archives of Canada
RCA	Royal Canadian Academy of Arts. Annual exhibitions held alternately at the Art Gallery of Toronto and the Art Association of Montreal
UBC	University of British Columbia
VAG	Vancouver Art Gallery
VSC	Vancouver Studio Club and School of Art

Chronology

Only a few important exhibitions are listed in the chronology along with a small number of studio and other exhibitions with which the author was personally involved.

1871
Born of English parents in Victoria, B.C., December 13.

1879
Baptised March 22 by the Reverend John Reid, Minister of the First Presbyterian Church, Victoria, B.C.

1886
Mother died: Emily Saunders Carr, born July 3, 1836; married Richard Carr January 18, 1855 at Eynsham Church, Oxfordshire.

1888
Father died: Richard Carr, born July 16, 1818 in Kent, England.

1888
Passed from Girls' Central Elementary to Victoria High School, by examination, in June, age sixteen-and-a-half. Completed the first year and is known to have been a much better student than she has given us to understand.

1890
Left for San Francisco in August or September to enroll in the California School of Design,* opened February 9, 1874 in a squalid wholesale district above the California Market on Pine Street. In 1893, while Emily was still there, the school moved into the Mark Hopkins mansion atop Nob Hill and the name changed to the Mark Hopkins Institute of Art.* It remained there until 1926 when it finally moved to the large, impressive, Spanish-style building high on Chestnut Street which the school still occupies today. She has always misled us about the name of this art school. Today it is called the San Francisco Art Institute not, as given in all other chronologies, the University of California School of Art, though it is still affiliated with the University of California.

* *These dates were previously thought to have been 1889 and 1894, though Emily says in her autobiography (*Growing Pains*, p. 134) that she studied for* three *years in San Francisco. I am indebted to Maria Tippett and the revised 1975 edition of* Emily Carr: A Centennial Exhibition *for these corrected dates. I do not question their accuracy as I understand that Ms. Tippett is in possession of Emily's San Francisco diary.*

* *Not the Mark Hopkins School of Art as heretofore described.*

1892-1893

Living with her sisters, Edith, Elizabeth and Alice at 1717 McAllister Street, San Francisco. The sisters spent about a year with Emily who is listed as a student at the University of California's affiliate, the Mark Hopkins Institute of Art, for the term 1893-1894.

1893

Returned to Victoria a week before Christmas.* Started drawing and painting classes for children. Her first classes were held in the dining room of the old Carr residence until Edith, the oldest sister, objected to the noise and disorder. Emily then took over the old cow barn, converting the loft into a fine studio. This was always her favorite studio. Even in later life she spoke of it with affection.

** These dates were previously thought to have been 1889 and 1894, though Emily says in her autobiography (*Growing Pains*, p. 134) that she studied for *three years *in San Francisco. I am indebted to Maria Tippett and the revised 1975 edition of* Emily Carr: A Centennial Exhibition *for these corrected dates. I do not question their accuracy as I understand that Ms. Tippett is in possession of Emily's San Francisco diary.*

1894

Probable year of first public exhibition in British Columbia—at the Victoria Fair, in October. Awarded first prize for her pen and ink sketches.

1898

First visit to the Indian Mission at Ucluelet on the West Coast of Vancouver Island, described fully in "Ucluelet," the first story in *Klee Wyck*. The mission was opened by the Presbyterians in 1894. This year love touched her life for the first and only time. She offered it to one unidentified man and rejected it from another: "Martyn," whose real name was William Paddon, scion of a pioneer Victoria family.

1899

Left for England in the late summer and enrolled at the Westminster School of Art, near Westminster Abbey, on September 18. Although Emily says she later joined night classes in design, anatomy and clay modelling, she registered for only two courses. Nearly twenty-eight years old, she was working in life classes for the first time. A copy of her receipt from the School shows her curriculum:

Westminster School of Art

Reg. No. 3322	Sept. 19, 1899		
Received from Miss M.E. Carr	£	s.	p.
Day life classes (6)			
Sept. 18, to Dec. 17	5		
(illegible) and White		18	
Entrance		2	6
	6	0	6

Spent the first summer sketching at Boxford, Berkshire. Then, unable to tolerate the noise and dirt of over-populated London and the stuffy crowded studios of the Westminster School of Art, she left for the St. Ives art colony in Cornwall where she spent a year studying in the studio of seascape painter Julius Olsson, whose assistant, Algernon Talmage, a landscape painter, encouraged Emily to work in the nearby Tregenna Woods. After another try at the London art school, she decided in the spring to go to Bushey, Hertfordshire, where she enrolled at the Meadows Studios of John Whitely. Then, in the fall of 1902, suffering from acute anemia or possibly incipient tuberculosis, she was forced to enter Sunhill Sanatorium, Nayland, Colchester, Suffolk, where she spent eighteen long miserable months. Returned to Bushey for three months before leaving for Canada.

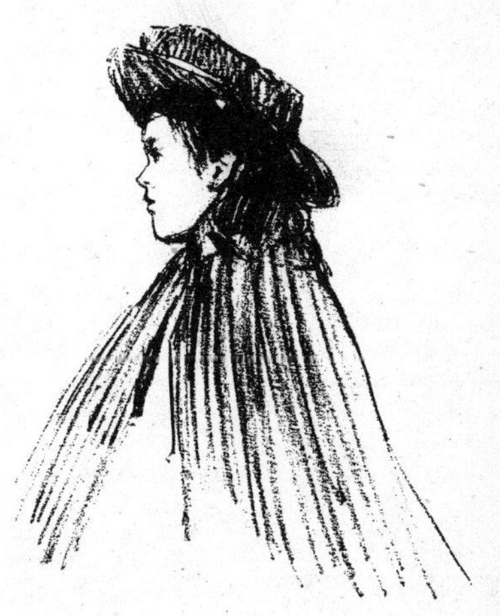

The Westminster School of Art was originally housed in the Royal Architectural Museum. The Museum, founded in 1851 as one of the projects stemming from the 1851 Exhibition, moved to 18 Tufton Street near Westminster Abbey in 1868 or 1869. The Westminster School of Art probably commenced in 1888. In 1903 the School was transferred to the London County Council to be operated as part of the Westminster Technical Institute in Vincent Square. It was then called the L.C.C. Westminster School of Art and endured under that name until a reorganization of technical education after the Second World War resulted in its cessation. The School was said to have had excellent instructors. W.R. Sickert, for instance, gave a course of lectures there just before the First World War.

Unfortunately, no records from the School have survived—at least not for the period prior to its removal to Vincent Square in 1903—so I was unable to discover any information about individual students during the period Emily was in attendance. Most of my information has therefore been drawn from *Growing Pains,* in which Emily gives a very full account of her life as an art student in England and France.

Vincent Square, where Emily lived for a time, has changed little since her day. It is very large and drab and the scrubby grass center is now used as a playing field. One side, nearest the Abbey, is architecturally good. One fine old building houses the Westminster College, which I suspect was the home of the old art school. But the rooming house where Emily boarded is gone. She could look across the courtyard into a hospital on one corner then; the hospital is still there but the adjacent building is modern. The "tuck shop" has also disappeared.

1904
Returned to Victoria October 14, spending eight weeks in the Cariboo en route.

1905
Living at home at 44 Carr Street (now the Emily Carr Arts Centre, 207 Government, a federally-designated historic site). Government Street, from Toronto to Dallas Road, was at that time named after her father, Richard Carr. It was changed to Government c. 1907.

Impressed with Emily's work, Alfred Watts, editor of the Victoria weekly review and newspaper *The Week*, commissioned her to do a series of cartoons for his paper. For eight months, March 25 to November 17, 1905, her amusing drawings and comments on federal, provincial and municipal politics appeared in seventeen issues of this paper.*

Rented a studio on Fort Street, corner of Craigdarroch Road, where large wrought-iron gates graced the entrance to Dunsmuir Castle. It was in this studio that she gave perhaps her first press interview to a reporter from the *Daily Colonist*.* She taught five or six pupils there—mostly from still lifes and casts. She also took them sketching, frequently to the old family home where they drew the chicken house, horse barn and cow barn,* so familiar to readers of Emily's stories of her early youth.

1906
Early 1906 (possibly late 1905). Went to Vancouver to fill the post of art teacher for the "Vancouver Ladies' Art Club"—in reality the young Vancouver Studio Club and School of Art. Rented a studio at 570 Granville Street and advertised for pupils. Her classes were highly successful and she held exhibitions of her pupils' work in her studio annually from March 1907 to March 1909 and a final one in December 1909. During these early years in Vancouver, 1906-1910, Emily was very active as a teacher and an exhibitor. She also sketched in Stanley Park, at the North Vancouver Indian Mission and in the summer, in Indian villages.

1907
August 10. Left on a memorable journey to Alaska.* Emily sketched at Skagway and Sitka on Baranof Island and decided to make a complete record of British Columbia totem poles. The trip resulted in the delightful *Alaska Journal* which was dedicated to Alice. They called it "The Funny Book." Alice was always Emily's favorite sister. She was born October 18, 1869 in

* The Week *"A Provincial Review and Magazine" was published in Victoria from December 1904 to May 1920.*

* *January 11, 1905: "Miss Carr Returns From Five Years Study Under English Masters." Emily gave an outline of her instruction in England and said she intended to paint again in Victoria and also teach. Her second press review, hitherto always called her first, was on February 18, 1905 in* The Week.

* *One of these pupils was Madge Wolfenden, now Mrs. James H. Hamilton, of Victoria. She was a close friend of Emily's from the very early days and had been one of Alice Carr's pupils. For many years she was on the staff of the legislative library and archives and continues to be active in all matters concerning the history of Victoria. Her drawings of the old barns on the Carr property, as well as one done by her brother Victor, are unique.*

* *In* Growing Pains, *p.279, Emily writes: "The first year I lived and taught in Vancouver my sister Alice and I took a pleasure trip to Alaska." This is not correct.*

Victoria and died in October 1953.

1908

Studio still at 570 Granville Street; boarded at 541 Burrard. Probably taught at the Crofton House School for girls. In a letter to Humphrey Toms,* whose aunts Dr. Jessie Gordon and Miss Mary Gordon founded Crofton House School in 1898, Emily writes: "I did at one time teach in Miss Gordon's school in Vancouver." From directory and other evidence, "one time" is thought to be 1908 to the end of the term in 1910, when Emily left for France. The Misses Gordon abhorred her later impressionist work and did not invite her to rejoin their staff on her return to Vancouver.*

* *August 2, 1933. Humphrey Toms was perhaps the one young man Emily never criticized. He became interested in her painting at the Island Arts and Crafts exhibition in 1932, met her the following year, and remained a loyal and helpful friend. He taught school, joined the Army in 1941 and served overseas. After the war he was with the Federal Department of Agriculture in Vancouver until his retirement.*

* *NGC, from a précis Emily made of her career, dated November 1, 1927: "the schools where I taught would not have me back."*

1908

Sketching trip to Alert Bay, on Cormorant Island, off the northeast shore of Vancouver Island. Emily seldom complained about the lack of comfort and hygiene in the Indian villages she visited, but the following description of the Indian reserve at Alert Bay a few years before she went there gives ample evidence of the unsanitary conditions she encountered:

> The unsavoury smell arising from the front of the Indian camp is getting to be a nuisance and causes annoyance and discomfort to people who have occasion to visit the east and who are obliged to use this road in going to the post office. The beach near the road is made a repository for fish offal and sewage matter of the worst description, the smell from which is enough to breed a pestilence. Wonder is expressed that the Indian Department permits such an undesirable state of affairs to exist.*

* *Victoria* Daily Colonist, *August 29, 1895.*

1909

Studio still at 570 Granville Street, but now lived at 634 Dunsmuir. Was one of the 20 founding members of the B.C. Society of Fine Arts, incorporated early 1909, and contributed to their first three exhibitions before leaving for France. She was among those entering the largest number of paintings in these early shows and her range of subject matter was very wide.

Definitely teaching at Crofton House School this year.*

* *Vancouver* Daily Province, *February 23, 1950.*

1910

Lived at 1035 Granville Street. June 20, held a farewell exhibition, tea and auction at the studio before leaving for France. Anne Batchelor, who took over the studio during Emily's

* *PABC,* Sister and I, from Victoria to London, *Memoirs of Ods [sic] and Ends.*

* Growing Pains, *p. 303.*

absence, exhibited with her.

July 11,* left for France accompanied by Alice. Stopped off in Calgary, with a one-week side trip to Edmonton to leave her sheepdog Billie with "Winnie" during her absence. Made further stops in Medicine Hat, Québec (July 30-August 12) and in London en route to Paris. In Paris attended the Académie Colarossi, but once more was unable to stand the hot, airless life-class rooms. Introduced to Harry (William Henry Phelan) Gibb, an English artist who had worked in Paris for years and was an exponent of the "new art" promoted by the modern artists and Gertrude Stein, he recommended her to the studio of John Duncan Fergusson, where he himself criticized. She studied there for a few weeks until a recurrence of the severe illness she had suffered in Vancouver, complicated by measles, put her in hospital for three months. Went to Sweden to recuperate. On return to Paris in the spring, she did not go back to the art schools, but joined a landscape-painting class that Gibb had formed in Crécy-en-Brie, near Paris. She later followed him to Brittany where she spent several months sketching in St. Efflam (named for a sixth century British or Irish hermit).

Just before returning to Canada, worked for six weeks in Concarneau with a "fine water colorist (Australian)."* This teacher, a woman, has never been positively identified but is thought to have been the gifted New Zealand artist Frances Hodgkins.

While in Paris in November 1976, I located all three addresses where Emily lived while attending art classes there. Rue Campagne Première, where she first took an apartment with Alice in the early fall of 1910, is a typical Latin Quarter street curving between Boulevard du Montparnasse and Boulevard Raspail, two blocks away from the famous Café du Dôme, a rendezvous for artists in Emily's day and later. Moved to 96 Boulevard du Montparnasse, also a short distance from Café du Dôme, but in the other direction, towards the Montparnasse station.

No. 96 is a magnificent, well-preserved, seven-story apartment house of *pierre de taille,* with fine ironwork balconies and an elevator. It is almost one hundred years old and consists of two buildings. The elegant street section changes dramatically back of the courtyard to a somewhat ravaged plaster and brick building with no elevator where the poorer tenants lived. I suspect Emily was among them, although the *concierge,* who had tended the house for over thirty years, had no memory of the Charbo family with whom she lived. Still later, just before returning home, she stayed at the Hôtel de Chevreuse, 3 rue de Chevreuse, between the Boulevard du Montparnasse and Notre Dame des Champs, immediately behind the internationally-known Jockey Club. The hotel, a modernized, six-storey, white plaster structure, still bears the same name. I also visited Crécy-en-Brie (the home of the famous French cheese), recently amalgamated with a neighboring village to form one community, Crécy-la-Chapelle. A picturesque town of about 3,000 inhabitants, it is beautifully situated in rolling hills, 43 km. from Paris, on a small, lovely river, *Le petit Morin,* which, controlled by quaint ancient locks, curls lazily through the town. Today Crécy-la-Chapelle is a retreat for Paris commuters, week-enders and summer residents, and not even the oldest inhabitants remember the days when it was invaded by artists such as Emily and the other members of Gibb's landscape-painting class.

1911

Paris. Had two paintings accepted by the *Société du Salon d'Automne* for their exhibition at the *Grand Palais* which opened on September 30. Emily has told us that the *Salon* was a "rebel" show and boasted that her pictures were hung alongside some of the great French moderns. Her friends were suitably awed, believing that a very special honor had been bestowed on her. But after reading the very long, comprehensive reviews of this important Parisian event in *Le Temps, Le Figaro* and *Le Matin,* I gained an entirely new insight into the aims, composition and function of these annual *Salon* shows. First of all, they were "open," that is, open to all artists and all types of art. Secondly, painting was only one section of an enormous, varied exhibition which filled the vast halls of the *Palais* with sculpture, furniture, decorative art, theater décor, tapestries, ceramics, jewellery, stained-glass windows, interiors, etc. The *Salon* also had an excellent tradition of retrospectives, and the critics devoted much of their space to those of 1911: Camille Pissarro and Henry de Groux. Few of the other painters mentioned in the press are remembered today, notable exceptions being Bonnard, Marquet, Vlaminck, Vuillard and, closer to home, Morrice.

Unfortunately, the "innovators" (fauves and cubists), including Emily, occupied only one small room in the *Palais,* and thus made up only a small fraction of the total exhibition. When mentioned at all by the critics (and never individually), they were attacked and ridiculed as *"illetrés"* who had not learned their lesson from Ingres.

It is sad to report that Emily's work went completely

unnoticed, even in a special article on the "minor poets" ("One Swallow Does Not Make a Spring") which gives a long list of unknown painters, many of them foreigners.* But it was at least gratifying to find scattered references to her name in the files of the Bibliothèque Nationale and a Carr listing in the prestigious *Allgemeines Lexikon der Bildenden Künstler des XX Jahrhunderts,* von Hans Vollmer.

* Le Temps, *October 1, 1911.*

November 11, returned to Canada,* but failed to establish herself as an art teacher in Victoria.

* *This is the date always given for Emily's return. Ira Dilworth first used it and others have taken it on faith. There is, however, a slight possibility that it may be incorrect since she participated in the Island Arts and Crafts Club exhibition held that year in Victoria October 5-8. None of her three entries bore a French title, however.*

First exhibition with the Island Arts and Crafts Club (later Society), and the first time she exhibited with any art group in Victoria. There is no evidence to suggest that she belonged to, or exhibited with, the forerunner of the Island Arts and Crafts Club, the B.C. Art Association, which held its first annual exhibition at the Victoria City Hall in September 1890.

1912

Early January. Went to Vancouver and opened a studio at Apt. 2-1465 Broadway West. Here, in March, she put on her second studio exhibition to show "all those interested in the modern French movement in art" the work she had done in France. On April 12, and subsequent Fridays during the month, her paintings were again on view at her West Broadway studio.

In the summer, made the first of her two major sketching trips to Indian villages in the Queen Charlotte Islands and on the upper Skeena River. Also returned to Alert Bay and related coastal areas.

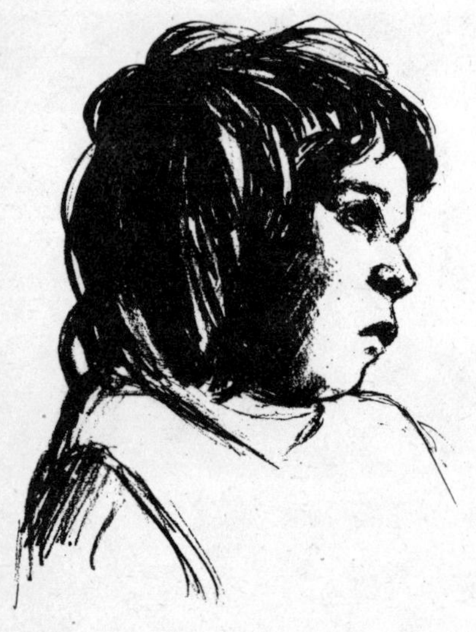

1913

April. Exhibited almost 200 Indian pictures at Drummond Hall in Vancouver. Except for impromptu showings of her work in Indian villages, and the exhibition in her Broadway studio the year before, this was Emily's first solo exhibition. It was also the occasion of her first public talk. Twice during her show she lectured on totem poles and her life among the Indians. In writing the text (of which no copy apparently survives) she sought the help of Dr. Charles F. Newcombe, who had pioneered scientific study of Indian culture in British Columbia. Though the exhibition was favorably reviewed in the press, Emily was discouraged about the poor reception of her "new art" and the dwindling of her classes.

Decided to give up teaching and returned to Victoria to live. On her share of the land she and her sisters had inherited from their father, Emily built a small apartment house (later called the

House of All Sorts) at 646 Simcoe Street, consisting of her studio and living quarters upstairs and two independent flats down. The original plans show only three apartments, but about 1928 a fourth, "the Doll's Flat," was carved out of her west-side rooms to produce more income. When rentals failed to support the house, she was forced to curtail her painting drastically and to take boarders, breed dogs, make pottery and hooked rugs in order to eke out a very slim livelihood. To help out, sister Alice gave a substantial mortgage on the house, but it continued to be a crushing burden for twenty-three hard years. In June, she moved into her newly-built house (a provincially-designated historic site since December 6, 1973) and held a combination "at home" and exhibition housewarming the same summer. *The Week* carried a long list of her guests, but made no mention of her pictures. Her strong, vibrant French paintings and bold new Indian work failed to impress either her guests or the reporter.

This same year, built a summer cottage in Oak Bay (a municipality bordering on the city of Victoria) at 494 Victoria Avenue.

1915

Possibly the first visit to Emily's studio by Dr. Marius Barbeau, ethnologist with the National Museum in Ottawa, after he heard about her 1912 sketching trip in the North from his Tsimshian interpreter in Port Simpson.*

Probably the year Emily opened her kennels. She had her first English bobtail sheepdog, Billie, as early as 1905, but started breeding them much later. Certainly she had sheepdogs in 1916 and had ceased to breed them before the end of 1923.* Her two kennels overlapped. Koko, the patriarch of her Belgian griffons, was purchased in 1919 and died in Lillooet in 1933. Woo, her mischievous Javanese monkey, was acquired in 1923 and died in Vancouver's Stanley Park zoo in 1938. Adolphus, the majestic Persian cat, lived longer than either—1914 to 1932.

** Barbeau is not always reliable about dates and his 1915 and 1921 visits to Emily's studio have yet to be firmly established. See chapter: "The Carr-Barbeau Mystery Story."*

** Emily Carr Arts Center, Emily to F.A.C. Redden, England, December 9, 1923: "I had to give up my sheep dogs . . ."*

1916-1917

Despite complaints about severe hardships at this time, Emily was able to spend this winter in California.*

** Emily Carr Arts Centre, Emily to F.A.C. Redden, late March 1917.*

1918

Early this year Emily contributed a series of cartoons to a Vancouver periodical, *The Western Woman's Weekly*. Vol. 1, no. 1 of this paper was published on her birthday (December 13) in 1917, and her large, spirited drawings began to appear the following month, on January 24, 1918. They were continued in the issues of February 7; February 21; February 28; March 21; April 4; April 18; April 25 and May 18. All are signed E.M.C. A tenth cartoon of similar technique appeared on September 28, but it is unsigned and was possibly done by another cartoonist.

In keeping with the tone of this publication, three of the drawings strongly support women's rights—the only time Emily showed a real interest in this subject.

A two-column write-up, with photograph of Emily and pets, also appeared in this paper (November 9, 1918) under the heading "Artists and Their Doings—Victoria Woman Artist."

1919

Edith Carr, eldest child (born February 5, 1856 in Alviso, California) died on December 11. She had been head of the family since the death of the father and was strongly resented by Emily.

1921

The Director of the National Gallery of Canada, Eric Brown,* first heard of Emily's work this year, probably through Marius Barbeau* who returned to Ottawa from the North in January or February* after a possible second visit to Emily's studio en route. Later, in October, Brown's attention was again drawn to her work by H. Mortimer-Lamb, Secretary of the Canadian Institute of Mining and Metallurgy, photographer and art connoisseur of Vancouver.

1923

Had a serious operation in November. In bed for more than two months.

1924

Mark Tobey, internationally renowned Seattle artist, probably stayed at Emily's boarding house for the first time early this year.** He somehow got her back to her easel, and his instruction renewed her enthusiasm for regular painting. He also encouraged her to enter four paintings in the *Ninth Annual Exhibition of the Artists of the Pacific Northwest,* Seattle Fine Arts Society, in April, where, to her delight and astonishment, she was awarded second honorable mention in oil. Seattle artists Viola and Ambrose Patterson, with other members of the faculty of the University of Washington, also began visiting Emily about this time.

* *Eric Brown, born at Nottingham in August 1877, was the first director of Canada's National Gallery, an office he held with distinction from 1913 until his death in early 1939.*

* *See chapter: "The Carr-Barbeau Mystery Story."*

* *Dr. Marius Barbeau, whose ancestors settled in Canada in the seventeenth century, was born in Ste. Marie de Beauce, Québec, March 5, 1883. He was educated at Laval University (where he studied law), and at the Sorbonne in Paris, and was the first French-Canadian to be awarded a Rhodes Scholarship. For his degree from Oxford University he wrote a thesis on "The Totemic System of the North West Coast." He also held an honorary doctorate from the University of Montreal. Before he died in Ottawa at the age of eighty-five, his name was known to every student of Indian culture in Northwestern B.C. He was also considered to be the dean of Canadian folklore. An ethnologist and folklorist with The National Museum from 1911 until his retirement in 1948, he collected Indian artifacts and totem poles from Northern B.C. for the National Museum.*

** *See chapter: "Mark Tobey to the Rescue."*

1925

Holiday sketching trip in September (". . . a most unusual proceeding for me"), perhaps also suggested by Tobey.

1926

Had an exhibition within an exhibition at the Victoria Fair. A newspaper critic pointed out that "Emily Carr was much better known as an artist in Victoria during the twenties than she would have us believe."*

* *Victoria* Daily Colonist, *August 18, 1926.*

1927

Taking a correspondence course with an American school of journalism: The Palmer Institute of Authorship in Los Angeles. Possibly enrolled late 1926. Flora Burns, who started the course with Emily, thinks so.

Twenty-six Indian oils, plus pottery and hooked rugs, included in the *Exhibition of Canadian West Coast Art* (Native and Modern) arranged by the National Gallery of Canada. Emily traveled east for the opening and also met Lawren Harris* and several other members of the Group of Seven.

* *Lawren Harris (1885-1970). One of Canada's finest painters. A moving force in the Group of Seven, The Canadian Group of Painters, and in British Columbia painting after his arrival in Vancouver in 1940. He exerted a strong influence on Emily and her painting and persuaded her to form the Emily Carr Trust of which he was co-trustee.*

1928

Sketched in the summer in the Queen Charlotte Islands and in villages along the Nass and Skeena rivers. For the first time she was able to work in Kitwancool, an inland village considered unfriendly to the white man. In November she exhibited the paintings done on this trip in her Victoria studio.

September. Mark Tobey spent three weeks in Emily's studio* giving instruction to her and several other Victoria painters in his so-called "master class." Emily organized this class to help Tobey financially.

* *People who lived in the House of All Sorts during Emily's boarding house days say that the boarders lived in all the rooms upstairs, including the attic. The studio was used as the dining room and Emily herself often had to occupy the basement or a tent in the garden.*

1929

June. Published an article, "Modern and Indian Art of the West Coast," in the supplement to the *McGill News*. Apart from Emily's cartoons and "jingles" in *The Week* and *The Western Woman's Weekly*, this is believed to be her only excursion into journalism.*

* *A review of an exhibition in the* Ladies' Review, *a supplement to* The Week, *Victoria, B.C., dated December 6, 1913 and initialed "E.C.," is attributed to Emily in the PABC; but neither the style, nor the vocabulary is typical of her writing. Madge Wolfenden Hamilton and I both believe that the critic was Edith Madeleine Cuppage, a part-time journalist who, for a time, was on the staff of the Vancouver* Daily Province.

1930

A big year for Emily. Her work included in the American Federation of Arts Exhibition, *Contemporary Canadian Artists* (traveling), which opened at the Corcoran Gallery, Washington, D.C.

First public solo show in the West since 1913, at the Crystal Garden, Victoria, sponsored by the Women's Canadian Club.

Gave her second public talk, "An Address," before the members of the Woman's Canadian Club on March 4th, to mark the opening of the exhibition.

Gave her third public address at a luncheon meeting of the Kumtuks Club for business and professional women on March 10th.

Second trip east to see Lawren Harris and the Group of Seven Exhibition in Toronto, in which she was an invited contributor for the first time.

First and only visit to New York.

Display of paintings, organized by Marius Barbeau, at the CNR ticket office in Ottawa. Though small, this was nonetheless Emily's first solo show in the East.

First solo exhibition at the Art Institute of Seattle, forerunner of the present Seattle Art Museum.

A studio exhibition and sale of pottery, the last of her Christmas sales, held annually since she started making pottery c. 1924-1925. She continued to hook rugs off and on until her illness in 1937.

1931

Included in the *First Baltimore Pan-American Exhibition* (traveling), Baltimore Museum of Art.

May. Spent almost three weeks sketching at Cordova Bay with the author.

September. Another long sketching trip (again with the author) to Goldstream Park, about twelve miles north of Victoria on the Island Highway.

From early December until the end of February 1932, worked with the author in her studio every afternoon doing exclusively portraits, still lifes and animal studies. The author's life portrait of her is now in the permanent collection of the Vancouver Art Gallery.

1932

May. Sketching trip for two weeks on Braden Mountain in the Metchosin hills, with the author.*

June. Sketched alone in rented rooms in a farm house on Cedar Hill Road, Victoria.

Received Honorable Mention for a painting exhibited in the *First Annual Exhibition of Western Water-Color Painting* at the California Palace of the Legion of Honor, San Francisco.

* *The Cordova Bay, Goldstream and Braden Mountain painting excursions are more fully described in the chapter: "Sketching Trips 1931-1942" and in* M.E.—A Portrayal of Emily Carr, *Clarke, Irwin & Co. Ltd., Toronto, 1969, both by the author.*

December. Held a four-artist show in the two lower flats of her House of All Sorts to give publicity to her proposed People's Gallery.*

1933

March. First of a series of exhibitions at the UBC Library, organized by Frederick J. Brand, Assistant Professor of Mathematics.* Exhibiting with Emily were Max Maynard** and the author. This was her first exhibition in Vancouver (except the 1929 BCSFA show) since 1913.

About this time, Frederick also read Emily's stories to his mathematics class—their first public reading. He then submitted them to Dr. G.G. Sedgewick, Head of the English Department, for criticism.***

May-June. Important sketching trip to the Interior which took her to Brackendale, Lillooet, Seton and Pemberton.

Late June. Purchased a dilapidated caravan trailer, "The Elephant," which, refitted to suit her needs, would revolutionize her sketching habits and be used for all future painting excursions until the end of 1936.

September. Second sketching trip to Goldstream Park in her newly-acquired van. The next spring it was towed to Metchosin where it remained—in four different locations—until 1938 when it was sold to a friend in Langford for $15.

Also in September: Amsterdam, Stedelijk Museum, International Federation of Business and Professional Women. Exhibition of Works by Women Artists organized by the International Committee of Fine Arts. A committee of three (including Margaret Clay)**** representing the local club, called at Emily's studio to select the exhibited painting.

November. Third trip East to Chicago and Toronto. The purpose of this trip was to see the exhibition at the Chicago World's Fair, "but," wrote Emily, "it was closed on my nose 12 hours before." To make the Chicago visit possible, the author persuaded Emily to let her have a large Indian painting (*Kispiox Village*) which she used to collect money from friends and organizations with the understanding that it would be donated to the Provincial Archives. Only $166 could be raised that difficult year, but it was enough to pay for Emily's trip. The painting was duly presented to the British Columbia Government by Frederick Brand in a small ceremony at the Parliament Buildings. For many years this gift was erroneously attributed to "a number of organizations." On Emily's death, it was the only Carr picture in possession of the Government.

* *See chapter: "The Collapse of a Dream—The People's Gallery."*

* *Frederick J. Brand, born 1905 in Falkirk, Scotland, came to Victoria in 1912 where he completed his early education. In 1925 he graduated from UBC with First Class Honors in Mathematics, after which he spent a year at the University of Washington in Seattle as a teaching fellow; two years at Jesus College, Oxford, as an Overseas I O D E Scholar; and a further year at the U of W before joining the Department of Mathematics at UBC, where he remained (with one year's absence—at Princeton—from 1933 to 1934) until 1940, when he joined the R C A F as a Navigation Instructor. F.J.B. and the author were married in New York in June 1934 and divorced in 1949, the marriage a war casualty. But our love and admiration for Emily have remained a bond and an exchange of memories about our association with her has been of great value to this book. Frederick now lives in Reading, England, and is also writing an "essay" which should contribute much to Emily Carr literature.*

** *Max Maynard, born in 1903 in India, came to Victoria in 1912, where he attended elementary and high schools and afterwards the B.C. Normal School, before starting his teaching career at the Lampson Street (elementary) School, Esquimalt. He graduated from UBC in 1937 and did graduate work at the University of Southern California (1938-1940). He was Acting Director of VAG in 1941, appointed to the English staff of the University of Manitoba in 1941, and left for Durham, N.H. in 1946, where he taught in the English Department of the University of New Hampshire until his retirement. He is now living in Peterborough, N.H. and devoting his time to painting, occasionally exhibiting in small solo shows. Max was a force in B.C. painting in the thirties and early forties and exhibited widely. For a time during the early thirties he had occasional visits with Emily, sometimes accompanied by Jack Shadbolt, and the three formed an uneasy* *friendship of sorts. Max was strongly influenced by Emily's work then and fascinated with her as a person, but now claims, with much truth, that her remarks about him in* Hundreds and Thousands *are "scurrilous."*

*** *Garnett G. Sedgewick, head of the Department of English, U B C., 1920-1948. Died 1949.*

**** *Margaret Clay, one of Emily's oldest friends, was head librarian at the Victoria Public Library from 1924 to 1952. As a girl, she was a pupil at Alice Carr's school and in the twenties and thirties was active in the women's liberation movement.*

1934

May-June. Sketched in Metchosin, first at Esquimalt Lagoon, then on the Strathdee farm, Metchosin Road. Worked in the same location in September.

Summer course in short-story writing at the Provincial Normal School, Victoria.

1935

April. Held a series of exhibitions in a downstairs flat of the House of All Sorts.

June. Sketching trip to Albert Head, Metchosin. Same location in September.

August. A two-day exhibition in the lower east flat of the House of All Sorts by request of summer school students at the Provincial Normal School. Open to teachers and students of the Summer School on one day and to the general public another.

October 22. Fourth and last public address, "Talk on Art," read before the students and staff of the Provincial Normal School.

November. First major solo exhibition in the east at the Lyceum Club and Women's Art Association, Toronto.

1936

Second major solo exhibition in the East at Hart House, University of Toronto.

January. Forced to dispose of the House of All Sorts owing to increasing financial difficulties and ill health. Having no money for urgent repairs, and no strength to cope with demanding tenants, Emily exchanged her twenty-three-year-old headache for a single dwelling at 1266 Oscar Street, which she immediately rented for $25 a month. For herself she found a ramshackle cottage at 316 Beckley Avenue, in the poorest part of James Bay, for which she paid $12 a month. The difference had to cover a good part of her expenses.

February. Second of Frederick Brand's exhibitions at the UBC Library, with nine other B.C. artists, five from Vancouver, four from Victoria.

Now writing regularly. Her stories, frequently read to close friends, were edited by the "listening ladies," Flora Burns* and Ruth Humphrey.*

June. Sketched again in Metchosin, but "The Elephant" was now closer to town, having been towed to a sheep farm on the edge of a yawning gravel pit. This was the location of her final two painting excursions in the van. The last was in September.

* *Flora Hamilton Burns, whose grandparents and parents knew the Carr family, became a close friend of Emily after her mother's death in 1924. Over the years, she edited many of Emily's stories and has written a number of articles on her life and work, among them one in* Clear Spirit, *published for the Canadian Federation of University Women by the University of Toronto Press, 1966, and the widely distributed "The World of Emily Carr," a catalogue introducing an exhibition of Emily's paintings from the Newcombe Collection (PABC) held at the Hudson's Bay Company stores in Victoria and Vancouver in 1962.*

* *Dr. Ruth Humphrey's friendship with Emily began late in 1936 while she was a professor of English at Victoria College; she is now an emeritus professor of UBC. She has written several articles about Emily, and her set of forty-four letters, written by Emily between 1937 and 1944 , was published in* The University of Toronto Quarterly, *winter 1972.*

August. Sister Elizabeth (Lizzie), born November 6, 1867, in Victoria, died on the 3rd. Because of the confusion in initials, Emily was at first reported dead, causing a flurry of telegrams between galleries and newspapers.

November. Invited friends and the public to view her work at 316 Beckley Avenue. Her last studio exhibition.

1937

January. Had her first heart attack. While in hospital, was visited by the respected art critic Eric Newton of the *Manchester Guardian,* who had been requested by the director of NGC to select fifteen pictures for inclusion in *A Century of Canadian Art* exhibition to be held at the Tate Gallery, London and for possible sales in the east. Realizing that Emily would have great difficulty paying her extraordinarily heavy hospital and medical bills, everyone pitched in and tried to help. In fact, 1937, with the assistance of NGC, was a wonderful year for sales.

Slow convalescence. Too ill to leave home throughout the year. Worked on her Indian stories while in hospital, then steadily until June or July, when she sent twenty (most published later in *Klee Wyck*) to Dr. Sedgewick for reading and criticism.

First solo exhibition at the Art Gallery of Toronto.

Exhibited in Paris at the *Exposition Internationale.*

House-bound much of the time, showed renewed interest in portraiture. Up to 1941 did occasional portraits of maids and a few friends, most during 1938-1939. Destroyed many during move in February 1940.

1938

July. Rented a cottage on Telegraph Bay Road, in the environs of Victoria. Relatively good sketching year.

October. First solo exhibition at VAG, five-and-a-half years after Frederick's exhibition at UBC had re-introduced Emily's work to Vancouver. The VAG show was organized by Nan Cheney* and hung by her with assistance from the author and advice from Jock Macdonald.*

Exhibited at the Tate Gallery, London, in *A Century of Canadian Art.*

November. Third of the series of exhibitions at the UBC Library, made up of pictures drawn from the solo show at VAG in October. First suggested and partly organized by Professor Hunter Lewis of the English Department, Emily soon quarreled with him and put the author in full charge.

* *Nan Cheney, a well-known painter whose portrait of Emily is now in the permanent collection of NGC, first met her in Ottawa in 1927. They corresponded from the start, and their friendship grew after Nan and her husband, Dr. Hill Cheney, moved to Vancouver in 1937. Her collection of 133 letters from Emily was acquired by the UBC Library, Special Collections.*

* *J.W.G. (Jock) Macdonald, a native of Scotland, began his career as an architectural draughtsman and textile designer before coming to Canada. In Vancouver he took over the Department of Design at the School of Decorative and Applied Arts, and inspired by his fellow-teacher, Frederick H. Varley, soon found his true vocation as a painter, becoming one of the nation's pioneers in abstract art. After 21 years in B.C. and a short stint in Calgary, he moved to Toronto in 1947 where he died in 1960, aged 63.*

At the end of this year. Ruth Humphrey introduced Emily's stories to Ira Dilworth.*

* *Ira Dilworth (1894-1962) had a varied and interesting career. In 1926, age thirty-two, he was already principal of the Victoria High School, and in 1934 became Associate Professor of English at UBC. He is, however, best remembered for his pioneer work with CBC, where he held important positions in Vancouver, Montreal and Toronto for twenty-four years, from 1938 until his death. He met Emily late in her life, but became successively her editor, co-trustee of the Emily Carr Trust and literary executor of her Will.*

1939

In hospital for one month with a second heart attack. Convalescence slow, but was finally able to go sketching in June.

June. Rented an old house on Millstream Road (Langford) where she worked for three weeks under ideal conditions, as "the ground all round (as far as I shall walk) is level."

September. Camped in a shack on Craigflower Road, not too far from town at the end of the Gorge bus line, but "it's all among bushes and trees, quite nice."

Represented in the *Contemporary Art* exhibition at the San Francisco Golden Gate International Exposition, and at the New York World's Fair.

1940

Emily's stories read on CBC broadcasts by Dr. G.G. Sedgewick on January 29 and February 5. On July 1, the first of two more programs was broadcast over the National Network, this time the stories being read by Ira Dilworth.* There were other broadcasts by Dilworth in 1941 and 1942, and probably later.

* *The dates for these broadcasts have been taken from Emily's writings since CBC did not reply to my letters of enquiry. They are, therefore, only presumed to be accurate.*

February 25. Moved to 218 St. Andrew's Street where she added a kitchen and bathroom to her sister Alice's house in order to have self-contained quarters. Her bedroom was the old dining room in Alice's school and her studio the converted classroom. This was a homecoming for Emily since Alice's cottage is built on what was the old family vegetable garden and the House of All Sorts is just around the corner.

May. Last sketching trip to Metchosin—again near the gravel pits, but without the van. She found a one-room shack and woodshed where she worked for about two weeks. Barely home, she suffered a stroke (on June 5) and was very ill all summer.

Exhibited in the International Business Machines Corporation collection, *Contemporary Art of Canada and Newfoundland,* at the Canadian National Exhibition in Toronto.

1941

Foundation of Emily Carr Trust, which established a permanent collection of forty-five of her finest paintings placed in trust as a gift to the Province of British Columbia. The date of this Trust has always been erroneously given as 1942, even by the trustees and VAG.

Published her first book, *Klee Wyck*. Ira Dilworth was instrumental in obtaining publication by taking a great deal of manuscript material (including the journals) to Toronto for consideration by Mr. and Mrs. (W.H. and Irene) Clarke, who made a quick decision to publish despite the many wartime difficulties and restrictions. Soon afterwards, they decided to publish some of the other material in a second book. W.H. Clarke undertook to publish trade editions of her books under the imprint of Oxford University Press (Canadian Branch), of which he was Manager, and educational editions under the imprint of Clarke, Irwin & Company Limited, of which he was President. Later the trade rights were purchased from Oxford by Clarke, Irwin for, I understand, $10,000. *Klee Wyck*, published by Oxford University Press shortly before Emily's seventieth birthday, subsequently won the Governor General's award for general literature.

1942

Her second book, *The Book of Small*, was published by Clarke, Irwin. As a child, Emily referred to herself as "Small" to distinguish herself from her next two oldest sisters, "Middle" and "Bigger." She continued this practice on occasion in later life, particularly after the publication of this book. It was also published in England.

June. Had a three-week working visit with Ira Dilworth in Vancouver.

August. Undertook her very last sketching trip. She rented a cottage at Mount Douglas Park and produced fifteen large sketches (and a number of small ones) in ten days. But she overtaxed her strength and, suffering another serious heart attack, had to go to hospital almost directly from camp. On discharge from hospital, she spent over five months in the Mayfair Nursing Home at 1037 Richardson Street.

November. Emily's Will, signed on the 30th, appointed Henry Graham Lawson (her lawyer) and Ira Dilworth executors and trustees, and William A. Newcombe* and Lawren Harris trustees of all pictures unsold at the time of her death. These were left in a special trust, funds from which were to be used for scholarships and the encouragement of art in British Columbia. They did not include the original forty-five true Trust pictures set aside in 1941.* Ira Dilworth was named the literary trustee. Alice inherited all real and personal property.

* *William Arnold Newcombe, son of Dr. Charles F. Newcombe, accumulated and preserved books, papers, photographs, Indian artifacts, etc, which, with the large group of Emily's drawings and early paintings and similar contributions from his father, make up the Newcombe Collection acquired by the British Columbia Government after Willie's death in 1960. Willie accompanied his father on many of his trips and did research in anthropology, ethnology and biology. He joined the Provincial Museum as assistant biologist in 1927. Although he and Emily had differing views on a great many subjects, they shared a deep-rooted love of nature, animals and Indians. He was her devoted friend and helper to the end.*

1943
First solo exhibition in Montreal at the Art Association of Montreal.

Last griffon (Matilda) died. Emily had already disposed of all her birds except the budgerigar Joseph, who remained with her in the nursing home (1942-1943).

June. Fifth and final solo exhibition at VAG.

Again in hospital, perhaps the result of overwork preparing for her June exhibition at VAG. Just before the ambulance came for her, she wrote to Ira Dilworth: ". . . pray for me and ask for me to die soon and quick. I'm so afraid of being a coward."

1944
Suffered another stroke which affected the use of her left arm. Again spent many weeks in hospital. Later, almost continuously confined to bed at home, but continued to write and even paint a little. Emily tells us of her terrible ordeal in a few lines: "Seventh time in six years I've been hustled off in that hateful white glass hearse. . . . I'm rather rebellious, for each return finds me a bit more groggy. I never quite catch up its cruel game, and I've had eight years of it."*

* *Emily to Humphrey Toms, March 12, 1944.*

This year, too, Emily finally reconciled herself to using a wheel chair: "I am going to effect a wheel chair—think of that! so I will be able to go up into the park to see the spring flowers, ducks . . ."*

* *Emily to Humphrey Toms, April 3, 1944.*

August. Dr. Max Stern, Montreal art dealer, called on Emily for the first and last time and immediately drew up a contract with her authorizing him to display her paintings in his Dominion Gallery—the first and only time she had consented to work on contract with an agent—except for pottery. In the fall he exhibited fifty-nine of her paintings.

Published her third book, *The House of All Sorts,* which contains stories about her house, tenants and trials as a landlady. A second section, *Bobtails,* dedicated to her sister Alice, describes her experiences breeding and selling more than 350 English sheepdogs.

1945
February. Worked on about thirty-five oil on paper sketches, preparing them for a show at VAG in April. It was never held. At the end of the month, exhausted by this effort she decided to seek a much-needed rest at St. Mary's Priory, a home for the aged run by Roman Catholic nuns in the old James Bay Hotel.

She took her typewriter and writing materials with her, but must have been too sick to work since she suffered pain and difficulty in breathing. She had a very bad attack in the morning of March 2nd, was given morphia, but died at 3:45 p.m., conscious to the end. The funeral was a rather hurried and grim affair attended by a mere handful of people. The Priory where she died was just two blocks away from the old Carr house where she was born.

During the scant week Emily was in the Priory, she wrote a few letters, the last one presumably to Ira Dilworth. It was dated just "Tuesday" in her usual manner.* Typically, too, she complained about conditions and service. But what shone through all her distress and pain was the great pride and satisfaction she felt in the knowledge that the Senate of the University of British Columbia had completed arrangements to confer upon her at the 1945 Spring Convocation the Degree of Doctor of Laws. Underneath her often-used words "humble" and "unworthy," Emily covered up a very healthy ego, which shows up, rather pathetically, in perhaps the last words she ever wrote: "I'm way off down a corridor where nobody ever comes and nothing ever happens. There's no bell if anything goes wrong. You go wrong by yourself. But then, they treat me like a half-wit (I know I am forgetful). Then, I want to shout, 'I'm nearly a Doctor! The University are making me one, so there!' " She says her final good-bye to Ira and ends her letter with: "What will Small's title be? Doctorette?" Thus, at the very end she reverts, as she so often did, to her childhood self "Small." She wanted her, too, to be honored.

** Emily died on a Friday, thus the Tuesday she wrote the letter would have been February 27th.*

Emily's funeral arrangements were handled by McCall Bros., whose records do not go back to 1945. The service was held on March 5th at their funeral home at 1400 Vancouver Street and she was buried in the family plot, Block H Plot 85 E. off Road 15 in the Ross Bay Cemetery. The only inscription then was the one word CARR carved on one end of the curb surrounding a grass plot. Emily's grave went unmarked until May 24, 1962 when a small ceremony took place at the graveside and a plaque was unveiled by Flora Hamilton Burns as a centennial tribute from the Victoria Branch of the B.C. Historical Association. The stone tablet is simply inscribed:

Emily Carr
Artist and Author
Lover of Nature

The plot is now choked by long grass and weeds and the neglected appearance of the grave presents a sad and forlorn spectacle for the Carr friends and fans who want to make a sentimental pilgrimage to the cemetery.

A final and touching tribute was read on the National Network 4:15-4:30, March 9, 1945, by Dr. G.G. Sedgewick. It ended thus:

> As artist, Emily Carr spent a good many years in a wilderness of neglect and disapproval. But it will be solacing to remember that she won honor, though not too much, in her own country before she died. Perhaps she got as much as she ever expected. But even if we British Columbians are not yet fully aware of it, our province has produced at least one thing more enduring than its brass or timber and more permanently valuable even than its 'provincial rights'!

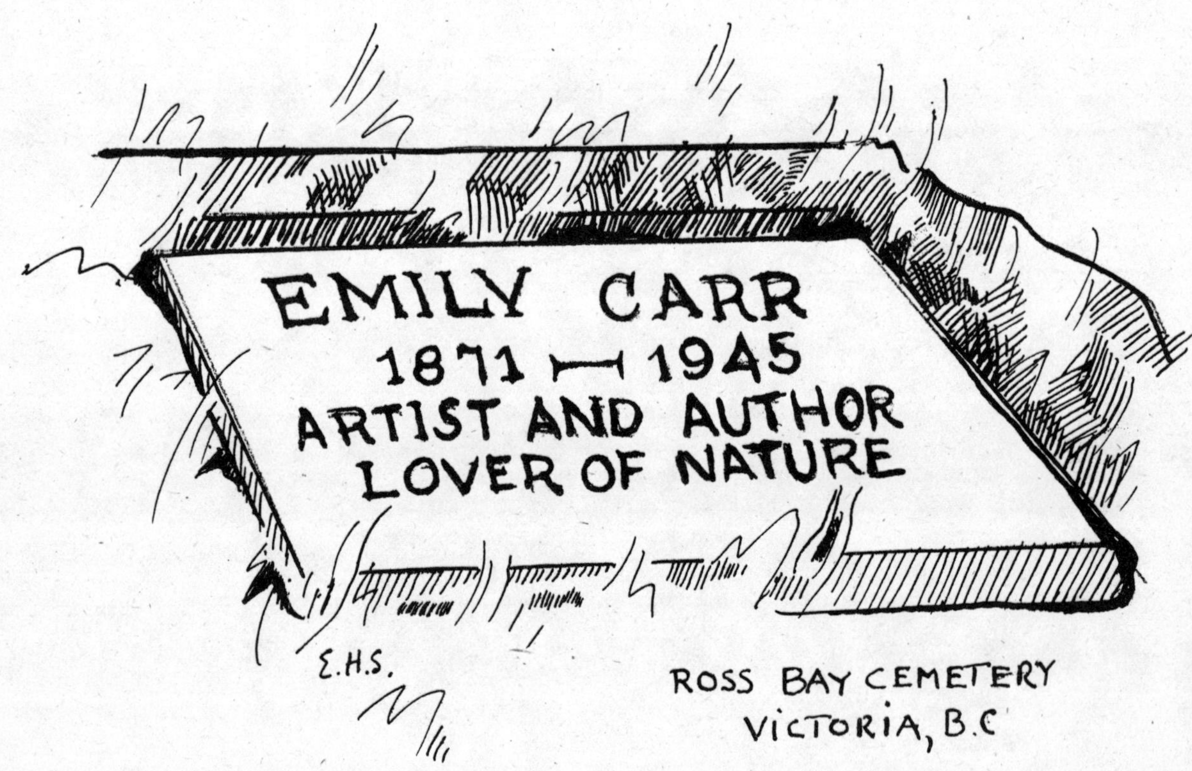

The Meeting and Marriage of Mr. and Mrs. Richard Carr

Fortunately, Richard Carr, a native of Kent, England, was much more methodical and precise about dates than his exasperatingly inexact youngest daughter Emily. He has left us a fascinating diary*—an exciting and romantic tale which reveals much about Richard in his youth. Indeed, by inference, we learn a great deal about Emily herself since, despite her vehement denials, she inherited many of his traits of character, both good and bad. More than the other children, she seems also to have resembled him physically, and thus was spared the long, sharp noses of three of the sisters. Even her talents were derived from her father: his eager interest in daguerreotype and determined efforts to earn his living as a photographer suggest a latent and undeveloped feeling for art. His natural ability for writing is unmistakable. A good reporter, he used his fine powers of observation and description with telling effect in relating his adventures on sea and land. In addition to this, he had wit, as had Emily. She was perhaps the more tart, but Richard, released by his sex and deckhand's attitudes from the inhibitions imposed on Emily by Victorian society, was racier. Yet a certain primness filters through, and in his rough seaman's way Richard Carr was a gentleman, just as Emily was very much a lady. Spelling was difficult for both, but Emily was a generation better and had had more schooling.

* *PABC*

Poor and uneducated, Richard left home at age nineteen to roam the world and seek his fortune. Reaching London in August 1836, he embarked on a steamer ("passage ruff") bound for "Calis" (Calais), the first leg of a thirteen-year vagabond voyage. Storm-tossed ships took him to many exotic, almost unknown and inaccessible lands which, despite grave perils, he explored fearlessly, alone, on horseback and on foot. In his description of one, Yucatan, it is evident that even Emily's love of animals, and her sympathy for Indians were also inherited from her father. He recounts how his dog "Spot," his faithful friend and companion for the next eleven years, frightened off brigands, cutthroats, dangerous animals and snakes while he slept. And he was indignant because of Mexico's treatment of the Indian. Still more reminiscent of Emily is his story of the birds he took home with him to England in 1861: "Have brought with me a dog and five mountain and twelve valey [sic] quail . . . my intention is to breed them. I have no doubt they will thrive well here." This is exactly the same story, in reverse, of Emily's plan, while in an English sanatorium about forty years later, to breed English songbirds there and bring them back to Canada.

Richard's long, adventurous wanderings ended in Guayaquil, "Equador," in 1848 when, after failing for the fourth time to establish himself in daguerreotype photography, he made the momentous decision that eventually led to his marriage, and to Emily's birth in Victoria in 1871. On October 21 we find the following entry in his diary:

> . . . news has got here that extensive gold mines have been discovered in Upper California and that labour is paid for at a most exorbient [sic] price. . . . I have got to leave here and perhaps shall do better their [sic] than elsewhere though the Americans I detest in all the time that I have been with them I have not become acquainted with one that could with propriety be termed a gentleman.

Thus Richard, like thousands of others, was lured to California by the gold rush fever. Late 1849 he settled in Alviso. He did not find gold in the mines, but in the provisioning of miners because, as he wrote, "those who did not dig took up goods [to the mines] and traded with those who did." He traded with miners and others until he eventually had a flourishing business which made him a wealthy man in a few years.

This, in brief, was Emily's father.

Much less is known about the mother. She remains a shadowy figure despite all that Emily has written about her love, devotion and untimely death—a blow from which Emily never fully recovered.

There is no one alive today who can tell us what Mrs. Carr was like. Aside from Emily's short description—"a small, grey-eyed, dark-haired woman with pink cheeks"*—only two photographs in the British Columbia Provincial Archives, taken while she was still young, give us any clue as to her appearance. A real brunette, her straight hair is coiled back severely from an unsmiling, thoughtful and attractive face. The features bear no resemblance to Emily's. She is petite and elegantly dressed. What surprises us most, however, is her apparent daintiness—a quality conspicuously lacking in her daughters.

* Growing Pains, *p.11*

Emily presents Mrs. Carr to us as a person of almost angelic virtues: a gentle, kind, loving mother and a patient, submissive, obedient wife. But we must be just a little wary. Her portrayal of her father as a martinet seems to me, particularly after reading his diary, somewhat distorted and unfair, and her account of his early life is less than accurate. Has she also described a make-believe mother? Was she covering up? The answers to these questions may never be known but, for me at least, this apparently meek, colorless and tiresome woman suddenly comes alive in the pages of Richard's diary. She emerges from between the lines as a warm human being with faults and failings like the rest of us. She begins to glow and have meaning.

From the outset, Richard's diary holds us spellbound; but the real jolt comes in 1854 when we read, unbelieving, that he met Emily's mother in California. This presents us with a dilemma since Emily has both said and written* that her father "went back to England, married an English girl and brought his bride out to California. . . ." And yet, there she is, in somewhat ambiguous circumstances, still unmarried. Few, if any, of Emily's old family friends knew that Mr. and Mrs. Carr had met in California, and none can now recall anything about Mrs. Carr's childhood and youth. Even Richard seems to conspire to keep her background a secret as he records nothing about her life in California or how she got there. Was she also in search of gold? Of adventure? Of a husband? Perhaps she came out on one of the bride ships which brought hundreds of girls, mostly orphans, from the old world to the new to start life afresh as wives of pioneer men.

* The Book of Small, *p.75*

A man of courage and resource himself, it is disappointing that Richard could not recognize and value the same qualities in his bride and write more fully and openly about their relationship. This was a perfect setting for an unusual frontier romance, and yet we can only conjecture about their meeting and their love and courtship. We feel cheated — our curiosity unassuaged. In fact, Richard mentions Emily's mother only once before their marriage—in four laconic words at the end of an entry late in 1854:

> Having on the whole been very successful since I have been in California have concluded to enjoy myself for six months or so in traveling. . . . Left San Francisco in the steamer "Golden Gate" for Panama. Miss E. Saunders accompanies me.

Since Miss Saunders is demonstrably none other than the future Mrs. Richard Carr,* we read this announcement with

* *Positively identified by a copy of the Carr marriage certificate in the possession of Frederick J. Brand.*

marked surprise. The image of a saintly woman is shattered and replaced by that of a lively, unconventional girl, who may, of course, have had in her the seeds of saintliness. She clearly left home young and alone, like Richard, as no father is ever mentioned and her mother lived in Freeland, Oxfordshire, five-and-a-half miles north-west of Oxford. Years later, on a visit to a Mrs. Quantack in Bristol, Richard wrote that she "was formerly in California. Emily and her used to live in the same house there."

Emily Saunders flouted the conventions for respectable girls when she accompanied Richard on his long holiday trip to England, even if marriage was planned on arrival; but her courage and initiative must be admired, as such a voyage in those days was arduous and full of risks and uncertainties. They booked first-class passage from San Francisco to Panama, then took a side trip to the Island of Tobago while waiting for the steamer "Valdevia," a "slow-propeller," to take them still farther south to Guayaquil, Ecuador, and several cities in Peru. Back in Panama, the hair-raising crossing of the isthmus began:

> Engaged mules to take me (and seven others) to the railroad station about fifteen miles from here. . . . The first part of the road passable latter part bad. mule sinks in the mud up to the girths of the saddle. . . . Left (summit and railway station) in cars for Aspinwall. On the road we had the pleasure of seeing the cars turned bottom up in two or three places, where they had run of [sic] the track on former occasions.

Even the intrepid Richard breathed a hearty sigh of relief when they reached the port of Aspinwall—now Colón. Boarding another ship there and traveling via Cartagena, Colombia, and St. Thomas, they landed at Southampton on December 31, 1854.

The next entry, on January 18, 1855, announces tersely:

> Got married at E[y]nsham Church, Oxon.

Emily writes that her father brought his bride to California in a sailing ship all around Cape Horn.* But this also is not true. Richard and Emily Carr went back to England together only twice. As described above, the first trip home was by steamer on the Pacific and, after crossing the isthmus, steamer again on the Atlantic. The return journey is not recorded, but it is evident that they took the same time-saving route, as Richard had only planned to stay away from his business for six months. He would just as certainly have been unable to resist the urge to log his adventures and the ship's progress had he traveled by sailing ship for the first time.

* The Book of Small, *p.75.*

However, in April 1861, when the Carrs went back to England a second time, planning to stay, they did sail around Cape Horn, presumably because they were burdened with two small children and household effects. Leaving San Francisco on a fast sailing ship, with only two other passengers on board, and "passing everything we came across," including many privateers, they "Hove too [sic] in Liverpool after a delightful passage of 96 days." This was their one and only trip on a sailing vessel. In 1863, disenchanted with England, they decided to settle in the New Land for good. Even with children, they again went by steamer to Colón and were fortunate, after crossing the isthmus, to travel from Panama to San Francisco on the "Constitution," "the largest and finest on the Pacific."

The Carr family returned to Alviso, where Richard had lived eleven years and three months, and where his two oldest children were born, but they stayed only briefly—just long enough to settle Richard's business affairs. For now he had a new dream, and a new destination, which would end his roaming forever and allow him to live in the New Land and under the British flag at the same time. He dreamed of Victoria.

The last leg of Richard's fabulous odyssey began on June 28, 1863 when he and his family boarded the SS "Brother Jonathon" at San Francisco and set sail for "Vancouver's Island." Landing at Esquimalt, they proceeded by stage to Victoria, a bustling town of 6,000 inhabitants, seven churches, three daily newspapers and high prices. The inflated prices were the result of British Columbia's own gold rush a few years earlier when at times, Richard writes, "as many as 3,000 people landed here in a day . . . on their way to the new gold mines of the Frazier [sic] river." He was "agreeably surprised" with the beauty of Victoria's location and immediately began clearing enough wooded land in James Bay to build the fine mansion in which Emily was born eight years later.

Although our knowledge of Emily Saunders Carr at the end of this saga is not appreciably greater than when we met her in Alviso, before she was a wife and mother, the overriding impression is that of an enterprising girl full of life and vitality. But she did not remain so for long. Marriage, the birth of nine babies, and tuberculosis quickly subdued her. Richard changed too. He was as successful in his "Wholesale Groceries and Liquors" business on Wharf Street in Victoria as he had been in California and, putting his carefree past behind him, he became a solid family man and respected burgher. But, according to Emily, he also became an autocrat and bigot.

Since our impressions of both parents have been largely formed by Emily's writings and conversations, it is refreshing and reassuring to meet in the pages of Richard's diary a very different and much more likable Mr. and Mrs. Carr.

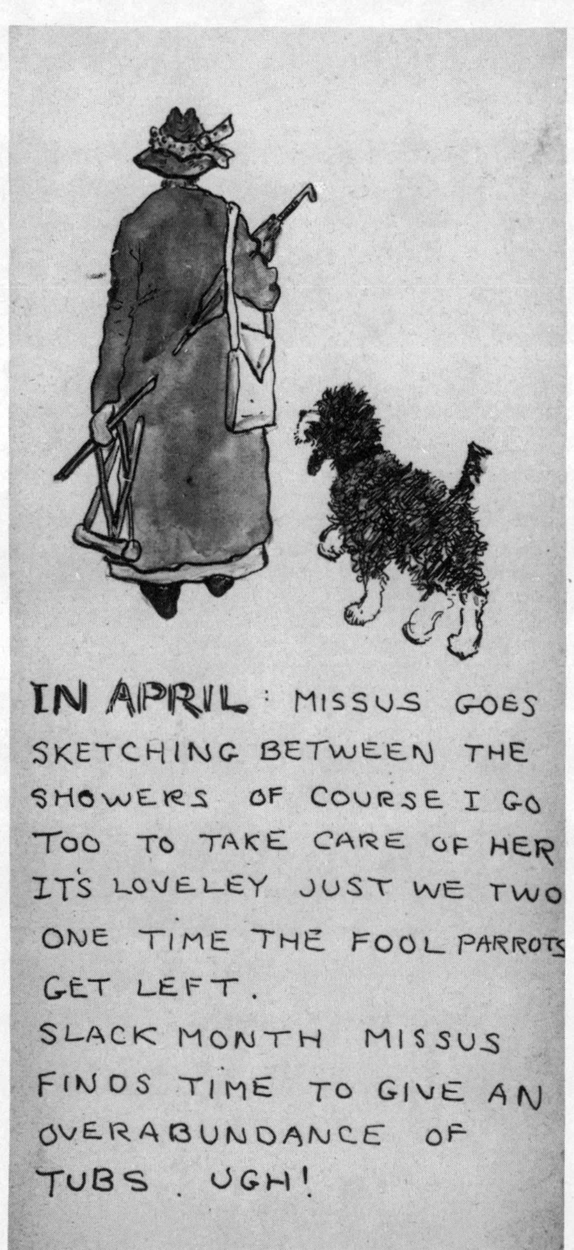

A Family Album

Mr. and Mrs. Richard Carr *PABC*

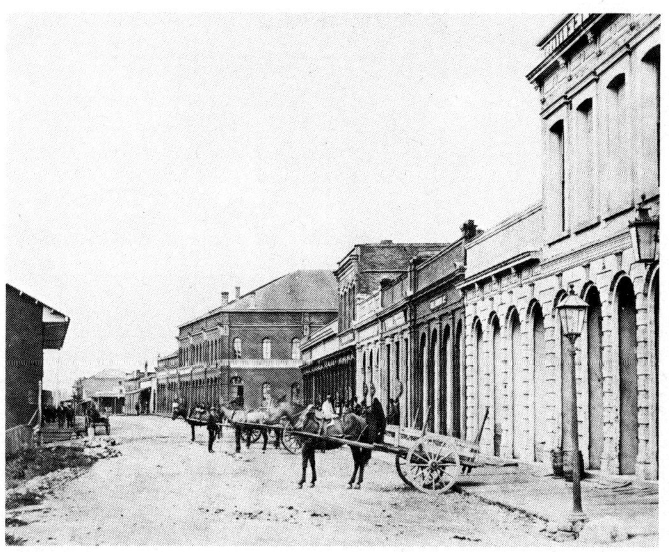

Richard Carr's store on Wharf Street, Victoria, in the 1870's, is the fourth building from the right. It is still in use.

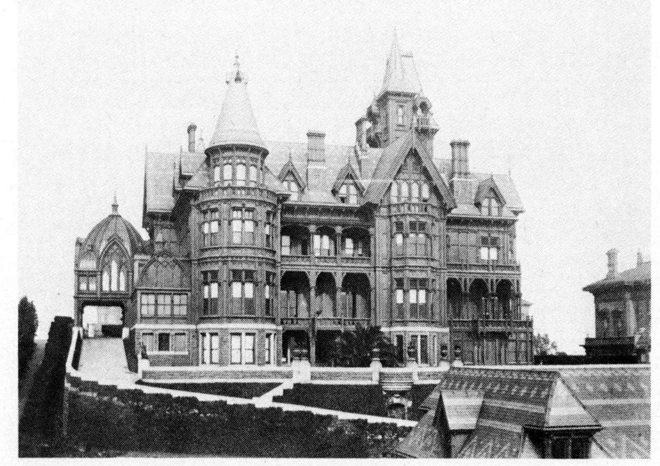

Old Mark Hopkins Mansion in San Francisco. Occupied by the Mark Hopkins Institute of Art in 1893, while Emily was still a student. Destroyed by fire in 1906, the school was reopened in 1907 in a building erected on the foundation of the ruined mansion. *Bancroft Library, U.C. Berkeley, California*

Architectural Museum in London, built 1869. It housed the Westminster School of Art commencing circa 1888. Emily Carr enrolled there 1899.

Architectural Association

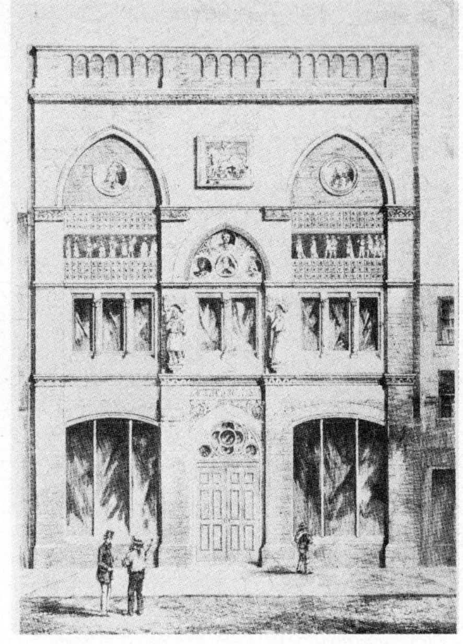

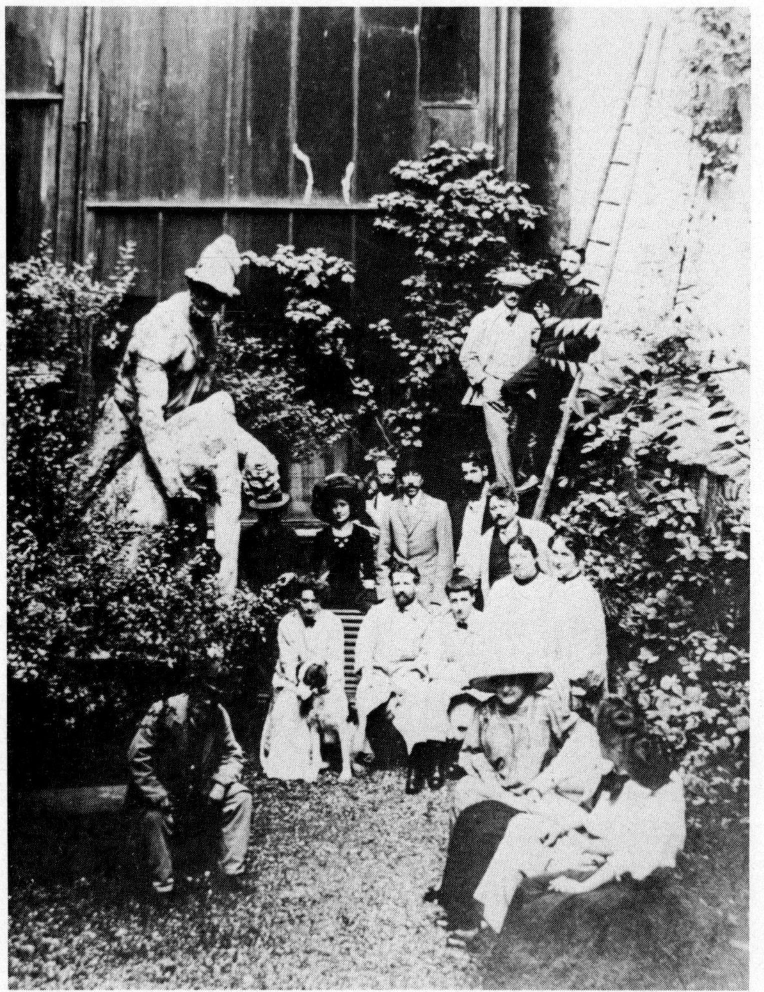

Teachers and students in the courtyard of the Académie Colarossi in Paris, which Emily Carr attended in 1910.

ACADÉMIE
COLAROSSI

ERNEST COLAROSSI Fils, Succr
10, Rue de la Grande-Chaumière

MÉTRO : Vavin, Raspail,
Notre-Dame des Champs.

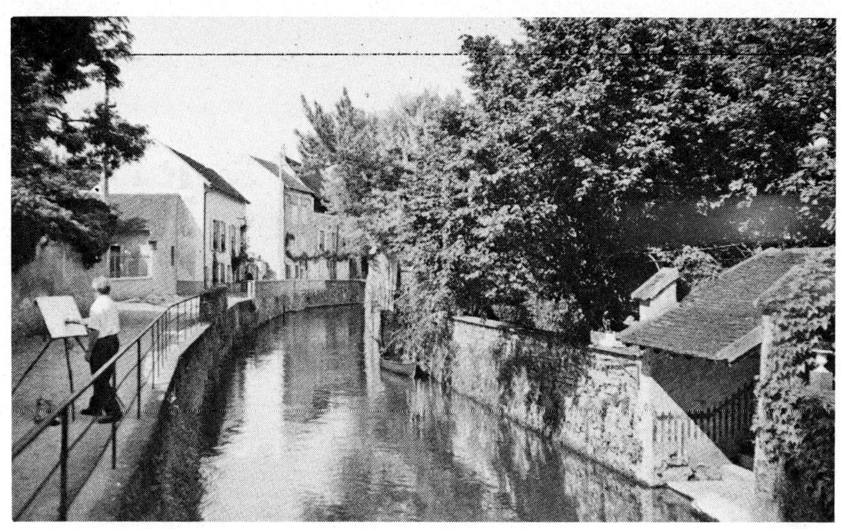

Crécy-la-Chapelle

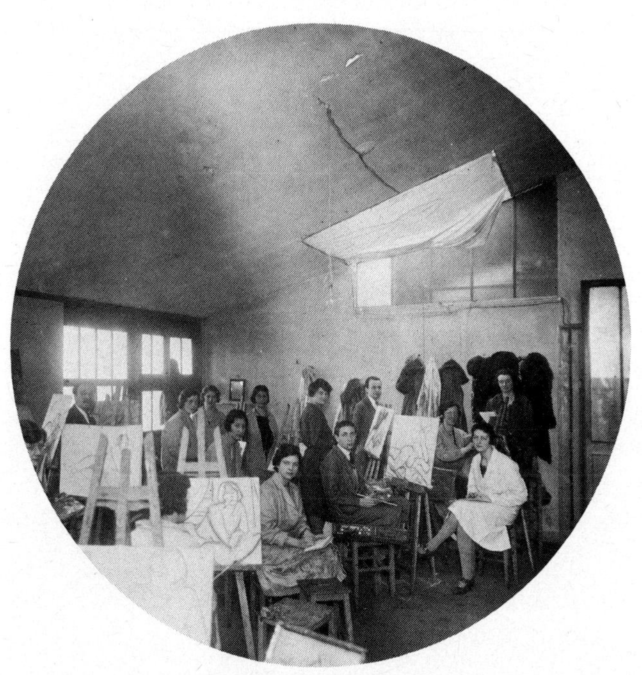

André Lhote's Paris studio

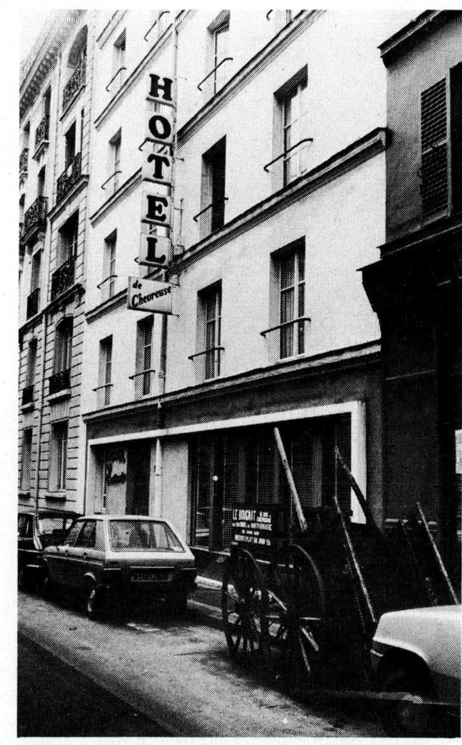

Hôtel de Chevreuse, Paris, where Emily Carr lived in 1911.
Canadian Embassy, Paris

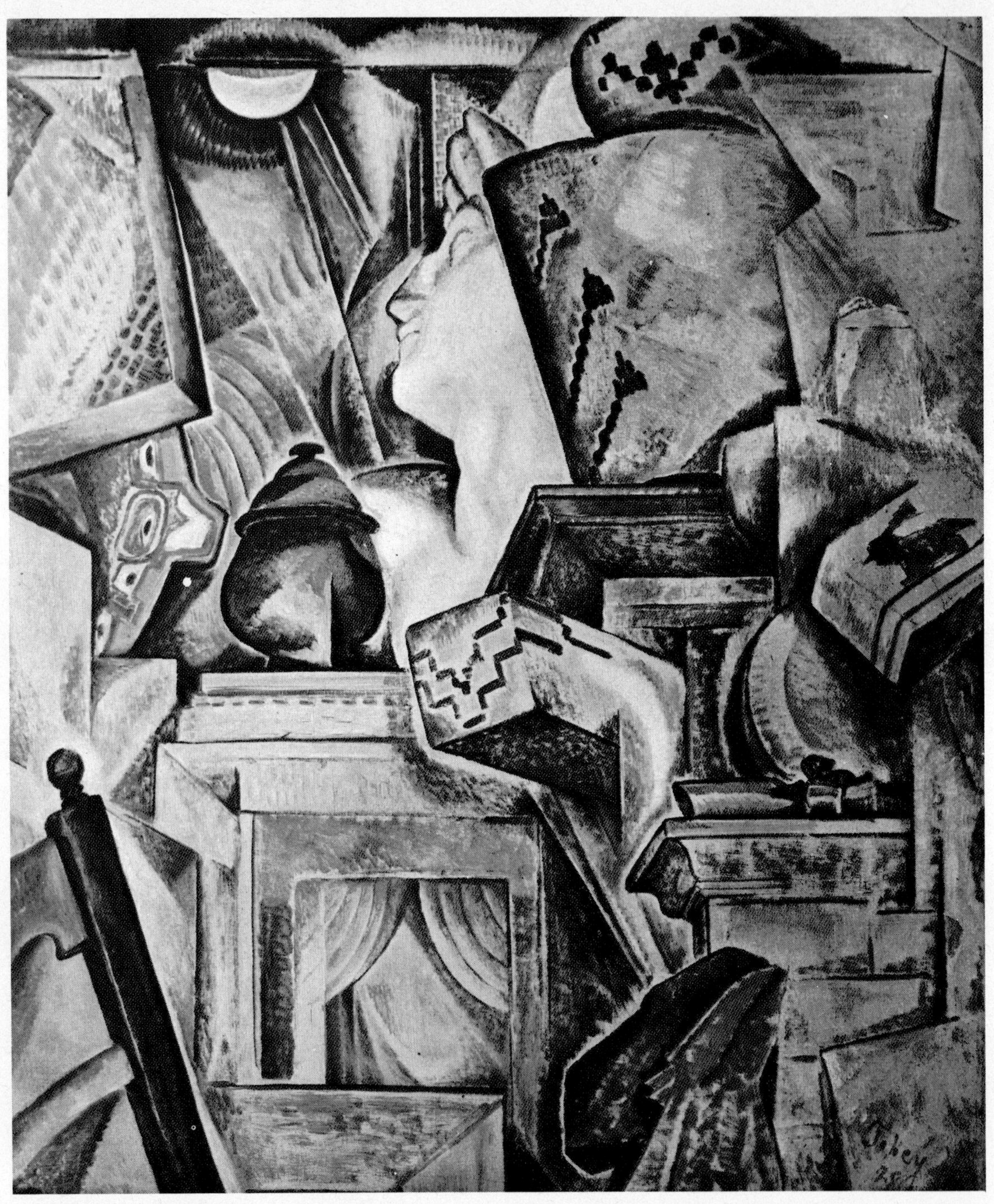

 Emily Carr's Studio by Mark Tobey, 1928 *collection: Mrs. Soren Juul, Woodinville, Washington*

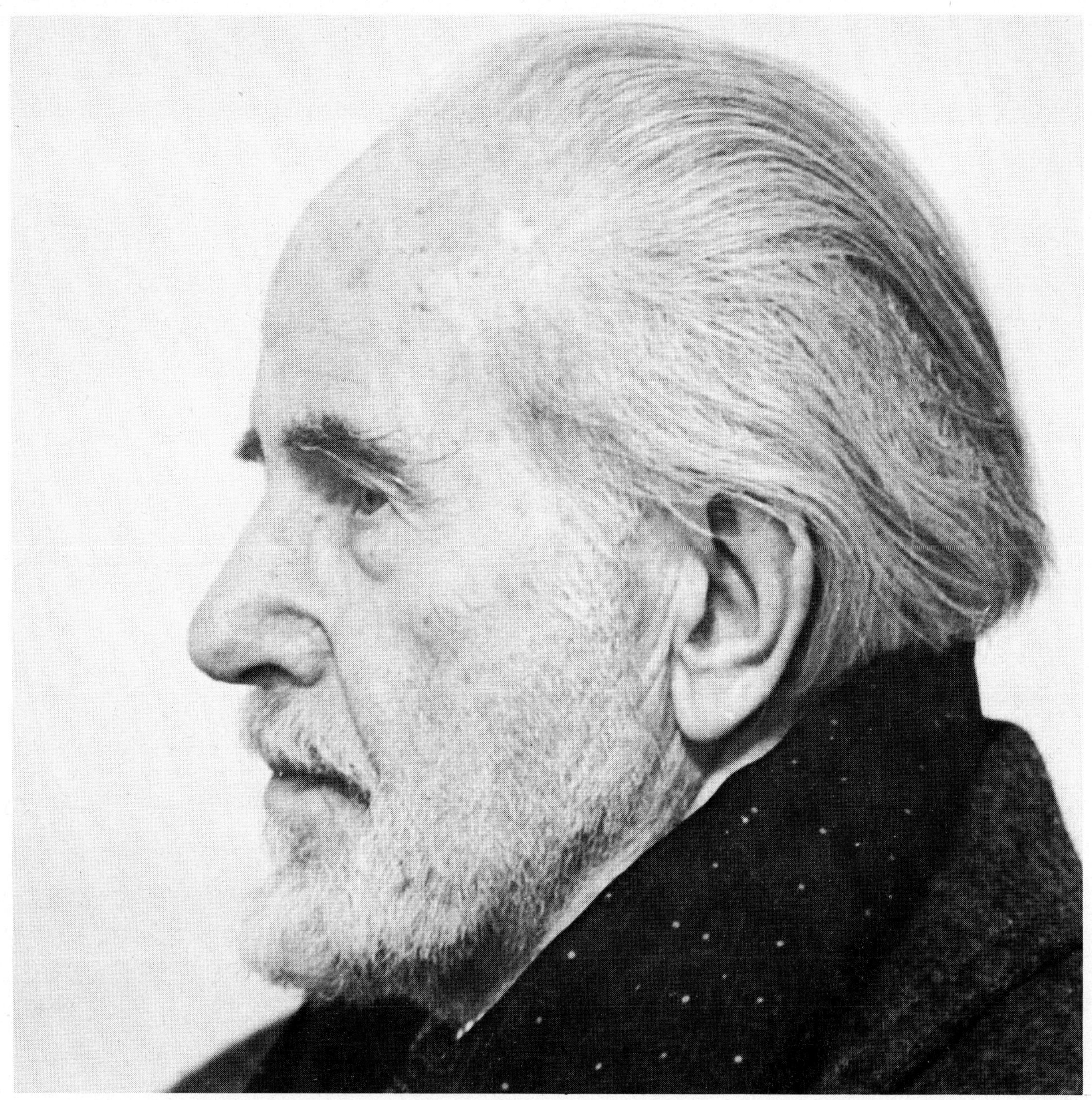

Mark Tobey in Basel, Switzerland in 1969 *Kurt Wyss*

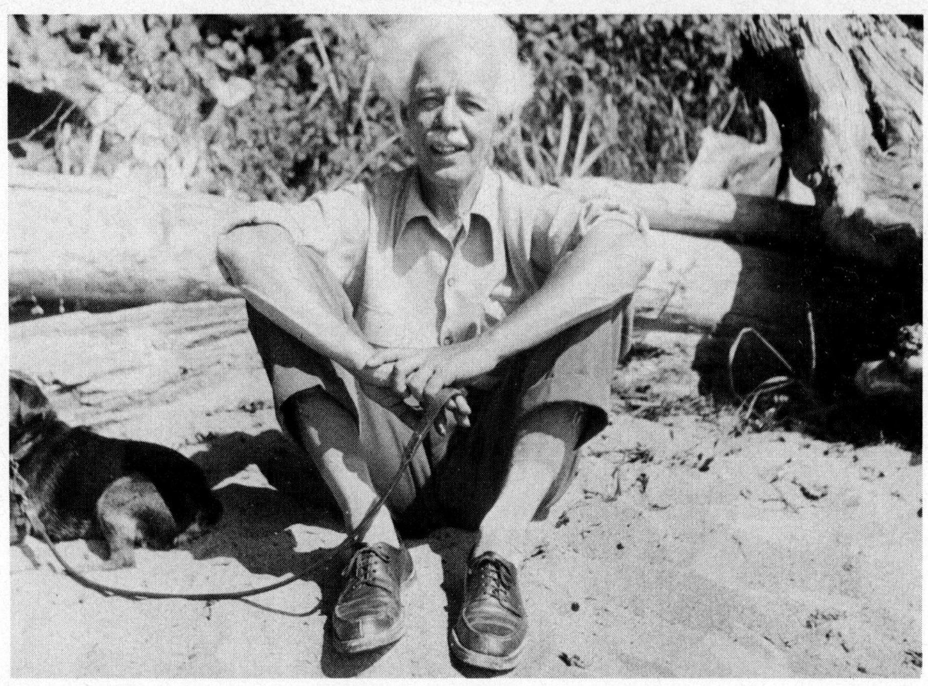

Lawren Harris in Vancouver, circa 1948. Photograph by his daughter Peggi Harris Knox.

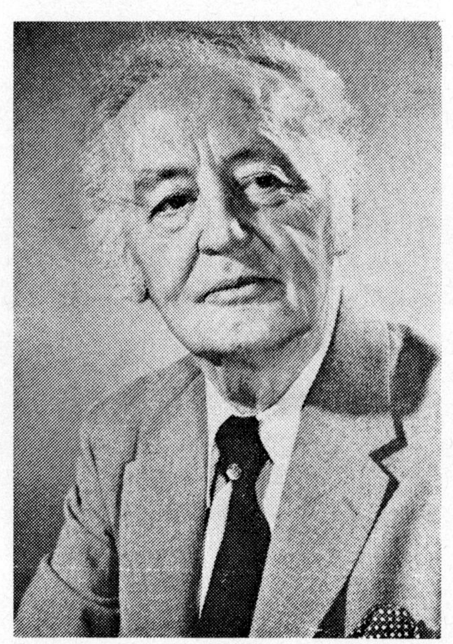

Marius Barbeau

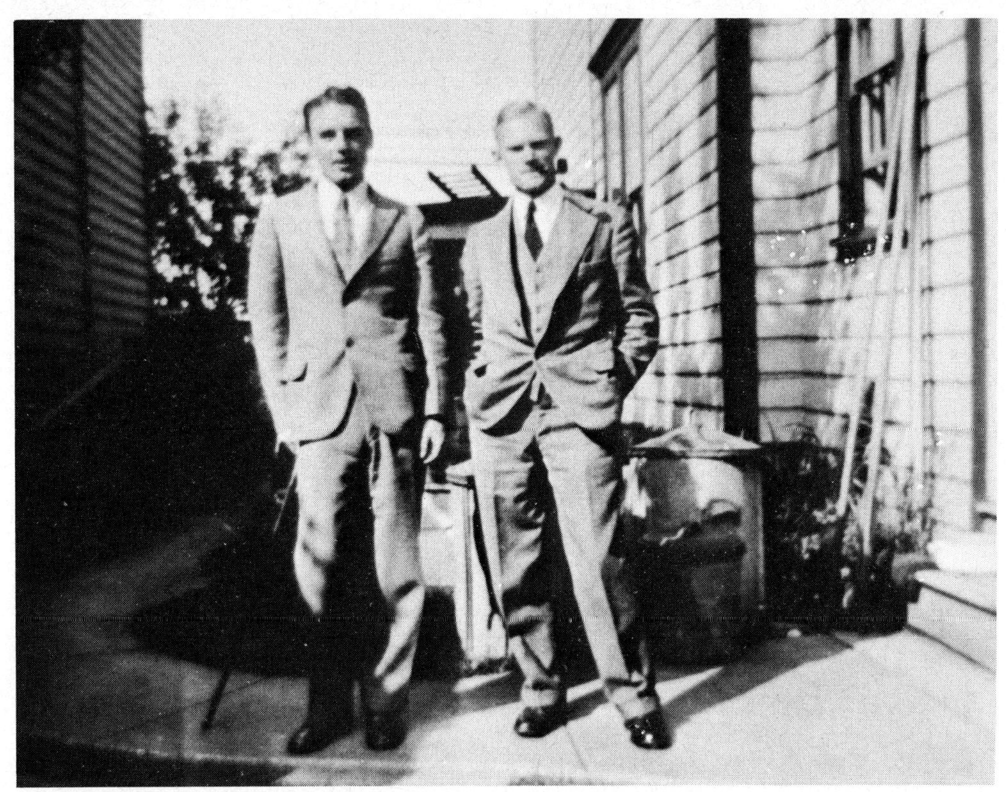

Frederick Brand and Max Maynard , circa 1930

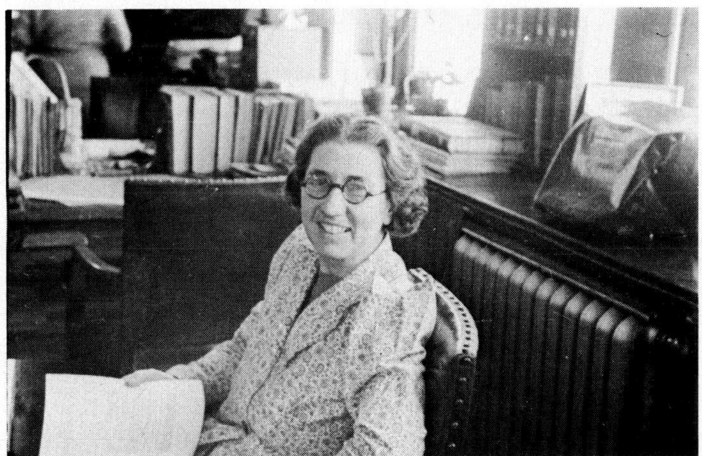

Madge Wolfenden, circa 1932 *Harold Walker*

Sketching Sites:

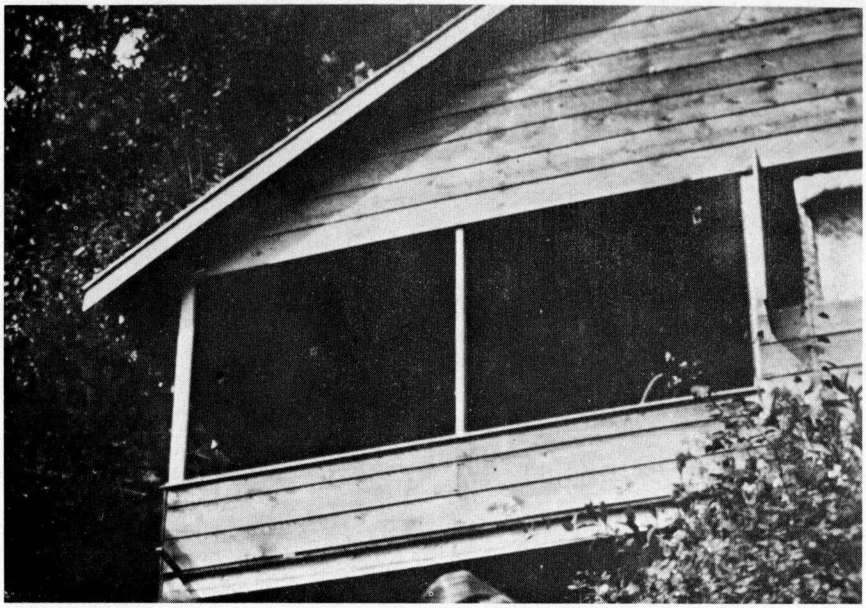

1. The Hembroff summer cottage on Cordova Bay Road in Victoria, where Emily and the author sketched in May 1931. Emily did many of her sea, log and beach studies from this veranda. *Photo by the author*

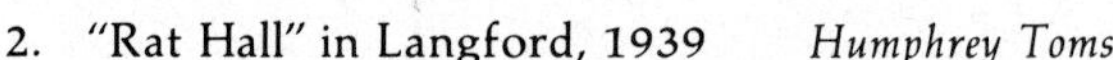

2. "Rat Hall" in Langford, 1939 *Humphrey Toms*

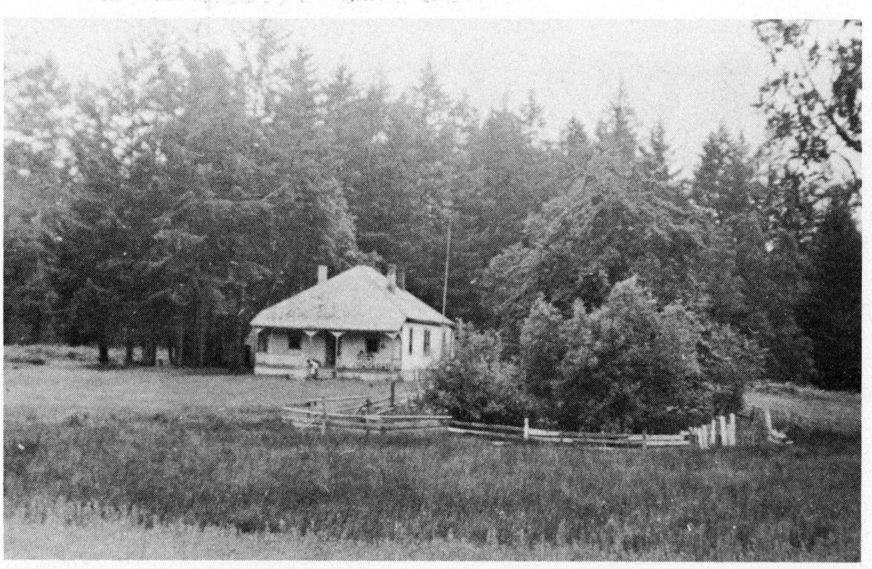

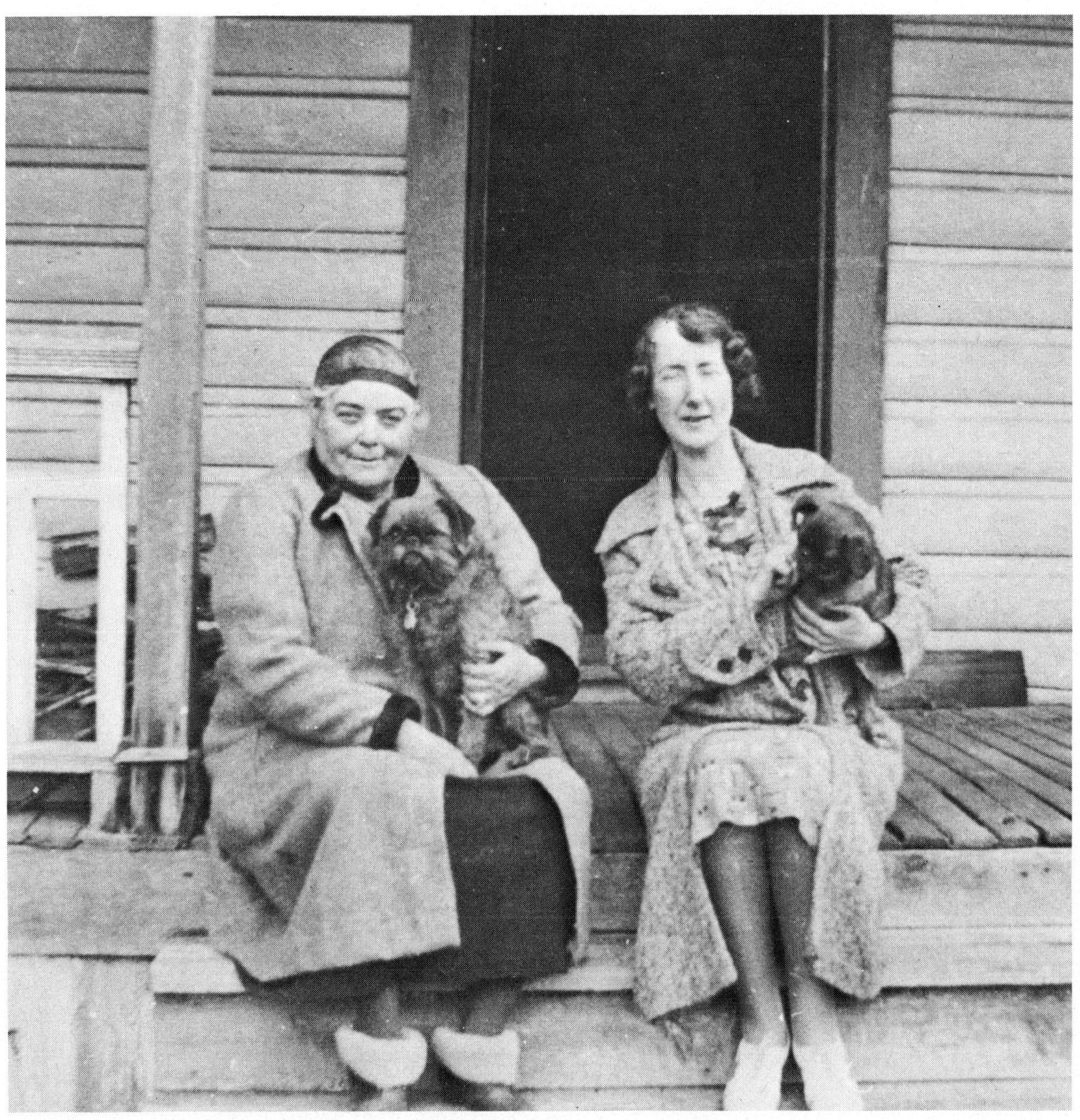

3. Emily and Flora Burns at "Rat Hall" in Langford, 1939. *Humphrey Toms*

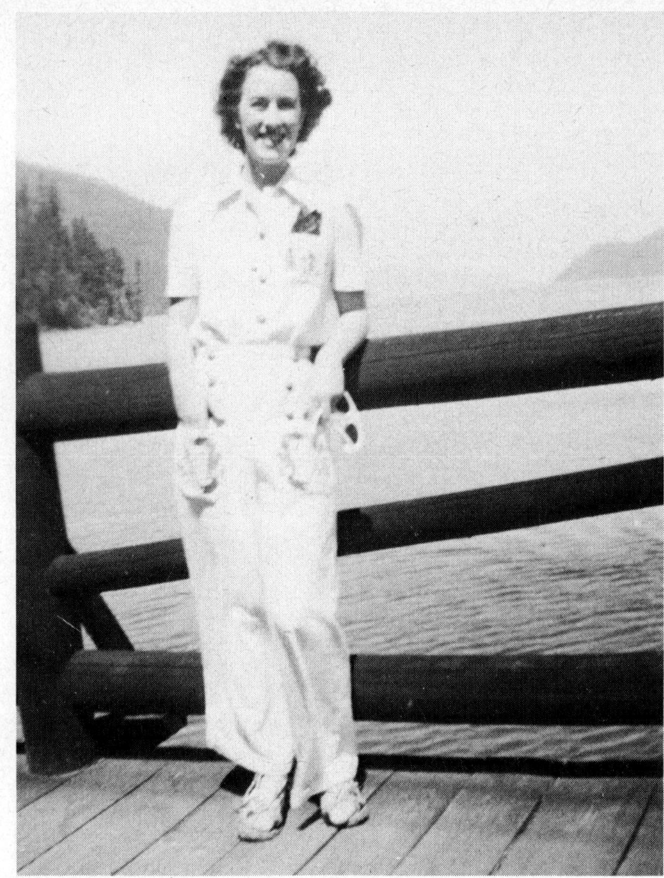

Phylis Dilworth Inglis

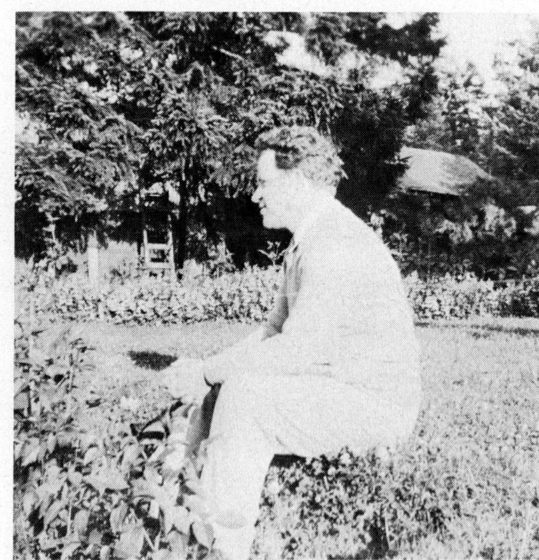

Ira Dilworth

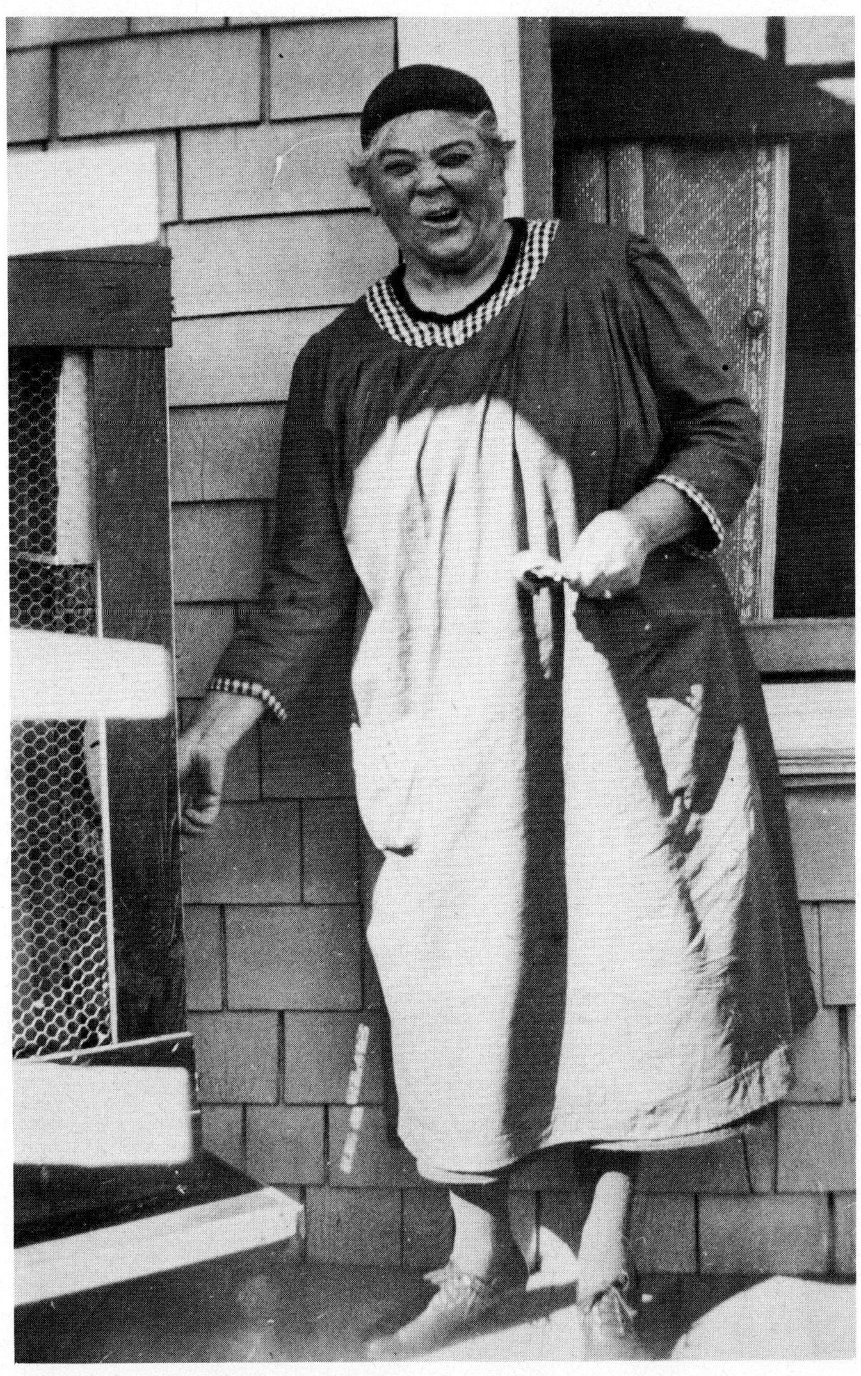

Emily Carr at 316 Beckley Avenue 1936-1940

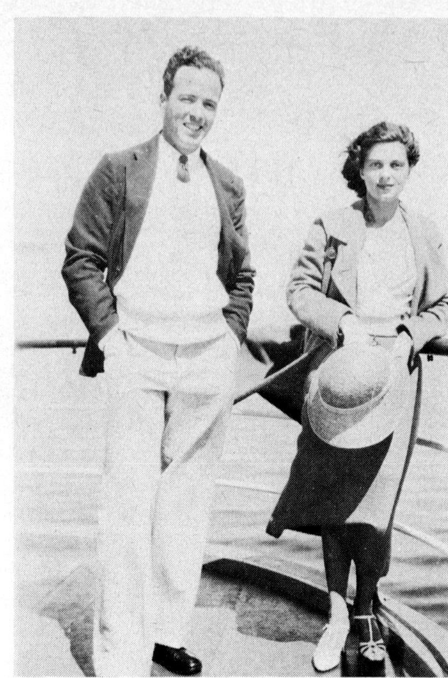

Jack Shadbolt and the author, 1932

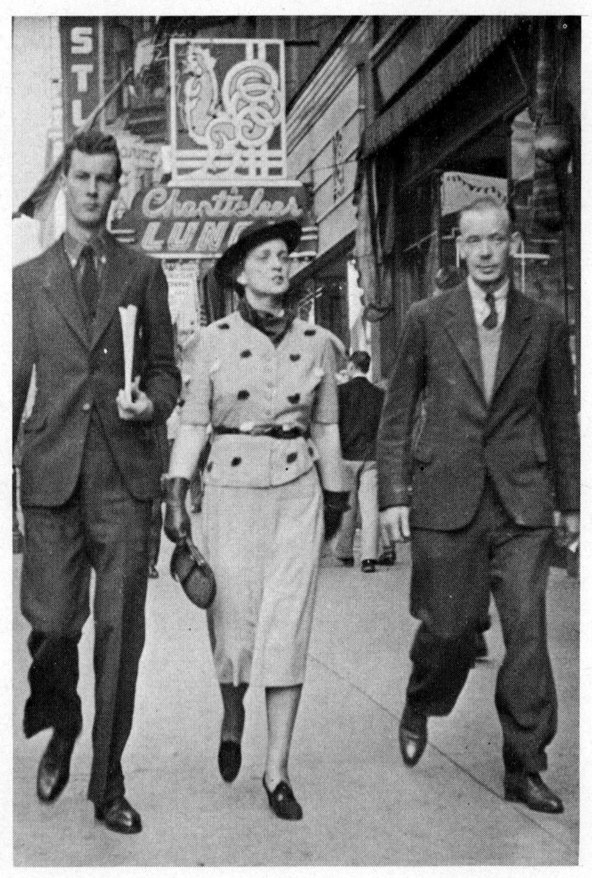

Humphrey Toms, Nan Cheney, J.W.G. Macdonald

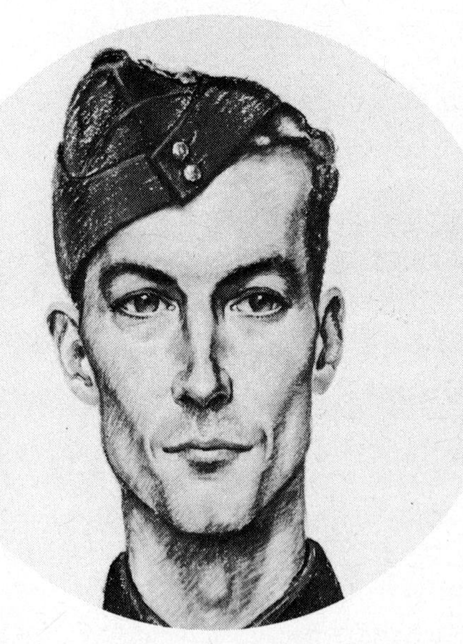

Humphrey Toms by Nan Cheney, 1941

Margaret Clay, circa 1960

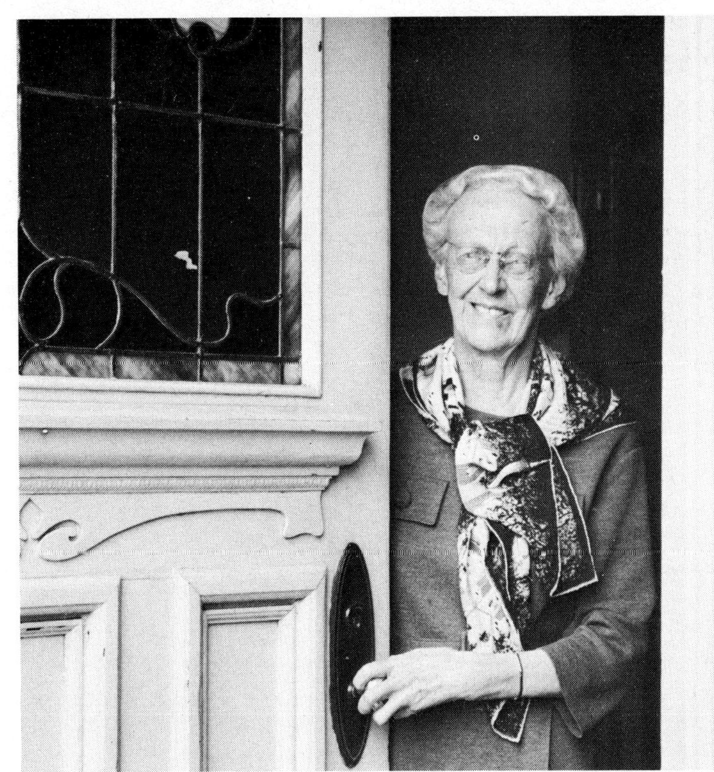

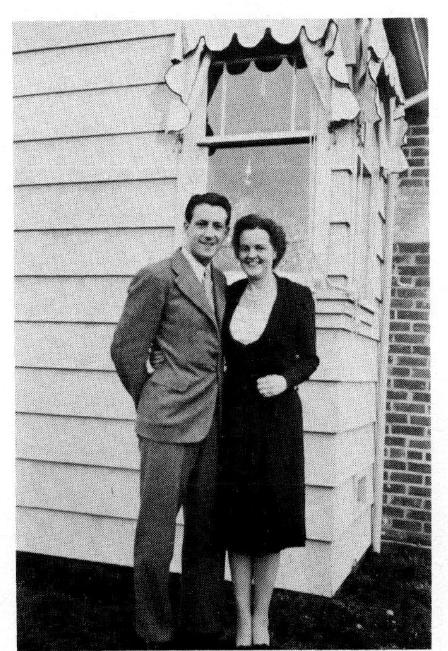

Jack and Edna Parnall, circa 1942.

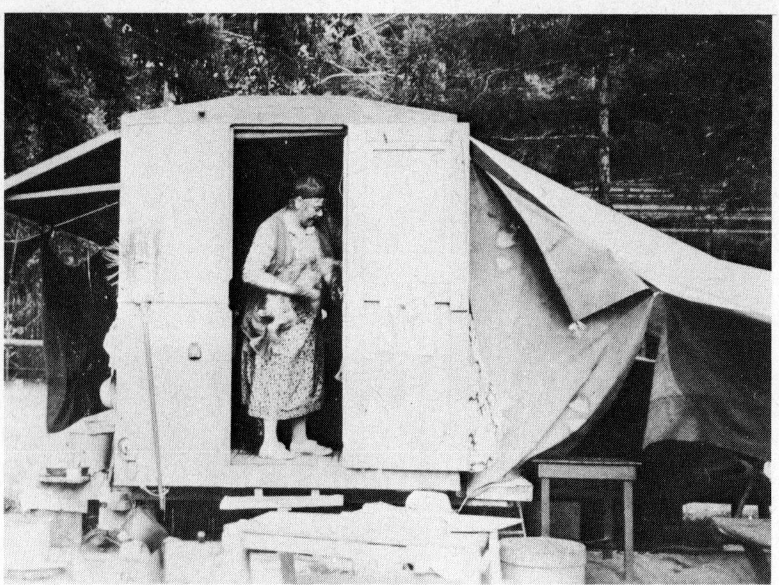

Emily and the "Elephant" in 1936 at Metchosin.
Helen Hembroff-Ruch

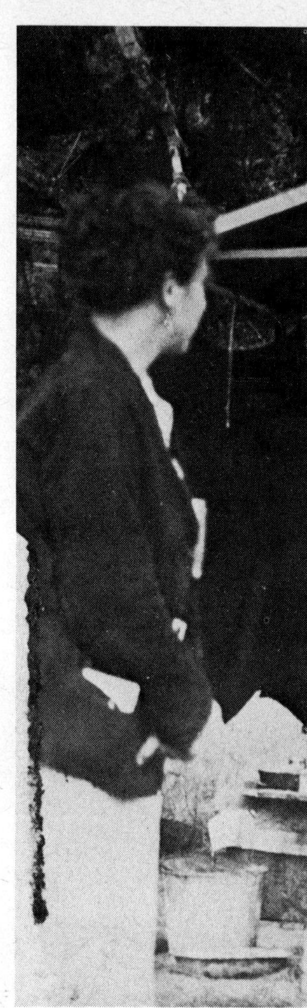

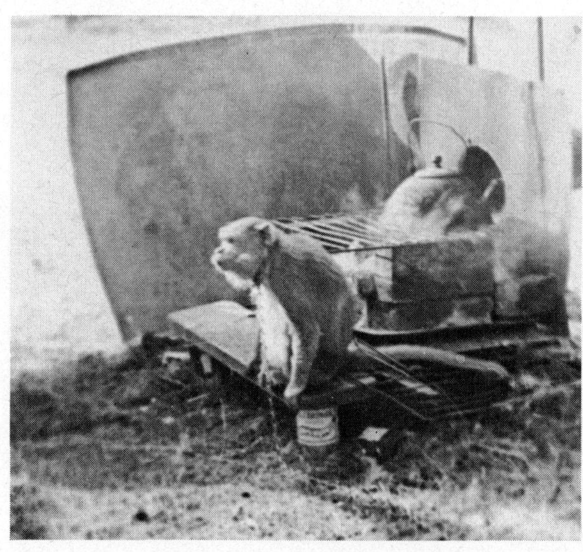

Woo warming her backside while waiting for tea.
Photo by the author

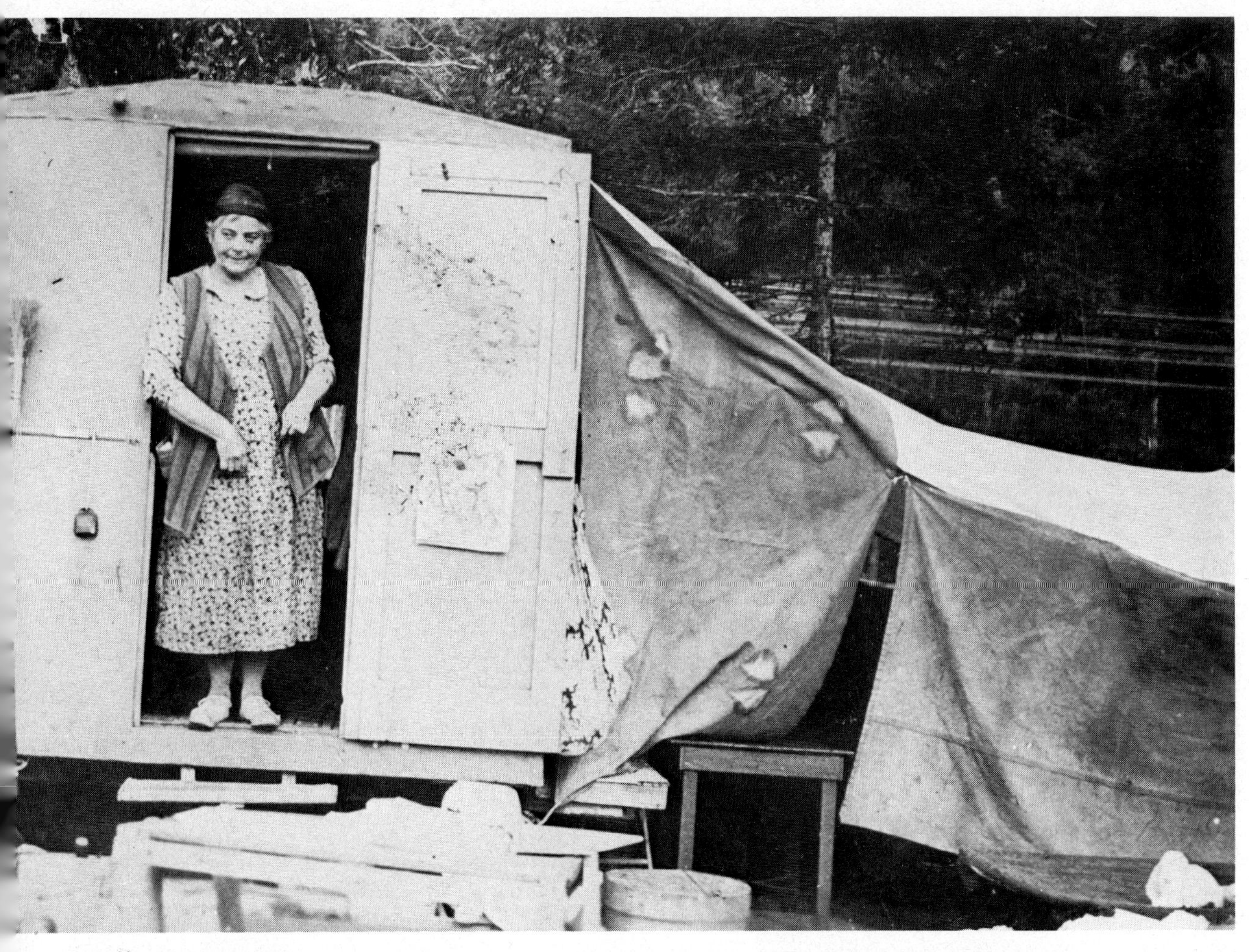

Emily with Ruth Hembroff-Herrington. Metchosin, 1936. *Edythe Hembroff-Schleicher*

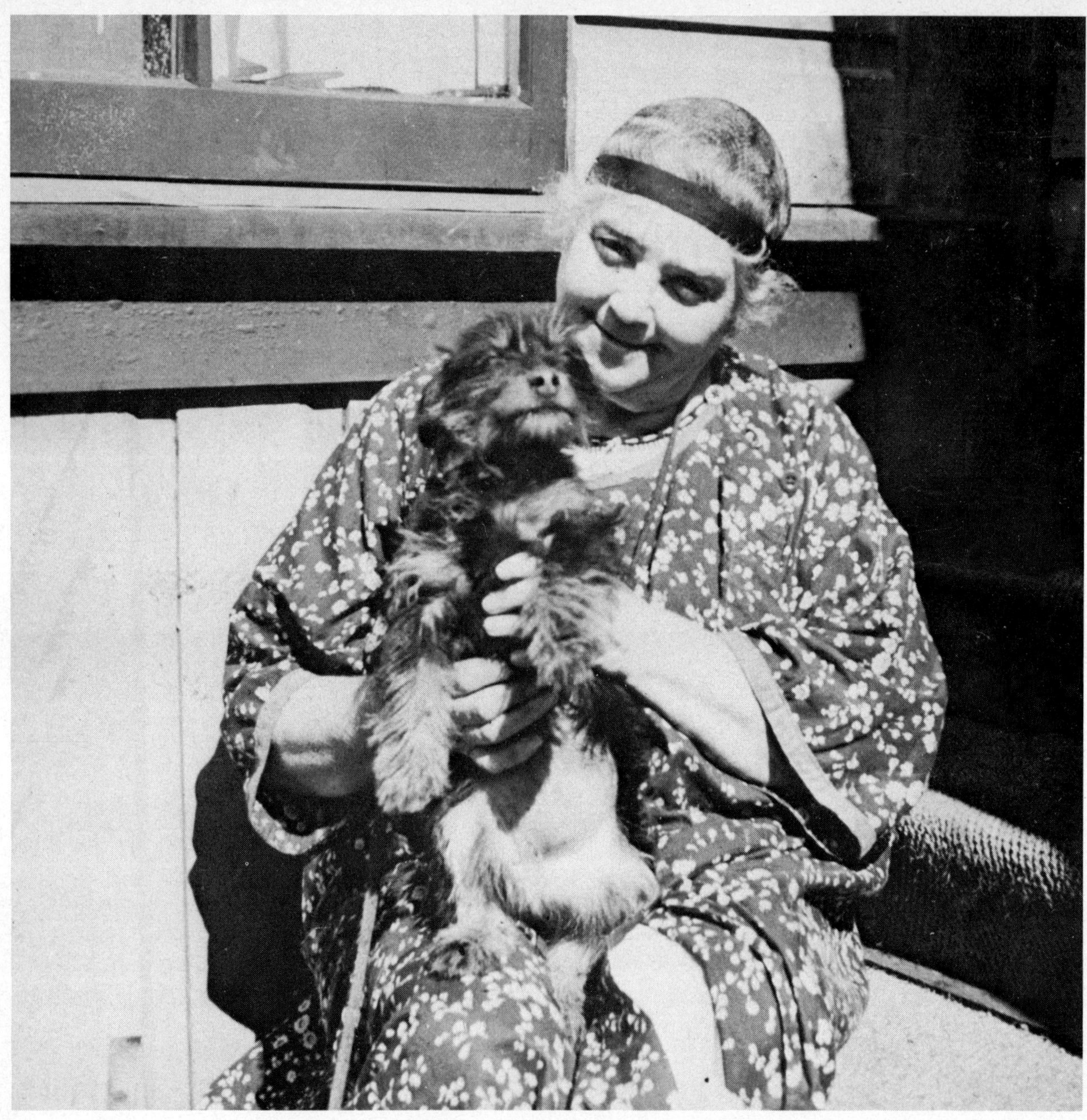

Cover photo: 1944

Last known photo of Emily Carr with the last of her dogs, on the veranda of the studio on St. Andrew's Street. Photograph by the author.

Emily Carr as a Painter

As a painter, Emily Carr was a prodigious producer—a late bloomer always racing against time. In her hurry to interpret for us, before time ran out, the great British Columbia forests with which she had so strong a sense of identification, her sketches, which literally flew from her brush, may sometimes appear a little careless, even breathless. But it is incredible how many important canvasses resulted from these sketches during her later years. She led us by the hand into her own special world of imagination and vision.

In her earlier years, Emily had also been a prolific painter, ready to face hardship and danger to bring back the fruits, mostly water colors, of long, arduous journeys to Indian villages in the north. Then came the happier, sunnier sketching trips to Crécy-en-Brie, near Paris, and Brittany, which produced her sparkling, impressionist French landscapes and interior genre subjects.

But, after giving up teaching in Vancouver to live again in Victoria, there was a gaping hole in the middle of Emily's career, from 1913 to 1927 (often called the "desert years"),* when she was too busy catering to the whims of boarders and tenants and focusing on other demeaning bread-winning activities to find much time, money, or even desire for regular painting.

She tells us that she stopped painting for about fifteen years,* and although we know now that she greatly exaggerated, we, her friends, believed her implicitly. We commiserated with her and, like a flock of parrots, indignantly repeated this presumed injustice. Yet not only was she not entirely ignored by the art world and public during these hard, lean years (when, most days being meatless, I suspect she subsisted largely on that appalling gruel she dished up for our breakfasts at camp, and those hard, flat, soda-tasting tea-biscuits, made in a fry pan, we had for supper),* she actually found time for considerable "recreational painting." Indeed, besides managing to fit in frequent painting excursions to Indian villages on Vancouver Island and the lower mainland in the summer, she apparently sketched off and on throughout the twenties at Sproat Lake, a few hours bus ride from Victoria, while visiting the owner of

* Emily Carr: A Centennial Exhibition *(1971 edition) p.26.*

* *Among other places, in* Growing Pains, *p.312.*

* *Mrs. Gertrude Ball, Victoria, who was Emily's boarder in 1925, says the Indian helper always brought her cold, stiff porridge and cold, soggy toast for breakfast, but found the other meals acceptable. She was, however, only 21 at the time and not very critical, being too enchanted when she woke in the morning to find a monkey swinging from the door handle and a cockatoo perched on the headboard of the bed to find much fault with anything.*

Klitsa Lodge, which at one time is said to have housed a collection of Emily's paintings.* During the twenties, too, she began working with Mark Tobey.

* Kelowna Courier, *December 8, 1959.*

In addition, she often packed her paint box and a bag of provisions and stole away from her domestic responsibilities to relax and sketch for a few days in her summer cottage in Oak Bay*—a pseudo-English municipality (later scarcely tolerated by Emily) whose residents still live complacently behind the "tweed curtain" separating them from Victoria, preoccupied with the past and their own superiority.

* *494 Victoria Avenue.*

None of Emily's friends ever saw this Oak Bay refuge, nor did she herself mention it. But rumors of its existence crystallized into concrete fact a few years ago when it was offered for sale and Emily's name was used for promotion. Soon afterwards, it was brought to my attention by the owner—an elderly lady who had lived in the cottage for twenty-four years. Local gossip had it, she said, that Emily had built it herself, nail by nail, in 1912, with the help of "one old carpenter," but had tragically lost it for tax arrears a few months after moving in. Well, the facts are not quite so pathetic as presented in the little old lady's tale. On searching the title, I found that Emily did indeed build the cottage herself (though in 1913, not 1912), that she kept it until 1919, then sold it (at a profit, I hope) with a clear title. But how curious that she could afford to build a cottage, or even a dog house, in 1913—the year she had to borrow money to build her House of All Sorts.* Yet she lived and sketched in Oak Bay intermittently for six years; and a few of the older residents in the area still remember seeing her walking to the beach, a canvas carry-all slung over her shoulder, dog at heel.

* Growing Pains, *p.310. It is also entered in the deed that her sister Alice had a $5,000 mortgage at 6% on The House of All Sorts as of January 21, 1916. Cancelled April 16, 1923. A talk with the family of the "one old carpenter" also revealed that this part of the story is correct.*

Although Emily destroyed much of her early work, there are still many paintings from this period in the homes of old Victoria families. Her contemporaries say that she also often sketched early in the morning in Beacon Hill Park during these "non-painting" years, and I know that she frequently painted the big, spreading orange-trunked arbutus tree in the garden of the old Newcombe mansion.* One of these pictures is dated 1923,* another, seen recently in a Victoria antique shop, 1919.

* *138 Dallas Road. The house fell into disrepair for many years but has now been at least partially restored to its original splendor and is used, at present, as a home for alcoholics. The beautiful arbutus tree still graces the property. It is now designated a Heritage House.*

* Arbutus Tree. *Collection: Mrs. T.G. Keir, Victoria.*

After 1913 Emily also found time to exhibit: Petulantly, but regularly, at the Island Arts and Crafts Society shows; once at the Victoria Fair; twice in Seattle; and twice in her own studio, though her entries were less likely to be Victoria landscapes than Indian subjects or strong, vibrant paintings done years before in France. Then, in late 1927, when her work was introduced to the East in the Canadian West Coast Art Exhibition at the National

Gallery, her fortunes changed overnight. She was catapulted onto the national scene, and the unproductive years were over.

All this adds up to pretty active inactivity, but however curtailed Emily's painting may have been during these fourteen years, she more than made up for it once she plunged into work in 1928. From then on she never looked back. She painted with unwavering singleness of purpose until illness stayed her brush, and when she died, her studio was crammed with pictures. She had sold scores by then, often for a pittance; she had given away many, sometimes on an impulse just because a friend, or even a stranger, had said a few kind words of praise at a moment when she needed heartening; and she also destroyed many others, usually in a fit of rage or frustration because a particular painting or sketch dissatisfied her.

Occasionally, too, she used her canvasses as packing merely because they were the nearest thing at hand. In the early forties, for instance, she bought an extremely highstrung Australian spaniel which she lovingly trained as a special gift for Ira Dilworth's mother in appreciation of his devoted help. When the day came to ship "Lady Jane" to Mrs. Dilworth, Emily needed something sturdy with which to line the crate, and, without a moment's hesitation or compunction, she grabbed a few old still-lifes, stuffed them into the crate along with the spaniel, nailed down the top and "Lady Jane" sailed away to Vancouver on a bed of early masterpieces which, I am told,* she treated with scant respect en route.

If Emily's exhibitions outside Victoria were rare at this time, it was largely because her purse was nearly always empty. Not infrequently she had to choose between food and cartage costs. No one who did not know Emily and see how she had to skimp to live could possibly understand such poverty. We read a lot about starving artists in Paris and other great art centers during her lifetime but it is doubtful if any worked so desperately hard and still remained so poor. Her father left his family well-off ($50,000 was a fortune in those days) but the finances were badly, if honestly, managed by Emily's guardian and her oldest sister, and the depression of 1912-1913 deprived the family of most of their inherited land.

Fortunately Emily's wants were few. Her animals were her one extravagance, and of these only the monkey and the griffon dogs were a drain on her resources. The birds and the huge bobtail sheepdogs she bred for many years were a good source of income. Despite her size, she was not a heavy eater, often fasting for several days at a time. She rarely spent money on clothes, and

* *By Phylis Dilworth Inglis.*

never took a drink other than a small glass of wine on festive occasions. She did not resort to drugs, as many in her circumstances might today, but only puffed on an occasional home-made cigarette.

Sales brought in little extra money until very late in her life since few people liked her work, and fewer still had any extra dollars to invest in paintings during the deep depression of the thirties.

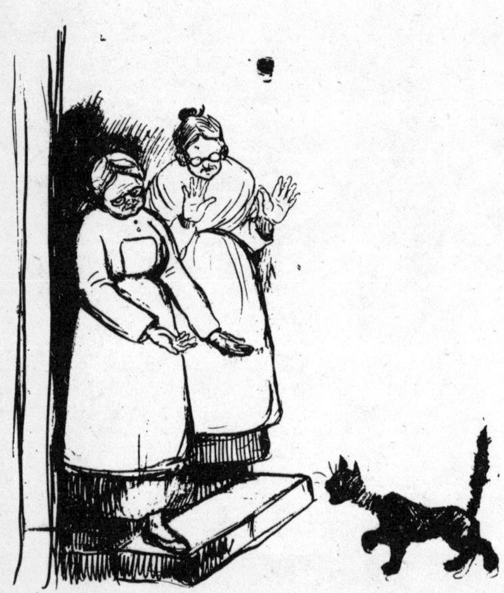

OH THE BEAUTIFUL DARLING! LET US KEEP HIM FOR OUR OWN AND LOVE HIM.

In other words, Emily could never cope with all her problems and wore herself out with household chores, tenants, animal care and the multitudinous tasks surrounding painting itself. An ingenious, if clumsy and impatient craftswoman, she made her own chassis, stretched and sized her canvasses, and mounted scores of field sketches herself—first on buckram, later on plywood or masonite. She also framed, in a fashion, both sketches and canvasses, and with Willie Newcombe's help, even made her own picture crates. No wonder the strain of overwork and worry taxed her strength to the breaking point and that she succumbed to a heart attack after making a supreme effort to move out of her burdensome house into an unencumbered cottage.

Regrettably, Emily was her own worst enemy. She could not work harmoniously with many people, and until the last year of her life, flatly refused to cooperate with an agent, although this would have left her relatively free to paint. After her 1938 exhibition at the University of British Columbia, for instance, before I packed her pictures, she asked me to leave a few sketches with Harry Hood, artist, art dealer, and proprietor of the Art Emporium:

> Mr. Hood wants some pictures left over with him. I'm not at all keen as I hate dealers and besides, they charge a terrific percent—nearly fifty I believe it is. I don't price high (he wants sketches) and you never know where things are. Pottery selling through agents used to give me the pip. I never tried pictures.*

Emily did try Hood, but the arrangement soon blew up and she struggled on alone—a struggle that ultimately broke her health completely.

* *PABC, Emily to author, (undated) November 1938.*

Love Unveiled (Martyn)

Had Emily, who was very attractive in her youth, felt able to marry Martyn, she could have lived in ease or even luxury, freed of all oppressive money problems. Martyn was a gallant "sweetheart," whose love "spilt over me and I let it spill, standing in the middle of the puddle of it, angry at being drenched and totally unable to accept or return it."* He proposed to her often, and pressed his suit so ardently that he followed her to England to propose again. But Emily sent him home, saying he disturbed her work. She could not marry him, she explained, because she loved another. Yet we know nothing of this other person except that he rebuffed Emily's advances.

* Hundreds and Thousands, *p.269.*

Memories of these two men remained deeply etched on Emily's heart, though in time she found consolation in the thought that compensation works out with absolute justice. But toward the very end of her life, when her emotions were quickened, she seemed to rebel: "Love *can* be unfair. I've been loved furiously and not able to pay back, and I've loved furiously with cold response. . . ."*

* *Phylis Dilworth Inglis collection, Emily to Ira Dilworth, (undated) probably 1943.*

These two half-loves, both concentrated in Emily's twenty-seventh year, were, I feel, her only true romances. As a curious young girl living alone with Emily in the woods, I would prod her with searching questions about early admirers as we wiled away a quiet evening in the glow of fire and lamplight. But apart from the tale of youthful infatuation with a fellow student at the San Francisco art school (which she then regarded as a "serious love affair"), I learned nothing more. Yet I did not feel she was being evasive.

A few authors, though, sensing that the public would expect something deeper, more passionate—even tragic—of Emily's turbulent nature, have either greatly intensified a known relationship, or created a new one. And even she, as an imaginative writer, realised how much a sentimental love affair would add to her autobiography. "I would like," she said, "to leave it [love] out altogether, but life wouldn't be complete, nor me *normal* without a touch of it I suppose." She also warns us, indirectly, about one future biographer, Carol Pearson, who, she says, "has always exaggerated dreadfully, awful things were always happening to her. I always took them with a grain of salt."*

* *Phylis Dilworth Inglis collection, Emily to Ira Dilworth, undated, (probably 1942).*

So let us accept Carol Pearson as an affectionate friend of Emily's, but not forget that she is a fantasist who has written a shockingly untruthful book.* In it along with a number of invented incidents, she discloses the drama of Emily's only true love!:

> She (Emily) told me many times the story of the one man in her life who had mattered, and who, years before, had gone off to war never to return. . . . There

* Emily Carr As I Knew Her, *Clarke, Irwin & Co. Ltd., Toronto, 1954. I do not deny Emily's genuine fondness for Carol Pearson when she was a young girl, and again in 1942 when she came to stay a month with Emily to help her over a severe illness, or that they corresponded in the*

interval; but I emphatically dispute the fairy tales she relates in her book about her very special "secret" relationship with Emily, that Emily had wanted to adopt her, and other misleading assertions about their friendship.

was a dear little pewter mug (I wept over this one; it had been given to her when she was eighteen, by the soldier who had been killed).

This would be 1890. So what war? The author does not say. The Sudan campaigns? Possible, but hardly likely. Did she mean the Boer war? If so, the soldier was killed before it started. And, what man? A phantom, I suggest, since Emily plainly states that she experienced love for the *first* time on her return home from Ucluelet—in 1898,* the year Martyn also declared himself.

* *Even if the soldier left when Emily was older than 18, he still could not have been the man Emily met and loved in 1898, since he rejected her. It must be remembered, too, that she was studying in San Francisco 1890-1893.*

Martyn, who became a wealthy man, could have protected Emily from the hardships of her austere spinster's life. But had she accepted him, what would have become of her indomitable will to express herself, against all odds, both in paint and in words? Would he have encouraged her? Would her original vision, her mysticism, all the qualities that go to make up a great artist, have been stifled? How could she have retained the deep feeling of regionalism, the local patriotism born and bred in her, which played such a vital role in her work, had she gone to the United States and become an American? She would have failed either as artist or wife, perhaps as both. As it was, she at least retained her affection for Martyn, and never quite forgot him. And Martyn never forgot her. Forty years later, Emily averred that he loved her still.

Martyn was not the true name of this likable and rather remarkable man. In reality he was William Paddon, of English-Irish descent, a member of an old Victoria pioneer family. His father, born in England and educated at Oxford University, was the Reverend Canon William Francis Paddon, for a time Rector of St. James's Anglican Church on Oswego Street in Victoria, where Emily and young Paddon could possibly have first met. In any case, something more than just friendship already existed between them by 1898, when they both traveled to Ucluelet on the "Willipa," a small Vancouver Island coastal steamer. He was the purser and she the only passenger. In the short factual description in her autobiography* of this normally stormy passage, Emily does not mention William by name—real or fictitious; but, if she was not too seasick, the "Willipa" may well have been the setting for "Martyn's" first declaration of his "immense love."*

* Growing Pains, *p.105.*

* *The purser's identity was established by combining several sources, but Mrs. Paddon's account of her husband's early life was the most revealing.*

I became interested in the history of the Paddon family several years ago when I lived on Paddon Street in James Bay. William Paddon's association with Emily soon came to light, and I learned much more about it when I met and talked with his second wife, Gussie May Paddon of Watsonville, California.*

* *Mrs. Paddon kindly gave me permission to use Martyn's true name for the first time. I submitted my text to her for approval and can thus vouch for its accuracy.*

The whole romance now falls into focus.

Mrs. Paddon confirms that her husband was deeply in love with Emily and as deeply crushed when she rejected him—which she did not only because she loved another but because she felt Paddon demanded more than she could give. Emily explains this years later: "He demanded *worship.* He thought I made a great mistake in not marrying him. He ought to be glad I did not; he'd have found me a bitter mouthful and very indigestible, and he would have bored me till my spirit died."*

* Hundreds and Thousands, *p.223.*

After returning to Victoria from his fruitless trip to England, William urged Emily to reconsider, but without success. Five years her junior, he finally decided that he was perhaps too young for her and left to seek his fortune in California with a friend and his wife. But the friend died, and William, feeling responsible for the widow, married her. This first marriage ended in divorce after years of wrangling over a property settlement, and he remained single for twenty-six years before marrying Gussie May when he was almost sixty-five and she twenty-nine. They had four children and a happy marriage, although Emily insists it was not.

William had earlier purchased a three-mile stretch of beachfront property on Monterey Bay, near Watsonville, ninety miles south of San Francisco, giving it the name it still bears, Palm Beach. It was on this beach that the couple met. William developed the land all around it, prospered in real estate and never returned to Canada. He died at the ripe old age of ninety-six.

Mrs. Paddon kept all Emily's letters to William for a long time, but eventually destroyed them, and though she never met Emily, she spoke of her with warmth and understanding. Emily, on the other hand, appears to have resented Gussie May, and to have been motivated by petty spite when she wrote that "[Martyn's] wife seems to pass through [his] letters a dumb, meaningless nonentity. . . ."* In fact, Emily remained possessive about her spurned lover, never wanting to relinquish him completely. She devoted eight pages of her autobiography to Martyn, and while working on the manuscript, paid this tribute to him:

* *Phylis Dilworth Inglis collection, Emily to Ira Dilworth, (undated) probably 1943.*

> Do you remember the nice things Martyn said about a mother's love? I was closer to Martyn that moment than any other before or since. He remarried three years ago after remaining single for *twenty-six years* and has a son eighteen months old of whom he writes most proud and delighted. . . . I've been writing a

Christmas letter to Martyn answering one received *five years* ago, written by him in '38. He was cutting up land, two thousand acres, making small homesites and towns. He loves doing that, he says he feels he is achieving something making small comfortable homes for the man of small means. I meant to answer his letter long ago but let it slip though he sends me a card faithfully every Christmas. Fifty odd years! All the same, I'm glad I did not marry him.*

* *Phylis Dilworth Inglis collection, Emily to Ira Dilworth, (undated) probably 1943.*

We are too. Perhaps we owe Emily's great collection to this decision.

Sketching in Indian Villages

In the summer of 1907, during a holiday and sketching trip to Alaska with her favorite sister Alice, Emily observed many deteriorating Indian villages along the coast. Her natural sympathy for the Indian aroused, she vowed to make as complete a pictorial record as possible of the bold housefronts, the clothing and customs of the West Coast Indians, but more particularly of their fast-vanishing, awesome totem poles, made by the coastal tribes of British Columbia and Southern Alaska. No other people in the world made carvings of identical meaning and conception and, fortunately, Emily realized this early.

She kept her promise. During the spring and summer, until she left for France in July 1910, Emily sketched in the vicinity of Vancouver, on Vancouver Island, in the Interior, and traveled alone, in any kind of conveyance, on land and on turbulent waters, to northern villages that were very difficult of access. She worked diligently and brought home sketches of great historical and anthropological value which she would later use to develop her powerful canvasses. Her most important Indian work, however, stems from her two landmark sketching trips to the Queen Charlotte Islands and the Nass and Skeena river areas in the banner years 1912 and 1928.

While visiting in Ottawa late 1927 to see her Indian paintings on display at the National Gallery, Emily gave a rare interview to the press* in which she described her visits to small unknown villages along the Skeena river in 1912:

* *Muriel Brewster, "Some Ladies Prefer Indians," Toronto* Star Weekly, *January 21, 1928.*

These paintings, now hung at last on the walls of the Canadian National Gallery, were first exhibited on the sunny walls of rough, Indian shelters, up the Skeena river, for always, before leaving a village, Miss Carr gave a picture show for the benefit of her subjects. "The queer thing was," she said, "that they wanted, above all things, to look at the back of every painting. When they found that there was nothing there, that I was not concealing anything from them, they were perfectly satisfied about my pictures, and they were most appreciative and friendly. In those days they had not learned to be avaricious, and they posed for me gladly, after they made sure that I was not bad magic.

At first they would not uncover their faces, but gradually they learned to trust me, and they would go on doing whatever the task of the moment happened to be, which was of course just what I wanted, and which enabled me to get my accurate record of their lives. Those who had known me before would tell the others about me—they would call out to the newcomers to come and see the woman making trees with her hands! They had seen people making pictures with a box, but never before with the hands. The idea about the hands led to a very funny fear which I had to remove; they were afraid that I was actually stealing the things that I was painting—the door of the house, the totem pole or the gateway; that I was transferring it bodily to my paper and that it would disappear when I left! Gradually I persuaded them that this was not the case. Danger? Oh no. There is no danger from the West Coast Indians unless some white man has given them "fire-water." They are fundamentally honest—until they are corrupted. It was for them—for the honor of the Indian—that I undertook this work. I love them! They are my friends!

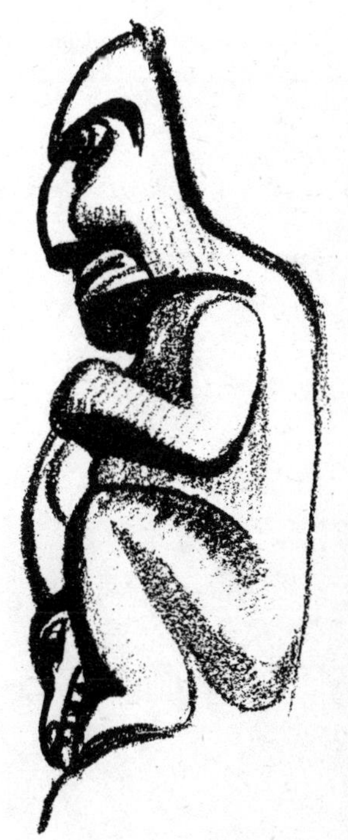

The Historic Sketching Trips of 1912 and 1928

Emily has explained many times why she considered our native Indians to be Canada's first "moderns." They deliberately distorted, she said, to strengthen their expression and convey their meaning. They believed that everything possessed its own spirit, and endeavored to depict that spirit, just as Emily tried to do while working in Indian villages from 1912 to 1930, but more especially during and after 1928, when her more mature style was marked by a new strength and conviction. About this time, too, influenced by both Mark Tobey and Lawren Harris, and feeling she had outgrown her Indian subjects, she decided to concentrate on the more creative task of interpreting the forests of British Columbia. Her Indian subjects were in any case disappearing. The Province was being stripped of its early aboriginal relics by museums in other countries, and in 1928 Emily was aghast to see that many villages were deserted and that the poles were rotting in high, dense undergrowth.

Emily has not, it seems, left us a first-hand account of her 1912 sketching trip, but does report on it in letters to Dr. C. F. Newcombe,* and to Provincial Secretary, Dr. H. E. Young.

** Dr. Charles Frederick Newcombe, a distinguished surgeon, psychiatrist and scientist, was born in England in 1851. Moving to Victoria in 1889, he interested himself in marine zoology, botany, paleontology and anthropology and left a fine collection in all these fields to the Provincial Museum. For about thirty-five years, Dr. Newcombe made countless journeys to remote Indian villages of the far North and became an internationally-known authority on Indian art. He greatly assisted Emily with photographs and valued advice on Indian matters and became an early supporter and patron.*

Soon after her return from the north, she wrote to the Provincial Secretary seeking to arrange an exhibition of her work in the Parliament Buildings. This was, I believe, the only direct appeal Emily ever made for assistance from a member of the Provincial Government:

> "I understand," she wrote, "that in the new wing of the Government Buildings in Victoria there is to be a room set aside for paintings of interest to British Columbia. I have been working for some years on a collection of paintings of Indian totem poles and villages of B.C. and have some very valuable material, some two hundred pictures. The object of my work is to get the totem poles in their own original settings. The Indians do not make them now and they will soon be things of the past. I consider them real art treasures of a passing race. . . . So far I have worked entirely by myself and at my own expense but I feel that I will probably need help to complete the work as the expense of traveling round out of the beaten track is heavy. I would like to get some backing from the Government. . . . I would be very pleased to show you what I have."

In his reply, Dr. Young states that it would be some time before the Government could establish an art gallery, but that he would ask Dr. Newcombe, an authority on such questions attached to his Department, to call on Emily to examine her paintings.*

** BCPM, Dr. Young to Emily, November 7, 1912.*

Thus encouraged, Emily took the initiative and wrote to Dr. Newcombe herself, inviting him to call at her studio in Vancouver to see the Indian work she had done that summer:

> "It is," she said, "still in the sketch condition but I have some excellent material for the winter's work. I was over in the Queen Charlottes and up the Skeena. I am

> making a special collection of Indian totem pole pictures. Knowing you are interested in the same, I would be pleased to meet you. I heard so many speak of you in the places I visited this summer."*

On November 30, Newcombe did call on Emily and subsequently reported to the Minister on "Miss Carr's Collection of Paintings of Indian Totem Poles" in an undated memo. He praised the accuracy in her representation of the carvings and suggested that the paintings would be of use in obtaining information about clan legends, especially for the Skeena river villages.

His assessment of Emily's paintings as works of art is much less enthusiastic:

> There are two sets of paintings. Some are in oil colors and the rest are in water color. To my mind they are too brilliant and vivid to be true to the actual conditions of the coast villages, at least. At close range it is seen that the materials used have been laid on with a heavy hand. On standing away at several feet distance, the colors blend and the roughness of the work is lost sight of. Another criticism I have to offer is that no standard of comparative size has been followed. Hence, in the case of the Haida places the short burial poles stand out as large as the high house poles, that is in different pictures.
>
> Summing up, I am of the opinion that if the colors could be toned down in new copies & if certain details of size & accuracy were corrected under proper supervision, many of Miss Carr's studies might be of interest and value as decorative wall paintings . . . except in very few instances the pictures do not show anything except totem poles and some of the houses. If the artist should be engaged to decorate the new Museum or to furnish a set of pictures, I think that an attempt should be made to supplement this deficiency and to throw more life into the scenes illustrated.

Unfortunately, Dr. Newcombe's report was read and forgotten, and Emily missed her one chance to become a mural painter. But though Dr. Newcombe was unable to do anything for Emily officially, his expert advice, his purchase of eight or nine pictures in 1913 and his abiding friendship were, in the long run, of more value than the financial aid she sought.

What a tremendous opportunity the British Columbia

* *BCPM, Emily to Dr. C.F. Newcombe (undated) 1912.*

Government had to acquire Emily's unique collection for a song. Because of Dr. Young's tragic decision, the collection is now scattered to the four winds and can never be re-assembled.

A delightfully witty description of Emily's 1928 sketching trip to the Queen Charlotte Islands and the Nass and Skeena rivers is contained in a letter to one of her closest friends, Flora Hamilton Burns.* The material is not entirely new: Flora herself has given a résumé of it in her own writings, and the trip is also documented in other sources. However, this letter, written on the spot, is more accurate than the stories which Emily told many years later. It has never been published in its entirety before, and should be compared with a similar one sent to Maud and Eric Brown about a month later* and with the two stories, "Greenville" and "Kitwancool," in *Klee Wyck*.

** I am greatly indebted to Flora for permission to use her letter.*

** NGC, Emily to Maud and Eric Brown, August 11, 1928.*

Written on July 19, 1928 from Greenville, a town situated on a nameless little river that flows into the Nass, the letter to Flora constitutes an exciting adventure story. The physical hardships Emily endured in getting to the almost trackless, isolated villages on or near these two great rivers, and in staying there to work, are almost beyond belief, especially when one recalls that the mere sight of a boat, big or small, made her violently seasick.

At the time of writing, Emily was living, she says, in the back rooms of a vacant school house, the school "marm" and her doctor husband being absent on summer holidays.* "I feel," she said, "like little Goldilocks occupying the bear's house in the woods and expecting them to come in any minute to ask what business I have here."

** Marius Barbeau describes this a little differently. He says that Greenville was a missionary village, and because Emily was not welcomed by the missionaries, she had to stay in an Indian house, with Indian people. He claims there were no totem poles left in Greenville in 1928, and that most of the Indians were away working at the Arrandale cannery.*

She had just completed a rough, exhausting trip up the Skeena and was eager to tell Flora about her adventures getting to Kitwancool, a terrifyingly remote village, rarely seen by whites, which she had long hoped to visit. She was deeply stirred by her experiences there, and gleeful that she had managed to bring back a bundle of excellent totem sketches, though she had encountered drenching rain everywhere. Once she had even crawled into leaky, dank Indian graves to seek shelter from the downpour but, she wrote, "I had to be careful the Indians did not see me (the living, not the dead) as it might have offended."

Too small and distant to be found on any ordinary maps, Kitwancool is situated inland from Kitwanga, on the Skeena, where Emily landed. To reach it she had to travel seven hours in a springless, rickety, lurching wagon, piled high with lumber and "three Indians and me on top." Emily sat in the middle enthroned on a sack of oats with her paraphernalia strewn all around her.

The jolting of the wagon made her hang on for dear life to anything she could grasp, including the Indians, to keep from being dislodged from her precarious perch. She clutched her small griffon dog, Ginger Pop, in her arms to prevent him from being flung overboard.

One of the Indians accompanying Emily was her guide. Another, "a gentleman just returning from three months in jail," was identified on arrival at Kitwancool as the Chief's son-in-law. To her surprise and relief, she was made welcome in the village and invited to sleep on the chief's verandah. The people were kind, and she acquired a very interesting insight into their way of life.

The large family of six adults and three children lived in a huge log house of only one room. But because the nine windows and two doors were kept open, it was airy and cool, quite clean, and the floors were "scrubbed white." Emily had a corner of the verandah all to herself which she curtained off with a canvas fly to ensure a little privacy, and when Mrs. Douse, the "chieftainess," produced a bed, a table and a rocking chair, Emily was able to make herself cozy and comfortable. Nearby two small babies slept in cradles slung from the rafters, and everyone passing by jerked the rope to keep them swinging. Two stoves kept the room warm and dry during wet weather.

Heavy rain forced Emily to stay with the Chief and his family for five days when she had only provisioned for two, and therefore all the food she had left for the last three days was hard tack and raisins. The Indians would gladly have shared their simple fare with her, but, "No, thank you!" she said, "I draw the line at Indians' food and beds!"

"But oh! goodness! the mosquitoes!" she moaned. Living in primitive conditions did not bother Emily, the steady rain did not daunt her, but the mosquitoes, which blighted the whole area, almost crazed her, and her ingenuity was taxed to the limit trying to outwit them with suitable protective clothing. Since they attacked her legs most, causing them to swell until they looked like "beef shanks hanging over my shoes," she tried using puttees made from strips of table oil cloth but, "they slipped and the beasts got in between!" She then devised long, loose canvas pants which hung down over her boot tops, and she painted with a cheesecloth bag over her head into which she had inserted a piece of glass to act as a window. She wore two pairs of gloves, one kid and the other "chamoisette," but the mosquitoes bit through both, never ceasing to torture her every minute she was out-of-doors. "It's terrible," she said, "trying to concentrate on 'significant form' or anything else for that matter with fiery stabs everywhere. They chew right through my khaki dress and I have to wear my hot coat and my khaki trousers. You fly-tox and smash day and night but that doesn't keep me awake as much as the fiery burning and itching of the bites I got while I was out. . . . It is not too bad while you are moving, but sit or stand still one instant and they mob you. It is most beautiful country but I wouldn't live here. In the winter it is very cold and in the summer this torment. Lazarus Moody, my Indian guide here stopped rowing his boat and enquired why God made mosquitoes. 'Well, I don't know,' I said, 'but it seems to me a bit of poor taste.'

"Lazarus took me for two awful and strenuous days on the Nass. The old villages are frightfully overgrown. Nettles, fireweed and bracken grew far over my head. You just have to burst your way through. Lazarus has lumbago and only one eye and is unfit to assist with my pack, so I have to bump along alone. He and his wife and child are the only souls in the village.

"I came up last Sunday from the Arrandale cannery at the mouth of the Nass River with an Indian and his two sons in an open gas boat. It is a lovely trip. There is a yellow rock half way up that the Indians call 'Nass's Tumtum' and Sam would have me sketch it. It is only a little rock and he ran his boat violently round and round it while the boys poked it with poles to keep the boat off it while I was supposed to draw it.

"My heart sank a bit when we got to Greenville and passed by the straggling, staring, empty houses. Sam (my guide) led the way to the empty school-house. It seemed such miles away from everything human, situated as it was in a willow swamp with tall, rank weeds overgrowing the entire path. The schoolroom looked so big and empty. I nearly turned and ran after Sam—but not quite!

"The first night was a bit creepy, everything cracked so. I clung to Ginger Pop as to a tower of strength and there was a squirrel living in the shed off the kitchen which helped some. Now I work and don't mind. I like the big school-room. It is so quiet to work in and I'm assured there's nothing worse than myself in the village. There are eight big stray dogs the Indians left behind. Poor dears! They've tried to hunt and got their faces full of porcupine quills. I asked Lazarus why he didn't try to pull them out, and offered to help, but he said they were very wicked dogs. However, I've made friends and there is a great wagging of tails when I go down to the village. One old female with a bad leg from poisoned quills is now a great pal and limps after me whenever I go out. She looks for her biscuit every day and is very gentle. A big, black brute also follows me and eats a biscuit. He has dreadful quills in his cheeks but so far I have not been able to touch his head. The old girl will let me do anything. . . .

"I hope to move on this week-end but there is no mail boat that touches here now that the people are away. I have had no letters since I left home and want them badly. There will probably be Indians up the river Sunday to see their potato patches.

"I leave here on the 27th and take a boat for the Queen Charlotte Islands. In Rupert on the 30th."

It was Eric Brown who made this venturesome, rewarding journey possible by arranging for free transportation. Before the pass was granted, she wrote to him outlining her proposed itinerary:

> I think the boat to Prince Rupert and rail to Jasper . . . would be a ripping help. . . . I want to branch off to several villages from Alert Bay and wonder if I could break the trip there. . . . The Indian agent there tells me there is still material in that part. Then I could take the boat from Prince Rupert to the Queen Charlotte Islands. . . . The Nass is also getatable from Rupert I think.* . . .

* *NGC, Emily to Eric Brown, March 27, 1928.*

Emily was thrilled with the results of this sketching trip, when she returned home with thirty large water colors, a few oils and a lot of notes. The oils, she said, were "messed up with the wet" so she found water colors a more satisfactory medium, both for painting and for carrying.*

* *NGC, Emily to Eric Brown, October 1, 1928.*

The Victoria Fairs

Even before Emily resolved in 1907 to document in paint the houses, poles and customs of the West Coast Indians, even before 1898 when she did her first watercolors and drawings in a native village, she was trying to bring her work to the attention of the public. But except at schools, church bazaars or other local functions and, after 1890, at the B.C. Art Association's annual exhibitions,* her only opportunity to exhibit in Victoria before the Island Arts and Crafts Club was formed in 1909 was at the old Victoria Fairs. These fairs go back a long way in Victoria's history and in Emily's history also, but her association with them has rarely been mentioned and never researched.

* *Emily could not have exhibited at their early exhibitions since she left for San Francisco about a month before the first annual exhibition opened at the Victoria City Hall in 1890, and was absent until Christmas 1893.*

The Victoria Fairs—often called the Victoria Fall Fairs or the Willows Fairs—make a fascinating story in themselves. They were extremely important events in early Victoria, more eagerly anticipated than Christmas. The main attraction was horse-racing, but there were also grand parades of livestock; band concerts; agricultural and industrial exhibition halls; arts and crafts displays; and, later, exhibitions of paintings. Special attractions were provided each day, all entries were judged, and about five thousand dollars was offered in prize money, some of it earmarked for awards in the art section.

These wonderful Fairs are all but forgotten today and I draw a blank stare whenever I mention them. Although they were primarily agricultural Fairs, organized by the B.C. Agricultural and Industrial Association, the Provincial Department of Agriculture has no record of them. There is little information about them anywhere. And yet, it was here that Emily started her exhibiting career!

The first Fair was held in 1861 in the market square on Broad Street, but owing to lack of space, was moved to land adjoining Beacon Hill Park in 1884. Since the park was only a few steps from Emily's back door, I like to think that, as a child of twelve, she first became interested in the Fair that year. She then had five full years to enjoy the parades of prize cattle and the exhibitions of animal drawings by just skipping across the street, before the Association moved again to a six-acre tract on Cadboro Bay Road in the Willows district which became the Fair's permanent home. The first Fair at the Willows Park fairground was held in 1891,* the last in 1941.

* *The first time that any enthusiasm had been aroused for a Fine Arts display: "The picture gallery . . . was thronged with visitors and admirers of local talent." The* Daily Colonist, *October 2, 1891.*

My feeling that these Fairs may have been important in Emily's development as an artist paid off handsomely quite soon after I started researching them. As the pages of very old newspapers flashed by me in the microfilm reader, the name "Miss E. Carr" suddenly appeared for the first time in a description of the Victoria Fair held October 2-6, 1894. Here is an excerpt from the *Daily Colonist* of October 4, which is of special interest:

> No fault could certainly be found with Miss E. Carr's capturing the first place in pen and ink sketches. A nicer little bit of work it would be hard to find. Her sketching is beautifully done and the little collection of hers is worth seeing.

To my knowledge, this date has never appeared on any exhibition list or chronology, and I at first regarded it with suspicion since it has been assumed that Emily returned from her studies in San Francisco at Christmas time in either 1894* or

* *Maria Tippett's catalogue for her exhibition at Simon Fraser University, Burnaby, B.C. in 1974:* Contemporaries of Emily Carr in British Columbia.

1895*—that is, after the Victoria Fair had closed. I therefore checked the passenger lists in the Victoria newspapers, but to no avail. I also wrote to Emily's art school in San Francisco, but the Librarian there could only say that all school records had been destroyed in the 1906 earthquake and fire, and that they are grateful for Emily's descriptions of their school in *Growing Pains* since they have little else.*

The date of Emily's return has since been established as 1893,* and thus she might have participated in the Victoria Fair in October 1894. However, it is possible that the "Miss E. Carr" who entered her pictures was not, in fact, Emily. Her two sisters, Edith and Elizabeth (Lizzie), could equally well have exhibited using the initial "E." Lizzie can, I think, be disregarded since, though talented, she appears not to have taken her "genteel" art lessons very seriously. But Edith was an experienced craftswoman, a well-known china painter who won first prize at the 1904 Fair, and a teacher of applied art. It is thus conceivable that she might have executed the prize-winning pen and ink sketches.

There is no doubt, however, about Emily's participation in the following year. When she exhibited at the 1895 Fair in September, she styled herself "Miss M. Carr," and so could not be confused with either of her sisters. That year she won first prize in pencil drawing, pen and ink sketches and, of all things, "painting on china!" Emily scorned china painting later in life and hated to admit that she had ever done any.

There were no Fairs between 1895 and 1901. Emily was absent from Victoria most of the time between 1899 and 1913, and they were discontinued again during the war and post-war years up to 1921. These gaps in no way endangered the pallid growth of the arts in Victoria, because the Fair exhibitions in those infancy years were pitifully feeble events. Although a few established professionals such as Thomas Bamford, Edward Shrapnel, and my first art teacher, Marjorie (Margaret) Kitto, contributed fitfully, little original, vigorous work was seen at the Fairs until Emily began exhibiting her post–impressionist paintings done in France. Only those of us who saw those early Fair exhibitions could possibly comprehend how truly banal they were. Everyone participated—school children, housewives, doctors, sailors, octogenarians. Acceptance meant nothing. A prize next to nothing. Some may wonder why Emily cared to show her work in such company at all, but one must not forget that she was always in search of a public. Although she loudly protested the attitudes of the Victoria art community, she

* *VAG catalogue* Emily Carr: A Centenial Exhibition *(1971 edition)*

* *The Librarian, Harry Mulford, is a Carr fan himself and has written an article about her entitled, "Growing Pains: Emily Carr and the Early Years of the San Francisco Art Institute." He is also stocking the school library with books written by and about her.*

* *VAG catalogue* Emily Carr: A Centennial Exhibition *(1975 revised edition)*

exhibited whenever and wherever she could.

Emily herself describes her next participation in a Victoria Fair exhibition:

> It was amusing the other day. I was in the Union Steamship Company asking about fares and the man said, "Did you see that lot of Indian pictures that was here some time ago?" I got quite excited and said, "No." and asked lots of questions. I thought they were photos probably. He was quite enthusiastic over them and I never dreamt of it being my things he was referring to till he told me they were up at the Agricultural Fair. Then I felt flat. "Well," I said, "I think you were the only one who did like them." "Well, I spent a whole half day with them," he replied.*

* *NGC, Emily to Eric Brown, March 9, 1928.*

The shipping agent's appreciation of Emily's work had reference to the 1926 Fair. She won no prizes that year, but seems to have had a section to herself, and perhaps did not compete. She was well represented and received good press notices:

> A second large individual collection is entered by Miss Carr, well known Victoria artist, whose powerful and characteristic interpretation in pigments of Indian village life and totemry has already brought her well-deserved fame.*

* *Victoria* Daily Colonist, *August 18, 1926.*

Emily waited until 1933 before exhibiting at the Fair again. Held that year in September, the art exhibition was put in charge of Arthur Checkley, one of the most active members of the Island Arts and Crafts Society, which had exhibited there as a group for the first time in 1927. After that date, the Society assumed responsibility for most of the Fair exhibitions and vastly improved both their quality and scope. Checkley urged Emily to cooperate with the Society and she finally agreed to let him have a "group of big oils." Following in her footsteps, several other Victoria moderns also agreed to participate, among them J. Delisle Parker and Max Maynard.

Arthur Checkley also organized the September 1934 Fair exhibition, giving Emily a whole section to herself. Egged on by her, Max and I also entered paintings, and one of mine won the dubious honor of first prize in oils—a new crisp, five-dollar bill.

This was Emily's last showing at the Fair, since she was by now too absorbed in her fall sketching trips to the woods to be bothered. She exited with her usual jibes at the members of the Island Arts and Crafts, who, though they may not have tolerated much innovation, at least rescued the Victoria Fairs from abysmal mediocrity.

The Victoria Fairs were originally known as the Provincial Fairs and were held in alternate years in Victoria and New Westminster until 1889, when New Westminster decided to hold their own shows. Separate exhibitions were held annually until 1924, and in 1929 a fire destroyed all the Fair buildings and records. In 1909, while living and teaching in Vancouver, Emily exhibited once at the Fair in New Westminster. She was not mentioned in the prize lists in the local *Columbian* newspaper, but her work was singled out for praise in the Vancouver *Daily Province*'s review of the exhibition.

First Solo Exhibitions*

** Some repetition from other chapters is unavoidable in order to describe the solo exhibitions.*

Excluding the small, early, outdoor displays of paintings in Indian villages, Emily's first solo show was held in her Vancouver studio in 1912. Her second, a large exhibition of Indian works, took place at Drummond Hall, Vancouver, in 1913, almost exactly a year later. Her third, in June 1913, was a house-warming exhibition to celebrate the opening of a new studio in her recently-completed small apartment house in Victoria.

But Emily and her advisers had miscalculated the income she could hope to receive from tenants in a depression year, and she was soon left with empty flats and a houseful of hungry boarders. She hung a few "nice" pictures on the walls of the studio cum dining-room for their benefit, but most of her important work was hidden away in the attic for many years. But as we all know, owing to a set of fortuitous circumstances, Emily's pictures were out of the attic and on the walls of the National Gallery by 1927, and she was back painting in the north again by 1928. The products of this fabulous sketching trip were put on view in her Victoria studio in November that year in her long-forgotten fourth solo show.*

** A Calgary writer, Archie F. Key, claims that Emily had a solo exhibition there in the twenties. However, since it is not documented and the date is uncertain, it is omitted from this list. (See Exhibition List I).*

But it was Emily's fifth solo exhibition, her "come-back" exhibition, held at the Crystal Garden in Victoria March 1930, that at long last brought her acclaim in her native city. Because it was sponsored, and promoted energetically, by the local Women's Canadian Club, it received a lot of publicity and was a mild sensation. People flocked down to the Crystal Garden to see her splendidly "weird" paintings, and Emily joined the crowd. She stood shyly, but slyly, to one side, unrecognized by most, very alert to all comment on her work. Much of it was derogatory, and she therefore blushed with surprise and pleasure when Max Maynard, who barely knew her then, congratulated her warmly on her paintings.

Seventeen years had elapsed since Emily's work had been shown publicly in Vancouver, and this 1930 show was thus her first solo exhibition in the memory of most people—certainly most Victorians. Even today it is often cited as her first solo show in the West.

The Art Institute of Seattle, not to be outdone, also hung Emily's work in 1930—her first exposure in a solo exhibition on the international scene. Carr exhibitions were now gathering momentum and she was soon firmly established in the West.

But what about the East? We know, of course, that Emily's "breakthrough" exhibition at the National Gallery of Canada in 1927 had established her reputation as an outstanding figure in Canadian art and probably led to the 1930 "come-back" Crystal Garden show in Victoria. But in 1927 Emily was only a contributor, albeit the principal one.

All catalogues give 1936 as the date of Emily's first solo exhibition in the East, but this is inaccurate. The exhibition catalogue *Emily Carr: Her Paintings and Sketches** lists only one solo show in the East in 1936—at Hart House, University of Toronto—but the Vancouver Art Gallery's 1971 centennial catalogue (and its 1975 revised edition) lists two exhibitions for 1936—at the Lyceum Club and Women's Art Association, Toronto, and at Hart House. However, neither catalogue lists anything for the year 1935, though this is the true date of Emily's first important eastern show. It took place at the Lyceum Club and Women's Art Association in November of that year. The Association itself was unable to give me the exact date, saying only that it was held "sometime between October 1935 and March 1936," but fortunately, I was able to fix the date precisely through an article, "The World of Art," in *Saturday Night** and a letter from Emily: "I am, however, having a show of sketches at the Women's Art Association in Toronto—last two weeks in November, I believe."*

Hart House has no record or recollection of its exhibition but it must have taken place very early in 1936, and was probably the same group of sketches that had been hung by the Lyceum Club and Women's Art Association a month or two before.

The Art Gallery of Toronto, with its showing of Emily's paintings in March-April 1937, placed third in this close race to mount solo Carr exhibitions in Eastern Canada in the thirties. They have made up for their relative tardiness by hanging her work regularly ever since.

Although these three exhibitions were indisputably Emily's first important solo shows in the East, an earlier, but

* *Published for the NGC and AGT by the Oxford University Press, Toronto, 1945.*

* *Vol. 51, No. 5, December 7, 1935 (See Exhibitions List I).*

* *UBC Library, Emily to Nan Cheney, October 25, 1935.*

much smaller show was held in Ottawa in 1930. It was hung in May in the Canadian National Railways ticket office on Sparks Street, and was arranged by Dr. Marius Barbeau. He called it a fairly large show, but critics used the word "display." Still, whether exhibition or display, it was a "first" for Emily in the East.

Since everyone contacted was skeptical of the idea that any such exhibition or display had ever taken place, trying to trace it led me up a lot of blind alleys. The CNR obligingly tried to verify it, but no records exist either in Ottawa or at their head office. The archivist in charge of the Barbeau Collection at the Canadian Centre For Folk Studies at the National Museum of Man in Ottawa also says that "there is no documentation in our archives to indicate that such an exhibit took place."*

* *See Exhibition List I.*

A retired CNR public relations officer and and well known journalist and art critic was kind enough to make enquiries, but he, too, drew a blank: "I'm sorry I can't uncover [the exhibition] because, as you say, it would be a feather in our [CNR] cap if the railway had given Emily her first."

The Sparks Street location was a last resort for Barbeau. He had tried to persuade the National Gallery to mount a solo Carr show, but it was against their policy at the time to display an artist's works during his or her lifetime, and they would make no exception for Emily. Besides, she had offended the Gallery in 1928 by expecting too much in the way of sales and service, and the quarrel possibly still rankled.

Barbeau did not feel that the CNR exhibition had greatly encouraged Emily, but he did manage to persuade the CNR agent to buy one or two of her paintings, and he himself bought another. This alone, from her point of view, was enough to spell success.*

* *"Portrait on Memory—Emily Carr" (unedited text).*

The Red-Letter Years 1927 and 1930

Any comment on Emily's early exhibitions would be incomplete without special reference to the years 1927 and 1930. These were the most important dates of the second half of her painting career, though it is difficult to say which was the more significant in terms of her sudden, dramatic climb to national and even international recognition.

Emily's rebirth as an artist in 1927 resulted from her participation in the National Gallery's didactic show of West Coast Indian culture, in which she emerged from a welter of interpretations as the most strikingly talented individual painter. For the first time since 1911, when her paintings were shown at the *Salon d'Automne* in Paris, Emily saw her work represented in a large, important exhibition. On this occasion, she appeared in the company of some of Canada's finest painters, among them a few of the Group of Seven. Her fond recollections of the visit to Ottawa to see the exhibition centered on her initial contact with members of this still controversial Group. These men gave her the will to "dig, delve and study" when she returned to her isolation in the West.

On meeting the Group—first Varley in Vancouver on her way East and then, respectively, A. Y. Jackson, Arthur Lismer, Lawren Harris, and J. E. H. MacDonald in Toronto*—she felt an immediate bond with them. This bond remained strong and steady for years until she finally outgrew their ideas, their ideals and their religion and trudged her chosen path alone.

Lawren Harris of course made by far the most profound and lasting impression on Emily, and they corresponded for years, exchanging views on art and religion. But even this close relationship suffered a temporary break when Emily rejected theosophy and tactlessly disapproved of Harris's divorce and remarriage.

But in 1927, there were still no clouds to disturb or dim this fast friendship which struck a deep inner chord in Emily and lifted her into serene "holy places." She read me some of Harris's letters as we sat before the fire in her studio on cold winter evenings, and I could see by her animated face what strength, inspiration and nourishment she drew from them.* The words of Lawren Harris, and the works of the Group as a whole, touched her very soul, and she felt as if a whole new world had opened up before her. With real feeling she said at the end of one letter, "God bless the Group of Seven!"*

As a result of the spin-offs from the West Coast Art Exhibition, 1927 became a red-letter year for Emily. She had no solo exhibitions that year and contributed to no others either in the East or in Vancouver, She even skipped the Arts and Crafts show in Victoria.* But the impact of her introduction to the Group of Seven caused a radical re-thinking of her spiritual values. Equally important, she could now count on the consolation, encouragement, support and understanding of her new eastern artist friends.

There was no immediate follow-up to Emily's success in 1927. The next two years proved to be an anti-climax, a time of limbo. She had only one solo show during the entire period and that she put on herself in 1928 in her own studio and at her own

* Hundreds and Thousands, *pp.3-7. In Emily's account of this trip in* Growing Pains, *she had either forgotten the order of these visits or changed it to suit her story. On page 317, she says that her escorts took her first to the studio of A.Y. Jackson, then to that of Lismer, then to J.E.H. MacDonald. Varley was, she said, away. Carmichael and Casson lived farther out of town, but she met them later. "Last of all," she recalls, "we went to the studio of Lawren Harris." Emily's autobiography is once again unreliable.*

* *Unfortunately, Lawren Harris destroyed most of Emily's letters before he died, and on his request, Emily burned all of his that were in any way personal. Ira Dilworth made the same request, but as she could not bear to part with his letters she kept them in a separate box plainly labeled "Give to Ira Dilworth when I die." Few are extant today.*

* *Emily took to blessing people liberally in her later years, a habit she learned from Harris. They blessed one another in their correspondence, then in turn blessed Ira Dilworth. What started as a sincere, religious greeting finally seemed little more than a mannerism, though in Emily's case at least, a genuine and earnest belief in blessing carried over from her childhood.*

* *Despite a listing to the contrary in VAG's Centennial catalogue (1975 edition, p.93). See Exhibition Lists II.*

expense. She contributed to only six group shows during this time: some water colors appeared at the National Gallery in January 1928* and nine paintings were entered in the Island Arts and Crafts Society show, Victoria, in the Fall. In 1929 she exhibited for the first time with the Ontario Society of Artists, Toronto, with the British Columbia Society of Fine Arts, Vancouver, and in the *Women's International Exposition* in Detroit. For Emily this Detroit show was the outstanding event of the year, partly because of the prestige of exhibiting abroad, and partly because it concerned women artists.

All in all, not a very impressive list for someone who had supposedly "reached the top."

Then in 1930 Emily rounded a sharp corner. Exhibitions began popping up all over the continent, most of them "firsts."

Eventful and fertile as 1927 had been, Emily's flash of fame could have dimmed, forcing her back into oblivion again. Only the seeds of her genius had been planted in the consciousness of Canadians at that time. They needed the germinal period of growth in 1928 and 1929 before their full flowering in 1930 in her more vigorous, mature style. 1930 was a year of triumph and solidification, an active year during which Emily firmly established herself as a major Canadian artist and achieved recognition in America as well with her inclusion in the important exhibition, *Contemporary Canadian Artists*, at the Corcoran Gallery in Washington. This exhibition later traveled to many other centers across the country and gave Emily and her totems considerable exposure in the United States before her first solo show south of the border opened towards the end of the year at the Art Institute of Seattle. She had also shown her work there somewhat earlier at the Sixteenth Annual Exhibition of Northwest Artists.

While gathering recognition abroad, Emily was having a bumper crop of exhibitions at home. She exhibited for the first time with the Group of Seven; was represented (for the second time) in the annual exhibition of the Ontario Society of Artists; and (also for the second time) in the annual exhibition of Canadian Art at the National Gallery. She also showed her work at the Palette and Chisel Club exhibition in Vancouver once more and submitted pictures to the Island Arts and Crafts show in Victoria.

When I met Emily in May, she was still agog about her success in Washington, D.C. and Toronto, and thrilled about her invitation to contribute to the Group of Seven exhibition. Nothing could have pleased her more. She said that she could ill

* *At the* Annual Exhibition of Canadian Art—*Emily's first appearance with this annual. It was never one of her favorites. In fact she wrote me some years later that she considered the painting in these annuals "repulsive."*

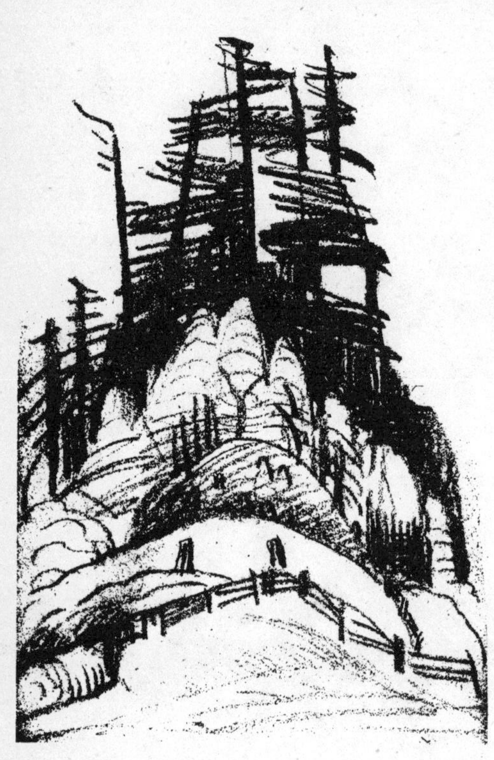

afford to go east again, but when Marius Barbeau obtained a railway pass for her and asked her to be a guest in his home, she packed her bags and left in a hurry. Fearful of feeling "shamed" when she saw her work hung in the illustrious company of her Group friends, she was buoyed up with hope and joy when she heard only congratulations and praise. Lawren Harris assured her she was making real progress, and A. Y. Jackson was "astonished" at the greater freedom of her work. Uplifted and stimulated, Emily plunged into work with renewed vigor the moment she arrived home.

Before leaving the East, Emily, on Harris's urging, visited the galleries in New York and saw for herself the works of leading American and French painters. In view of the importance of this second trip east—the Group show, her stay with the Barbeaus, and her only trip to New York—it is mystifying that not a single comment about it appears in her journals. In fact, almost the whole of this super-year is excluded, the first entry being dated November 23. At first I thought a big chunk of 1930 had been excised by the publishers for reasons best known to themselves, but Phylis Dilworth Inglis, who was involved in the editing of the journals, has told me that nothing was omitted except a few pages of vitriolic criticism of two friends.

My own feeling is that 1930 was too busy and satisfying a year for Emily to bother with notes. She tended to write when she was sick, or alone, seeking the solace and comfort of words; but in 1930 she had little time to herself. Since I met her early that year and saw or telephoned her almost daily after her return from the East, I like to think that I brought enough camaraderie into her life to help keep her active and content.

Emily writes in *Growing Pains** that she made three trips to Eastern Canada during exhibitions of the original Group of Seven to which she was an invited contributor. But her memory failed her. She visited the East in November-December 1927, April-May 1930 and November 1933, and the only time she saw her paintings hanging with those of the Group was in 1930. In 1927 there was no exhibition by the Group, and by 1933 it had expanded to become the Canadian Group of Painters.

* *p.324.*

Emily "slipped across the line" to visit New York in April 1930 staying a week with an old friend* on Long Island before facing up to the hubbub of noisy Manhattan and the fatigue of "doing" the art galleries. Accustomed to an impoverished existence in Victoria, she was amazed and appalled at the extravagances of the Long Island millionaires, and felt like a modern Cinderella plopped into a fabulous fairyland.

* *Mrs. Cozier, an English friend who had earlier farmed in Victoria. At the time of Emily's visit to Long Island, the Coziers managed an estate there.*

The following week, during her round of the modern galleries in Manhattan, Emily studied intently the paintings of the most famous artists of the day—Kandinsky, Braque, Archipenko, Van Gogh, Picasso and many others. Some, she said, had "gripping power," and she was moved by their great strength and beauty. Others she found contrived and artificial, striving for sensation and effect. On the whole, though Emily's visit to New York was a significant event, it was not a significant painting experience. She met few artists, and none who made a lasting impression on her—not even Georgia O'Keeffe, an overpowering personality with whom she talked at the Stieglitz Gallery* and whose work she admired. Emily disclaimed any influence, but perhaps she did find something meaningful in O'Keeffe's painting that later crystallized in her own. Paul Duval, the noted art critic, contends that her painting *Forest, B.C.* is reminiscent of canvasses by O'Keeffe. He also makes the interesting observation that Emily, Georgia O'Keeffe and Käthe Kollwitz are the feminine big three of modern art.*

* *Georgia O'Keeffe must have spent considerable time at the Stieglitz Gallery (owned by her husband). I also listened to her there a few years later as she sat like a queen, on a velvet settee, surrounded by admirers.*

* *Paul Duval, "Emily Carr's Art is a Growing Art,"* Saturday Night, *November 3, 1945.*

Suddenly Emily felt uprooted and homesick for her beloved British Columbia woods, and even for the problems of her House of All Sorts. After all, New York in 1930, with its abstractionists, was not Paris in 1910, when the post-impressionists and fauves made such an impact on her "seeing" that their influence was evident in her work for years after her return home. However, later critics, and a few friends, noted the influence of Van Gogh, which Emily herself half acknowledged. It is most noticeable in the 1934-1936 sketches done while she camped in her van in Metchosin painting agitated, swirling skies, and in the seascapes painted about the same time from Dallas Road near her studio.

Although Emily rushed out, bought and eagerly devoured anything recommended by the Group artists, such as *The Canadian Art Movement* by F. B. Housser; *Yearbook of the Arts in Canada* by Bertram Brooker; *Modern French Painters* by Jan Gordon, and books by Roger Fry and Clive Bell, she was on the whole bored and impatient with books on art, particularly art history, and had little curiosity about the lives of famous painters. Van Gogh was a rare exception. She read his biography, *Lust for Life,* avidly, but found it "*disgustingly sexy.*" She gloried in his work, but was revolted by his living habits, his exploitation of his brother Theo, his craving for money, and his love affairs. Still she thought him a genius, or rather a victim of his genius, and his paintings provided the one truly moving emotional experience of her stay in New York.

Her lesser attraction to Picasso is not unexpected. After reading Gertrude Stein's *Picasso*, she summed up her reaction in a letter to me: "Rather interesting though I'm not particularly drawn to him. Enormous, brutish women and collections of inanimate material. She [Stein] says he was not interested in the soul—that was something else again. Well, it seems to me that without a soul, a spirit, things do not exist. If you take that away, what have you but straight man-made mechanics? Only *design*. Only arrangement of ornament. There are, however, some very interesting things in the book well worth thinking about. . . ."

Another artist in whom she developed a more typical interest about the time of her New York visit, possibly because of a religious kinship, was the nineteenth century English poet William Blake. A well-thumbed, much underscored volume about his life, his lyrical verse and sublime illustrations, inscribed "Emily Carr New York 1930" was among Emily's literary treasures inherited by her sister Alice, who later gave it to Flora Burns. Emily was not above quoting Blake when she wanted to get me out of bed at camp. "Blake said, 'Energy is eternal delight.' Let's get busy."

Emily had toiled so hard in San Francisco, London and Paris, always subordinating pleasure to work and rarely going out without her sketch sack, that it is almost impossible to imagine her as a light-hearted tourist. But that is what she was for a short time in New York. The recollections of her sight-seeing in *Growing Pains* are entertaining, but the on-the-spot impressions written in a letter to Flora are still better, and of course fresher. Two paragraphs from the letter are enough to set the tone:

> From Hotel Martha Washington in New York.
> See where I am? Truly it is a mighty city. I drew near to it with great fear and trembling. The brick and mortar overpowered me, but I've got quite brave and see so much of wonder and greatness. It has such a huge spirit to present to me and it's so clean. So *quiet* for its bigness. People are so happy-looking and are so courteous and kind if you want any information or advice and even the elevator men go slow to accommodate cranks. Of course I have not dared any of the very highs, about six or seven stories is all I can bear. These *toppers* are *awful*! I admire them from the bottom.
>
> I am just going out on a rubberneck wagon to see the sights. Mrs. C. [Crozier] and I went on one yesterday and it was well worthwhile. The roof is all glass so

you can see the 'scrapers' and the talk-man does his job well. The traffic is really wonderfully managed.... My Martha Washington Hotel is funny. It's for women and is stuffed with old tabbies. It's like a home for the aged though there are also some young women. Men are allowed in the dining-room and come in millions because the food is exceedingly good."*

* *Emily to Flora Hamilton Burns, April 28, 1930. I am indebted to Flora for permission to quote from her unpublished letter.*

Yes, 1930 was an exciting year for Emily—an eventful year highlighted by three landmark exhibitions (her first solo shows in Victoria, Eastern Canada and the United States), and her rewarding, stimulating trip to Toronto and New York. How fortunate I was to meet her at such an auspicious time.

1930 seems a fitting place to end *my* narrative of Emily as a painter and to let her pick up the threads herself in the regular entries in her journals, begun at the end of 1927. She continued this vivid record until March 7, 1941 when her painting days were nearly over and in it poured forth her innermost thoughts about her work and about people, art and religion.

Emily's death in 1945 was timely, for it coincided with the end of an epoch. Even if she had not been incapacitated by illness, she could never have accepted nor understood the upheaval in Canadian art which followed the Second World War. She deplored Lawren Harris's conversion to abstract art* (though she later grudgingly agreed that it was the right and natural development for *his* work) and would have looked with horror on later dramatic experiments that changed the direction of the country's art.

* *PABC, Emily to author, (undated) December, 1937. "Well, time has come for Lawren to change, but I will confess to disappointment in the change." See also: Exhibition List II; 1937, Art Gallery of Toronto (Canadian Group of Painters).*

When she died, however, Emily was still regarded by many as an audacious, *avant-garde* painter of lyrical landscapes characterized by sweeping, swirling rhythms and brilliant, incandescent color. This would have pleased her, for she always loved to shock. Though official recognition came late, she also had the satisfaction of knowing that she had eventually won her lonely, desperate struggle for acceptance. Thus the story of Emily Carr as a painter, grim as it was in spots, did have a happy ending.

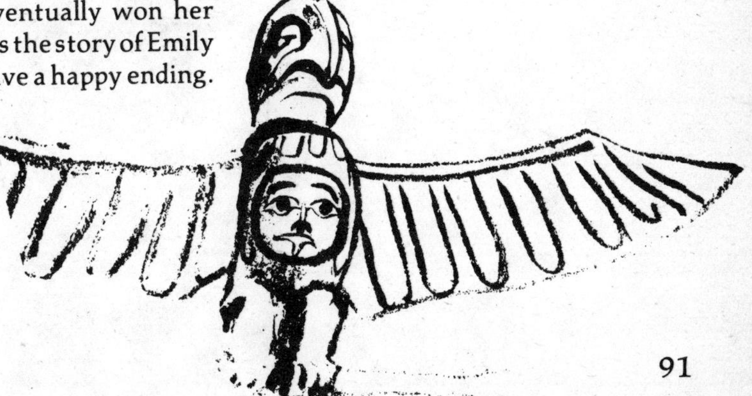

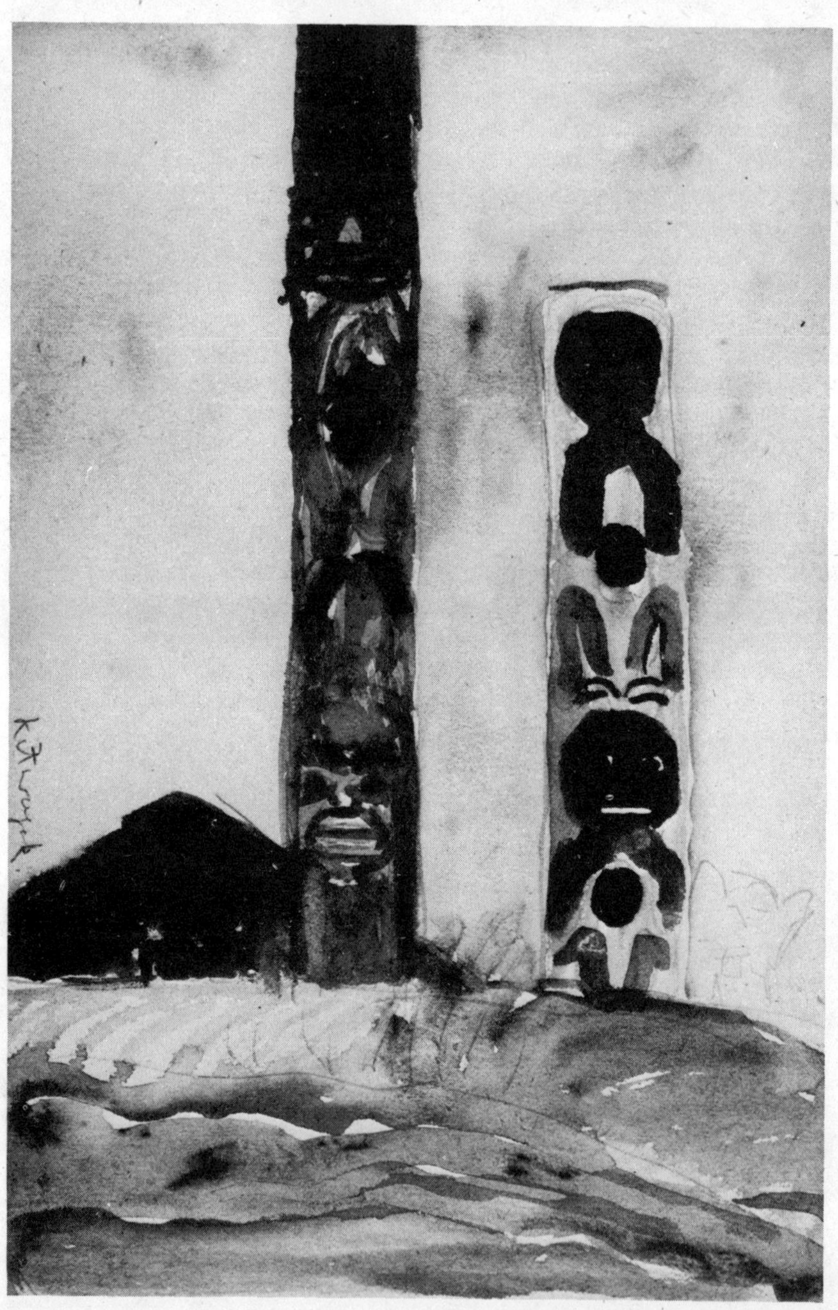

Emily and the Indians

tl'iiw'ik—A Linguist's Dilemma

"Did Emily Carr feel superior to the Indians?" a few people now ask. Critics and readers at the time of the publication of *Klee Wyck* certainly did not feel so. Not a shade of suspicion can be detected in a single review.

Nor did Emily's friends ever question her affinity for the Indian in those early years. We accepted her beliefs implicitly, commending her on her great understanding of, and sympathy for, the native people. She championed the Indian at a time when the rest of us* were looking in the other direction–away from a guilty conscience. She went among them without fear and established a communication of sorts. Most of her friends did not—and I blush now for our obtuseness, our snobbery, our indifference. In those days undernourished Indian women with long raven braids and broad, brown faces, enveloped in dirty shawls, went from door to door in Victoria and Vancouver trying to sell their beautiful handwoven baskets for a pittance. We bought their baskets, but only after beating down their price, and we were prouder of our successful haggling than of the baskets themselves.

* *The Newcombes, father and son, and Marius Barbeau are three exceptions.*

Emily at least had contact and compassion. She felt at home with the Indians and was, she insisted, accepted by them. She liked many, had regard for a few, and love for one—her longtime friend from the Indian Mission in North Vancouver—Sophie. Despite the harsh living conditions in the villages where she sketched, she enjoyed their way of life, reveling in the unaccustomed freedom she found among them and drawing comfort from their quiet strength. Her maternal affection for them and her deep and abiding respect for their totemic art shine through her stories like a beacon.

But Emily professed "love" for the Indians. Was it the kind of love she would give to a white person? Was she vitally concerned with their welfare? I think not. She deplored the passing of the old ways, the gradual loss of their ancient arts and, as an artist, the destruction or removal of the totem poles; she lamented the fatal intrusion of the white man who had taken their land, destroyed their traditional way of life and separated them from their religion, culture and customs. But she did not contemplate any action which might have helped her friends to alleviate their hard lot. She did not wish them to change. She liked them as they were—children of nature, close to the earth, the woods and sea, guided by the sun and the tides.

Recently, I began thinking back on Emily's life with the Indians, as far as I knew it, and vividly recalled conversations I had had with her about her trips to Indian territory—especially in 1928. For the first time, a disturbing doubt began to creep into my mind and, in retrospect, I sensed a definite, though subtle, condescension towards the natives and decided to re-read her haunting Indian stories.

After years of neglect, I opened my dusty, dog-eared autographed copy of *Klee Wyck,* and was startled. Had time changed the stories so much? They now seemed as outdated, remote and innocent as the twenties themselves when Emily last lived with the Indians. Her genuine, but immature interest in them now took on a patronizing tone which had escaped me before. Friends, like myself, who first listened to these stories in her studio, and had the happiness of seeing them in print in 1941, were also unaware of this flaw then—a measure, perhaps, of how much the general consciousness of such matters has risen in the intervening years. The stories remain little literary gems—as witty, imaginative and original as before—but they now seem quaint, a little unreal and the humor sometimes rankles since it is often at the expense of the Indians. Because of our dramatically changed attitudes to racial problems today, we are much more sensitive to *their* feelings and *their* needs and rights, whereas we enjoyed the book uncritically thirty-five years ago.

It was never Emily's intent to belittle the Indians. The condescension that now dates the book was instinctive and unconscious. It was also inevitable because of her upbringing. Only the perspective of time allows us this new insight into her character and her relations with the Northwest Coast Indians.

Emily's innate feeling of superiority toward the Indians reveals itself in many ways. Her love for them, while exaggerated for literary effect, seemed genuine enough on first reading of *Klee Wyck* in 1941; but on re-reading, it appears benign and patronizing—the kind of love one might bestow on children, servants or "inferiors." Feeling wronged and rejected as an artist herself, she was quick to recognize the injustices suffered by the Indians, but her sympathy and indignation did not penetrate deeply. She tried harder than most to rid herself of prejudice, but her conservative background and sense of caste, belonging as she did to a pioneer family of money and privilege, prevented her. Still breathing the air of colonization, she could not, with the best will in the world, have regarded the Indians as her equals. The social barriers between them could never be entirely removed. Her feeling for them was similar to the paternal affection of many Americans for the negro at about the same time—an "Amos and Andy" love for the blackface provided he entertained them, was useful to them, and kept his place.

It is more than likely, too, that Emily neither sought, nor wanted, true equality. In her experience, equality usually led to friction. Until very late in life when, desperately ill, despondent and dependent, she allowed herself to be dominated by two strong, male friends, she had played the dominant role in most of her relationships. Possibly she got along better with the Indians than with her peers precisely because she could not regard them as her equals; and her association with them bolstered her ego because they were childlike and a little subservient.

Seen against this colonial background (and Emily was a proud pioneer), the condescension, while regrettable, does not really shock. It is not, I think, imagined. Others, too, have noticed it, among them an ethnologist and a curator of linguistics. Two educated Indians with whom I spoke, were almost contemptuous of Emily's view of their people; but George Clutesi, the talented Indian painter and writer from Port Alberni, who met Emily shortly before her death, was not so sure. He felt that he did not know her well enough to form a true judgment, particularly as he remembered her more as an old, tired, sick woman than artist, writer or champion of Indian rights. He admired *Klee Wyck*, he said, but feared he might be too conditioned to the white man's feeling of superiority to have recognized it in Emily's book. Perhaps, he mused, his own reputation as a painter and writer influenced her to treat him with more interest and respect than a fellow Indian without accomplishments. Clutesi and his wife had tea with Emily several times after Margaret Clay introduced them, and he found her to be "civil" and understanding, although somewhat formal and stiff. But, altogether, a "person of meaning."*

Why, if she loved the Indians, did Emily rarely talk about them after ceasing to sketch in their villages? Why did she seldom see Sophie, even when she had the opportunity? Why did she never entertain them in her home? In the memory of her closest friends, Clutesi, whom she met so late in life, was the only Indian to be invited to her studio.

Emily's deep-seated romanticism found the perfect outlet in the Indians and her anecdotes about them. She also made

* *Quoted from an interview with George Clutesi.*

considerable use of literary license and distorted events and dialogue to create an impression.

In "Ucluelet," for instance, the first story in *Klee Wyck*, after introducing herself as "a fifteen-year old school-girl" when in reality she was a mature woman of twenty-six, Emily describes how the Indians came in a body to welcome her on arrival at the Mission House in Ucluelet. The advent of a white person was a rare event in 1898 and the Indians would wish to observe the social formalities required by custom. But her description of the chief's behavior would better fit a chimpanzee than a human being. The chief, she wrote, "perched himself on the top of the missionaries' drug cupboard, his brown fists clutched the edge of it, his elbows taut and shoulders hunched. His crumpled shoes hung loose as if they dangled from strings and had no feet in them. The stare in his eyes searched me right through. Suddenly he lifted them above me to the window, uttered several terse sentences in Chinook, jumped off the cupboard and strode back to the village."

Emily is here sacrificing too much accuracy to unbecoming humor. Even calling the chief "Old Hipi" smacks of condescension. With his highly-developed sense of ceremony, a chief, according to experts, could not have acted with such incivility. He would have made a formal call on Emily as a sign of respect to a visiting white person and, because she was staying with the missionaries—the most important if not the most loved people in the community—he would probably have worn his potlatch hat as a mark of rank.

By 1898, an Indian chief might have addressed Emily and the missionaries in intelligible English, but she chose to have "Hipi" speak, more colorfully, in Chinook, although Nootka was his native tongue. But when writing her story, she no doubt recalled that missionaries usually learned Chinook Jargon rather than Nootka as it was a practical, simplified trade language used by many tribes to facilitate communication among them. Therefore, everyone at the welcoming ceremony understood Chinook, except Emily.

Chinook Jargon, I am told, has largely lost its influence today and English has taken its place. If two Indians from different tribes met, say, in Victoria, they would now use English as their common language, even though Nootka is basically the Island language. The Nootkan family of closely related languages extends from Cape Cook on the upper West Coast of Vancouver Island down to Port Renfrew, and is found again on the tip of the Olympic Peninsula in the State of Washington. It includes three main languages and many dialects.*

* *I am indebted to two Curators of Linguistics at the British Columbia Provincial Museum, Dr. Barbara S. Efrat, head of the Linguistics Division, and Robert Levine, for most of my information about the Vancouver Island Indians.*

The Indians in Ucluelet spoke Chinook to the missionaries, but to Emily alone they spoke "dumb talk." They called her "Kleewyck," a word that exists in both Nootka and Chinook Jargon. When she asked, with gestures, what the name meant, they pulled up the corners of their mouths with their fingers to delineate a smile. The name "Kleewyck," "The Laughing One," stuck. It became Emily's second name, the name of her pottery, and the name of her first book.

We wonder how she arrived at the spelling. The missionaries may have helped her, but perhaps she just put into the English alphabet the sounds she thought she heard. There was no written language among the Northwest Indians before the arrival of the white man, and linguists are still working on a practical alphabet. Spelling of Indian geographical names, as we know them, is thought to have originated among explorers and scientists who were influenced by their own language—English, French, Spanish—when spelling Indian names for their own use. As there was no alphabet from which Emily could transliterate into English, she, like the explorers, had to depend on sound. Considering her ineptitude for languages she did remarkably well, although "The Laughing One" is a little too strong. "The Smiling One" would be more accurate, and "Kleewyck" should be written in one word, not two.

The form "Kleewyck" is the anglicized version of a word from one of the Nootkan languages. Linguists would transcribe it as ƛ̓i·w̓ik– "always smiling." It is composed of the stem ƛ̓i·xʷ "to smile, laugh," plus the suffix -'ik- "given to, fond of smiling." In more practical alphabet symbols it is written Tl'iiwik the true spelling of Emily's beautiful name.*

* *Quoted from* Nootka Texts *by Edward Sapir and Morris Swadesh. Information quoted in the Tsishaath dialect (Port Alberni).*

There are other reflections on the Indian in *Klee Wyck* besides the caricature of Chief Hipi, although I am not certain whether her use of the words "squaw," "Injun" and "crone" should be construed as such or not. Most British Columbians in pioneer days, and even into the thirties, used these words frequently, and always disdainfully. We were unthinking, but shameless, racists. The so-called "squaw laws"—laws discriminatory to women—were almost a byword. Emily was as much aware as the rest of us that these words, often used as a calculated insult, could be offensive to the Indians, but somehow in her book they seem innocuous and kindly meant. "Crone" is more admissible to most readers than the others. When Emily described white women as crones, as she did on occasion, ridicule was apparent and intended. But her Indian crones are just

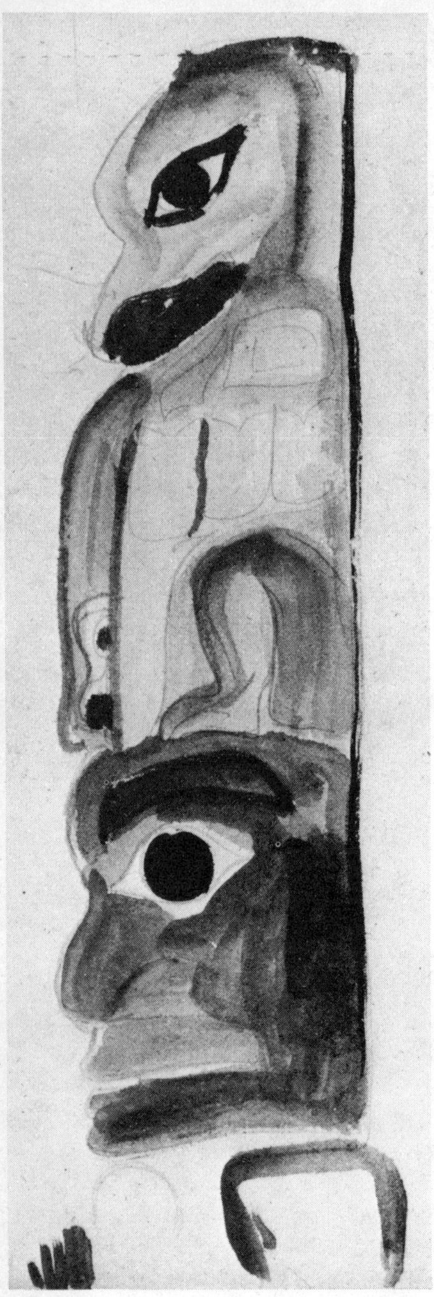

pitiable, wrinkled, shrunken old women with claw-like fingers squatting on the earth floor weaving cedar fiber into mats. There are no racist overtones. In fact, I doubt if Emily would have understood the word racism as it is used today. For her, the Indians were just simple, guileless people, good companions and guides on her sketching trips, and most important, good carvers. As a story-teller rather than a precise recorder of facts, she found them ideal subjects, and she was innocent of any conscious condescension when she made them the butt of her sometimes trenchant humor.

Another example of Emily's intuitive feeling of superiority and separation was her habit, even in Indian territory, of underlining the fact that a man was Indian by saying that she saw "the Indian Tom," or that she had bequeathed her painting materials to "the Indian Clutesi." She often stresses race before mentioning a name. Nor was she always flattering to the Indians as a people. In one of the most intriguing stories in *Klee Wyck*, "Kitwancool," she describes a harrowing, bumpy twenty-mile journey atop a pile of lumber loaded on her conveyance of the moment—a broken-down primitive wagon. Three men sat on two coal-oil boxes in front of her and one of them, Aleck, son of the Kitwancool chief, was treated like a hero. On arrival at the village, people came rushing out to welcome them, making a great fuss over the "hero-man." But he was no hero to the Mounted Police. He had, they told Emily on her return, gone in on the wagon with her to Kitwancool straight from jail, "a fierce, troublesome customer." What was Emily trying to suggest when she indicated that a whole village hero-worshipped a villainous character whom she referred to as a "jail bird"?

For me, as a linguist who earned her bread and butter from languages for over twenty years after an abortive career as an art teacher, the most painful reflection on the Indian in *Klee Wyck* is Emily's persistent use of an invented jargon. This kind of gibberish is degrading to a people who could express themselves in two and sometimes three languages. Emily knew only one. She could never handle accents, still less dialects or vernacular, and her jargon introduces an uncomfortable note into the Indian stories and creates a dilemma for a linguist.

We know, of course, that Emily's concern for Indian culture was centered almost exclusively on their poles. She showed little interest in their music or dances, somewhat more in their ceremonies and legends, but none at all in their languages. However, though most of her Indians spoke a curious fractured English, she was quick to notice—or was told—that the letter

"R" does not exist in the Indian languages of the North West, usually being supplanted by "L." A good example of this is the title of her touching story, "The Hully-up Paper."*

In her writings in general, Emily has tended to put garbled English into the mouths of people of different background or race. Most Victorians, in the days when Chinese men wore coolie hats and pigtails, and the women hobbled down Government Street on tiny, bound feet, spoke to their gardeners, cooks and houseboys in a home-brew pidgin. But while this, too, was motivated by caste, it was more justifiable than in the case of the Indians, even though most lived on reserves. For the Chinese in Emily's childhood, and even in mine, lived a mysterious life of their own, cut off from the rest of the city, and learned only scraps of sing-song English.

But to the many Japanese, East Indians, and others of oriental extraction, and the handful of Negroes in Victoria, we spoke normal English. But not Emily. In "Art and the House," a story in *The House of All Sorts,* she has the young Negro coal-carrier—who had attended local schools—saying, "Dat monk in de basement slam de winder ev'time de sacks come fo' to empty. What us do?"

Emily, as we know, had no interest in any language. After spending almost a year and a half in France, she had, she said, a basic vocabulary of a dozen or so words, which she promptly forgot. Therefore, because she was no linguist and had a poor ear for sound, the English spoken by the Indians in *Klee Wyck* must be approached with some skepticism. In the twenty-one stories which make up the book, the Indians speak good, or intelligible, English in seven, fractured English in ten, a mixture in one. There was no conversation in three of the stories. Two Indians stand out as shining examples in their literate use of English—Jimmie and his wife Louisa of the proud Haida tribe in the Queen Charlotte Islands, who guided Emily to the wave-pounded villages of Tanu, Skedans, Cumshewa and Chaatl in 1912. They were the aristocrats of her Indian acquaintance. They lived in a well-furnished house and had some pretense to English culture. Most of the others spoke pure gibberish. In one of the longest stories, "Salt Water,"* there is a curious blend of school and broken English in the same family. After a stormy, wave-tossed passage, the uncle anchored his boat in Skedans Bay. "Can we go nearer?" Emily asked. He shook his head. "No can, water floor welly wicked, make boat bloke." Two pages later, when they had landed on the beach, the niece cries out in impeccable English, "It (the boat) is driving for the reef!" Since this incident (almost

* The Heart of a Peacock, *Oxford University Press, Toronto, 1953.*

* *It is interesting to note that Emily herself had a great deal of trouble with this story and did not consider it entirely successful. She wrote to Ruth Humphrey on May 8, 1938: "I've been wrestling again with 'Salt Water and a Woman' (an earlier title). . . . It's reactions to, on, over and under the sea poorly done, I'm afraid, but I've put lots of honest grind on it. Am typing it for the*

third time. . . . I do seem to find such cartloads of new faults with each re-reading, as tho' I could never get it clear or right on paper."

accident) took place in 1928, it is likely that the uncle would also have spoken adequate English.

There is more confusion a few pages later when a Norwegian seine boat comes to their rescue. The big Norwegian sailors, "with long beards like brigands," spoke good English as they yelled, "Hurry! Hurry!" The captain, as he later stood in the doorway to Emily's cabin, spoke not only good, but colloquial English.

"Wants a few minutes to midnight—then I shall put you off at the scows."

"The scows?"

"Yep, scows tied up in Cumshewa Inlet for the fish boats to dump their catches in."

"What shall I do there?"

"When the scows are full, 'packers' come and tow them to the canneries."

"And I must sit among the fish and wait for a packer?"

"That's the idea."

"How long before one will come?"

"Ask the fish."

Curiously, the only Anglo-Saxons around, Smith and Jones on the scow (probably English, judging by Smith's use of the word "nipper" when referring to Emily's Ginger Pop), spoke ungrammatical English, somewhat better than the Indians, but with none of the polish of the Norwegian Captain:

"Us'll have first go," said Smith.

Then, later:

"You've et well; how'd you like a sleep?"

A nameless little person, of unknown nationality, whose speech defies all analysis, then enters Emily's cabin, like a gnome from a fairy tale. He remains a shadowy little creature who watched over Emily. His few lines do not help to identify him.

"Come you please, lady."

"I do wish you good sleep lady."

"Please, lady, nobody do sleep when at night we go."

"Quick, go! Man do be mad."

Despite the drama of this exciting tale and Emily's inimitable description of the many calamities that befell her on this disastrous sketching trip, her linguistic adventures left me dazed and I was thankful to see her finally scrambling up the ladder to the canners' wharf and hear an ordinary Canadian voice shouting down at her peremptorily,

"Come on there. What's the matter down there? . . . Hurry!"

Indeed, what was the matter?

Contact with the white man and civilization altered in 1862, when a major smallpox epidemic decimated the Indian population. The survivors abandoned their noble totem poles and huddled together in larger villages, such as Skidegate, Masset and Greenville. These were called missionary villages and each had a store, a school, an Indian agent and a church. But the poles were disappearing there too—the reason Emily found Greenville so disappointing for sketching in 1928. The missionaries were determined to stamp out the "heathen" languages of the natives, and English was compulsory in the schools. In fact, many Indian children were subjected to corporal punishment if they were heard speaking their own language. Therefore, Indians born after about 1880, including "Old Hipi," must necessarily have had some fluency in English, and the Indians Emily met while sketching in 1912 and 1928 had still less excuse for massacring the English tongue.

In the charming story "Wash Mary," in *Klee Wyck,* Emily succeeds in giving us, with pathos and humor, a vivid word picture of Mrs. Carr's washerwoman. It is told with such economy of means that her life story is encompassed in two-and-a-half pages of text. The only discernible discrimination is in the sobriquet itself. Mrs. Carr, being a kindly woman, used the word sympathetically, but it is doubtful that she would have called a white woman "Wash Mary." More subtle is the question of language. The Carrs knew that Mary spoke English because, as a good Catholic, she had left the Songhees' reserve to live in Victoria "as white people did." Yet either in fact, or because Emily colored her story later, little Emily's mother taught her to say "chahko muckamuck" so that she could call Mary to dinner. The sound intrigued Emily and she hung around until noon, then skipped across the yard calling out this rather unappetizing Indian summons as she ran. This became almost a game between the two and little Emily liked to watch Mary wash the suds from her brown arms, dry them on her full skirt, and hurry expectantly to the kitchen.

Of course, had Emily just announced "dinner is ready," or even "come and get it," Mary would have hurried just as fast and understood just as well. But then we would have been deprived of this engaging little anecdote.

Sophie's English, Emily said, was "good enough" unless her husband Frank was present, when she became as "dumb as a plate," embarrassed because she did not have his "school English." But Emily is downgrading her friend to make a better story, as Sophie lived at the North Vancouver Mission and would be expected to speak English there. We thus have one more example of Emily's desire to keep her Indian friends, and characters in her stories, as Indian as possible—Indian according to her concept—a little primitive, a little exotic, really grown-up children. Once more she used poetic license when she quotes Sophie as saying during their first meeting, "Money no matter. Old clo' 'waum skirt—good fo' basket." But Emily was not consistent. At times Sophie spoke surprisingly well, and then would lapse into broken English again and say, "My mad fo' boy bloke my plitty glave flower,"—only doing that well, Emily explains, because, in her fury, she forgot to be "shy of the English words."

The use of such burlesque language, whatever the reason, is unfair to the Indians, as they could do much better. Sophie proved this when she wrote to Emily on August 6, 1915, from North Vancouver:

> My dear Emily
>
> I would only be too glad if I could go, but I am not feeling well. The waves make me sick. So you must not feel sorry about it.
>
> I would bring the mat or send it but because the lady is not sure to buy it. The Indians are not like the white people, the lady is not allowed to go alone any place.
>
> Don't be too sorry about it though I can't help it. I'd like so much to go but I don't like the sea voyage.
>
> Your dear friend,
> Sophie Frank

Two things are clear from this letter: (1) That Sophie could write (and presumably speak) reasonably grammatical English, obviously learned at school. (2) That she did not make a single spelling error, and could probably spell better than Emily!

Possibly the finest and most sincere tribute Emily ever paid to the Indians was not in *Klee Wyck,* where she often distorted the truth and humiliated the Indian to heighten humor and intensify dramatic effect, but in a piece of straightforward reporting, "Modern and Indian Art of the West Coast," published in the supplement of the McGill News, in June 1929.

When the Europeans arrived in the eighteenth century, almost every sheltered bay and cove along the southwest coast of Vancouver Island, and some of the outer islands, already had a settlement. Fortunately there were still many left to explore when Emily first began sketching at Ucluelet and other West Coast villages in 1898. But most were difficult to reach, and she describes in this article the terrifying experiences she had getting to them and the hardships she endured to stay there and sketch. She also explains the development of her work—from the early days of casual sketching, for the pure joy of painting, to the day she was startled into realization that the Indian way of life was rapidly passing and that it behooved her to reproduce their great, carved poles on paper while they were still standing straight and proud. She worked from dawn to dusk in a race with time.

But the real essence of Emily's article is her profound admiration for Indian art. She reminds us that it is the oldest art in Canada but, at the same time, far more "modern" in spirit than anything else in the West. To her, it was vital, alive, free and unfettered. The artists, she said, searched beneath the surface for the hidden thing, which is felt rather than seen—the "reality," the underlying spirit. She strove to express this mysterious spirit faithfully in all her later work. She acknowledged the carver's keen eye for beauty and symmetry, and envied his infinite patience and deep desire for self-expression—with no thought of recompense, reward or fame. Pride in the totem he was striving to represent was all the compensation he needed.

In one short paragraph Emily sums up, without pretense, the warmth of her feelings for the Indian. It is simple, sincere, and seems to come right from the heart:

> My own work has been humble enough, and it falls very far short of what I wish it could be. But it has been done largely amongst the Indians, and so I have learned a good deal about them. I have always loved these people of whom there were a great many about Victoria when I was a child; and several reservations. Frequently the Indians camped round on the beaches in the course of their travels up and down the coast in their great canoes and often I used to wish I had been born an Indian.

But, like a pendulum, Emily often swung from one extreme to another—from joy to sorrow, from love to hate, from friend to foe. Her sentiments for the Indians also vacillated. She venerated their art, struggled ceaselessly to interpret it and was able to convince herself for years that her regard for the people almost equaled her awed admiration of their poles. True, she liked the Indians, enjoyed living among them for short periods and bemoaned sincerely the deleterious effects of white civilization on their way of life. But when she attempted to convince *us* of her "love" for the "dear" Indians, it became less credible. In a burst of romantic feeling, she endowed them with virtues they did not always possess. We hear little of their negative qualities—little, that is, in her public writings.

But in 1928, while making preparations for her last sketching trip to the North, in a moment of truth, speaking more as an annoyed woman than a legend, she complained to Marius Barbeau that the Indians had become difficult. "I understand more than most the unlimited patience and perseverance, against odds and discomfiture one must go through to get it out of them. . . ."* A month later, she wrote to Barbeau again this time accusing the Indians of being avaricious, ". . . the Indians do charge so tremendously."*

* *Emily to Marius Barbeau, January 28, 1928. Marius Barbeau Collection, Canadian Centre for Folk Studies, National Museum of Man, National Museums of Canada, Ottawa.*

* *Ibid. February 27, 1928.*

Emily criticizes the Indians still more severely towards the end of her life in *The Book of Small* when she compares the Indians with the Chinese to the advantage of the latter:

> It was the Chinese man but the Indian woman who shouldered the burden. The Chinaman's wife was back home in China. The Indian rolled leisurely and with empty hands, behind his squaw. A cedar-root burden basket of her own weaving was slung across the woman's back, steadied by a woven pack strap worn across the chest. Women of some tribes wore the strap across their foreheads, pushing their heads forward against the burden's weight.
>
> The Indian squatted upon each doorstep to rest. The Chinaman never rested—he kept up his mechanical jog-trot all day. He lived frugally, sending the earnings of his brown, calloused hands and his sweating toil home to China. The Indian wasted no sweat on labor — he took from nature those things which came easiest. What money he earned he spent in the nearest store immediately, exchanging it for whatever pleased his eye or his stomach. The Indian's money circulated; he had no idea of its value nor of saving it. The satisfying of immediate needs was enough for him. . . ."*

* The Book of Small, *p.107.*

The key to Emily's perplexing attitude to the Indian is perhaps to be found in one of her own statements: "The white man more or less understood the childlike Indian; he belonged to his own hemisphere. The Oriental eluded him." *

* The Book of Small, *p.108.*

Emily Pauline Johnson,* famous as the Mohawk Princess, Tekahion-wake, has been censured by some contemporary critics* for her failure to interpret the Indian to the white man

* E. Pauline Johnson *1861-1913.*

* *N. Shrive, "What Happened to Pauline?"* Canadian Literature, XIII *(1962).*

satisfactorily. This verdict on another indomitable woman applies equally to our Klee Wyck. It is fair to say that the image of the Indian Emily bequeathed to us is sentimental, somewhat demeaning, and unreal; and that the book *Klee Wyck,* although autobiographical, is a blend of fable and fact.

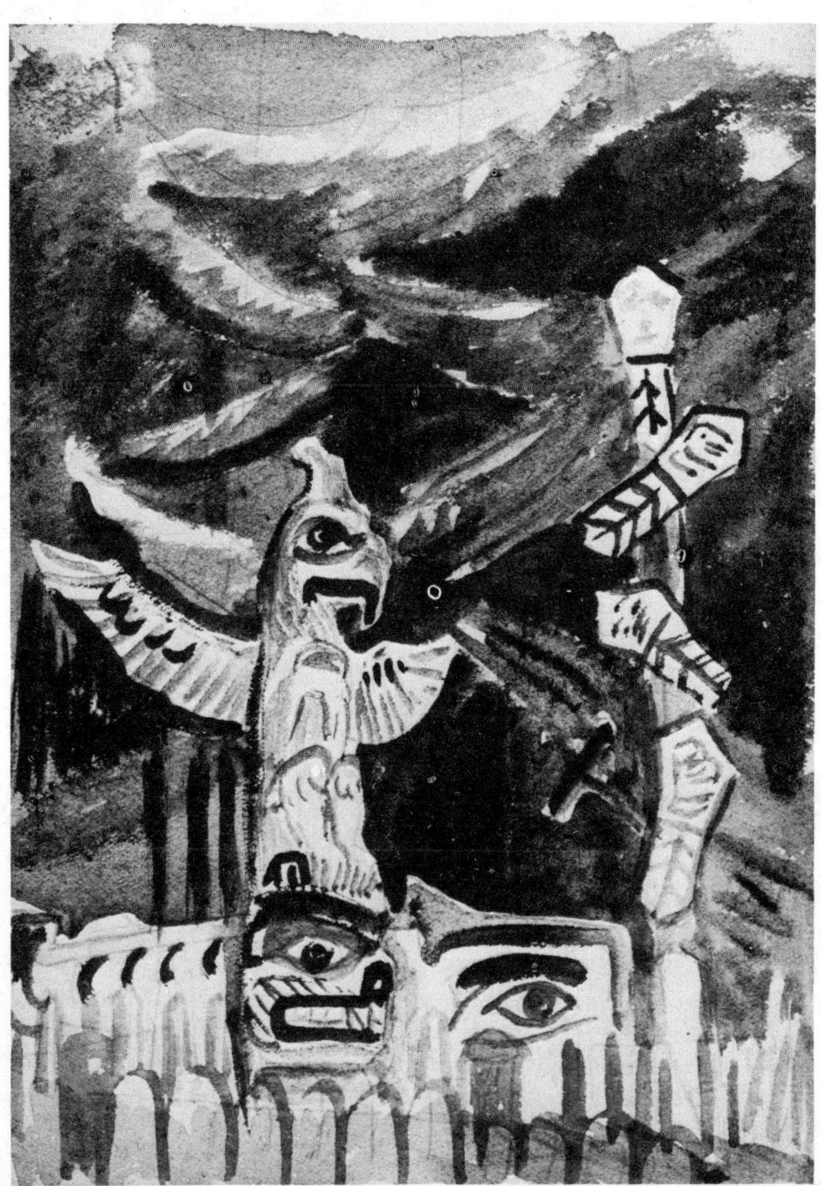

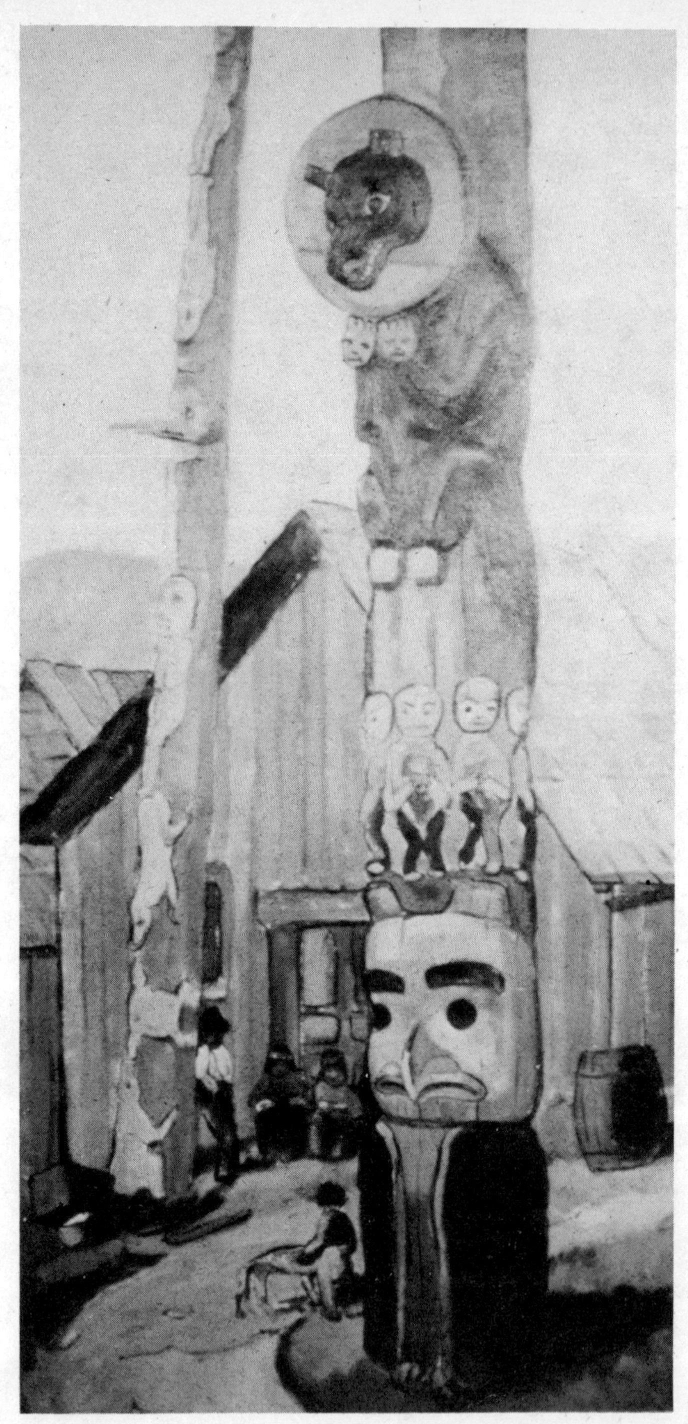

The Bear and Moon Totem.
collection of F. Schaeffer, Toronto

The Carr-Barbeau Mystery

Who "discovered" Emily Carr? This question was raised but not fully or convincingly answered in a recent essay by that title in the *Journal of Canadian Art History*.* Even in her summation, the author of the essay leaves us stranded amid a fresh series of questions. Yet the essay provides considerable substance for rumination and also for argument, since the author has made it a point to challenge the claim of Marius Barbeau to be Emily's discoverer. My aim is to contribute to the substance of the argument, to vindicate Barbeau and to eliminate all question marks but one—an enormous, almost indelible brute that resists any effort at erasure.

I approach my subject with sentiment (because of my feelings for Emily), with respect (because of my admiration for Barbeau's learning) and with humor (because both had so much of it).

The essay under discussion is prefaced by a résumé of the accepted and perpetuated version of the Emily Carr discovery story, familiar to most of us. But the crux of the matter, upon which the whole paper depends is:

> This long perpetuated story of Emily Carr's "discovery" may well be questioned. . . .

The gist of the questioning is of course a skeptical examination of the popular version of the story, and of the claims that have been made by and for the "discoverers" of Emily: Eric Brown, former director of the National Gallery of Canada; H. Mortimer-Lamb, Vancouver mining engineer and art connoisseur; and Dr. Marius Barbeau, former ethnologist at the National Museum of Canada. Curiously, no credit is given in this context to Mark Tobey—that somewhat imperious master from Seattle who has emphatically declared that, "there would have been no Emily Carr if it had not been for me." This is naturally only a half-truth but, in a sense, he also qualifies as a "discoverer."

But who deserves the honors at home? After scanning the merits of the three Canadian candidates, the essay, somewhat perplexingly, hands the distinction of discovery to Emily herself:

> The real discoverer (if one can use the word) was Emily Carr herself. She contacted Barbeau through whom she subsequently met Brown.

* The Journal of Canadian Art History, *Vol. 1 No. 2 Fall 1974. by Maria Tippett.*

To me this is a bit like saying that it is not the diver but the oyster that is the discoverer of the pearl. But surely whatever else may be involved in discovery, in the arts it is a matter of sensitive recognition. No artist can discover himself. Though he may *present* himself, he has to wait for the moment of recognition from some other person or group of persons. Thoughtful readers of the essay are likely to feel that it was begun with a much too simplistic notion of what "discovery" involves.

If Tobey is kept out of the running, the leading contender for the title of "discoverer" is, in my view, Marius Barbeau, who, though consistently underrated or overlooked by the critics, has never been bashful in claiming this honor for himself. Criticism has long acknowledged the debt Emily owed to the influence of Brown, Lawren Harris, the Group of Seven in general and, more speculatively, Tobey. But Barbeau's image is still shadowy behind the inscrutable totem poles that brought him, the scientist, and Emily, the painter, together. He did not profoundly influence the development of her art, as did the others; but his great knowledge of Indian lore was invaluable in showing her a new way of seeing and feeling the Indian world which for a time cemented a strong bond between them. Many of Barbeau's books, and Emily's first book, are memorials to the native Indians and native artists of the North Pacific Coast.

Barbeau (1883-1969) had an impressive background. He was an ethnologist and folklorist with the National Museum from 1911 until his retirement in 1948; he was a Rhodes scholar and the author of more than fifty books and countless monographs and articles. His name is known to every student of Indian culture in Northwest British Columbia. Such qualifications cannot be lightly brushed aside, though opinions about him are divided and debatable. Many who knew him laud and love him, often speaking of him with bemused perplexity as if holding back a humorous tale. Most are persuaded of his sincerity, honesty and seriousness of purpose. But a few challenge his accuracy and even his integrity. Are they justified, because all the facts do not as yet jibe, in calling such an eminent and respected scholar a hypocrite? Or perhaps even a liar?

The author of "Who 'Discovered' Emily Carr?" does just that. Neither word is explicit in the text, but running through the essay is a faint, but audible, obligato of moral accusation. It is not my wish, however, to engage in polemics with the author, but only to present a little more evidence that may help to defend this most winning and energetic of all Emily's friends, who has so unfortunately become a controversial figure in Emily Carr research. Although he has long been credited as the man who "forged the first link of the chain which . . . brought both Miss Carr and her pictures to Ottawa,"* the essay implies, not too obscurely, that Barbeau is a trouble-maker and himself helped to create this myth by claiming to have visited Emily's studio in 1915, 1921, and 1926. These generally-accepted dates are disputed, particularly the first two, proof of which would automatically put Barbeau ahead of the field.

* *Muriel Brewster, "Some Ladies Prefer Indians,"* Toronto Star Weekly, *January 21, 1928.*

My interest in Barbeau as a distinctive and unmistakable personality in his own right grew slowly. For years I thought of him as Emily's "discoverer" in 1915 and as an active member of her entourage during the more intense phase of their friendship from October 1926 to June 1928. But Emily was always the dominant figure. In studying their relationship more closely, however, I had trouble in keeping Barbeau in second place. He was too ebullient for that. He compels attention; his books compel attention; and his words arouse in us a keener appreciation of the Indians, their villages and their totem poles than Emily's pictorial records have ever been able to do. However sketchily he may be drawn in writings about him, his voice from the past is insistent and, in all fairness, we must listen to him as we listened to Emily's other well-known friends who, in 1927, helped Barbeau to give the big push that enabled her to emerge from her cocoon of isolation on the West Coast.

According to the essay, Emily and Barbeau did not meet until, or more likely after, 1926 when she "pointed herself out to [him]." This contradicts Barbeau's story that he first heard of her from his Tsimsyan* interpreter at Port Simpson in the early months of 1915 and visited her the following spring. The assumption has much to support it but is, I feel, overhasty, based as it is on two inconclusive letters:

* *Tsimshian*

1. Emily to Barbeau, October 23, 1926(?), inviting him to visit her studio. Suggested evidence that they did not meet before this date.
2. Barbeau to Brown, October 3, 1927. Suggested evidence that: (a) Emily did not meet Barbeau even in 1926 and (b) she did not meet Barbeau before Brown.

*Letter of October 23, 1926(?)**

This letter is a most damaging piece of evidence since it appears to furnish incontrovertible proof that Emily and Barbeau did not meet until at least October 1926. Emily describes her Indian sketching trips as if to a stranger, invites him to visit her, and gives him instructions on how to reach her studio from the CPR wharf.

* *Marius Barbeau Collection, Canadian Centre for Folk Studies, The National Museum of Man, National Museums of Canada, Ottawa; Emily to Barbeau, October 23 (no year date given).*

There must be an explanation for this ambiguous letter, but perhaps the links with hard evidence are so obscure that they may never be found. For the time being, Barbeau's defense is left with a strong conviction of his innocence, but a weak case. It must be remembered, though, that his two previous assumed visits to Emily were not a conspicuous success. She was busy, distracted, took little notice of him, and no real rapport was established. Is it therefore not possible that Emily, in this troublesome letter, took refuge in the stiff Victorian formality she so often adopted when she did not know a person well? Perhaps she believed that Barbeau had forgotten his way to her studio after the elapse of so many years. Perhaps (and knowing her ways, I feel this is not at all unlikely) she had even forgotten all about him. She may even have forgotten his name, and not realized that she was addressing a man she had already met.

This letter must be read with a sharp eye if certain nuances are not to be overlooked. In the essay, for instance, it is arbitrarily dated 1926, without explanation or note, although my copy of the same letter bears no year date. The year was no doubt determined, or assumed, from Emily's reference to a series of five lectures Barbeau was giving on the Northwest Coast Indians at the University of British Columbia in Vancouver from October 21-27, 1926.* A similar series was given at the same place in the same month (October 6-12) in 1927.* Now, is it not possible that Barbeau, always in demand as a speaker, might have given other lectures at the University in connection with his earlier visits to the West Coast? I think this is a distinct possibility which future historians must explore, although I could find no reference to any lectures in *The Ubyssey* in 1921. Nineteen-fifteen, the assumed year of his first visit, will be even harder to research since *The Ubyssey* was not founded until 1918. For now, my case must rest upon supposition.

Even if posterity agrees that Emily introduced herself to Barbeau and not conversely, as I claim, and that they first met as late as 1926 or even 1927, their meeting could not have led to her discovery and recognition had Barbeau not been aided by a unique set of fortuitous circumstances. Although the popular version stresses that Barbeau was the first to sense her great potential as a painter, and recommended her work to Eric Brown, the Director of the National Gallery, it was only Brown's decision to include her paintings on Indian themes in the Exhibition of Canadian West Coast Art, Native and Modern, at the National Gallery in 1927 that brought about her sudden and dramatic acceptance on the national art scene.

* The Ubyssey, *Vol. IX No. 7 Vancouver, October 19, 1926.*

* *Ibid Vol. X No. 2 Vancouver, October 4, 1927.*

*Letter of October 3, 1927**

The date of this letter is used as additional evidence to support the suspicion, conveyed in the essay, that Barbeau did not meet Emily even in 1926:

> In writing to Brown in October 1927, Barbeau did not mention having met Carr or owning any of her paintings. . . . There is no evidence to show that Barbeau met Carr's 1926 invitation. . . . If such a meeting took place he did not tell Brown in his letter of October 3 . . .

Now why in the world should Barbeau have reported to Brown on October 3, *1927* that a meeting had (or had not) taken place almost a year before? During this interval they had had many opportunities to discuss Emily and her work in Ottawa and there was surely no need for Barbeau (unaware that he would be on trial in the future) to recall, in correspondence, any of his previous visits to Emily.

Moreover, there is some fairly explicit evidence on hand to show that Barbeau did see Emily in 1926. For one thing, she informed him in November (1927) that:

> The [pottery] bells are finished and I am shipping them today. I have only the address on the letter heading you wrote me last year but I suppose it will be right now.*

The above passage is proof at least that Emily and Barbeau corresponded in 1926, and in the circumstances, it strongly indicates that a meeting also took place.

The bells were almost certainly seen, and ordered, in Emily's studio during a visit documented by Barbeau himself in his letter to Brown October 3, 1927:

> I will go and see her on the 14th, after my series of lectures at the Univ. is over.

Also in this letter we find another ambiguous statement that shows Barbeau at his bewildering best:

> I saw 4 of her [Emily's] paintings at Hazelton. . . . They were certainly from a genuine artist.

Should we interpret this passage to mean, as the essayist obviously does, that Barbeau had not seen any of Emily's works in her studio, before he went to Hazelton? Definitely not. This answer is not dictated by my avowed and definite bias for Barbeau, but by common sense. It was just by chance that he ran across these particular four paintings in Hazelton during his summer on the Nass and Skeena rivers, and as he had only arrived in Vancouver from Hazelton shortly before writing to

* *NGC, Barbeau to Brown, October 3, 1927.*

* *Marius Barbeau Collection, Canadian Centre for Folk Studies, the National Museum of Man, National Museums of Canada, Ottawa; Emily to Barbeau, November 3, (1927) Barbeau seems to have used these bells as gifts. He gave one, in the form of a bird, to Mrs. Douglas Leechman, who donated it to the Art Gallery of Greater Victoria in 1972.*

Brown, it was also by chance that he mentioned them in his letter.

A parting pot shot is aimed at Barbeau:

> Nor does Carr mention in any of her published writings that she met Barbeau before Brown. [that is, before September 1927]

This is true. But it means little since Emily's writings are spotty. Inexplicable blanks occur (perhaps owing to the editing of her journals) just when we are anticipating an interesting entry. In her autobiography, *Growing Pains,* for instance, aside from a brief anonymous reference to Tobey, she does not name a single person connected with her professional life from 1913 to 1927 when Brown bursts dramatically into the story. So why should she make an exception for Barbeau? Along with Brown and other friends in the eastern art world, he is mentioned in her journals, *Hundreds and Thousands,* in a vivid description of the opening of the Canadian West Coast Art Exhibition and the events surrounding it, but is omitted entirely in her entries for 1930, a year when he played an important role in her life and career.

Her only other book in which Barbeau could have been mentioned is *The House of All Sorts.* The studio in this house is where his meetings with Emily took place; but the house itself, her tenants and her animals were the subjects of this book, and only one friend, Eric Brown, is identified by name.

This is not surprising. Emily wrote these books very late in life when she had neither seen nor corresponded with Barbeau for over ten years;* but Brown, to whom she remained grateful, was still fresh in her mind. Moreover, she usually forgot her friends quickly when they were at a distance or ceased to be of use or interest to her; and when she turned away from the Indians to seek future inspiration in the forest, soon after her visit to Barbeau in 1930, she also turned away from him. He was expendable; his star sank rapidly; and she had little reason to revive her memories of him when she wrote her books.*

The inferences that Emily did not meet Barbeau before September 1927, that is, after she met Brown, are dubious and unfair without more evidence to substantiate them. If we are to believe Barbeau's story (and most of us do), he induced Emily to get down her pictures from the garret in 1926 and then carefully selected and set aside sixty of them, from which Brown made a final choice when he and his wife Maud visited her that September.*

Thrilled at the prospect of having her scorned paintings

* *Except for a note of congratulations from Barbeau on the publication of* Klee Wyck *and Emily's acknowledgement of April 1942.*

* *AGT, Barbeau to Grace Pincoe, Librarian, AGT, August 28, 1945: "We (Emily and Barbeau) did not afterwards keep in touch as we had done for awhile. . . . Nan Cheney . . . could tell much about those years."*

* *AGT, Barbeau to Grace Pincoe, August 28, 1945. Barbeau gave the figure of 80 in this letter, but repeated 60 in the CBC broadcast of December 3, 1957.*

exhibited at long last, and awed that the prestigious National Gallery of Canada should wish to display them, Emily had to hustle to get them packed and shipped early enough to ensure their arrival in Ottawa in time for the opening of the Canadian West Coast Art Exhibition. She was exhausted by the time the last crate had been nailed shut:

> Oh, what a job! It is well I did not realize or I fear I would not have had the courage to undertake it. . . . The man had very little sense, and I worked like two men myself. In fact I had to go to bed all in at 7 o'clock both Monday and Tuesday nights and I felt as if I never wanted to see a picture again.*

* *NGC, Emily to Eric Brown, September 28, 1927.*

The exhibition was being arranged by the National Gallery in cooperation with the National Museum, and Barbeau, as ethnologist for the museum, was working in close association with Brown. He also functioned as Brown's talent scout while in the West and, in this capacity, called on Emily and viewed the work of other British Columbia artists such as C.H. Scott and F.H. Varley of Vancouver. He was especially impressed by the latter's mountain sketches, selected a few to send East and recommended to Brown that they also be included in the exhibition.

Others besides myself have come forward in defense of Barbeau, notably Maud Brown, whose testimony is unique in that she was present when Barbeau told Brown about *meeting* Emily. She says so in a letter to me* and in her book, *Breaking Barriers.** The essay refers to Maud's book, but the key sentence is inexplicably overlooked:

* *F. Maud Brown to the author, May 19, 1975.*

* *F. Maud Brown,* Breaking Barriers, *The Society for Art Publications, 1964, p.103.*

> Before the second trip [1927], however, Marius Barbeau . . . had given Eric [Brown] some valuable information. He told of an artist he had met in British Columbia, named Emily Carr.

"*Met*" is, of course, the decisive word here.

Because Maud followed these events as they unfolded and knows what happened, while the rest of us might write pages of supposition and still guess wrong, she should, I feel, have the last word on the order in which these two men met Emily. She sums it up this way:

> Barbeau discovered Emily Carr and Eric started her painting again. Honours divided.*

* *F. Maud Brown to the author, May 19, 1975.*

And what of the third candidate, Harold Mortimer-Lamb? He is still trailing, even though A.Y. Jackson credits him with being "the first person to realize the potentiality of Emily Carr's work. . . ."* But although Mortimer-Lamb was one of the first to

* *A.Y. Jackson,* A Painter's Country, *Clarke, Irwin Co. Ltd., Toronto, 1964.*

promote Emily, drawing her to Brown's attention as early as October 24, 1921,* Barbeau also claims to have told Brown about her Indian paintings the same year—in January, after his visit with her and return to Ottawa from his 1921 field trip to British Columbia.* In the race to discover Emily, this would put him nine months ahead of Mortimer-Lamb.* Still the important thing is not who got to Brown first, but how Brown reacted. And he proved to be resistant to Mortimer-Lamb's enthusiasm, but receptive to Barbeau's recommendation.

There is little solid evidence to support Barbeau's story of meeting with Emily in 1921, much less in 1915. He himself seems to deny both when writing for publication in 1932:

> An interesting find was made at this time* of a Western Canadian painter so far unknown who had not yet been recognized by her own community—Emily Carr of Victoria.*

But this remark is vague and seems to refer to the National Gallery's late discovery of Emily rather than his own, because he has insisted elsewhere that he not only discovered Emily but was *reputed* to have discovered her. As proof, he mentions the invitation he received from Ryerson Press to write a short book about her for their art series.*

Regrettably, most of Barbeau's descriptions of Emily, her studio and her pictures were given in old age when his memory was blurred by time, and events tend to overlap. And yet his recollections give the impression of reliving an actual experience, not just repeating what he had later read or heard. The most engaging version of the story of his three visits to Emily's studio, in which he describes pets and paintings, rug hooking and pottery making in a sprightly style, was taped for a CBC radio broadcast in 1958.*

First Visit—1915

While in Victoria in 1915 Barbeau stayed, he said, with an old friend, Dr. C.F. Newcombe, an acknowledged authority on Indian art, who was also a friend of Emily's. Newcombe arranged a visit between the two, but only after warning Barbeau that he would find Emily queer and unfriendly—which he apparently did. Still, despite errors and fuzzy details, Barbeau's account of his initial encounter with Emily sounds genuine, and the "spooky" studio comes alive with rightly identified animals. But they were obviously sparring and felt little attraction for one another at first. Barbeau has confessed as much:

> I went away without definite impressions or a lively interest in her and her accomplishments.

* *NGC, Brown to H. Mortimer-Lamb, November 23, 1921.*

* Geological Surveys of Canada *(1920-1921).*

* *Walter J. Phillips, a well-known artist who did some fine wood engravings of Kwakiutl carvings, also called Brown's attention to Emily's work at an early date—1927. (From a telephone conversation with Mrs. Phillips in Victoria in 1977.) Three of Phillips's engravings are published in Barbeau's* Totem Poles, *Vol II, pp.459, 460, 461.*

* *1927, when the NGC was preparing for the* Canadian West Coast Art Exhibition.

* Marius Barbeau, "The Canadian Northwest—Theme for Modern Painters," Magazine of Art *(American Federation of Arts), Washington, Vol. XXIV, No. 5, May 1932.*

* *"Emily Carr, Painter and Writer," CBC Recording, December 3, 1957. This book was never written.*

* *"Portrait in Memory—Emily Carr," CBC broadcast April 9, 1958.*

Second Visit—1921

This visit was more congenial than the first, but Barbeau still felt uncomfortable among so many strange pets, particularly objecting to a noisy crow that flew around freely. But again they failed to establish a meaningful relationship, and Emily still refused to show or discuss her Indian work:

> Of painting and pictures no mention from her just then. Still I saw totem poles hanging on the wall in her studio.

Third Visit—1926

The suspicion and indifference that had marred the earlier visits had dissipated by 1926, and Emily even invited Barbeau to stay in her boarding house as a paying guest. But he, a fastidious man, begged off: "I preferred staying in my second-class hotel." Emily even mellowed enough to open up her "long, narrow, black box not unlike a coffin,"* which contained many of her sketches and also served as a room-divider between studio and work area. She pulled out one sketch after another and discussed her work with Barbeau for the first time. In his enthusiasm, he completely forgot his distaste for the strange birds and beasts and the dangling cobwebs that had previously distracted him:

> I was getting acquainted with her work and then, too, she felt I had a genuine interest [in it] which she didn't meet elsewhere. I was interested in these pictures because they were rather faithful interpretations of the totems I had seen. . . . They were mildly impressionistic, but . . . I liked impressionism in painting. Besides, my interest in her had developed since my earlier visit.

This new-found harmony was rudely disrupted by Mrs. Galloway, a friend Barbeau had brought with him,* when her young daughter was bitten by Woo, Emily's small Javanese monkey:

> There was a big fuss. Mrs. Galloway was afraid the child would get blood poisoning, as the King of Bulgaria had just been bitten by his pet monkey and had died.* Emily Carr was annoyed at this fussy woman. She said, "No, Woo has clean teeth—no danger there."

To a friend like myself, who knew Emily well—and Woo all too well—this rings absolutely true. It is almost precisely what she indignantly said to a young friend of mine who was also bitten by Woo. Emily pounced on him in a fury because he had insulted Woo and her "clean teeth" by rushing off to a doctor for

* The House of All Sorts, *Clarke, Irwin & Co. Ltd., Toronto. First paperback edition, 1967, p.89.*

* *The Galloway story has a follow-up which adds credence to it. In March 1928 Barbeau wrote Emily that Mrs. Galloway and her daughter were visiting his home in Ottawa. (The Marius Barbeau Collection, the National Museum of Man.)*

* *This statement is not historically accurate.*

an injection of anti-tetanus.

It is noteworthy that Woo, the *enfant terrible* of the studio, is only mentioned in Barbeau's description of the 1926 visit. Had he described her antics in 1915 or 1921, all his testimony would have to be questioned because she only acquired Woo in 1923. But in 1926 Woo was very much present.

Still more miscellaneous evidence has turned up in support of Barbeau's visits:

1. A reporter for the *Toronto Star*,* after interviewing Barbeau at the National Gallery while the Canadian West Coast Art Exhibition was still on the walls, quotes him as saying:

   > When I first saw Emily Carr's pictures . . . [they] were hidden all over her house . . .

   Since both Emily and Brown were bound to read this statement, it is extremely unlikely that Barbeau would claim to have visited Emily if he had not done so.

2. Barbeau's letters to
   a) Grace Pincoe, August 28, 1945.*
   and Ruth Humphrey, November 27, 1957.*
3. Barbeau's two radio broadcasts:
   December 3, 1957 and April 9, 1958.

   In these four documents Barbeau either describes or lists all three of his claimed visits to Emily's studio.
4. Corroboration by Nan Cheney, long-time friend of both Barbeau and Emily (in a conversation with me), and by Maud Brown (in an interview with me in September 1974).

Another of Barbeau's supporters is Seattle artist Viola Patterson, who told me that Barbeau was both friend and student of her late painter husband, Ambrose, in 1908 in St-Jean du Doigt, France. The Pattersons lost touch with him over the years, but contact was apparently re-established in 1929* when Barbeau went to Seattle. They also knew Emily well, but although they visited her regularly from the early twenties to the early forties, their paths never crossed Barbeau's in her studio. However, Viola would be very surprised, she says, if Barbeau did not meet Emily during those early years because he knew about her and was vitally interested in her kind of totem art. But sadly, like other friends, Viola can produce no proof.*

The most confusing aspect of Barbeau's reminiscences is the lack of uniformity in his dates. He has given both 1915 and 1916 as the date of his first visit, and either 1920 or 1921 for the

* *Muriel Brewster, the* Toronto Star Weekly, *January 21, 1928.*

* *Maria Tippett claims that this 1945 letter contains the only evidence that Barbeau visited Emily before October 1926. Of course there is more.*

* *Barbeau's letter is a reply to Ruth Humphrey's of November 20, 1957, in which she requests biographical material for use in her article on Emily Carr for the* B.C. Centennial Anthology, *then in press.*

* *Ambrose Patterson to Barbeau, June 1929*

* *Viola Patterson to the author, May 30, 1975.*

second. But he never wavers about 1926, perhaps because this visit was so much later, and more significant, than the first two.

In an attempt to eliminate these inconsistencies, I consulted the *Summary Reports of the Geological Surveys of Canada** and learned that Barbeau did not come to the West Coast in 1916, but did spend a period of three months in the early part of 1915 at Port Simpson, British Columbia, on Tsimsyan* field work. He also undertook a seven month investigation in the field of ethnology of the Gitksan tribes, still farther north in the Province, from June 1920 to January 1921, visiting Victoria on his way home as was his custom.

In the summer of 1926, he was once more in the North restoring totem poles at Kitwanga, and in 1927, again in the summer, he was in the Nass and Skeena areas making a study of native music in cooperation with Dr. Ernest Macmillan, then of the Toronto Conservatory of Music. He did not visit British Columbia in 1928, but in 1929, during the summer field season, he completed his ten-year survey of the Tsimsyan* tribes. As far as is known at present, Barbeau's last studio meeting with Emily took place that year. He did not return to the West in 1930.

At least at certain periods, especially during and after the Canadian West Coast Art Exhibition (1927 and 1928), Barbeau worked devotedly to further Emily's career. He was remarkably generous in money matters, and encouraged the National Gallery, the National Museum, the Department of Indian Affairs, collectors such as F.N. Southam, and his own friends and colleagues to purchase her paintings. He himself acquired at least four, possibly as many as nine,* the best known being *Bear and Moon Totem*, one of Emily's finest early works which he saw for the first time on the wall of her studio in 1921.* Because he had a special interest in this picture, having seen and studied the pole it depicted *in situ* while working with the Gitksan Indians in Kispiox, he always hankered to possess it. But his first opportunity to buy it only came in March 1928 when the Canadian West Coast Art Exhibition, in which it had been included, completed its tour and returned to the National Gallery.* Barbeau had bought a smaller, less expensive painting of two Hazelton totem poles during the early days of the exhibiton, but was able to exchange it for *Bear and Moon Totem*.* He also persuaded the National Museum to buy a small $50 picture of the Gitraldo pole, the tallest totem pole at Hazelton. As far as I can discover the *Bear and Moon Totem* was the only Carr painting sold during the entire three months the exhibition was on view in Ottawa, Toronto and Montreal.

* *Department of Mines, Anthropological Division—Ethnology and Linguistics, Ottawa. (Summary Reports for the years 1915-1930.)*

* *Tsimshian*

* *Tsimshian*

* *There were definitely three in his possession in November 1927 (see* Hundreds and Thousands *p.10: "Three of my things were on Barbeau's wall . . .") and in 1928 he purchased* Bear and Moon Totem. *There were also, Barbeau said, a forest subject bought in Emily's studio in 1928 (sic) and two other pictures "in her new style" acquired in the studio in 1929. One or two were also purchased in 1930 while Emily was in Ottawa.*

* *"Portrait in Memory—Emily Carr."*

* *NGC: Approximately 40 items of miscellaneous pottery in two cases and four hooked rugs were displayed at this exhibition along with 26 oil paintings.*

* *Barbeau purchased this canvas direct from Emily for $100.(Barbeau to Emily, June 16, 1928.) It was priced at $150 in the exhibition catalogue.*

Although the bear and moon totem story sounds perfectly credible, a routine check was made of Barbeau's title against those in the exhibition catalogue. Imagine my consternation and dismay when I did not find it! "Aha," his detractors would have said, "Barbeau is up to his old tricks again." For one dark, doubting moment, I was tempted to agree with them but then, ashamed of my sagging faith, I started to search for reasons by writing to Charles C. Hill, Assistant Curator of Post-Confederation Art at the National Gallery, who has never failed to come to my aid. Once again, Charlie ransacked the dusty files in the vaults of the Gallery and, among other material, turned up two very revealing lists which, complementing as they do the exhibition catalogue list I had already consulted, tell the whole story of Barbeau's purchase:

1. "List of Indian Oil Paintings Loaned to Ottawa by M. Emily Carr."
2. "List of Emily Carr's (Oil) Paintings of the West Coast now in the Keeping of the National Gallery."*

** The water colors, not shown in the 1927 exhibition, are enumerated in a separate "keeping" list.*

List No. 1, which gives the titles and prices of the paintings in Emily's handwriting, is the authentic, original list and, to my joy and relief, there, under No. 11, I found the lost title of Barbeau's picture: *Bear and Moon Totem*, Kispiox, $100. One up for Barbeau!

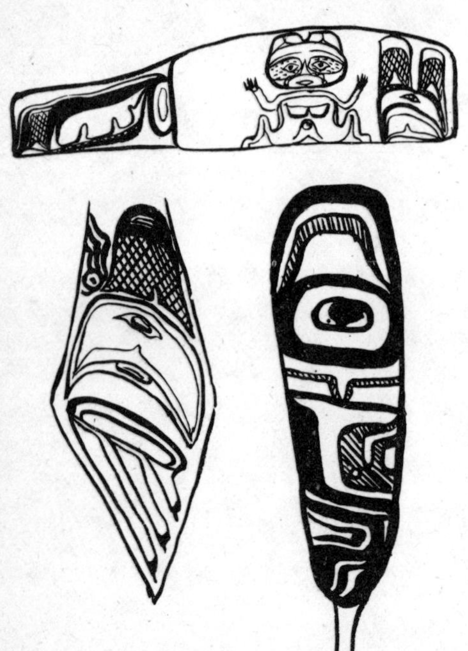

What still lacks clarification is why the National Gallery completely disregarded Emily's list (No. 1) in compiling their own two lists, that is, the "Keeping" list (No. 2) and the final exhibition catalogue list. In both, Emily's titles have been entirely and inexcusably dropped, many prices have been increased, some doubled. The "Keeping" list gives only the names of the Indian villages as titles (probably corrected and updated by Barbeau), and the exhibition catalogue duplicates this procedure except for the addition of the words "totem poles" to a few of the village names. Only one real title was listed, No. 10 *Graveyard Entrance, Campbell River*. But even this is changed from Emily's title, *Grave, Campbell River*, which should have been retained since it suggests quite a different theme. However, the "Keeping" list, misleading and inaccurate as it is, contributes something: Beside listing No. 13 *Gitsegyulka* $150 is the notation: "Sold C.M. Barbeau."

The lists are so muddled that any comparison is virtually impossible, though a close examination of titles and prices does reveal that No. 11 *Bear and Moon Totem*, Kispiox, on Emily's list, becomes No. 13 *Gitsegyukla* on the "Keeping" list and ends up as

No. 13 *Kispayaks Totem Poles* in the exhibition catalogue. How is that for a juggling act?

It is *Gitsegyukla* (Kitseukla on Emily's list, Gitsegyula in the exhibition catalogue) that misleads because this village is confused on the "Keeping" list with Kispiox as the site of the *Bear and Moon Totem*. However, the right village, if not Emily's title, has been restored in the exhibition catalogue, but with a new spelling—*Kispayaks*. Kispiox is a town at the junction of the Kispiox and Skeena rivers (population 222 in Emily's day), the home of two clans, Raven and Bear. Between 1870 and 1911 its name was spelled in thirteen different ways, Kispiox being the latest version.* So why then was Emily's almost correct spelling, Kis[h]piox, changed to Kispayaks?

Was Barbeau, the expert on British Columbia Indians, largely responsible for the changes and errors in the National Gallery lists?* Yes and no. He must have helped compile them and probably edited the spelling and listed the villages. But I feel convinced he would not have tampered with Emily's titles. Certainly in his own writings he invariably used her original title for the *Bear and Moon Totem.**

Barbeau also purchased numerous examples of Emily's pottery and, during his 1921 visit to her studio, two or three hooked rugs of Indian design. One decorated the floor of his office at the National Museum and another, which he spontaneously presented to Eric Brown, was on the floor of the Director's office at the National Gallery for many years until, much to Barbeau's expressed annoyance, it was completely chewed up by moths. He also found outlets for the sale of Emily's pottery in several eastern cities, kept an eye on her water colors held at the National Gallery, and made sure that the publisher of his book, *The Downfall of Themlaham,** paid her $25 for the right to reproduce *Bear and Moon Totem.*

In 1950 Barbeau also selected nineteen of Emily's 1912 paintings as illustrations for his two-volume work, *Totem Poles.** But this was several years after her death. The last time he was able to help her in a practical way during her lifetime, and in all likelihood the last time he saw her, was in 1930 when he obtained a railway pass for her trip east to see the Group of Seven exhibition to which she had been invited to contribute. He also arranged a display of her work in downtown Ottawa* while she was in the city and, best of all, invited her to be a guest in his home.*

Nan Cheney, a frequent visitor at the Barbeau home when she lived in Ottawa, has given me an amusing account of Emily's

* Handbook of Indians of Canada, *Geographic Board of Canada 1912, printed by C.H. Parmelee, printer to the King's most Excellent Majesty, Ottawa 1913.*

* *The three Kispiox titles disappear from Emily's list, two reappear in the exhibition catalogue. One Gitsegyukla title disappears from the "Keeping" list and does not reappear.*

* The Bear and Moon Totem, *Kispiox, ex collection C.M. Barbeau, is now in the collection of Fred Schaeffer, Toronto, who has fortunately restored Emily's meaningful title. He writes: "The true name was always known to me through [Barbeau's]* The Downfall of Themlaham *and* Canadian Landscape Painters *by Robson, where it is reproduced in color and correctly titled." Mr. Schaeffer acquired this painting in 1970 from Barbeau's family.*

* *The Macmillan Company of Canada Ltd., Toronto 1928 (first edition). The Hurtig Publishers, Toronto 1973 (new edition).*

* *Bulletin 119—Volumes I and II. Anthropological Series No. 30, King's Printer, Ottawa, 1950-1951.*

* Ottawa Citizen *May 13, 1930.*

* *Barbeau has said in his unedited taped reminiscences for "Portrait in Memory—Emily Carr" that he procured a railway*

pass for Emily to travel east in 1927, and that she stayed in his home then. This is not correct. He has confused the two dates.

stay in the Barbeau's fine old red brick house, and in particular, of the spare bedroom she occupied while there. All the furniture had been fashioned by Barbeau's father many years before and Nan clearly remembers a large, high wooden bed which had shelves behind it loaded with religious objects, among them a statue of the Virgin Mary. The mattress was slung on canvas strips and the bed, Emily reported, squeaked and skidded ominously every time she moved so that she spent many sleepless hours fearing that the Virgin would topple over on her head.

Painfully modest, Emily was always intent on reaching any bathroom invisibly, and sometimes enlisted the help of a friend in order to do so; but the problem was magnified in the Barbeau household as their bathroom was situated off the landing some distance from her room. To avoid being caught *en négligé,* she would first reconnoiter, glance right and left, then hasten down the hall with her quick little steps, only to encounter another problem. For the door had a large frosted glass pane and Emily was sure that her silhouette could be plainly seen by the passing family. To make matters worse, the door had no lock and the fear that Monsieur Barbeau himself might burst in unannounced kept her in suspense. Apart from these anxieties, she greatly enjoyed the delightful French-Indian atmosphere of the Barbeau home. She found sincerity there, culture, and a "joyfulness that catches you up."

It is disappointing that Barbeau's family, including his son-in-law, an artist and craftsman who helped him in field research and in museum and photographic work, cannot contribute any information that would be useful in my quest for answers to the Barbeau mystery. My scheduled interview with Madame Barbeau in Ottawa fell through at the last moment owing to her advanced age and illness, and her daughter, Dalila, though grateful for my interest in her father, regrets that she cannot give me the material I require as they have not kept a family archive.

The principal purpose of my defense has been to mitigate the effect of the essay in question, which many will feel is ungenerous towards Barbeau. If he was at times in error (and he was) we should, I think, graciously and charitably assume that the error was not caused by mendacity.

Never reluctant to talk or write about themselves, Emily and Barbeau nevertheless left almost everything unsaid about their own productive relationship. Linked professionally by common interests, and engrossed in them, they were forthright personalities with a magical quality. Barbeau was not less colorful than Emily. Nan Cheney, who liked and admired him, as Maud Brown did, also found him diverting. He was said to be impish and unpredictable. On the occasion of his visit to Vancouver in 1939, she wrote to a friend:

> Barbeau has been here and is as funny as ever—had a pink homespun suit and a blue rayon tie and his hair long . . ."*

Nan Cheney and Maud Brown were Barbeau's friends, and they believe in him. Others, from coast to coast, have known and loved him.* I esteem and respect him. Best of all, Emily greatly profited from her meetings with him—whenever they took place. Does not such an outstanding man and scholar deserve our faith until the evidence eventually turns up which will vindicate him?

* *Nan Cheney to Humphrey Toms, July 10, 1939.*

* *F. Maud Brown,* Breaking Barriers, *p.103.*

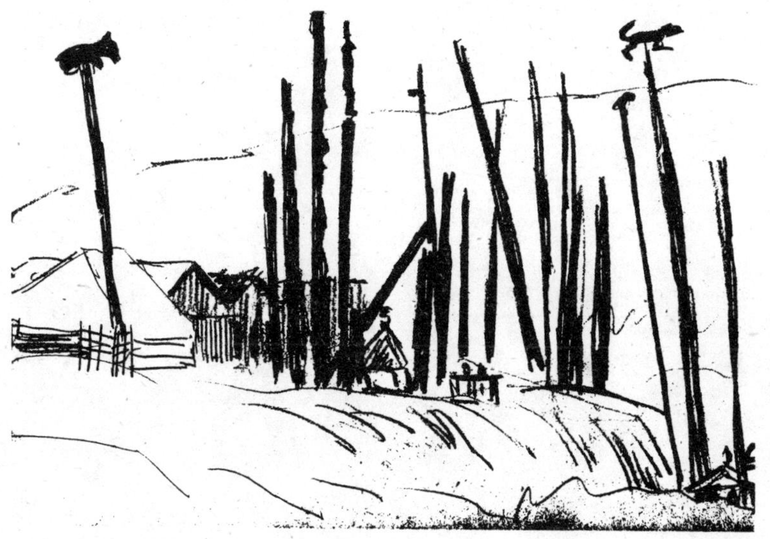

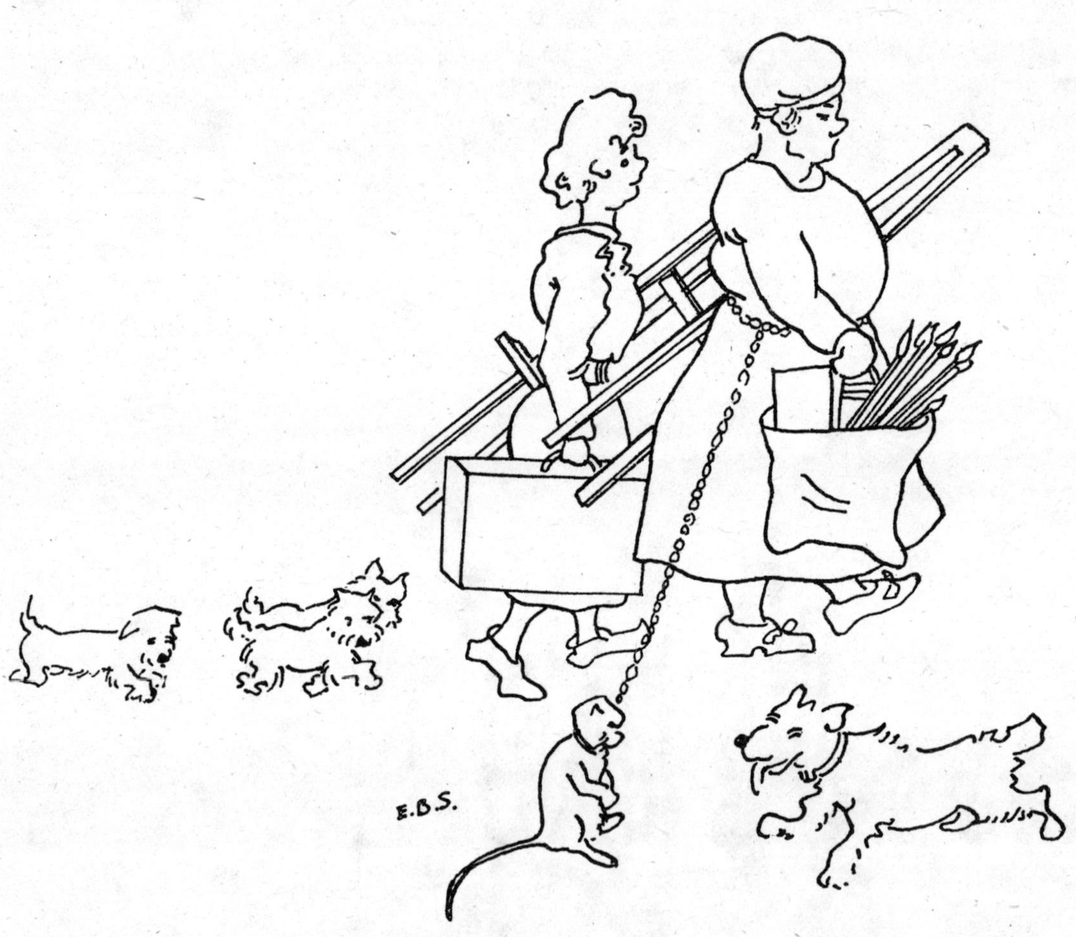

May 1931 Emily and Edythe off for a day of sketching. in Cordova Bay. *Edythe Hembroff-Schleicher*

Sketching Trips

Early Sketching Trips 1898-1930

It would be impossible to trace all Emily's early sketching trips, since there were many unrecorded ones of short duration, usually to Indian villages. The majority of these casual trips took place between 1906-1910 while she was living and teaching in Vancouver, particularly after her Alaska journey in 1907. For it was on her way home from Alaska that she decided to "picture totem poles in their own village settings, as complete a collection of them as I could."*

* *Growing Pains*, p.283.

During the next two summers, and the spring of 1910, before she left for France, Emily therefore traveled "in anything that floated in water or crawled over land" to almost inaccessible northern Indian villages to record their totem poles. She also worked in small communities on Vancouver Island and Alert Bay, in the interior of British Columbia, and on the north shore of Burrard Inlet. In 1912, on her return from abroad, she embarked on a major sketching trip to the Queen Charlotte Islands and the Skeena River area. Even after giving up teaching and settling permanently in Victoria in 1913, she still found time in the summer or fall to travel to nearby villages. Then in 1928, her second major sketching trip took her to the Queen Charlotte Islands again. She also penetrated into deserted villages on the Nass River and painted the most powerful of all her totem sketches in Kitwancool in the upper Skeena region. Another important trip, to the northern half of Vancouver Island, took place in 1929, followed by a brief one to the same general area in 1930.

The following is a short summary of Emily's earliest sketching trips:

- 1898 Ucluelet, Vancouver Island
- 1906-1910 During these years she made trips to northern B.C. and others to Indian villages on the lower mainland, the interior, Vancouver Island and Alaska.
- 1907 Alaska
- 1908 Alert Bay, B.C.
- 1909 Lytton, B.C.; in August she sailed "for the North"—possibly Alert Bay.*

* *PABC*, Studio, Billie's Calendar 1909. *August: "All woes forgot. Sail for the North on a sketching tour . . . round Indian villages."*

* *Emily's well-known water color* Indian School at Lytton *is dated 1910, but if she was in Lytton in 1910 it had to be before May (not a normal time to go sketching) as this painting was shown in the British Columbia Society of Fine Arts exhibition in Vancouver that month. It is more likely that the water color was painted expressly for this exhibition from a 1909 sketch.*

* *NGC, Emily to Eric Brown, March 27, 1928: "I want to branch off to several villages from Alert Bay . . ." (Her plans may have been changed later.)*

1910 Alert Bay and possibly Lytton.*

1912 The Queen Charlotte Islands and the Skeena River area; Alert Bay.

1928 The Queen Charlotte Islands and along the Nass and Skeena Rivers; Kitwancool; possibly Alert Bay and nearby villages.*

1929 Friendly Cove and other villages on the northern half of Vancouver Island, including the Kwakiutl villages of Koskimo and Fort Rupert.

1930 Fort Rupert and possibly other neighboring villages.

Nineteen thirty marks the beginning of my personal knowledge of Emily's sketching trips since I was with her constantly that year after she returned from her visit to the East toward the end of May. I recall her departure up-island in August and a quick return because of bad weather. She was tired, disappointed, unenthusiastic about the material she brought back and determined not to go so far afield again. Her last trip among the Indians was in fact her shortest.

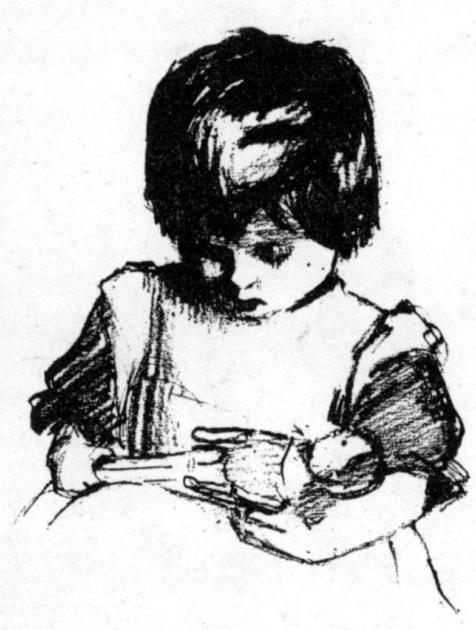

In contrast, the 1929 trip was exciting and rewarding. Emily's zest for work can be sensed in the forceful, geometrically articulated sketches she produced this year, one of which was later developed into a famous canvas, *Indian Church.* But little is known about the trip itself—how, for instance, she reached and lived in such desolate places. Friendly Cove, about ninety nautical miles north-west of Ucluelet, where she first worked with Indian material in 1898, is situated on the south-east end of Nootka Island in an inlet off the rugged west coast of Vancouver Island which is lashed by mountainous seas. One wonders how Emily, clutching her painting gear and small griffon dog, could have been lowered into a bobbing Indian canoe to be paddled ashore. The natives must have been just as curious, if not as apprehensive, as the day two centuries ago when Captain James Cook, R.N. sailed into Friendly Cove on his famous voyage of discovery. Emily's landing will never be marked by a bicentenary celebration like Captain Cook's, but in her small, determined, intrepid way, she, too, was a tough explorer who deserves to be commemorated.

* Friendly Cove, B.C. *Collection: Mr. and Mrs. Harold S. Foley, Vancouver.*

* *The lighthouse is on Miguel Point on the north-west shore when entering Nootka Sound.*

Unfortunately, all too little work in circulation dates from this trip, though at least two water colors of the church at Friendly Cove are extant, and a third shows a view of the cove itself.* Another large water color, *Captain Jack's House, Friendly Cove,* is now in the collection of the Vancouver Art Gallery, and a sketch, *Nootka Lighthouse,** which Emily either gave or sold to the lighthouse keeper, E. Fish, is one of the 1929 water colors which have recently turned up in auction sales.*

* *In Vancouver, March 17, 1977. Sold for $8,500.*

This preamble brings us to 1931 and the beginning of a detailed description of Emily's future sketching trips. This was the year I first accompanied her into the woods. I subsequently worked with her in the field a number of times (the only person to have done so) and later visited most of the camp sites where she sketched alone in her van. The following is a complete list of her sketching trips from 1931 to 1942.

Sketching Trips 1931-1942

1931
May
CORDOVA BAY

Emily and I began sketching together soon after we met in May 1930. At first we only did quick sketches while resting on a log on the beach, or on a bench in the park, during our walks with the animals. Later we went off for the whole day with picnic basket and paint box. But it was not until May 1931 that she invited me to accompany her on a full-scale field trip lasting almost three weeks. We chose Cordova Bay* because of the free roof provided by my family's summer cottage, situated half way between beach and road on a steep slope of heavily wooded property. But the woods around Cordova Bay were not silent or remote enough for Emily. Civilization seemed to intrude everywhere, and we soon gave up trying to find suitable "woodsy" material and turned to beach and shoreline for inspiration, usually sketching from the verandah. This was Emily's first attempt to interpret seashore and sea-drift intensively. On the whole she was disappointed in the sketches she took home from this trip, but she nevertheless developed a few fine canvasses from some of the beach and log studies when she reworked them in the studio. *Cordova Drift* is the best of these.

* *For a full description of this trip see:* M.E.—A Portrayal of Emily Carr, *pp.27-29. The address where we sketched is 4945 Cordova Bay Road, but the Hembroff summer cottage has long since disappeared. However, the original Dilworth cottage, next door at 4947 Cordova Bay Road, still stands. Eva, Edna and Phylis Dilworth were childhood friends.*

1931
September
GOLDSTREAM PARK

Four months after returning from Cordova Bay, Emily and I were off on another sketching expedition—this time to Goldstream Park,* about twelve miles distant from Victoria on the old Island Highway. Sketching material was infinitely better here, but living conditions infinitely worse. Squeezed into a

* *For a full description see:* M.E.—A Portrayal of Emily Carr, *pp.32-34.*

miniature ramshackle garage flush with the highway, we had to walk about a mile to the park each day loaded down with gear, and trailed by panting griffons and an indignant monkey. Only my terrier, Paris, enjoyed the tramp. He bounded on ahead yapping excitedly from sheer *joie de vivre.*

Despite the trials of our cramped, primitive living quarters, the stay at Goldstream was carefree and happy because Emily, in those days, could still chatter, laugh and even sing. We lived in perfect harmony with one another, the woods, the animals and the birds. And of all Emily's sketching trips, this was the most successful. Although she had painted cedars before (as shown in the conventionally-treated water color *Wood Interior* dated 1909), in color, line and mood she regarded them as new material, a new experience, and a challenge in 1931. The park itself, encircled by damp, often dripping woods, was somber, except for the moss-covered "Flats" near the road where the sun could peek through the widely-spaced giant cedars. The "Flats" were gay with sunshine during much of our stay at Goldstream and thus we were able to work long hours until the sun suddenly dropped down behind the bulk of Mount Finlayson leaving us in the dusk.

On good days, Emily did three, sometimes four, large manila paper sketches. On others, she varied her routine by doing smaller oils, or perhaps a charcoal drawing. One day, while she was concentrating on painting, I drew several thumbnail sketches of her instead of trees, and these I still have. One shows her perched precariously on, and bulging over, a tiny sketching stool, hat on head and a lapboard on her knees. This was the last year she used such a board for small sketches. The following spring she changed her painting gear and sketching technique and worked exclusively from an easel.

1932
May
METCHOSIN (The Metchosin Hills, also called Sooke Hills)*

This trip was almost as prolific as the preceding one at Goldstream, but still more enjoyable as an outing because of our commodious and entertaining living quarters. The rolling hills, in which we snuggled, were glorious in color and form, and we had absolute solitude except for a few curious, friendly deer and a bear. An old and formidable friend of Emily's, Mrs. McVicker* had lent us her tumble-down, but delightful "hunting lodge." Unused for years, it was situated in a small clearing high up on Braden Mountain.* To get us there, my long-suffering father had to risk his car on an almost overgrown logging road off the

* *For a full description of this trip see:* M.E.—A Portrayal of Emily Carr, *pp.39-43.*

* *Mrs. Maude Eighmey McVicker, a Klondike pioneer who came to Victoria early in the century and established the town's first antique shop on Fort Street near Douglas.*

* *Braden Mountain: One and one-half miles due west of Humpback Lake; two and one-*

narrow, bumpy Humpback Road which links the old Island Highway (and Goldstream) with Metchosin. Primitive though it was, we adored the place and gladly coped with wood-chopping and an intractable stove and fireplace. It was here that Emily perfected the new sketching technique which, evolved largely for practical reasons, formed the basis of a completely different approach to her work. The cheap standard-size manila paper she was to use for sketching almost exclusively from then on provided a large painting surface on which to develop her woods subjects; it also simplified exhibiting, storing and framing. Contrary to belief, this is the only time Emily camped in an isolated, thickly-wooded area during her trips of the thirties and forties. In the lower parts of Metchosin, where her van was stationed from 1934 to 1936, the setting was unexpectedly rural, with only fringes or clumps of trees. But Braden Mountain was dark and sombre. The forest pressed in on our campsite from all sides. Emily herself vividly describes this trip at some length:

half miles south-west of Goldstream. Elevation: 1500 ft.

> Edythe Hembroff and I are rusticating among ants, verdure and wood ticks. It's glorious, exhilarating, soothing, ticklesome and inspiring all at once. Edythe promptly took flu . . . was reduced to wormliness for three days but is round again. I just love this spot. It is completely isolated and Papa Hembroff took our things [illegible] and drove us out here under my locating. You can't anywhere approach the door with a car and we had to lug the victuals and bedding and sketch stuff very far. He left us at the snake fence and fled. . . . Our cabin is log and very old. Two rooms and a passage connecting same with a door each end and cyclone whipping through down the gulley. We are 1000 ft. above sea level and everywhere are hills not too heavily wooded but that you can scramble over them. There is a waterhole among the bullrushes and we have to carry the water a long way. In fact, everything is primitive and completely inconvenient. There's a junk cookstove which we ignore and cook splendid meals over a huge open brick fireplace in the other room. A huge black iron kettle and a mammoth steel frypan are our choicest possessions. We sketch all day and sleep all night. I get up at six a.m. and go out onto the hills . . . really I've completely forgotten I have a house or tenants or a garden or relatives.*

Many of Emily's so-called rain forest paintings originated from this trip, including her masterpiece, *Grey.*

* *UBC Library, Nan Cheney Collection, Emily to Nan Cheney, May 15, 1932.*

1932
June
CEDAR HILL

Barely home from Braden Mountain, Emily went alone in June to a new sketching site on Cedar Hill Road where, for a month, she rented two rooms in an old farm house near the Mount Douglas woods. Again, as in May at the hunting lodge, she cooked her meals on an ancient brick hearth. But this trip was of short duration. Emily herself tells us why:

> . . . then in June I went a short way out (Cedar Hill) carrying with me six dogs (a new mother with three pups three days old) and the monk. Had rooms in an old farm house and cooked on a brick hearth as out of date as Abraham. We had three scorching days and then a wet spell in which I dawdled round the woods and got a chill and returned home ignominiously to bed. I did not get much out of that trip . . ."*

* *UBC Library, Nan Cheney Collection, Emily to Nan Cheney, October 22, 1932.*

Despite Emily's short stay at the farm house, her presence was noted and remembered. Ever afterward it was referred to as the Emily Carr House by the residents of the area. I tried to locate it in 1975, but was told by a neighbor that it had been demolished the previous year to make room for a housing development. Emily usually went to the woods twice a year, but in the fall of 1932 she was too busy and occupied with her People's Gallery to get away. Her next trip was in May 1933.

1933
May-June
INTERIOR OF B.C.

Emily's mountain sketches, and the fine canvasses, such as *Houses Below Mountain,** derived from them are the products of this important trip. Leaving Victoria on May 15, she visited Brackendale, Lillooet, Seton and Pemberton in her search for mountain themes before returning home about a month later. Her own account of this journey,* hilarious in spots, tragic in others (death of her beloved griffon Koko) describes hauntingly her struggle to interpret her new and overwhelming material: "Oh, these mountains, great bundles of contradiction, hard, cold, austere, disdainful, remote yet gentle, spiritual, appealing! Oh, you mountains, I am at your feet—humble, pleading! Speak to me in your wordless words! I claim my brotherhood to you." Not long after Emily's return to Victoria, one of her fondest dreams came true. Before the end of June she became the proud

* *Collection: Dr. and Mrs. Max Stern, Montreal.*

* Hundreds and Thousands, *pp. 34-40.*

owner of her "Elephant," a caravan which would be used for all future sketching trips until, and including, the fall of 1936.

1933
August-September
GOLDSTREAM PARK

Despite the high enthusiasm with which Emily undertook this second visit to Goldstream Park in her newly-acquired caravan, it was not one of her most successful. In her eagerness to try out the van, she started sketching earlier than usual, about mid-August. Everything went wrong. She had to select a site more suited to the cumbersome van than to herself, her companion* was difficult, and the picnickers disturbed her. Until the seventh of September she couldn't rise even "a tiny bit above the mundane." But the next morning was joyous, "sun blazing, whole woods laughing . . . calm radiance everywhere," and she did a few good sketches before sinking back into terrible loneliness and depression. Homesickness finally drove her home a week later feeling defeated and unhappy about her entire season's work. "Not one uplifting statement," she said. "Only muddled things."

* *Afflicted with encephalitis, Henry Brand, Frederick's young brother, was an extremely nervous boy.*

Emily summed up her impressions of the Goldstream trip in a letter to me:

> September was wretchedly wet and cold. . . . The Flats are nice for warm weather but very damp and too many Sunday picnics there. Henry made the first part impossible to work and then the weather broke. I did sketch but nothing startling. The Flats strike me as incongruous. The immense trees are of a different time and place to the other stuff. There is no second growth to fill the gap. It is being very spoiled by gravel and wood trucks. In and out all the time mutilating and destroying roads, peace and growth.*

* *PABC, Emily to author, October 4, 1933.*

1934
May-June
METCHOSIN

In mid-May the "Elephant" was towed from Four Mile House, where it had wintered, along Metchosin Road as far as Lagoon Road, then down a steep hill to Esquimalt Lagoon. There it was unceremoniously dumped by the haulers on a small patch of soft soil just above the high-water mark on a glittering white sand beach. Emily had been dubious about leaving the silence and shade of the woods to camp on an open beach,* but once the trials of settling in were over, she loved the Lagoon with its wide sweep of shoreline and strange, long, narrow spit. A lightly-wooded hill rising steeply behind the van provided all the trees she needed, and an unobstructed view over a placid sea to Esquimalt and beyond inspired some of her best sea and skyscapes. A diminutive stream, which Emily delighted to listen to, trickled down the bank, rippled over the rocks, and then gurgled into the soft black earth surrounding the van. And although she was far from suspecting it, this innocent-looking baby stream was to be her undoing. For after about a week of exhilaration and good work, the rains came down hard, swelled the trickle to a torrent and flooded Emily's campsite. She confided to her journals on May 24: "Oh the misery of living in this slop! The water lies all round the van. I can't stand it."* She also complained to Willie Newcombe:

> That spot got unbearable for water. . . . I moved Saturday and the "luggers" had a terrible time dragging the old elephant out of the bog but eventually we got here. It is Mr. Strathdee's place on Metchosin Road just before you get to Lagoon Road. He offered me a corner and we are very comfortable.*

Once the ponderous "Elephant" had swayed up the hill, it squatted on the Strathdee farm in a large open field circled by sheltering trees. Long waving grass partially hid its ugly underpinnings. Dried out and happy again, Emily painted steadily until about June 20th, and despite the Lagoon *contretemps* enjoyed one of her more successful outings.

In the mornings Emily worked near the van in the shade of "gracious great pines" painting glorious, swirling, dome-like skies (to add to the skyscapes done on the beach) or a distant row of trees. In the afternoons, to escape the glaring sun, she trudged across the road to the calm woods which had been liberally logged, leaving a lot of frivolous little pines, but few giants. Here she did the first of her stump studies which would continue to interest her as long as she sketched at Metchosin. Her main subjects this year were pines, stumps, sky and space.

Back in the studio, Emily thrilled to her summer sketches and found them a joy to work on. "The job," she said in her journals, was to "keep them up, up, up, to keep the praise in them bursting, rising, passing through the material and going beyond and carrying you with it. . . . I wonder what I have learnt on this trip? I guess it is a matter of infinitesimal daily gain."*

* *For the first and last time.*

* Hundreds and Thousands, *p.124.*

* *PABC, Emily to Newcombe, May 30, (1934).*

* Hundreds and Thousands, *pp.135-136.*

1934
September
METCHOSIN

Again at camp on the Strathdee farm early in September.* Because of bad weather, Emily could only work intermittently at first, but by the middle of the month was painting full blast. The subjects were the same as in May and June—high, blue sky, a straggle of distant pines, and stumps—but parched yellow grass in the foreground now supplanted the green of spring. The whole area was bursting with material and when she left for home on September 29th, she took twenty-one sketches with her.

* *Ibid, p.145-150.*

Compared with the 1931 and 1932 trips to Goldstream Park and Braden Mountain, Emily's output had sharply decreased. But she would never again match the productivity of those earlier years.

1935
June
METCHOSIN (Albert Head)

Emily was still in Metchosin in 1935, but had moved the van a little farther along Metchosin Road toward Albert Head, about eighteen miles from Victoria. Although this was her most distant location from town during the three years she worked in Metchosin, the nearest and farthest camps—1936 and 1935—were not more than two miles apart. The 1934 site was in between.

After "a little maneuvring and adapting of the tent and windbreak canvas, and the stovepipe adjusted to the wind, and the elements accepted as part of the game,"* Emily had solved her domestic problems and started to work. A row of second-growth trees, which sprang up before her every time she opened the van door, began to tease her, and she painted them over and over until she was able to unlock their secrets. The relationship between the trees and sky troubled her until she realized that the sky is just as important as the earth or the sea in working out a thought. Even in this supposedly remote place, Emily was at all times close to the road and to people. She could hear voices from the nearby well, and when sketching in the woods, she was always conscious of the jangling of sheep and cow bells. Only a yellow grain field, bounded by a wire fence, separated her from the highway where flocks of turkeys liked to strut.

* Hundreds and Thousands, *p.186.*

At Albert Head, both spring and fall, Emily reverted to the 1931 studies of rushing undergrowth and worked in a jungle of woods. She also continued to paint her active, swirling skies, which many friends and critics found reminiscent of Van Gogh.

Suddenly, during her last week at camp, Emily was filled with gloom and foreboding and lost her will to paint. Her heart heavy, feeling tired of the struggle, she was glad to return home on July 4. She was disappointed in her spring sketches: "Subject not enough digested. Spirit not enough awake."

1935
September
METCHOSIN (Albert Head)

Back at Albert Head in the fall, Emily continued her studies of jungle undergrowth. She worked in the core of a "great forest" where the tangled growth had been undisturbed for untold years, making it almost impossible to find a space wide and clear enough to sit and work without drowning in a sea of salal and bracken. But at the end of the season, Emily still had not found a mode of expression for jungle undergrowth. "It just sticks at paint," she wrote, "as if the coming and going of mystery were abhorrent to paint."* Health may have played a part in her unresolved struggle with "perfectly ordered disorder" because, as she wrote to me between two visits to her camp, she was feeling miserable the last week of her stay in the woods:

* Hundreds and Thousands, *p.201.*

> Still sitting in my field. There were five days of *complete pour* but I sat on. Used to tuck myself up on the bed, put tins round to catch the drip and work, read, write and watch the rain come down. It's assorted now—dew, shine, blow, cloud. I'm working, but have not been feeling good. . . . I did get as far as my woods to-day. Other days I have been working in the dip beside the van. The sea and sky have been naughty; sulky and drab with fog. I have been changing my size because only two shapes in an exhibition of sketches gets very monotonous. I did a *bad* square this morning and a small wretch this afternoon. Both rubbish but I did real study on them so don't care."*

* *PABC, Emily to author (undated) September 1935.*

Just after breaking camp on September 30, she wrote to me again:

> The last week at camp was *awful.* Such towering wind, rain and dullness the last three days. I gave up and made no attempt to work. . . . I had a headache much of the time latterly out there and I think the wind aggravated it. . . . I did only about six or seven sketches

> after you were there. Spent two days down back in the woods to try and elude the wind.*

* *PABC, Emily to author (undated) October 1935.*

Two interesting visitors came to the van to meet Emily this fall of 1935—Murray and Frances Adaskin, both musicians from the East. I drove them out to Metchosin, and it was obvious that they enjoyed Emily. Strangely, they felt diffident about asking to buy a water color (as they had planned to do) and only obtained one ten years later, after her death, when Lawren Harris selected for them the particularly fine water color, *Indian Church.*

1936
June
METCHOSIN (Spencer's sheep farm)

Instead of going to the Saanich peninsula to sketch as she had planned, Emily decided at the last moment to keep the van in Metchosin, but had it towed nearer Victoria to Spencer's sheep farm. There it was propped up on the clifftop overlooking the huge pit of Producers Sand & Gravel Company which she thought "a splendid spot to camp—complete, extra excellent." In fact, this was her favorite of all the Metchosin locations.

Its predominent characteristic was space: "Great scoops out of the gravel pit, wide scoops of sea." Emily did her second series of fine sea and skyscapes here, as well as the majority of her stump and root paintings.*

* *The same subjects she painted in 1934.*

Feeling better than in 1935, Emily was anticipating a bumper crop of sketches but, alas, a deluge started soon after her arrival and continued almost without interruption until the end of her stay. She was imprisoned in her van for days at a time—writing and reading, but not painting. Her vexation shows in this letter:

> Thank you for fire permit. One certainly feels very *safe* from *fire* this weather. Disappointing for work but otherwise rather amusing (sitting dry surrounded by water). . . . It's a *lovely* spot, loads of ant hills (but not aggressive ants) no humans round and comfortable camp when dry.*

* *Emily to Humphrey Toms, June 9, 1936.*

Emily needed all her sense of humor to sit out the drip, drizzle and saturating pour of the first week on the farm, although one mellow, cloudless evening, she was able to get outside the van long enough to paint a sketch—a slash of blue sea in the mist with a glowing, grey-green stretch of grass and two stumps and a bush in the foreground. She was "fairly happy" over it. The following week, with the exception of one day of "exquisite" weather, when she "sketched in fits," was as watery as the first. By this time, she was beginning to slump into despondency and was bitterly lonely because, other than the baker, not a soul had as yet called at her camp. However, the third week, the weather changed to great heat ("the earth has forgotten all about the sousing it recently received") and Emily finally got into her stride and did a quick series of superb sketches of open spaces, burnt stumps, sea and sky. As soon as Frederick and I arrived in Victoria for the summer, we immediately drove out to Metchosin to see Emily and her spirits promptly revived. She even sang as she and I traipsed off into the woods to work together for an hour or two.

Our last visit, accompanied by my sisters, Ruth and Helen, was on July 2 when we took our best photographs of Emily—two of them now familiar pictures showing her in the door of her rickety van. Humphrey also came out, pedaling the long distance as usual, and adding gladness to Emily's heart by purchasing a sketch, the original of *Above the Gravel Pit,** one of her better known canvasses. She wrestled with the gravel pit many, many times before succeeding so well in Humphrey's sketch.

* *Collection: The Vancouver Art Gallery 42.3.30, oil on canvas 30"x 40".*

This outing lasted exactly one month (June 4 to July 4), a little longer than most. But at the end, Emily was in a hurry to get home because she had undertaken to start a sketching class about the 11th.

This is surprising news as no one, not even Emily herself, ever mentioned this class. I myself had forgotten about it, but now, a passage in her journals, a letter to me and, more importantly, a newspaper clipping have jogged my memory. Just before Emily's departure for the country, a classified advertisement appeared in the Victoria *Daily Colonist,* under "Education:"

> Sketching classes, July, August, Emily Carr.
> Write 316 Beckley Street.*

* *Humphrey saved this (undated) clipping.*

Emily insisted when she left Vancouver in 1913 that she would never teach again. However, in 1936, she was more desperately in need of money than ever before and, too old and ill to go back to pottery making or dog breeding, she decided to organize a sketch class as her final resort.

I doubt that many pupils applied for her class, but there must have been at least two, since Emily wrote to me the day before Thanksgiving that "I only had my class six weeks. Miss Paterson, one of the females, is now in Vancouver. . . ." She again mentions "one of the females" in her journals: "My pupil is scrubbing away, making a blue sky, two sunny houses, and a bit of a plum tree. She is happy. I am trying to get behind her eyes and poke them out into space."

Another interesting sidelight thrown on this Metchosin sketching trip is contained in a letter Emily wrote to Humphrey when she ran out of paint:

> I enclose $1.00 bill. Will you go to Prior's hardware and buy me a 2 lb. can of Green Seal Zinc White paint. It is *I think* .40 per lb. and the postage would not be more than .20.*

* *Emily to Humphrey Toms, June 9, 1936.*

This proves what I have always contended, that Emily used ordinary white house paint in order to economize, at least after 1930. But her colors were of good quality. No matter how poor she was, she always managed somehow to import Cambridge paints from England.

1936
September
METCHOSIN (Spencer's sheep farm)

By the sixth of September, Emily was back at the Spencer farm for her annual fall sketching trip, but she was still grieving for her sister Lizzie who had died early in August. She worked well at first, but the visit was short (the shortest on record) and there are fewer notes and letters to document it than any other.* There is nothing about it in her letters to Nan Cheney, and Ruth Humphrey's correspondence started only in 1937. Emily did not need to write to me from camp as I was in Victoria. I visited her only once before she was driven home by rain on the twelfth, and it is unlikely she had other visitors as the time was too short.

* *Less than two-and-a-half pages (259-261) in* Hundreds and Thousands.

This was the last time Emily used her beloved van, since a few months later she suffered the crippling heart attack that would revolutionize her sketching habits. The poor old unwieldy "Elephant" was not easy to dispose of. No one wanted it. However, in 1938 the owner of the Millstream cottage where Emily sketched in 1939 finally agreed to buy it for $15. Back in the studio, Emily worked on her summer Metchosin sketches, reliving them all. Despite the downpour in June and the greatly curtailed camping trip in September, she felt that she had made progress in 1936—that she had had an uplifting experience and had seen things a little more as a whole. Some sketches she did not touch at all. She had made her point, she thought, and was afraid she would only bungle them in reworking.

The day before Thanksgiving, Emily wrote me about her summer's work:

> Have been painting. . . . I want to sort of sum up this

year's sketching and get them [the sketches] ordered . . . and then start canvasses with a clean slate. I hate a lot of unfinished stuff around and, another thing, I like to find definitely what my summer's work was about before trying to "canvas." You are generally, I find, going for some specific thing but if you leave it in the air it stays there until they [the sketches] are pulled together and mounted so that you can meditate on them. I am very keen on getting down to some canvasses. I feel I should soon now.*

* *PABC, Emily to author (undated) October 1936.*

1937

Emily was too ill to leave home throughout 1937. In the spring, she was slowly recovering from her January heart attack. Although she was able to paint a few canvasses in the fall, she could only work intermittently and the doctor insisted on considerable bed rest. I invited her to visit us in Vancouver so that she could recuperate without domestic worries, but she replied: "So, I am sorry that I shall not be at your party of hen painters for Nan [Cheney]. I really think I had better not [visit Vancouver] by my feel. But he [the doctor] said perhaps next year I'd be able to go out sketching."*

* *Emily to author, October 4, 1937.*

1938
July
TELEGRAPH BAY ROAD (Cadboro Bay, Victoria)

In May or June, before leaving to sketch in the country, Emily worked for a week in a nearby park just to keep her hand in. "MacDonald Park," she wrote, "is lovely with new green and I'm studying there with joy."* She had rented a cottage for the month of July from Mr. Godfrey of 3975 Telegraph Bay Road, but simplified his address to:

> last house before the sea. Postal address c/o Godfrey's milk farm

* *Emily to Ruth Humphrey, May 9 (postmark June 9), 1938.*

Although changed now, the old family home still stands. Mr. Godfrey is also still there but, over ninety years old, and frail, he is guarded from interlopers by an understandingly protective family. The whole Cadboro Bay area was farmland in Emily's day, but is a purely residential district now, and Telegraph Bay Road is lined with fine homes. Emily's cottage, which was very close to the Godfrey cow barn, has long since been demolished but was located where a modern house now stands at 4010 Lockhaven Drive. Emily delighted in her rural cottage, except for its proximity to the cow barn and the bull tethered to it. The farm was peaceful and she enjoyed resting under the spread of a big maple tree outside her door. After living in the van for several years, the cottage seemed enormous with its large kitchen-parlor and two bedrooms—completely furnished except for cooking utensils and bedding. It also had a touch of luxury to which she was unaccustomed—a private toilet, a cold water tap of its own, and even a meat safe. Oddly enough, Emily fails to mention this visit to Telegraph Bay in her journals, but she at least wrote several entertaining descriptions of her surroundings to Nan Cheney. In her first, just a postcard, she wrote: "Love camp. Have quit letter writing for a spell (receiving only). Working hard—weather variable—cottage comfortable—cows soothing—health fair." In a later letter, she spoke of her tremendous joy to be in the woods again, and added:

> I've done quite a lot of work sloshing away. What I shall see when I open them out at home I quail to contemplate. They are taken straight from my board to a high shelf and never looked at once. . . . The cows are another joy. I am sure I have far more in common with them than with the ordinary society lady; flop-tailed, skulking old hussies [but] at least their jaw-chewing is silent and unmalicious.*

Emily had more visitors than usual at Telegraph Bay, perhaps because she was close to town. I rushed out to see her for a quick cup of tea before leaving to take a course in egg tempera painting at the University of California at Berkeley, and Frederick had several visits with her which she told Nan she enjoyed. Even W.P. Weston of Vancouver came by, and Humphrey cycled out as was his custom. He reported that Emily refused to show him her sketches but told him she had done over thirty. The pastoral, idyllic setting of the Godfrey farm, so close to the dark blue waters of the Strait of Georgia, made it the most scenic and delightful of all Emily's sketching sites.

Home again in August, Emily seemed doubtful about the quality of her July sketches. At first, when she studied them on the wall of the studio, she was thrilled; but later she complained that when she went to work on them they shriveled away and looked mediocre.

Although Emily's health continued to improve, she was afraid to risk another sketching trip that year. Moreover, her first solo exhibition at the Vancouver Art Gallery was to be held in October and she was frantically busy preparing for it. She was close to exhaustion late in September when she wrote me, "I am

* *UBC Library, Emily to Nan Cheney, July 25, 1938.*

beginning to crawl out of my fatigue. When those crates got off, I was too tired to take a long breath even."*

* *PABC, Emily to author (undated) September 1938.*

1939
June
LANGFORD (Millstream Road)

After suffering another heart attack early in 1939, Emily was in the hospital for a month and then unable for some time to make the slightest effort without pain and shortness of breath. Consequently, when the doctor finally told her late in May that she was well enough to return to the woods, she was jubilant. Aided by friends with cars, she scoured the countryside for a suitable cottage on a flat piece of land with a flat forest nearby and found one on Millstream Road in Langford (between Victoria and Goldstream Park). She rented it for a month and moved in on the eighth of June. It was a real ugly duckling of a place, but it looked beautiful to Emily because of the cost—only $7.50 a month for six rooms, big verandahs back and front, and fifteen acres of complete privacy. Soon after settling in, she wrote to Nan Cheney: "Edythe and Fred came out to see me and I have invited them to supper on Wednesday. They have their little toy car with them."* This toy car, an M.G., took us back and forth to Emily's Millstream cottage several times during her stay there, and we became quite attached to the ugly duckling despite the rats and the drafts. Humphrey Toms, with whom I recently reminisced about Emily's life at Langford, remembers that, "she found this square shack on Millstream Road. Later she dropped me a line to say where she was and how to get there and I bicycled out. . . . She told me with glee that she had well behaved rats as co-tenants so I promptly christened the shack 'Rat Hall.' I took several snaps with my box brownie.* . . . About 1972 I got my brother to drive me along Millstream Road from the 'new' highway to the old Island Highway. 'Rat Hall' was still there but much painted and prettied up, and likely raised onto a concrete foundation. Its squareness is still obvious and it sits further back on the property than its more modern neighbors."*

* *UBC Library, Emily to Nan Cheney, Monday (probably the 12th) 1939.*

* *Humphrey's photographs of "Rat Hall" were taken on June 24, 1939.*

* *However, when Humphrey, Frederick and I went out to Langford again in 1975 to photograph the house, we were unable to find it.*

Humphrey also showed me a letter Emily had written to him about "Rat Hall": "Lovely out here and the habitation completely successful, weather less so—Mondayed on Sunday to fool the rain. In bed most of 1st week, done quite a bit of work—nothing breathtaking—some scribbling also. Air excellent and appetite unfortunately (for the waist line) large. Complete privacy—frog music at night—I am peppered with bites, few mosquitoes but those wee no-see-ums and the whole Royal family of Ants who have all cut their teeth. We don't leak except chimneys. A family of young rats live in the field under my window, pretty ones who live on the hay. I have the big dining room for bed-studio, better studio than at home.*

* *Emily to Humphrey Toms, June 19, 1939.*

Emily enjoyed the sojourn at Langford "mightily" despite poor weather. She devoted herself to painting when the weather was fine, to writing when it was wet, and got a lot of good work done. At the back of the camp was a logged-off clearing and at the front a wood with great yellow-green mossy rocks. She came home with "nippy" ideas and was soon producing canvasses from her Langford sketches. Some of them, among others *Yellow Moss* and *Mossy Rocks,* were exhibited at the Vancouver Art Gallery in her second solo show there the following November.

1939
September
CRAIGFLOWER ROAD (Victoria)

Emily camped much of September in Mrs. Shadforth's shack on the Gorge, near Craigflower bridge in the outskirts of Victoria. Although her cabin was next door to the Cameron Car Wrecking lot, this did not unduly disturb her because the cabin was set far back on the property in a peaceful setting, out of sight and sound of the road. It was just big enough to hold Emily; her maid, Florence; the dogs; and her beautiful blue budgerigar, Joseph. A few steps from the door was a bit of woods that supplied good sketching material. Since I could not visit Emily that September, I have no personal knowledge of this outing, but it is fully covered in her journals* and in letters to friends. She wrote to me the day before she broke camp:

* Hundreds and Thousands, *pp.305-308.*

> It is a lovely spot—quite quiet, quite private, quite wild, rather rough and hilly, so I've had to be more "put" than any of my other places and I get up late and go to bed early as the cold autumn damp, when the sun is *not,* about knocks me. But I have found good study. At first, I was too war-upset to work well but last week got in good swipes. . . . Our cabin is very comfortable—one good-sized room. I have not minded sharing with the youngster [the maid Florence] as much as I feared. She is decent that way. Just dull and self-centered as the present youth are. . . . I have had very few visitors out. Did not ask other than my sister and her friends and Flora [Burns] once. . . . Well, I must get up and do my last sketch. That will make twenty this trip, of sorts, not all A.1. New trains

of thought perhaps, waked by autumn, war and atmosphere. These mid-days are mystifyingly illusive. There's lots of wasps.*

* PABC, Emily to author (undated) September 1939.

1940
May
METCHOSIN

This was Emily's only outing in 1940 and immediately preceded her incapacitating stroke on June 5.* There are few extant references to this last visit to Metchosin and it is not mentioned in her journals. I did get out to see her once, but the visit was short as I could not leave my invalid mother for long. Still I recall clearly the superb location of Emily's flimsy shack in the enclosed grounds of a proud, aloof manor house near the familiar pits. I found her working hard, apparently well though tetchy, and humorously boastful about living on an estate. A few scraps of information and description have turned up in letters to other friends. One, to Nan Cheney, was written while Emily was still camp hunting: "Well, I'll see what offers I can find of up-to-date *modern* equipped shacks. Oh for the dear late van, but I am glad I have not the care of her just now."* Then twenty-five days later, after she had settled into her new quarters, she wrote to Nan again: "I came out to camp a week or more ago. Found a one room and woodshed in Metchosin. It is very comfortable in a park-like private property and I'm doing good work. . . . I shall probably stick out one more week, now all my stuff is out here."* Later still, after describing the effects of her stroke to Ruth Humphrey, she merely adds: "So glad I got in some sketching before smit."*

* *This date is deduced from Emily's letter to Ruth Humphrey of July 2 (1940). She writes: ". . . 4 weeks tomorrow since I collapsed." This event is strangely reported in* Hundreds and Thousands, *p.324, and would seem to be out of context. It is entered under the date of March 6 in a subsection entitled "Later." The next entry in October 23.*

* *UBC Library, Emily to Nan Cheney, (postmark) May 1, 1940.*

* *UBC Library, Emily to Nan Cheney, May 25, 1940.*

* *Emily to Ruth Humphrey, May 25, 1940. (This date is incorrect. Perhaps* June *25, 1940?)*

But the best report comes from Humphrey:

> I took Emily and her sister [Alice] out in a U-Drive car to look for a place in the middle of May, and settled her in a shack near her beloved gravel pits at Metchosin. I was practice-teaching in the neighborhood and got off the teachers' bus the last Friday afternoon I was there and went in and had tea. She was purring like a kitten, had done two sketches a day in the first two days and toddled me around the estate. The country out there is all quite flat, so is very suitable for her and she has her girl Florence . . . and her dogs. She intended to stay as long as she could.*

* *Humphrey Toms to Nan Cheney, June 7, 1940.*

After the stroke, when she was feeling stronger, Emily got out her May sketches to study them. They were high in key with lots of light, and she was moved by the spring tenderness they evoked. She wondered how she could have done such joyous things when she was so torn up by the war.*

Gradually Emily regained her composure and her health and spent happy, contented days working, hoping hard she would be able to get back to the woods once more in the fall. But when September came, she was still too weak to face the rigors of camp life, especially as she needed all the energy she could summon up to complete and mount the May sketches for her third annual solo exhibition at the Vancouver Art Gallery. But by October 16 she had signed the last of them and was ready for the November opening.

* Hundreds and Thousands, *pp.324-325. It is not known how many sketches Emily did on this trip.*

1941

Although Emily was again in reasonably good health and spirits, there was to be no sketching trip for her this year. She was busy with visitors and her publishers in the spring, and after a nasty upset in mid-summer, she collapsed and had to give up all work for several weeks. Afterwards she painted and mounted sketches when she could and managed to put together her fourth annual solo show at the Vancouver Art Gallery in October. But it was too late then to camp in the country.

1942
August
MOUNT DOUGLAS PARK (LITTLE CORDOVA BAY)

For Emily the highlight, the real "gladness," of the year 1942 was her final sketching trip to Mount Douglas Park, a protected area of tall trees crowding a mountain with a parkland across the road leading to Cordova Bay, where she and I had sketched eleven years before.

Still feeling fairly perky as the new year unfolded, Emily was absorbed in her plans to work in the woods; to visit Ira Dilworth in Vancouver to seek his assistance in the revision of her manuscript for her second book, *The Book of Small;* and to hold still another exhibition at the Vancouver Art Gallery. To clear her calendar for these three major events, she did her "practice" sketching early, going to the woods on two separate days in May.* In May she was also busy in the studio readying three large canvasses for a Vancouver show in the fall.* Then, in June, toward the end of her pleasurable and profitable visit with the Dilworth family, she suddenly announced to Ira: "I must go home. The forest still has something to say to me."

Heedless of her doctor's warning, Emily rented a cabin at Mount Douglas Park in August. Tucked askew behind a popular

* The Clearing, *frontispiece in* Growing Pains *and a gift to Ira Dilworth mid-1942, was painted on one of these days. It is now in the National Gallery of Canada Collection.*

* *This exhibition did not take place because, as Emily put it, she "busted herself."*

tea room, and thus invisible from the road, the cabin was hemmed in by giant trees on the mountain which towered over it. And from the tea room squatting at its base, where Emily had most of her meals, she could look through the trees of Mount Douglas Park and see the calm waters of Georgia Strait beyond.

The great pines, cedars, firs and hemlock of the mountain and park did indeed have something to say to Emily—something urgent, something spiritual, as if they were aware it would be their last message. But they whispered it gently, almost joyfully, the dark foreboding gone; and the mood of the fifteen large sketches, and a few smaller studies, done in her ten-day stay at Mount Douglas is sober, serene, sublime. Emily, of course, brings a touch of typical humor to her description of this final sketching trip:

> Two more sketches yesterday and a walk (sizable).... This cabin is BLISS—tar paper and shiplap—scenery peeking in through the knotholes and windows. Door never closed—occasional yaps of iced agony from the sea bathers below. I breakfast in bed and go to the tea room for others. It is a happy comfortable little park used by plain people.... This place is full of cedars and their colors are terribly sensitive to change of time and light. Sometimes they are bluish *cold* green then they turn yellow *warm* green. . . ."*

* *Phylis Dilworth Inglis Collection, Emily to Ira Dilworth, August 2, 1942.*

In another letter, written almost a year later, Emily returned to the subject of the Mount Douglas woods: "... the work [I] did last summer . . . is rather sombre [but] that was the character of the woods thereabout. But they were not *sad*. It was a very happy session in my cabin at Mount Douglas Park."* The old fever of creation had taken possession of Emily while in the woods, and in her enthusiasm she both over-worked and over-walked. This excessive exertion utterly exhausted her before long and brought about renewed and, finally, constant heart pain which forced her to pack up and leave ahead of schedule. She explains:

* *Phylis Dilworth Inglis Collection, Emily to Walter Gage, May 14, 1943. (Walter Gage, former President of the University of British Columbia, was in the thirties a colleague of Frederick's in the Department of Mathematics.)*

> Came home very ill (overdid I 'spose). Had thrombosis (clot of blood in the artery of the heart) and nearly died. [It was] considered remarkable, with my other heart trouble too, that I squeaked through. That is 6 weeks ago. I am still in bed, was in hospital 2 weeks. Specials and all that stuff. Tried home (could get no help and had 2 nurses) so came here for a month or more [Mayfair Nursing Home]. After that what???*

* *Emily to Humphrey Toms, September 26, 1940.*

In 1975 I returned to Little Cordova Bay (as early Victorians still call it) to roam in the Mount Douglas woods and to see if Emily's cabin still stands. It does—but now it is a shed serving the needs of a thriving restaurant, and the kindly Mrs. Edward's tea room is no more. As I explored this familiar spot, thinking of Emily and her final sketching trip, I was amazed that she could have worked there at all in her precarious state of health. The little cabin is on an incline steeper than she should have tried to climb, and she could not have entered the woods at that point since they cover a mountain. I came to the conclusion that she could not have worked in the woods at all, but only in the park across the road. There she could have painted the forest above her cabin from safe and level ground, or else made her own forest from a clump of trees in the park itself—which she so often did in Metchosin.

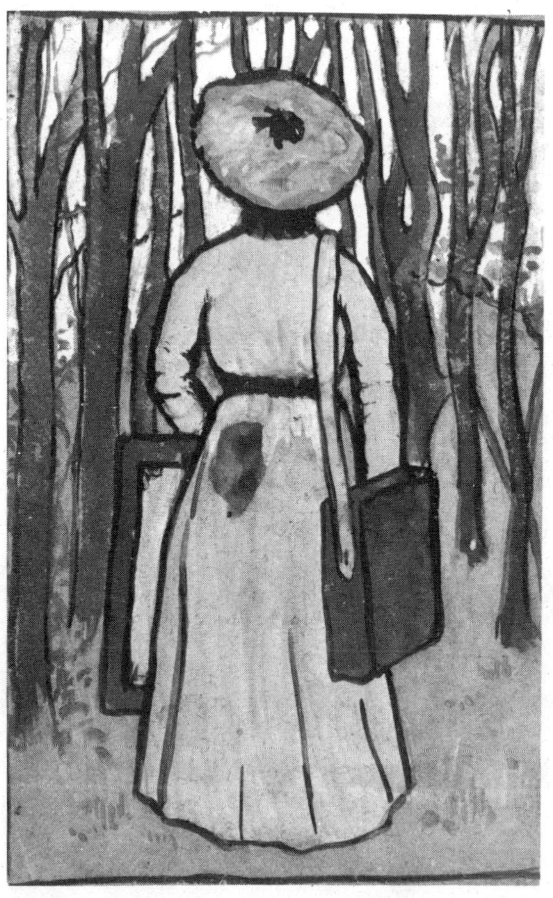

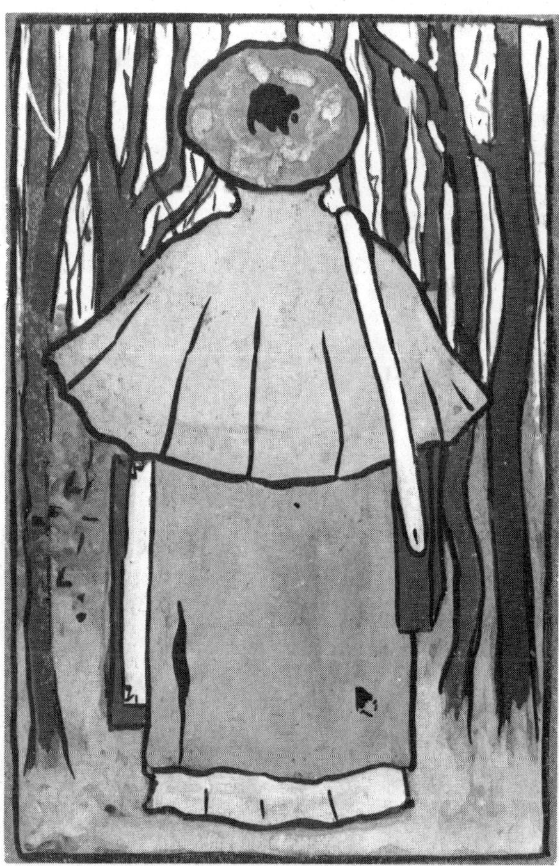

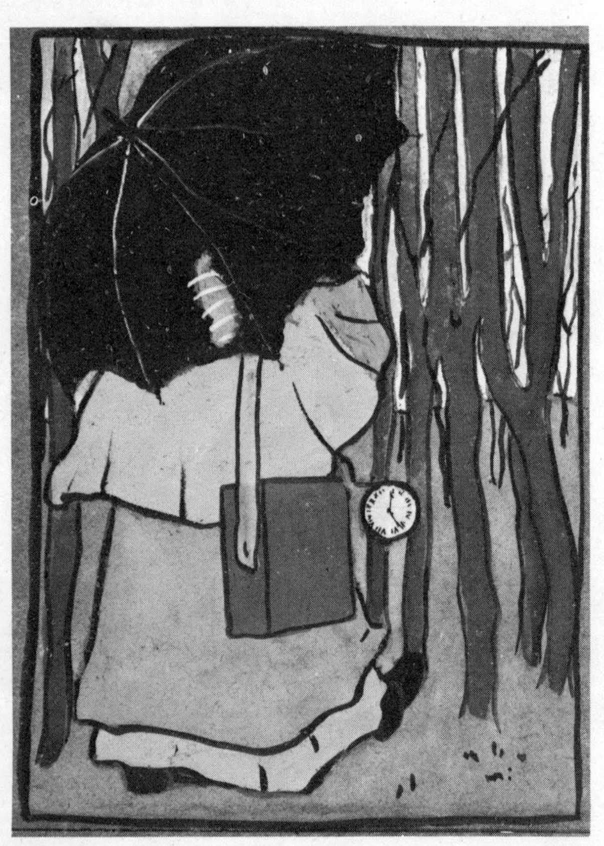

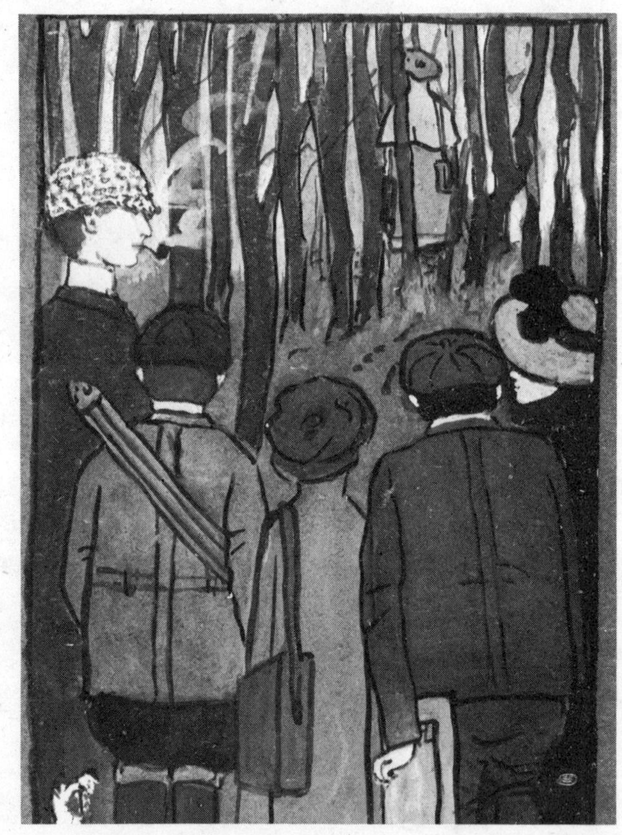

The Errant Emily Carr Trust

Most people, I suppose, would loosely define the Emily Carr Trust as a collection of the artist's finest paintings now housed in the Vancouver Art Gallery. A few, more knowledgeable, might recall that she had bequeathed a number of these Trust paintings to the Province of British Columbia. Extremely few, even of those who work in, or hover around, the Art Gallery, could be more specific; and no one as yet has troubled to unearth, and untangle, the true, confused facts.

My own curiosity was aroused when I noticed that the number of pictures said to make up the Trust was prone to discrepancies. The Vancouver Art Gallery gave differing figures (even in the same Gallery Bulletin) as to the number of works in the collection; the National Gallery gave another figure, and the Vancouver newspapers differed with both. The trustees often contradicted themselves and each other in giving out information and Emily frequently disagreed and added her own version.

The Emily Carr Trust, when initially established, was composed of only forty-five of Emily's best paintings—those she intended as a gift to the Province. She directed that these pictures, less any sold by the trustees, should be used to form a permanent collection to be known as "The Emily Carr Picture Collection."*

* *The Emily Carr Trust: 2(d) The trustees shall . . . select such of said (original Trust) pictures as they shall see fit as a permanent collection to be known as "the Emily Carr Picture Collection."*

When the Trust was terminated in 1966, this Collection had grown to 164 pictures: forty-seven oils; thirty-one oils on paper; twenty-nine water colors; forty-two charcoal drawings and fifteen brush drawings. These figures can be verified from the schedule to the agreement made on February 1, 1965 between the trustees, the Vancouver Art Gallery and the Art Gallery of Greater Victoria. The same figures appear again in the agreement dated March 1, 1966—between the same trustees and galleries—which terminated the Trust.*

* *Trustees John E.A. Parnall and Alistair Bell who succeeded Ira Dilworth and Lawren Harris respectively.*

Section A of the 1966 agreement states that the trustees are trustees of certain paintings (called the "collection") executed

In 1973, when the Trust Collection was catalogued again, the total number of pictures remained the same, but it was found that the classifications in the previous list were, in some cases, not accurate. Therefore, the exact listing of the Vancouver Art *by Emily Carr which collection includes but is not limited to those paintings and other works of art listed in the schedule.*

It is expressly stated in this document that the pictures may not be sold, although under special circumstances a picture, or pictures, may be disposed of by gift only to another public library, museum or archive in British Columbia.

Gallery's present holdings in the "Emily Carr Picture Collection," according to information received in February, 1975, is: thirty-nine oils on canvas; twenty-six oils on paper; thirteen oils on board; twenty-nine water colors; forty-two charcoal drawings and fifteen brush drawings.

How many pictures the Collection actually comprised when the Vancouver Art Gallery acquired it in 1946 is more difficult to determine. The Gallery has virtually no records on the subject. There is nothing on file as to exactly when, and by whose authority, the Gallery assumed custody of the Collection. It has no record of the handling of the Trust by the two original trustees, Lawren Harris and Ira Dilworth, and there are no early lists on file of the pictures in the Collection. What the Gallery did say is this:

> There were originally 170 works in the Trust but six were subsequently disposed of by the trustees . . . although this is not so stated.*

Well, it can be so stated now.* I have located the six paintings and find that all *were* disposed of by the trustees. Five were sold in 1956 to the Glenbow Foundation in Calgary (which became the Glenbow-Alberta Institute in 1967) and the sixth was sold a little later to the Beaverbrook Art Gallery at Fredericton, New Brunswick.* The paintings for Glenbow were selected by both Dilworth and Harris, but the latter handled all correspondence and completed the sale. Since Dilworth was not in Vancouver when the second sale was made, Harris alone chose the sixth painting, an oil on canvas, *Cape Mudge: An Indian Family with Totem Pole,* painted in 1912.

During my correspondence with the Glenbow-Alberta Institute, a curator confirmed their 1956 purchase, gave me a list of the titles and, to my surprise, said there was nothing on the work sheets under "remarks" to indicate that the pictures bore the "Emily Carr Trust" stamp.* Since all original or true Trust works must have the marking "Emily Carr Trust" on the reverse of canvas,* a closer examination of the canvasses was suggested. Sure enough, after removing the cardboard backing of the paintings, the curator found an oval marking "Emily Carr Trust" in black paint on all five paintings.

Only three of the titles; *Kitwancool; Lillooet, Indian Village;* and *Masset Pole** exactly match those of original Trust pictures. The other two paintings, *Base of Kitwancool Pole* and *Among the Firs,* like *Cape Mudge* in the Beaverbrook Art Gallery (which also bears the Trust marking), were, however, among the forty-seven pictures in a "permanent (not for sale) collection," established later by the

* *In reply to my letter of May 10, 1974.*

* *Through the kindness of former trustee J.E.A. Parnall in releasing correspondence between Ira Dilworth and Lawren Harris.*

* *The Beaverbrook Art Gallery does not know the exact date of purchase, nor the price paid for their painting, since this information is not included in their permanent record on the painting. Their collection was only formed in 1959 and the painting, therefore, bears the accession number 59.29. The catalogue number at VAG before the sale was EC42.39.*

* *Date the pictures were received at Glenbow: December 12, 1955. Date accepted: June 26, 1956.*

* *Works left to the Scholarship Fund in Emily's will should only bear the small rectangular "Emily Carr" stamp on the face of the picture, not the "Emily Carr Trust" marking on the reverse.*

* *There are two titles* Masset Pole *(Q.C.I.), but the Glenbow Pole can be identified by size.*

trustees. To form this collection, they took at least twenty-four identifiable paintings from the original Trust and added their own selections to this nucleus to make up their new permanent collection. It is difficult now to compare the original Trust list with the trustees' list because the latter is undated, some of the titles were changed, and no sizes were given. The list was subject to revision by agreement between the trustees, and all forty-seven pictures, whether from the original Trust or not, are now marked on the back "Emily Carr Trust" or "Ira" [Dilworth].*

** Also, on the canvas or on its frame each is marked with the Roman Numeral "I" and its own serial number written out in words. The I possibly stands for "Ira."*

One wonders what motivated the trustees to add so many pictures to their "permanent (not for sale) collection" and to fuse the original Trust works with it. Had they sold so many that they needed to bring the collection back to approximately its initial strength of forty-five? Lacking a date, we can be certain only that the Trust was restructured before December 1955, since all the paintings sold to Glenbow were still on this list.

Nonetheless, the original Trust pictures require special treatment and should not have been merged with any other collection. They were, as Emily has repeatedly said—and the trustees have confirmed—her gift to the Province of British Columbia and, as far as possible, should be re-assembled in a permanent "Emily Carr Picture Collection" as she directed. Moreover, the forty-five original Trust pictures are possibly the only ones that have a right to the official "Emily Carr Trust" marking.

Negotiations for the sale of the paintings to Glenbow were conducted by Lawren Harris and Dr. Douglas Leechman* who was instrumental in persuading the Calgary Gallery to buy them. In a Glenbow memorandum of November 29, 1955 he reports on his first contact with Harris:

** Director of Glenbow Foundation.*

> Dr. Lawren Harris showed me five of the very best Emily Carr canvasses in the reserve collection in the Vancouver Art Gallery. This Gallery has two large rooms devoted to a permanent collection of Emily Carr's work and these five canvasses would have been included had there been more room. . . . Dr. Harris is holding them for us at a very reasonable price.

This is a curious statement. Why, we may well ask, was there not enough room in the Vancouver Art Gallery for Emily's best works—for at least the three original Trust pictures? And why were the five canvasses in a "reserve" collection when all of them were on the trustees' list of "permanent (not for sale) paintings?" If space was the problem, despite the existence of the Emily Carr Memorial Galleries, less important pictures could have been sacrificed.

The sheaf of letters exchanged between Harris and Leechman,* containing the history of the purchase, also makes strange reading at times. For example, in a letter written in January 1956, Harris says that the Vancouver Art Gallery "does not own the Emily Carr paintings. The Province of British Columbia owns them . . ." But if the Province owned them, how could Harris have sold them—on his signature alone? He also wrote that, "Ira Dilworth and I are the trustees of the Collection with the power to sell some of the paintings." Why some? Does he mean a certain number of paintings, or that some were specifically excluded? And why, since the whole Collection had then been in the custody of the Vancouver Art Gallery for ten years, did it not have sufficient control over the administration of the Trust to object to or veto the sale of those prime canvasses? Another statement made in Harris' letter of December 24,1955 is equally puzzling:

> I know the trustees will not allow any other paintings to be sold except the five you (Glenbow) have. It took years to get the release of these five. They are by far and away the best Emily Carr paintings outside the permanent Art Gallery collections.

* *Copies of some of these letters kindly supplied by the Glenbow-Alberta Institute. Calgary.*

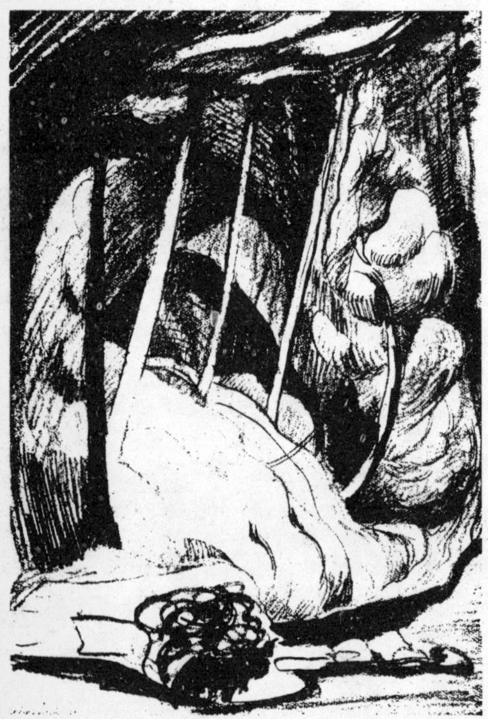

But why did Harris require a release? From whom? From Dilworth?—did he protest the sale? From the Vancouver Art Gallery? Hardly likely. The rightful owner (according to Harris), the Province of British Columbia, was not consulted. Also, why were these five paintings "outside the permanent Art Gallery collections?" Surely, as Trust works, they were at the very heart of the Gallery's permanent Collection.

We badly need a fuller account of the handling of the Trust. Perhaps in the future, unearthed gallery files or original trustees' papers may yield enough information to answer these questions. So few restraints were placed on the trustees by the conditions of the Trust or Emily's Will that they had authority to do whatever seemed best—at least before the Vancouver Art Gallery assumed responsibility for the Collection. They were busy men, and there was no need, they thought, to write everything down. Decisions between these two good friends were therefore made in informal conversations or personal letters, which worked admirably during their lifetime but leave us guessing today.

From the moment he met Emily in 1927, Lawren Harris took her under his wing, helped her in many crucial situations and always acted in what he considered to be her best interests, before and after her death. Ira Dilworth, too, was unselfish in his devotion. But Harris, especially, because he was greatly interested in promoting the training of talented young painters, interpreted Emily's Will to mean that priority should be given to the Scholarship Fund, and in his great enthusiasm was ready to sell even the original Trust pictures to support it. Artists badly needed such assistance then, and the trustees could not guess that Emily's paintings would become such a priceless asset to the Vancouver Art Gallery and the Province of British Columbia. But hindsight makes us wonder if perhaps the trustees did not misinterpret Emily's wish and intent by allowing some paintings she had set aside for the people of British Columbia to be sold to another province. The decision, though well-meant, was shortsighted. In order to foster the talent of a few, the paltry sum of $10,000 was accepted for the five paintings sold to Glenbow.* The sum was minimal, and many of the scholarship recipients are forgotten today. But the paintings will be admired and enjoyed for untold years—by Albertans, not British Columbians.

* *The Glenbow-Alberta Institute declined to divulge the price paid for their paintings. I found it elsewhere, and apologize to the Institute for making it public.*

Let us revert to the May 1974 letter from the Vancouver Art Gallery, already discussed in relation to the six paintings sold by the trustees in 1956, to examine another statement in it: "there were originally 170 works in the Trust. . . ."* How should we interpret this remark?

* *See also VAG's catalogue* Emily Carr: A Centennial Exhibition *p.5 (1971 edition), p.6 (1975 edition).*

If "originally" means there were 170 works in the Trust when it was formed, this is wrong. The number was, of course, only forty-five.

If, on the other hand, "originally" refers to the date the Collection was transferred to the Vancouver Art Gallery, the number 170 is still wrong. It has been contradicted by the Gallery itself in its Bulletin of June 1946.

But if "originally" means the number of pictures contained in the Trust when it was terminated in 1966, then 170 is right—less, of course, the six paintings sold earlier—not "subsequently."

To add to the general confusion, there are various other statements, made at various times, by various people. In the *Souvenir Catalogue of Exhibitions* opening the new Vancouver Art Gallery in 1951, with its increased facilities, including two Emily Carr Memorial Galleries, Lawren Harris erroneously states that Emily left 170 paintings and drawings to the Province of British Columbia, as well as 500 works to be sold to establish the Emily Carr Scholarship Fund.

But in 1958, in the catalogue accompanying the first major exhibition of Trust paintings at the Art Gallery of Greater

Victoria, Harris wrote that he, Dilworth,* and Emily together had selected 200 works as a gift to the Province which would eventually be housed at the Vancouver Art Gallery.**Of the remainder, he said, 500 plus had been reserved for the Scholarship Fund and thirty to forty for specific requests.

Then again, according to a summary of the proceedings at the official opening on May 1, 1946 of the Emily Carr Memorial Exhibition, as printed in the Art Gallery Bulletin of June 1946, Harris said the Emily Carr Permanent (or Trust) Collection consisted of eighty-two oils, twenty-seven water colors and fifty-seven black and white drawings, a total of 166 works. But the President's report (1945-46), in the same issue of the Bulletin, said that "some 157 choice examples of her [Emily's] art" were presented to the Gallery. And so it goes, on and on. Nothing tallies. Considering the astronomical prices of Emily's paintings today, and the great potential value of the Collection even then, the continual misplacing, misquoting and miscounting of the Trust pictures seems scarcely credible.

Ira Dilworth was closer to the truth when he reported in the Art Gallery Bulletin of May 1942 that Emily had left eight canvasses and sketches to the people of Canada [sic], of which forty-five had been designated a permanent collection, not for sale. Proceeds from the sale of the others, he said, were earmarked for a fund to care for and house the permanent collection and to establish a scholarship fund.

In the same Bulletin, Dilworth announced that the whole Collection was to travel east immediately to assure wartime safety of the pictures. Still earlier, Harris, too, had been concerned about the safety of the Collection and was trying to make arrangements to store the pictures in the basement of the Empress Hotel in Victoria or, failing that, in the Hotel Vancouver.* But after the beginning of hostilities with Japan, when air raids seemed imminent, the trustees hurriedly changed their mind and requested the Art Gallery of Toronto to take over the safekeeping of the paintings at once.* One lot of Trust pictures (eight crates) had already been sent direct from Emily's studio to the Parliament Buildings for safekeeping.*

To trace the wartime travels of the Collection between its departure from Vancouver in 1942 and its return early 1946 is well-nigh impossible, as adequate records are not available. However, entries of Carr paintings in the shipping register of the Art Gallery of Toronto show that sixty-two of her paintings, in eleven boxes, were received there for storage on April 21, 1942. They were exhibited in London, Montreal, Toronto and

* *With Lawren Harris, Ira Dilworth was a trustee of the Emily Carr Trust, as well as literary executor of her Will. But the Will also appointed two "Trustees of My Pictures"—Harris and William A. Newcombe of Victoria. The overlapping of trusteeships is confusing, particularly as Dilworth assumed Newcombe's duties about a year after Emily's death. It is not known why Newcombe appointed Ira Dilworth to act in his place as second "Trustee of My Pictures" but in May 1946, Harris wrote to Newcombe: "The lawyer suggested it would be best for all concerned if you wrote and signed a statement that you appointed Ira Dilworth, Regional Director of the CBC of Vancouver, to act for you as a trustee of the Emily Carr pictures with myself. He thinks your agreement to permit Ira to act for you should be regularized, made legal."(PABC)*

** *It is not explicitly stated in Emily's Will that she intended her Picture Collection to be housed in VAG, but her letters imply this. It is obvious when she writes "Vancouver" that she means VAG, as, for instance, in one written December 26, 1942 to the Rev. F.E. Tomalin: "My studio is closed. . . . I have been in a nursing home for five months. The main portion (of my pictures) are now traveling in the East and will eventually make their home in Vancouver.*

* *Nan Cheney to Humphrey Toms, February 20, 1942.*

* *Vancouver* Daily Province, *February 11, 1943.*

* *Phylis Dilworth Inglis Collection, Emily to Ira Dilworth, April 19, 1942.*

Ottawa during their stay in the east and the last shipment of her work—twenty-nine pictures in six boxes—was forwarded to the Vancouver Art Gallery on May 2, 1946.

Emily's own comments on the original selection of pictures for the Trust add a little to our knowledge of its development, but also contribute to the general perplexities. What she says is both intriguing and revealing and plainly shows that a small spark of discord—triggered by the Trust—had crept into her relationship with Harris towards the end of her life.* This is unexpected as Emily's faith in, and devotion to, her "beloved Trustors" (Harris and Dilworth) had been unshakable for years.

* *Also because of Emily's growing dislike of Lawren's second wife, Bess.*

Emily obviously felt that Lawren Harris was too wealthy to be capable of understanding her own large, ever-present and very real fears about simple financial security. Though she greatly admired and respected him, they did not always see eye to eye, as she frankly admits in an undated letter written about this time: "Lawren and I disagree on a lot of points about art, and whole-heartedly agree on others. Did I tell you he is for having that *filthy* Emily Carr (portrait) of Nan's hung in the Trust shows? I kicked like a steer and he has given way, but *without* approving."*

* *From the National Gallery of Canada Annual Reports 1944-45: "Gifts and Bequests—Portrait of Emily Carr by Nan Lawson Cheney. Bequeathed by the late John Frederick Bligh Livesay, Toronto."*

Before her death, Emily added about thirty-five paintings to the original Trust but her letters show that she took a definite stand against the inclusion of her water colors during her lifetime.* They were consequently only added by the trustees after her death, along with the black and white drawings. She was annoyed with Harris for insisting that she part with the water colors because she "had already given thirty to thirty-five pictures, which grew to fifty, swelled to eighty and then swallowed up the water colors too. . . . I don't even see that Trust room built. It's Lawren's rose-colored specs."

* *All letters mentioned in this paragraph are to Ira Dilworth.*

Emily felt that the popularity and relatively low price of the water colors made them a sure source of income and a hedge against mounting medical costs and, less than two months before her death, she was still opposing their inclusion in the Trust: "No, I do not intend to present the water colors to the Trust. I know they (the trustees) have been good in giving me monies from sales during my lifetime, but they have a good many more (pictures) in keeping than were actually *given* to the Trust. They were only given because I considered the Trust had a better chance to sell them than I.* That is, beyond the fifty [sic] given outright to British Columbia. . . . All my good canvasses were taken. I have only scraps and sketches left to income on. I am not needing the money for the present as I told you but in my

* *The trustees sold some pictures to help Emily during the last years of her life, but not the Trust pictures.*

shape there are doctors bills and drugs all the time and one never knows what else, when. Or, there is Alice. . . . Oh! Isn't money filthy!"

Here is one of Emily's more interesting, and accurate, comments on the Trust:

> Did you know I presented 80 canvasses to the Nation, that is to British Columbia? They are in trust, Lawren Harris and Ira Dilworth are the trustees. Forty-five will be kept for a permanent collection, housed in Vancouver, the rest sold as opportunity offers for upkeep and support of the rest. They are now housed in the Toronto Art Gallery till the Japs are sat down, then they will be returned to the West. It was quite a turn-out of the studio but there is quite a lot left, and I'm not quite through yet (painting).*

* *Emily to Humphrey Toms, June 15, 1942.*

No list appears to have survived of the thirty-five canvasses Emily added to the Trust, as a further gift to British Columbia, less than a year after it was established. Certainly no legal document was drawn up to list and regularize the gift as in the case of the original forty-five Trust pictures. But Emily's remarks in the above letter are noteworthy since they confirm that the forty-five original canvasses were intended to be kept for a permanent collection (which they were not) and that the added paintings were to be sold for their upkeep as need dictated.

All the information given so far about the Trust was acquired from documents, letters and press extracts. Now it is time to turn to people. The first person I contacted, more by chance than design, was Alistair Bell, well-known Vancouver artist and former trustee, who was very obliging and helpful. He explained that the Trust was transferred from Lawren Harris and Ira Dilworth to himself and J.E.A. Parnall in 1962* and that they (Bell and Parnall) signed the document of March 1 1966* which terminated the Trust and conveyed all their legal interests in the Collection to the Vancouver Art Gallery. All works available for sale had been disposed of before Parnall and Bell assumed the trusteeship, leaving a bank balance of $8,923.11. During the remaining four years of the Trust, this money, plus accrued interest, was spent on scholarships and routine legal fees.

* *One document, in which Lawren Harris and Ira Dilworth appointed Parnall as trustee, was signed on February 5, 1962, and the other, in which Parnall and Harris appointed Bell as trustee, was signed on February 6, 1962.*

* *Copies of the 1962 and 1966 documents were kindly made available by J.E.A. Parnall.*

The legal arrangements concerning the Trust contained some obvious loopholes until its termination transferred possession of the pictures to the Vancouver Art Gallery and ratified what had been for years a "fait accompli."

But it is precisely these loopholes that make the earlier

history of the Trust, during the quarter century before Parnall and Bell became trustees, so interesting and tantalizing. The many obvious blanks are difficult to fill in at present, but Lawren Harris, like Emily, was a prolific letter writer and it is suspected that many of his letters are still in private hands. Apart from the previously-mentioned Glenbow correspondence, scraps of useful information have turned up in a few letters from Lawren Harris to Willie Newcombe (about the financial state of the Trust for about a year after Emily's death) and to Dr. Max Stern (about sales and pricing of her pictures at his Dominion Gallery in Montreal after 1944). Harris's letters often end with "Ira agrees," suggesting that he regarded himself as both secretary and treasurer of the Trust. In fact he says so in a November 1946 letter to H.O. McCurry, then director of the National Gallery: "The E.C. Trust . . . is . . . a purely philanthropic trust and as its treasurer (Gawd save us) I do my best to keep the accounts and collections up to the minute." But he always consulted Ira Dilworth before making an important decision.

All four trustees were self-sacrificing, able men who worked hard at a thankless task, but the original two were Emily's close friends and advisers and took a great personal interest in the Trust. Because she had such implicit faith in both, arrangements among them, usually made informally over a cup of tea in the studio, were not recorded and their decisions, and reasons for them, are lost to us forever.

After Emily's death, the administration of the Trust made still greater demands on the trustees who, in a determined effort to build up the Scholarship Fund, economized in all possible areas by trying to do everything themselves. Perhaps they assumed too many responsibilities and should have had a business man on the "team" to help lighten the load and produce more efficient accounts and records. It is possible, of course, that more complete records *were* kept but later lost or destroyed. In any case, the Harris family has no record among Lawren Harris's papers* of the handling of the Trust nor did Ira Dilworth's heir find any Trust documents among the Carr papers she inherited.*

At last, however, we do have something tangible to work on—six important legal documents which have been traced, assembled and studied for the first time. They are basic to this study and solve many problems, doubts and inconsistencies. They are:

1) The Inter Vivos Trust

2) The Will Trust

* *According to Mrs. James H. Knox, Lawren Harris's daughter, of West Vancouver, who kindly assisted me.*

* *As confirmed by Phylis Dilworth Inglis.*

3) & 4) Two separate documents transferring the trusteeship from Ira Dilworth and Lawren Harris to John E.A. Parnall and Alistair Bell respectively

5) An agreement between the trustees (Parnall and Bell), the Vancouver Art Gallery Association and the Art Gallery of Greater Victoria

6) An agreement between the above trustees and galleries terminating the Trust

Four of these indentures have already been referred to in connection with the transfer of trusteeship in 1962 (3 and 4) and the composition of the Trust Collection on termination of the Trust in 1966 (5 and 6). By far the most important documents, the Inter Vivos Trust and the Will Trust (1 and 2) have been separated from the others in order to give them fuller and individual consideration here. First of all, the Inter Vivos Trust must be disentangled from the Will Trust with which it has always been identified owing to some overlapping in certain aspects. In fact, the Will Trust is usually held to be the Inter Vivos Trust, and this mistake has given rise to many errors and misunderstandings, including the correct date of the Emily Carr Trust itself.

The Inter Vivos Trust was made by the law firm of Crease, Davey, Lawson, Davis, Gordon and Baker of Victoria, predecessors of the present Crease and Company, of which D.J. Lawson, Q.C. is a partner. It was a particular pleasure to meet Mr. Lawson when I called at his office, as he is the grandson of James Hill Lawson, Emily's guardian, and the son of Henry Graham Lawson, who, like Emily, died early 1945. Just "Harry" to her, he was her lawyer and one of the two executors of her Will.*

For thirty-three years, no one, apparently, had asked to see, or use, the Inter Vivos Trust document, and Mr. Lawson himself seemed surprised to find it still in the office files. He generously agreed to let me have a copy after I had complied with a few simple conditions.

The date of the Inter Vivos Trust, never questioned, has invariably been given as 1942—even by the trustees. Yet the correct date of the document—and therefore of the Emily Carr Trust—is July 15, 1941! Only the supplement was signed in 1942 (November 25). But except for the total exclusion of Alice Carr from the terms of the Trust, effected by small deletions in two sentences,* there are only two insignificant alterations to the original text, which have no bearing whatsoever on the main

* *The other was Ira Dilworth. To recapitulate: Dilworth was:*
a) Co-trustee, with Lawren Harris of the Inter Vivos Trust.
b) Co-executor, with Henry Lawson, of the Will Trust, plus literary executor.
c) Co-"Trustee of My Pictures," with Lawren Harris, after replacing Willie Newcombe in 1946.

* *In compensation, Alice was left all Emily's real and the residue of her personal property in her Will dated November 30, 1942. She*

provisions.

A discussion of the fine points of the Trust would be tedious, and hazardous, too, without having a lawyer nearby to interpret them. But one paragraph, at least, is completely clear to the average citizen, whom it also directly concerns:

2(b), p. 1 At their (the trustees') discretion from time to time to exhibit any or all of such pictures and to charge an admission fee to see the same;

except that the words

"... and to charge an admission fee to see the same"

have been struck out in the supplement. Does that mean that we, the public, are entitled to a refund of all admission fees we have paid over the years to see Emily's 1941 Trust pictures? After all, both Emily and the trustees have said over and over again that these particular pictures belong to us, the people of British Columbia, not to the Vancouver Art Gallery. They constitute a great gift, by a great woman, to a grateful Province, and it would interest many of us to know how legally sufficient Emily's wishes and conditions are today, and exactly which forty-five pictures she bequeathed to us. A schedule of these original pictures follows—with approximate sizes, in inches and notes by the author:

also received a large valuable painting as a gift, about which Emily wrote: "I have given (Alice) now that big canvas in my studio over the table. Lawson put a reserve price of $500 on it. It is hers any-time to sell or to will if she wants and where she wants, but she is out of the other pictures and therefore cannot will them back to the nieces."

Schedule of the forty-five original Trust pictures.

TITLE	*SIZE*
INDIAN SUBJECTS	
Masset Pole*	50 by 21
D'Sonoqua	(not given)
The Yan Poles	33 by 23
D'Sonoqua with Cats	43 by 27
Raven	44 by 33
The Crazy Stair	42 by 26
Totem Mother, Kitwancool	42 by 26
Totem Mother 2, Kitwancool	36 by 20½
Kitwancool	40 by 32½
Old Time Coast Village	49 by 35
B.C. Indian Village	(not given)
Three Totems	(not given)
Silhouette	49 by 35
Indian Village, Lillooet	(not given)
Totem	23 by 17
Skidegate Eagle 1	25 by 12
Skidegate Eagle 2	25 by 12

* *Note that there are two titles* Masset Pole *on this list. It would seem that* Masset Pole *(50 x 21 in.) was sold, or perhaps renamed, as it is not listed in the Schedule of 1966 when VAG assumed custody of the Collection. Nor was it exhibited under this name in the 1971 Centennial Exhibition.* Masset Pole *(27 x 44), however, is the missing No. 29 on the 1966 list. It was sold to Glenbow in 1956.*

D'Sonoqua—water color	17½	by 12½
Skidegate Totem	25	by 12
Skidegate Totem	25	by 12
Indian Raven	31	by 16
House Front with Boat	36	by 25
House Front, Gold Harbour	36	by 25
Mortuary Pole—water color	29½	by 10½
Crying Totem	30	by 15
Beaver Pole Masset	30	by 34
Masset Pole	27	by 44

OTHER SUBJECTS

Tree Trunk*	50	by 21½
Forest	46	by 29
A Rushing Sea of Undergrowth*	44	by 27
Sea Drift at the Edge of Forest	44	by 27
Old and New Forest	44	by 27
The Little Pine	44	by 27
A young Tree	44	by 27
Among the Trees	44	by 27
Scorned of the Sky*	(not given)	
Above the Gravel Pit	(not given)	
The Path	44	by 27
Vanquished	49	by 35
Forest	44	by 35
Pemberton Meadows	(not given)	
Village in the Hills	(not given)	
Tall Boles and Small Trees	27	by 29
The Blue Bough	36	by 30
Strangled in Growth	25½	by 19

* *VAG has incorrectly catalogued this oil on canvas as* Tree *(42.3.2). This has caused confusion and duplication of title as there is a second* Tree *(42.3.63), an oil on paper sketch, in their Collection. See chapter "Notes on Six Emily Carr Paintings."*

* *First exhibited at VAG, October 1938, as* Sea of Growth *(a woodscape)—no doubt Emily's own title for this painting.*

* *Note inaccurate title. Emily tried to express in paint just the opposite sentiment in the correctly named:* Scorned as Timber, Beloved of the Sky.

The Inter Vivos Trust states that certain restrictions would be binding on the Vancouver Art Gallery, as trustee for the public benefit of the pictures received under this Trust, were they to sell one of the Trust pictures. In such a case, they would be bound to utilize the proceeds of the sale for the purposes specified in the Trust, that is, for the care, insurance and upkeep of the pictures or for leasing or building a gallery to display the pictures or for the purpose of promoting art education among Canadian artists. On the other hand, the Vancouver Art Gallery would actually own any pictures received under the Will Trust and would be entitled to the proceeds of any sale. These provisions, however, have been superseded by those of the 1966 agreement which expressly state that the pictures cannot be sold.

Finally, to ensure that the difference between the two documents is fully understood, brief summaries follow:

Inter Vivos Trust:

On July 15, 1941, Emily transferred forty-five of her pictures to Ira Dilworth and Lawren Harris as trustees. The terms of the Trust are that the trustees—

a) may sell some or all of the pictures if they think fit;
b) may exhibit the pictures;
c) may sell such pictures as they see fit to form a permanent collection to be known as the "Emily Carr Picture Collection," and until there is a suitable building or space provided for housing them, to loan the pictures to any government, municipality, individual, organization, institution or art gallery.
d) may use the capital and/or income of the Trust to promote art education among Canadian artists.*

There is also a provision for appointment of new trustees.

Will Trust:

On November 30, 1942, Emily appointed William A. Newcombe and Lawren Harris the trustees of her pictures and gave all the pictures which she owned at her death to them upon the trusts mentioned. It should be noted that this transfer does not include the forty-five pictures set aside under the Inter Vivos Trust.

The picture trustees under the Will have the right to sell them or alternatively may give all or any of them to any public gallery in British Columbia.

They also have the right to use monies arising from sales for the teaching of art in British Columbia or the founding of a Scholarship Fund to enable art students residing in British Columbia to further their education.*

When Emily died and the Trust provisions came into full effect, Dr. Max Stern, as an art dealer, was instrumental in carrying them out. In close cooperation with the trustees, he disposed of most of the Trust pictures released for sale, the proceeds thus realized adding materially to the Scholarship Fund. He also became the principal private collector of Emily's paintings.

Yet Stern only met Emily once—about six months before her death. He visited her studio in August 1944, not because he

* *Although the Trust document stipulates "Canadian artists," later documents restrict scholarships to "British Columbia artists."*

* *I owe a debt of gratitude to Mr. Lawson for supplying this précis of the two documents.*

was greatly interested in her work, but on behalf of a client who had authorized him to purchase a painting. On arrival in Victoria, unannounced, he telephoned Emily, and being assured that she was feeling well that day, hopped into a cab and hurried out to St. Andrew's Street. She was sitting outside waiting for him, well wrapped in a blanket, with a cat beside her.

Once inside the studio, Emily began to pull out one painting after another from the racks. "I was speechless when I saw the first one," said Stern. "The pictures were much more modern than I had expected—stronger and more powerful and emotional than anything I had seen on this continent." In his excitement he told Emily that he no longer wanted just one picture, but enough for a whole show, and he asked if he might organize an exhibition of her work in Montreal. Emily quickly agreed but, in her blunt, honest way, warned him that her paintings might not sell. Stern brushed off this objection and selected sixty on the spot which were displayed later in the fall at his Dominion Gallery.

In the light of the tremendous success of this exhibition, and the one following it in 1945, as well as the sharply escalating prices of Carr pictures ever since, it is obvious that Dr. Stern has made a very handsome profit on his investment. But it must not be forgotten that up to 1944 no one else had wanted to risk a solo show of Emily's work in a commercial gallery. This should be borne in mind when reading Dr. Stern's contract with Emily* because at first glance it appears that he drove a hard bargain with an impoverished, elderly and desperately ill artist. Stern is naturally an experienced and astute businessman, as well as a competent judge of paintings, and would not, for instance, agree to cover the cost of insurance. Since Emily could not afford to do so, the pictures traveled to Montreal uninsured. Had they been lost, damaged or destroyed (and Emily's water colors were badly damaged once in transit from the National Gallery to Victoria), Emily would have been ruined. Quite apart from such possible disasters, had the exhibition itself been a failure, she would have had to pay part of the loss from her own pocket. But other than this, and the insurance clause, the terms of the contract seem fair, and neither Emily nor Stern had the slightest cause for complaint about this exhibition—her first real attempt to work with an agent.*

** PABC*

The agreement is reproduced here only as a matter of historical interest. No criticism is implied. On the contrary, Dr. Stern is to be congratulated. Owing to his successful promotion of Emily's work, the last five painful months of her life were

** This does not apply to Emily's pottery and rugs, and she did experiment briefly with an agent for her pictures in 1938.*

greatly eased financially. She also had the proud satisfaction of knowing that she had at last won true fame as a painter as well as a writer.

Contract between the Dominion Gallery, Montreal and Emily Carr, dated August 4, 1944.

> I [Emily Carr] confirm the following agreement according to which I give the Dominion Gallery, of Montreal, Quebec, the below-mentioned paintings on consignment for a period of one year, fixed at the below-mentioned prices which I have suggested, less one third net for me under condition that if Mr. Ira Dilworth and Mr. Lawren Harris are not in favor and so advise me, I am at liberty to cancel it in writing within two weeks from to-day.
>
> The paintings are not to be insured. I take the full risk on myself. Furthermore, I am willing to pay one third of the costs of crating, transportation and exhibition. I only have to pay anything if not more than $300.00 of [sic] my paintings are sold, and my share should not be more than $100.00 . . .

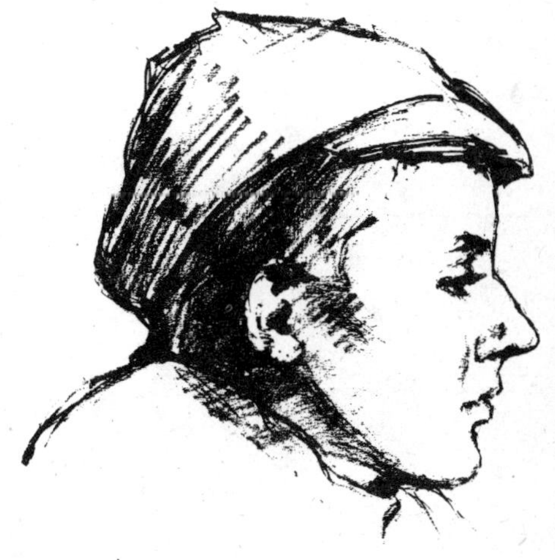

Fortunately, these terms of the contract did not have to be implemented. Stern congratulated Emily on the spectacular outcome of her Dominion Gallery show and offered to pay for all future crating and shipping—but not for the mounting of her paper sketches. The mounting, he said, could be done in Montreal (on masonite as it neither splits or warps and is fairly reasonable) and the cost then deducted from the receipts of future sales.

Stern mentions the Trust pictures for the first time, it seems, when he told Emily in October 1944 that the trustees had authorized him to sell some of the Trust pictures still being stored at the Art Gallery of Toronto.

Considering the astounding prices Emily's work commands today, it is pitiful to note in retrospect how slowly the Scholarship Fund grew from the sale of her Trust pictures, in spite of the fact that purchasers were plentiful. The Dominion Gallery was commissioned to sell enough paintings to support the Fund (as well as the Collection) but at the time of Emily's death prices were still unbelievably low—most well under $100—and, of course, one-third of the proceeds went to Stern.

On September 11,1945, the Trust account had a balance of only $4,036.23; in April 1946, $12,812.00; in January 1948,

$13,519.88. By January 1956, it had risen to $17,982.89, largely attributable to the sale of the five paintings to the Glenbow Foundation. How much was finally realized from the sale of pictures, or exactly how much was paid out in scholarships would be difficult to determine, but the trustees were satisfied that Stern had done a careful, considered job of pricing.

Whatever the amount collected, it sufficed to support a modest scholarship program to encourage and develop British Columbia talent. According to Lawren Harris, by 1956 the Fund had enabled ten young artists to continue their studies abroad (out of which eight had been most successful) and ten more one-year scholarships were planned after the windfall of the Glenbow sale. The first to be awarded an Emily Carr scholarship was Joe Plasket,* a teacher, whom Dilworth and Harris chose on the strong recommendation of A.Y. Jackson, who wrote that: "[he is] to my mind, the young painter with the greatest possibilities in British Columbia today."

* Vancouver Sun, *July 27, 1946, "Plasket Awarded Carr Fellowship."*

After vainly enquiring of the Vancouver Art Gallery exactly when they assumed custody of the "Emily Carr Picture Collection," and how many works it comprised at that time, I found at least a partial answer in the Vancouver press. The *News-Herald* and the *Daily Province* (both of May 2, 1946), after adding their own inaccurate totals of Trust pictures to the growing list of discrepancies, told a fascinating story about the formal presentation of the Collection to the Art Gallery.

The *News-Herald,* for instance, writes that "The world's finest collection of paintings by Emily Carr became the property of the citizens of British Columbia Wednesday night (May 1) when the Emily Carr Memorial Exhibition was formally opened at the Vancouver Gallery. On behalf of the trustees of the estate, artist Lawren Harris presented the Collection of 157 [sic] oil paintings, water colors and drawings to the Province. Dr. G.M. Weir, Minister of Education, accepted on behalf of the people of the Province and turned over the Collection to the City of Vancouver. Alderman John Bennet placed the Collection in the custody of the Vancouver Art Gallery. W.H. Malkin, President of the Art Gallery, accepted the Collection and said that, in the near future, a wing would be added to the present building to provide a permanent home for the Collection."

The *Daily Province,* after giving its own inaccurate estimate of the total number of Trust pictures presented to the Gallery (159), noted that the black and white drawings were selected for the Collection by the trustees after Emily's death. The water colors were not mentioned, but, as already shown, they, too, were added to the Collection after she died.

The curious thing about this presentation ceremony is that it is almost completely undocumented. Emily had always said, in a surge of emotion, that she was giving her pictures to the Province of British Columbia, but she never pinned it down in any legal sense. In fact, British Columbia is not mentioned in the Trust document, and only in relation to art education and scholarships in her Will.*

The gestures of gift passing at the opening ceremony of the Memorial Exhibition in Vancouver were therefore more symbolic than factual since no records exist to prove that the Province or the City of Vancouver ever had physical possession of the Collection. In fact they only had titular right to it for the few minutes it took to make two short speeches.

The Minister of Education to whom I wrote requesting an explanation of Dr. Weir's speech, and a copy of it, referred my letter to the Provincial Archivist who replied, in part:

> There is no indication that the Provincial Archives was involved in the arrangement between the trustees of the Collection and Dr. Weir, who held the portfolio of Provincial Secretary and Minister of Education at the time . . . a search [was] made in the orders-in-council and the records of the Provincial Secretary's office which failed to produce any documentation on this matter. (Letter dated December 6, 1974.)

A similar letter was received from the City of Vancouver Archives which only added to the ambiguity and was, moreover, incorrect on all counts in stating that:

> We have checked with the Legal Department and with the City Clerk's office at City Hall in an attempt to discover some documentation regarding the transfer of the Emily Carr Collection to the citizens of Vancouver. We found nothing, not even a reference to the 1967 [sic] agreement by which, supposedly, the Board of Trustees [sic] handed over complete responsibility for the Collection to the Vancouver Art Gallery. (Letter dated January 13, 1975.)

It must therefore be assumed that the Collection was solely under the control of the trustees at all times and that for good reasons of their own, perhaps to make the gift look more official and the ceremony more impressive, it was presented by two consecutive speeches to the Provincial Government and the City of Vancouver before finally being transferred to the custody of

* *In the Trust document Emily simply "assigned and transferred" the 45 original Trust pictures "unto the trustees." In the Will she "gives unto the 'Trustees of My Pictures' all my pictures and paintings belonging to me at the date of my death."*

the Vancouver Art Gallery.

Although Emily has frequently intimated that she expected her pictures to be ultimately housed at the Vancouver Art Gallery, she does not expressly say so in any official document. The trustees, it seems, acted on her verbal wishes rather than on any written instructions or legal directives and, in the end, the Vancouver Gallery was *their* choice as much as hers. In fact, her ideas about the final disposition of the Trust pictures was still vague in 1941 when she seemed to be thinking more in terms of leasing, or even building, a gallery to house her Collection. But she was more explicit in her Will when she stipulated that:

> the trustees may . . . give any of such pictures and paintings to any public art gallery now or hereafter existing in the Province of British Columbia.

Vancouver was the logical choice at the time, but it is conceivable that the Collection might have gone to Victoria had it had a fireproof gallery and adequate storage facilities. Emily herself says so: "[The Trust] *should* have come to Victoria only Victoria is too hopeless. She could never have bothered to arrange or house, all her top men are ossified."*

* *Emily to Humphrey Toms, June 15, 1942.*

It is conceivable, too, that Ira Dilworth, as a former Victorian, might also have preferred his home town, since he, like Emily, had deep roots there. Thus, when Victoria finally obtained the requisite gallery facilities, he wanted Emily's birthplace to at least share in the Trust Collection, and the Art Gallery of Greater Victoria gained a stake in it partly because of his influence. Victoria had at last awakened to its lost opportunities. It had long felt irked that Emily had not bequeathed her paintings to her native city, conveniently forgetting that its citizens had shown more derision for, than interest in her work during her lifetime. She had always keenly resented their attitude, and when the gift of her Trust pictures was announced in the press, the lack of reaction infuriated her. Her agitation, spewed forth in a letter to Ira Dilworth, is expressed by so many underscorings, insertions and jerky sentences that editing was required to make it intelligible:

> Except for Mrs.Parker not one allusion has been made in my hearing to the Trust. Some weeks ago, when the gift of eighty pictures to British Columbia was told and noted in the paper, no remark was made. I don't *really* care. I *don't.* Still, I thought it was general that one's *townspeople* (who have known you since you were born) offered congrats to one of the members of their community who had met with a measure of

success. It makes me feel further away than ever from people to see how *little* these things matter. The reviewers and big shots who *did* matter *did* (offer congratulations) but *personal* friends (beyond one or two in Vancouver) didn't. Well, it's good for one's conceit. Although one does not care about fuss, one likes honest appreciation. Is that conceit? Victorians, or rather I should say, the *only* Victorian who made a remark . . . said the pictures should have been left to Victoria, not Vancouver. The artists, Victoria artists, hate me and my works and are mute.*

* *Phylis Dilworth Inglis Collection, Emily to Ira Dilworth, June 30, 1942. Mrs. Parker was the mother of a prominent B.C. artist, J. Delisle Parker.*

At last, thirteen years after her death, Emily won the tardy recognition, admiration and affection of her fellow Victorians—even of the most recalcitrant oldtimers—and returned to the city of her birth in triumph. The way had not been easy. An early step, perhaps the first, was taken by then curator Colin Graham of the Art Gallery of Greater Victoria. With real foresight, and aided by Lawren Harris, he saw an opportunity to gain access to the Trust Collection by pressing the authorities to add a fireproof wing to the existing gallery as a centennial project. Enthusiasm for the project gained momentum and soon public demand for the new wing mushroomed into a lively campaign with the slogan, "Bring Emily Home!" This theme won the support of all and the press, too, took up the hue and cry.

One reviewer reported that prospects for the construction of a fireproof wing for the Gallery as the city's centennial project had improved since the trustees agreed to share the "Emily Carr Picture Collection." Estimated cost of the new building was $55,000, but no gallery, he claimed, no matter how wealthy could buy such a collection. Victoria, he continued, had been put in an ignominious position. When visitors to the Gallery requested to see their Carr paintings, they had to be told that Victoria, where Emily Carr had lived and worked, was the only city in Canada whose gallery did not have one Carr picture.*

* *Victoria* Daily Colonist, *April 30, 1957.*

Two unsuccessful briefs were submitted to the Municipal Centennial Committee, but the third, read by prominent Victorian and collector of Carr pictures, Major H. Cuthbert Holmes, was accepted and the Centennial wing was built. For Victoria this was a fitting conclusion.

Emily came home on September 30, 1958 when the first major exhibition of her Trust pictures in her native city was opened at the Art Gallery of Greater Victoria.* She has returned almost annually ever since.

* *A small selection of Trust pictures was exhibited, along with others from the NGC and private collections, in the Little Centre in 1946.*

The Art Gallery of Greater Victoria received certain

guarantees under both the 1965 and 1966 agreements with the trustees and the Vancouver Art Gallery which "permitted the Victoria Art Gallery at all times to have and display a portion of the collection, such portion to be not less than twenty-five per cent of the whole, and in such a manner that it shall be possible for the entire collection to have been displayed in the Victoria Art Gallery, over a reasonable period of time not to exceed twelve years."

The Vancouver Art Gallery retained technical ownership of the pictures, but the agreement amounted to virtual joint ownership by the two galleries. *

* *Unless it can still be established that the Province of British Columbia owns them.*

As early as March 26, 1943, long before these two agreements had been reached, even the director of the National Gallery had expressed interest in the Trust pictures:

> I sincerely hope it will be possible to provide a permanent home in the Art Gallery of Vancouver for the 40 [sic] pictures now under the control of the trustees. It would be both a happy and logical development, although the National Gallery itself would not be averse to considering such an opportunity. . . . I feel safe in saying that I rank Miss Carr in the same group as Tom Thomson as one of the most individual Canadian artists this country has produced.

Later, there was even some discussion about providing a room in the new National Gallery building for the permanent display of Emily's work. What a triumph for her that the National Gallery of Canada should consider offering a home for her Trust Collection.

Six months after Emily's death, in a letter to Willie Newcombe, Lawren Harris makes a rare comment on his attitude to the Trust and his plans for it. Because this passage sheds some light on the future handling of the Trust and its termination, it is quoted at length:

> I must confess that I have not thought of it as a trust in perpetuity. After receiving your letter I re-read Emily's will and really do not think that she considered it in those terms, nor did she, so far as I can remember, in conversations we had about it before she died.
>
> There is this about it also—you and I are no longer youngsters and if one or both of us 'pop off' whose hands will we leave it in? Frankly, I wouldn't know.
>
> Then too it would mean that we would have to

> invest the money—that I wouldn't like to do for outside of Gov't bonds I wouldn't know what was safe—and Gov't bonds would not yield enough each year to carry out any assistance we determine upon so as to make it effective. We could not really assist a young artist unless we enabled him or her to use his or her full time in painting for at least a year . . .
>
> I would also favor that we plan, if we can do so, to use the whole amount of the trust in our lifetime. I have seen a good many benefits unwisely used so that their result was ineffective—mediocre talents assisted with no fruitful results. I think we can avoid that—but I cannot see that we can leave it in other hands. . . .
>
> I have been thinking also about assisting art education in B.C. I have a few rather hazy ideas but until I discover something worthwhile I won't bother you with them. I have discussed the Trust with Ira and he agrees that we should not consider a Trust in perpetuity.*

* *PABC, Harris to Newcombe, September 18, 1945.*

Lawren Harris's wish to see the Trust terminated during his lifetime came true; but for reasons of health, he was unable to administer it during the last four years of its existence. He died in January 1970 having served as Emily's trustee with exemplary devotion for twenty-one years. Ira Dilworth, less intimately involved with the Trust than Harris, was nevertheless an active worker for it and only relinquished his co-trusteeship shortly before his death in 1962.

Though the Trust was organized, developed and administered by these two "beloved trustors," it was not conceived by them. "I think," said Ira Dilworth, "this idea was Emily's own idea, not the idea of me or Lawren Harris. Emily wanted to do something to help young* painters in Western Canada* and this was her way of doing it."*

* *"Young" was frequently used by the trustees, but never by Emily. It is doubtful that she would have approved this distinction.*

* *Canada, Western Canada and British Columbia have all been used at various times.*

* *"Portrait in Memory—Emily Carr," CBC broadcast, April 9, 1958.*

Yes, this was Emily's way of doing it. She never regretted her decision but the final parting from her Trust pictures, when she actually saw them being crated and carted away from her studio, was a painful wrench that shook her to the very core. She has tried to explain this:

> *Nobody* . . . knows what it has cost to see them [the pictures] go. . . . Don't call me fine, noble, Canadian, patriotic—I *am* Canadian, but first and hardest I am *just* a woman—a poor old artist-woman and all ache'd up over parting. I *want* Canada to have them and I'm

glad to have done it for her, but I *can't* feel *exalted*. . . . I had never before realized the relationship between one's pictures and oneself. Maybe the Indians were right [and that] something of you can get trapped forever in the picture as long as it lasts.*

* *Phylis Dilworth Inglis Collection, Emily to Ira Dilworth, April 18, 1942.*

Addendum

Admiring, as I do, the three trustees appointed by Emily (Ira Dilworth and Willie Newcombe I knew well personally, Lawren Harris casually) and being myself intimately enmeshed in the background of the Trust, I find it difficult indeed to judge their performance as trustees. That they invariably acted in good faith and in the best interest of the Trust as they saw it, is unquestioned; but one wonders if they acted in its true spirit in deciding to dispose of some of the original forty-five Trust paintings in order to devote the proceeds to a Scholarship Fund. This, they felt, was the rightful interpretation of Emily's wishes and Harris, in particular, worked with zeal and enthusiasm to establish a program of awards which produced, he told Dilworth, most gratifying results:

> When the cheque for $10,000 comes in tomorrow* the Trust will have $17,982.89 for future scholarships. What a difference that will make to the Province, its art and artists.
>
> We have awarded 11 scholarships to date. One [of] them was awarded ½, Walter Korner* paying the other half. Looking over their names and the achievement of each, I would say the awards have justified themselves, justified Emily's gift in really a remarkable way. The new Director of the National Gallery was here in the fall. [He] visited the artists' studios and stated that the most outstanding painting being done in Canada to-day was in B.C., in Vancouver, and with 2 exceptions the painters were all Emily Carr scholarship awardees (if that's the word).*

Ira Dilworth felt also that, "Emily would be most gratified" that "so many people have been helped by the Trust."*

And yet, Emily's words, repeated over and over, still ring, rather hauntingly, in our ears like a litany: "The main portion of my work I have given to British Columbia for all time as a permanent collection."*

* *From the then Glenbow Foundation.*

* *Dr. Walter Koerner, Vancouver businessman, art connoisseur, philanthropist.*

* *Lawren Harris to Ira Dilworth, January 15, 1956.*

* *Ira Dilworth to Lawren Harris, January 23, 1956. Both letters courtesy of J.E.A. Parnall.*

* *Emily to the Rev. Tomalin, December 26, 1942.*

Note

The catalogue numbers of the Glenbow Carr paintings are composed of Emily's initials, year of accession, and the individual picture number, that is: CE.56.2.3. (Kitwancool). The Vancouver Art Gallery's catalogue numbers, when the Trust was terminated in 1966 were similarly composed, except that *their* Trust date "42" was substituted for the accession number. *The Masset Pole* (Q.C.I.), for instance, bore the catalogue number EC42.29 in Vancouver and CE.56.2.1. in Calgary after the sale. But the catalogue numbers of Trust pictures at the Vancouver Art Gallery have a different style now, the initials having been dropped. The original Trust picture *A Rushing Sea of Undergrowth* is thus catalogued at present as No. 42.3.17. However, since "42" is neither the customary accession date, nor yet the year of the Trust, would it not be preferable to change the year of all *true* Trust pictures to "41"? In this way we would know at a glance exactly which pictures were designated by Emily as her gift to us—to the people of British Columbia.

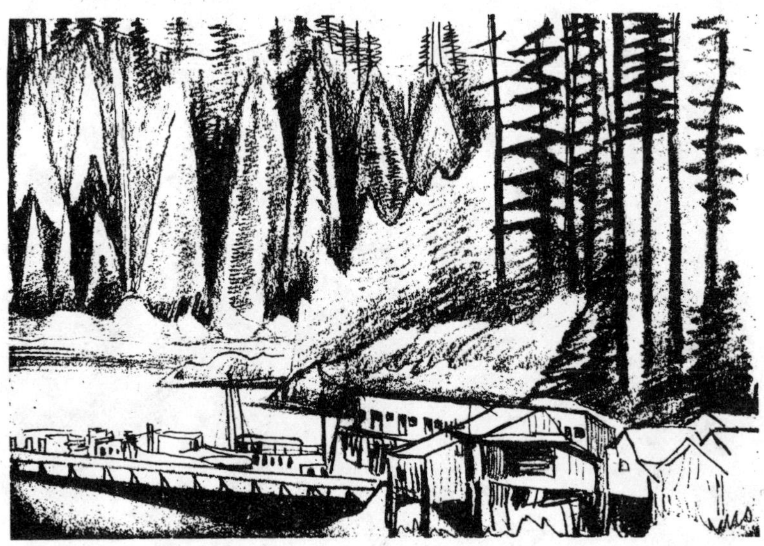

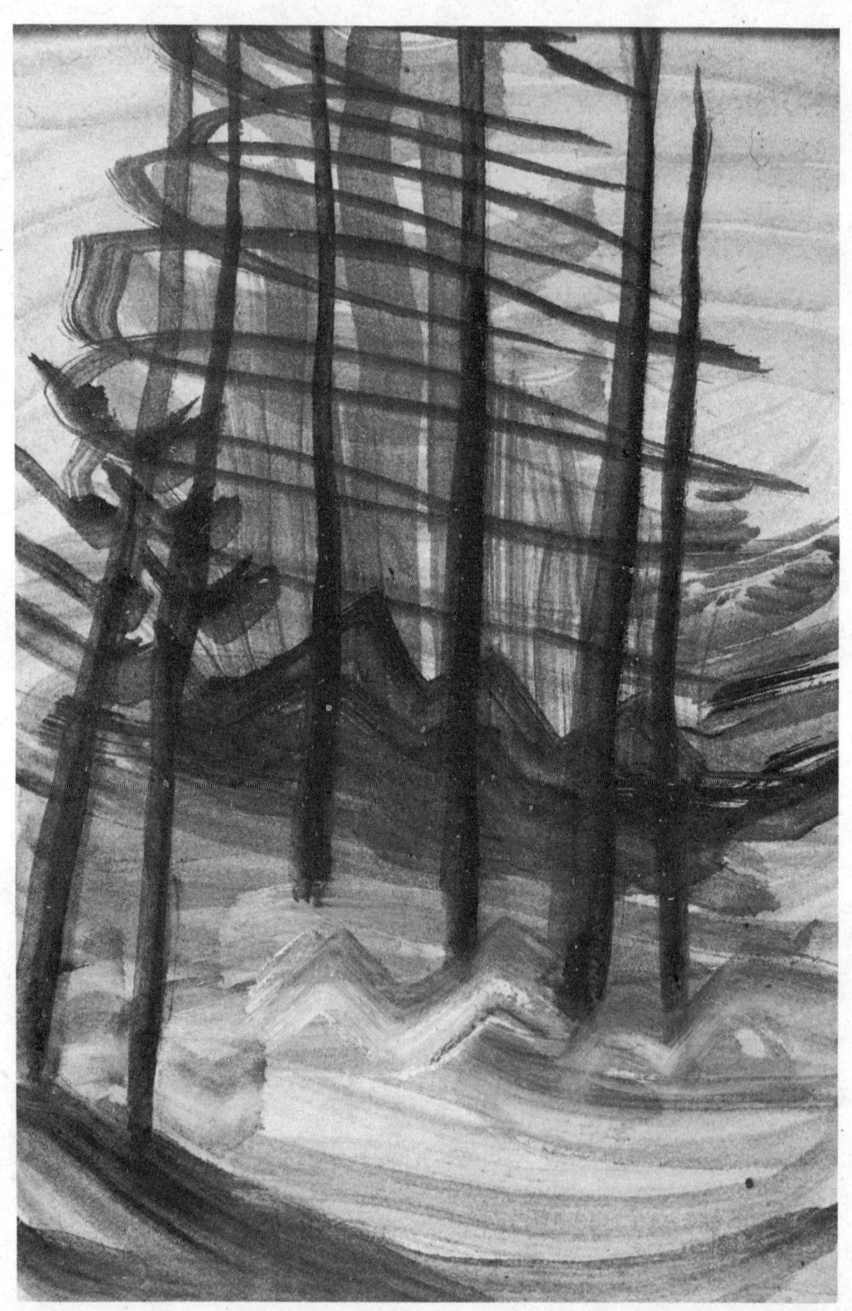

Sources of Error

Introduction

This little word, "Error," has grown into a book since the day, unsuspectingly, I undertook to research Emily Carr's life and career. The realization that so many errors about her and her work were in circulation came to me slowly—not, in fact, until 1968 when I began to prepare my first book for publication.* That was the year *Carrs on Wheels* got rolling—the first touring show of Carr works organized by the Extension Service of the Vancouver Art Gallery. The exhibition catalogue—*Emily Carr 1871-1945*—contained, I noticed, some misinformation, which of course would be dropped off all along the three circuits of the exhibition route—to the Okanagan, the Kootenays, and Northern B.C. and Nanaimo. This gave me pause, and I wondered if these same errors were to be found elsewhere. They were—in almost everything I read, and it occurred to me that really basic research was needed. The National Gallery had never got round to it, and after a quarter of a century of privileged custodianship of the Emily Carr Picture Collection,* the Vancouver Art Gallery, long regarded as the *fons et origo* of all Carr information, had still done pitifully little to research its most valuable asset—Emily. It had not lived up to its reputation.

* M.E.—A Portrayal of Emily Carr.

* *See chapter "The Emily Carr Trust."*

I asked myself: Dare I, a non-professional, attempt to do what the Vancouver Art Gallery had failed to do in almost three decades? My qualifications were not formal, nor recognized. My training had been largely in painting and languages. Still, years of intelligence work had heightened my powers of observation and taught me to be a good tracker and patient burrower. My long association with Emily, as a close friend and companion in the field and studio, was a unique asset. After reflection, and in the belief that the Vancouver Art Gallery, in committing itself almost exclusively to the most experimental, *outré* art of today had badly neglected Emily, I decided to try to rescue her—even at the risk of bringing a hornet's nest about my ears.

* *The exhibition catalogue published by the National Gallery of Canada and the Art Gallery of Toronto to celebrate the important 1945-1946 retrospective exhibition of Emily's work. Oxford University Press, Toronto, 1945.*

* *First published in 1967, the catalogues referred to in this review are:* Emily Carr: A Centennial Exhibition, *first revised printing 1971 and second revised printing 1975.*

Catalogues as a Source of Error

Although I "collected" errors from then on, and noted that publications such as *Emily Carr: Her Paintings and Sketches** contained many; I did nothing much about my "mission" until 1971 when the Vancouver Art Gallery also published an exhibition catalogue, *Emily Carr: A Centennial Exhibition.** But then I snapped to attention and haven't stood at ease since.

The Vancouver Art Gallery catalogue, superficially more scholarly than its eastern progenitor, is possibly less accurate in detail because it is more ambitious and interpretive. Moreover, it was published twenty-six years later and therefore has far less excuse for its errors. These errors, it seems, cannot be due to lack of money since the catalogue was handsomely funded and two staff members, besides the author, were "heavily involved in the preparation of the exhibition."

Neither catalogue is the definitive work it was intended to be. Both provide an informed study of Emily's painting, but the biographical sketches are not basically accurate, the chronologies are badly researched and the exhibition lists are lean and poorly presented. Both catalogues have long been regarded as a Carr Alpha and Omega and have been widely quoted—error along with truth.

Fact or Fiction

Long before the contents of these publications were known, Emily had created her own little comedy of errors, which, because we all believed her implicitly, and therefore failed to check her exactitude, became embedded in much future Carr literature.

Emily's date of birth was one that she delighted to recall—a mid-December day of icy, howling winds which piled snowdrifts high against the window of the room where midwife, mother, and a row of curious sparrows peeking in awaited her delayed arrival. Emily has anchored this date to the boundless love she bore her mother who, in giving life to a dallying, reluctant child, saw to it that she inherited the moral force to face it.

This one date is inalterable in Emily's story. Even had she wished, she could not have manipulated or concealed it. But even before her baptism took place, her imagination had quickened and she began withdrawing into that curious little world of make-believe which, though greatly enriching her enquiring mind, led her to treat chronology lightly and embellish the events of her life with the imagery of an artist.

In the opening line of her autobiography, Emily recollects that her baptism was an unpleasant memory: "I was a little over four years of age. My brother was an infant. We were done together." But if Emily's memory of her baptism was unpleasant, it was also false. No less a person than her father says so. In his diary he records that Emily and her younger brother Dick (Richard Henry) were both baptized by the Reverend John Reid on March 22, 1879!* It was thus the gurgling infant Dick, born October 20, 1875, who was four years old—Emily was eight!

* *This is confirmed by Emily's baptismal certificate. The First United Church in Victoria (previously the First Presbyterian Church, where Dr. Reid served as minister from 1876 to 1881) has, however, no knowledge of Emily's baptism since, owing to a disastrous fire, their records only date from Vol. II—1884-1912 though the church was established in 1861.*

Who can say why, starting with her baptismal story and continuing throughout the early part of her autobiography, Emily deluded herself (and us) that she was much younger than she was? She said she was twelve when her mother died, although she was almost fifteen, and when she begged her stern guardian to send her to California to study art, she was eighteen, not "sixteen, almost" as she claimed. She would have done better to tell the truth since the elderly Scottish gentleman, her guardian, sorely troubled about his responsibility, hesitated to send "a little girl" like Emily to a city as big and wicked as San Francisco. A few years after her return from the South she visited the Indian Mission at Ucluelet and nonchalantly described herself as a "fifteen-year-old schoolgirl" when she was in reality a mature woman of twenty-six.*

* Klee Wyck, *p.3.*

Emily's baffling habit of shedding time, in a droll desire, I suspect, to maintain a girlish image, is strangely untruthful, as is the account of her education and the story, told to commiserating readers and listeners, that she virtually had to give up painting for about fifteen years in the prime of life to stoke the furnace and feed her "greedy," ridiculed lady boarders. She said, too, that only Lizzie, Alice, she herself and Dick were born in Victoria, though another boy, Thomas (who survived only five months) was also born there. But possibly the most improbable statement in her autobiography is that her two oldest sisters, Edith and Clara, were born in England, though both were native Californians, born in Alviso. Some deep-seated reason must have dictated this falsehood—a cloaking sort of refuge sought by a rebellious, unhappy child who, subconsciously, desperately needed to believe that these two resented sisters, especially Edith, were of a different nationality from the other sisters and brother. Emily even quotes Edith as saying, "I too was born in England." She accused her oldest sister of punishing her and her brother every day with a riding whip, "a swishy whip [that] cut and curled around our stockinged legs very hurtfully."* But old-timers scoff at this "nonsense." Edith, they say, was a kindly, respected member of the community interested only in charitable works and the welfare of her family.

* Growing Pains, *p.16.*

Another "fact" which still sticks like glue to every mention of Emily's studies in San Francisco is the erroneous name of the school she attended. She repeats over and over that she went to the "San Francisco School of Art," yet when she enrolled it was called the California School of Design. While she was still a student there, the name was changed to the Mark Hopkins Institute of Art when the school moved from its old Pine Street location to the imposing old Mark Hopkins mansion atop Nob Hill, the site of the present luxury hotel of the same name. The art school has had many ups and downs, and many names since Emily's day. When I studied there it was The California School of Fine Arts.

With the notable exception of Richard Carr, Emily's methodical father, whose adventuresome past she thought advisable to purify a little, her family was as airily disregardful of dates as she was. Sister Alice, for instance, like Emily, said that they had traveled together to Alaska in 1906, instead of the following year; and when Edith died the surviving sisters noted in her obituary that she had resided in Victoria since 1864. The excellent Mr. Carr once more set things right by recording in his diary that he and his family arrived at Esquimalt on July 5, 1863 and then "proceeded by stage to Victoria, a distance of three miles, and put up at St. George's Hotel,"* where he paid $2.50 a day for his family of four.

* *PABC,* The Diary of Richard Carr.

And so it goes, on and on. One must have the eyes of Argus.

Pseudonyms, of course, are not errors, but it is well to know that Emily made use of them—the reason it took so long to identify her persistent suitor, "Martyn." And it has only recently come to light that her dearest friend in England, "Mrs. Radcliffe," was in real life Mrs. Redden.

Why, one wonders, did Emily elect to mask the identity of these two key figures in the story of her young womanhood? Since only she could know how much the attributes of these two friends were adjusted, and how freely their conversations were interpreted in order to write a humorous, readable and salable book, only she could say why she felt it necessary to disguise them. Probably she feared that by disclosing either too much or too little truth, she could embarrass or wound the families of her friends, or even her own, as all three were well-known in their respective communities.

Besides many perhaps inconsequential inaccuracies of date, and some very personally construed, intensified facts, in certain areas of Emily's life one also finds delusory errors in which she projects an outsize image of herself that goes beyond truth or reason. It is necessary to know her well to recognize the clues, but they are there.

She always vociferously professed, for instance, to hate journalists and asserted that she would suffer no intrusion into her private life. But this was pure play-acting, because deep down, never admitted, she welcomed publicity, even sought it. Several examples come to mind, but perhaps one of the most telling dates from 1940 when she readily, indeed eagerly, agreed to let me ask an old friend, Ken Drury, then editor of the Victoria *Times,* to assign a good reporter to interview her. Ken sent Ruggles, and Ruggles, predictably, drew Emily's wrath on sight, as she energetically confessed to me later:

> I'm sorry, Edythe, but I was just beastly awful. She was such a total *fool*—I could have taken to my bed with pip. She stayed one and one half hours and did not have any idea how even to *ask* things leave alone understand. . . . I told her about work but said, "Now look here, I *won't* tolerate a lot of mawkish personalism." Then she sat down (I took her into the cold room so that she should not stay, but she pranced all over the house *unbidden*). "Now," she said, "I want some of your personal history." "Well, you don't get it," I said. "I am *Canadian born* of English parents, and proud of the fact. That is enough for your confounded paper. The rest is my business. Good Day! I'm busy!"

Yet with all her expletive-laced vexation, Emily, we notice, gave Ruggles a very long interview. She even allowed her to return, and purred like a contented kitten when a flattering illustrated article was published.

Nevertheless, Emily would have genuinely, deeply and bitterly resented the publication of her personal letters and posthumous prying into her private life and thoughts. I, for one, have experienced nasty twinges of conscience when digging into her life, her work, even her soul, since I truly believe that her plea for privacy should have been respected, and at least her more intimate letters burned as she requested. But the convenient word "research" has allayed all such qualms—mine, and those of other friends who have either sold or bequeathed Emily's letters to public institutions. Only Lawren Harris who destroyed all her letters before he died, has kept faith with her.

Was Emily a High-School Dropout?

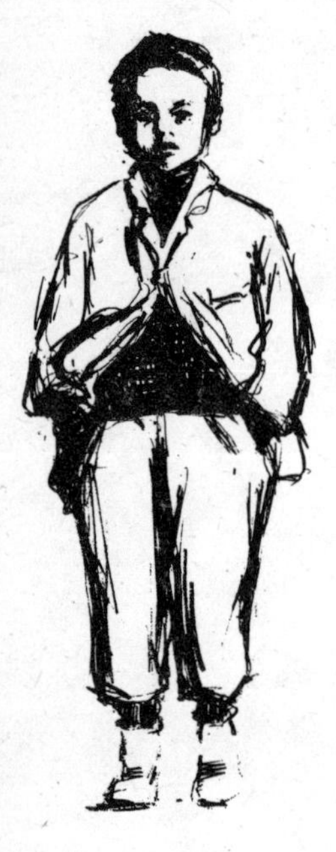

Another area in which Emily has wilfully misled us is her early education. As a young girl she hated school and got into a great deal of trouble for drawing faces on her fingernails, pinafores and textbooks, and was sometimes relegated to the dunce stool. She seems to have been a rebellious child in school, as she was at home, but later, as she moved up a few grades, she undeniably developed into a bright pupil, though she insisted that she was bored with academic subjects and brought home poor report cards.

The instruction she received in public schools was enlightened compared with that of her friends attending private schools, because these were run by ultra-English, impoverished spinsters of dubious scholastic background who taught the girls little but good manners, social graces and Christian virtues.

Usually critical of her father, Emily later in life applauded his decision to withdraw his younger daughters from the "Ladies' Deportment Academies," where "[their] brains remained empty," and enroll them in public schools, despite strong criticism from other parents. "Father," she said, "was proud that all his children, with the exception of me, were good students by Canadian standards."

Emily need not have excluded herself from her father's pride in his children, even though she was not brilliant like her sisters, particularly Alice. When Alice graduated from high school in 1889, she won prizes or high marks in all subjects plus "a Provincial Roll of Honor for Deportment."* Emily was never commended for her deportment, nor did she win any honors or prizes when she passed from elementary to high school at age sixteen-and-a-half in 1888.* Nevertheless, she was far better educated than most Victoria students of her age, irrespective of sex.

* *Victoria* Daily Colonist, *June 28, 1889.*

* *Ibid, June 27, 1888.*

Emily told me, and other friends, that she had "skipped a year of high" to study art in San Francisco,* but the facts contradict this. Instead of skipping a year, she completed only a year (1888-1889)—in the Junior Division of first year high taught by R. Offerhaus. It took three to six years then to finish high school, and Emily therefore needed about three more years to complete her program. A student graduated whenever he succeeded in passing the final examinations (which could be taken at any time), the average student requiring four years. However, in giving up formal schooling, Emily was not the high school dropout in today's sense of the term, because she

* *Emily put it a little more amusingly in a letter to Ira Dilworth of November 7, 1941: ". . . and [I] had never even wriggled through 'High.' "*

continued studying in her specialized field for many years. But late in life, when she began to write seriously, and was appalled at her scant knowledge of basic literary skills, she seemed to regret her 1889 decision: "If only I were better educated, but how I *hated* school! It takes a genius to write without education."*

* Hundreds and Thousands, *p.160.*

The only *official* records prior to 1892 are the *Public Schools Reports* published annually by the Department of Education. The report for 1888 shows that Emily was one of only thirteen girls who passed the high school entrance examination in June of that year from the Victoria Girls' School on the Central School Reserve.* She was not promoted routinely, but passed the obligatory external examination, held in four chief centers of the Province,* which required above-average ability. In fact, for a boy or girl to reach high school at all in those days was an unusual academic achievement.

* *The author is indebted for much of the information gathered on British Columbia schools in Emily's time to Dr. Peter L. Smith, Dean of Fine Arts, University of Victoria. Dr. Smith is the author of* Come Give a Cheer, *a Centennial History of Victoria High School, published early in 1976.*

* *See the Victoria* Daily Colonist, *December 5, 1893, for a description of the British Columbia examination system.*

When Emily denigrates her school performance it is all too easy to believe her—and everyone has—because of her known difficulties with the mechanics of writing which she laments at length in her autobiography and letters. To the end of her life she was never able to master the spelling of a handful of words, but this only adds to the charm of her letters and underlines her originality. Some of her most persistent errors were: *buisy* and *buisness, maybbe, shure* and *inshurance, diddn't* and *agoe.*

On publication in 1969 of Emily's letters to me,* and in 1972 of others to Ruth Humphrey,* the respective editors had to decide whether or not to retain her unorthodox spelling. In both cases punctuation and spelling were finally regularized on the ground that they might provoke a little ridicule at the expense of a highly-gifted and humorous woman. This decision was no doubt rightly taken, but how much more amusing and lively the original letters are with their erratic punctuation, underscorings, profuse exclamation marks and the delightfully misspelled words given above.

* M.E.—A Portrayal of Emily Carr. *First publication of Emily Carr's letters.*

* University of Toronto Quarterly, *Vol. XLI, Number 2, Winter 1972, University of Toronto Press.*

Curiously, and rather touchingly, all these spelling errors were learned from her father, whose influence seems to have been stronger than that of her teachers because exactly these same errors recur throughout his highly descriptive diary. In March 1861, during the long weeks of shipboard monotony traveling with his family from California to England around Cape Horn, Richard Carr took over the education of his two eldest daughters and tells us that: "Emily [Mrs. Carr] and the children [Edith and Clara] are seasick . . . a cow on board supplies us with an abundance of milk and, having plenty of sheep, pigs and poultry, the table is well supplied with provisions. The children are learning to read. I am schoolmaster and the progress they are making is quite flattering to me."* Is it not more than likely that father Carr also supervised Emily's homework years later and thus influenced her spelling?

* *PABC*, The Diary of Richard Carr.

Since Emily liked to picture herself as a misunderstood child, she took an almost perverse pleasure in belittling her own learning abilities. Like many other younger children progressing through the school system in the wake of more proficient siblings, she felt inferior to her two older sisters, and even late in life, while writing her autobiography, this youthful grievance still rankled: "My sisters . . . were good students. When I moved up a grade the new teacher said, 'Ah, another good Carr.' But they were disappointed."*

* Growing Pains, *p.16.*

Also late in life, Emily reflected on her indifference to dates, titles and time:

> I'm afraid I can't give much data regarding the Emily Carr Trust pictures. I never kept one date from birth to death. I had no "periods" that I know of. I simply went ahead and worked. Perhaps after a few years I saw more so I showed more. My work just naturally grew out of study—events like going to Paris and like seeing work of the Group of Seven impressed me undoubtedly—but as to what year I did it in or what particular picture they influenced I cannot say. I have forgotten the names of most of my pictures. They were only stuck on because in exhibitions there has to be a catalogue. I can't even say if I have reached the "final period" . . . The only definite statement I can give is that I went on working and got what little I did by letting it grow itself, forgetful of time.*

* *Phylis Dilworth Inglis Collection, Emily to Ira Dilworth, late 1942.*

EMILY CARR: A CENTENNIAL EXHIBITION

An Exhibition Catalogue (1971) Cover Portrait

The powerful self-portrait of Emily on the cover of the catalogue shows her barrel-like body, in her habitual painting garb, planted as solidly and squarely within her composition as the great Lillooet mountain she struggled so long and hard to paint in 1933. It is not a very good likeness. The face is too stern and hard. But what is strikingly Emily is the indomitable spirit shining through the unaccustomed spectacles.

The portrait belongs to a private collection in Montreal and is surrounded by a double ring of anonymity. Few people know the name of the owner—not even, I am told, the Vancouver Art Gallery which obtained permission to reproduce the portrait. Dr. Max Stern, of the Dominion Gallery, Montreal, could identify the owner if he chose, but considers such a disclosure would be a breach of confidence. He did tell me, however, that the portrait was one of the paintings he had selected for his 1944 exhibition of Emily's works, and that it had been sold then to a Montreal resident.

It really is not very important, or pertinent, who owns this painting, but the secrecy surrounding it aroused my bloodhound instincts. The scent finally led me to the Montreal Museum of Fine Art's Stable Gallery where a self-portrait of Emily was hung in May-June 1959. It was loaned from the collection of Mrs. Emma Frankenberg, Montreal, and is probably the catalogue cover portrait since, to my knowledge, no other self-portrait of Emily has been in circulation since her death.

It is an oil on paper sketch 34 x 23 in. and is signed "Emily Carr." In the caption beside a small reproduction of the picture in the catalogue (Carr 1971 no. 95), the date is given as circa 1934-1935—demonstrably too early; but in the text itself it is given as circa 1938 which may well be right. Although I myself am unable to put an exact date to this portrait, I feel I have collected enough material to reduce the uncertainties to the outside limits of June 1938 and early June 1940. An educated guess would shrink the margins from the fall of 1938 to February of 1939, and a considered opinion would narrow the doubt still more to January or February 1939—my presumed date.

Ordinarily the style of signature would have some bearing on the dating of Emily's paintings because, though she played with signatures as she did with words, a loose sort of pattern is still discernible. But in the case of the cover portrait, the signature is of no assistance since it is highly unlikely that the sketch was signed when painted.

Emily began dropping the letter "M" from her signatures more and more frequently in her later years, and almost entirely after the death of her sister Elizabeth (Lizzie) in 1936. But before that, and especially before the death of Edith, there had been confusion with the three "E" sisters and Emily introduced the "M" to distinguish herself from the other two. The "M," of course, stands for "Millie," the nickname used exclusively by the family and old friends. In fact, some oldtimers who purchased early paintings still maintain that they own a "Millie Carr" to emphasize that their pictures are not to be confused with the later "aberrations" of "Emily Carr."

However, many of the earlier pictures painted before Lizzie's death also bear the plain "Emily Carr" signature. Most of these, like the cover portrait, remained unsigned until Dr. Stern insisted that all works he had selected for his 1944 exhibition, from whatever year, be signed before shipment to Montreal. Emily, therefore, put "Emily Carr" on everything set aside for crating.

But let's review Emily's career as a portraitist (if such it can be called) for guidance. She did occasional portraits throughout her life, starting with one of her father when she was a child. It is reasonable to assume that she drew or painted other members of her family, and perhaps also friends or Carr domestics such as Bong the Chinaboy or Wash Mary the washerwoman. She drew faces in her scribblers, and I am sure that she took an impish delight in lampooning her teachers, pompous elders, or the detested missionaries on their knees in the parlor. For she was a clever caricaturist. Then, of course, because she was devoted to her dogs, birds and assorted pets, there was a constant stream of animal studies during her youthful years.

At the age of eight, she did a drawing of the family dog Carlow, using a charred stick from the fireplace and a split-open paper bag as her materials. In 1909, while living in Vancouver, she did the familiar water color of her first, faithful sheepdog, Billie, who accompanied her everywhere for sixteen years. She also did a group of exquisite figure studies in the same medium; portraits of Chinese and East Indians and, also in 1909, an excellent water color likeness of her sister Alice (The Schoolmistress) seated at her desk in the classroom.*

The following year (1910), just before leaving for France to study, Emily painted engaging sketches of Indian children at

* *Reproduced in the centennial catalogue, p.19 (1971 and 1975 editions).*

Lytton, B.C., and on her return to Canada seventeen months later, she brought with her from Brittany a bundle of spontaneous, sparkling sketches executed in her new style. Among them were gay village and interior scenes depicting Breton women going about their daily chores.

The most charming portrait of all is a delicate, almost-unknown pen and ink drawing, done in an intricate cross-hatching technique, of eighteen-months-old Jenny Lawson, the younger daughter of James Hill Lawson, Emily's guardian. She wears a quaint little stiffly starched dress with a ribbon on her shoulder, and was certainly Emily's youngest and most cuddly model. Emily herself was barely twenty years old when she did this drawing, from a photograph. It betrays the sentimental side of her nature, ordinarily so scrupulously hidden.

The most surprising portrait is one Emily did of herself in 1899 in England. This self-portrait (perhaps her first) is a striking likeness, punctiliously executed in smooth, rubbed charcoal and, compared with the casual, almost carelessly painted cover portrait (probably her last) it resembles a Dürer more than a Carr. It is so unlike anything else I have seen by Emily that I would be tempted to doubt its authorship had it not been authenticated by her grand-niece.

Emily never showed a sustained interest in the human face or figure. For long periods she did none at all. During her mature years, she really only concentrated on portraits once—in the winter of 1931-1932 when she and I worked daily in her studio for three months doing nothing but heads, still-lifes and a few animal studies. We did portraits of one another, portraits of young diabetic children sent over from Alice's school as wriggling models, and self-portraits. But the cover portrait is not one of them. Nor was it painted in "circa 1934-1935" (the centennial catalogue date) since, stylistically, it belongs to a later period. Besides, the "specs" on her nose prove that it post-dated June 1937 because it was then that her oculist first prescribed painting glasses: "I've always fought them. Dirty brutes—cost $20.00 too . . ."*

* *Emily to Ruth Humphrey, June 26, 1937.*

After acquiring her caravan in 1933, Emily was far too busy with trees, stumps and skies to be interested in humans. But after her heart attack in 1937, when she was housebound for months at a time, she again turned to people for inspiration and began to paint her long-suffering maids, as they came and went with startling rapidity, and a few friends. Some of the maids' portraits survive, but those of the friends were tossed on Emily's super bonfire of 1940 when she was weeding out four years' accumulation in the cottage before moving to Alice's house. She says so in a letter to Humphrey Toms, who had asked Emily if he might buy the sketch she had done of him in the fall of 1938:

> "Re portrait," she replied, "no can do. I rid myself of all unnecessaries and failures at the time of move. If one thing is most reproachful and painful it (is) a failure portrait."*

* *Emily to Humphrey Toms, April 5, 1941.*

Also in 1938, sometime after Emily's sketching trip to Telegraph Bay in July, she did two portrait sketches of her current maid, Shirley Duggan. One, *The Spotted Apron,* turned up in a Toronto gallery in 1955, was valued at $1,500 (a fabulous price then) and said to be one of her most important works. But when first exhibited in Stern's 1944 show in Montreal, it was one of the pictures that did not sell. Shirley thought the portrait unflattering and was, in any case, completely bewildered by Emily's ideas on art, and not at all keen on the pictures that were "harder to understand." "For instance," she said, "there was a picture that showed a tree painted from the inside looking out. That was what Miss Carr said it was."*

* *Victoria* Daily Colonist, *May 29, 1955.*

Emily did other portrait sketches around this time, perhaps of earlier maids Louise, Flora and Connie Rogers because in February 1939 Shirley who, surprisingly, had not yet left, was helping her soak off old sketches from their buckram backing in the bath-tub preparatory to mounting them on plywood. The same month, Humphrey wrote that, "She [Emily] has framed some of the portrait sketches and has mounted all of them so that they may be shown privately somewhere! She talks about washing out my face and doing it again, which I think is a good thing."*

* *Humphrey Toms to Nan Cheney, February 18, 1939.*

During these years, Emily did portraits of several friends besides Humphrey. Frederick Brand was one, but his was never finished. In 1942, she worked hard to get a good likeness of Phylis Dilworth as a special gift for Ira, but was so dissatisfied with the result that she criss-crossed it with angry, black lines and tore it up in a fit of anger and disgust. Phylis was anything but sorry to see the painting destroyed because, as she told me, "Emily made me look like a red-haired horse."

So when did Emily do the cover self-portrait? I think it likely that it was among the batch she soaked in the bath-tub in February 1939 after finishing it earlier that year or late 1938. Humphrey has described a self-portrait done about this time which fits the cover portrait exactly: "I want some day to acquire her self-portrait. Rather severe, but very like Emily [is when] disturbed, in her painting smock, glaring at an intruder through her specs."* Several years later, Emily herself commented characteristically on the portrait when Humphrey asked to buy it: "That fierce sketch of me? I'spose it is still in the rack. It is so long since I went through them."*

* *Humphrey Toms to Nan Cheney, June 7, 1940.*

* *Emily to Humphrey Toms, April 3, 1944.*

There is one more piece of evidence to support a later date than mid-1938. On July 8 of that year, the Director of the National Gallery wrote to Emily: "I liked Nan Cheney's portrait of you. I would like to have a Uffizzi self-portrait gallery of Canadian artists and if it ever comes off and you don't want to do one of yourself, this would do admirably." This is admittedly vague, but the text does intimate that Emily did not yet have a self-portrait available for inclusion in Eric Brown's gallery. Perhaps the letter even prompted her to paint the one we have.

Everything suggests that the cover portrait is the one discussed in these pages. The facts dovetail too neatly to leave much room for doubt. But for the time being, the date must still be left with a question mark, though happily, a much smaller one. The winter 1938-1939 has to be very close.

On December 31, 1940, Emily wrote her last words on the subject of portraiture:

> I hate painting portraits. I am embarrassed at what seems to me to be an impertinence and presumption, pulling into visibility what every soul has as much right to keep private as his liver and kidneys and lungs and things which are coated with flesh and hide. . . . The better a portrait, the more indecent and naked the sitter must feel. An artist who portrays flesh and clothes but nothing else, no matter how magnificently he does it, is quite harmless. A caricaturist who jests at his victim's expense does so to show off his (the artist's) own powers, not to portray the subject. To paint a self-portrait should teach one something about oneself. I shall try.*

* Hundreds and Thousands, *p.330.*

Did these random thoughts, so late in Emily's life, perhaps lead to another, as yet undiscovered, portrait?

Text Of The Catalogue

I do not intend to discuss the contents of the centennial catalogue in the manner of a reviewer. That is not my function—I am a researcher, not an art critic. Therefore, I shall limit myself to uncovering apparent errors and commenting on those parts of the material which, in my opinion, require clarification.

The first error occurs in line one of the text (page three) and it happens to be in French, as are several others later on, including two French place names. Although minor, these errors nevertheless detract from the general scholarship of the catalogue. The cavalier attitude to French in British Columbia is regrettable, and in this case particularly so as the French have honored Emily in their prestigious *Grand Larousse encyclopédique* (1960). Under "Canada (peinture)" she is one of the very few artists mentioned:

> . . . d'autres paysagistes vont suivre, que l'impressionisme puis le fauvisme orienteront: c'est Emily Carr (1871-1945), auteur de délicats paysages de l'ouest canadien . . .

While reading in the library of the *Centre culturel canadien* in Paris a few years ago, I came across another reference to her in the *Nouveau Petit Larousse* (1969) which contains a knowledgeable article on "L'Art canadien." Only two modern painters were selected for special comment, one French and the other English Canadian—Pellan and Emily Carr.

On page four it is indicated that Emily gave only two public talks in her lifetime. The revised catalogue does not mention the number. My total, however, is four: The first was in Vancouver in 1913 while her exhibition of Indian works was in progress at Drummond Hall; the second was an address to the Victoria Women's Canadian Club in March 1930; the third was also in March 1930 to the Kumtucks Club in Victoria, and the last was a talk read before the students and staff of the Provincial Normal School, Victoria, on October 22, 1935.* She did however, receive (but decline) at least two more invitations to lecture. One came early (1925) from the committee of the B.C. Art League in Vancouver,* and the other, surprisingly, from the Island Arts and Crafts Society in Victoria not long after her two successful talks to the above-mentioned women's clubs.*

Also on page four, paragraph 5, there is another statement that needs clarification: "There was nothing in her family environment to suggest art as a vocation or even as a serious interest." However, Emily's father, though uneducated, had an interest in, and feeling for, art. He encouraged Emily to draw, and all his daughters took art lessons. Edith, a teacher of applied art, put on an exhibition and sale of her craft work every Christmas in the old family home. Lizzie was at least eager enough to stick to her lessons and paint flowers, and Alice

* *See chronology for more details concerning these dates.*

* *Vancouver City Archives, Gallery Committee, B.C. Art League Minute Book, October 26, 1926.*

* *PABC, Island Arts and Crafts Society Minute Book, February 15, 1932.*

showed more than usual promise. When she graduated from high school in 1889, she was mentioned in the *Colonist* description of the ceremony: "*The 'Girls' Own Paper!* the production of the Misses Tite and Carr,* was read and listened to attentively. The cover of the paper is a work of art. The clever fingers of Miss Carr have drawn an excellent combination of the whole of the studies of the girls. The artist deserves the heartiest congratulation."

* *The article makes quite clear that Alice, not Emily, is the artist.*

All this surely adds up to an environment in which art, even serious art, could flourish.

On page five we read: "Even in 1942, three years before her [Emily's] death, when the Emily Carr Trust was formed which set aside one hundred and seventy of her best works for the Province of British Columbia . . ." The information about the Trust contained in this remark is inaccurate, but contradictory statements about the Trust crop up everywhere and in fact, this study was originally prompted by my desire to present a more reliable record. I have therefore made it the subject of a special chapter, "The Emily Carr Trust."

The name of Emily's art school in San Francisco is given erroneously in the chronology and in the text (page eight). The name is corrected in the revised edition, but its name after the school moved to the Mark Hopkins mansion is wrong, as is its present name. The catalogue also states that she spent five years studying in California, but Emily says in *Growing Pains* that it was only three. Moreover, the text and the chronology give two different dates for Emily's return to Victoria, 1894 and 1895 respectively. The dates of Emily's stay in California have been amended in the revised edition to 1890-1893, but only in the chronology, not in the text.

It is true, as we are told in the last paragraph, page eight, that Emily converted the loft of the family cow barn into a studio when she formed children's art classes after her return from San Francisco. But this was not the immediate solution to her teaching problem. The revised text notes correctly that Emily's first classes after her return were held in the old Carr residence. She utilized the dining room for the purpose.

On page nine, Emily is said to have attended the Herkomer Art School in Bushey, Hertfordshire when in fact she worked under John Whitely at the Meadows Studios. The revised text corrects the error.

On the same page, we are told that she was suffering from pernicious anemia when she entered a sanitorium in Suffolk in 1902. But according to medical opinion, pernicious anemia in those days was always fatal. She was overworked and her resistance was therefore very low so it is more likely that she developed a tenacious secondary anemia. Since her mother and brother both died of tuberculosis and she herself was forced to spend eighteen months in a T.B. sanitorium, she may have been suffering with incipient tuberculosis. The revised text omits the nature of Emily's illness.

On page ten, the catalogue states that Emily took a studio in Vancouver in 1905, though the chronology allows that it may have been early 1906. This is the year she contributed a series of cartoons and jingles to a Victoria newspaper, *The Week*. Since the last cartoon appeared late in the year (November 17) and since Emily always spent the Christmas season with her family, it is unlikely that she left for Vancouver before the end of December. Notices in the Vancouver press indicate that she arrived there in January 1906. The true significance of the year 1905 is overlooked in both editions.

There is ample additional proof that Emily spent the year 1905 in Victoria, some of it pictorial. Her old friend, Madge Wolfenden Hamilton, one of the five or six pupils in Emily's class in her Fort Street studio, has saved four fascinating, well-executed charcoal and pencil drawings done at that time. She also has a pen and ink sketch of the old cow barn studio, done c. 1897 by her brother Victor—an earlier pupil of Emily's. She tells me that Emily's pupils in 1905 often worked in the studio from plaster casts or still-lifes, but when the weather was fine, they were taken to the old family residence on sketching trips. Her four drawings were all done there.

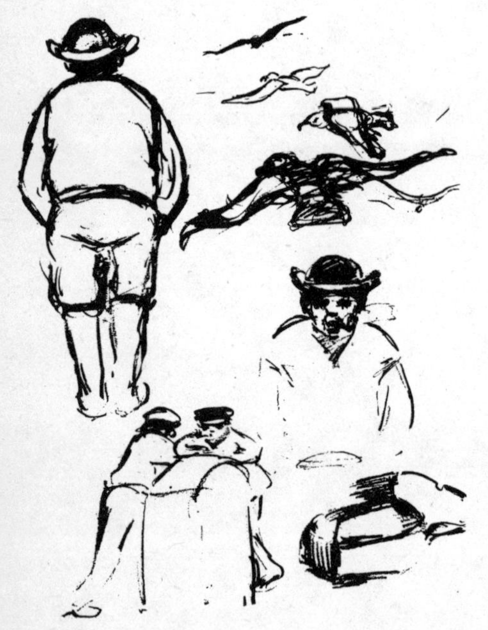

These drawings are historically important as they are possibly the only extant pictures of the old cow barn, the horse barn, and the hen house built by Richard Carr at a cost of $103.25 in 1864—all so familiar from Emily's stories in the *Book of Small*.

Still on page ten, Emily's trip to Alaska is wrongly dated 1906, but is correct (1907) in the chronology. In the text the trip is rightly confined to Skagway and Sitka on Baranof Island, whereas in the chronology the Yukon is added to her itinerary. This is wrong, though a scenic side-trip took her as far as the border. The year of the Alaska trip is correct in the revised text, but Baranof Island is misspelled in both catalogues.

It is the inconsistency between text and chronology that is so puzzling. Another example is the location of three northern villages, given in the chronology as the Queen Charlotte Islands. The text locates them correctly in the Skeena district.

On page eleven, the caption under the photograph states that she visited the Cariboo region of British Columbia on her way home from England in 1909 instead of 1904. In the text Académie has no accent, Salon D'Automne reappears, and Crécy-en-Brie and St. Efflam are misspelled. With the exception of Salon D'Automne, these errors are corrected in the revised edition.

Note: The French place names have been corrected in the revised catalogue, but one stubborn error, "Salon D'Automne" still appears in two places.

On page twelve, the catalogue says that Emily built a four-suite apartment house in 1913, but according to the original house plans, there were only three—two self-contained flats downstairs and Emily's studio and living quarters, including a maid's room, upstairs. In this instance, though, the catalogue is simply repeating what Emily has herself written in *Growing Pains.* It also repeats Emily's claims that she was unable to paint for fifteen barren years after building the House of All Sorts because she was forced to earn her living in a variety of uncongenial ways. This story is at least misleading and in repeating it, the catalogue (both editions) helps to perpetuate another of Emily's exaggerations.*

Let us now look at the delightful photograph of Emily and her pets on page thirteen.* In the original caption these are said to be Woo (the Javanese monkey), "Cocoa" (should be Koko), and Ginger Pop, two of her small Belgian griffon dogs. But the dogs shown are enormous, shaggy, bear-like English bobtails. The monkey turns out to be a cat—her old veteran Adolphus. In fact, not one of the animals mentioned under the photograph is present in it. The picture itself is dated c. 1930 which is patently impossible judging from Emily's dress and coiffure alone. Circa 1916 would be very close. In the revised edition the names of the animals have been omitted.

* *In note two, page twelve, Willie Newcombe is said to have been one of the Trustees of Emily's estate. This is incorrect. (See chapter, "The Emily Carr Trust.")*

* *Corrections of the captions under the above photographs, and of other items, were contained in my letter of November 26, 1973 to the Director.*

In paragraph two, the title of the exhibition *Canadian West Coast Art (Native and Modern)* is given incorrectly, as it is in the chronology. It is, however, right in the exhibition list. In the revised edition, the title is correct in the text and chronology, but wrong in the exhibition list.

Also on page 13 (and on page 14 of the revised text), it is stated that the National Gallery purchased several of Emily's water colors from their 1927 Exhibition of Canadian West Coast Art. This is wrong. (See Exhibition List III and Emily Exonerated, Part II.)

On page fourteen, we find the statement: "In a year or so [after Emily's heroic trip up the Nass and Skeena rivers and to the Queen Charlotte Islands in 1928] she had worked through the Indian material and she turned to the forests. The summer sketching expeditions were henceforth to the deep forest, the sea edge, Goldstream Flats . . ." In truth, Emily never "worked through" her Indian material. She had scores of undeveloped sketches and returned to the Indian motif off and on until the early forties. And she made two more trips to Indian territory (1929 and 1930) before deciding to turn to the woods for inspiration—partly on the advice of Tobey and Harris. She did not however sketch in the woods in the summer—a season she disliked—but usually in her favorite months, May and September. And the forest was not "deep." (See chapter "Sketching Trips.")

On page fifteen, the photograph of Emily standing in the door of her van in Metchosin in 1936 is wrongly credited to the British Columbia Archives, but through no fault of the Gallery. The picture was taken by me, but circulated by the Archives, in good faith, until the error was brought to their attention. Emily's van pictures are among the most popular and frequently reproduced. I have three, and only know of one other—a particularly fine one taken by Mrs. Morley, whose initials I have forgotten. It is reproduced in *Growing Pains,* but not identified.* Emily did not like it and, in a letter to me, protested my plan to use it for publication: "I must say, personally, I do not think that photo suitable. There is such a gang of people in it who do not bear on the subject or have any point as far as I can see for the article."

** The photo shows Miss Morley with a dog in her lap and Joyce Maynard, a sister of Max Maynard, in the foreground.*

Also on page fifteen, note two, Frederick Brand is said to have read Emily's stories to his classes at the Victoria College instead of at the University of British Columbia.*

** Corrected in the revised edition.*

On page sixteen, in both catalogues, we find one of the more inscrutable errors made by the Shadbolt-Tippett team: "In [1944] another exhibition in Montreal at the Dominion Gallery gave [Emily] the one practical success of her life-time; fifty-seven out of the sixty were sold."

There is a discrepancy between Emily's list of the paintings she forwarded to Montreal and those listed in the Dominion Gallery catalogue, but by a process of correlation I was able to identify her list positively as referring to the 1944 exhibition. Dr. Stern had just one undated catalogue but indicated that it too referred to this exhibiton. Here is a breakdown of the pictures exhibited and sold:

According to Emily's statement of August 4, 1944 she contracted to send Stern	60 pictures
Forgot to crate one (No. 24), thus forwarding to	

Montreal	59 pictures
Exhibited October 19-November 4, 1944	59 pictures

According to Stern's statement of February 10, 1945, unsold at the end of the exhibition were nineteen paintings, nine oil on paper sketches and twelve water colors, a total of forty. Therefore, not "57 out of 60" were sold, but 19 out of 59.

However, one oil on paper sketch (Emily's cover portrait) and three water colors were sold early 1945, thus increasing Emily's sales for the exhibition and up to February 1945 to a total of	23 pictures

This clearly indicates that the number fifty-seven is an error, surprising in view of the evidence available.

NB: At some later date, Dr. Stern himself purchased for $250 gross the most expensive painting in the exhibition: *The Mountain,* which is reproduced in the centennial catalogue, p. 43.

On page thirty, in both catalogues, the last paragraph is devoted to Mark Tobey and his recognized influence on Emily's painting. However, I disagree with one sentence: "In the early fall of 1928 Mark Tobey, who was to visit her on several occasions, gave a short course of classes in her studio." The 1928 classes are not in doubt, but there is no evidence to suggest that Tobey ever visited Emily again, though he did occupy her studio in 1930 while she was away in the East. (See chapter "Mark Tobey to the Rescue.")

It is pointed out on page thirty-nine, in both catalogues, that Emily left Indian themes about 1930 as a major preoccupation . . . "[and] turned to the forests themselves. Harris had recommended this step but she would probably have taken it in any case for the totem poles, in taking her into the deep woods had revealed for her a more comprehensive world of creation." This order, I think, should be reversed, because the totem poles did not take Emily into the deep woods. She was always in or near woods from the moment she was born. She grew up with her beloved pines and sought out the coolness and solitude of the woods long before she ever saw a totem pole. Clearly, too, the suggestion of "deep" woods is misleading. As she describes and paints them, the poles were either silhouetted against sky or mountain, as at Kitwancool and Cumshewa, or stood in the open before houses, or along beaches as at Skedans and Yan.

Although they could be partly submerged in lush undergrowth, they did not stand in the forest, which served largely as a backdrop. Emily could have painted all her totem poles without going into the woods or even very near them. She wanted to record the poles for posterity, but once this mission was fulfilled, she turned away from them and went back to the woods for inspiration.

Also on page thirty-nine, in both catalogues, Emily's first sketching trip to Goldstream Park is analysed. I happen to know more about this trip than anyone else because I was there, working beside her every moment of the day, either in camp or in the field, for over two weeks. Some of her most important sketches—and the paintings composed from them—originated here. I could never forget them because we displayed and discussed them each evening before dropping exhausted into bed, and again in the first light of morning. I knew them all like children. I think I still do.

Doris Shadbolt writes that *Grey* (Carr 1971 no. 69) "is the most important of several paintings and sketches done in a monochrome of black, grey and white originating in the first Goldstream visit . . ." I agree fully about the importance of *Grey*, but not about its time and place of origin. *Grey* was reworked from a sketch done when Emily and I set up camp on Braden Mountain the following spring (1932), in a forest much more remote and jungle-like than Goldstream. This oil on paper sketch was purchased the same year by John McDonald of Vancouver, who sensibly got Emily to sign it before leaving the studio, though he insists that she added the date herself without coaching. This makes him the proud owner of one of the very few dated sketches of that period. It is reproduced in the centennial catalogue (Carr 1971 no. 77), is dated 1932, and bears the unimaginative title *Forest Interior*—so christened by John himself because Emily had not named it. Curiously, both sketch and canvas are signed "M.E. Carr." This may mean nothing at all, but on the other hand could indicate a signature fad of the moment..

While it is true, as stated in the text, page thirty-nine, that the forest in Goldstream is of a particular character, one has to be familiar with the park to realize that it is made up of two quite dissimilar parts divided by a stream. It is therefore misleading to say of the park as a whole that "the experience is not of choking jungle growth, but of dry vaults deep under the living ceiling of foliage . . ," since this description only applies to the section adjoining the road. These "dry vaults" are popularly known as

"The Flats" because the huge stand of towering arrow-straight cedars springs from a flat carpet of golden moss (or did in 1931) without any entangling underbrush of "choking jungle growth." Emily was fascinated by these giant trees—said to be the oldest living things in Canada—as she felt they were "of a different time and place." But when she sought a change of pace, place and material, we simply set up our easels on the other side of the little stream which is of quite different character from the Flats. There the woods have the aspect of a true rain forest—high, dense and almost impenetrable undergrowth, wave after wave of salal and bracken. Although we did not work in the damp, soggy, forbidding "rain forest" side of the park as often as in the vaulted spaces between the big cedars, Emily did do a number of "rushing undergrowth" studies there—her first.

Usually writings, plays, films and talks about Emily depict her as a sombre, dedicated and rejected genius sketching alone in a vast, remote, silent rain forest. The ominous word "rain" trickles off pen or tongue lovingly, as if it explains everything—her genius, her desire for isolation, her determination to overcome obstacles, her eccentricities, and her need to commune with God and nature. I wonder if the idea of Emily and the rain forest originated in the Vancouver Art Gallery? If not, it was popularized there. Over the years it has become almost a label—a false label.

Doris Shadbolt uses this expression several times in the catalogue text. On page six, for instance, she opines that "her [Emily's] isolation has also a bearing upon the two great themes of her mature work: The Indian forms and the vast British Columbia rain forests."

This is pure fantasy. Emily never worked in a true rain forest in her life—certainly not after I met her early 1930, about the time her compelling interest in the forest began. This is precisely why I have stressed, above, that the part of Goldstream Park where she did her "rushing undergrowth" studies in 1931 has only the "aspect" of a rain forest. Like all other woods she worked in, it is close to civilization—in this case only a few steps from the main Island Highway and a picnic ground.

After 1930, I either shared or visited all Emily's extended sketching trips or visited her at their location near Victoria, with the exception of Esquimalt Lagoon, Craigflower Road and her final one in Mount Douglas Park.* Even these latter places I know. Esquimalt Lagoon is a popular beach where we went a few times for a picnic lunch and a day's sketching; Craigflower Road is in the outskirts of the city, not in the woods, and having spent

* *See Chapter "Sketching Trips 1931-1942."*

my summers as a child near Mount Douglas Park, I know the woods there intimately. They are criss-crossed by trails and one hears the laughter of people. Back of Emily's cabin, the trees abruptly climb a small mountain, far too steep for her sick heart. Thus, of necessity, she had to skirt the mountain while painting, only working around its edges. So where are the rain forests? Only in people's imaginations.

Nor did Emily yearn for isolation. After purchasing her van, solitude was forced upon her since it was barely big enough to accommodate her and her pets. But she was happy whenever I could drive out to spend a day working with her, or perhaps a night sleeping under the canvas fly. She also welcomed Humphrey when he pedaled out to her camps, and she encouraged other friends, among them Frederick and Flora Burns, to visit her as often as they could. She even sought out neighbors, any neighbors, just for company and a chat.

For this reason, it is often difficult for friends to recognize Emily in books or articles by people who did not know her, even in the excellent and beautiful, prize-winning docu-drama produced so efficiently by Nancy Ryley for CBC last year. Nancy had a sincere interest in Emily which developed into real affection as the film progressed. But she did not listen to old friends enough and overdid her portrayal of Emily as the lonely, misunderstood and soulful genius. For Emily did not brood constantly about her art, nor have noble, serious thoughts all the time. Her gaiety and humor are too often overlooked or underemphasized, as is her need for companionship. If she was isolated at times, it was not in a rain forest, and not by choice She enjoyed people—even if she sometimes flew at them—and she wanted friends desperately.

Cordova Bay, Goldstream Park and Metchosin, where Emily did most of her sketching in the thirties, are all lightly wooded. But Braden Mountain, the site of our 1932 excursion, was covered with a dense, somber, solitary forest of high trees and lush undergrowth, except for a few enchanting clearings where the sun spread a warming glow over the cool, yellow-green spring grass. Yet it was not a rain forest. Emily's own description makes this clear: "We [Edythe and I] are 1000 ft. above sea level and everywhere are hills not too heavily wooded but that you can scramble over them."*

What people do not realize is that Emily could sit in front of a clump of trees and paint a forest. So let's explode one more myth and get her out of that fictional rain forest forever.

* * * * *

* *UBC Library, Emily to Nan Cheney, May 15, 1932.*

The last section of the catalogue, devoted to "The Work As a Whole" and "Assessment," deserves generous praise as a fine piece of critical writing. Few could assess Emily's work better, or write about it more effectively; and I think it only fair to acknowledge the merits of this chapter before resuming my thankless task of exposing errors in the "Chronology" and the "Exhibitions," which follow the main text.

CHRONOLOGY

The catalogue chronology is perhaps adequate as a general guide, but it is poorly researched and contains many small errors as well as important omissions. See the author's chronology for corrections and major additions. Attention has been drawn to any still unverified dates.

EXHIBITIONS

The exhibitions lists are broken down into three categories—Solo, General and Canadian Societies. Most noteworthy exhibitions are recorded with correct dates, but they are bare of comment and little effort has been made to put them in order. Thus a December exhibition may well precede one held in January, and this is particularly the case with exhibitions held outside Vancouver. There are, however, too many omissions, especially the early exhibitions. Emily's studio shows, for instance, have not been untangled and only two are listed—one misleadingly. The Canadian Societies list is sloppily put together: The Vancouver Studio Club and School of Art exhibitions are incomplete and the name is wrongly given. The British Columbia Society of Fine Arts listing contains several errors (although all catalogues were available) and the Island Arts and Crafts Society, Victoria, is credited with only five of their fifteen exhibitions which included Emily's work.*

* *The errors in the Canadian Societies list have been largely eliminated in the revised edition of the catalogue.*

BIBLIOGRAPHY

The bibliography, which concludes the text of the 1971 centennial catalogue, is drawn largely from Marguerite Turpin's commendable and useful work* and has been only minimally expanded in the revision: Ms. Turpin's own bibliography is listed there, as are Emily's two last books. Four articles about Emily have been added (one by Doris Shadbolt and three by Maria

* The Life and Work of Emily Carr (1871-1945), *A Selected Bibliography*, *UBC, Vancouver, January 1965.*

Tippett) and, finally, two more catalogues. That is all; and yet so much more was written about Emily between the publication dates of the two catalogues. I myself collected many titles over the years, but then decided that the bibliography was not really my concern.

A very special regret, though, is that it contains no French sources; yet many articles have been written about Emily in French, and still more translated into French, including the 1971 Emily Carr exhibition catalogue. A few that come to mind are: "L'Art d'Emily Carr," by Graham McInnes, published by Guy Sylvestre, *Gants du Ciel*, Ottawa, 1945: "Des Horizons nationalistes—Emily Carr" (which I picked up at the Centre culturel canadien in Paris; no date or publisher given); and *Québec Histoire*, Vol. II, No. 1, Automne 1972; "Biographie d'Emily Carr (1871-1945)" Peintre et Ecrivain de la Colombie Britannique, by F. Lefebvre.

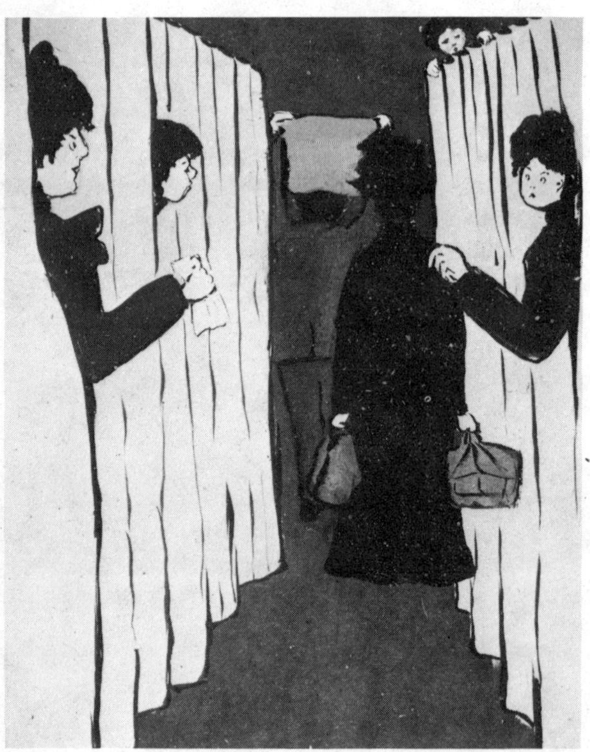

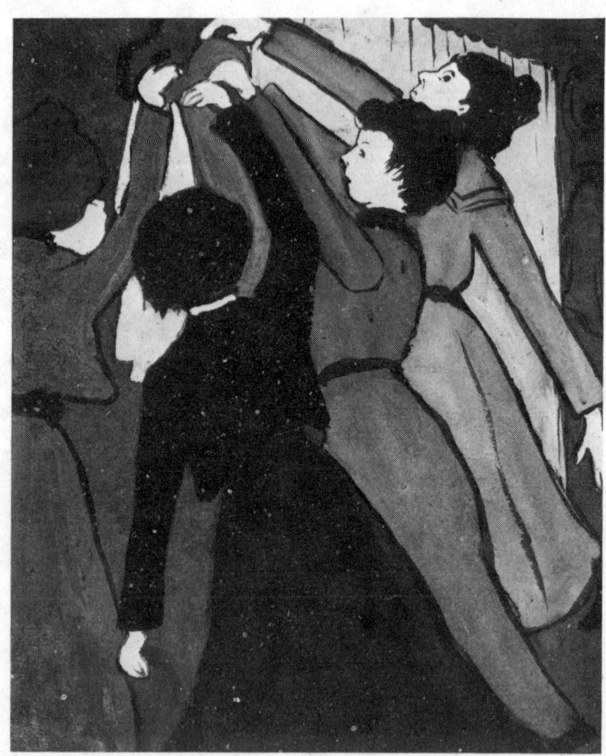

EMILY CARR: A CENTENNIAL EXHIBITION

An Exhibition Catalogue Revised Edition (1975)

The revised edition of the 1971 centennial catalogue is out—at a most painful moment for me, caught as I am between my finished critique of the earlier version—already in the hands of the publisher—and the reluctant necessity of starting all over again. But since the 1975 edition still contains enough error to require comment, I must follow through.

The design of the new catalogue has been altered very little except for an improved white cover and Harold Mortimer-Lamb's photograph of Emily on page seven instead of Knight's. The text has been completely re-typeset, but not greatly modified. A few dates and facts have been corrected in the biographical sketch and two or three notes added. In the final section, "Her Work," devoted to an evaluation of Emily's painting, many changes have been made, but most very slight. A number of words and doubtful dates have been omitted. The biggest change, however, is the price! Seven ninety-five for a catalogue that fell apart after a week's use.

Despite the improved elaboration of the text and increased accuracy of the lists, I do not think it advisable to scrap my critique of the 1971 catalogue, because this is the one that most people have read and still refer to. Moreover, the critique has not lost its value as reference material, particularly as many errors it points out have not been detected and therefore not corrected in the revision.

Many of the corrections in the new catalogue must be credited to Maria Tippett, a Carr researcher who assisted with the revision. In providing new dates for Emily's departure for California (1890) and return home (1893), she has made an important contribution to its accuracy. I had been unable to verify the previously assumed dates (1889 and 1894) even though I corresponded with Emily's old art school in San Francisco and scanned all passenger lists and personal items in Victoria's *Daily Colonist* and *Times* for these particular years. All to no avail. Emily's name is not there. Without any proof, I am quite willing to accept Ms. Tippett's new dates since I understand that she is now in possession of Emily's San Francisco diary, given to her by an old friend of the Carr family.

Oddly enough, the new dates, listed in the chronology, are not revised in the text. On page ten, they are still given as 1889 and 1894, and Emily's term of study in San Francisco as "three years." Why the quotation marks? Three years is correct according to the new dates.

The name of the San Francisco school Emily attended is now correct in the chronology and on page ten, but incorrect on page six. In other words, the inconsistencies noted in the first edition continue in the second.

There is also a new wariness in the updated catalogue—an unwillingness to risk error in doubtful areas, such as the nature of Emily's serious illness in England. On page five, paragraph three, reference is again made to the address Emily gave in Victoria in 1930, but this time care is taken to avoid specifying that it was "one of, it appears, her only two public talks." On page forty-two, in another cautious move, seven canvasses have been stripped of the dates assigned to them in the earlier catalogue (same page). Another example is the complete elimination of Marius Barbeau from the new chronology, though for a time he was a very important person in Emily's life. Even if doubt still exists as to the exact dates of his visits to Victoria, he cannot be disregarded. There is, too, a reluctance to be specific, particularly in the exhibition lists. Years are given, but rarely months; and, despite treading gingerly, the authors have overlooked a considerable number of errors in the 1971 catalogue. A few have even been added.

The most significant errors to escape the revisors' vigilance concern the Emily Carr Trust. Strange that neither thought to examine this crucial date. Other uncorrected errors are:

1. The catalogue spelling of: Salon d'Automne; Baranof Island; Skidegate.

   The spelling of Indian place names has been generally up-dated and standardized, but there are two schools of thought as to whether the new or old should be used in areas pertaining to history or art, such as the titles of Emily's paintings. My own feeling is that Emily's spelling should be retained if it was right for that period. However, if she misspelled the names through indifference, sloppiness, or inability to catch the right sounds, the titles should be changed. A few place names which fall into this category are *Tanu* (Emily's Tanoo), *Kitseguecla* (Emily's Kitsegukla or Kitseukla) but more particularly *Skidegate,* as this name appears so frequently in the catalogue. Skid*e*gate (not Skidigate) is right—and has been as far back as 1899.

2. Emily spent "another five [years] in San Francisco," page four. This is not in accordance with the new dates in the chronology nor with the statement "three years" on page ten.
3. "Her family had never produced an artist or even known one," page five. Not true. (See critique of the 1971 edition.)
4. Emily is still in the "rain forest," page eight. (See critique.)
5. Emily built a "four-suite apartment at 646 Simcoe Street," page thirteen. Not strictly in accordance with fact—nor the original plans of the house. (See critique.)
6. The comment about Dr. Marius Barbeau, page fourteen, is open to question. Needs qualifying.*
7. In note, page fourteen, Willie Newcombe is said to have been one of the trustees of Emily's estate. He was actually one of the two "trustees of my pictures" appointed by Emily in her 1942 Will. (See chapter "The Emily Carr Trust.")
8. Page fifteen: "In times of urgent need, she sold paintings to her friends for fifteen or twenty-five dollars." This has been changed from "five or ten dollars" in the earlier edition. I personally know of quite a few friends who only paid the lower prices.
9. To say that Emily's caravan "was hauled by truck to some spot where she could work in solitude," page fifteen, is misleading. The van had to be left wherever the truck could deposit it—by the side of a good road, near a driveway, or in an accessible flat field. (See "Sketching Trips.")
10. It is still wrongly suggested, if not definitely stated, page sixteen, that Emily's first major solo show in the East took place at Hart House, University of Toronto, in 1936. (See Exhibition Lists.)
11. Harry Gibb, correct on page twelve, is spelled Gibbs in the note, page twenty-four.
12. Mark Tobey is still not accurately presented, page thirty. (See critique.)

* *See Maria Tippett, "Who 'Discovered' Emily Carr" (or: "The Discovery of Emily Carr"—the title used in the catalogue).* Journal of Canadian Art History, *Vol. 1 No. 2 (Fall) 1974. Also: the author's reply to the above article, the chapter, "The Carr-Barbeau Mystery Story."*

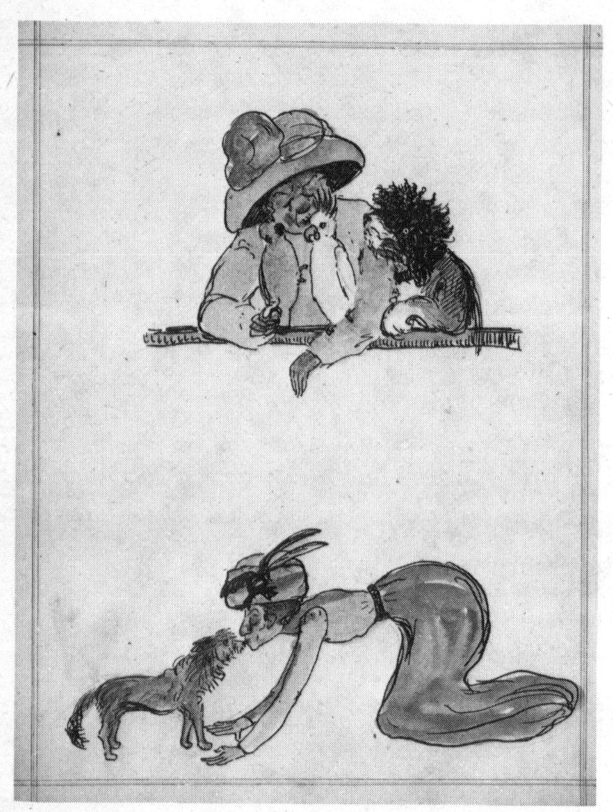
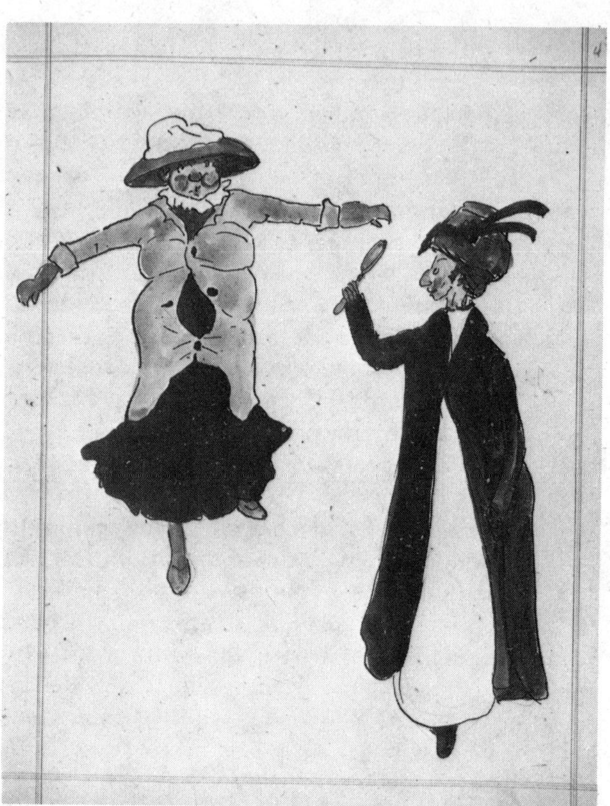

An Exhibition Catalogue
Revised Edition (1975)

Suggested Changes in CHRONOLOGY

1890 The real name of the art school Emily attended in San Francisco has finally come to light. However, its later name, changed while she was studying there, was the Mark Hopkins *Institute* of Art, not *School* of Art as given. The present name of the school is also wrong. It is now called the San Francisco Art Institute.

1905 Emily did not teach at the "Ladies Art Club" in Vancouver (1906). This is a fictitious name used to mask the real title of the group she worked with: The Vancouver Studio Club and School of Art.

1907 Emily did not visit the Yukon during her 1907 trip to Alaska.* Her *Alaska Journal,* composed of entertaining verse illustrated by comic water color cartoons, and dedicated to her sister Alice, was the record of the sum of her impressions of this trip. The *Journal* has disappeared from view since Alice's death in 1953, but is rumored to be "in the East," possibly now owned by Emily's publishers. Emily and Alice set forth on August 10 on the SS Princess Royal, Ketchikan being their first important stop. Then on to Skagway where they spent a week. Emily sketched there and followed the old Klondyke trail in a miniature train of the White Pass and Yukon Railway as far as the Yukon border. Leaving Skagway on the SS Jefferson, they traveled to Sitka on Baranof Island (where Emily again did some work) before boarding the SS Dolphin for the return journey via Juneau, Wrangell, Nanaimo, Seattle.*

* Growing Pains, *p.280.*

* *Although I—and a few other friends—have seen the* Alaska Journal *no one thought to take notes. The above itinerary is therefore based on excerpts from it published in a series of articles in the Victoria* Daily Colonist *in 1953 by James Nesbitt.*

1911 "November 11, returned to Victoria." This date is generally accepted, but there is some evidence to dispute it. (See author's chronology.)

1913 The House of All Sorts was not a boarding house when Emily took possession in June. (See author's chronology.)

1917-1928 "Bred sheep dogs, made pottery." Emily was breeding her Bobtails in 1916 (perhaps a year earlier) and had ceased to breed them in 1923. She only gave up making pottery on a large scale in 1930. (Documented in author's text.)

1921 Mortimer-Lamb is given credit for drawing the attention of Eric Brown of the National Gallery of Canada to Emily's work. But it is likely that Marius Barbeau was the first to do so—a few months earlier. (See chapter: "The Carr-Barbeau Mystery Story.")

1924 Date incorrect. Emily enrolled in the Palmer Institute of Authorship's Correspondence Course in short story writing late 1926 or, more likely, early 1927.*

* The Heart of a Peacock, *Ira Dilworth's preface, p. xiii.*

1930 Emily did not exhibit at the present Seattle Art Museum, but at its forerunner, the Art Institute of Seattle. Her one trip to New York should not have been omitted here.

1933 Did not sketch in the Sooke Hills in the spring, but in the Interior. (See "Sketching Trips.")

The People's Gallery episode is misdated. The year was 1932.

1934 Sketched only two weeks at the Esquimalt Lagoon in May—not May-June. After being flooded out, the van was stationed on a farm on Metchosin Road. (See "Sketching Trips.")

1935 The sketching site "in woods" in September is decidedly vague. As in June, she spent this month working at Albert Head.

1936 Did not give up her boarding house when she moved to 316 Beckley Avenue (not Street). She had ceased taking boarders 1925 or 1926.

1939 There were not "several" sketching trips this year, only her usual two. (See "Sketching Trips.")

1940 Did not move "next door" to her sister Alice. Emily took over Alice's old classroom and dining room and added a new kitchen and bathroom to make a self-contained unit. But there was a connecting door between their quarters and they both lived in one house.

"Had a heart attack in March, a stroke in May." The year is wrong for the heart attack, and the month for the stroke. The correct date for the former is March 1939 (the date used—without the month—in the text of the catalogue, page fifteen, thus contradicting the chronology once more). This date is documented elsewhere in the author's text.

The "stroke in May" was on June 5. (See "Sketching

Trips," May 1940.) Other documentation exists.*

1942 The ubiquitous error about the Emily Carr Trust.

1944 According to the Dominion Gallery catalogue 59, not 60, pictures were hung. Sold 57? So it is always said, but a letter from the Gallery director to Emily (February 10, 1945) states that considerably fewer were sold.

* *Humphrey Toms to Nan Cheney, June 9, 1940.*

EXHIBITIONS

The exhibition lists in the 1975 edition, presumably revised by Maria Tippett, are considerably improved over the 1971 edition, but still fall short of the mark. The wariness pointed out in the text is also evident in the lists. No risks are taken. Indeed, to explain or excuse any errors or important omissions, the lists are prefaced by a remark stating that they are not definitive. No, they are not. Once again, little attempt has been made to list the exhibitions in chronological order as to months in the Solo and General categories, and there are far too many omissions. The Canadian Societies exhibitions, however, are much more precise than before because previous errors in exhibition listings for the British Columbia Society of Fine Arts in Vancouver and the Island Arts and Crafts Society in Victoria have been largely eliminated. They should never have existed at all since catalogues for both Societies were available.

Curiously, two bonus exhibitions have been added to this edition. These will be pointed out in the comments below as will the continuing errors in Emily's studio shows. For closer dating, augmented lists and more information see the author's exhibition lists.

Suggested Changes

SOLO EXHIBITIONS

1913 First studio show in Victoria is omitted.

1930 Art Institute of Seattle, not Seattle Art Museum.

1933 Edmonton. Not a solo exhibition. Two other artists exhibited at the same time, though they were grouped separately.

1934 I can find no record of a studio show in February. The

only reference to one is in *Hundreds and Thousands:* "I wonder if I should open the studio to the public for two days . . ." Emily obviously changed her mind as the subject is not mentioned again. The private showing in August, however, did take place, but it was *really* private—more a party than an exhibition.*

* *See* Hundreds and Thousands, *p.145; also the author's Exhibition List I.*

1935 The April exhibition (really a series of exhibitions, as three different ones were hung) was not in the studio, but in one of Emily's flats downstairs. But there were two exhibitions in 1935—the second one in August—also downstairs.

1936 The Lyceum Club and Women's Art Association exhibition took place in November *1935.*

1937 Toronto, March-April. Since this was Emily's first solo show at the AGT, its omission is inexplicable, particularly as it was listed in the earlier catalogue.

1938 A solo exhibition at the University of British Columbia took place as listed, but two others at UBC, in 1939 and 1940, are not mentioned.

1940 Toronto, the Art Gallery of Toronto.

This was not a solo show. Maria Tippett (if she revised the list) should not have slipped up here since she herself wrote to AGT requesting xeroxes of catalogues for Emily's exhibitions in 1937, 1940 and 1943 and was informed by the Gallery that 1940 was not a solo show.

1945- *Emily Carr: Her Paintings and Sketches*

1946 Besides being held at the Art Gallery of Toronto and the National Gallery of Canada, as listed in both catalogues, this important memorial exhibition was shown at the Art Association of Montreal early 1946 and at the Vancouver Art Gallery in May 1946, but this is not noted in either edition.

GENERAL EXHIBITIONS

It is strange that Emily's first exhibitions anywhere—1894 and 1895 at the Victoria Fairs—are not listed in either of the catalogues. In fact none of her Victoria Fair exhibitions is mentioned.

1927 The title of this exhibition, right in the text and chronology, is wrong here. It should read: Exhibition of Canadian West Coast Art (Native and Modern).

1932 It is not strictly correct to call this a studio exhibition.

It was a four-artist show held in the two lower flats of the House of All Sorts.

1943 Andover, Massachusetts, Addison Gallery of American Art *Contemporary Painting in Canada.* Opened in Andover September 18, *1942.* Later circulated.

1944 The title of the New Haven exhibition should read: *Canadian Art 1760-1943,* not 1916-1943.

For the many omissions in the Vancouver Art Gallery's list of General Exhibitions (a number originating in their own Gallery) see the author's expanded list.

SOCIETIES EXHIBITIONS

1906 The name of this Society is inaccurate throughout the list. It should read: The Vancouver Studio Club and School of Art. The catalogue listing is: Vancouver, Studio Club, May and October, which is wrong on two counts: (1) Emily did not contribute to the show in May. The press reported only a "showing of old china and lace," and this is therefore one of the two previously-mentioned "bonus" exhibitions. (2) The fall show of this Club was in November, not October. (See author's Exhibition List II)

1909 Emily contributed to the listed June-July exhibition of the Vancouver Studio Club and School of Art, but also to the unlisted fall show in October-November.

1927 This is the second "bonus" exhibition in the Societies list, because Emily's name does not appear (even in the crafts section) in the 1927 Island Arts and Crafts Society catalogue as stated in the 1975 Vancouver Art Gallery list. Nor is she mentioned in the Victoria *Daily Colonist* review of the show (October 25, 1927).

1933 The Canadian Group of Painters had *two* exhibitions in 1933, not just one as listed. The first exhibition ever held by the Canadian Group took place in Atlantic City during the summer. Their first exhibition in Canada was held at the Art Gallery of Toronto in November.

1934 Overlooked was a Canadian Group of Painters exhibition at the Art Association of Montreal—selections from the Toronto show of November 1933.

1936 The Canadian Group of Painters exhibition this year was held at the Art Gallery of Toronto in January and the National Gallery of Canada in February, as listed, but also at the Vancouver Art Gallery in October.

1939 The exhibitions of the Canadian Group of Painters and the Canadian Society of Painters in Water Color are incompletely recorded in the Vancouver Art Gallery list for this year. (See the author's Exhibition List II for details.)

1942 The Canadian Group of Painters traveling exhibition this year was shown at the Art Gallery of Toronto, the Art Association of Montreal and the National Gallery of Canada, as listed, but also at the Vancouver Art Gallery in January-February 1943—not listed. Strange that this Gallery so often omits itself.

Summary

Although the 1975 edition of the Vancouver Art Gallery centennial catalogue is markedly superior to its predecessor, it is still too flawed to be considered an authoritative work. In other words, this revised edition, produced at great expense and involving a number of people is still inadequately researched and will require further updating.

This is not to suggest that I consider my version flawless. Far from it. I have had to write a do-it-yourself book with no help (except archival), minimal advice, almost no critical reading by friends, and, due to the time factor, comparatively little, though excellent, professional editing. It was done at great personal sacrifice and even, despite grants, with considerable loss of income.

I have made many friends while gathering information; but will all of them still be friends, not foes, when they read my criticism of the Vancouver Art Gallery and a few writers on Emily Carr? That is my one concern. I think of myself as a mild, accommodating person not easily roused to ire (I had to be to live with Emily), and will be disconsolate if even one friend finds me unfairly condemning, or even unduly harsh, in my judgments. But if pounding at the Vancouver Art Gallery doors does not gain me a hearing to plead Emily's case, I have no choice.

The writers of the catalogue can only profit from my house-cleaning, since one of them at least, Maria Tippett, has a tendency to take one minor point (or document) and expand on it until it becomes disproportionate to other more certain facts.

She is young, she will settle down and, in time, do the same credible, and creditable, reporting on Emily that she has done on British Columbia landscape painting as co-author of a recently published award-winning book; and as Doris Shadbolt has always done in the field of criticism.

I therefore invite them both, and any other zealous Carr researcher, to analyze and interpret my findings minutely and to tell me, derisively if they like, if and where they think I have gone wrong. I will welcome well-founded corrections in the name of Emily. I only ask them to be a little indulgent about dates. I have had to find, write, evaluate, copy, revise, recopy and proofread so many that a few lost or scrambled ones may be inevitable. Otherwise, so be it.

EHS versus VAG

"Cool it," cautioned Humphrey when he learned that I had a few criticisms to make of the Vancouver Art Gallery—IN PRINT! "Don't get into a flap. Do you want the welcome mat pulled out from under your feet?" "I've never noticed one," I retorted, "at least not since the thirties when I was an active member of the Gallery, frequently exhibited in their glistening new galleries, and won a modest bronze medal, which I still prize." But my love affair with the Vancouver Art Gallery is over. Emily has come between us.

Humphrey, that young cyclist friend of Emily's, whose affection for him she sometimes measured with a ruler (yards and yards of him) is too charitable to judge others severely and, therefore, does not wholly agree that the Vancouver Art Gallery management should be castigated. But then, he has long been out of touch with the Gallery and has not read my grievances since I did not wish to embarrass him with any involvement. Nor has he my undying preoccupation with Emily and her work, and is not therefore so easily roused to indignation. He is quick to point out that although the so-dubbed progressive exhibitions and events promoted by the Gallery these many years do not appeal to him personally, he recognizes that the younger generation, which now looks on Emily as an 'Old Master,' demands just such diversified programs. I concur completely. Forward-looking galleries do not mark time and look on the greats of yesteryear as sacred cows forever.*

But my quarrel is not with management as such. It would be both insensate and improper for me, a raw layperson, to even

* *As for example, the Vancouver School of Art's faculty and students' demand for the renaming of their institute, now called the Emily Carr College of Art (Victoria* Colonist *February 1, 1978).*

touch on this topic, particularly as the management of the Vancouver Art Gallery is reputed to be both vigorous and imaginative. Nor could, or would, I disparage the achievements of Doris Shadbolt, author of the Emily Carr centennial catalogue, in her former position as Associate Director of the Gallery, respected as she is as one of Canada's best curators of contemporary art.

No, my criticism relates to one area only—Emily Carr, and it is sad indeed that the Gallery and I have been unable to coexist amicably within it. But as Emily's friend, as observer and as Carr researcher, I am also entitled to express an opinion and allege that the Gallery, while squeezing every drop of prestige and popularity from the priceless Trust Collection, has shown a singular lack of responsibility as its privileged custodian. My reproaches are three:

1. Curatorial neglect:
   a) Errors abound, particularly with reference to the Emily Carr Trust. It did not even occur to anyone on the Gallery staff to go down to the stacks to make a definitive count of their Carr holdings before 1973. Until recent years, the Gallery had little on file about Emily's paintings or exhibitions. I ran into a blank wall when seeking information.
   b) The Gallery has completely lost the identity of the group of original Trust paintings specifically set aside by Emily for the Province of B.C. and named in the Trust document. These paintings, and others added to the Trust both before and after Emily's death, are now loosely lumped together in the Vancouver Art Gallery permanent collection. (See chapter The Emily Carr Trust.)
2. Physical neglect: Much more difficult to substantiate and assess because I did not have free access to the Carr archive. But considerable damage has occurred.
3. Underexposure: Elimination of the Carr Memorial Galleries and reduced size of fewer exhibitions. The last time I saw a Carr

exhibition at the Gallery it consisted of perhaps a dozen pictures hanging along the corridor upstairs.

1. *Curatorial Neglect*

When I first read the Gallery's 1971 catalogue, *Emily Carr: A Centennial Exhibition,* I was dismayed to find both mistakes and misjudgments. Fact was sometimes fallacy; French askew; Indian villages sometimes misplaced; exhibitions lost; inconsistencies frequent. In a word, the catalogue was not the scholarly work one would expect from a Gallery which had housed Emily's picture collection for a quarter of a century.

In a gesture of friendly cooperation (Humphrey please take note), I wrote to the then Curator, Doris Shadbolt, and expressed in general terms my appreciation of the catalogue, especially the quality of the writing. But I also drew her attention to several errors.* The reply acknowledged the praise, but overlooked the corrections though, as a trained curatorial person, and one who welcomes objective criticism (her words) she no doubt noted them. Even without taking notes she knew that I had had a very close working relationship with Emily and would be a special, prime source to tap when a revision of the catalogue was being contemplated. But I was never approached. Nor was any other old friend of Emily's—any one of whom could have made interesting comments on the first edition and worthwhile suggestions for the second.*

My admitted *idée fixe* about setting Emily's record straight prodded me to further study, which exposed further errors. They in turn prompted me to write to the Gallery again *two* years later, this time to the then Director, Anthony Emery.* His reply, very righteous, very superior and lofty, left no room for doubt that, in Gallery arithmetic, two letters, even though so widely spaced, added up to meddling; and he also made it clear that I had become *persona non grata* at his Gallery when he brushed me off arrogantly in one curt sentence: "There can be little benefit to you in continuing this correspondence."* This same ill-mannered director had earlier kept me standing in his office, offering no word of apology or thanks when I pointed out two errors on the walls of the exhibition (there were more, but I had not done sufficient research at that time to recognize them). Would any other gallery have been so petty? So unconcerned about accuracy? How different was the attitude of important galleries in eastern Canada. I had a wonderful working relationship with all. The staff assisted me courteously and welcomed

* *Author to VAG, October 4, 1971.*

* *Before publication of the 1971 catalogue, Flora Hamilton Burns had been asked to write a short biography of Emily for inclusion in the text, but very unfairly to Flora, since she put considerable time and effort into her contribution, it was not used. Instead she was only given credit for "helpful information."*

* *The author to Director Anthony Emery, November 26, 1973. Emery's acrimonious departure from VAG when his conditions for the renewal of his contract were not met made news in Vancouver in the summer of 1974. Director for seven years, Emery claimed he had been ousted by an elitist board of trustees because he was "pandering to another élite, the great unsoaped who had no money to offer." (Vancouver* Sun, *November 6, 1974.) The "other élite" obviously interested Emery more than Emily.*

* *VAG, Anthony Emery to author, December 4, 1973.*

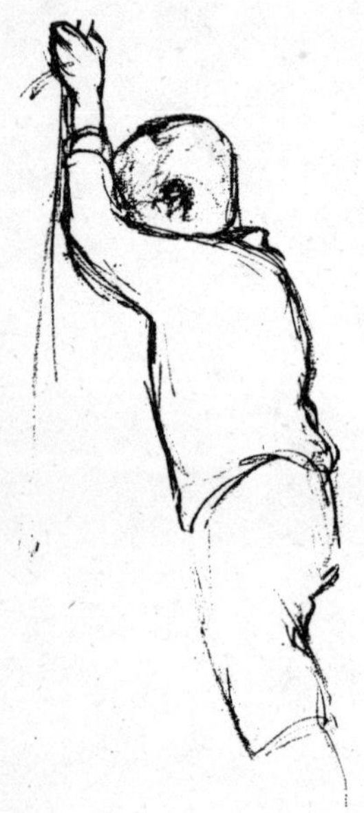

any information I could contribute about Emily. Suddenly, in a flash, I comprehended what should have been a self-evident truth: The Gallery professionals, in their unwisdom, preferred to be wrong with insiders than right with outsiders. Another Holy Alliance.

These two letters from the Gallery lit the fuse that set off my completely independent investigation which soon revealed that this institution had failed to meet many of its obligations toward Emily. And though I hesitated to test wits with professionals, I really had no choice but to knuckle down and review the Emily Carr Trust and the centennial catalogue myself. I breathed a mighty sigh because the prospect was frightening, necessitating as it did, besides emending the text, the compilation of an enlarged, corrected chronology, greatly expanded lists of exhibitions and a classification of Emily's sketching trips—never documented before. All in all a tedious, provoking, demanding task which spawned a dizzying accumulation of dates that eventually bogged the mind and blurred the eye. Unlike gallery staffs facing a similar problem, I had to work quite alone without benefit of assistant, typist or the indispensable proofreader. Yet it was not exactly dull work as it put me in touch with many interesting, dedicated people in galleries, museums and libraries across Canada, in the United States, in England, Scotland and in France. And in an attempt to keep it from being dull for the reader, and to make the long columns of dates more palatable, I have enlivened the text with comments from books and press notices, and with Emily's own pithy remarks from letters to friends.

Scouting for "lost" exhibitions was also an exercise in exasperation because many, even important, ones were shown, and circulated, without an accompanying catalogue, or even a list. And often if a catalogue did turn up, it bore neither a year date nor the name of the city in which the exhibition was held. Frequently not a word was put on file or in the press. But fortunately, at least the National Gallery now stipulates that all catalogues and exhibition posters be provided with such basic information. Future researchers will rejoice.

As this chapter unfolds, it will be clear, I think, that the Gallery's research of Emily's life and work was far from adequate. Its statements about her, her collection, the Trust, her exhibitions, in polished mellifluous English, have an authoritative ring, but the bell often rings without a tower, as witness the history of the Trust. In all fairness, however, it must be admitted that the Gallery's appalling record-keeping during the years it should have been accumulating information about the Trust and exhibitions was typical of most smaller Canadian galleries. They all had grave financial problems in the thirties and throughout the war, and struggled along on minute budgets and with equally minute staffs. As late as 1950, Doris Shadbolt reports, record keeping in many areas of the Gallery's operation was minimal or nil.

True. But when Emily's pictures found a home in the Gallery, the depression and the Second World War were in the past and galleries were burgeoning, and flourishing, all over Canada. Surely by then there should have been a solid item in the budget for the conservation of Emily's pictures and a start on basic research. At least after the mid-sixties, when the Canada Council began pouring money into art museums, and the Vancouver Art Gallery presumably got its share, the initial grants for special projects would have ideally fitted a program dedicated to the study of the Emily Carr Picture Collection.

2. *Physical Neglect*

While the Vancouver Art Gallery's neglect of Carr records is positive and provable, physical neglect of the paintings is difficult for me to assess as I was not in the Province in the fifties, not seeking information in the sixties, and not able to gain access to the Carr archive in the seventies. I was not precisely refused access. In fact, Director Emery, softening his original stand, invited me to go through the Carr archive at my convenience.

A visit finally became convenient in 1975—only after Emery's resignation and departure. I had asked Humphrey to accompany me, but when we, Mutt and Jeff, arrived at the desk and asked to see the Carr paintings, no one present in the Gallery that day seemed to have the authority to grant permission. There was some hesitancy and doubt, but eventually a man in a white smock was summoned from the nether regions and we trotted down the stairs behind him not, as expected, to the stacks, but to a small bare room nearby where we were invited to sit on small bare chairs. From these chairs we viewed Humphrey's favorite canvas, *Above the Gravel Pit,* and two Indian water colors and an oil on paper sketch that particularly interested me at that moment, all brought in at some inconvenience by Mr. White Smock, who was polite, but cool. Still I had not come from Victoria just to see a few pictures I was already familiar with; and since the ex-Director's invitation to "go through the Carr archive at your convenience" was not honored and we felt unwelcome, we terminated our "inspection" hurriedly—mission unfilled.

Emily's pictures, I believe, are carefully stored now in areas of controlled temperature and humidity. Many canvasses have apparently been restored, and oil on paper sketches de-acidized by competent conservators in order to preserve as long as possible the cheap manila paper. The Gallery, of course, cannot be held responsible for the deterioration of the papers caused by time, but unfavorable storage conditions in the early years have undoubtedly greatly hastened the progress of decomposition. When the Gallery accepted the custodianship of the Trust paintings in 1946, there were no adequate facilities for housing them; and until 1951 when the new Gallery addition was built, they were stored in cases in an ordinary commercial warehouse.* Hearsay (reliable hearsay) has it that even in the sixties the Trust pictures were still carelessly stacked. I cannot vouch for that, but I myself saw three damaged oil on paper sketches on exhibition at the Art Gallery of Greater Victoria in December 1971, two noticeably torn in one corner. Shocked, I drew them to the attention of the then director, Colin Graham. I also noticed, when examining the backs of unhung Carr paintings at the same Gallery before another exhibition opened there in July 1976, that a few large original Trust paintings were still being crated and sent on tour without any kind of protective backing. One of Emily's finest oil on paper sketches, *Tree,** has at one time been ripped from corner to corner and the mended scar is plainly visible and mars the painting. One friend who saw this painting in Charles C. Hill's National Gallery traveling exhibition, *Canadian Painting in the Thirties,* wrote to ask me if I knew why *Tree* was so torn. Would the Vancouver Art Gallery please tell us?

* NGC, *Lawren Harris to McCurry, July 4 (1946).*

* *VAG (42.3.63)*

Whatever the degree of neglect and damage in early years, whatever the sum now being spent on the preservation of the paper sketches at the Provincial Archives as well as at the Vancouver Art Gallery, if one takes the long view nothing helps or matters. The present scientific conservation of the pictures can at best retard their impairment. Some of the early water colors, painted on good quality rag paper, may, with care, survive; but the prognosis for the cheaper papers is dim. Nearly half a century old now, the oil on paper sketches will disintegrate at an ever-increasing rate and Emily's spirited and spiritual paper statements will probably crumble into dust before *their* centenary has been reached.

3. *Underexposure*

The amount of exposure due to the Trust Collection is, I suppose, a matter of opinion. Emily's priority was sky high in 1946 when the Gallery ecstatically accepted the Trust Collection. Five years later we were all still star-gazing when two new Memorial Galleries were specially built to permanently house Emily's pictures.

But then came rapid and radical change and Emily's priority diminished. Post-war art was on the march. The artistic awakening begun in Montreal and Toronto had reached Vancouver which soon became one of the major art centers in Canada. But Emily's art typified the end of an epoch of romantic landscape painting and the impatient younger generation, during the exuberant period that followed, was determined, as is natural with the thrust of youth, to experiment with new forms and new means of expression. Led by Jack Shadbolt—once in Emily's thrall—whose influence as both painter and teacher is proverbial, the new breed made the Gallery a showcase for their own work. Tuning in to the strong beat of more sophisticated trends from New York and California, they rejected Emily's spiritual, passionate concern with the British Columbia landscape and interpreted its awesome immensity in cold, intellectually-conceived abstractions. So intent was the Gallery in de-regionalizing the art scene in Vancouver that it had little time, thought or space for the most regionally-minded of all British Columbia painters—Emily. Gallery policy went overboard with the artists and by 1960 Emily's pictures were relegated to the basement. Perhaps, in one way, this was just as well as she would have felt out of place and quite unnerved in the weird world of happenings upstairs.

After 1960 Emily's paintings continued to be shown at the Gallery, of course, and a selection of her work was seen in many centers across the country and in a few in the United States. But according to the Vancouver Art Gallery's own catalogue, not a single comprehensive solo showing of her work was held in their galleries between the memorial show in 1946 (which they have forgotten to list) and the centennial show in 1971. This represents lamentably little exposure considering the size of the Trust Collection and the stature of the painter. Emily's paintings were being stamped *démodées* and downgraded—grossly if one goes along with the original intent of trustees Harris and Dilworth and the founders of the new gallery and not with the negation of it by later management. For the main cause of underexposure was the suppression of the two Emily Carr Memorial Galleries around 1960. Today they are simply called the East Gallery and the Video Room and the more recently-appointed staff are unaware that they were both at one time devoted solely to Emily's work. Senior staff who recall the opening and dedication of the Memorial Galleries argue that there was good reason for the conversion of these galleries to other uses—simply that the space was sorely needed. But was it right to oust Emily? Was it even legal? I myself am guided, and think others should be guided, by a statement made by Lawren Harris, Chairman of the Exhibition Committee, in the Souvenir Catalogue for the opening of the new Vancouver Art Gallery in 1951:

> Because of the great value of these works of art to the city of Vancouver, to this province and country, the Council of the Art Gallery decided to build an addition to the Gallery in which to display the Emily Carr paintings and drawings. Donations for this purpose were first received from Mr. J.S. McLean of Toronto and Mr. H.R. MacMillan of this city, both of whom realized that the paintings of Emily Carr embodied the character and spirit of the B.C. landscape and Indian motifs in unique and enduring works of art. Other donations, both from individuals and corporations followed the initiative of these two donors.
>
> The two Emily Carr Memorial Galleries will undoubtedly be the outstanding feature of the new Gallery for the Emily Carr collection is the best and most comprehensive collection of paintings and drawings by an outstanding Canadian artist to be *permanently* hung on the walls of any Canadian art gallery, and is bound to attract visitors from many parts of the world.
>
> She thus left two great gifts *to this province*, an occurrence which would be unique in any land, and one that more than justifies the memorial galleries *donated in her name.* (Italics are the author's.)

Harris emphasizes three points in his catalogue statement: (1) That the Memorial Galleries were to be a permanent feature of the Vancouver Art Gallery; (2) That funds had been solicited from wealthy donors on the understanding that the two galleries would be built to honor and display Emily's paintings and drawings; (3) That the Collection belongs to the Province, not to the Art Gallery of Vancouver.

But when the Memorial Galleries were phased out, was the

Province consulted? No. Were the people of British Columbia asked to express an opinion? No. Perhaps it is still not too late to investigate and force a reversal of this unfortunate decision when the Gallery moves to new and more spacious quarters in the Vancouver Courthouse.

Ironically, while artists with their new and radical perceptions were outgrowing Emily's influence, the public, after scoffing for decades, suddenly awoke and developed a fond and absorbing interest in her paintings, her books and her foibles. But they were too late, since by then her pictures were no longer on permanent display. During the twelve years, after 1962, when I worked as a volunteer "sitter" at the Art Gallery of Greater Victoria, I was amazed at the gathering momentum of curiosity about Emily and her paintings. Tourists from other provinces and the United States seldom knew the name of any other West Coast painter. They all asked questions about her, they all wanted literature about her. She had become British Columbia's most famous citizen outside our borders.

I had one final encounter with the Gallery before renouncing my cause and fleeing in full retreat. I had done what I could for Emily and errors but was beginning to react emotionally to the put-down and the turbid thinking of the upper echelons of the staff. I had barely completed my critique of the 1971 catalogue when I heard that the Gallery would soon be publishing its second revised printing. Feeling that such overlapping of research was wasteful in terms of both effort and money, I wrote once more offering to put my findings at the disposal of the Gallery if requested. This time I sent my letter to the President of the Gallery, who did not bother to reply.* Completely taken off guard by this new development, I was now forced to review not one catalogue but two, a complex and unsatisfactory undertaking.

I wish this protracted contretemps with the Vancouver Art Gallery could have been avoided,* as it will no doubt lead to acrimony and counter charges. Considering the trial I must have been to Doris Shadbolt, her conduct, unlike that of the Director and President, was correct, if evasive. She maintained her composure and was pleasant and placating throughout my *mésentente* with the Gallery. Her attitude on the whole was that of a patient, sorely-provoked schoolmarm rapping an unruly emotional schoolgirl over the knuckles. Yet looking back, I detect a concerted effort to freeze me out of the Gallery as I, the closest of Emily's friends during the thirties, was the only one not invited to the opening of the centennial exhibition. Why?

* *Author to Mr. Roy Jessiman, President of the Vancouver Art Gallery, November 14, 1974. However, Doris Shadbolt did write.*

* *I specifically exclude the Registrar, W.W. Thom, and the Librarian, Jean Martin, who at all times willingly gave me what little information they could—or were allowed to.*

Because my knowledge of Emily far overshadows theirs, because I was a threat to their complacency, and piqued professionalism is a hard condition to cope with. Not that it is a matter of great moment. My one obligation is to Emily; my one concern the elimination of errors circulating about her—many stemming from the Vancouver Art Gallery's 1971 centennial catalogue.

The importance of the Emily Carr Picture Collection to the Gallery can scarcely be exaggerated, and is emphasized by an article, "Gentle Vibrations," which appeared in the October 1, 1973, issue of *Time Magazine:*

> In recent years the gallery [Vancouver Art Gallery] has concentrated on being a center of activities rather than a repository of art treasures. This is partly by necessity: apart from its major Emily Carr holdings, the gallery's collection is not distinguished.

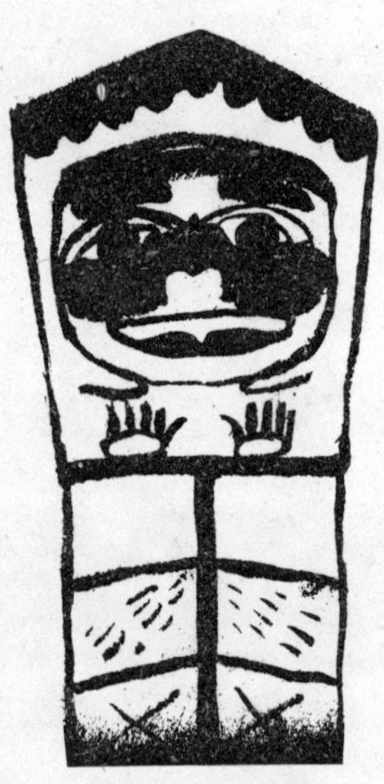

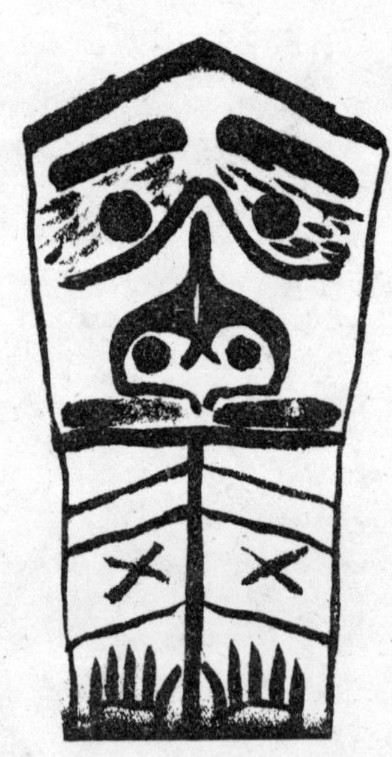

Dating and Signing of Emily Carr Paintings

The dates of all paintings in the Emily Carr Trust Collection indicated as "circa" were assigned by Doris Shadbolt. Though she is very competent, this difficult undertaking was, I feel, too great a responsibility for any one person, no matter how expert. Doris herself admits, in the Centennial Exhibition catalogue, that the task was complex and delicate: "Therefore any attempt to deal with the problem [dating] while utilizing the existing factual data, must rely heavily on stylistic evidence."

Since the factual data were, it seems, insufficient, and as reliance on stylistic evidence amounts at best to educated conjecture, why did the Gallery not seek other resources in an effort to obtain the most exact dates possible? No doubt Jack Shadbolt was extremely helpful, since he knew Emily, though superficially, and is, of course, very knowledgeable about her work. But her more intimate friends, who have the all-important personal experience of Emily and her paintings, could have supplied additional information. Their contribution would have complemented Doris's professionalism and minimized the "grey" areas. I, for one—and Nan Cheney for another—could have put a definite year, even an exact month, to many paintings and, because of my sketching trips with Emily, could have identified many of the places where the sketches originated. Memory not being infallible, there would have been a few blanks, uncertainties, even errors, but the Gallery would have profited by drawing on "living sources." How many galleries have such an opportunity when researching a famous deceased artist?

A number of people have speculated about Emily's aversion to dates and even signatures, especially during her magnificent mature period, 1930-1942. Some suggest that she did not sign and/or date many paintings because she rarely felt she had entirely succeeded in interpreting her material and tended to put her work aside to finish later after fresh study. But, engrossed in a new sketch or canvas, she continued to put off the day. Others claim the lack of signatures and dates was due to sheer carelessness or indifference. But the reason, I know, went much deeper.

Emily had a fixation about progress which impelled her again and again to show her work to those friends whose judgment she trusted, in the hope that they would praise her *latest* paintings. But wanting, or so she insisted, an absolutely honest, objective opinion, she hesitated to show her invited critics dated paintings knowing they would praise "fresh" work in order to please her. She tortured herself until the verdict came. If recent sketches won approval, she was jubilant and encouraged; but if an earlier work was admired, she felt she was "slipping" and despaired. Her reaction to a "crit" from Lawren Harris helps to clarify these anxieties: "I observed that he turned back to former canvasses often with epithets like 'swell,' 'grand,' 'beautiful,' and the later canvasses he was perhaps more silent over. I wonder if the work is weakening and petering out."* Similar sentiments were expressed in a letter to a friend: "Mr. Robson liked the last thing I did greatly—it's a 'woodsy.' It is always so gratifying when they like the latest (people whose opinion counts . . .)"*

* Hundreds and Thousands, *p.327.*

* *Emily to Ruth Humphrey, August 22, 1937.*

Contrary to belief, Emily was very conscious of dates, since she feared the effect of time on her work; but she never worried about chronology except in the sense that she was determined to look ahead—not back.

The fear of "weakening and petering out" developed only during Emily's mature years, after she had renounced Indian themes and became preoccupied with the more creative task of interpreting the solemn British Columbia woods. Certainly she had no hesitation in affixing signatures and dates to totem poles or early water colors. Indeed, looking back, we note that she signed many of her paintings before 1930—among them early works from her student days in San Francisco and England, from sketching trips to Ucluelet (1898), Alert Bay (1908 and 1912) and from her period of residence in Vancouver (1906-1910). Numerous French paintings, both water colors and oils,* and sketches in both media done in the north in 1912 and 1928 are also signed. Many, particularly between 1909 and 1928, are also dated. However, after 1930, though Emily signed most canvasses and some oil on paper sketches (but the latter only for exhibitions or on demand when selling to galleries or private collectors),* she virtually dropped the practice of dating. The Vancouver Art Gallery's centennial exhibition catalogue lists fifty-eight paintings done after 1929, of which only four (nos. 77; 106; 111; 120) are dated. Three are canvasses. Only one oil on paper (no. 77; *Forest Interior,* a special case previously mentioned) bears a date—1932.

* *Before Emily went to France in 1910, she painted, with rare exceptions, exclusively in water color. The earliest oil (on card) reproduced in the VAG Centennial exhibition catalogue (no. 22) was done in Brittany in 1911. From then on she used both media (usually water color in the field and oil for developing her themes in the studio) until 1930. After that the water colors dwindled perceptibly until 1932 when they ceased entirely. Emily's sketching medium from then on was oil on paper.*

* *All other oil on paper sketches bearing a signature were signed ("Emily Carr") in 1944—usually lower right.*

But even when a painting is provided with a signature it is sometimes difficult to determine whether it was affixed on completion of the work or added late in Emily's life as an afterthought, though the style of signature is a good guide.* But with the exception of the original Trust pictures (all signed by 1941) and those signed by request of the Curator of the Vancouver Art Gallery for Emily's later exhibitions there, much of her work, including most of her oil on paper sketches, was unsigned until the last year of her life. Then, in 1944, pressed hard by Max Stern of the Dominion Gallery of Montreal, Emily settled down to whole sessions of signing almost everything in the studio that lacked her mark. She acknowledges her debt to Stern for her new awareness of the necessity of signatures: "One good thing he did for me. He made me get busy and sign *everything*. You know that is a bad fault of mine."* In an excess of zeal Emily at times went too far. In a few cases, she absent-mindedly signed lower right after having years before signed lower left, thus presenting us with the anomaly of double signatures, as in the water color *France* and the oil on paper *Untitled (Trees and Sky)*. Unfortunately, however, Stern did not make Emily aware of the importance of dates.

* *In general sketches bearing the signature "Emily Carr" were signed in 1944 under the direction of Dr. Stern, whereas those whose signature includes an "M" were signed when sold (or sometimes, when exhibited) in the thirties.*

* *Phylis Dilworth Inglis Collection, Emily to Ira Dilworth, undated letter 1944.*

Emily's hectic last minute signing activity at least benefited Stern's fall exhibition in 1944 and all posthumous exhibitions, starting with two memorial exhibitions in 1945—one at Stern's Dominion Gallery and the other, a comprehensive retrospective, *Emily Carr: Her Paintings and Sketches,* at the Art Gallery of Toronto (traveling). In fact, of the seventy-nine oils shown in Toronto, only one, *Indian House Interior With Totems,* was unsigned (though only sixteen were dated). Of the twenty-five water colors, only three were unsigned (only eight were dated). Of the twenty-two oil on paper sketches, only two were unsigned (none was dated). Emily somehow overlooked all her fine charcoal studies as none of the thirty-six shown was signed nor dated, and only two of the fifteen brush drawings bears a signature—none a date. On the other hand, in the 1971 Centennial exhibition at the Vancouver Art Gallery, 120 works were shown, but only 106 were signed and thirty-two dated. So Emily's *"everything"* was not quite all.

Remarks concerning Emily's painting chronology were taped by Marius Barbeau for a CBC radio program in 1958.* They are obscure, which perhaps explains why they were deleted from the final script. But in the original text he says:

* *"Portrait in Memory—Emily Carr."*

> Yes, she had gone north in 1912. She didn't mention the date. I put dates on her pictures. But she was vague about dates and never mentioned any. Except

> that now I notice that on the pictures of the 1912 period, she often has the date 1912 . . .

Did Barbeau really put dates on Emily's 1912 paintings? On other Indian paintings? It is far from impossible* but, since his memory was confused in his old age (he was seventy-five at the time of the program), we cannot place too much reliance on his statement.

** Barbeau helped prepare Emily's 1912 paintings for exhibition at NGC in 1927. (See chapter "The Carr-Barbeau Mystery Story.")*

I should confess that I also added something to Emily's paintings. I did not date any (more's the pity), but I did sign some. Except in the case of four paintings which she gave me,* I signed them in her studio, with her consent, with her brush and after a little practice. But nonetheless it was another hand than hers. Still, I felt that it was better to have a "dictated" signature on the pictures than none at all and my action at least authenticated them in the broad sense of the word. I have never suffered any remorse.

* *A canvas* Joy; *a seascape* From Dallas Road; *a small unnamed " woodsy" sketch on plywood; a portrait of myself painted by Emily in 1932 (oil on paper).*

Another artist, Myfanwy Spencer Pavelic, whom I had known as a girl and who became a close friend of Emily's in the forties, also signed paintings for her. Myfanwy was discretion itself, never having told a soul about the signing incident until March 1975 when she and I discussed our friendship with Emily in a taped conversation in her studio. I questioned her specifically about the signing since I knew, from a letter Emily sent to me in Ottawa, that she had helped prepare Emily's paintings for her last solo exhibition at the Vancouver Art Gallery in 1943. Emily herself confirms this in another letter:

> If I feel better bye and bye when Myfanwy comes home, maybe I can get her to get my paints and those Mount Douglas sketches and do the few bits needed *here.** My sketch bag has never been unpacked since Mount Douglas. I rammed all sorts of things in after my valises were full I remember, so it will be a putrid mess.*

** A nursing home at 1037 Richardson Street.*

** Phylis Dilworth Inglis Collection, Emily to Ira Dilworth, (undated) early 1943.*

Myfanwy admitted on tape,* I am sure a little reluctantly, that she had indeed signed a number of paintings because Emily was in a nursing home at the time, too ill to make even the small effort required to sign her name. Myfanwy also made a few minor changes to certain areas of several sketches that had been bothering Emily. She clearly remembers working on a small patch of bracken in the lower left-hand corner of one sketch, though could not recall just how she altered it other than to change the color a little.

** The text of this article, as it concerns Myfanwy, has been read to, and approved by, her.*

These paintings were the product of Emily's last sketching trip to Mount Douglas Park the year before, and she was lying in bed worrying about getting them signed, crated and shipped to Vancouver in time for the opening of her exhibition in June. Myfanwy's help enabled her to meet the deadline.

She showed me a crude little plan Emily had drawn of her studio so that Myfanwy could locate her sketch sack in a mass of debris and bring it along with the Mount Douglas sketches. Myfanwy found the sketches and painting materials, brought them to the nursing home and signed, she thought, twelve to fifteen sketches under Emily's close supervision. If this number is correct it would mean that virtually the entire output of Emily's last sketching trip to the Mount Douglas Woods was signed by a friend.

Another curious (and useful) little anecdote about dating stems from Emily's last Indian paintings. According to the Centennial exhibition catalogue, this series of paintings was completed "circa 1942," many years after she had given up Indian themes. Yet it was not renewed nostalgia for Indian villages, such as she experienced while writing her Indian sketches for *Klee Wyck,* that compelled her to return to totem subjects so late in life. It was a new, surprising, and uncharacteristic ulterior motive—publicity for *Klee Wyck.*

When Oxford University Press was preparing *Klee Wyck* for publication and planning advance publicity and promotion in 1941, W.H. Clarke, the Manager, wrote to the Director of the National Gallery of Canada suggesting that "a traveling show under the auspices of the National Gallery might arouse a great deal of interest in Miss Carr's work as a painter, if it were held at the same time as our publicity campaign in connection with her first two books (*Klee Wyck* and *The Book of Small*). I know Miss Carr will provide a number of her paintings and if to these a number in the National Gallery could be added, I am sure a very interesting one-man collection could be sent out." *

* *NGC, Clarke to Director, June 16, 1941.*

The Director replied in part: "I recognize the fact that it would be a very desirable thing to have an exhibition of Miss Carr's painting touring Canada at the time the books are published but our difficulty is that we have a definite rule against 'one-man' shows of the work of a living artist at the National Gallery."*

* *NGC, Director to Clarke, June 17, 1941.*

The Director then suggested that a show might be arranged along the lines of the 1927 Canadian West Coast Art Exhibition by combining the work of several other artists with Emily's, but after a further exchange of letters the whole idea was dropped.

In the meantime, either prompted by the publishers or on

her own volition, Emily had started working on Indian canvasses in order to have new totem paintings ready for the promotion of *Klee Wyck* should exhibition plans materialize. By July 6 she had "five new Indian ones nearly finished."* Perhaps she had hoped to do more, but she collapsed once more early in August and had to give up all work for several weeks. When she recovered, publicity plans had changed. There was no more talk of a National Gallery traveling exhibition and Emily decided to use the five Indian canvasses, plus a dozen new non-Indian paintings and a few sketches, in her Fourth Annual Exhibition at the Vancouver Art Gallery in October.

* *Emily to Ruth Humphrey, July 6, 1941.*

Thus, we now have a definite date, as well as a motive, for these last, and possibly best, of Emily's Indian paintings. The "circa" can be scrapped, and a firm date assigned. All five (perhaps even seven) paintings were completed in 1941.*

* *There was no catalogue nor even a list for this exhibition and none of the three reviews available.*

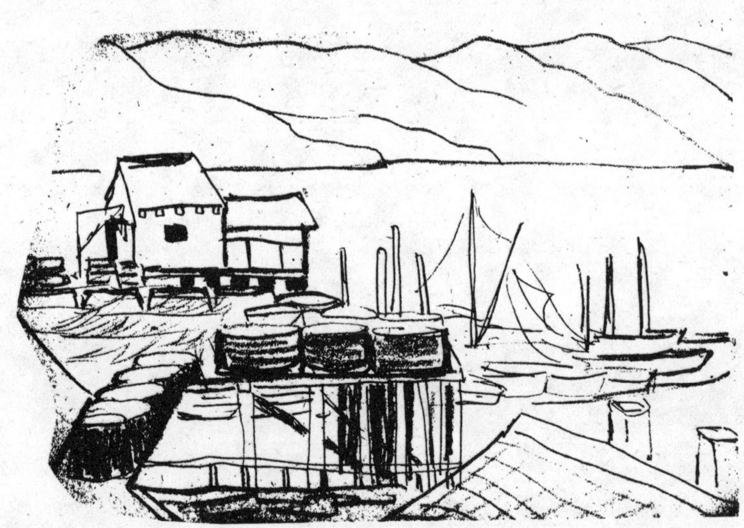

Mark Tobey to the Rescue

The Vancouver Art Gallery's centennial catalogue* sums up Mark Tobey's* considerable impact on Emily's painting career in one short paragraph—just enough to whet the appetite and make one wish for more. The subject is intriguing, as is the story of their personal relationship. Too little is known of either.

* Emily Carr: A Centennial Exhibition, *p. 30 (1971 and 1975 editions).*

* *Mark Tobey was born in Wisconsin in 1890. He left the U.S.A. to live in Basel, Switzerland, in 1960. He died there in April 1976 after most of this study was completed.*

Tobey himself, with typical and delightful braggadocio, was always the first to insist that his influence on Emily was profound—that he had "liberated" her. He put it bluntly: "There would have been no Emily Carr if it hadn't been for me."* This is a grossly exaggerated claim, partly motivated by spite, as Tobey never quite forgave Emily for failing, in her autobiography, to give him the credit he felt was his due. From then on he bristled whenever her name was mentioned, his pique being almost childishly transparent in such statements as:

* *Victoria* Times, *March 25, 1957.*

> She is not the only one I started on their way to recognition. I am not interested that my name be associated with hers as regards her fame, but I can't stomach those who write astonished that she could, living in Victoria at that date, all alone, suddenly become the strong painter she became. I merely quarrel with the lack of scholarship.*

* *NGC, Tobey to Donald Buchanan, received April 15, 1957. Donald Buchanan (1908-1966) was associated with the NGC for more than thirty years—Trustee from 1963 until his death. Director of Talks CBC before 1947 and editor of* Canadian Art *for almost fifteen years.*

The story of Emily and Mark Tobey is a tragedy in miniature. They were both dedicated artists overflowing with talent and energy, seeking incessantly to expand their horizons. Of basically similar views, aesthetic and theological, they also shared a struggle between the spiritual and the material. They had so much to give the world of art and, more particularly, one another; and yet, although each maintained that there could be no break between art, religion and personal life, this fine theory, under the strain of a tense working relationship between two dynamic, temperamental people, sometimes exploded into acrimony. Then Emily, a good actress, played the tragedienne and Tobey reacted with burlesque (he had done a brilliant series of burlesque drawings just before he met her), and tempers flew. But one day, after several such outbursts and a lot of soul-searching, Emily went to Tobey and announced, a little shamefacedly, "You win!"*

* *As told by Tobey to Colin Graham, Director Emeritus of the Art Gallery of*

Greater Victoria and their expert on Tobey—a personal friend since 1957. He is the author of the catalogue accompanying the exhibition Mark Tobey in Victoria, *held at the Gallery December 16, 1975-February 1, 1976. He visited Tobey in Basel not long before the latter's death.*

Emily gave up taking boarders late 1925 or 1926, a date so close to Tobey's visit and his exhortations to free herself that it can hardly be coincidental.

Before Betty Bowen's recent lamented death, she was the Seattle Art Museum's authority on Tobey and the author of the catalogue for their exhibition Tobey's 80*—eighty paintings for his eightieth birthday. In the spring of 1976, she also arranged the Museum's exhibition held to celebrate Tobey's eighty-fifth birthday. She visited him in Basel as late as December 1974.*

Published by the Museum of Modern Art, New York, 1962. At time of publication, Seitz was Associate Curator, Department of Painting and Sculpture Exhibitions at the Museum.

Tobey was the right man at the right time. Without his energetic push, which jolted her into action, Emily might never have escaped from the stifling trap of her boarding house.* She has acknowledged his influence more than once, but it is up to us to determine the degree. I for one accept Tobey's own claim that it was profound.

We must also attempt to determine the number of times Tobey visited Emily—as opinions vary sharply here too—and to surmise how much time they devoted to study. I have used letters, Emily's own writings and friends' accounts to bring this subject into sharper focus. Unfortunately, I had no access to Tobey's private papers, as I had to Emily's, and therefore run the risk of presenting the story too much from her point of view.

I only wish I had known Tobey personally. He is said to have been a vital personality whose followers and devoted, enthusiastic friends were legion. He was, they say, brilliant, highly complex, volatile and unpredictable—the adjectives go on and on. I have at least had the privilege of talking with some of his friends, two of them—Betty Bowen* and Colin Graham—intimate friends, both very knowledgeable about Tobey as a man and as an artist.

Feeling that Tobey himself would be the logical person to clarify his whole relationship with Emily, I wrote him two letters. Alas! He did not reply to either. When I complained to Betty Bowen, she explained that I could not expect a miracle—that Tobey had not written letters for several years, often did not open the ones he received, and that his memory had failed badly. With a sigh, I realized I was years too late in approaching him and would have to limp along without his help.

However, with the aid of friends and the admirable book *Mark Tobey*, by William C. Seitz,* from which biographical material has been drawn, it is possible to piece together, probably for the first time, an account of the relationship of these two giants which is something more than mere guess work. Unfortunately, Seitz, for all his impressive scholarship, did not discover Tobey's relationship with Emily. His only mention of Victoria is to list Tobey's exhibition at the Gallery there in 1957. Even in his commentary on Tobey and the Northwest Coast Indians, he takes a giant's stride from Seattle to Alaska, straddling the whole of British Columbia and ignoring Emily in Victoria. Did she fail to make any imprint at all on Tobey's life? Very little, it would seem, or Seitz would have noted it. Yet many people in Seattle who knew Tobey also knew something of Emily—and still do.

Since timing is an essential factor in assessing Tobey's influence on Emily, his visits to Victoria must be established at the outset. In all, they extended over a period of thirty-five years because his affection for the city itself outlived Emily. For him Victoria was a haven from the pressures and noise of big city life on the mainland. He enjoyed its slower pace, its quaint tea rooms, its unpolluted air and its English atmosphere. (Is it possible that his acclimatization in this atmosphere had any bearing on his later decision to move to England?)

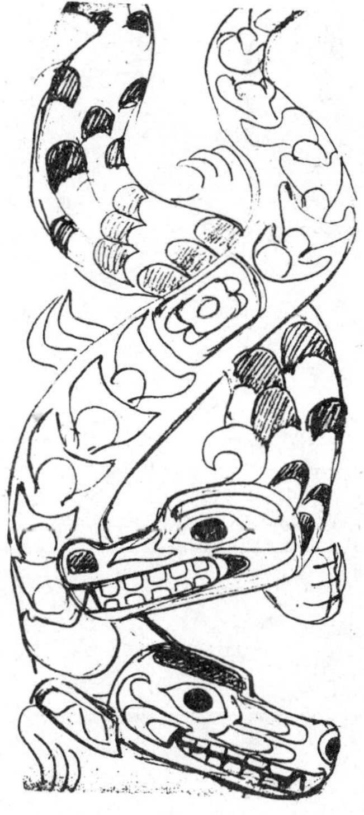

Our only real concern here however is to determine the dates of Tobey's actual sojourns in Emily's house. In my view there were only three:

1924 First visit, as a boarder. A working visit.
1928 Second visit—held his so-called master class in Emily's studio.
1930 Third visit, most of it during Emily's stay in the East. (Probably not a working visit. Emily would be too busy with travel plans to settle to painting.)

I have found no proof, or indeed suggestion, that Tobey visited Emily before, between, or after these dates, although he could have seen her early 1925, before he went to France; late 1927, when he returned; or in 1931 before his trip to Mexico which preceded his departure for England to take up residence there.

At least we know the reason *for* these visits. Tobey sought out Emily's boarding house for rest and relaxation and is said to have been accompanied by other Seattle artists. And why not? They were all poor. Tobey, for instance, was paid $2.00 a class for his teaching, from which the school took $1.20—and Emily gave them lodging for $2.00 or, de luxe, $2.50 a week and good lunches or suppers for thirty-five cents. She also knew how to provide the right atmosphere. Tobey has said that they had "many fine times and many discussions on paintings."*

* *NGC, Tobey to Donald Buchanan, received April 15, 1957.*

The 1928 date has been abundantly verified by Emily, her friends and Tobey himself, who has also written that he stayed in her studio in 1930. But the 1924 visit is unsubstantiated, and was deduced by the following reasoning:

1) It could not have taken place before 1922 as Tobey, after a very short and unsuccessful marriage, decided to leave New York that year. He settled in Seattle after finding a job as a teacher at the progressive Cornish School, starting with four pupils. It is not likely he would leave until he got established there.
2) A visit in 1923 would, perhaps, have been possible,

but the evidence points to 1924. Kate Mather,* a close friend of Emily's and usually a reliable informant, says that Tobey *first* came to Emily's boarding house while she herself was living there between 1924-1927.* Since Tobey was absent from Seattle from June 1925 to late 1927, 1924 seems the only possible date. He was perhaps accompanied by Teng Kuei, the Chinese student at the University of Washington whom he had met the year before and who introduced Tobey to Chinese brush work.

3) Additional evidence for the year 1924 is Tobey's statement that he met Emily in Seattle between 1922 and 1925 and visited her in Victoria soon thereafter.* Since Emily exhibited in Seattle in April 1924, and Tobey, along with Seattle artists Ambrose and Viola Patterson, encouraged her to do so,* he must have met her there earlier in the year and come to Victoria before the exhibition took place.

Still supposition? Perhaps. But these three points add up to reasonably firm evidence that 1924 was the year of Tobey's first visit.

Tobey was in Seattle most of the time from late 1927 to 1931 when he left for England to become resident artist at Dartington Hall, a school and cultural center in Devonshire where he also taught. He remained there until 1938. Like Victoria, Devonshire became a sanctuary from the clamor of big American cities, and later from the over-stimulation of a trip to Europe and his crucial visit to China and Japan in 1934. He was in Seattle again in 1939 and most of the forties—developing white writing, multiple space and moving focus—but nothing indicates that he and Emily met again during all those years. I myself believe that he saw her for the last time in April-May 1930, but that they corresponded until he left for England. His last recorded letter* was written in November 1930, shortly before Emily's first solo exhibition in Seattle opened on the 25th. The letter did not specifically mention the exhibition, but Tobey, the teacher, filled it with critical suggestions, perhaps prompted by a preview of her unhung work. He urged her to pep up her work and get off the monotone, even exaggerate light and shade. She should, he said, watch rhythmic relations and reversals of detail and make her canvas two thirds half-tone and one third black and white.

This was indubitably Tobey's last "lesson." When Emily held her second solo show in Seattle in 1943, there was no

* *A salty character, a psychiatric nurse from Winnipeg who retired in Victoria to live in The House of All Sorts. For many years she sold Emily's pottery and rugs in her handicraft shops in Banff and the East. She purchased five Carr paintings which now belong to the Glenbow-Alberta Institute in Calgary, and owned a very large collection of Emily's pottery.*

* *Emily has also confirmed that Kate Mather "lived in my house for three winters . . ." (Emily to Ira Dilworth, undated letter, presumably 1942.)*

* *NGC, Tobey to Donald Buchanan, received April 15, 1957.*

* *Viola Patterson to author, March 24, 1978: "I feel sure that Tobey would have encouraged her (Emily) to enter the (1924) Northwest Annual, as we also would have done."*

* Hundreds and Thousands, *p. 21.*

letter—no comment. Such is the outline of dates and events that linked these two exceptional people—disappointingly meagre pickings.

During Tobey's first sojourn with Emily, he did not paint and meditate as he had planned because he quickly became interested in the talents of a "greatly gifted woman who was frittering away her time making pottery and ash trays and painting still lifes." He "freed" her, he has told us, and got her "out of the dishpan," back to her easel, the park, and the beach. She became his enthusiastic pupil and he began to exert a decisive influence on her work which has been underestimated by almost everyone except Tobey himself. He taught her, he said, "the principles and concept of form" which she finally understood "after a great struggle." He further insisted that it was impossible for a woman living her circumscribed life to have developed as she did toward conceiving her great swirling canvasses and wonderful tree forms without someone to show her the way. "I was that someone . . . for some unaccountable reason she turned against me . . ."*

* *Victoria* Times, *March 25, 1957.*

Kate Mather angrily challenged Tobey's statement, saying it was enough "to make Miss Carr turn in her grave." But she conceded that the instruction he gave Emily during the week he spent in her house had influenced her to some extent and that he subsequently returned to give a master class in her studio when she was again his pupil:

> I was living with her at the time he first came to her boarding house. I have been a friend and admirer of Mark Tobey ever since but Emily Carr would have been great if she had never heard of him. She owes much more to Lawren Harris. . . . Tobey is up to his old tricks, the big I AM. He is too big an artist to resort to this claim of making Emily Carr, but I have no doubt he sincerely believes it himself now. He is capable of just that!*

* Ibid, *March 26, 1957.*

Flora Burns also objected to Tobey's remarks but admitted that Emily had greatly profited from his teaching and had enjoyed their discussions and long hours of work together. She was striving, Flora said, with Tobey's help, to master the theory of abstract art, and though often moved by the work of others when she perceived its underlying truth, she was never drawn to abstraction as a medium for herself.*

* Ibid, *April 4, 1957.*

Although Emily and Tobey worked together with mutual respect and relative harmony at first, a rupture was inevitable. He was as wise in the ways of the world as she was innocent. He had come to "pure art" by way of the tough and merciless route of commercial art in Chicago and New York, while Emily plodded along through one art school or landscape class after another. She was a good, but not brilliant student, sometimes enthusiastic about her instructors, but not really stimulated until she went to France. Until late in life she was a follower, whereas Tobey was a leader and innovator—an individualistic and experimental artist who found his themes everywhere. Both made teaching an important part of their careers, but Emily had long since given up her classes when she met Tobey in 1924, while he was new to this enriching experience. An inspired and inspiring teacher, he was able to provide the guidance Emily so desperately needed at this juncture of her life; and though nineteen years her junior, he threw himself into the development of his new "pupil" with ardor and authority. Initially Emily was unperturbed by his overbearing conduct being too impressed and invigorated by his unorthodox mode of teaching to be critical. It was only later that they quarreled. In this year of liberation, he opened up a whole new world for her to paint in.*

His teaching technique, which he himself described as a "sort of receptive method,"* was peculiarly his own. Older students, among them Emily, were told to "start with the imagination" then "go out and look at things, to study them, and that will stimulate your retentive memory and your retentive memory will bring it back to your imagination again."

Their first clash came on the subject of form. Tobey told Colin Graham that he had had to battle with Emily to get her to accept his views on form. He had evolved a system of volumetric analysis of forms combined with the pressure of light areas against dark, and vice versa, based partly on his study of El Greco. He infuriated Emily by accusing her of hiding behind the bulwark of impressionism. But in the end her resistance crumbled because she needed his help to assimilate such radical concepts intellectually.

Tobey had not yet achieved international fame when he met Emily. In fact he was only beginning to enjoy a national reputation about the time of her death.* When he first came to her studio, he was just entering on his long career of experimentation and was engrossed in the study of Chinese calligraphy, a technique that had little appeal for Emily. Curiously enough, living as she did on the fringe of a Chinese community, her work was, and would remain, totally unaffected by Oriental influence.

Who can say how indelible was the impression Tobey made

* *Both NGC and VAG acknowledge Tobey's influence on Emily's work. In the* NGC Catalogue of Paintings and Sculpture, *edited by R.H. Hubbard, University of Toronto Press, 1960, vol. 3,* Canadian School, *Hubbard writes in the introduction that she (Emily) met the Group of Seven (in 1927) and was shocked into action on seeing the large canvasses of Lawren Harris. Returning, she began to paint in the austere manner, using totem poles as motifs for canvasses such as "Blunden Harbour" (1928). In the years following, her art underwent a phenomenal development (probably affected by contact with Mark Tobey of Seattle) which gave evidence of the liberation of an ardent spirit. (Author's note: The date given for* Blunden Harbour *is incorrect.)*

* *William C. Seitz,* Mark Tobey, *p. 46.*

* *1944 beginning of national reputation. 1955 beginning of international reputation. (Both dates taken from* Mark Tobey.*)*

on Emily during that first week of instruction? She took it hard, it had impact, but it did not dramatically change her manner of painting overnight. Perhaps she still had little time for painting; perhaps she found it difficult to apply Tobey's theories without his guidance and was content to let them simmer. In any case, although she exhibited in Seattle and Victoria during the twenties, there is a very small body of work originating between his two teaching visits in 1924 and 1928 on which to base an opinion. The Vancouver Art Gallery's centennial exhibition, for instance, did not include a single Carr painting from this period. The aftermath of the early instruction appeared to be little more than the gradual elimination of post-impressionist overtones from Emily's work, a greater emphasis on form and a more disciplined composition. She was slow to absorb Tobey's instruction and gestation may well have lasted four full years until, in round two, with an assist from Lawren Harris, Tobey found her so much matured that he was able to propel her, suddenly and magnificently, into the dynamic painting of the late twenties and early thirties.

In their social moments, Emily and Tobey were, of course, silently assessing one another. Poles apart in some ways, they found they had some remarkable similarities. They both left school at an early age to further their art training, but Tobey's family was poor and he had to go to work when he abandoned high school. Except for a perfunctory course or two at the Art Institute of Chicago, he was self-taught. Emily, on the other hand, grew up in relative luxury and could afford to go to art schools in San Francisco and London before becoming semi-independent.

They were both brought up in strict Protestant homes surrounded by a large family to whom the idea of professional art was to some extent alien. But Tobey was more fortunate than Emily in his home environment because he had the total backing and understanding of his father in his determination to become a painter, whereas Emily's father, though interested in her art, only encouraged it as a pastime or preparation for a teaching career. Anything else would have been less than respectable for a girl of her sheltered upbringing.

Tobey and Emily collided repeatedly on the subject of artistic values—and even on such minor issues as his living habits—but because she had been cut off from the mainstream of art for so long she was, for a while, a receptive, sometimes docile, pupil and he was able to quicken her interest in modern art expression.

Another bond, perhaps the strongest, was their profound, shared concern with religion and a consequent search for spirituality in their art. At the beginning this concern seemed to unite and compose them, but it later proved to be the strongest of the wedges that drove them apart. Tobey had embraced the Bahá'i World Faith in 1918, a key event that deeply affected both his life and development as an artist. To Emily his faith seemed as unorthodox as his teaching, but it did influence her own religious sentiments since she also was seeking a new, positive and personal belief. But Tobey was unable to convert her, just as Lawren Harris was unable to convert her to theosophy a few years later. Before she died, Emily had finally resolved her soul-rending religious conflicts alone by re-affirming her stand on the side of Christ and returning to the Anglican fold.

In the late twenties, the ubiquitous Marius Barbeau, noted ethnologist and admirer of Emily's Indian work, bounced into the already confused story of Emily and Tobey and stirred things up still more. Unfortunately his recollections about both, made late in life, are highly-colored and, I feel, distorted. In taped reminiscences,* he mentions a visit to Seattle, where he met Tobey, and though no specific date is given, it is now known to be 1929.* The garbled text, edited, goes like this:

> When I was there [Seattle] I went to see an American painter named Mark Tobey. I had heard of him from Emily Carr herself on my last visit to see her.* She told me about them, those American painters—that they would come to visit her from time to time to spend their vacations. They would drink and have [illegible] if they needed it. Tobey had advised her to abandon the totem poles in her pictures and turn to something else. To look inside herself. They had said, "Look at what you *feel* and paint it!" That was their point. They were right. She was to prove it. But at that time it was much too early for her to understand. She said she despised them because they drank. Their discussions lasted all through the night and in the morning she ejected them. She didn't want to see them again in her house. I don't think she ever forgave them because they had rejected both her and her totem poles. What they wanted her to do was something that was still undone and that she might not want to do. But after her visit to the East when she saw the work of the Group of Seven, whom she admired so much, and after having talked at length

* "Portrait in Memory—Emily Carr," a CBC broadcast, April 9, 1958 (unedited text). By kind permission of Elspeth Chisholm, narrator and producer.

* Ambrose Patterson to Barbeau, June 1929.

* This no doubt refers to Barbeau's presumed visit to Emily's studio in 1929.

> with Lawren Harris, who tended to abstraction himself in his interpretation of mountains and landscape, she began to understand a little better. She was facing a transitional period. Her creative period was still ahead. . . . Curiously enough Lawren Harris . . . gave her the same advice in letters. This she could endure. It was not fighting. It was not Mark Tobey. It was Lawren Harris, a friend who had understanding and sympathy for her.

Was Barbeau merely gossiping? Did some of Tobey's Seattle friends really imbibe too much and occasionally become too rowdy to be welcome guests in Emily's prim boarding house? It is unlikely that Tobey drank to excess, if at all, as I am told that there is a Bahá'i injunction against the use of alcohol. But even if all were non-drinkers this would not preclude the possibility that Emily ordered them out. Noisy discussion late at night would alone be enough to incur her wrath.

We have read and heard so often that Emily turned from totems to trees about 1930 on the recommendation of Lawren Harris, that it has become an undisputed, indeed unassailable, fact. Yet here is Barbeau, who knew the period intimately, giving prior credit to Tobey. He is probably right because we have previously heard rumblings that Emily's preoccupation with totem themes caused friction with Tobey, even though he was "very keen," she said, on the summer's work she brought home from the north in 1928. She had at last accepted his views on form, but still resisted his advice and that of other Seattle artists, including the Pattersons,* to renounce her Indian motifs and seek a new source of inspiration.

* Ambrose Patterson, professor of painting at the University of Washington 1919 to 1947 and his wife Viola, also a painter who held the same position, on the retirement of her husband, from 1947 to 1968. Both visited Emily several times a year.

Since Tobey was a man of intellectual attainments, sensitivity and curiosity, everything in his environment affected him to a greater or lesser degree, and totem poles and other Northwest Indian artifacts were an occasional subject matter and a plastic influence after his arrival in Seattle. He was also a diligent collector of all primitive art, but was not, it seems, caught up in enthusiasm for Indian themes to the degree that Emily was.

Perhaps the unusually small format of most of Tobey's paintings, his media (largely tempera or water color) and the general delicacy of his work precluded any real interest in the massive physicality of totem poles and the assertive greens surrounding them. Tobey's poles seem almost ephemeral compared with Emily's.* He was not concerned with accuracy of detail—his subjects were drawn largely from idea and memory

* As, for example, Drums, Indians and the Word of God, *tempera 18½" x 13⅞", painted 1944. Collection: Herman Schulman.*

and were often mystical—whereas she felt a duty to the Indians to record their poles faithfully, no matter how imaginatively she might, in later years, treat the undergrowth that swirled around them.

Shortly after Emily's death, Colin Graham had occasion to go to her studio and was surprised to see three or four small entirely non-objective paintings consisting solely of abstract intersecting planes. Only their deep green color, of the kind she used in the late twenties, seemed to allude to forests as the subject matter.

It is difficult to see where this cubist influence came from if not from Tobey. Certainly not from Lawren Harris or the Group; just as certainly not from books as she read little on art subjects and was impatient with art terminology. She has related that she once went to a lecture on art history and then fell asleep in the middle.

However, in her quest for knowledge of *l'art nouveau* in Paris, Emily had come under the influence of the post-impressionists and fauves and may have been startled into an early awareness of cubism, as two of her teachers, Harry Gibb and John Duncan Fergusson, were exponents of Cézanne and may have introduced her to the work of Picasso and Braque. But it is more likely that she first investigated cubism under the tutelage of Tobey in his 1928 master class. He had belatedly made what he called his "personal discovery of cubism" one night at the Seattle Cornish School just prior to meeting Emily, but appears to have communicated his discovery to her only after returning from abroad in 1927, freshly invigorated by his contact with Parisian cubism and abstract art in general. Tobey's cubism in 1928, Colin Graham believes, was of a more solid kind. His well-known study of Emily's studio,* for instance, is of an almost sculptured nature. In teaching his class, however, he possibly went back to the pre-war analytical phase of Picasso's and Braque's cubism.

After the master class, Emily literally exploded into creative activity, and the break with her painting past was abrupt and dramatic. She began composing large-scale, powerful canvasses such as *Big Raven** which was reproduced on an Emily Carr Centennial six-cent Canadian postage stamp, issued February 12, 1971. Twenty-seven million stamps were printed. In 1928, too, the influence of Tobey and Harris overlapped, and the heavier, more formalized paintings Emily produced were partly the result of Harris's example and partly of Tobey's teaching. Tobey, says Seitz, knew something of the monumental light and shade of Michelangelo.

* Emily Carr's Studio, *oil on canvas 29¾" x 24¾", 1928. Collection of the late Soren Juul. Acquired in Seattle long ago, presumably because of the personal interest of Mrs. Juul's family in Tobey. Her father, Horton C. Force, was Secretary of the Board of Trustees of the Seattle Art Museum for many years and Mrs. Force was one of the handful of women in Tobey's first class after his arrival in Seattle.*

* Big Raven, *oil on canvas 34¼" x 45", 1928/29. Collection: the Vancouver Art Gallery (42.3.11).*

It is hard to say which painter's influence was the more dominant in terms of the pure structure of her painting, but Harris's, as we know, was the more lasting—possibly because Emily had a smooth friendship with Harris and a tempestuous one with Tobey.

Tobey's cubist influence is also noticeable in many of Emily's forest paintings of the late twenties and early thirties in which precise geometrical lines and figures make their appearance. Her folded foliage and draped forest pictures are also typical of this period and are strangely reminiscent of the linear undulations of some of Tobey's paintings, such as the 1929 oil, *Before Form.** However, while everything Emily knew about cubism and abstract art at that time was *absorbed* from Tobey, her method remained her own. She rarely experimented with ideas or depended on memory, but needed a "fresh" subject before her, or at least her own sketch of a fresh subject. She and Tobey strove for the same universal themes, but Emily battled both ill health and the elements to find them in the woods from nature.

** Collection Mrs. Horton C. Force, Seattle, 33¼ x 44½.*

The master class was entirely Emily's idea. She told me, and other friends have confirmed, that she invited a few Victoria artists to form a class in order to help Tobey, who, she said, "was completely on his uppers." After he had finished his instruction and gone, Emily wrote an enthusiastic letter to Eric Brown:*

** NGC, Emily to Eric Brown, October 1, 1928.*

> Since my return home, I have been very busy. . . . I had just got straightened out when Mr. Tobey, an American artist, came over from the States for three weeks. He was on his way to Chicago where he is to give an exhibition of his paintings. He is a man that interests me very much, very modern and very keen. He was over in Europe last year and made good use of his time. He has been teaching at the Cornish School in Seattle. I think he is one of the best teachers I know of. He gave a short course of classes here in my studio and I felt I got a tremendous lot of help from his criticism. He was very keen on my summer's work and his crits I feel will be very useful in the working out of many problems connected with my summer's work, which I hope to do this winter. I am as hard at work as my household cares permit me to be. How I wish I had *nothing else* to do but paint!

Emily managed to round up five or six painters for Tobey's class, but I have only been able to trace two. One, Ina D.D. Uhthoff, a respected art teacher in Victoria for many years, whom Emily describes anonymously in her journals,* told me

* Hundreds and Thousands, *p. 172.*

personally about the 1928 class and how much it had inspired her. The other, George Napier, Provincial Assistant Public Works Engineer and Department Manager of Railways, was a "Sunday painter" of considerable ability. Always interested in Emily and her work and distressed that she was too poor to pay for proper painting materials, he took lessons from her and bought a few paintings in order to help without offending. He met Emily in 1922 and they were on very friendly terms. The lessons were held on Sundays and afterwards the Napier family joined the two artists in the studio for a cup of tea. They and the animals munched on delicious cookies Mrs. Napier never failed to produce from her sewing basket, and they all looked forward to the following week.

Unhappily, like so many of Emily's friendships, this one, too, did not endure. Napier inexplicably incurred her displeasure, and the good relations, the fruitful lessons and the cozy teas all came to an abrupt end in 1929. But Napier has passed on his recollections of this remarkable class to his niece* and also told her that he not only paid Tobey's return fare from Seattle out of his own pocket but also reimbursed Emily for a good part of her boarder's expenses.

* *Since George Napier's long and close association with Emily is not generally known, I have quoted quite liberally from an interview with his niece, Ms. Peggy Bartholomew, a tapestry specialist in Victoria.*

It is amusing to follow the course of the relationship (it could scarcely be called a friendship) between Emily and Tobey because it was bound to be stormy. Two such peppery, egotistical and determined characters—he a suave cosmopolitan of commanding appearance, she, though outwardly unconventional, a puritan at heart—could not conceivably live and work together without mounting discord. When the clash inevitably came, Emily's former words of praise and appreciation quickly soured and turned to vilification, though she tempered her remarks about him later in life when the sting was gone.

In sharp contrast to Tobey and—if one believes Barbeau—his unruly friends, Seattle artists Ambrose and Viola Patterson and a few of their faculty colleagues enjoyed relaxed weekend holidays in Emily's House of All Sorts and maintained a tranquil, durable friendship with her until the early forties when her swiftly deteriorating health made further visits impossible. Emily, I think, was even more impressed by their university background than by their reputation as vanguard painters who, like her, were experimenting with the techniques of post impressionism and *l'art nouveau* in the stimulating atmosphere of the Seattle art community. With tongue in cheek, she describes the "sedate" behaviour of her University of Washington guests:

Many artists from Seattle visited my studio—

> professors, art teachers—often spending weekends. It amused these staid educators to stay in a house in which there was a live monkey.

These Seattle friends, Emily recalled, loved going on a picnic with Woo and were not above stalking grasshoppers on their hands and knees on the grassy slope of Beacon Hill Park to appease the appetite of the diminutive, scarlet-aproned monkey: "The professors [then] dusted their learned knees, pleased that their offering had been accepted."*

* The Heart of a Peacock, *Oxford University Press, Toronto, 1953, pp. 202-203.*

If both Emily's and Barbeau's versions of the Seattle artists' behavior seem exaggerated, it must be remembered that each, in his own way, was an unabashed story teller. The truth no doubt lies somewhere in between.

Although Viola Patterson could not remember the exact year Emily and Tobey met, she clearly recalls Emily's reactions to him. She had, Viola said, a very high opinion of him as a teacher and painter, was fascinated by his brilliant conversation, but thought rather less of him as a human being. For one thing, Emily felt that Tobey had taken advantage of her by making too free use of her painting materials when she could ill afford to buy enough for herself. But according to Viola, Tobey was a most generous man who thought nothing of "borrowing" from artist friends as he was always glad to "lend" them whatever he had. Emily did not see it that way and was "riled."

Betty Bowen recalled that Tobey was deeply hurt and offended that Emily had "done him in" by failing to mention him in her autobiography.* He showed Betty the newspaper clipping in which he claims to have "freed" Emily,* and refused to recant. He conceded, though, that they had had a number of "exchanges" during which Emily had stormed out of the room in a rage, refusing for some time to resume their customary master-pupil roles.

* *He was however mentioned, anonymously, as "an American artist"—in less than seven lines—in* Growing Pains, *p. 324.*

* *Victoria* Times, *March 25, 1957.*

Never a painter, Betty attended Tobey's classes just to listen and learn, and she remained one of his many "enthusiastic and adoring friends" all her life. She found him "maddeningly contrary, sometimes impossible, but an impulsively generous, compassionate and gentle man—so stimulating that even in his worst moods he was a more exhilarating companion than anyone else she knew. His friends, she said, consisted of a vast spectrum of types, from wealthy, cultivated, famous people to the most downtrodden and scruffy.* Betty was convinced that even his closest friends had no real inkling of the number of people with whom they shared him.

* *In* Mark Tobey *Seitz writes: "He is fascinated by skid-row drifters that haunt the Pike Place Public Market in Seattle."*

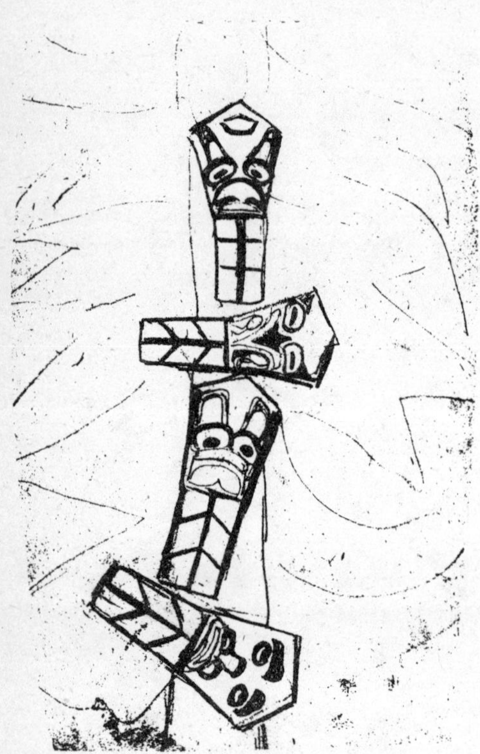

Like Tobey, Emily tended to compartmentalize her friends, rarely mixing painters, musicians, writers or professors. Having few friends, this was no problem for her, but Tobey had a large circle of loyal admirers in all walks of life. One of these was Colin Graham.

Colin met Tobey in 1957 when, as Curator of the Art Gallery of Greater Victoria, he was able to persuade the by then internationally renowned artist to allow the Gallery to mount an exhibition of his work. This was a major show which Colin said "other galleries would have given their eye teeth to get." In fact, the following year, Tobey was honored with the most prestigious award Europe can bestow—the grand international prize at the Venice Biennale, the only American to receive it since Whistler in 1895.

Colin's description of Tobey is, like Betty Bowen's, panegyric—so different from Emily's that it is hard to reconcile the two. But Emily, who often failed to draw out the best in people and was at times a harsh and biased critic, never found the key to Tobey's psyche—nor he to hers. He himself told Colin that they had "fought like cats and dogs."

Colin sees Tobey as an intellectual painter who made a decisive impact on those he met in a quiet, persuasive, but still authoritative way. Colorful rather than flamboyant, he was not nearly as arrogant as press articles indicate, nor as mercenary as Emily thought. A world spirit and the soul of generosity, Colin has observed none of the "mean spirit" Emily depicted.

> "Tobey may well have been much more peppery as a young man when Emily knew him than in his genial expansive years as an acknowledged master," Colin admitted. "Furthermore, I had no occasion to cross him, as Emily did, and hence knew only the milder sides of his nature. Certainly he could be testy, and could, and frequently did, expatiate virulently on what he considered the desecration of man's psyche by technology. But I have known numerous Americans who have had close associations with him, and without exception, they speak with deep affection of him as a man of marvellously generous spirit with a deep concern for others. His anonymous benefactions to young artists, both in terms of time devoted to them and hard cash given them surreptitiously, have been legion. In Basel, for example, I found that he wanted more money than he was getting because it meant he would have more to give to

struggling Basler artists. A totally unknown young Seattle woman painter who visited him while touring had an envelope pressed into her hand when leaving: It turned out to be about $500. Tobey had an extremely wide acquaintance with leading artists, musicians, philosophers etc., both in Europe and the U.S.A. It was my privilege to read many of their enormously respectful and often very affectionate letters to him. I suspect that Emily brought out the worst in him and he in her."

Tobey has told at least two people that he painted a portrait of Emily. He made the disclosure in 1957—the year so much information about her appeared in the press on the occasion of his visit to Victoria. He mentioned it to Colin then, and a month later to Donald Buchanan: "I painted her portrait which I guess she has destroyed as she turned against me in a fury. . . . I do regret the loss of the very fine portrait I did of her."*

* *NGC, Tobey to Donald Buchanan, received April 15, 1957.*

I fear Tobey is right. The loss of this unique painting is tragic since he was a good portraitist. But did he do a recognizable likeness of Emily? It would be fascinating to see how Tobey, the cubist, handled his pupil in paint.

His influence waned as suddenly as it peaked—all in 1928. The same year, even before Tobey's master class took place, Lawren Harris had begun writing Emily his long "fatherly" letters of advice and encouragement and, better suited to her temperamentally, soon gained the ascendancy. There were no fireworks or flourishes in this new solid friendship with Harris, an estimable man, fine painter and convinced theosophist, but how lifeless and pedestrian it seems compared with the *élan* of her relationship with Tobey.

Strangely, Emily never acknowledged the spiritual side of Tobey. She only saw his surface qualities and insisted he had no soul. But more intimate friends found him all soul, and the feeling persists that she somehow missed the boat and was the loser in this potentially rewarding friendship. Subconsciously she may have felt that he was beyond her grasp intellectually, and was perhaps disturbed and inhibited because she was not, like Tobey, articulate in expressing her attitudes in words. He was a remarkable and romantic figure who had much to offer Emily aside from his teaching; and since they shared so many beliefs, both in painting and religion, he might have helped to make her later years richer and more meaningful. But all this was lost in a tempest of petty quarrels, and Emily was not docile or patient enough to sit at the feet of one master forever.

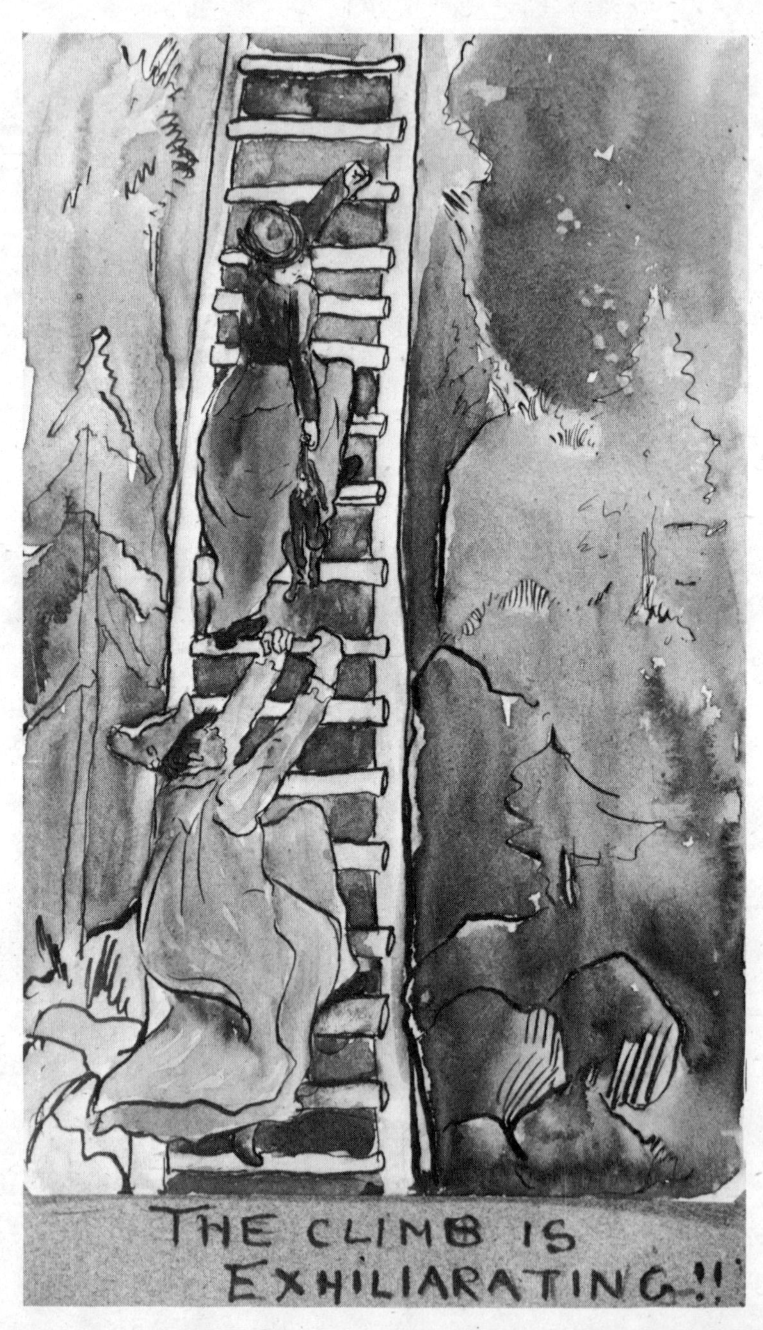
THE CLIMB IS
EXHILIARATING!!

Emily Exonerated

Part 1

The Case of the Seven Photographs

The last place one would expect to find a fairy tale is surely in the learned *Bulletin of The National Gallery of Canada;* and yet such a tale appeared in its pages not too long ago.* The heroine is Emily Carr, whose early arduous travels to British Columbia's forbidding northland to sketch the native Indians, their boats, their painted house fronts and, above all, their totem poles, have become a part of her legend.

* Bulletin 25/1975, The National Gallery of Canada, *"Emily Carr's Blunden Harbour," pp.33-37, by Maria Tippett.*

Now we learn (and herein lies the tale) that Emily's tribulations in Indian territory were still greater than we had supposed because, while traveling by stage or wagon over difficult terrain, and by gasboat or canoe over treacherous waters, she had to lug around not only a bulging sketch sack, but also a heavy camera and a supply of photographic glass plates. "Carr," so this fable goes, "had begun to take her own photographs in 1912 on her excursion to the Queen Charlotte Islands and the Nass and Skeena Rivers."

Nor is the proverbial happy ending wanting. We glean between the lines that our heroine's fortitude, her long hours working alone in uncanny surroundings, and her exacting labors with cumbersome photographic equipment eventually bore bright fruit in the colorful oils, such as *Tanoo, Q.C.I.;* Kwakiutl House;** and *Totem By The Ghost Rock*** that were developed later in her Victoria studio from 1912 field sketches and her own photographs.

* *Collection PABC, oil on canvas 43" x 67"; signed lower right: M. Emily Carr; inscribed and dated lower right:* Tanoo Q.C.I. 1913.

* *Collection VAG (Carr 1971 No. 44) oil on card 23½" x 35¾", 1912.*

** *Collection VAG (Carr 1971 No. 37) oil on canvas 35" x 44½", 1912.*

This is luscious legendary material which, unless brought into proper focus, will cling to Emily's already distorted image forever. Indeed, the *Bulletin* essay is so permeated with errors, in reasoning as well as in fact, that mounds of material have had to be gathered and sorted to get at the truth.

"History," Max Beerbohm writes, "does not repeat itself. The historians repeat one another." Nothing could be truer of the Emily Carr story. It has been told and retold; hashed and rehashed; each historian has drawn on the same stale and often inaccurate secondary sources.

But Emily in the role of photographer is news, and would be arresting news and a welcome departure from the stereotyped pattern of Carr reporting, if it were true. But it is not. It merely illustrates the myth-making faculty of still another Carr writer who, disregarding the voices of Emily's contemporaries, and Emily's own voice from the past, rushes headlong into a new discovery, "Emily the photographer," basing the creation on a vagary spun from erroneously reasoned material. Because it had all the aspects of a *find* this material was recognized as good copy and presented in the *Bulletin* essay without the precaution of independent investigation.

The *find* is said to consist of:

Six photographs in the [British Columbia] Provincial Museum which can be attributed to Carr by reason of their very close similarity to specific paintings of the artist.* But do these photographs** provide sufficient evidence to contradict Emily's often expressed views on photography, and her friends' views on Emily as a photographer? Assuredly not. Admittedly, a few scattered references to Emily on the reverse of these photographs and in the work sheets of the Ethnology Division of the Museum could possibly prompt the unwary into reaching false conclusions or making inaccurate attributions. However, I hope to make this issue clear by drawing on the observations of Emily's friends, my own memory, and the following evaluation of the seven photographs. For study purposes they have been divided into two groups:

1. Five photographs (PN5539,5541,5542,5543,9680) were made from 5 x 7 glass plates, and taken in Tanu and Skedans in the Queen Charlotte Islands in 1912. They "were probably taken with the same camera and probably by the same photographer."*** They are not of very good quality and are somewhat blurred.
2. The remaining two photographs (PN2807, 2240) were printed from negatives of the same size and type, and are transparent sheet film, not glass plates. They were taken at Tsatsisnukwomi* at the entrance to Knight Inlet, also in 1912. They are of better quality than those in Group 1, and were likely taken by a different photographer.

With the exception of one (PN5543), all above photographs bear an undated, penciled inscription on the reverse stating the location of the subject totem poles or houses. All inscriptions are initialed "M.E.C." and all are in the same handwriting, which, however, bears no resemblance to Emily's.

* *NGC Bulletin 25/1975, "Emily Carr's 'Blunden Harbour,'" Note 6.*

** *Author's note: There are seven, not six photographs in this group in the Ethnology Division of the BCPM. They are:*

- *PN5539 Skedans, Q.C.I. (1912) Haida. Emily's drawing board can be seen in the lower right corner.*
- *PN5541 Tanu, Q.C.I. (1912) Haida. View of three totem poles and three house fronts. Centre of section facing north.*
- *PN5542 Tanu, Q.C.I. (1912) Haida. Same view as PN5541. North part of section facing east.*
- *PN5543 Tanu, Q.C.I. (inscribed 1929) Haida. "Flood story pole. Highest (carved) pole known . . . in the Q.C.I.*
- *PN9680 Skedans, Q.C.I. (1912) Haida. Inscribed on reverse: "East End." "Emily Carr photo."*
- *PN2807 Tsatsisnukwomi (1912) Kwakiutl. Easel shown in right lower corner. Large house; belongs to MEquilla (or moon). Four carved posts in front, D'Sonoqua in top row and male figures below. Large sisiutl reaching across the entire house front.*
- *PN2240 Tsatsisnukwomi (1912) Kwakiutl. House front.*

*** *I am extremely grateful to Dan Savard, Photographic Technician, Ethnology Division, BCPM, for his generous and invaluable assistance in all technical matters pertaining to these photographs. Although acquired with the Newcombe Collection after W.A. Newcombe's death in 1960, no extensive curatorial work has as yet been done on these photographs and the word "probably" is still advisable in assessing them.*

* *There are several spelling variants of this name, as of most other Indian place names.*

The exception, a view of "Tanou" (a rare spelling) bears the puzzling inscription, "By E.C. Stevens 1929." However, Emily was not on the Queen Charlottes that year, nor is the handwriting familiar. Thus, despite the 1929 date, this photograph obviously belongs to the 1912 Queen Charlotte Island group, and has been classified with it because:

1. The glass plates are similar
2. The grass is the same height
3. The inscription on another print of this subject is written by the same hand that inscribed the 1912 photographs.*

* *The fact that the "Stevens" print (PN5543) is numbered consecutively with PN5541 and PN5542 in the Ethnology Division, BCPM, and that PN5541 and PN5543 are numbered consecutively (24435 and 24436 respectively) in the PABC, also indicates that they were filed at the same time, from one source.*

Possibly all these inscriptions and initials are notes made by a member of the Museum staff, but more likely by W.A. Newcombe who, as co-trustee of all pictures and paintings in Emily's estate, may have wished to retain and catalogue the photographs for the Newcombe collection, while identifying them as Emily's property. But one thing is certain. Emily herself did not annotate them. Even the spelling is tell-tale. For she would have written "Tanoo" and "centre" not, as inscribed, "Tanu" and "center."

The fact that Emily's easel is shown in two prints* does not necessarily indicate that she was the photographer. It is merely evidence that she was in the vicinity. Perhaps she was eating lunch; perhaps cooling off in the shade of a tree; perhaps swatting mosquitoes, or even wading in a brook or off the beach, as she so often did when sketching. It would have been impossible for her to have taken at least one of the pictures because she herself is the subject of it! Oddly enough, Emily's revealing presence in this Tanu photograph* is not recorded in the *Bulletin* essay. Yet there she is, standing before her easel in the middle foreground painting a large sketch of the now familiar three-totem theme, a plump figure attired in her habitual northern painting garb and coiffed and masked with flowing mosquito netting. Two women sitting behind her on logs watch her at work.

* *PN5539, 2807.*

* *PN5541.*

Her companions on this sketching trip were Jimmie and Louisa, her Haida guides, and poor little "Miss Missionary," whom Emily and the two Indians treated roughly. The two women were undoubtedly the friends shown with Emily in the Tanu photograph, because no one else was in the party. No one else shared the "bitter-sweet of the overwhelming loneliness" of the villages except Jimmie. And Jimmie, a jack-of-all-trades of above average education, accustomed to act as guide and interpreter for roaming scientists and artists, had presumably acquired a certain useful and profitable knowledge of photography. Since he was the only one of the quartet not in the picture, it is logical to assume that he took this photograph plus the others in the Queen Charlotte Island group.

In the other two Tanu photographs depicting the three totem poles and house fronts against a background of coniferous trees,* the tall grass partially obscuring the poles is the same height. But in *Tanoo, Q.C.I.,* Emily's striking oil of the same subject painted the following year, the grass is so much shorter that the crest figures are exposed to the base of the poles. Emily explains:

* *PN5541, 5542.*

> Beyond the little point there were three fine house fronts. A tall totem pole stood up against each house, in the centre of its front. When Jimmie cut away the growth around the foot of them, the paint on the poles was quite bright. The lowest figure of the centre pole was a great eagle; the other two were beavers with immense teeth—they held sticks in their hands. All three base figures had a hole through the pole so that people could enter and leave the house through the totem.*

* Klee Wyck, *p.20.*

This quotation proves beyond doubt that Emily could not have painted her 1913 Tanu canvas from the photographs because these do not show the anatomical features of the lower crest figures that are so clearly visible and carefully delineated in sketch and painting. In fact the painting gives us a completely new and personal interpretation of Tanu. We see the poles in their entirety; the house fronts modified to meet the demands of design; the position of the logs on the reduced strip of beach contrived to give greater play of line; and the diagonal treatment of the freshly-cut grass, the rocking trees and racing cumulus clouds all add movement and interest to this fine, creative composition.

To claim that Emily took these photographs and later developed similar oil paintings from them shows a basic ignorance of her work and her work methods. There are of course similarities, even close similarities, but also basic differences. Whether by camera, brush, charcoal or pencil, totem poles and house fronts have to be reproduced from one particular vantage point for maximum effect. Like a nude or portrait, they are usually painted *en face.* Emily's oil on card, *Kwakiutl House,* for instance, is said to have been painted "with the aid of a watercolor sketch, *Tsatsinuchomi* [sic] . . . and a photograph taken in that village in 1912. . . ."* But even a superficial examination reveals

* *The spelling given here is misleading.* Tsatsinuchomi, B.C. *(VAG) is the title*

that the oil bears a very much greater resemblance to the field sketch than to the photograph. The same applies to the oil on canvas *Totem By The Ghost Rock,* which is totally unlike the photograph of the same subject, and to *Skedans, Q.C.I.*, one of Emily's largest and best oils of this period, which was hung at the National Gallery's exhibition of Canadian West Coast Art in 1927.* This painting is so completely different from the photograph that no comparison can be attempted. The high rocky hill that dominates the composition is much farther seaward in the photograph than in the painting, where it serves as a dramatic backdrop for a dozen or more weatherbeaten, wind-tilted totem poles that have been compressed into about half of their photographic space to make a tighter composition. The deep impression this weird, wild, deserted scene made on Emily as she sat on the beach sketching it can be sensed in her vivid description:

of a water colour of a single eagle totem (Carr 1971 No. 43) whereas the water colour in question is Tsatsisnukomi, Tribe Klawatsis *(VAG) (Carr 1971 No. 42). The photograph referred to is PN2807.*

* *As was* Tanoo, Q.C.I. *and* Totem By The Ghost Rock.

> Skedans Beach was wide. Sea-drift was scattered over it. Behind the logs the ground sloped up a little to the old village site . . . and a battered row of totem poles circles the bay; many of them were mortuary poles, high with square fronts on top. . . . Some of the mortuary poles were broken and you saw skulls peeping out through the cracks. . . . They (the poles) were in a long straggling row the entire length of the bay and pointed this way and that; but no matter how drunken their tilt, the Haida poles never lost their dignity. . . . They were bleached to a pinkish silver color and cracked by the sun, but nothing could make them mean or poor, because the Indians had put strong thought into them and had believed sincerely in what they were trying to express.*

* Klee Wyck, *pp.27-29.*

The Group 2 photographs (PN2807, 2240) of the Kwakiutl village Tsatsisnukwomi (New Vancouver), at the entrance to Knight Inlet,* are more difficult to analyse than those of Group 1. But the two negatives are of the same size and type, which suggests that the pictures were taken by the same photographer, though this time we have no clue as to his identity. However, since these two photographs are of fairly good quality, Emily's authorship, it seems to me, can be effectively ruled out owing to her known slipshod approach to all things technical.

It is therefore folly to state so flatly that Emily started taking her own photographs of totem poles in 1912. Such a notion is diametrically opposed to my memory of her and the

* *Tsatsisnukwomi is within sketching radius of Alert Bay where Emily is known to have worked in 1908 and 1912. Curiously, at least two oil paintings signed and dated 1912 (Carr 1971 Nos. 34 and 35) are up-dated copies of her own work: two water colours done in 1908 (Carr 1971 No. 9 and 10). However, the style of the paintings* Tsatsisnukomi, Tribe Klawatsis *and* Kwakiutl House *(Carr 1971 Nos. 42 and 44) with the same theme as the Museum photograph PN2807 makes them the product of the 1912 trip.*

opinions of Emily's other old friends who, on being questioned, said they had never known Emily to use or mention a camera. They recalled how Emily longed, each spring, to return to the old Indian villages, and later to the woods, because it was the "fresh meat" she brought home in her field sketches that formed the groundwork of her studio canvasses.*

* *BCPM, Dan Savard to author, April 26, 1977 (after several discussions about these photographs): "In short, after re-examining the photographs in our collection there is no evidence that Emily took these photographs."*

Frederick Brand, who knew Emily better than any of the other young men who sought her out in the thirties, sums up our collective feelings about Emily and a camera:

> No, I never saw a camera in Emily's house or hands. The two "objects" just do not go together—Emily and a camera. It's a laughable-absurd-stupid suggestion.*

* *Frederick shared Emily's apartment briefly in 1932 and for several months in 1933. He learned a great deal about her at that time.*

Nor, apparently, did Emily show any 1912 photographs to Dr. Newcombe, the anthropologist who assessed her Indian sketches for the British Columbia Government on her return from the north, though photographs would have interested him more than Emily's art.*

* *Dr. C.F. Newcombe, father of W.A. Newcombe. Report to the B.C. Provincial Secretary, December 1912.*

In the end it is Emily herself who tells us, in her own inimitable way, that she did not take her own photographs. In 1928, in an interview with a Toronto press reporter she said: "They [the Indians] had seen people making pictures with a box, but never before with the hands."* In other words, it was the scientists who used a camera to make a record of British Columbia's totem poles, but Emily used only her hands and a brush.

* *Muriel Brewster, "Some Ladies Prefer Indians,"* Toronto Star Weekly, *January 21, 1928.*

Two years later, in an address given to the Victoria Women's Canadian Club, Emily was still more specific about her disapproval of the camera as a painting aid:

> "Certain of the camera's limitations are now universally admitted. The camera cannot comment: The camera cannot select: The camera cannot feel, it is purely mechanical. By the aid of our own reinforcement we can perceive roughly what we desire to perceive and ignore, as far as is physically possible, what we do not desire to perceive. No work of real value is produced by an artist unless his hand obeys his mind. The camera has no mind."

In a familiar fairy tale of yore, gnomes or elves used to come at night to repair shoes left in a kindly old shoemaker's shop. Well, in this more modern tale, it is my hope that a few friendly gnomes or elves at the National Gallery will come at night to repair Emily's image. She has been accused of something she abhorred—copying, ... N... Gallery should set this right. How about it ...

Part 2

The Missing Water Colors

Another opinion expressed in the *Bulletin* essay under discussion also requires comment. We are told, but without supporting evidence, that Emily was repeatedly hindered in her work by a dearth of sketch material on which to base the elaboration of the Indian motif in her studio canvasses. But what about the vast number of water colors and charcoal drawings done during her recurrent journeys to Indian villages between 1898 and 1930? No hint is given as to what happened to these sketches. Such assumptions about Emily's life and work must be discouraged. They are too often wrong, too often inspired by an impulsive enthusiasm for discovery rather than for literal fact. They have disillusioned me with biography in general, and forced me into the uncomfortable, unwilling role of critic which I would not feel competent to fill except for one thing: I knew Emily. I lived with Emily; I believe that I understand her as well as anyone could; and I have studied her life minutely. On the basis of these studies and first-hand observation, I know that Emily never lacked the sketches she needed to develop her large oils, and am therefore perplexed to read that:

> After Carr's "discovery" in 1927, material to paint from did not become any more plentiful than before, though access to Newcombe's photographs allowed her to supplement her small collection.

This passage gives no clue as to whether "material to paint from" refers to photographs or water colors. And why the emphasis on the date 1927? It has no significance for Emily's career as it concerns production, and, besides, she had had access to Newcombe's photographs since she met him in 1912. But the idea of a deficiency of sketch material has been planted here and must be watched.

Of necessity Emily had to consult photographs occasionally to ensure accuracy of totem figures or the Indian designs she used on her pottery and rugs. But with one notable exception (the previously discussed *Blunden Harbour*), she did not, I believe, ever draw on photographs for the themes of her canvasses. Why should she have? Her own water color sketches gave her far better guidance than any photograph: The general controlling idea had already been determined; the composition worked out and pruned of non-essentials; crest figures boldly delineated to preserve totemic detail; and colors recorded—all on the spot. Later, in the studio, she frequently had little to do except copy and enlarge her own water colors, though at times she did several versions of one sketch that particularly stirred her imagination.

Emily regarded many of her field sketches as studies unsuitable for reworking into canvasses but nevertheless had an abundance of good ones to fall back on. As early as 1913, she already had almost 200 Indian pictures ready for exhibition, many "still in the sketch state." She painted relatively little between 1913 and 1927, but still managed to work in small Indian communities often enough to considerably augment her growing pile of water colors and other sketches in her "black box."

This long black coffin-like box, which doubled as a room divider in Emily's studio, was the repository for her sketches; and it was from this box, in 1927, that she selected twenty prime water colors (along with oils and panels) for shipment to the National Gallery of Canada by invitation of the Director, Eric Brown. Ten of these were framed by Brown and hung in the Gallery's *Third Annual Exhibition of Canadian Art* which opened on January 24, 1928.*

* *NGC, Brown to Emily, January 14, 1928. "Regarding the water colors, I have framed up ten of them and shall include them in our Annual Canadian show which opens on the 24th." (See also chapter "The Carr-Barbeau Mystery Story.")*

The black box also contained about thirty large water colors (as well as a lot of notes and a few oils) that Emily brought home from the North at the end of the summer of 1928—all excellent painting aids. Yet the essay persists that:

> Carr was often hard-pressed for material from which to paint. Though she traveled north during the summer of 1928 and gathered "quite a bunch of work" it was not sufficient. Paintings from the 1927 Indian and West Coast exhibition [sic], still held by the National Gallery were requested from the gallery's director: "Please Mr. Brown . . . may my watercolors be sent home to me as soon as possible—I want some of them to work from. . . ."*

* *NGC, Emily to Brown, October 1, 1928.*

This statement contains several inaccuracies, including the reference to the National Gallery's famous 1927 exhibition, correctly titled *Canadian West Coast Art.*

For one thing, the source of the quotation "quite a bunch of work" is not, as the author indicates in a footnote, a letter from Emily to Brown dated April 29, 1928, for how could Emily have known in April how much work she would be bringing home at the end of the summer? (If this is a typographical error, however, my full sympathies are enlisted. I shudder to think what may happen to my own dates and notes.)

Also, in her letter to Brown, for which the author gives the date "October 1928," Emily could not have been requesting Brown to return the water colors that had been exhibited at the *Canadian West Coast Art* exhibition because:

a) Only oils were exhibited at that show*

b) Her twenty water colors (less five that had been sold in the East) were returned to her in mid-April, 1928.

Emily was, in fact, demanding only the return of the eight water colors which were damaged in transit to Victoria in April and then returned by her to Ottawa for insurance appraisal.* This error of interpretation is the basis of the whole fallacious argument concerning Emily's lack of sketch material.

Emily could be sly. She did not suddenly need these damaged sketches—she had had most of them since 1912; seven fine examples had been returned from the National Gallery; and there were bundles more of them in the studio, including the thirty odd new ones she had brought back from the North about a month before. No, it was money she needed, and it was primarily her impatience to see her claim settled ("what have they [the insurance people] decided to do for me?") that prompted her to ask for the return of her pictures. When the insurance cheque for $200 arrived, she was jubilant. "How I wish some old duffer would buy [the pictures] outright," she wrote Brown wistfully.

There is one more quotation which, in fairness to Emily, must be questioned:

> Carr was again strapped (author's note: for painting material) in the autumn of 1930. She had been asked by the Seattle Art Institute to stage a solo exhibition in late November. By mid-November she was still working very hard in order to prepare thirty-two canvasses for the Seattle show. Even after her preparation of the Seattle show, she continued to find material where she could.

What is meant here by "preparing?" In this context it appears to imply that Emily had to scrounge around to assemble a sufficient number of sketches to paint thirty-two canvasses—a Herculean feat indeed, even had she had months instead of days at her disposal. But she herself told a friend that she was "some busy" getting thirty-two canvasses "off" to Seattle* and she

* *See Chapter "The Carr-Barbeau Mystery Story."*

* *National Museum of Man, Emily to Barbeau, May 5, 1928. "Did you know that the watercolors were ruined on the way home . . . eight are all spotted with oil marks. . . . Mr. Brown wrote me this a.m. to send them all back to Ottawa. . . . they are of course unsalable tho' will be all right for notes. . . . I want to use some of them.*

* *UBC Library, Nan Cheney Collection, Emily to Nan Cheney, November 11, 1930.*

meant precisely that. "Off" to Emily signified the usual last minute retouching, but the real work was finding, repairing and painting enough rickety frames to equip her exhibition—a time-consuming, arduous task.

I feel eminently qualified to describe Emily's activities at this particular moment because I was with her almost daily, involved as we both were in two other exhibitions that took place almost simultaneously—the Island Arts and Crafts Society Annual in Victoria and the Northwest Artists Annual in Seattle. I drove Emily and her entries for the former show to the reception center, and we packed our paintings for Seattle in the same crate to reduce expenses. I also helped her prepare and ship her solo Seattle exhibition.

The time factor alone precluded any possibility of painting new canvasses for Seattle. Emily visited friends there, for a few days I think, at the beginning of November in order to see the Northwest Artists exhibition,* and on return she only had two weeks to work on her Seattle solo show. Fresh oil paintings (and they were all oils) would not have dried, let alone hardened, enough to crate and ship by the 18th.* Consequently, Emily's problem was not shortage of painting material, but shortage of time.

* *UBC Library, Nan Cheney Collection, Emily to Nan Cheney, November 11, 1930.*

* *UBC Library, Nan Cheney Collection, Emily to Nan Cheney, November 11, 1930.*

Emily's water color collection reached its peak in 1930, a few months before the opening of her Seattle show when she returned from her last trip to Indian territory—this time to the Kwakiutl villages of northern Vancouver Island. From then on she painted no more in water color, and her collection gradually decreased during the thirties as she gave away some of her pictures to friends, burned many, and sold a few for a pittance. Sales picked up during the early forties, largely through Lawren Harris's devoted efforts and Dr. Stern's successful exhibition of her work in the fall of 1944. Twenty-eight water colors were on view in his Dominion Gallery and all, eventually, were sold.

Yet when Emily died the following year, the Newcombe Collection alone contained 108 water colors, or sketches done with a water color treatment. She bequeathed many more (along with oils and drawings), in trust, to Lawren Harris and Willie Newcombe as "Trustees of My Pictures," who sold a considerable number themselves. Others were disposed of by Dr. Stern at the time of his second solo exhibition of Emily's work in 1945. When the Vancouver Art Gallery assumed custodianship of the Emily Carr Trust Collection in 1946, the trustees added all unsold water colors and charcoal and brush drawings. There are also uncounted dozens in private hands, many purchased by or given to old friends of the Carr family well over a half century ago.

So where was the shortage of water colors? Emily, who was awash in them, would arch her quizzical eyebrows in astonishment.

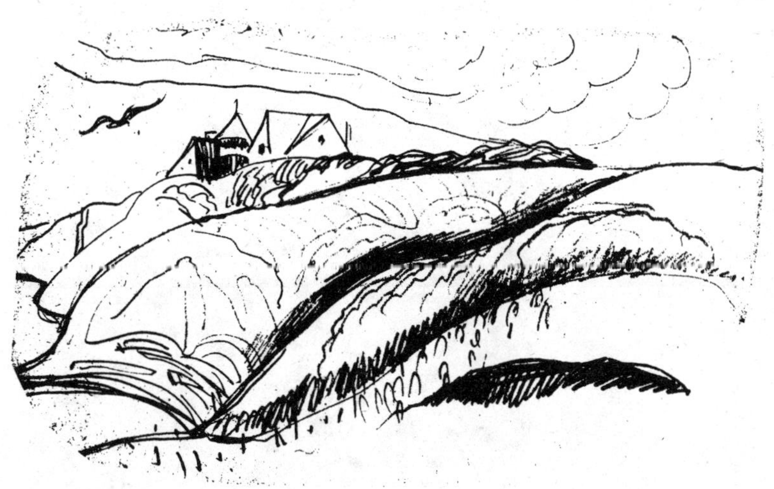

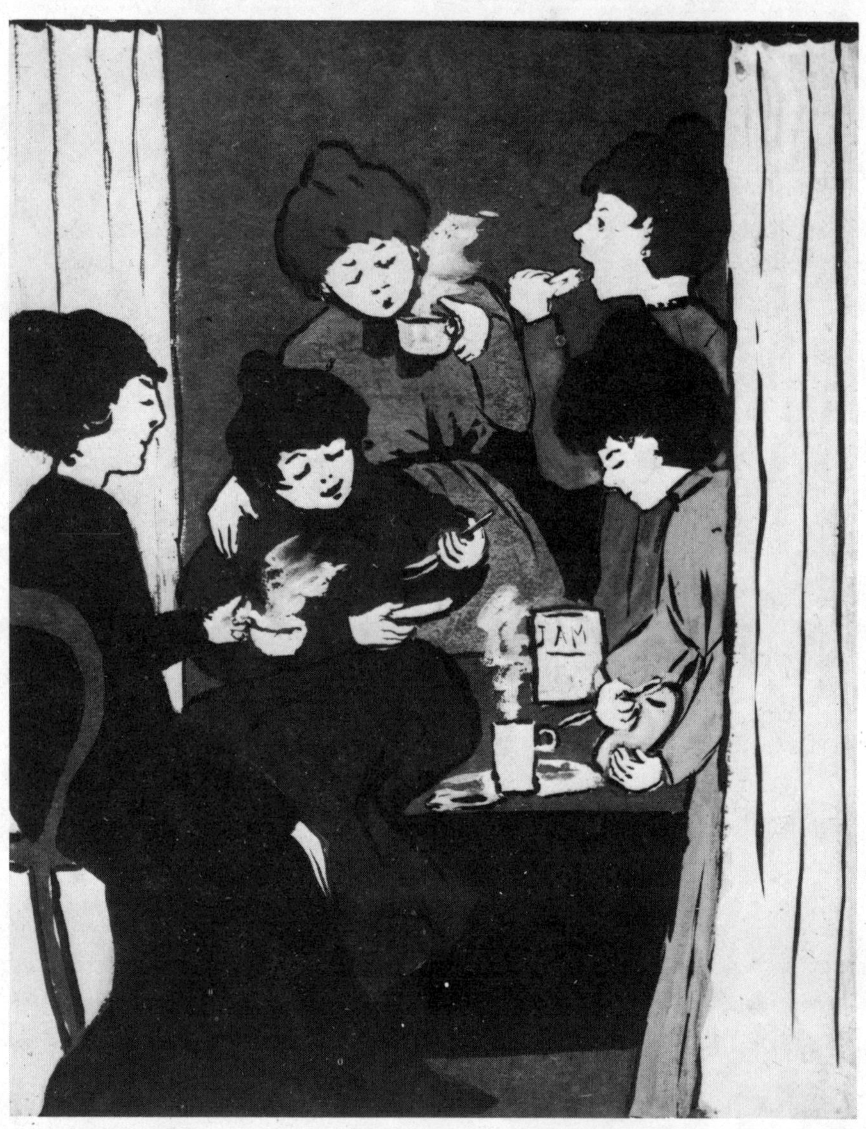
JAM

The Collapse of a Dream—the People's Gallery

While Emily Carr's proposed People's Gallery was being discussed in Victoria in 1932, she held a four-artist exhibition in the two lower flats of her House of All Sorts to give it publicity. She also had meetings in her studio with friends and supporters to plan ways and means of financing this project which wholly engrossed her attention at the time. This is one of the several reasons why an informed explanation of it should be given here, as errors of fact and interpretation are still in circulation.

The date of the abortive People's Gallery, and the exhibition connected with it, is nearly always given as 1935—even by the Vancouver Art Gallery.* The confusion arises from the fact that there was indeed an exhibition that year in the House of All Sorts—two of them to be exact—but they had nothing to do with the People's Gallery. By 1935 the agony of the People's Gallery was long since over.

There had been other exhibitions in Emily's house before this very special, though ill-fated one in 1932, but they had been held upstairs in her studio, since at least one of the two downstairs flats was always occupied. But now both "Lower East" and "Lower West" on the main floor fell vacant simultaneously and she had space for the first time to think in terms of a gallery. In the strict sense of the word, it was not a studio exhibition at all.

Fortunately Emily was an old hand at arranging her own exhibitions, forced as she was to display her work in the studio since she could never afford to exhibit in a commercial gallery. However, aside fom the practical aspect of these shows—the hope of selling a few paintings—she actually enjoyed having the public and friends flock to her studio, though she complained each time about the prodigious amount of work involved and the utter weariness afterwards. She enjoyed still more her informal tea-exhibitions when, one by one, she pulled out her latest sketches from the racks, clapped them on an easel and invited opinions from her assembled friends. But her "duty" teas, when she showed carefully selected (more conservative) pictures to members of the despised and ridiculed Island Arts and Crafts Society, always raised her hackles. An amusing description of one such "exhibition" was contained in a letter to me:*

* Emily Carr: A Centennial Exhibition *1971 edition, p.90. In the 1975 edition, p.90, it is changed to 1933—also wrong. The final collapse of the Gallery occurred at a meeting in January 1933, but it was started in 1932. (See chronology.)*

* *PABC, Emily to the author (undated) March 1939.*

> I don't think I've written since my Arts and Crafts tea? I invited nine old crones—all I know now in the Arts and Crafts Society—last Tuesday. They all hate each other and I expected bloodshed but we got over it with no red, mainly because Miss Crease could not come. I showed sketches, I invited them for 3.30 and all came within five minutes of the time! Then they all jammed into the sitting room and tead. It went off very well but I was tired. Had rather thought of an evening for some younger people but felt unequal. The old crones were pretty awful. Such silly little remarks. What you would expect canaries to make, but not so sweet. Complimentary fluff but no understanding about work or feeling and, being deaf, you know I don't hear half that is said.

Emily described this same tea-exhibition just as entertainingly, in a letter to another friend:

> Next Tuesday I am planning inviting six gikes into tea to view the pictures (nearly all Arts and Crafts stiffs). I believe some of same are at dagger points to the others so the day *may* end in bloodshed. Anyhow it will reek with sniffings—but there you are. Females are feline—it even comes out in budgerigars. All the hens are fighting tooth and nail, stealing each others nests *and* husbands. It's awful being J.P. in an aviary. I never realized until now that Parsons *do* earn their marriage fees.*

* *UBC Library, Emily to Nan Cheney, March 2, 1939.*

Emily's usual practice whenever she had a studio show was to insert a small, free-of-charge notice in the social column of the local newspapers inviting the public to come to her studio to view her work. They nearly always responded, which never failed to amaze her as she was convinced that Victoria hated her and her work. One wonders today how many came just to wile away a tedious afternoon or evening, or perhaps out of sheer curiosity since her studio was often a topic of gossip and always remained a strange and intriguing world for most people.

Although Emily and her work were already well-known in Victoria's art circles in 1932 (often for the wrong reasons), it took the People's Gallery proposal to introduce her and her paintings to the general public. For she managed to make her dream gallery a very lively issue for over two months. She was so absorbed and occupied in publicity for it, and in planning the opening exhibition, that she gave up her usual fall sketching trip—a rare exception.

The exhibition had to be organized first. Emily had a carpenter cut a door between the two lower flats in her house which gave her six well-lighted rooms to display the work. She herself was to be the chief contributor, but the choice of three other artists to exhibit with her was a ticklish matter. She had always vehemently supported the young moderns in Victoria—Jack Shadbolt, Max Maynard and myself, and wanted to ask us to participate. But in her determination to put on a popular show, and after a struggle with her conscience, she compromised her artistic principles and invited three very conservative painters: Robin Watt, a portraitist; Mrs. Fitzherbert Bullen, an English woman who favored pretty cottage scenes and, after the withdrawal of a flower painter, Lee Nan,* a Chinese boy whom Emily sponsored for a time, who painted Oriental birds and flowers in water color. Emily occupied one room with Indian canvasses and hung her "new and disliked work" in the two kitchens. The three others divided the rest of the space.

* *I have not been able to trace Lee Nan. No one in Victoria's Chinatown remembers him today. Even most of Cormorant Street, where he held his own exhibitions, has disappeared with him.*

Emily firmly believed that her motives for organizing a People's Gallery were purely altruistic, and was convinced that only the "common folk" or "humble people"—the butcher who delivered her meat, the coal-carrier, the milkman, her baker—were genuinely interested in art. As pointed out elsewhere, Emily, despite herself, was always class-conscious and could never have accepted these same tradesmen as friends, or even equals, but the naive notion "popped into [her] head" that they desperately needed a gallery that would enable artists to respond to their longing for meaningful art. She wanted to open a gallery that would be a warm and pleasurable place to visit on raw winter days; and she wanted it specifically for honest working people—not for snobs, dabblers, dilettantes or supercilious members of the "Arts and Crafts." But though Emily decried the attitudes of this group, some of whom would tolerate no innovations and denounced her work, she was nonetheless unable to quite break away as they were "of my own class . . . an extremely exclusive set."

A few friends* wisely tried to dissuade her from the whole idea, feeling it to be impracticable during the depression. How could the city administration pay out about one hundred dollars a month for rent and maintenance when people could not even pay their taxes to keep their homes? Who would control the finances and supervise the gallery? The friends also knew that Emily was a poor business-woman—unaware of the financial hazards of such an undertaking—and they were doubly fearful of the outcome since Emily had no reserve of capital to fall back

* *Frederick J. Brand, Assistant Professor of Mathematics at the University of British Columbia was one. Jack Shadbolt, who also tried to help Emily, may have been another.*

on. They felt that she exaggerated the "genuine" interest of the man in the street and certainly over-estimated the backing she could hope to obtain from the wealthy and influential. But Emily threw herself into this project body and soul, and most of us finally went along with her, propelled by the sheer force of her infectious enthusiasm.

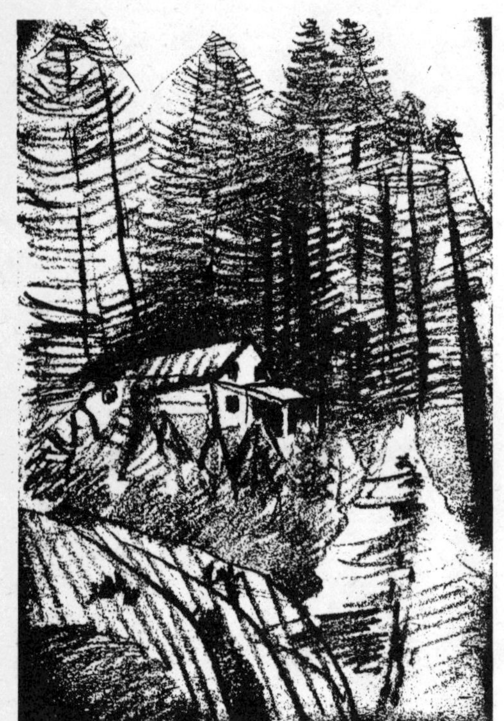

It is strange that Emily makes no mention in her journals of this attempt to establish a gallery, though the whole concept of a People's Gallery was close to her heart. The journals have no entries between September 28, 1931 and November 3, 1932. When she started writing again in November and December 1932, while these activities were taking place, there was no report at all. She only mentions her scheme very briefly in January 1933, but by then it had completely folded.

Emily's motives for initiating the gallery project were, I believe, twofold. She warmly believed in the idea she was promoting, but sometimes, when talking to her alone, I could sense the fear and the hard economics in which her idea originally took root. Her main source of income was rentals and she could find no tenants. She had no money. She was weary of the struggle to maintain her house. She was worried about the future. Therefore, had she been able to interest the city, or an influential group, to underwrite the expenses of founding and developing the gallery, she would have been successful on three fronts: assured income from the two lower flats; freedom from tenant troubles and irritations; and the excitement and interest of contributing to the success of a venture that was her brainchild.

Emily worked hard to publicize her scheme. She outlined her proposals in a written report which was read at the first meeting of interested people. The plan seemed to gather momentum for a while, and the friends and well-wishers who had rallied to her cause did their limited best to support her. It was further discussed at another meeting held on December 14 and reported in the press under the heading, "People's Gallery Plan is Under Consideration":

> A plan for the creation of a people's gallery, which would be open to the public seven days a week and in which pictures of all types, conservative, progressive, oriental, children's and many others would have impartial opportunity for exhibition" was considered by a representative group of Victoria citizens that met last evening at the studio of Miss Emily Carr, 646 Simcoe Street, at her invitation. At the end of a

> lengthy discussion, Jack Shadbolt, chairman of the informal proceedings, was named convenor. . . . others taking part in the discussions were Miss J. Crease, Mrs. Fitzherbert Bullen, Miss Agnew, Max Maynard, Miss Hembroff, Mrs. Nairn. . . . The cost of ninety-five dollars monthly was estimated to be the approximate cost of operating such a gallery.*

* *Victoria* Daily Colonist, *December 15, 1932.*

Emily also composed a form letter which she typed and sent to people whom she particularly hoped to interest. Willie Newcombe's copy, to which she has added the footnote: "Come and boost a mighty *Boost* for the *National Gallery*" still survives* and reads:

* *PABC.*

> Please can you spare time on Wednesday next, December 14, at 8:15 p.m. to attend an exhibiton of pictures to be given at 646 Simcoe Street, corner of Douglas (just below the Kiwanis pool) and to discuss with me the possibility of converting the lower portion of the premises 646 Simcoe Street into a small art gallery for the people of Victoria, for which it is well situated and well suited.
>
> Perhaps you may think that this is a poor time to propose such things, and certainly it would not seem the time to approach the city and its over-burdened tax-payers. But these days, perhaps as never before, the people need things that will turn their minds, even for a brief spell, from money perplexities. In the winter months the band does not play in the park. A short spell in the gallery would break the monotony and induce the growth and better understanding of art among our citizens, especially if short talks were added also.
>
> It is not a costly undertaking that I propose and if the various clubs and societies of Victoria as well as interested individuals could see their way to each give a very little financial help and a big bit of kindly interest, I feel we might develop something worthwhile and very fine.
>
> Exhibitions could be changed fortnightly and would comprise conservative, progressive and children's work.
>
> The exhibition to which I invite you next Wednesday evening will be drawn from the work of four outstanding artists. I earnestly ask of you to

come and to examine the idea yourselves.

Sincerely, M. Emily Carr

Poor, dear Emily! Her hopes of having a studio upstairs free of worry and encumbrance and a publicly-financed gallery downstairs to display, and perhaps even sell, a few paintings were quickly dashed. "Perhaps," she said despairingly, "if taxes go on increasing and rentals decreasing, the city will get the house anyhow. For nothing!"

She wrote a pathetic lament on the demise of her People's Gallery to Eric Brown, Director of the National Gallery:

> She's dead. There was a meeting two nights ago when she should have been decently buried as *'we'* (the workers) wished. But *'they'* (the talkers) insisted on pricking another kick out of her so the obsequies are postponed until next week when the 'talkers' will fail to turn up and the 'workers' will have to be corpse, parson, hearse and pallbearers all conglomerate. . . . The Lieutenant-Governor was approached as a patron and he said it was a fine scheme and he heartily approved. But, on the small, simple scale suggested, he could not think of lending his name to a little thing in a private house in a quiet district. Now, if we would buy a *city* lot, put up a fireproof building of fine appearance, I suppose aiming to outdo Vancouver, he *might* be willing to lend us a set of Dürer's drawings he had. He knew at least twenty people in Victoria who would subscribe $500 each. I notice he did not give names nor tap his own cheque book. . . . Well, anyhow, I'm not sorry I tried. It's set some thinking and some day, somehow, something may come of it.*

* *NGC, Emily to Eric Brown, January 20, 1933.*

But will it? Suggestions have been made, articles written, but after the elapse of more than forty years nothing has come of it, and it may soon be too late.* The house is now in a sad state of repair, crumbling in spots, but still waiting stubbornly, in its prime location adjacent to Victoria's lovely Beacon Hill Park, to fulfil Emily's dream. The great painted Indian eagles which she always felt protected her and her house for the twenty-three years she lived there, still spread their wings over the inside whitewashed roof of her attic eyrie where she sought solitude and peaceful restoration in times of despair. When she moved out, she consoled herself with the thought that the eagles would watch over her house forever since they could not be removed

* *Since writing this chapter, an elegant, if very small Emily Carr Gallery has been created by the B.C. Provincial Government in an artistically restored building on Wharf Street: Victoria. Opened to the public on July 8, 1977. (See: PABC brochure, "A Cluster of Sunburst—Our Emily" by the author.)*

without tearing off the roof. But time and neglect can remove them too, and will, if something is not done soon to restore and preserve them as they are deteriorating rapidly. They have also become invisible eagles—almost inaccessible to would-be viewers due to the extensive alterations made to the house when Emily left. False ceilings were installed, leaving the eagles only a crawl space to brood over, and the ladder-like stairs which led to the attic from both hall and studio were ripped out.

The House of All Sorts is now a provincially-designated historic site and it is the hope of Emily's friends and admirers that the Government will buy and restore it, and open it to the public for suitable uses, preferably in accordance with Emily's wish. The people of the Province and especially the citizens of Victoria, owe her that much.

But back in January 1933, in despair about the collapse of her dream project, Emily poured out her heartfelt disappointment and bitterness in fifteen stanzas of touching, jingling verse. A few will suffice to show her complete disillusionment:

(1) Young Ideal was seeking a lodging
And by luck she came my way
"May I come in? Do you want me?
I'd love to come to stay.

(2) Her face was as fair as the morning
Eyes blue as the Heaven above
For the Father of her was Vision
and the Mother of her was love.

(5) And when we were well acquainted
My little Ideal and I
I called to folks about me
The lowly, the middle and high

(9) They took my simple Ideal
and decked her in gaudy gear
They swathed her in convention
and bound her with doubt and fear

(15) Like bulbs in a winter garden
Tucked safe in their sodden black bed
Little Ideal lies silent and dormant
Sleeping safe till spring comes—
No! Not Dead!

Although Emily's verses end on a note of optimism, she never forgave Victoria for not supporting her in 1932. Ten years later, when writing her third book, *The House of All Sorts*, she retells the story of the People's Gallery. The account has mellowed a little with time. The fire, the ire, of the great thirties decade had receded by then, illness had sapped her energy, and she describes the unhappy events of that time with a measure of detachment. Possibly she even thought, as her friends did, that it had all turned out for the best since a rented gallery in her house might well have caused her more frustrations, agitation and noise—to which she was unusually susceptible—than two flats full of tenants.

In this new version of the People's Gallery, some details have become blurred and a little distorted, others forgotten. The sting, the bitterness have been replaced by telling sarcasm intended to shame the Lieutenant Governor, the Mayor, the Superintendent of Parks and, in general, all wealthy and influential citizens of Victoria. However, the main attack, as spirited as ever, was reserved for her favorite scapegoat, the Island Arts and Crafts Society, whose members she had petulantly refused to invite to her People's Gallery. She cannot resist one more jab:

> The Club held exhibitions, affairs of tinkling teacups, tinkling conversation and little tinkling landscapes weakly executed in water colors. None except their own class went to their exhibitions. A baker, a coal-carrier! Good gracious!*

* The House of All Sorts, *p.92.*

Emily was hard on the Island Arts and Crafts—as intolerant of the members as some of the members were of her. But many of them had a sincere and honest approach to painting, some timidly admired Emily's work and, as a group, they at least went to the trouble and expense of organizing annual exhibitions—which Emily nearly always attended and in which she nearly always exhibited.

The People's Gallery exhibition was considerably less successful than Emily recalls, somewhat over-enthusiastically, in her *The House of All Sorts.* There was a fairly satisfactory turn-out, but certainly no throng. In fact, when she re-opened it to the public for three days between Christmas and New Year's, only one person came the first day, four the second and fourteen the third.* She degraded the Lieutenant Governor's "set of Dürer's drawings" to "two small etchings," and failed to mention that both downstairs flats were empty for several months, and that the consequent serious reduction in her income was one of her main reasons for promoting the Gallery at all. She simply states: "I closed the connecting door between the suites and again rented Lower East and Lower West as dwellings." Just like that! As if it had been a matter of choice and that renting, before and

* *NGC, Emily to Eric Brown, January 3, 1933.*

after the Gallery affair, had been no problem at all.

If Emily were alive today I am sure she would wish to see her house used as a revived People's Gallery to house exhibitions for ordinary people. But in the thirties, she was far too Victorian in her attitudes to be consistently for the people all the time. She could be for them one week and then, annoyed perhaps by the butcher, berate them the next. Eleven years after her Gallery's collapse, for instance, in a letter of advice to a young friend,* she expressed views diametrically opposed to those she had professed in 1932:

> The (Vancouver Art) Gallery seems very active. I don't know if I think the messy public masses are a great advantage to art. They just go to stuff tea and be entertained. I think a few thoughtful souls progress art more. Does their babbling trash *mean* anything?

The whole story of the People's Gallery is full of contradictions. But then, as we all know by now, Emily was full of tantalizing contradictions herself.

* *Myfanwy Spencer Pavelic.*

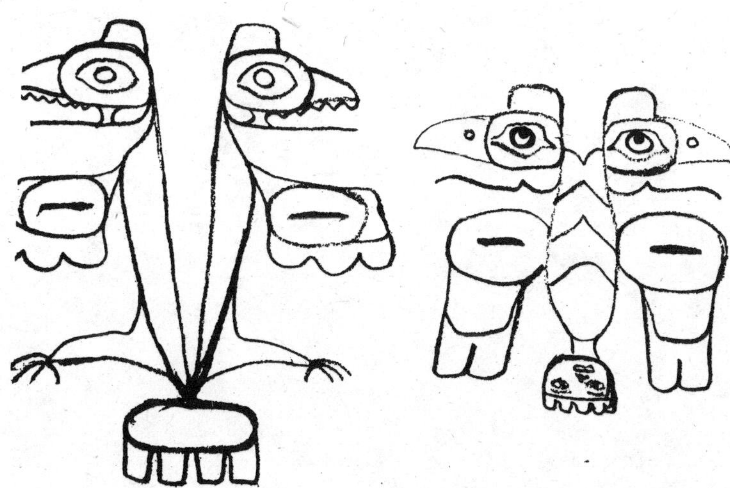

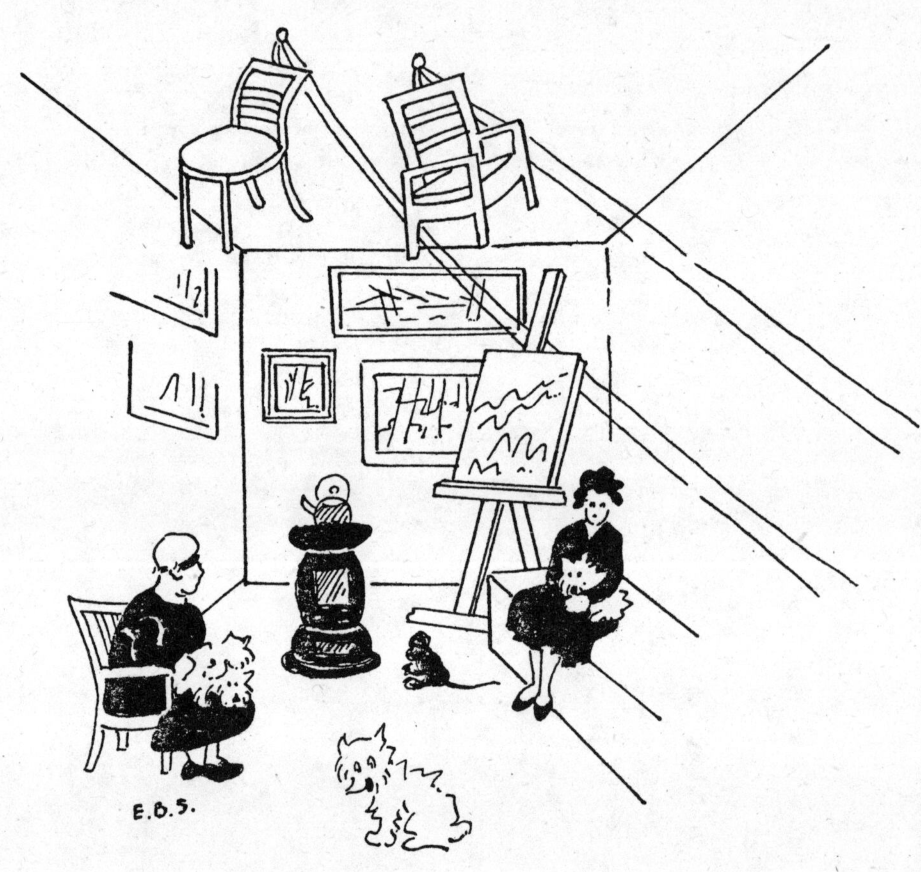

Emily and Edythe in the studio at Simcoe Street. (House of All Sorts) Edythe Hembroff-Schleicher

Notes on Six Emily Carr Paintings

The "Notes" that follow found their way into my book by sheer chance—through a misunderstanding with Charles C. Hill of the National Gallery of Canada while he was in Vancouver supervising the installation at the Vancouver Art Gallery of his impressive exhibition, *Canadian Painting in the Thirties*. For anyone like myself who was painting during that decade, "fascinating" would be a better adjective to describe it. My only regret is that so few of my painter friends in Vancouver qualified for inclusion in the exhibition or in the text of the exhibition catalogue. But at least Emily comes first in Charlie's list of the three figures who dominated painting in British Columbia during that period. Fred Varley and Jock Macdonald are the other two.

Charlie telephoned from Vancouver to say that he would like me to appear in a half-hour film being produced jointly by the National Gallery and the National Film Board to be made up of a series of interviews on the painters selected for his exhibition. He wanted me to do the Emily Carr segment and, or so I thought, to discuss during the interview the six Carr paintings in his exhibition. He said he would be over in Victoria in a few days with a crew and was sending me a catalogue immediately.

I took on this assignment less than willingly as the dating of the six exhibition pictures (which is what it amounted to) would involve me in a very sensitive and complex area. However, by working practically night and day, I was ready for Charlie when he and his two film-makers arrived—over an hour late as they had queued up for the wrong ferry.

Charlie had a bad cold and I was nervous. The film crew was busy pushing furniture around to make room for their equipment when I suddenly became aware, from their conversation with Charlie, that I was not expected to dispense wisdom on the subject of Emily's paintings, but only to reminisce about her as a friend. I was stunned that I had done so much unnecessary work because of a stupid blunder, but this explains why I now have these unplanned and unused "Notes" on hand. I feel they are too useful to discard or stow away in a filing cabinet to be forgotten, particularly as Charlie says they are helpful, and have therefore decided to reproduce them here, in the full knowledge that they may be of little general interest. I apologize for any repetition of material used in "The Sketching Trips," but there must inevitably be some overlapping in these two areas.

After working with catalogues for more than three years—longer than it took Charlie to prepare his exhibition—I claim to be something of an authority on the subject. Many catalogues seem so hurriedly put together, lack essential data and make dull reading. But Charlie's has none of these faults. He examines the art of a whole decade, comments on it with authority, and has produced a catalogue that is scholarly, highly professional and, at the same time, very readable. It amazes me that he has been able to research so many painters, so exhaustively, in so short a time, when I have had so much trouble with one. However, since I still know Emily better than he does, perhaps, on the basis of these "Notes," he will decide to use some of my dates for his six paintings in any future revision of his catalogue, instead of depending too much on those assigned by the Vancouver Art Gallery.

NOTES ON SIX EMILY CARR PAINTINGS

Selected by Charles C. Hill
Assistant Curator, Post-Confederation Art
The National Gallery of Canada
for his exhibition

CANADIAN PAINTING IN THE THIRTIES

arranged by the National Gallery of Canada

This exhibition was shown in 1975 at the National Gallery of Canada, Ottawa, the Vancouver Art Gallery and the Art Gallery of Ontario, Toronto. A reduced version traveled to Calgary, Edmonton, Saskatoon and Montreal.

Reproductions of the six paintings appear in Charles Hill's exhibition catalogue nos. 28-33.*

* *Exhibition catalogue* "Canadian Painting in the Thirties" *by Charles C. Hill. The National Gallery of Canada for the Corporation of the National Museums of Canada, Ottawa, 1975.*

GREY c. 1931 *My date: 1932*
canvas
NGC cat. no. 28
44 x 27½ in.
provenance: purchased from the artist c. 1937*
VAG (Carr 1971 no. 69)
collection: Mrs. Charles S. Band, Toronto

* *1937 is the exact date. See* Hundreds and Thousands, *p.287.*

The original signed and dated sketch for this painting was done in May 1932 when Emily and I were sketching on Braden Mountain which towers over the narrow road linking Goldstream Park and Metchosin, where she did most of her sketching in later years. The sketch was purchased the same year by John McDonald, Vancouver, one of Emily's small group of devotees in the thirties. The canvas derived from it, *Grey*, was also painted in 1932, probably in the fall.

The sketch for *Grey* was nameless when John purchased it and he himself gave it the title *Forest Interior*. This is unfortunate as it duplicates the title of a sketch (Emily's choice this time) shown at the University of British Columbia Library in March 1933.

Done in a monochrome of black, grey and white, this canvas, *Grey*, was at first one of Emily's favorites. Five years later though, when it was purchased by Charles S. Band, the first important collector to acquire Carr paintings, she had already begun to have reservations. When Band, wavering in his selection, asked Emily if *Grey* was one of her first choices, she replied: "Yes and no. I did like it and many people have liked it, but since painting it my seeing has perhaps become more fluid."*

* Hundreds and Thousands, *p.287*.

TREE

c. 1931 — *My date: 1931*
canvas — VAG date: c. 1929-1930
NGC cat. no. 29
50¾ x 22 in.
provenance: The Emily Carr Trust, 1942 [sic]
VAG (Carr 1971 no. 64)
VAG cat. no. 42.3.2

The dates of all six Carr pictures in the National Gallery exhibition agree with those assigned by the Vancouver Art Gallery, with the notable exception of *Tree* (cat. no. 29).* Charlie Hill did the right thing when he changed the date from c. 1929-1930 to c. 1931. In fact, he could have safely omitted even the "circa," as 1931, in my opinion, can be regarded as a completely verified date. Unfortunately, the name of this canvas has been changed and it has thus ended up in VAG, and therefore in Charlie's exhibition, with the wrong title. This is a pity, as it is confusing to find two pictures out of six, in one catalogue, with the same name. No one could say now when, why and by whom the name was changed, but perhaps more work on exhibition catalogues would provide a clue. But my probing so far has

* *Not to be confused with cat. no. 31 in the exhibition catalogue which has the same title.*

yielded the surprising fact that in 1941, when this canvas was selected as one of the Emily Carr Trust pictures, it was called *Tree Trunk* and was No. 1 on the list of non-Indian subjects. The size given on the Trust list (50 x 21½ in.) does not exactly tally with Charlie's correct dimensions (50¾ x 22 in.), but the painting has been given other measurements over the years and these two are remarkably close considering how casually all Trust pictures were measured initially. The trustees recognized nothing under one-half inch—indeed, most sizes were quoted in round inches.* Besides, Emily rarely used such a long, narrow format. The only other true Trust picture which approximates it in size is an Indian subject, *Masset Pole* (50 x 21 in.)*

* *VAG, for instance, negligently gave no measurements at all for the long list of paintings placed in their custody by the Trustees in 1966.*

* *There were two paintings* Masset Pole *in the Emily Carr Trust list. The second one, however, was sold to the Glenbow Foundation in December 1955. The Trust measurements for the picture were 27" x 44". Glenbow's were 42½" x 27".*

I suggest, therefore, that this painting be re-named *Tree Trunk*. The title is historically accurate and eliminates confusion.

According to the list of exhibitions for this *Tree* (cat. no. 29), it was shown for the first time at the Island Arts and Crafts exhibition in Victoria in 1932. The listing, however, is preceded by a question mark. But in view of the change of title, and the very strong probability that *Tree* was called *Tree Trunk* throughout the thirties as well as in 1941 and perhaps later, I believe that the 1932 listing for this painting can be transferred, without question mark, to *Tree* (cat. no. 31). In my opinion, *Tree* (*Tree Trunk*) was first exhibited at the University of British Columbia Library in 1933.

Tree, or *Tree Trunk* hung in the most prominent place in Emily's studio—near the fireplace on a large windowless wall opposite the big north window. From the time she finished it in 1931, to 1936 when she gave up the House of All Sorts, it was permanently on display in the select company of such other famous favorites as *Vanquished, Big Raven, D'Sonoqua of the Cat Village,** *Totem Mother* and *Blunden Harbour*. It only disappeared from its accustomed place to travel to a very occasional exhibition.

* *Also called:* Zunoqua of the Cat Village.

Charlie recognizes that Emily would have rejected any identification of sexuality in her work, but in the belief that one can unconsciously express sexual symbols in painting, has written in his catalogue the following interesting passage about the two paintings so far discussed in these "Notes":

> The glowing interior fires of *Grey* contrast with the external thrust of *Tree* (c. 1931, cat. no. 29). Almost surreal representations of female and male sexual energies, they are the most intense and concentrated expressions of Emily Carr's vision of the dynamism of her natural surroundings.

Emily could never understand the comments of critics.

They amazed her: "They find things in my pictures I never even thought of," she said. She was even more blunt after reading Dr. Sedgewick's review of her work exhibited at the University of British Columbia in 1936: "What rubbish these critics are!" When she was painting the towering cedars at Goldstream, such as *Tree* (or Tree Trunk), with their long hanging fronds and scraggly branches, they reminded her of ancient bewiskered men. She tried to express the surge and growth of the big trees, their seeming immortality and everlasting existence with God. Her thoughts, while painting them, were solely religious, and therefore, any implied manifestation of sex, no matter how well considered, is, to me, a jarring note in Charlie's criticism. But I protest this mildly, as I myself do not fully understand what is meant by "almost surreal representations of female and male energies. . . ." Emily would have understood it still less, but the word "sex" alone would have been enough to infuriate her. She would have made mincemeat of the critic (meaning Charlie) or at the very least have "stuck him with a hat-pin"—a weapon she would have liked to use on many a contemporary critic.

However, Charlie is not the only person to see sexuality in Emily's painting. As I recall, Jack Shadbolt has said much the same thing. But Lodewyk Bosch, a writer and painter from Holland, was the first to voice such a daring opinion—daring that is for the early thirties. Bosch exerted considerable influence on the young modern artists in Victoria for a time and his studio in town became an exciting rendezvous. But Emily remained aloof. However, after she and I returned from camp in 1931, I gained permission to take Bosch to her studio to see her Cordova Bay sketches. Unfortunately, not realizing how prudish Emily was, he was tactless and gauche enough to suggest that he detected phallic forms in her beach and log studies. Emily took off like a rocket, showed Bosch the door unceremoniously and never allowed him to return. Thereafter she always referred to him as "that Dutch Turkey," which was a little hard and unforgiving as he was among the very first to show intelligent and even prophetic appreciation of her work. In a newspaper article in 1930, he stated that he was "staggered" on seeing such imaginative and creative work in British Columbia and could not believe that Canada remained so totally indifferent to Emily's powerful and inspired work.

A RUSHING SEA OF UNDERGROWTH

c. 1932-1934 *My date: 1935*
canvas
NGC cat. no. 30
44 x 27 in.
provenance: The Emily Carr Trust, 1942 [sic]
VAG (Carr 1971 no. 84)
VAG cat. no. 42.3.17

Because I have a rather special knowledge of this canvas, I feel competent to disagree with the date assigned to it by both the Vancouver Art Gallery and Charlie. It was first exhibited at the Vancouver Art Gallery in October 1938 as *Sea of Growth* (a woodscape), evidently Emily's early name for it, but by 1941 when it, too, was selected as an original Trust picture, it already bore its present title. After the Vancouver Art Gallery show was over, I myself hung this painting, and many others drawn from the Gallery show, in the Library of the University of British Columbia at an exhibition held there in November, as Emily had put me in full charge of arrangements. I had often seen this canvas in her studio and when working in Toronto in 1974, also saw the undated sketch, *Untitled* (forest landscape),* from which it was derived. Though I did not see either of them being painted, I cannot accept the relatively early date assigned to them.

* *In the collection of University College, University of Toronto, and hangs in the Women's Union on St. George Street. It was purchased from the Fine Art Galleries, Eaton's College Street, by Marion Ferguson, then Dean of Women, University College, on April 22, 1949. (Sybille Pantazzi, Librarian, AGO, to author July 4, 1975).*

I have no real proof to offer for my date (1935), but I was intimately connected with Emily during 1932-34, saw all her work, and honestly feel that neither the sketch nor the canvas was done then. She did many such undergrowth studies and, though it is easy to confuse them after so many years, I know that most of them were painted the year *before* and the year *after* the assigned dates, that is, 1931 and 1935.

Emily made her first experiments with rolling and weaving salal and bracken in the so-called rain forest part of Goldstream Park in September 1931, and intensified her study of the subject when working out of her caravan near Albert Head in 1935. I feel, rather than know, that the sketch was done then (1935) and the canvas soon after. The glimpses of a vivid, bright blue sky behind the pines in the canvas are typical of her 1935 work and she was never as preoccupied with jungle growth before or after.

Let's examine the years 1932 to 1934 suggested by the Vancouver Art Gallery and Charlie as the date of origin. In May 1932, in the remote wilds of Braden Mountain with me, Emily was painting the much bigger trees of a deeper forest than shown in this painting. As an exception, she did no field work at all that fall. In the spring of 1933, she was painting the mountains of the Interior and it seems highly unlikely that the sketch was done there. It could perhaps have been painted during her second trip to Goldstream in August-September 1933, but knowing from visits to her then, how and what she painted, I believe this can be ruled out. She did little work at all during this visit to Goldstream and none that satisfied her. It was one of her least productive field trips and she worked entirely in the "Flats," or the big cedar side of the stream. The "jungle" was farther away from the van.

The 1934 sketching trips are equally doubtful as "The Elephant" was located first on a beach and then in an open field on a farm. The woods she worked in then had been logged over leaving only spindly trees and stumps as material for Emily. There was no underbrush.

Instinct, memory and reasoning tell me that Emily painted *A Rushing Sea of Undergrowth* from a 1935 sketch after returning from camp in the fall. It was perhaps done in November. At any rate she wrote in her journals on the 28th of that month: "Working on jungle. How I want to get that thing! Have not succeeded so far but it fascinates."

Whether or not my assumed date, 1935, for both sketch and canvas is accepted, it is much more accurate than the c. 1932-1934 date so far assigned to it.

TREE c. 1932-1933 *My date: 1932*
oil on paper
NGC cat. no. 31
35 x 23⅜ in.
provenance: The Emily Carr Trust, 1942 [sic]
VAG (Carr 1971 no. 87)
VAG cat. no. 42.3.63

There is not much I can say about this oil on paper sketch with any degree of certainty. I recall seeing Emily painting it, but cannot say where or when. However, it is not typical of her 1931 or 1933 work at Goldstream Park and I would therefore opt for 1932. It was probably painted on Braden Mountain in May of that year, and first shown at the Island Arts and Crafts Society exhibition in Victoria the following October. (See *Tree* cat. no. 29)

OVERHEAD c. 1935 *My date: 1936*
oil on paper
NGC cat. no. 32
24 x 36 in.
provenance: The Emily Carr Trust, 1942 [sic]
VAG (Carr 1971 no. 105)
VAG cat. no. 42.3.69

The subject matter is the clue to the dating of this oil on paper sketch. It could not have been done in 1935 as the view from Albert Head, where she camped that year, is quite different. Even the 1934 site would have shown a broken coast line. But in 1936, the row of hills across the bay (actually Victoria with the buildings left out), which runs straight across this picture, is what Emily would have seen from her location close to the Spencer sheep farm and the gravel pit—her nearest sketching site to town. My date, therefore, would be 1936.

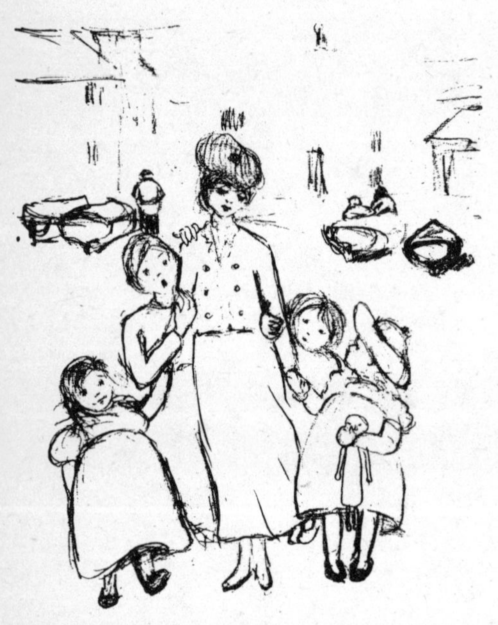

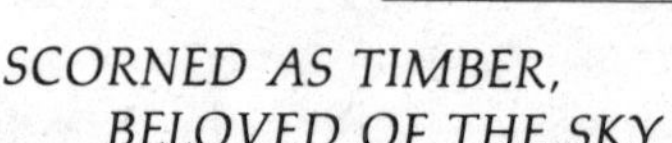

SCORNED AS TIMBER,
BELOVED OF THE SKY
c. 1936 *My date: 1935*
canvas
NGC cat. no. 33
44 x 27 in.
provenance: The Emily Carr Trust, 1942 [sic]
VAG (Carr 1971 no. 108)
VAG cat. no. 42.3.15

Scorned . . . is a painting I watched grow in Emily's studio once she let me look behind the dust sheet. She never allowed anyone, even me, to see a canvas in its beginning stages. She first worked briefly from the sketch, but as soon as she had taken her central and controlling idea from it, she usually discarded it and developed the canvas without referring to it again. Many changes were generally incorporated into the final work, and it was only when she felt that she had progressed beyond the point where criticism could influence her that she removed the dust sheet from the painting to invite comment.

Emily often talked about this canvas, as the idea she had tried to express was important to her. The little rejected tree, striving mightily to reach heaven itself, lifted her spirits and was meant to lift ours.

Once again I differ with the NGC and VAG dating of this canvas, though only by one year. The sky treatment at first suggests 1934 or 1936, Emily's two great sky years, but an examination of the 1935 *dated* canvas, *Loggers' Culls* (Carr 1971 no. 106), reveals exactly the same spindly tufted pine as in *Scorned....* In fact, the theme of *Scorned...* was in all likelihood lifted from the same sketch as *Loggers' Culls*. Now, if the canvas *Scorned...* had been painted in 1936, it could scarcely have been exhibited at the University of British Columbia early February that year—which it was*—particularly as Emily was visiting me in Vancouver in January.* No, both the sketch and canvas were painted in 1935, as were others of similar subject, such as the canvas *Odds and Ends* (Carr 1971 no. 116), collection: the Greater Victoria Public Library. Charlie Hill lists October 1938 (the Vancouver Art Gallery) as the date *Scorned...* was first exhibited, which is not correct.

* *See Exhibition III List.*

* Hundreds and Thousands, *pp.217-218.*

Loggers' Culls was also first exhibited in 1936 when it was accepted (one of three entries) for the *Contemporary Canadian Painting* exhibition, arranged on behalf of the Carnegie Corporation of New York for circulation in the southern dominions of the British Empire.

Emily herself has led us astray on the date *Scorned...* was first exhibited. In an undated entry in her journals, which, however, follows the entry of February 8, 1935, she writes that this canvas* had recently been exhibited along with *Blunden Harbour*. But the date of the entry should be February *1936*.* There were no Carr exhibitions at all in British Columbia in 1935 except two she put on herself in The House of All Sorts. Something is inexplicably wrong with this entry as the original journal is a continuous document from February 8 (1935) dating through several separate passages to a section which bears the heading "March."*

* Hundreds and Thousands, *p.171. Emily does not give the exact title, but her description makes it obvious that* Scorned *... is the picture under discussion.*

* *This conclusion is further strengthened on p.172 when Emily writes: "I had visitors, an artist that also showed at the Vancouver show ..." She refers here to Delisle Parker who was a contributor to the UBC show in 1936.*

* *Memorandum of April 21, 1976 from Ruth DonCarlos, Trade Editor, to W.H. Clarke, Executive Vice President of Clarke, Irwin and Company Limited. The original journals were then in the possession of Clarke, Irwin.*

Everything Emily says about *Scorned...* points to our February 1936 exhibition at the University. She writes that *Blunden Harbour* and the "little spindly tree," (in *Scorned...*) were selected for special comment by a professor of English at the University* and blasted him for his criticism of the latter painting:

* *Dr. G.G. Sedgewick, Head of the English Department at UBC in 1936 who selected the two paintings for criticism. (Victoria* Times, *February 23, 1936.*

> The criticism was flowery.... the fact that the canvas was a sky study entirely missed them (that is the critics).... They called it "the thicket." It was only incidental. The sky was the subject.

In my opinion, the above analysis is abundant proof that 1935 is the correct date for both sketch and canvas. The evidence of *Loggers' Culls* alone is enough to verify it, even without the added proof of the 1936 University exhibition.

Emily believed that she had not managed to get her point across about the skyscape *Scorned* . . . as everyone, critics and viewers alike, thought the subject to be the slender little pine. To my mind, this striving and determined tree symbolizes all Emily's own striving and aspirations—both in painting and religion. In 1945 the noted critic, Paul Duval, claimed it to be one of her most important pictures and called it the artist's spiritual self-portrait. But Emily herself did not consider she had painted a really successful canvas. She wondered if it was not "her stupidity in blundering to the point" that prevented the beholder from seeing the sky as the subject. Why then did she focus attention on the tree in the title?

Whatever the subject, and whether or not she failed to help us see it, this superb painting has inspired at least one poet to express his feeling for it in verse. California-born Charles Lillard wrote "*Scorned as Timber—Emily Carr 1872 (sic) - 1945*" in 1973.*

It is of interest to note that the title of this canvas on the original Trust list is: *Scorned of the Sky*. Emily was trying to express exactly the opposite sentiments in her correctly named *Scorned as Timber, Beloved of the Sky*.

* Prism International, *Vancouver, B.C., Spring 1973.*

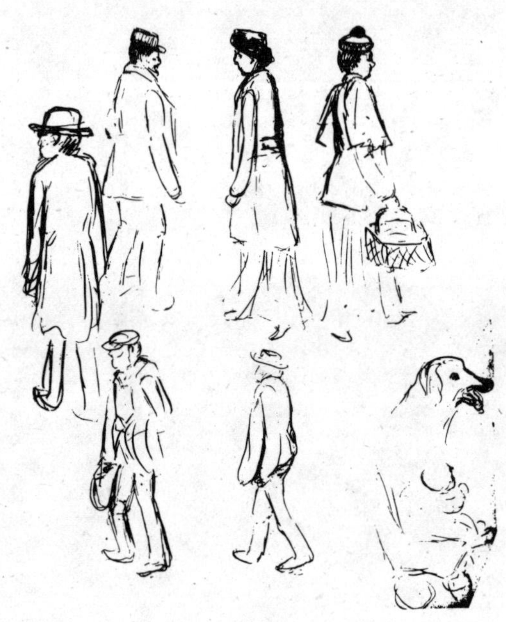

Emily Carr — "Canadian People's Artist"

The People's Art Gallery has not yet been resurrected, and may never be, but, behold—a "People's Artist" has arisen in its place! Evidently influenced, and misled, by Emily's choice of name for her gallery, Barry Lord, a writer on art subjects, has published a "long-awaited" book, *The History of Painting in Canada; Towards a People's Art*,* and one section of it is devoted to "The Achievement of Emily Carr." It starts with the painting of the native people and continues to the present. This section, or excerpts from it, was published in Vol. 1 No. 1 of *Warpath*, "Canada's National Patriotic Quarterly of Cultural Struggle." *Warpath* is a new Maoist periodical now on sale at Canada's newsstands.

* *NC Press, September 1974.*

To set the tone, they feature two cover articles: (1) "Imperialist Publisher Searching for Canadian Suckers" and (2) "Emily Carr, Canadian People's Artist." I couldn't believe my eyes when I saw this latter title, and when I read the article, I was stunned. How could any serious student of Emily Carr be so wrong? How could Lord so disastrously misinterpret the material and the substance? To sponsor a People's Art Gallery in no way means that one automatically becomes a people's artist. This was far from Emily's thought or purpose. Actually, she was willing, right from the start of her gallery scheme, to sacrifice her proclaimed radical principles by compromising with the "establishment" in her choice of the other three artists contributing to the opening exhibition. Instead of inviting the "moderns," whom she habitually supported, such as Jack Shadbolt, Max Maynard or myself, she deliberately selected a portraitist, a painter who specialized in English cottage scenes, and a young Chinese boy, Lee Nan,* who painted oriental birds and flowers. She felt that they would be more acceptable to the committee and the people she hoped to influence.

* *Spelled Lee "Nan" in* Hundreds and Thousands *and Lee "Nam" in* The House of All Sorts.

Poor Emily! When will they leave her alone and just let her be herself! She was a near genius, but not a true intellectual and certainly not a crusader. She had no grandiose message to impart, only wanting to give us an understanding of the Indian and his art and, later on, to describe on canvas her joy in the woods. We, in Victoria, were familiar enough with the woods and thought in our casual way we knew them. But it was her interpretation that revealed them to us. She never struggled for anything in her life except for the technical means and the power to express her vision and, necessarily, for plain bread and butter. She was not a protester in any political sense. In fact, she died as she was born: A true "Victorian" in her attitudes, a vague monarchist politically, loyal to king and country, protesting only the harshness of life and the stupidity of man—particularly of her fellow Victorians and the local amateur artists. She didn't fight *for* people, she was too busy fighting against them, and she played the role of a martyr more convincingly than that of a militant. Characterizing her as a revolutionary painting propaganda pictures is the height of absurdity. Barry Lord's image of her is deformed and he has distorted the truth in an attempt to fit her into a Maoist mould. But she is too individualistic, too large to fit. She is an original, and a pleasure to her friends because she cannot be, in any way, classified.

This deluded party-man begins his article with a motto of Mao-Tse-Tung:

"Dare to struggle! Dare to win!"

These imperatives apply only to political action and could have no appeal to Emily. She had her rebellious side, when personal freedom was in peril; and she was a pioneer in spirit and in her Indian art. But in social manner, social thought and all her ethical and political loyalties she was, out and out, conservative and temperamentally incapable of toeing any party line.

Instead of reading Mao, whom she assuredly never heard of, Emily was immersed in Walt Whitman's *Leaves of Grass.* She read few books at any time; she rarely left her own house and garden, except to go on sketching trips. She never attended a political meeting in her life. In fact, she scolded her young friends for going to hear Tim Buck and felt that my study of the Russian language was somehow a little treasonable.

Emily had a very definite code of behavior. Men did not loll in her presence and women were ladies who sat rather primly on a straight chair with their legs neatly crossed at the ankles. Although a little eccentric in her own dress, for practical reasons and because not everything fit her rotund form, she disliked anything that smacked of bohemianism in others and expected conventional clothing. Pants for women were not yet accepted in those days, but I wore them for painting and picnicking. But not with Emily. Not even in the woods. She was not above trying to dictate a small thing like my hair-style, saying that I had been "badly influenced" by my family when I cut my long hair, as my "crown of braids looked so ladylike."

Emily even reprimanded me, instead of supporting me, when I lost two jobs in quick succession in Vancouver. I was inexperienced as I had not been permitted to work before I was married. My father and the "system" always reminded me that it wouldn't be fair for me to apply for work as I would be depriving a poor girl (or worse still, a *man*) of a livelihood. But an Assistant Professor was certainly not rich in those days and I felt poor enough after marriage to seek work with a clear conscience.

I was first employed, in Vancouver, as an art teacher in a well-known private school for genteel young ladies and was just as genteelly dismissed when I deviated from the Princess Louise-approved course of drawing that the school subscribed to. The pupils' papers were marked in England according to principles that denied them freedom of expression, but I wanted to show them the satisfactions of creative painting. The school did not share my point of view. The headmistress was English and wanted the instruction, and the girls, to be as English as possible. There was considerable friction but I managed to hang on until the end of the year when I put on a display of the girls' work in the school gymnasium. It was not considered satisfactory. I was not asked to return.

When I told Emily about my dismissal, instead of being sympathetic, she berated me roundly for being irresponsible. "A job is a job in these hard times," she said. "You should have compromised temporarily with your conscience in order to keep it." In so admonishing me, Emily forgot that she had not followed her own advice years before when she was summarily dismissed from her post as art teacher with a Vancouver club (or so she said) because she refused to conform; and, like me, she had not been asked, after her return from France, to resume teaching duties at the same girls' private school where I had taught. But then, one could afford to show much more independence in 1912 than during the tough thirties.

My next job was as sign-painter and window-dresser for a large women's wear store on Granville Street. I had a dark, stuffy studio in the upper reaches of the filthy building, across the hall from a real sweat shop where a dozen dressmakers were squeezed into a small, airless, badly-lighted room. The plight of these exploited women roused my sympathy and all the militant instincts I had inherited from my Australian cousin who, at the peak of her highly successful career, laid down her palette and brushes to champion the cause of women and lead their marches down the streets of Canberra. While not inciting the dress-makers to strike (God forbid!), I did urge them to protest their deplorable working conditions and demand changes and slightly higher wages. Again I was fired, this time not so genteelly. As before, Emily maintained that I had erred, and thought that I had made things worse for the women.

Is this Emily's alleged interest in communism? Or socialism? Or any kind of social awareness? No! Emily did not fight for workers' rights, women's rights, Indians' rights or even, effectively, her own rights. She scrapped a lot with anyone who crossed her, and often blew up like a fire-cracker in the face of derision, abuse or obvious injustice, of which she suffered more than her fair share, but she was incapable of sustaining her anger, or her interest, long enough to conduct a campaign, call a meeting, march with a placard, or otherwise try to improve her lot, or the lot of others, through public or popular action. Her nature and her upbringing would have made such a course repulsive to her. It would not have been "decent." Besides, she was too engrossed and occupied in her own private world.

Like most women of her time, Emily suffered both hardship and discrimination because of her sex. Male artists often assured her patronizingly that she painted very well "for a woman." Others told her flatly that professional painting was not an occupation for a woman; they were not good enough. When she was forced to give up painting and teaching, because she refused to "debase her art," her only means of livelihood was what she could earn at home, and she finally resorted to taking in boarders. She hated "doing for the boarders" and suffered from the necessity of stifling her tormenting creative urges during the fourteen years her painting was so sharply curtailed.

But she did not dislike housework as such. Indeed, she took a certain pride in managing her house well, felt that physical labor developed character, and continued to boast about her culinary accomplishments long after she was able to give up cooking for others. Consequently, Lenin's words, as quoted by Lord in *Warpath:*

> In most cases housework is the most unproductive, the most savage and the most arduous work a woman can do. It is exceptionally petty and does not include anything that would in any way promote the development of a woman,

would have been largely lost on Emily. She would have paid scant attention and gone on with her daily chores. True, she grumbled a lot about the tenants, the hungry furnace, the shoveling of snow and coal, but she accepted her lot stoically, philosophically, and even got some satisfaction out of it.

A few Canadian women were, of course, fighting for emancipation in Emily's time, but none interested or inspired her; not Nellie McClung,* whom she met; not even her life-long friend, Margaret Clay, who was an ardent worker for women's rights. It is a little strange that Emily was not more of a feminist since women's liberation was a contemporary issue in the twenties and even earlier. All she did, apart from drawing a few cartoons supporting the cause of women in 1918 for the *Western Woman's Weekly* in Vancouver, was to stick up for women *painters* in conversation and in one passage of her journals.* Most people had very decided opinions about it, including wits like folk philosopher Will Rogers, who said, "Imagine the idea that a woman couldn't live happily at home and have an active mind."

* *Nellie McClung was a prominent Canadian suffragette, writer and Alberta MLA, elected in 1921, who retired to Victoria where she lived until her death in 1951.*

* Hundreds and Thousands, *p.287.*

Dr. Margaret Clay, former head of the Victoria Public Library, knew Emily as a girl and continued to see her once every ten days, when in the city, throughout the twenties, thirties and even later. She supports my claim that Emily gave no thought to women's rights, although she tried to interest her in the subject during their cozy suppers together. Emily did not even want to listen.

In connection with her pioneer work in this field, Margaret has told me a story* about one of her experiences which ought to have incensed even Emily. Amusing as it may seem today, it was anything but a laughing matter for the concerned women involved.

* *Margaret at first asked me not to repeat this story, as she felt it might be misconstrued as a reflection on the police. I persuaded her to let me do so, however, on the grounds that the police were not responsible for the action, but were only carrying out the orders of the Mayor or some other higher authority.*

A group of women protesters in Victoria, Margaret included, organized a large but orderly demonstration in 1917 and were marching purposefully down Yates Street, past the Library, placards aloft, when the police intervened. Instead of letting the women continue their planned march through the city to the parliament buildings to demand a meeting with the premier, the police maneuvered them in the opposite direction toward Chinatown behind the City Hall. But this area was also Victoria's red light district and the women were naturally indignant when they were herded in there before being dispersed. Did the city fathers in those days consider that female protesters and prostitutes were "birds of a feather"?

Nor can Emily be credited with either the will or the desire to help the native people solve their social and economic problems. In a sense they helped her more than she helped them. In telling Marius Barbeau about her sketching trips to their villages and her determined efforts to paint their totem poles before they were removed to museums or rotted in the bush, she aroused his interest in her work. Thus the Indians started a chain of fortuitous events, begun in remote villages of the north, which finally led, via Barbeau and Victoria, to the halls of the National Gallery of Canada in Ottawa.

No one will deny that Emily made a noble contribution to Canadian art in general and to the pictorial preservation of Indian artifacts in particular when she faced danger and real hardship sketching in isolated areas of British Columbia. She was a brave woman, a determined woman, a dedicated woman. She stood guard over Indian culture and shared with us her respect for it. British Columbia owes her a debt of gratitude for the rich heritage of Indian paintings that she has bequeathed to the Province in the Emily Carr Trust. It was in this way that she championed the Indian cause; by friendship and artistic endeavor—but though she felt a warm bond of sympathy for the Indians, as she did for all those she considered underdogs, the thought of taking up the cudgel to obtain political action on their behalf never occurred to her. She deplored the lack of cleanliness and hygiene in many villages, and often held her nose while painting, but really did not want to change the Indians. She liked them as they were. In fact, she strove against change, feeling that contact with the white man would bring about their downfall and destruction. Her attitude was maternal and she would not like them today with their new boldness (this would, I believe, have been her word). The dispute between the Indians and the Canadian administration, and the use of threat and force would have shocked her.

Perhaps the most extraordinary part of Lord's article is his interpretation of one of Emily's most widely-known canvasses, *Blunden Harbour*.* He claims that she painted this picture with the new insight gained from contact with the Group of Seven and that its meaning is clear: "These austere figures [the three almost life-size carved figures standing on the dock of a Kwakiutl village], full of dignity, show us the strength of the native peoples, their ability to fight back. They stand as guardians on the dock, an identification of this village and a warning to unfriendly visitors. The rage of the native people at the destruction of their proud civilization can be sensed in the raised fist closest to us, and in the determined expression on the three carved faces."

** Purchased by NGC early 1937. It is the most frequently reproduced of all Carr pictures.*

Everything that the author reads into this painting is wishful thinking. Surely the expression on the face of the largest totem figure is benign, and his arm seems to be raised in a gesture of welcome or greeting.* There is nothing menacing in his stance. His hand is cupped, but is certainly not the clenched fist of communism. There is absolutely no political statement in this canvas, or in any other Carr canvas. To be facetious, this critic has carried too much sail in approaching Blunder Harbour and his analysis could only be taken seriously by a hard-core radical wearing blinkers.

* *Another well-known canvas, which formed part of the Major Cuthbert Holmes' collection and was recently sold at auction in Victoria for $26,000, depicts a similar totem figure and bears the title,* The Welcome Man.

If he had actually seen Emily painting this picture, as Frederick Brand and I did, his theories would collapse like a pricked balloon. In all honesty he would have to retract his conclusion that this work is "essentially social realist in character."

What I saw was a plump, elderly little woman sitting* stolidly before her crude, home-made easel bringing to life the theme of *Blunden Harbour* on a large 51 x 37 in. canvas. Not knowing it was going to be such a famous work, let alone a symbol of communism, she did not even bother to stretch a new canvas for it, but worked on an old, somewhat bumpy picture that had been over-painted with flat white.*

* *Emily had to sit as much as possible to paint as she always had painful and slightly deformed feet. She had to have a toe amputated when studying in England as a young woman.*

* *At least partly on my suggestion,* Blunden Harbour *was x-rayed at NGC in September 1975. It proved to have an underpainting as I thought—a forest study done, in my opinion, in 1932.*

She was not happy, I think, that I had caught her painting the three dynamic totem figures on the wharf in the foreground from a small black-and-white photograph attached to the right support of her easel with a thumb tack. She created her own sky and background, but took no liberties with the figures themselves, copying them faithfully in detail. She did not approve of copying—especially for students—and rarely used photographs as a painting aid; but late in life when she could travel no more to Indian villages, she occasionally had to refer to a photo to depict her totem themes accurately. And because she had never been to Blunden Harbour and the subject made a deep impression on her, in this case she had to depend on the help of a camera.*

* *See chapter "Emily Exonerated" and* M.E. A Portrayal of Emily Carr, *pp.55-56, both by the author.*

As Emily painted, I observed no agitated movement, perceived no agitated thought. She worked quietly, endeavoring to convey the weight and immensity of the carved figures and what they meant to the Indians and to herself—in a religious and spiritual but not political sense. Emily reiterated again and again, until it became almost a litany, that she strove only to interpret the underlying spirit of her subject. For her there was no art without religion, and this painting is therefore more a prayer than a protest.

Just as Barry Lord was wrong about Emily's studio, so he also errs on several other, if minor, points. Emily did not, for instance, ever paint on brown butcher paper. She was poor, but always managed to buy vast quantities of cheap manila paper, and it is rubbish to say that she was a "social outcast at the age of forty-two," as she always had a small but faithful group of friends and admirers. Also, Mr. Lord, Emily did *not* go east in 1931.

To sum up: Emily was neither for nor against the struggle for emancipation and equality of workers, women or Indians. She was scarcely conscious of its existence. It was never a topic of her conversation. She was exclusively occupied with her own struggle for recognition as a painter and a writer.

Many labels, big and small, have been pinned on Emily in the last few years, mostly by individuals and groups who have tried to use her as a propaganda tool for their own ends. One that is often mentioned of late is "environmentalist." None of us was conscious of danger to the environment in the twenties and thirties. The world seemed big enough and clean enough for all to enjoy, and the word "pollution" was not in current use. In the pure sea air of Victoria, no one thought of it at all.

Emily was a naturalist, almost a nature-worshipper, and she instinctively respected and loved the great British Columbia forests and the clear-running rivers and streams. Littering, or any kind of destruction, was abhorrent to her and she was pained and shocked by the ruthless devastation caused by logging operations. But, again, she bemoaned this without resorting to any kind of political action. Any seeming protest about wanton destruction of woods in some of her paintings, such as *Logged Leavings, Odds and Ends* and, a favorite, *Scorned as Timber, Beloved of the Sky,* was quite unconscious. There are those who suggest that her stump pictures are also protest works, although I know that Emily first worked on stumps, while sketching at Metchosin, as studies in form, just as she got "good study" from the logs at Cordova Bay.

It is interesting to note that people, even at the other end of the world, have taken up this protest chant. When Emily's painting, *Loggers' Culls,* traveling with the *Exhibition of Contemporary Canadian Painting,** arrived in New Zealand in 1938, the reporter who reviewed the show for the *Chronicle* in Wanganui wrote: *Loggers' Culls* shows another aspect of the [logging] industry and, although the principal interest in the picture is probably the wind storm in the sky, there is a forceful reminder in the foreground of the taking away of the good trees and leaving of the slender saplings that are not worth cutting down."

This is part of a new twist in the appreciation of Emily's art. She deplored the ravages of landscape by industry, but not on

* *NGC 1936, arranged on behalf of the Carnegie Corporation of New York for circulation in the southern dominions of the British Empire. (See Exhibition List III)*

canvas. When she was painting in a wood, her mind was on other things. Spiritual things. Joyful things.

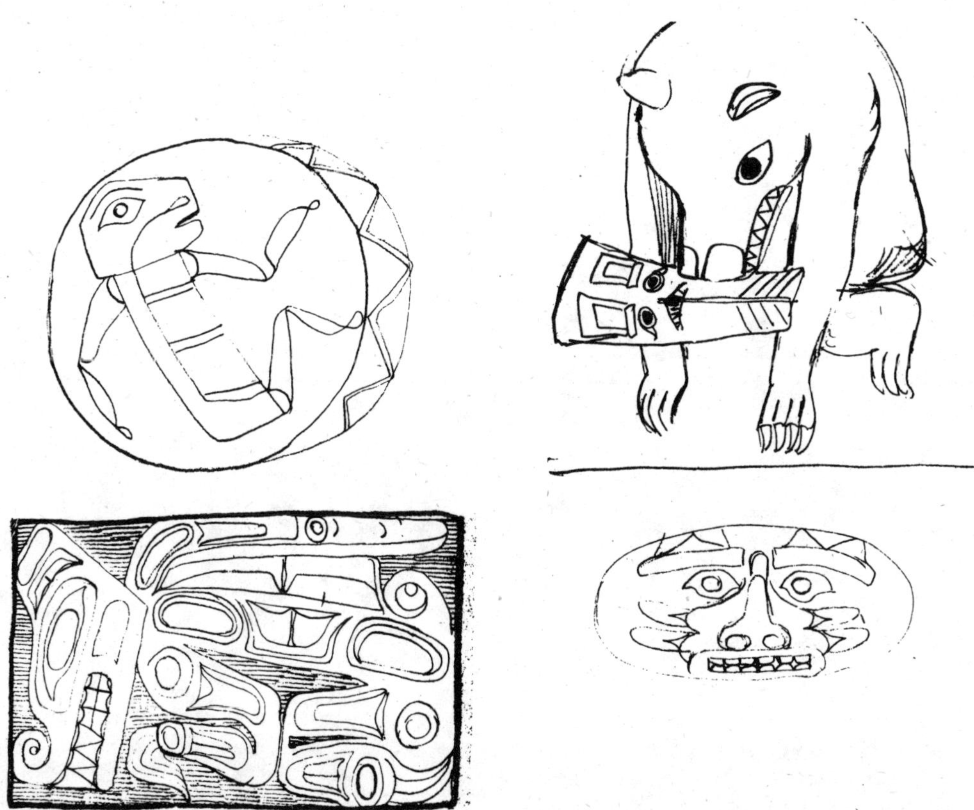

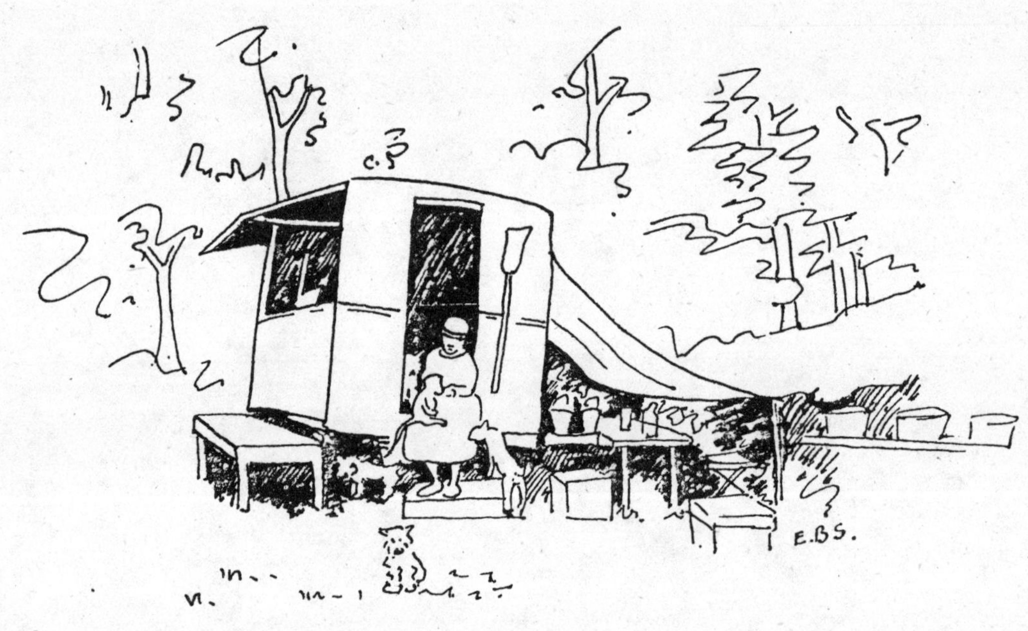

Emily at Metchosin. *Edythe Hembroff-Schleicher*

Emily Turns to Writing

For Phylis

I have read Emily's "sketches" many times, both before and after publication. I watched them grow, story by story. I witnessed her anguish as she struggled for expression, as she worked and re-worked the text, "peeling" it down to its very essence and worrying about her poor spelling and erratic punctuation. She was humble about her talent in those early days, and deeply troubled and confused about the mechanics of writing, feeling that her workmanship was shoddy.

Emily wrote off and on all her life, but in 1928, after many years of greatly diminished creative activity, the whole tempo of her existence suddenly speeded up and, encouraged and invigorated by her new Group of Seven friends, she drove herself relentlessly both in painting and writing. But a heart attack slowed her pace in 1937. Her painting curtailed, she began to concentrate more and more on writing.

But as early as 1924, Emily had turned to one close friend, Flora Hamilton Burns, for help with her stories. For several years she was the only person who knew Emily was writing and she became her critic, teacher and editor. Then late 1926 or early 1927,* in an attempt to bolster Emily's confidence, she enrolled with her at an American school of journalism and helped get her off to a flying start with her first assignment, a later version of which was published as "In the Shadow of the Eagle" in *The Heart of a Peacock.* Flora also assisted her with the typing and, as Emily's handwriting was always a stumbling block, she was the first to rejoice when Emily finally bought an antique clattering typewriter and learned to type, in a fashion, herself.

Emily called Flora her "listening lady," a title she retained until Ruth Humphrey also became her editor some years later, after which Flora was dubbed "listening lady No. 1," and Ruth "listening lady No. 2." But Emily liked to read her stories to other friends as well and, as soon as I met her, I was pressed into service as "assistant listening lady." Among other "assistants" were Nan Cheney, Margaret Clay and Frederick Brand—the only regular male listener among our little coterie of admirers.

* *In* The Heart of a Peacock, *p. xiii, Ira Dilworth proves that Emily was taking this correspondence course in 1927 but it is possible that she enrolled at the end of 1926—Flora's date.*

He was also the first person to read Emily's stories in public—to his students at the University of British Columbia. When they responded with interest, he took the manuscripts to Dr. Garnett G. Sedgewick for a professional opinion and later, of course, Garnett, then Ira Dilworth, read a selection of them on radio broadcasts. Finally, through the efforts of the latter, many of Emily's best Indian stories were edited and published in 1941 in her first book, *Klee Wyck*.

The stories in *Klee Wyck*, like the others, were done over and over. They look deceptively simple, but Emily sweated out their production. So quick in paint, she was painfully slow in writing, and although her talent is obvious to all, it would never have been developed without her grim determination. She forced herself to take a typing course, working with a class of young girls who smirked at her plump, badly-dressed body and clumsy fingers. Even in 1934, sixty-two years old and still eager to learn, she attended night school classes at the Provincial Normal School summer session, conducted by Mrs. N. deB. Shaw. She turned out to be the star student in the class! One of her Indian stories, "The Hully-up Paper,"* was warmly praised for its fine literary style and captured the first prize. Other Indian stories, appearing seven years later in *Klee Wyck*, won a much more coveted honor—the Governor General's medal for general literature.

* *Published in* The Heart of a Peacock.

After the publication of *Klee Wyck*, the function of the "listening ladies" as critics almost ceased. Emily still read them a story occasionally, but more and more she came to depend on Ira Dilworth's advice alone. As she was very fond of both Flora and Ruth, her conscience troubled her at first, but she soon rationalized the switch, and in silent gratitude for their long and loyal help, she bequeathed the manuscript of "D'Sonoqua" (the wild woman of the woods) to Ruth and that of her biography to Flora—not because she thought them of value, but just as keepsakes. However, since the publishers later objected to such impediments on Emily's material, she "disinherited" them—a little sadly, but irrevocably.

About this time, too, Emily wrote a rare criticism of her critics:

> Don't think I am disloyal or ungrateful to Flora and Ruth. In the beginning they helped me tremendously, but there came a time when we got to an impasse. . . . I couldn't read my thing to Ruth and Flora without being embarrassed. More by what they didn't say than what they did. One of them wanted me to be

hard and historical, the other mushy and sentimental. My literary shortcomings seemed so blatant. I needed help and I did want to use clean, good English with right meaning words. But I rebelled at having values only obtainable by direct, actual contact with Indians and wild places battened down by academic conventions.*

Close to Christmas 1941, Emily again reverted to the subject of her "listening ladies:"

I've always thought of myself as ordinary and illiterate. Flora always made me feel that and so did Ruth sometimes. I mean—like when they struck out my colloquialisms and slang sometimes that I didn't even know I was using.*

When Ira Dilworth became Emily's editor, late 1938 or early 1939, he criticized and discussed all her stories, but did not correct or change them as much as the "listening ladies" had. In fact, Emily and Ira both state emphatically that he never rewrote a single line of her material.* She explains:

I have been preparing MSS for the next book. Ira told me he thought "Bobtails" would not require much going over but I found *millions* and billions of things I wanted to straighten out and clarify. . . . If I only knew the *rules* of the game better. I have to work over and over to make the words run with any kind of smoothness. If one could only go direct (word their meanings first shot)! My editor will not change or allow to be changed one word. He goes over punctuation and points out some things if he thinks I have not made a meaning clear, but he *never* rewrites or rewords me. When Mr. Dilworth saw (previous) corrections he made me take them all out and go back to my own way though, being a professor of English, he made me *see for myself*.*

About a year later, Emily reverted to the same topic:

I have made big strides on the MS. I am cleaning it, it is all done except a couple of final readings. Mr. Dilworth sent me a wonderful crit on the last. High praise in some spots, severe *criticism* in others. A very frank go-over. *That is what I like* and what makes me *respect* a good stiff crit (not sugar and water nothings).*

Before Emily's stories were at last assembled in a published book, they had done a lot of traveling and caused her much anguish as, like everything else, she took her writing hard. We,

* *Phylis Dilworth Inglis collection, Emily to Ira Dilworth, (undated) probably early 1941.*

* *Phylis Dilworth Inglis collection, Emily to Ira Dilworth (undated)*

* *In the preface to* The Heart of a Peacock *Dilworth states that he made no changes except ordinary editorial work such as punctuation, paragraphing and the like.*

* *Emily to Myfanwy Spencer Pavelic, January 7, 1942.*

* *Emily to Myfanwy Spencer Pavelic, (undated).*

her friends, listened to them one by one, and discussed them "learnedly." We found ourselves caught up in her delightful autobiographical writing, in which she recalled people and events from her own life so long before we knew her. Our favorites, her childhood recollections, were revived through the eye of "Small," who, Emily said, was "just a phantom child, made up of memories and love."* Best of them all, and closest to Emily's heart, was "The Cow Yard"* which, after completion in 1934, we urged her to submit to a magazine. On the advice of an old family friend,** she chose an English publication, *The Countryman*, which seemed a suitable vehicle for anything to do with farm animals. To everyone's disappointment, it was returned as being "not just their type," her first dispiriting rejection. Later, as her manuscripts accumulated, she sent them off in all directions to all possible magazines. Back they came: "The Cow Yard" and "Peacock" from *Atlantic Monthly*; others from *Macleans*. No regrets and no explanations. Even her prize-winning "Hully-up Paper" was rejected by the *Saturday Evening Post*. Later still, her stories were turned down by both Macmillan and Ryerson Press.

* The Heart of a Peacock, *p.xv.*

* *Emily to author (undated) November 1936: "I am enjoying Miss Humphrey so much. . . . she has given me such good help and ideas. . . . Cow Yard she condensed a lot, leaving out heaps. It spoils the Cow Yard for me but helped me a great deal in seeing how to tackle other things."*

** *Madge Wolfenden Hamilton. In 1936, when the old Carr house was sold after Lizzie's death and all furnishings disposed of, Madge bought the large, antique mahogany bed from the master bedroom in which Emily was said to be born. It is still in use—cut down to three-quarters size.*

Emily was deeply discouraged and felt, rightly, that her material was of no interest to the magazine-reading public of the day. She complained to her journals:

> They want blood and thunder, sex and crime, crooks, divorce, edgy things that keep them on the *qui vive*. . . . I can't write that stuff. I don't want to learn. I won't. So I guess my little homely tales of creatures and things will sit in my box forever. I want the money dreadfully, but I don't want dirt money.*

* Hundreds and Thousands, *pp.159-160.*

Emily struggled on, more than ever conscious of her technical shortcomings, as one senses in this cry of despair:

> "Often I wonder at the desire in me being so strong, and drivelling out in such feeble words and badly constructed sentences."*

* *Ibid p.160.*

But Emily was never a quitter. Not as a painter and not as a writer. She worked under conditions of illness, great pain and frightening financial worries that would have crushed anyone else. During the last few years of her life, when she was in and out of nursing homes and hospitals, writing sustained her, both financially and morally. With all her great fortitude, she needed this crutch. Writing became a necessity. A release. Her creative urge still nagged, refusing to be stilled by other activities.

Marguerite Turpin has written in her Carr bibliography* that the sketches in *Klee Wyck* were written at various times

* The Life and Work of Emily Carr (1871-1945), *A Selected Bibliography published by the School of Librarianship, UBC, Vancouver, January 1965.*

when Emily traveled into the lonely places of forest and village, seeking Indian subjects. Others agree with her. However, this conclusion would be difficult to substantiate as Emily has consistently said that most of her Indian stories were either written or revised while she was convalescing in the hospital in early 1937, and that they were posted to Dr. Sedgewick for criticism in June or July.* About the same time she told a friend that she had written the stories entirely from memory:

> Writing about village after village, all as *exactly alike* as they are TOTALLY DIFFERENT—sets one digging for the difference. . . . Things come to me clearly over the time—guess they sunk in O.K. Of course sketching in the places helped.* . . .

A few years later, in a letter to Ira Dilworth, she again says quite categorically that, "I never made a note about my Indian trips. I kept a sort of running account which I sent to Alice thinking she would keep them . . . anyhow they were all burnt as soon as received. Of course I should have asked her to keep them for reference."

But after her 1928 sketching trip to the North, Emily said that she returned home with "a lot of notes."* The only explanation for this apparent contradiction is that the 1928 notes were probably sketch book jottings (color, Indian legends, designs, totems) to aid in reworking her sketches into studio paintings, and not descriptions of the villages themselves that could have been used later in her written sketches.

Yet the question is still puzzling, and knowing Emily's penchant for half-truths, one wonders if something is eluding us. Could memory alone, plus a keen eye and colorful imagination have given us these vivid accounts in such a wealth of detail—without notes? She was unusually perceptive and observant, but could she store up all the minutia she noticed for use in her stories so many years afterwards? Probably not. There must have been some material to jog her memory, if not what she formally called "notes." She was an inveterate letter writer, and although Alice purportedly destroyed all the letters she received, a few friends like Flora or Maud and Eric Brown recognized the uniqueness of theirs and preserved them. Emily could easily have used these letters for reference. Her story "Kitwancool," for instance, with very little editing and some embroidering, could have been lifted almost intact from either of these letters.

Emily's very first Indian story was written, it seems, in 1933 on her return from Toronto, where she had stayed with

* Hundreds and Thousands, *p.291. In Emily's entry of June 24, 1937 she writes that she had already sent her Indian stories to Dr. Sedgewick. According to her dating, they must have been posted between June 14 and 24. But in a letter to Ruth Humphrey of July 21, she states that ". . . I am sending what I have done to Dr. S. tomorrow or thereabouts." Since several entries in* Hundreds and Thousands *are incorrectly dated, it is likely that Ruth's letter is the more reliable.*

* *Emily to Ruth Humphrey, (postmarked) June 22, 1937.*

* *NGC, Emily to Eric Brown, October 1, 1928.*

Bess and Fred Housser. Fred, who wrote *A Canadian Art Movement*, on which Emily depended so heavily, was the first author she had ever known. He encouraged her to write, praised the story she sent him for comment, but criticized her construction.*

Then, in 1936, when Emily first met Ruth Humphrey, and early 1937, before Ruth left on an extended trip abroad, they worked together on several of Emily's Indian stories. Before her departure, Ruth accompanied Eric Newton, respected art critic for the *Manchester Guardian*, to the hospital to visit Emily, and finding her in the depths of despair, he managed to instill in her the courage and will to get well and work again. "Get better," he admonished in parting, "these hands are too clever to lie idle."* "These hands," thus encouraged, were soon very busy writing and revising the seventeen stories Emily completed during the next six months.

Fate took a hand here. Eric Newton, who had never even seen a British Columbia Indian, became, in a sense, the father of *Klee Wyck* as he gave Emily the determination to create in words what she was no longer able to do in paint. Before the year was out, all the sketches the book was to contain needed only final editing, a publisher and a name.

But before publication finally took place, Emily's Indian stories led a life of adventure. All three copies of "D'Sonoqua" went astray for a long time in 1937, Emily blaming Ruth for losing one during her travels. When the copies eventually turned up, Emily was contrite: "Did I abuse you?" she questioned Ruth. "I'm a low toad." The remainder of the stories were in and out of the hospital with Emily, then lying around, neglected, in Garnett Sedgewick's topsy-turvy study in Vancouver. After that, they languished in the East for almost a year before the publishing house returned them. Frustrated, Emily wrote to Ruth towards the end of May 1938:

"I've been roaring mad. Those miserable Ryerson Press people have coolly told me they have lost my twenty Indian sketches and five short stories.* They have moved and say very calmly they 'are sorry' but so it is, isn't it vile? . . . makes one swear they will give up trying to send out."

The more one reads, thinks, or writes about Emily, the more one is filled with admiration for her unremitting perseverance. During the hard years after 1937, she worked at both her painting and writing against almost insuperable odds. Her books would never have seen the light of day had Emily not stubbornly made up her mind to write—even in hospital when she was desperately ill; even when rejection slips came in as fast

* *Frederick B. Housser, noted writer on Canadian art and closely associated with the Group of Seven. He also wrote on theosophical subjects, and is credited with having introduced Emily to Walt Whitman, whose* Leaves of Grass *was her daily spiritual sustenance for many years. When she spoke of "Fred Housser's Whitman" in her writings, she was referring to "The Creative Man" an unpublished manuscript which only appeared in print (in* The Canadian Theosophist- *May 15 and June 15 1947) after her death under the title "Whitman to America." The Group of Seven introduced Emily to Housser's* A Canadian Art Movement *(The MacMillan Co. of Canada Ltd., Toronto 1926). After a divorce, Bess Housser married Lawren Harris.*

* Growing Pains, *p.357. It should be noted that Emily's two versions of the Eric Newton story vary considerably in detail in* Growing Pains *and* Hundreds and Thousands.

* *Meanwhile, Emily had increased her Indian sketches to twenty, added five or six other stories (depending which account one reads) and had submitted them to Ryerson Press on February 7, 1938.*

as she could send her stories out; even when the "crits" of her editors were discouraging or confusing. Almost anyone else would have given up in despair when her Indian stories were lost, but Emily, a lioness when roused, harried all the Ryerson Press executives with a constant stream of bristling letters until, in sheer desperation, they instituted a mammoth search and finally located the typescripts. Someone, in the disruption of moving day had lined a box of school books with them as packing! It is almost a miracle that *Klee Wyck* survived in the face of all these obstacles.

Nineteen-thirty seven, Emily's most prolific writing year, was also Dr. Sedgewick's year in her writing life.* She was a little disenchanted with editors at that point, and tried for a time to work alone. She had outgrown Flora's corrections, Ruth was away, and Ira Dilworth had not yet been introduced to her stories. Although she continued to seek help from friends, she needed a qualified editor who could give her good hard "crits," and after Frederick had shown her manuscripts to Dr. Sedgewick, she became obsessed with the idea of enlisting the aid of this brilliant and popular professor. But because she stood in great awe of him, she persuaded Frederick and me to act as unwilling go-betweens. Garnett had the best of intentions when he agreed to criticize Emily's work, but trouble was bound to brew because he was pretty much a law unto himself around the University of British Columbia, and an incorrigible *mañana* person. Students and professors alike fell under his spell and accepted him as he was. But not Emily, that is, not for long.

At first, after sending her stories to Vancouver, she was so impressed by Sedgewick's reputation as a critic and his position as Head of the English Department that she awaited his comments with quite untypical patience and restraint, hoping he would eventually devise a magic formula that would transform her unwanted manuscripts into marketable gems of literature. Her faith in him was as great as it was naive. But as the months dragged by, it turned sour; and when she took off her rose-colored spectacles, she suddenly saw Sedgewick as an ordinary mortal with his fair share of shortcomings. By November she was beginning to berate him roundly (to me) and demand her sketches back, with or without criticism: "No word from Dr. Sedgewick. . . . I don't care how learned a professor he is, he is a *rude* man." In December, after I had tried to pacify her and tactfully prod Garnett into action she wrote to me again:

> You were lovely to answer so quickly and so nice and explaining and I learned a lot by your pulling out of

* *Emily's four editors, in order of appearance, were: Flora Hamilton Burns; Ruth Humphrey; Garnett Sedgewick and Ira Dilworth.*

> memory the drift of what Dr. Sedgewick said. Yes—you did say he admired and was congratulatory etc., but that was not what I was after and wanted to know about. Perhaps I wanted to know more about the working side and wherein I could get ahead by being shown up my failings. . . . I wrote to him after I got your letter and never peeped you had mentioned his speaking of [the stories]. . . .
>
> He answered briefly that he was delighted with them, that he feared they would not find a *big* audience but that they deserved it . . . that he had been very pressed for time and that *'criticism of this sort is not an easy business!'* You know, that surprised me. I had thought of his reading and correcting like a school mistress doing the day's class exercises: Scoring out words or sentences and scribbling 'bad,' 'clumsy,' 'unconvincing,' and such like in the margin. I never thought of a Professor of English having anything but 'easy business,' when it came to beginner's work. I felt a bit ashamed I'd been impatient and given him extra when he was busy. I told him so and will just let the whole business drop. . . . I believe he thinks they are not twaddle so that heartens me. That is what I wanted more than anything to find out. . . . You *cannot* tell yourself.

This subdued and repentant mood was of short duration. Emily finally blew up and pushed me into the center of the controversy:

> I am going to ask you a favor. . . . It is to get in touch with Dr. Sedgewick and say I have asked you to bring my MSS over with you. It is useless writing to the brute. He has not sent me a word and I wrote over two weeks ago asking for my things and I *want* them, whether he has bothered to do them or not. I think he's an old *fraud* and I don't want any more dealings with that kind. I want my MSS and I want them now—all of them. I want them, even if I only burn them. . . . Perhaps he has *lost* them or some such thing. Well, he can just find them.

In the end, Frederick and I had the uncomfortable mission of going to Sedgewick's home to collect the manuscripts, and my sister Helen, who was visiting us in Vancouver, took them back to Emily in person. Dr. Sedgewick had no real criticism to make of the stories. He thought them very sharply etched, matter and manner well fused and said they needed no revision other than that routinely supplied by any publisher's editor. He felt they should be published for the select few who would appreciate them.

This was pretty lean comment for an eager writer who had waited on the *qui vive* for months to hear Sedgewick's verdict. However, he helped her in other ways and soon became a staunch and vocal admirer of both her painting and writing. He also purchased three of her sketches. Emily gave him a fourth and his sins were forgiven.

Although couched in general terms, Dr. Sedgewick's appraisal of Emily's stories did much to hearten her; and Ira Dilworth, who would soon be center stage in her life, and assume full editorial responsibilities, did still more to heighten her self-confidence. At times she continued to lament her lack of technical knowledge, but had ceased to regard this as an insuperable obstacle to forceful and meaningful writing. Here and there she gives glimpses of her work methods, more especially for her *Klee Wyck* stories, but a year or two before her death, while revising the manuscript for *Growing Pains** she decided to include her impressions of New York, on Lawren Harris's suggestion. She had already described her student days in both London and Paris and Harris felt that New York, as one of the "big three" art centers, should not be omitted, even though her visit there was short. Emily admitted that the scraps of description she had jotted down while in New York were not of much value, but felt that by adding a little to them and drawing on memory for the rest, she would be able to give a reasonably accurate account of her stay in the big city. "It is," she said, "all made up of tiny incidents. No big grand doings. I tried to show the growing and that all those tiny happenings contributed to the whole."

Klee Wyck is generally considered to be Emily's best book, though some critics and most friends prefer *The Book of Small*. *Klee Wyck* was popular from the moment it appeared, the first printing of 2,500 copies being sold out in a few months. The best measure of its success is that the publishers increased the first printing of Emily's second book, *The Book of Small*, to 4,000 copies, more than they had ever printed in a first edition.*

Emily wrote *Klee Wyck* to honor the Indians, but felt, on publication, that Ira Dilworth should share the honors equally. She expressed her gratitude to him in an undated letter in 1941: "The tribute they (the critics) paid to *my editor* (Ira) and *literary critic* gave me *more* satisfaction than what they said of me.

* *Emily to Myfanwy Spencer Pavelic (undated). ". . . as a section (of the autobiography) is given over to Lawren and his work, I felt it only fair he should read it. It is also dedicated to him. . . . Lawren wrote me yesterday having read the first part (San Francisco Art School (sic)). He wrote in glowing terms—loved it."*

* *Phylis Dilworth Inglis collection, Emily to Ira Dilworth, June 3, 1943. Emily said she had received this information in a letter from "Mr. Bill Clarke."*

Such a great share of *Klee Wyck's* glory is *yours* by *right*. It just made all the difference. No matter how *deeply* I felt the things (and I did feel them deeply) your dusting them of clumsy impediments was of inestimable value. What a lucky woman me! I am so glad, glad, to have been able to pay tribute to the dear Indians and to the loveliness of our Far West."

Although *Klee Wyck* is dedicated to Sophie, this was not Emily's original intention. Long before she finished the Indian stories that make up the book, she had started writing her autobiography which she at that time planned to dedicate to Sophie—jointly with Eric Brown, whom she wished to honor as a friend and as director of the National Gallery. These two good friends died the same year—1939—while Emily was in the hospital.

Lawren Harris, of course, tried to persuade Emily to write her autobiography, but it was Eric Brown who initially discussed it with her and coaxed her to make a start. She worked hard on the book, even completing the first draft, but ran into problems which she outlines in a letter to the distinguished British Columbia poet, Dorothy Livesay Macnair:

> Eric Brown mentioned a biography [and] thought it might be helpful to other Canadian students . . . [so] why not do it myself, or let someone else. . . . [He then] suggested two writers in Victoria, Mrs. Legri Shaw and Gwen Cash, two women who know very little of me. . . . So I began, meaning to send it to Eric Brown for criticism later. . . . I finished it [but] parts need re-writing. . . . As one's life and work are closely woven, it meant I was obliged to bring in my family's indifference to my work. I read the first part of my writing to my only close relative remaining (a sister) . . . and she was *very angry* about it. If I could not do it *honestly* I could not do it at all and the emotional stress was very bad for the angina pains. My sister is going blind and I felt she had enough to bear without the other. So the MS I have not looked at for several years. Some day I may re-write it. Some day I may tear it up?*

* *Undated, but definitely written early 1941.*

Ms. Livesay Macnair had approached Emily for permission to write her biography, but Emily replied, "Thank you for your interest, but let me die first."

Others perhaps also wanted to write Emily's life story. Certainly, according to her, Max Maynard did, but he indignantly denies this today.

It is interesting to speculate on the dedications of Emily's books: Sophie was transferred from the autobiography to *Klee Wyck; The Book of Small* was dedicated to Ira Dilworth; *The House of All Sorts* to Bill and Irene Clarke, Emily's publishers; Lawren Harris was given the autobiography, *Growing Pains;* Dr. David Baillie, her longtime family doctor, was remembered in *Pause: A Sketch Book.* But Eric Brown's name is missing from this roll of honor. It was he who encouraged her to write the autobiography, but he was dead and forgotten before it was finished.

The Heart of a Peacock is dedicated to Victoria Anderson and Viola Morris, two Australian women who called themselves "The English Duo." Superbly fine singers, they came to Vancouver during the war and stayed for several years. Ira Dilworth, who attended their first recital, was so enchanted with their singing that he offered them a contract for a series of broadcasts on CBC. This dedication is puzzling and unmerited, crowning as it does such a fleeting friendship, most of it on the airways, but since *Peacock* was published eight years after Emily's death, and the manuscript then belonged to Ira, it is hard to say whether the choice was his or Emily's. However, Phylis Dilworth Inglis, an accomplished musician herself, and also a friend of the "Little Ladies," as Emily called them, told me, after a moment's reflection, that she believed the dedication had been Emily's own wish.

Of all the Indian villages described by Emily in *Klee Wyck,* Kitwancool most aroused my curiosity and captured my imagination. It provided the material for one of her most vivid stories, for long, spontaneous informative letters and for some powerful Indian paintings. In her book, in the studio among friends, or in the woods, Emily delighted to retell (among others) the story of her bold conquest of this "hostile" village from which—so the Mounted Police reportedly told her—the Indians had chased away missionaries and driven off surveyors with axes.*

Who would wish to contradict Emily? Or change her colorful account of this trip? Who could? No one else had the courage to go in and find out. So why look at cold statistics? Let alone go after them? Certainly not in a desire to detract from Emily's unique achievement, but simply, in my case, from force of habit. For several years now I have been following in her tracks wherever they led and when they took me to Kitwancool I was curious and paused long enough to gather a little intriguing information.

Kitwancool (kit—"people of," wan—"place of," ‡kul—

* *The hostility and suspicion with which whites were regarded in some villages was caused in large measure by a law of The Indian Act of 1886 which made potlatching illegal. Indians charged with taking part in a potlatch often served prison sentences.*

"small" or "narrow") are a small Indian tribe whose village, of the same name, is situated in a mountainous region on the Chiltach river, a tributary of the Skeena, about half way between Kitwanga* and Kitwancool Lake. Justly famed for its totems, and its coolness towards intruders, the village in Emily's day was accessible only by trail. But officially,* "hostility" is reduced to "coolness," and a Census of Indians undertaken by the Department of Indian Affairs in 1912 makes the Kitwancool Band look still less threatening. The population for that year was forty-six—of which thirty-six were Anglican and only ten pagan. In the Annual Report for 1914, the people of this band were said to be "intelligent and energetic and, notwithstanding their isolated condition, have made fair progress. [They] are temperate and moral." In 1917—getting closer to the date of Emily's visit—the Kitwancool were described as "law-abiding, industrious and making steady progress along the lines of civilization."

* *Kitwanga is the revised, standardized spelling. It was previously Gitwangak or, as Emily spells it in* Klee Wyck, *Kitwangak.*

* Histories, Territories and Laws of the Kitwancool, *Anthropology in B.C. Memoir No. 4 1959, British Columbia Provincial Museum.*

If Kitwancool was Emily's favorite Indian village, Sophie was her favorite Indian. She is a very special case. Emily not only dedicated *Klee Wyck* to her, but also honored her with one of the stories and the frontispiece—a portrait of Sophie painted in 1914.

I never met Sophie, but because I had read and heard so much about her and had studied her portraits, I formed a definite image of her in my own mind. But today, with a much fuller knowledge of Emily's whole life—not just the segment I shared with her—I am not sure that I understood her relationship to Sophie at all, though it is clear that an enduring affection, if not friendship in the accepted sense, existed between them for years. When Emily was inundated with congratulatory messages and excellent reviews on *Klee Wyck,* she thought of Sophie, and her part in it, and wondered how much all the fanfare would have touched her gentle heart. Knowing Sophie's modesty and unassuming ways, she concluded that it would have been of small moment compared to the deep undercurrent of affection between them. But why? This strange affinity is mystifying. I once asked Emily to explain it and her reply was as artless as the friendship itself: "She is good. I love her."

This now strikes me as over-simplification. How could Emily, with her conservative, protestant background, have developed deep, spiritual ties with a semi-literate, primitive woman whose only interest in life, aside from her Catholic church, seemed to be her twenty-one dead children and their equal number of tiny tombstones? She wove beautiful baskets, but there her talents stopped. It must have been her qualities of calm gentleness and staunch loyalty that touched Emily. Indeed she may have had need of them. Perhaps, too, it was a relief to have an uncomplicated person like Sophie for a friend, with whom she could not quarrel. Sophie asked nothing in return for her affection. She was a model of submission—as a wife, as a friend, as an Indian.

Still, had Sophie lived in Victoria, supporting herself as a maid, or a washerwoman like "Wash Mary,"* rapport between them would have been unlikely. Emily's maids, washerwomen and gardeners were servants to whom she was usually kind, sometimes sharp, but never intimate;* and the Indian helper she employed when she ran her boarding house in the twenties never became a friend. She reveals something about her attitudes to household help and tradesmen in a passage of her journals written in 1934: "Well, I had the chimney swept today and the sweep and I had a long conversation over politics and religion. Fancy a few years back talking to a sweep about Jesus Christ and the state of Russia and communism and soul-stirring things!"*

To the end of her life there was always an invisible barrier between Emily and those who served her. Indeed, at times, her sense of social caste bordered on snobbery. Just as she was a little condescending looking down the social scale, so she could be a little obsequious looking up. A good example of this is the flurry caused by Lady Tweedsmuir's visit to her studio on Beckley Avenue,* and Emily's later desire to give her a complimentary copy of *Klee Wyck*, even though she only had six copies at her disposal:*

> Tell me, she asked Ira Dilworth, shall I send her K.W.? And where and how? How do I address her? You remember—I ran out of the cottage and grabbed her paw . . . so she needn't expect much more from me in the way of manners.

Whether or not she actually sent the book is not known. I hope the idea was abandoned as this was not Emily at her best, willing as she was to overlook old friends to give a copy of her first book, from her meagre supply, to a Lady she had only seen for an hour in her whole life.*

But no feeling of class distinction is discernible in Emily's relationship with Sophie. Perhaps it was the mother in her (". . . all woman, maternal from the soles of her feet to her black Indian hair") that attracted Emily, because her maternal instinct, too, was very strong. One sees this in the protective love she

* *One of the stories in* Klee Wyck.

* *As late as 1942 Emily still sometimes referred to her maids as "servant girls."*

* Hundreds and Thousands, *p.156.*

* *PABC, Emily to the author, August 7, 1937. This letter contains an account of Lady Tweedsmuir's visit.*

* *The publisher had sent Emily twelve copies, but she gave half of them to Ira Dilworth in the belief that he was entitled to share half of everything concerning the book, including praise and honors.*

* *Lady Tweedsmuir came only once and stayed about an hour selecting a sketch. The chauffeur, however, came back a second time to return the sketch for signing and a third time to pick it up again. He also did a little private business on the side by persuading Emily to sell her antique copper warming pan (which hung just inside the front door) for $5.00.*

showered on animals, a few underprivileged persons, or a young girl. Curiously, she did not like children. She thought, and said, she did. She gave them cookies and tried to be kindly. But her patience soon wore thin and she became restless and irritable. Some of the children in Alice's school were terrified of her.

Only one thing disturbed the otherwise smooth tenor of friendship between Emily and Sophie. As a devout Catholic, Sophie was saddened and troubled that Emily was not of her faith, even though she sometimes accompanied her to church. She worried about it in silence for a while, but finally summoned up enough courage to speak to the priest. To her relief, he told her that a good woman like Emily was just the same as a Catholic.

Oddly enough, despite Emily's expressed affection for Sophie, she made little attempt to see her—at least later in life—even when the occasion presented itself. After 1930, I believe they only met twice: Once, by chance, in Brackendale in 1933, and once, by design, in 1934 when Emily was in Vancouver and found time to slip over to North Vancouver for a "satisfactory and happy" visit with Sophie. "I love Sophie's smile of welcome," she wrote. "It is just as dear, perhaps dearer, now that her countenance is abbreviated by losses."*

* Hundreds and Thousands, *p.117.*

But they could have met again in 1936 when I drove Emily to North Vancouver to visit Varley's studio and asked if she would like to call on Sophie too. She demurred. Then, when she was visiting Nan Cheney, who lived on the North shore, she had another opportunity. But Nan says Emily never mentioned Sophie. And yet, when *Klee Wyck* was published almost three years after Sophie's death, Emily wanted it to be a monument to her Indian friend.

Perhaps "Indian" is the key to this baffling relationship, as it seems that Emily was as much attracted to the symbol in Sophie as to the woman. Ira Dilworth may have sensed the same thing:

> There is a great, almost epic sweep in *Klee Wyck*. One feels space in it. In spite of the fact that things at times are so clear and vivid, there is another sense in which they are symbolic, general, almost abstract. Sophie, for instance, is so deeply, vividly depicted that she becomes a real person and yet in a way she is a symbol and type of her race.*

* *Phylis Dilworth Inglis collection, Ira Dilworth to Emily (undated) early 1942.*

Emily lived in a dream world for weeks after *Klee Wyck* first appeared shortly before her seventieth birthday. Congratulations poured in from all over Canada, and only half-believing, she was swept along by a wave of praise and acclaim. Nothing had prepared her for this, and nothing in her experience as a painter could compare with it. Indeed, real fame as a painter still eluded her when she became famous overnight as a writer. To her amazement, she was invited to become an honorary member of the Victoria Branch of the University Women's Club, which further honored her with a mammoth birthday party to celebrate the publication of her book. During the party, letters of congratulation were read from many prominent Victoria citizens, including the Lieutenant Governor, the Mayor and other city officials and dignitaries. Many clubs and other organizations sent best wishes.

When Emily rose, at first shaking with fright, to thank everybody for being so kind to *Klee Wyck*, she said a rather curious thing: "I did not write *Klee Wyck*, as the reviewers said, long ago when I went to the West Coast villages painting. I was too busy painting from dawn till dark. I wrote *Klee Wyck* one year ago (that is, 1940) in the hospital." But Emily had forgotten. Her book *Klee Wyck* was born, as she said, in the hospital, but in 1937, not 1940.

This party was a very proud occasion for Emily—so proud that she devotes a disproportionate number of pages to it in her autobiography. But then, who can blame her? Success was all the sweeter for being so long delayed.

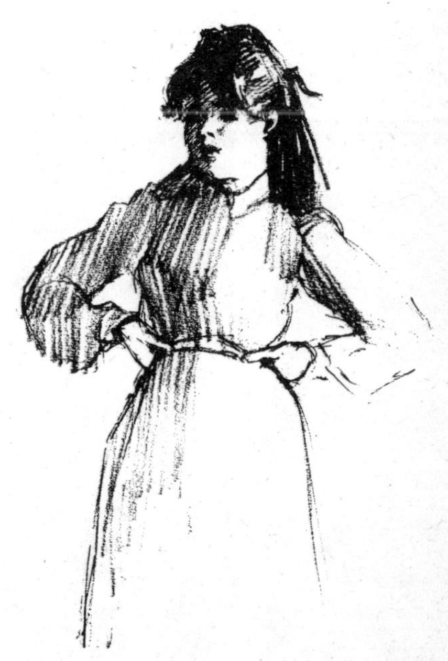

The reviews were also congratulatory. One eulogy followed another. Ira Dilworth, who had written the foreword for *Klee Wyck*, now took up his busy pen again to write two articles for *Saturday Night*. In one he states:

> There is a poetic quality in everything she writes. It reveals itself in the economy of detail used, the rigid selectivity which she practises, the sense of rhythm and form evident in the shaping of her sketches, her insistence upon the exact word and her skill in finding it. There is in her writing a pictorial quality which one is quite prepared to find in the work of a painter. There is in both her painting and writing a sweep, an almost elemental quality, very vigorous, very masculine. It is a spirit akin to that of her favorite poet, Walt Whitman. . . .

Lawren Harris also wrote a review of *Klee Wyck*, "Emily Carr and Her Work," attributing to it ". . . a timeless quality" and stressing that the written sketches were worthy companions of Emily's painted sketches: "Both go to the heart of the matter seen and experienced," he said . . . "The depiction of a scene or incident or mood of nature in these sketches is sometimes so startling in its vividness that it passes beyond description and

* The Canadian Forum, *December 21, 1941.*

* *Then Literary Editor of the Montreal* Gazette.

* *Then Literary Editor of the Toronto* Globe and Mail.

* *Both quoted passages are excerpts from Emily's undated letters. Ruth Humphrey disputes their accuracy. She does not recall any such conversation about the radio review and states that she took her own copy of* Klee Wyck *to class to read some portions of it to her university students as an example of undecorated and effective writing.*

* *The first (undated) written late 1941, the second on June 30, 1942.*

becomes evocation."*

The well-known writer and critic, Blair Fraser,* was unstinting in his praise:

> In these pages we meet an artist, whatever her medium, and to meet her is a rare privilege. It's also a privilege, as she makes you aware, to meet her Indian friends, such as Sophie. She likes them, herself—without sentimentality, and with full respect. She respects their ancient culture, their way of life, their language and faith; their art, as expressed in the totem poles, she admires unreservedly.

Blair Fraser's counterpart in Toronto, W. A. Deacon,* claimed that Emily's book had "no rival in charm," and finally, Dr. G. G. Sedgewick, broadcasting a review of *Klee Wyck* over CBR, was exceptionally warm in his praise:

> One by one, the sketches get home, some gently and humorously, some pathetically, others with a kind of sinewy power. Each one of them strikes fire from some facet of this region's life or appearance. . . . they pungently SMELL of the West Coast, particularly of Vancouver Island—of the cedar trees, the tides, the mists, the hills, and—very pungently indeed—of the Indian villages.

This radio review pleased and flattered Emily immensely and she was indignant with Ruth Humphrey (one of the few times, as she regarded Ruth as one of her staunchest friends) because she neglected to phone immediately to applaud it. Emily waited impatiently for a week and then, unable to restrain herself, called to ask Ruth's opinion: "Oh!" said Ruth. "Didn't I mention it? I didn't think it as good as his reviews generally are." "Well," retorted Emily, "Lawren and Ira thought it fine." Being cross with Ruth, she boiled over in a letter to Ira Dilworth: "She (Ruth) asked to borrow my copy of *Klee Wyck* for her pesky school kids—rather cheek, I thought."*

Emily's exhilaration and happiness about the reviews, the birthday party and the official accolades suddenly collapsed and a reaction set in. She was accustomed to scorn and ridicule, particularly in Victoria, and took an almost masochistic pleasure in torturing herself about the supposed indifference of her friends. She slipped once more into her familiar role of martyr, and in two letters to Ira Dilworth, poured out her dissatisfaction and disappointment:*

> 1. How grand and lovely everyone is to me and you about *Klee Wyck*. Did I sound as if I had expected more

when you asked me to-day? Oh! No! I did not expect half so much. It's only Victoria. I feel a little chilled, but Victoria is like that always I think. Really I have *very* few friends here. . . . Flora Burns is the only intimate friend in Victoria who has been warm about *Klee Wyck*. Some people have made me feel I did sort of a brag writing. Edythe* was nice enough yesterday, but a little patronizing. Nan said a lot of stuff about having been privileged to hear some of *Klee Wyck* long ago in MS and always knew etc. But the joke is she *went* to *sleep* once when I read one to her and I never did read another.* . . . Bess* did not send me one line. Lawren did, but his was quite *individual*.

2. Congratulations on the medal-winning.* But for your help *Klee Wyck* would not have seen the light of day and would not have got the Governor General's pat on the head. There was a piece in the Saturday *Times*, a mention in the *Sun* and *Colonist*, and I heard it on the CBC news this a.m. Not one, either friend *or* foe (other than Alice and old Mrs. Marks) have rung up or commented—not even Flora. And it was out last Saturday, and this is Tuesday. . . . Do you wonder I turned in on myself? You can see surely what your sympathetic help and appreciation has meant to me? Don't you think Bess and Lawren might have written a word? Bess took *weeks* even to *acknowledge* the book *Klee Wyck* when I gave a copy to them. People I gave *Klee Wyck* to in Victoria, thinking they were my special friends, never even said the plain decent word "thanks." It was the indifference of *old* friends (people who have know me *all my life*) and members of the art society, who one would rather expect to hear from, who have completely ignored me and my works. Every kind word I got came from newer friends, most from Vancouver, or from complete strangers. Well, it makes the *thing itself* even more worthwhile *doing* somehow and the people less worthwhile. One concentrates more on objectives than on the froth. One separates 'blitherbags' from real.

But old friends *did* write, or visit, or telephone. Emily says herself that I went to her studio (especially to congratulate her) and that Flora Burns phoned. Just as certainly, Nan Cheney, Ruth Humphrey, Frederick and Humphrey Toms either wrote or called; and it is unthinkable that old family friends such as

* *The author.*

* *Nan Cheney. This, of course, is not true. Nan quite often listened to Emily's stories.*

* *Bess Harris.*

* *This refers to the Governor General's Award for General Literature. The Earl of Athlone was then Governor General. Emily later wrote less appreciatively about the medal she won for* Klee Wyck*: "My name and what for are scratched on it with measly gilt letters. . . ."*

Margaret Clay and Madge Wolfenden Hamilton would overlook such an important occasion. Even Jock Macdonald, whom she did not know well, wrote her "a long palavery letter saying he found *Klee Wyck* very sad." But Emily had expected to be the center of an excited and an admiring group of friends and acquaintances, and when this did not happen, the old friends had to bear the brunt of the blame.

She felt hurt again the following year by her friends' imagined failure to congratulate her on *The Book of Small*. She bemoaned "Small's flop": "It's been out ten days and not one comment, not one notice, not one ring-up (just a note from Ruth). Two casual comments on her jacket by Edythe and Nan. Gee! It has cut!"

Gradually, however, her spirits rose as praise for "*Small*" began to surface early in 1943: "Good reviews continue to come in about '*Small.*' " She had even recovered her usual buoyant sense of humor: "There was a horror in the *Colonist* Sunday. *Had me up painting in the woods at 4 a.m. this last summer.* Can't you see me? Performing feats that would fell an ox."* Then, almost exactly a year later, Emily was able to even boast about "*Small's*" reception: "Mr. Clarke tells me she is the *only Canadian* book to be published in wartime London. She is that yellowish paper with a white cover, quite neat. She has had some very good reviews."*

* *Emily to Myfanwy Spencer Pavelic (undated) 1943.*

* *Emily to Myfanwy Spencer Pavelic (undated) 1944.*

The last few years of Emily's life would have been almost unrelieved suffering and gloom had she not been able to write. Her books were the companions of her old age when she could paint little—then not at all. She worked on her stories at home, in the hospital and the nursing home—wherever and whenever she had the slightest respite from pain. It is quite likely that she was still writing when her fatal heart attack struck in the morning of March 2, 1945.

After 1937, when Emily concentrated on and finished her Indian sketches, she worked haphazardly for several years on her non-Indian stories (not yet organized into book groupings), on her autobiography, and on her journals. Because she inevitably became discouraged if she got a hard "crit" from one of her editors, and rewrote and retyped her material over and over, she would put one story or chapter aside to cool while she struggled with another. Her writing was thus in no sense chronological. Her last book,* for instance, written as *Birds* but renamed and published posthumously as *Pause: A Sketch Book,** was started in January 1938, more than three years before her first book was published. Emily has described her progress with *Pause*:

* *Except for the long-delayed journals.*

* Pause: A Sketch Book, *with illustrations by the author, Clarke, Irwin and Co. Ltd., Toronto, 1953.*

Am getting on with my new yarn at last. It is a lump of incidents & description of life in an English San (I was in one for 18 months). Maybe it's dry, maybe it's grim, maybe it's no good at all, maybe it's worked round the gamut of woes and come out amusing—I can't tell. I started its second typing yesterday, then after another thorough weeding & cleaning, I type it out clean. . . . Will get Miss Burns to correct spelling & punctuation, & tap it out myself.*

* *Emily to Ruth Humphrey, January 31, 1938.*

All through the late thirties and early forties, whenever she could hold a pencil in her hand, or peck out a few words on the typewriter, Emily maintained her grim determination to write, despite repeated heart attacks and two strokes. While in the Mayfair Nursing Home during a long enforced stay after her near-fatal heart attack in 1942, she describes the plucky effort this cost her:

*Small** is expected out by the end of the month. Mr. Clarke already has a third book in mind. . . . I have been working (much as they will allow). They insist on *much* rest but find if I am able for it writing calms me. In getting up, bodily movement, or much talking I am not a success. At lying quiet in bed I can do *some* writing. I had intended doing up some *old stuff* in here, but a pesky bunch of ideas got into my brain & the correcting has not been tackled yet.*

* The Book of Small, *published 1942. Emily's second book.*

* *Emily to Ruth Humphrey (postmarked) October 13, 1942.*

Emily's third book, *The House of All Sorts,** begun in 1937, grew slowly as she added one lively story after another about friction with her tenants and the subsequent upheavals in her apartment house and studio. The second half of the book, "Bobtails," dedicated to her sister Alice, and comprising twenty-five humorous sketches about her famous English bobtail sheepdogs, was completed only in January 1943 while she was still recuperating in the nursing home. "The *Bobtails,*" she wrote at the time, "are traveling with Mr. Dilworth. He said he was going to read the MS on the plane. . . ."*

* The House of All Sorts. *Clarke, Irwin and Co. Ltd., Toronto 1944.*

* *Emily to Myfanwy Spencer Pavelic (postmarked) January 15, 1943.*

By December 1943, Emily had also finished her autobiography—her "Biog," as she called it, and Nan Cheney commented on it: "[Emily] has written her autobiography which she gave to Ira and he let Bess and Lawren [Harris] read it. They say it is really good in spots. It must be *very* egotistical and of course is not to be published until after her death."* Emily, herself commented—enthusiastically:

* *Nan Cheney to Humphrey Toms, December 2, 1943.*

If you ever read my Biog: you will see I think that I did love *country* England. It was London & the English

> worship of traditions that riled me. My publisher, Editor & Lawren Harris, the only three I have allowed to read the biog, say she beats *Klee Wyck*, *Small* & the rest. It should be my best thing to be published. Personally I think it very bad taste to publish an autobiog till you're dead.*

* *Emily to Humphrey Toms, March 12, 1944.*

The "Biog," or *Growing Pains*,* Emily's fourth book, was the first to be published posthumously. Despite her glowing predictions, this did not prove to be her best book. In fact, it contains many inaccuracies. Madge Wolfenden Hamilton, who is better qualified than anyone to comment on Emily's "growing-up" years, has written an interesting review of it.*

* Growing Pains, *Oxford University Press, Toronto, 1946.*

* The B.C. Historical Quarterly *(Vol II, 1947, pp.63-64).*

Growing Pains was followed seven years later by Emily's fifth book, *The Heart of a Peacock*,* and her sixth, *Pause: A Sketch Book*, both published in 1953. The final section of *Peacock*, "Woo's Life," gives us twenty-three delightful sketches about Emily's petite, mischievous monkey. After Emily's 1937 heart attack, Woo lived a full year in Vancouver's Stanley Park zoo before she died of natural causes at the ripe age of fifteen. On Emily's urging, Frederick and I—and Nan Cheney too—visited her there several times and found her looking indecently naked without her bright pinafore, but happy with her own kind—not recognizing us nor pining for Emily.

* The Heart of a Peacock, *Oxford University Press, Toronto, 1953.*

Emily's journals, *Hundreds and Thousands*,* were not published until twenty-one years after her death, partly, I think, for technical reasons. Ira Dilworth had started editing them but, in indifferent health for several years, had only completed about ninety pages before he died in 1962. His niece, adopted daughter and heir, Phylis Dilworth Inglis, assisted the publishers to finish the work.

* Hundreds and Thousands, *Clarke, Irwin and Co. Ltd., Toronto, 1966.*

Almost as an after-thought, and in an effort by two publishers to squeeze the very last commercial drops from Emily's writing, two final slim volumes appeared: *An Address by Emily Carr*, in 1955;* and *Fresh Seeing*—two addresses by Emily Carr—in 1972.*

* An Address by Emily Carr, *Oxford University Press, Toronto, 1955.*

* Fresh Seeing—*Two addresses by Emily Carr, Clarke, Irwin and Co. Ltd., Toronto, 1972.*

An Address by Emily Carr was offered to mark the tenth anniversary of her death, and the erection by the Historic Sites and Monuments Board of a memorial plaque in front of the house where she was born in Victoria. Ira Dilworth, who unveiled the plaque at a small moving ceremony on May 11, 1955, also wrote the introduction to the book. The address was given on March 4, 1930, at a meeting of the Victoria Women's Canadian Club at the Crystal Garden (see chronology) and was, says Ira, significant as it and notices in the contemporary press of Victoria, show a degree of public interest in Emily and her work which "has perhaps not always been recognized as existing at so early a date as 1930." He did, however, err in writing that "An Address" was Emily's one formal public talk.

Dilworth's error is pointed out in the later book, *Fresh Seeing*, but Doris Shadbolt, who wrote the excellent preface, herself errs in saying categorically that "not only are these the only two public talks on art Emily Carr ever gave, one feels they were the only talks she had it in her to give." The first part of this statement is incorrect (see chronology), and the second is surely a matter of opinion.

In this little book, Emily's extremely unimaginative titles ("An Address" and "Talk on Art") have wisely been changed by the publishers to "Fresh Seeing" for the 1930 speech, and to "The Something Plus in a Work of Art" for the talk given before the Provincial Normal School students and staff on October 22, 1935.

In the preface to *Fresh Seeing*, Ms. Shadbolt writes:

> This publication of Emily Carr's two talks on art is an indication of the renewed interest in that great Canadian woman stimulated by the passing of the centennial anniversary of her birth in 1871.

Even after publication of her very successful books, Emily was unable to keep up with her soaring medical and hospital costs. She expressed grateful relief when her publishers in 1944 sent her advance royalties on *The House of All Sorts*. A little later, she received another check for $300 along with the happy news that the sale of her books had at last caught up with her advances. "What would I have done without my children?" she asked. But the royalties from books, and the accelerated sales of paintings was still not enough, even with her small regular income,* to support herself, help Alice, and pay for her "flighty" maids who came and went with upsetting regularity. Emily's financial situation remained precarious right up to the day of her death. She never achieved the ease of complete security. Less than two months before she died, she was still anxious: "I may have to sell [her manuscript for *Hundreds of Thousands*] before the time comes to publish."

* *Only $25 monthly rental (less taxes and expenses) from the house she had acquired in 1936 in exchange for her House of All Sorts, plus about $10 monthly income from bonds inherited from her sister Lizzie (also in 1936) and, a bitter pill for her to swallow, $15 a month from a wealthy niece who started these payments after the death of Lizzie whom she had previously helped.*

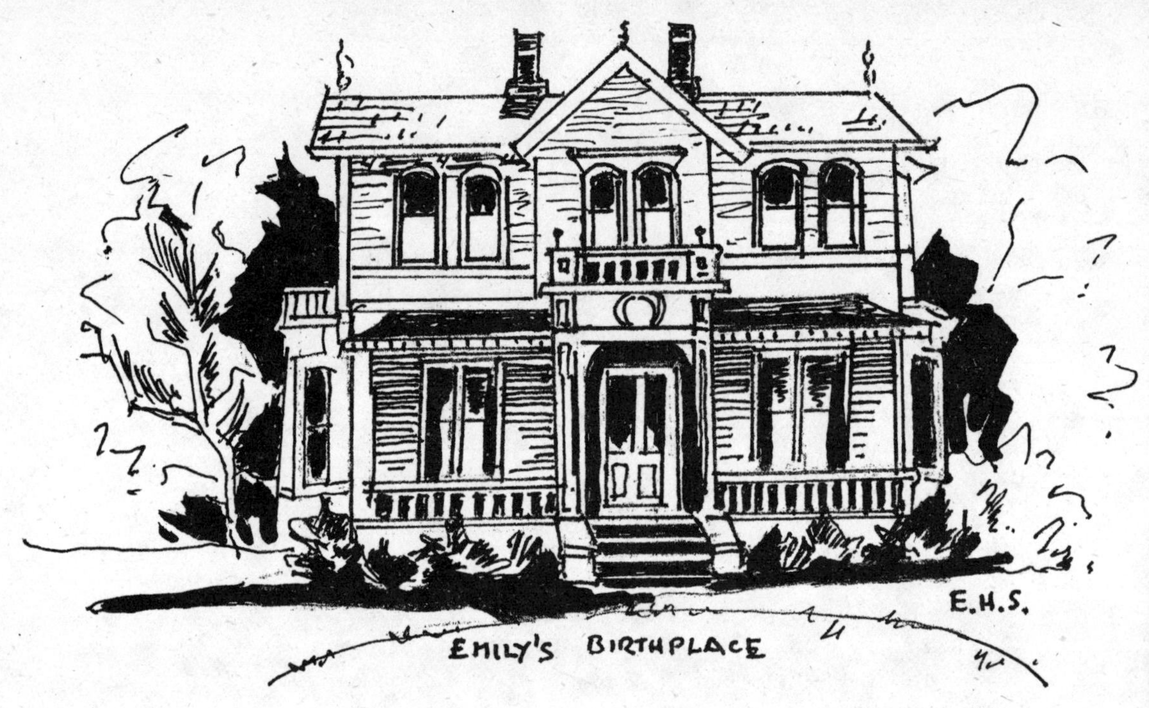

1871-1913 207 Government Street
Birthplace

Farewell

So farewell Emily! Despite your sometimes irascible, sometimes ungenerous behavior, those of us who knew you well, loved you well. We admired and supported your rare dual talents, and respected your integrity, your honesty and your grim determination to surmount the many obstacles that beset your life and work. After thirty years, we miss you still.

1945—March 2, died, age 74
St. Mary's Priory,
now: James Bay Inn
270 Government Street

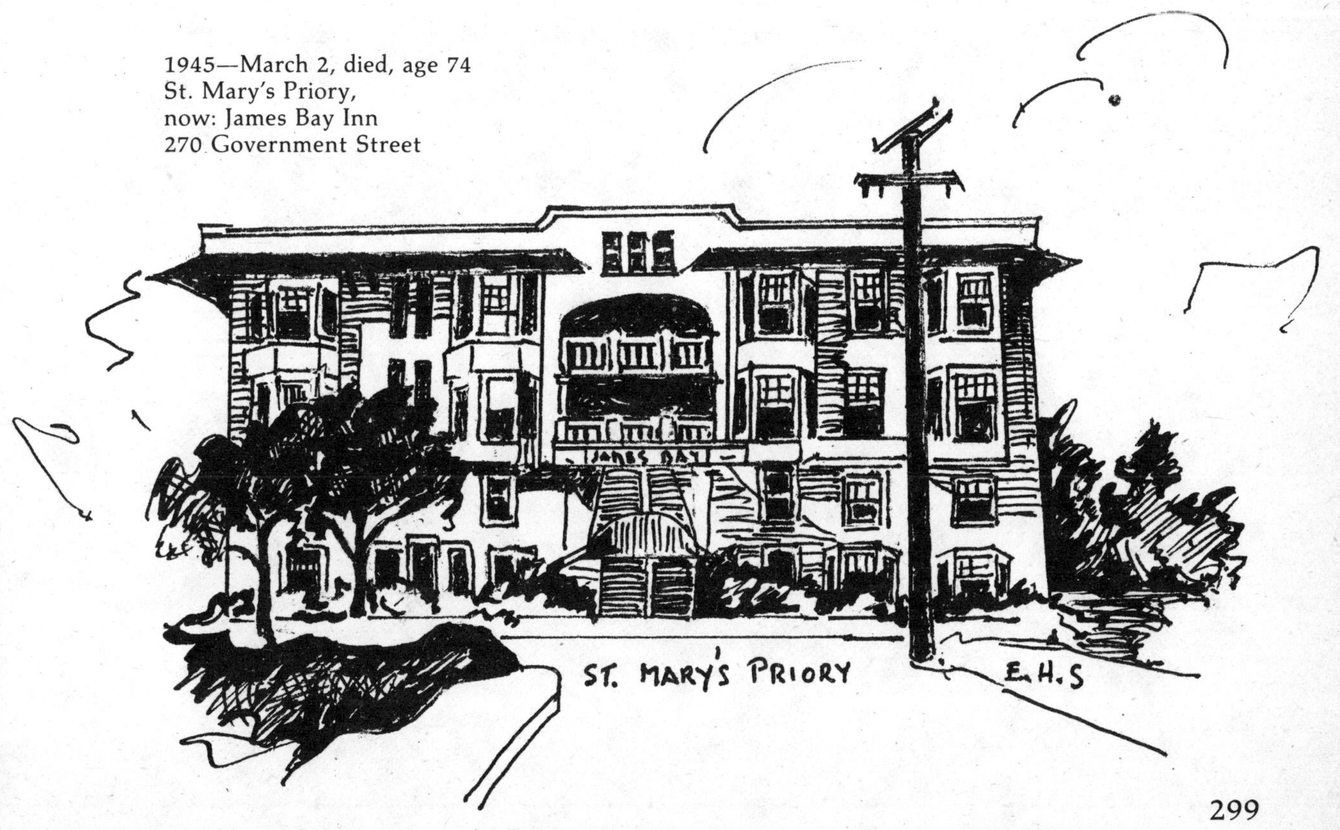

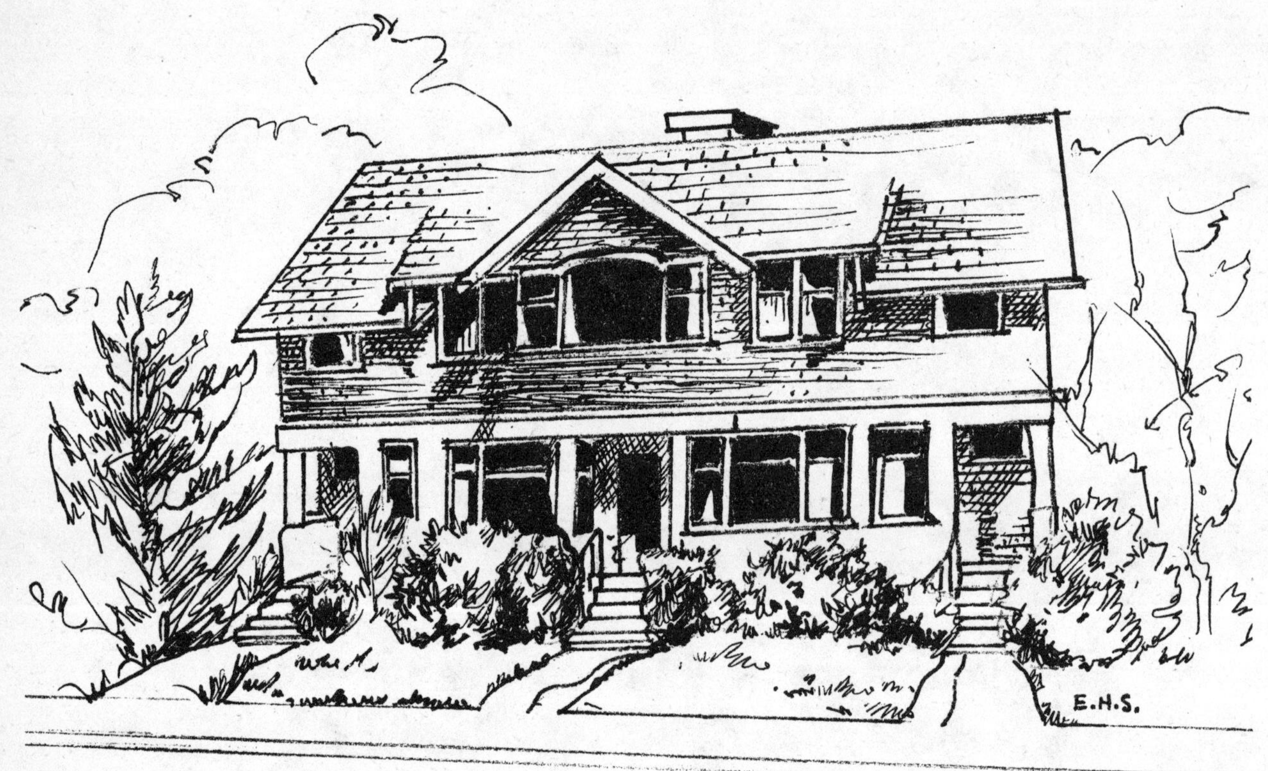

1913-1936 646 Simcoe Street
"House of All Sorts"

A History of Emily Carr's Exhibiting Career

An Annotated Catalogue

NOTE

It is recognized that the style of these exhibition lists is inconsistent and does not always conform to the usual format. However, this seeming lack of professionalism is intentional. It is the author's aim, apart from accuracy, to avoid the usual bone-dry lists and make them chatty and readable by introducing whatever interesting odds and ends that came to light for any given exhibition. Titles, prices, etc., are only given occasionally as a guide to the reader.

I Solo Exhibitions 1912-1945

Exhibitions which took place during her lifetime, with a few added for special reasons—up to 1972.

* * * * *

For Frederick J. Brand and Nan Lawson Cheney who got things moving for Emily in Vancouver.

* * * * *

1912
Vancouver **#2-1465 West Broadway** **March 25**

First exhibition held in her studio after returning to Victoria from France in November 1911, and to Vancouver in January 1912. It attracted about sixty guests—friends and others interested in the "new school of art." It was also the first of many solo exhibitions held in her various studios until the last one in 1936. About seventy of her paintings were on view for one day. The *B.C. Saturday Sunset* gave its write-up considerable space saying that "Miss Carr's at home and exhibition . . . was a great success, many of her guests being most enthusiastic over the 'new school' of art." The Vancouver *Daily Province* of March 25 wrote that: "The pictures are interesting as indicating the trend of recent French work in the direction of brilliant color and a certain distaste for detail. By the use of almost pure color, Miss Carr obtains some startling effects of light, and her technique is of great breadth and vigor." Emily's paintings were again on view in her studio Friday evening April 12, and each successive Friday until the end of the month.

These evenings were remembered six months later by W.C. Nichol writing in the *Daily Province* of September 14, 1912: "This year she spent in the wilds and last year in the foremost studios in Paris. Last winter her Friday evenings in her delightful studio were an inspiration to art lovers, who considered it a privilege to see some of the work of the new French school—'the modern movement' as it is sometimes called. It is hoped that Miss Carr will again this winter throw open her studio to allow her friends the privilege of seeing sketches of some of the remote corners of the northland."

1913

Vancouver Drummond Hall April 15-19

First large public showing of Emily's work—almost 200 pictures. Said to be the largest collection ever assembled by one artist on Indian themes—a very valuable record of a passing race. Many of these paintings were done during the summer of 1912 on a two-month sketching trip to Indian villages in the Queen Charlotte Islands and along the Skeena river. Others were large canvasses painted from on-the-spot sketches. Now painting more in oils, her work was characteristic of the bolder colors, simpler forms and freer brushwork she had learned in France. This exhibition was also the occasion of her first public talk. The *News-Advertiser* reported on April 13, that she lectured on her Indian work and the Indians themselves on Wednesday and Friday evenings.

Victoria in the studio, 646 Simcoe St. June

Shortly after her Drummond Hall exhibition, Emily returned to Victoria to live. She had built a small apartment house and studio and hoped to devote herself full-time to painting while the tenants paid off the mortgage. She opened this House of All Sorts in June with an "at home" and exhibition of her latest work, which included Indian paintings and some done in France. The people of Victoria were shocked by her use of totem poles as subjects and by her strong colors and unfamiliar shapes. The freshness, brilliance and charm of her French paintings went unnoticed. The newspapers listed the guests present at the function, but ignored the pictures.

c. 1928-1929
Calgary gallery unknown month unknown

The only solo exhibition of Emily's works in the twenties (apart from her studio show in Victoria) was held in Calgary. But when? Where?

I first learned about this early exhibition from an article, "Prairie Painting in the Dirty Thirties" in *Arts West* Vol. 1 No. 4 1976, in which the author, Archie F. Key, stated:

> An Emily Carr show came to Calgary in the mid-twenties. At that time when she was rejected by Victorians, a local women's club purchased one of the works for presentation to a newly founded Civic Collection of fine art.

After reading this article I wrote five letters to Calgary, but am not much wiser today. An exhibition undoubtedly took place there in the twenties, and a water color, *Gitwangak* (29¼" x 20½"), is known to have been purchased by a local women's club. But details are lacking because no early records survive. The painting was in the permanent collection of the Calgary Allied Arts Centre from 1946 to 1969 when the Centre was closed and its assets taken over by the Glenbow Foundation. This Foundation has since changed its name to the Devonian Group of Charitable Foundations and is the present owner of the picture. But they also know nothing of its background.

However, through another source, the National Gallery of Canada, I learned that *Gitwangak,* one of the twenty Emily Carr water colors held at the National Gallery early in 1928, was sold and forwarded to Calgary before mid-April. It was apparently hung in Emily's solo exhibition which, therefore, could not have taken place before the end of April 1928—not, as Archie Key has written, in the mid-twenties.

1928

Victoria in the studio, 646 Simcoe Street November

A still larger and more important studio exhibition was held in the House of All Sorts to display the work Emily had done in the summer of 1928 in Indian villages in the Queen Charlotte Islands and along the Nass and Skeena rivers, although some of her pictures done in France were also hung. Visitors admired the paintings and pottery in which, "she has preserved in such interesting form the fantastic art of the Haidas and other Indian tribes. The collection makes a weirdly barbaric display . . . making it easy to imagine oneself in some of the lonely villages along the Skeena, Nass or the northern shores of the Queen Charlotte Islands. Informed explanations given by Mr. Wm. Newcombe of the Natural History Museum, one of the foremost authorities on the West Coast Indian, served to give a livelier interest to the various details of the exhibition, as did Miss Carr's own description of the hospitable Indians amongst whom she spent many an interesting summer." (*Daily Colonist,* November 29, 1928.)

1930
Victoria — Crystal Garden Gallery — March 4-6

Exhibition by Emily Carr
Sponsored by the Victoria Women's Canadian Club.

A talk Emily gave at a meeting of the Women's Canadian Club at the Crystal Garden on March 4 to mark the opening of her first solo gallery exhibition in her native city was given wide publicity in both Victoria daily papers. The *Times* said in part: "The foregoing summarizes the earnest plea made by Miss Emily Carr . . . for a greater spirit of tolerance and understanding towards the modern artist who, striving to portray not merely the photographic delineations of Canada's beauty, but the very spirit and soul of its majestic appeal, deserts the traditional school of art for that of the impressionist.

"Miss Carr's plea was made the more forceful by the exhibition of her pictures. . . . Two distinct phases in the development of her art were apparent in the collection, the first, while virile and powerful in design, tending more to the 'photographic' interpretation of scenes of the Indian villages on the west coast and in other parts of the Province, while her later work showed a groping after and a conception of the spirit underlying the primitive art of the Indians, as expressed in her amazing studies of totem poles."

That the exhibition was an unqualified success was demonstrated by a record attendance at the Club meeting and the eagerness of Victorians to see her paintings, perhaps because, as Emily so typically said in her address: "Modern art may stir and irritate the onlooker, but isn't it more entertaining and stimulating to feel something unpleasant than to feel nothing at all—just a void?" Originally intended as a one-day exhibition, due to its popularity, it was held over until the 6th.

Ottawa **CNR ticket office, Sparks Street** **May**

Exhibition by Emily Carr

Dr. Marius Barbeau, who arranged this show, has said that it was held "upstairs and downstairs in the CNR ticket office." However, the Ottawa *Morning Citizen,* in its review, said in part: "An interesting visitor to Ottawa just now is Miss Emily Carr of Victoria, who may be said to be the West Coast representative of the newer Canadian School of painting. Miss Carr has devoted her talents mainly to interpreting the British Columbia scene and particularly the West Coast Indian villages and totem poles. Some examples of her work were on display in the windows of the CNR ticket office and attracted a good deal of attention." Whether an exhibition, according to Barbeau, or a display according to the review, it was Emily's first exposure in the East in her own show and thus an important event.

Seattle **Art Institute of Seattle** **November 25-January 4**
(forerunner of the present Seattle Art Museum)

Exhibition by Emily Carr

Emily's first solo exhibition on the international scene. She wondered how the Seattle art world, especially Mark Tobey, would react to her pictures and stewed about lack of news in her journals when no one telephoned her the day following the opening: "Well forget it old girl, I guess your work is only humdrum . . . just a little sideshow of the gallery for the month." Emily had expected her exhibition to be the main event of the month and was crestfallen that it had "flopped." But she perked up quickly a week later when reports started trickling in. There had been a great division over her work, she was told. People were either for or against it. Some thought it crazy—others were thrilled. The Director himself wrote that no one came or went away without saying *something,* which was exactly the kind of publicity Emily had hoped for.

The Victoria *Daily Colonist* wrote on December 4: "Miss Carr, by special invitation, has sent a collection of her paintings of British Columbia Coast Indian totems, villages and people. . . . The exhibition will continue until January 4 after which the pictures will be sent to San Francisco and Los Angeles to be shown. . . . In Seattle a group of ethnologists is also evincing a special interest in Miss Carr's work." The Museum has no catalogue of this exhibition.

Victoria in the studio, 646 Simcoe Street December

Exhibition and sale of pottery.

This was the last of Emily's annual Christmas sales and the first one I attended. Very few people came the two afternoons and evenings her work was on view and few sales were made—about a dozen bits of pottery and no pictures.

1931

Victoria in the studio, 646 Simcoe Street December

Emily wrote to Nan Cheney on December 14: "Yes, I gave a tea before my pictures went East as several had asked to see them. I gave no specials—just put it in the paper and left it to the public. To my surprise both afternoon and evening the studio was full. Of course some hated it but on the whole many expressed interest . . ."

1934

Victoria in the studio, 646 Simcoe Street July

A garden party and exhibition of sketches done the month before at Esquimalt Lagoon and the Strathdee farm at Metchosin for twenty-five to thirty summer session students of the short story class at the Provincial Normal School. Emily was stunned at the pop-eyed and shocked reaction of the students to her work: "Nobody knew what to say so there was that awful silence in which one tosses sketch after sketch on the easel hooks with nervous haste and wants to sink through the floor. Then someone breaks the silence with a horrid, 'What's that supposed to be?' " (*Hundreds and Thousands,* p. 139)

Victoria in the studio, 646 Simcoe Street August

A combination exhibition and purely private party given in honor of my sister Ruth Hembroff Herrington who was visiting from New Haven. One of the three guests from Seattle was my younger sister, Helen Hembroff Ruch. The three from New York were Frederick Brand, Jack Shadbolt and myself, all three of us having recently returned from a year's study in the East. The two from Paris were J. Delisle Parker and his mother. Delisle had also been studying abroad. John McDonald may also have been there but I can really only guess who the other "twenty-five souls" were. During the "exhibition," my sister Ruth purchased a sketch. Emily asked only $5.00. Years later it was sold to Dr. Stern in Montreal.

1935

Victoria in the studio, 646 Simcoe Street April 2-7

A series of exhibitions held in a downstairs flat of the House of All Sorts. Emily reported that it had been far beyond her expectations, and that some 200 people came and, on the whole, were keenly appreciative and interested in the work. During the first two days she showed thirty early Indian paintings. It is not clear what was displayed on the third day, but by the fifth day the third and last exhibition had been hung—modern landscapes and her later Indian works which, she said, looked somehow lacking and dark: "Maybe I am tired and that's the reason. How completely alone I've had to face the world, no boosters, no artist's backing, no relatives interested, no bother taken by papers to advertise, just me and an empty flat and the pictures." (*Hundreds and Thousands,* p. 176.) Feeling bone-weary and dispirited throughout these shows, Emily nevertheless came to the happy conclusion that they had been very worthwhile.

Victoria in the studio, 646 Simcoe Street August

A two-day exhibition held in the lower east flat of the House of All Sorts by request of the Provincial Normal (Summer) School. It was open to the general public on Sunday, August 4, and to teachers and students of the Summer School on the 5th. "Very well attended," wrote Emily. "Could one sift the entire sayings and conversations that passed in that flat today during those three hours, putting sincerity in one pile and insincerity in the other, which pile would mount higher? It is hard to be absolutely sincere. I believe people were absolutely sincere in their appreciation of the exhibition being open to the public free of charge. They like to get something for nothing and to satisfy their curiosity. A few were sincere in their liking of the work, but the insincere pile mounted high when it came to the work. One feels very strange, very callous." (*Hundreds and Thousands,* p. 189.)

Toronto Lyceum Club and Women's Art Association November

Exhibition by Emily Carr

This was Emily's first major solo exhibition in the East, a milestone for her. As she confided to her journal on October 19, she was very excited about it: "I have known for some days that I was to have an exhibition in Toronto at the 'Women's Art.' I felt a little thrilled about it—a chance to see if my work means anything to the outside world. The West is an absolute blank when it comes to ranking one's work." (*Hundreds and Thousands*, p. 201.) This was an exhibition of fifty sketches. Emily was very hard up at the time and unable to pay for shipment of large, heavy pictures. She agreed to show at the Lyceum Club and Women's Art Association only because the sketches, ". . . are on paper and light and inexpensive to transport." The exhibition was very successful and given almost heady praise in a fine review by Graham McInnes, "The World of Art," in *Saturday Night* (December 7, 1935). Emily was so touched and pleased that she said she was "dreadfully embarrassed and blushed up" when a friend read it to her. She wrote me (March 8, 1936) of Yvonne McKague Housser's delayed reaction to the show. Mrs. Housser had said that the pictures were well received and that Lismer had given a lecture on modern art while they were still on the wall. She also reported that Professor Helford, Head of Fine Arts at the University, and the Instructor in art at Upper College were both impressed. Fred and Yvonne Housser were "thrilled." Emily felt that her paper sketches represented a very important aspect of her work. Actually she did not look on them as true sketches but, mounted on board or buckram, as a permanent part of her picture collection. She made the following comment on them in 1942: "Yes, I *know* the sketches have spontaneity and freshness. I thought Lawren [Harris] did not approve of them—doubted their permanency at first, being paper. I feel I owe half of any knowledge I have gained to these sketches." (Emily to Ira Dilworth, April 19, 1942.)

1936

University of Toronto Hart House probably early Jan.

Exhibition by Emily Carr

This was Emily's second major solo exhibition in the East. It followed closely on the heels of the first, at the Lyceum Club and Women's Art Association, and it is believed that the same pictures were shown. But much less is known about it. In fact, it is the most hidden of all Emily's more important shows as it is not mentioned in her journals nor in letters to friends. Hart House itself was unable to give any helpful information. In reply to my inquiry, the Programme Advisor wrote on May 22, 1974: "To the best of my knowledge and according to our records, there has not been an Emily Carr exhibition at Hart House." It is strange that he did not at least mention the very favorably reviewed exhibition of twenty-six of her works at Hart House in October 1963.

Victoria in the studio, 316 Beckley Street November 17

Two days before this show took place in Emily's small studio in her rented cottage, she wrote to me: "On Tuesday I am having a few people in to see my summer sketches. Rather an ordeal, and it remains to be seen how it will work out in the cottage. I shall use the two front rooms and studio and show the sketches on an easel in the kitchen, being my biggest room. Hope Woo comports herself decently. . . . I wish you and Fred could be here to help me. Alice is coming. There will probably be around fifteen. One or two are uncertain and Margaret Clay, Ruth Humphrey and Miss Bruce are bringing people as well. So there may be room for all of us in the pantry *or* the walls of the cottage may burst. Well, all part of the game and nothing is *all* nice." In the end about twenty-five guests came. In one room were modern oils, in one Indian mixed periods, and in the studio woods things. The sketches were shown in the kitchen. The people were seated at one end of the room, the lighted easel was at the other. One man sat on the stove, fortunately not lighted. Emily showed about twenty-five 1936 sketches. This was Emily's last studio exhibition. About two months later she suffered her first heart attack and was never able to show her work publicly in the studio again.

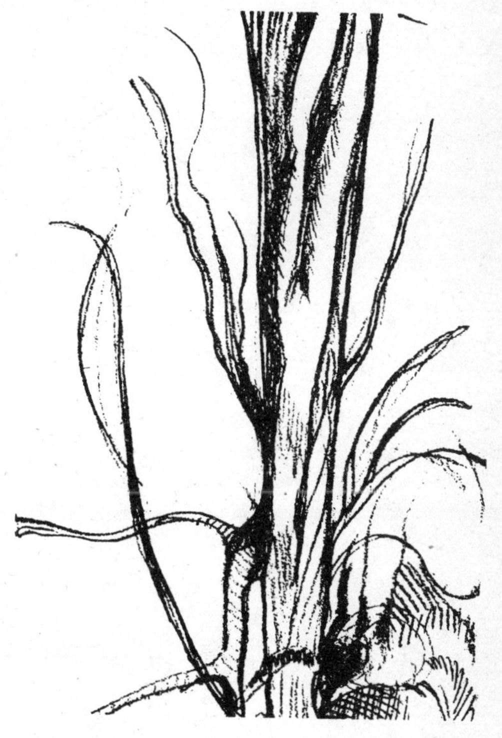

1937

Toronto Art Gallery of Toronto (East Gallery) March-April

Exhibition by Emily Carr

Emily's first solo exhibition in the Toronto Gallery. It is not listed in AGT exhibitors' file, nor in the Gallery Bulletins, catalogues or Annual Report files. The only mention made of it was in the Minutes of the Exhibition Committee and newspaper clippings reviewing the show.

Emily seems confused about the composition of this exhibition, as nothing was sent direct from Victoria and she had no control over it. Since there was no catalogue, only a list secured in 1945, it is still not known whether the pictures sent East for Charles Band* were included or not. If not, only nineteen paintings were on view—sixteen oils and three water colors. Emily commented on this exhibition: "As far as I can make out my things sent to [Band] are in Toronto where my one-man show was. They have asked to keep the balance for a year, hoping to sell more or use them in exhibitions and I guess they may as well. I don't pine for them back." (Emily to Ruth Humphrey, [postmarked] May 28, 1937.)

Emily also mentioned that about twenty canvasses were

* *Charles S. Band, a member of the Council of AGT and the first collector to recognize Emily's talent and purchase her works.*

collected from Toronto and Ottawa, and that she got two good press reviews and a check for $50 for a canvas.

1938

Vancouver Vancouver Art Gallery October 12-23

Exhibition by Emily Carr

Finally, the first solo exhibition at VAG (twenty-eight oils were listed, but No. 29, *Edge of the Woods,* was added in handwriting). The moving force behind this exhibition came first of all from Eric Brown, then Director of NGC, who had helped Emily so much in 1937 after her heart attack by requesting Eric Newton, noted art critic for the *Manchester Guardian,* to select fifteen of her paintings for shipment East to show to prospective buyers. Many were sold and Emily was thus enabled to meet her mounting medical costs. At the end of 1937, still wanting to assist Emily, Eric Brown wrote to Nan Cheney, an Ottawa artist who had recently moved to Vancouver: "I hope she will have enough [money] for some time to come and I imagine that you could perhaps help her to arrange a representative show of her work for next winter." Nan was therefore the one who got the show rolling although A.S. Grigsby, the Curator of VAG, was glad to cooperate. Nan, J.W.G. Macdonald and I hung the show (Emily to Nan Cheney, October 17, 1938.) Emily was bubbling with excitement about the whole thing and worked feverishly to prepare, mount and frame the paintings she had selected. She commented frequently on the coming exhibition in letters to both Nan and me as far back as August 15: "And I'm *tired* as the Devil trying to prepare my show in October . . ." On September 13 she wrote to Nan again: "Had to get my work off to Vancouver. . . . Your own shows are frightfully harrowing. It is *good* for you to see your stuff hung but meeting the onlookers—horrors!!" Then, once more to Nan on October 4: "Now the stuff is off (or packed) I can live again. It has laid me low—like a toppled mountain." She continued on October 11: "The show opens tomorrow. . . . I guess perhaps it is best that I can't go to Vancouver as money's a bit tight and all just now. My frames etc. cost $20.00 and I do not expect there will be any sales. This money-root-of-all-evil business, isn't it a curse? Unless I make an occasional sale I really have *very* little to live on." At the last moment, Emily changed her mind and did go to Vancouver after all, staying with Nan and Hill Cheney. She reported to me: "Glad I saw the exhibition. It is good for one and sits their conceit down bump. I saw many things in my work I wanted to pull up on."

Emily was jubilant and almost unbelieving about the success of her first VAG show when she received a cheque from Grigsby for $172.00. It was well reviewed in the press. The *Daily Province*, for instance, reported on October 13: "Judged by this show, no other painter has come so close to the heart of the province. Although at first glance the pictures appear to be merely forest scenes, a closer study reveals forms, color and light which drive toward a fundamental conception of B.C. as a growing organism."

There was a great deal of correspondence about this exhibition—Emily wrote to all her friends, and friends wrote to one another. One such letter was sent by Nan Cheney to Humphrey Toms: "I have been so excited about Emily's exhibition . . . the show was a tremendous success. . . . She sold eleven pictures and the gallery is very pleased that I urged them to take a chance—in fact I am patting myself on the back that everything went off so well after my *year* of working Emily up to the idea and the gallery up to the point of inviting her. However I understand that Professor Lewis is taking all the credit and when the show went out to the university, the speeches to the students were to the effect that *they* had *just* discovered this genius and no one else had ever heard of her. I was more than amused—however, she sold a lot out there and that is the main thing after all." In her elation about the outcome of her show, Emily also wrote to Eric Brown: "I believe you will be interested to know that VAG gave me a one-man show last month and that the Vancouver people were most kind and appreciative. Ever so many went and many went several times. I had such lovely letters from people I knew and some I did not telling me what the things meant to them personally. These are much better thanks than the space-filler write-ups in the papers by people paid by the line with nothing in their heads or hearts. Of course it was not Victoria. Victoria is just art-hopeless, but it warmed my heart coming from as near home as Vancouver. What made me so pleased about it was the fact that I had been able to make their own Western places speak to them. If they [the pictures] had been shown in England or France it might have been only the picture technique or something that interested them. But the fact that the spirit of the places they know said something to the people who lived in them made me very happy." (NGC, Emily to Brown, November 24, 1938.)

Vancouver University of British Columbia Library Nov. 1-4
Exhibition by Emily Carr

Comprised of twenty-four paintings drawn from Emily's show at VAG the preceding month, plus ten from private collections, this exhibition was originally the idea of Assistant Professor Hunter Lewis of the English Department UBC. He completed the arrangements with the University and took charge of the publicity, but working with Emily was a different matter. They inevitably clashed and she refused to cooperate with him. In an undated letter written in October, she gave *me* full authority to take over: "I would have thought that Vancouver had had enough 'Emily' without encoring the dosage. If it is just for that Hunter Lewis—no! (I don't like him.) For you—yes! *Show* if you want to. Go ahead and have a University show! . . . I am afraid it will give you a lot to do and you already seem so rushed. I hope H.L. will help and not get some malady that will leave the heavy end to you. Why is that man such a crimson waver to my bovine nature? The dealings I did have with him were small and mean personally. I scarcely know him, though, and I'm a *cat.* I leave the authority to you, not him, and you will see they are re-packed right—no padding; only cleats to keep [the pictures] taut."

This was Emily's first show of her own at UBC. The other two (1933 and 1936) she had shared with other painters. I cannot recall why Frederick did not organize this one as he had the others, but he wrote the review of the exhibition in the University students' newspaper, *The Ubyssey*, giving a short biographical sketch, a description of her painting and of her work methods in the caravan: "She goes out in differing light of morning, afternoon and early evening, to make the large paper sketches in oil, examples of which are on show in the library. These, always completed at a sitting, are scarcely ever retouched." Emily really bubbled over in her first letter to me after the show: "I am simply *overwhelmed* and my head turning clean round hind before on my neck, with all the nice things said and done. I'll be uppish soon. I am so glad for your sake and Hunter Lewis's as well as my own that the exhibition was a success and am glad that the students enjoyed it. Dr. Sedgewick has always been *very nice* to me and Hunter Lewis too although why he should is beyond my comprehension as my behaviour had not warranted it. . . . I know the pictures were well hung at the gallery and university, thanks to the Brands and Cheneys and Grigsbys, not forgetting the military staff of the gallery."

A few days later she wrote to Frederick: "I was astonished at how many sales were made. In fact my breath is not back yet from jumping off on a honeymoon with surprise. Now I can settle to work again. The last few weeks have been hecticish with so many letters to write and all the surprise sellings and compliments. I bought a hat just before the ex and now it won't fit." Still later she wrote another fine letter of appreciation: "Thank you a million for everything. The crates came back this a.m. . . . I think you and Fred have been wonderful and I am grateful from the bottom of my heart and am so glad that the students and faculty enjoyed the pictures. It's just grand about the sales. As to cracking—I do not think there is the least fear. The sketches are mounted on *heavy* three-ply and you can't crack that. Perpetual wet can cockle it but no picture is exposed to perpetual wet. Far better than the muslin back and more permanent. The UBC article, I think, was fine. Perhaps it made me a trifle 'pioneer' about there being no mode of travel except canoe but still, that *is true* of some of my side trips and I think the Brands did fine by me and that really is a revolting job (the writing up) especially when their victims kick like me."

1939

Vancouver University of British Columbia Library probably July

Exhibition by Emily Carr

This is another "lost" exhibition as the only reference to it that has so far turned up is in a letter dated August 6, 1939, from Nan Cheney to Humphrey Toms. Apparently the exhibition had just taken place and was a solo show, perhaps for summer students. Nan was in charge of this show, but she cannot recall the date. She wrote at the time: "The exhibition at the University was a flop due to that stupid Riddington (the then Librarian). It was not advertised, even round the University, and of the 700 students only twenty turned up for Weston's lecture. It was an awful lot of work—actual physical labor and Riddington was too superior for words—considered he was doing us the greatest favor, etc. I haven't been so mad for years. . . . *Never* again. They can whistle for the next show. Don't tell Emily. It might upset her. I can explain what is necessary when I see her."

Vancouver Vancouver Art Gallery November 7-19

Exhibition by Emily Carr

In this second solo exhibition at VAG, forty works were shown including Emily's favorite Indian painting *Totem Mother: Happiness,* a gift to Myfanwy Spencer Pavelic a few years later, and her all-time favorite *Juice of Life,* priced incredibly low at $50.

Many others were painted from sketches done at Langford the previous June and at her Craigflower Road camp on the Gorge in September. Emily may not have considered *Juice* her best picture (she was often a poor judge of her own work) but it was her favorite for sentimental reasons. A gift to Ira Dilworth in acknowledgement of her gratitude and affection, it had a special meaning for her: "I understand the vague weariness of theosophy. It is ether not blood. [Others] maybe can feed on ether but you and I need a thicker 'Juice of Life.' " Nan Cheney wrote that this show was a tremendous success despite the bad times: "I hung it early one morning and Ross Lort, the architect, was so impressed he thought the gallery should buy the whole show and keep it as it stood for a permanent collection of Emily's work. Not so the founders, and Mr. Stone in particular, who raved and ranted and said they were a disgrace." Emily worked hard for this show as usual, and described her preparations in an undated letter to me: "Wow! Busy woman me! Got my material from the mill yesterday, mounting boards, frames and framing for mounted sketches, and have been working furiously with the priming coat. Today the house smells to Heaven and I ache. . . . If I am able to manage it, I plan to come up for a couple of days, probably to see it hung and started. . . . I don't know why (war I suppose) but I feel rather as if it will be a flop. . . . Have still some painting to finish. Have a good many out at present (13) . . . so, taking out all the ones shown in Vancouver last year it makes quite a bit of work getting together a good show. You know I am always opposed to showing old chestnuts. I think an artist's duty is to give the public his up-to-date work. Don't you?" Emily was exhausted when she wrote to Nan Cheney on October 30: "Am not going to expense of printed catalogues. Am I foolish? I am all in—dead tired. Have been at it strenuously. These one-mans do mean a lot of work that must be done by you and no one else. . . . I have cut out the finish on one or two pictures."

1940

Vancouver Vancouver Art Gallery November 5-17

Exhibition by Emily Carr

Emily's third solo exhibition at VAG finally opened as planned, but for a time it was in doubt due to her slow convalescence after a stroke in early June. However, by the end of July, she was *hoping* to have her "annual" on the reserved dates, as she had already mounted a lot of sketches from the previous year. By the middle of September, she was well enough to begin mounting those she had completed just before she collapsed and, one month later, she had reached the signing stage. Forty-two paintings were shown.

Nan Cheney described the exhibition to Humphrey Toms on November 17th: "Emily's show is on now and simply *glows* from those dingy old gallery walls. This is the first one I have not been able to hang, but they look very well. Only five canvasses and all Indian so I doubt if she sells them—in fact no sales so far. But it is going to UBC for a week. She needs someone there (all shows do) to talk them up a bit." After the show was over, Nan wrote again: "She sold five pictures . . . she thought she should have sold more and wrote Grigsby and me an awful bleat about it. But you know what she is like—always biting the hand that feeds her. I smoothed him down with an explanation about her moods." Emily had written Nan earlier: "Was glad you liked the show. It was my first intimation of what it looked like. However, [Grigsby] dropped me a line that there were *many visitors* on Armistice Day and people thought it my best yet in Vancouver. . . . I am putting the final touches on three good-sized pictures—ready for *next* year's show." Emily's final comment on this show was: "The exhibition was successful, people more enthusiastic than usual. I had nice letters and sold five, more than I expected, especially as it was during the Community Chest drive. I felt this time particularly anxious it should be a bright, happy, springish show these war days, as a little booster to the spirits, and it seemed to work."

Vancouver University of British Columbia Library November
Exhibition by Emily Carr

Hunter Lewis, who had earnestly tried to help Emily by writing reviews of her work, buying a picture and attempting to organize the 1938 UBC exhibition, could do nothing right in Emily's jaundiced eye. After her snubbing in 1938 when she put me in charge of the show, he surfaced again in 1940 and decided to try once more. Frederick and I had left Vancouver by then and do not know the circumstances, but the show, despite ruffled feathers and insults, was somehow hung and declared a success. We can only guess what went on to provoke another outburst in a letter to Nan: "That *fool Hunter Lewis* wrote me a spiel. He is absolutely undependable, full of excuses, etc. I detest the man. Suffered extreme meanness at his hands. However, as there are other men on the faculty I'spose they might keep him up on the ex. No *Fred and Edythe* this time, no Nan in Vancouver, no nobody, no nothing. Not even an old me to poke my nose round the corner." Emily was soon mollified, however, when she heard the news that two sales had been made. Hunter Lewis was an extremely polite man and deferential to Emily in his dealings with her. He tried in every way to please and promote her, but in doing so, only succeeded in provoking her. It is hard to understand how some people, for no reason at all, aroused instant and lasting antagonisms in her. She was, of course, furious with Hunter for paying more for the beautiful frame he bought for her picture than for the picture itself.

1941
Vancouver Vancouver Art Gallery October 21-November 2
Exhibition by Emily Carr

Emily's fourth solo exhibition at VAG. Twenty-eight works. She started working hard for it in August, had a nasty upset about the middle of the month and had to take two weeks rest. But she got the pictures off in time despite her agitation about Grigsby's departure and Max Maynard's appointment as interim Curator: "Would never have had one [a show] this year had I known how things were going." This unwillingness to cooperate with Max (she disliked Max and Jack Shadbolt because of their supposed arrogant treatment of me and my painting)* blew up into a storm after this exhibition when Max had good solid crates made to return Emily's paintings in place of the flimsy, damaged ones in which they had been received. Emily wrote him a "stinker" about the way her canvasses had been returned, saying she could not re-use the heavier crates because of increased shipping costs. Max was so upset he was unable to ignore the tongue-lashing and, in return, wrote her a "snorter." From this time on their relations steadily deteriorated. Emily was very close to her seventieth birthday when this show took place. The idea of reaching "three score and ten" had bothered her for some time as she wrote to Ruth Humphrey as early as February 13, 1938: "... curious how we hate that backing down. I shall refuse to paint after 70—think it is indecent, and folks say, 'Pore old thing, it amuses her, but of course . . .' "

"Palette" (pseudonym for the well-known painter J. Delisle Parker) reviewed this show for the *Daily Province* on October 23, saying in part: "Miss Carr's majestic interpretation of British Columbia landscape, especially of forest scenes and totem poles, maintains all the customary force and appeal. Although closely related in general character to the pictures by the painter shown in four special exhibitions in the past few years, the present display creates a different note. The style seems to assume a more stately tempo and has less of a fascinating but rather

* *Emily also told Ruth Humphrey that this was the cause of her dislike. Max today agrees that he may have been arrogant, but says he was quite unconscious of it at the time.*

disquieting movement. And there is greater insistence on the Indian subject matter. . . . Thus the present exhibition is linked with a book of stories appearing this week . . . entitled *Klee Wyck*. Four colored reproductions of the artist-author's work accompany this unique group of sketches based on local Indian characters and their villages."

Contributing to the success of the exhibition was a lecture on it by Jack Shadbolt who was given a rough time by a lively protestor who refused to leave the room when asked to do so. The *Sun* reports that: "Mr. Shadbolt extolled the virtues of the pictures of the artist which hung on the walls around him. In their gloomy formlessness he could see unmistakable values for posterity, though it was plainly evident that not all of the audience agreed with him." (October 25, 1941.) The *News-Herald* of October 21 also comments on the Indian canvasses: "Some uncanny sense has enabled Emily Carr to catch on canvas the eerie, sinister feeling of the totem. She seems to see it and paint it as it emotionally affected the Indian. . . . Nine years ago Emily Carr was refused a showing of her painting in local exhibitions. Today she is the top ranking Canadian artist and is represented in the National Gallery of Canada and in galleries in England."

Toronto Lyceum Club and Women's Art Association December

Exhibition by Emily Carr

Toronto *Telegram*, December 20, 1941: "An exhibition of pictures by Emily Carr was held at the headquarters of the Women's Art Association on Prince Arthur Ave. Many of the paintings were loaned by Charles Band and Douglas Duncan."

1942

London, Ontario London Art Gallery November 13-December 31

Exhibition by Emily Carr

There was no catalogue for this exhibition but, according to the *Gallery Bulletin* (Exhibitions 1942-1943), "A group of more than 60 paintings by Canada's foremost woman landscape painter and author of the current best-selling book *Klee Wyck* was exhibited . . ." It would be interesting to know from what sources the London Art Gallery acquired thirty-six Carr paintings—if indeed they did exhibit sixty—as only twenty-four were sent to them on October 29th from AGT. These same twenty-four paintings were then forwarded to the Art Association of Montreal in January 1943 for their first solo Carr exhibition.

This is a confusing series of exhibitions as the galleries in both London and Montreal have virtually no records to document them. Dr. Clare Bice, then Curator at the London Art Gallery, remembers the exhibition well and says that the paintings "were all poorly framed and really looked quite pathetic." None, he said, was sold.* It was a very impromptu exhibition since Lawren Harris wrote at the last moment to ask if any space could be made available. There was no specific schedule. Only its purpose was clear: Lawren Harris's desire to sell a few paintings to help Emily. He made the same request of other centers "in the East."

* *My list of the twenty-four paintings shipped to the London Gallery from AGT includes two paintings which merit comment: (a)* Indian House Interior *and (b)* Scorned as Timber Beloved of the Sky.
(a) Although this painting should have gone forward to Montreal with the rest of the exhibition, since no paintings were supposedly sold, it does not appear on the list of "23 Emily Carr Pictures in Montreal" attached to AGT Curator Martin Baldwin's letter of January 8, 1943, to Arthur Lismer of AAM (from the files of AGT). This suggests that this picture was in fact sold in London, despite what the Gallery remembers today.
(b) One of Emily's most famous paintings and the subject of a poem, "Scorned as Timber, Emily Carr 1872 [sic] - 1945," by Charles Lilliard. (Prism International, Vancouver, B.C., Spring 1973.)

1943

Montreal Art Association of Montreal (now MMFA) January

Exhibition by Emily Carr

The following reply was received from the MMFA about this badly-chronicled exhibition: "Upon checking again this file of the first one-man show Emily Carr had at the Museum, we were unable to find a list of works, but do know that there were thirty-three of them, twenty-four having been exhibited at the London Art Gallery, the show closing December 31, 1942. The other nine had been sent direct from AGT."

Although this exhibition is described in the VAG centennial catalogue as "a matter of prestige" for Emily, facts do not support such a glowing report. It was not a large-scale, carefully planned exhibition like the one following it in Toronto, but a small, hurriedly-put-together show of paintings in crude, homemade frames, most sent on from London, at Lawren Harris's request. It could not have been regarded as a very special event by AAM as they did not print a catalogue, or even prepare a list. However, Arthur Lismer A.R.C.A. did give a lecture, *Emily Carr and Her Paintings,* on January 8, and it was the Gallery's opening show of the year.

Toronto Art Gallery of Toronto February

Exhibition by Emily Carr

No catalogue was printed for this large and important exhibition but there is a list of the ninety-two oils and water colors shown, sixty-one of which were from the Emily Carr Trust. The other thirty-one paintings were from galleries or private sources. All Emily Carr Trust pictures shown were being stored at AGT for safekeeping during the war. (See: "The Emily Carr Trust.") Nan Cheney's letter of October 18, 1942 to Humphrey Toms gives us a little background information about this exhibition: "Her exhibition is not to be held in Toronto until February and she refused to have my portrait of her included. I am not surprised, knowing Emily." Emily inexplicably turned against this excellent portrait although she had praised and liked it (with a few small reservations) when it was painted in November 1937. She also complained that the Gallery, "tried to have me fix dates and [give] rubbish for the catalogue. I don't know one date of me from birth to death. Makes me sick to be perioded like furniture and china." Nevertheless, she eagerly awaited news of the show and was disappointed when it was slow in arriving: "No one has written to me or sent cuttings to me, but Ira says Lawren had a letter from A.Y. Jackson that it looked fine and filled three galleries." (Last two quotations are from letters to Myfanwy Spencer Pavelic.)

"Palette" describes Emily's "notable success at Toronto" in the Vancouver *Daily Province* of February 11, 1943: "The display represents the first comprehensive of her works, with additions from private sources, to be seen in Toronto." Critic Pearl McCarthy of the Toronto *Globe and Mail,* refers to Emily as one of the half-dozen most honored artists in this country: "It is difficult to imagine how anyone can be proof against the powerful impact of these paintings. Miss Carr is apparently not only at home in the world of aesthetics but is just as surely in touch with nature."

Vancouver **Vancouver Art Gallery** **June 11-24**

Exhibition by Emily Carr

Twenty-seven works. In August 1942 Emily went on her last sketching trip to the Mount Douglas woods and completed fifteen large manila paper sketches and a number of smaller studies which she hoped to have ready for another annual exhibition at VAG that fall. But she suffered a very serious heart attack almost immediately after her return home from this over-strenuous trip and her Vancouver show had to be cancelled. She therefore showed these sketches in 1943—in her last exhibition at VAG. She knew it was to be her good-bye show, and was sorry it seemed rather sombre. "But," she said, "that was the character of the woods thereabout. But they were not *sad*. It was a very happy session in my cabin at Mount Douglas Park." Lawren Harris was enthusiastic: "Fine, fine, swell!" he kept repeating. "She's an amazing person, going on constantly." He was very impressed with the strength and, at the same time, the delicacy of Emily's latest work. (From a conversation with Ira Dilworth in June, 1943.)

It was a dreadful ordeal for Emily to finish and ship this

show to Vancouver in time for the opening. She started preparing for it in May, but was feeling "pretty miserable." "[I] hound myself to the easel for an hour or two. Will be so glad when the show is boxed and off." Shortly after writing these words, Emily was taken to the Jubilee Hospital where she was "good and big sick." She wrote about her problems to Myfanwy Pavelic: "The exhibition got done and is hung. Lawren and Ira came over to Victoria and we three had a glorious two-and-a-half-hours. I got up next two days and did finish bits of [the pictures] and then I collapsed. But the work was done. Willie [Newcombe] shipped and the others hung the final 'Emily one-man!' Ira thinks it is the best show I've had in the West."

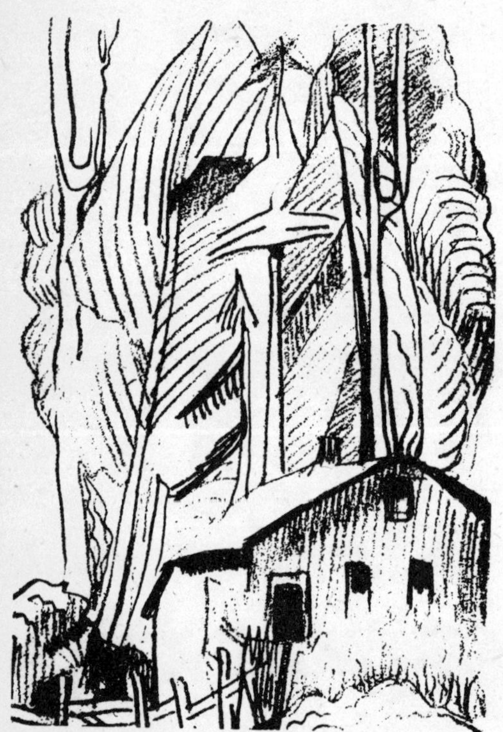

Nan Cheney did not agree with Ira: "Emily had a small show in the water color room downstairs and made $250.00. It wasn't half as good as in former years, but [it is] remarkable that she was able to do anything last year."

The Vancouver *Sun* critic agreed more with Ira than with Nan: "Victoria's Emily Carr, whose work both as an artist and writer has received such wide acclaim during recent years, is holding her fifth one-man show at the art gallery. There is something courageous and remarkable in the spectacle of this woman, no longer young and in very poor health, painting with such profusion and with growing power at an age when many are laying down their tools and slackening in the mental concepts.... The pictures on display are all landscapes and most of them have been painted in the vicinity of Mount Douglas Park near Victoria. The artist's preoccupation with tree subjects, especially wood interiors, are again the predominant features." Praise was heaped on Emily by friends and the press after this exhibition, but none of it made her as happy as Ira's comments had done after the 1942 sketching trip: "The work is actually very impressive. You have brought back from these woods in your sketches something that is true, exact, highly imaginative and impressionistic and yet almost literal too. By which I mean, that this work is a faithful, honest portrayal of what you saw and felt out there.... I thank you for letting me have a first look at them. I must see them again.... God should vouchsafe to you moments of calm vision and power to translate some part of your vision to others."

Seattle Seattle Art Museum August 25-October 3

Exhibition by Emily Carr

Emily's second solo exhibition in Seattle. No catalogue. Like so many others, this exhibition was arranged by Lawren Harris.

Emily wrote to me in Ottawa about this show—somewhat sketchily: "The Vancouver Art Gallery is considering sending my show entire to Seattle. They are holding it over while considering, or rather while Seattle considers. They have a nice little gallery over there." Certain customs problems were involved and Emily made a lot of fuss and a few conditions about it. Her concern stemmed from her experience with her 1930 exhibition in Seattle when the Canadian customs tried to charge her duty on frames she had failed to declare in advance, although no one would be tempted to smuggle in American frames had they had any resemblance to Emily's. She herself broached this subject in a letter to Grigsby, the Curator at VAG: "I had a one-man many, many years ago in Seattle—mostly Indian stuff. I remember it gave me a *terrible* amount of bother but I had no one to help me." She asked if she would have to pay duty on pictures bought by Americans and thought they should pay the full Canadian price. There is little information available about this exhibition in 1943. Emily was wretchedly ill at the time—too concerned about her private troubles to give it much thought. She did not even bother to make her usual comments in letters to friends, except for the two small references above.

1944

Montreal Dominion Gallery October 19-November 4

Exhibition by Emily Carr

It was a lucky day for Emily when Dr. Max Stern, well-known Montreal art dealer, called at her studio in August 1944. Almost unbelievably, Stern was not acquainted with Emily's work at that time, though she had had large, successful and well-publicized exhibitions in both Montreal and Toronto the previous year. He was bowled over when he saw her paintings: "I have never seen anything like it in Canada before," he said. He persuaded Emily to allow him to put on a comprehensive showing of her work in his Dominion Gallery in the autumn, and immediately drew up a contract for her to sign—after selecting sixty paintings for shipment to Montreal. Fifty-nine were hung. Sales were good. Among those purchased were Emily's self-portrait reproduced on the cover of VAG's centennial catalogue and *Indian Village, Alert Bay* for the permanent collection of AAM. (See chapter "Text of the Catalogue" for full details of the composition of this exhibition and a popular misconception of it.)

The exhibition covered all aspects of Emily's painting career from her first sketching trip to the Indian village of Ucluelet in 1898 to her last sketching trip to Mount Douglas

Park in 1942. Several portraits were also shown. Before Dr. Stern finally decided to risk a Carr exhibition, he asked Arthur Lismer's opinion. Lismer advised against it: "The pictures were interesting," he said, "but without sales value." Yet the exhibition turned out to be by far Emily's greatest practical success.

Stern wrote to Emily on September 5: "We shall arrange your exhibition in October and shall most probably show at the same time one French and two other English artists. However, the main room of our gallery will be given to your paintings and water colors. . . . The transport, so far, was not too expensive—thanks to light crating—namely $42.50." The *Montreal Star* wrote on October 20: "The exhibition which is now open at the Dominion Gallery shows some of the best work of the B.C. paintings of Emily Carr. Oil paintings by Miss Carr have often been shown here and some of these are in the collection. These show the native villages and scenery of her native province and have a value, in addition to their pictorial worth, in leaving records of Indian life and surroundings which are fast disappearing. Miss Carr's water colours have been seldom seen in exhibitions. A number of them are in this collection and are even more admirable than the oil pictures. Some of them are Canadian but many, and they are among the best, are of places and people in France. Some portrait sketches are notably good." This was Emily's last exhibition. She died four months less two days after it closed. When Stern first proposed sponsoring it, Emily was doubtful because of her dislike of Montreal. However, she did not deliberate long and was soon writing to Ira: "As Lismer and Jackson work with him, I 'spose he is O.K. and of course it is advisable to rid myself of as much as I can and not leave the junk on Alice. How different one must feel when they have anyone who *cares* to leave things to."

1945
Toronto **Art Gallery of Toronto**

Emily Carr: Her Paintings and Sketches (Memorial Show)

Circuit:	AGT	October 19-November 19, 1945
	NGC	December 8, 1945-January 8, 1946
	AAM	January 24-February 10, 1946
	VAG	May 1-26, 1946

A great retrospective of Emily's work—in four major galleries. According to the *NGC Annual Reports 1940-1950*, the exhibition comprised 265 works, but the exhibition catalogue,

Emily Carr: Her Paintings and Sketches, lists only 177. The paintings are numbered 1-265 in the catalogue, no doubt accounting for the seeming error in the *Reports,* but there are unexplained gaps in the list between the oil paintings and water colors: 79-101; between the water colors and oil sketches: 125-151; between the oil sketches and charcoal drawings: 172-201; and between the charcoal and brush drawings: 236-251.

The exhibited pictures were: seventy-nine oils; twenty-five water colors; twenty-two oil on paper sketches; thirty-six charcoal drawings; fifteen brush drawings; that is, 177 pictures. *Indian Village, Alert Bay* (purchased by AAM from the Dominion Gallery in 1944) was chosen for the cover plate—why is a mystery because it is an early work, not typical of Emily's best painting. She would have been displeased, just as she always was when NGC exhibited the three early water colors they had purchased in 1928. She felt such work did her an injustice and she complained to Eric Brown on October 19, 1934: "They [NGC] keep as representative of my work, and show among the work of Canadian artists, those two [sic] miserable old water colours done more than 20 years ago. When there are slides here from Ottawa, I am shamed. There has been comment on it and some indignation. Mr. Lismer himself told me I was miserably represented. I would prefer to be left out altogether."

The chronology and exhibition lists in the catalogue are incomplete, far from accurate and no attempt has been made to assign dates to the pictures. In general, it is a disappointing piece of scholarship considering its august sponsors. And yet, an attempt *was* made at the time to compile a definitive work on Emily, as can be seen from a NGC letter sent to Lawren Harris on April 16, 1945: "I am very interested in the proposal for a memorial exhibition of the work of Emily Carr and I agree that the catalogue should be *THE* work of reference on this artist. It will take some time to make a thoroughly successful job of it . . ." The introduction to the catalogue states that NGC and AGT, in presenting this exhibition, did so in order to show not only the already familiar quality of Emily's vision, but also the development of that vision, and the presence of it in her most intimate impressions as well as in her greatest conceptions. Lawren Harris draws particular attention to Emily's charcoal drawings as they had never previously been exhibited: "In these drawings we find her widest range of expression in experimentation."

Dudley Dell wrote in *Mayfair,* October 1945: "I have seen at the Art Gallery of Toronto the paintings and drawings which will be on exhibition there for a month. . . . These will form the first public showing of Emily Carr's works since her death, and by the arrangement which is planned for them they will provide the first opportunity ever given of following the development of her work and personality from first to last. . . . There is much that will be new, even to most of Emily Carr's devoted admirers."

Montreal **Dominion Gallery** **November 10-28**

Emily Carr Memorial Exhibition

A Montreal critic wrote on November 13 that the work of the late Emily Carr was now getting recognition for its importance to Canadian painting: "In this exhibition both early and late works by Miss Carr are being shown. . . . Some excellent Brittany scenes and studies of French peasants are among them (early paintings) and the water colors are particularly good. . . . The pictures painted on her return to British Columbia still show Miss Carr as an impressionist, and many fine studies of totem poles . . . were made at this time. . . . Miss Carr's last pictures show her as no longer so much concerned with the outsides of scenes or things as with her own sensations in their presence. These are the most distinctive of all her works. Most of them are inspired by forest scenes, pictures full of color, light and mysticism, some of them not easily understood."

The *Montreal Gazette* (November 10, 1945) also praised Emily's work: "The oils and water colors which fill the main rooms give a good survey of her development and present a good offering of items which will gratify widely different tastes. A number of the paintings, however, are in her later manner which, according to the bulk of opinion, most convincingly reflect her sturdy independence, lively imagination and marked individuality." This exhibition was a still greater financial success than the previous one organized by Dr. Stern in 1944 and provided a considerable sum to swell the coffers of the Emily Carr scholarship fund. Although a copy of the catalogue survives, it contains only a biographical sketch and reproductions of her self-portrait and four other paintings. If a list of exhibited works ever existed, Dr. Stern is unable to produce one today. He did, however, kindly send me an extract from his sales book for the exhibition period, which contains surprising information. First of all, whatever the number of pictures exhibited, 103 were sold and, unbelievably, seventy were spoken for before the show even opened. Perhaps many of them were purchased by Dr. Stern himself for his fine and large private collection.

Toronto **Fine Arts Galleries, Eaton's College St.** **November**

Emily Carr

As soon as the above Montreal show ended, another, comprising forty-five paintings, was opened at Eaton's. A half-page ad in the *Globe and Mail* of November 30 announced that, "an exhibition and sale of paintings by Emily Carr, one of Canada's foremost artists, is now open." It was arranged in cooperation with the Dominion Gallery of Montreal, which was acting for the Emily Carr estate. Any money paid to the estate for the paintings was to be used for the art education of young British Columbia artists. A 1939 tribute to Emily by Eric Newton, then art critic for the *Manchester Guardian* and *London Times*, was used for publicity purposes and ran as follows: "If the word 'genius' (a word jealously guarded by the critic and used only on very special occasions) can be applied to any Canadian artist, it can be applied to Emily Carr."

1945-1946

Ottawa **National Gallery of Canada** **December 8-January 8**

Emily Carr: Her Painting and Sketches (Memorial Show)

Not all the works shown in Toronto were sent on to Ottawa. Fourteen oils; twelve water colors; two oil on paper sketches; ten charcoal drawings plus all brush drawings were withdrawn or abstracted. Some were held in Toronto and others not shown for various reasons.

The Director of NGC, H.O. McCurry, reported to Lawren Harris on December 10: "The Carr exhibition opened here on Saturday and I must say the exhibition makes a great showing. I was not much impressed when I saw the exhibition in Toronto, but I imagine this was due to the arrangement and overcrowding of the galleries. Here we have it spread out and the whole thing is most impressive. Her work has taken on a new significance to me and I begin to appreciate your enthusiasm."

1946

Montreal **Art Association of Montreal** **January 24 -February 10**

Emily Carr: Her Paintings and Sketches (Memorial Show)

The AAM was always in the dog house as far as Emily was concerned. And perhaps with reason. In August 1939, after "dallying a year," Emily heard that the Museum had at long last decided to organize her first solo exhibition there and wanted the pictures "in a mad rush"—by the third week in September. Professor A.H.S. Gillson of McGill University, Chairman of the Exhibition Committee, was very keen to make this an outstanding show, and had prevailed on his committee, at a special meeting, to go ahead with it despite the war. But he did not realize what it would be like to deal with Emily when she felt pushed or when her feathers were ruffled. She complained about "those rude Easterners" upsetting her plans and was difficult about the selection of pictures. In the end, although the Montreal show was actually "assembled, named, priced, dusted" and waiting to go forward on schedule, the whole arrangement fell through due to wartime restrictions. Emily never quite forgot or forgave Montreal. She wrote to me late September: "Well, Montreal is off. Door slammed for good, after wires of 'yes' and wires 'no' and airmail communications* and letting poor old Willie do all the crating." Ironically, it was an exhibition of *my* work that Gillson, then a Wing Commander*, finally sponsored, not Emily's. Fate dictated that both he and I would turn up at No. 1 Air Navigation School at Rivers, Manitoba, a year later—he as Chief Instructor and I as an Air Force wife. Because of his mathematical background and interest in art, he and Frederick were kindred spirits from the start, and it was no time at all until they had the walls of the Officers' Mess adorned with my paintings.

* *It is difficult to realize that airmail was not in general use in Emily's days. She only resorted to "airmail communications" in a real emergency.*

* *Later promoted to Group Captain. After the war he was Dean of Arts at McGill, then President of the University of Manitoba.*

Even when Emily's first solo show at AAM was eventually hung in 1943, she was not mollified, because the invitation to exhibit did not come spontaneously from the Museum but as a result of Lawren Harris's pressure on them, and several other galleries in the East, to show her work while the Trust pictures were still in Toronto. He hoped to help Emily by promoting sales. It is perhaps not generally known just how much Harris did to assist Emily during these hard years because he kept in the background and his efforts went largely unnoticed. Emily herself did not realize how much he contributed to her welfare. Incredible as it may seem, when AAM was again approached by Harris in 1945, the President, Dr. C.F. Martin, was still doubtful about cooperating with AGT and NGC in mounting a four-city memorial show. He expressed his views in a letter to Director McCurry of NGC on November 29, 1945: "I have had a letter from Lawren Harris urging us to take on the Emily Carr exhibition, and from the wording of his letter I take it that he would be much aggrieved if we do not hold the show here. I have a feeling that our own Committee and a good many members of the Council would not be much in favour of that exhibition. They may be all wrong but I would be most grateful if you would give me some kind of inkling as to whether they are wrong and whether the exhibition in your opinion is really as important as Harris seems to think. I note it is being held in Toronto and Ottawa, but there has been so much propaganda about Emily Carr in the last year or two that I don't want to be too much influenced by that as an incentive to holding the exhibition here."

McCurry did not then have the same admiration for Emily's work that his predecessor Eric Brown had had, nor the same friendly feeling for her as a person. In fact, until the 1945 Memorial exhibition was hung at NGC, he did not like her work at all. He therefore replied to Dr. Martin's letter on November 30 with some caution: "All things considered, I would be inclined to have the exhibition if you can fit it into your program. I do not believe it is as important as Lawren Harris thinks, but I am sure Montreal would be disappointed if they do not have the opportunity of seeing it. In these controversial matters, I take the view that it is a public gallery's job to show the people what is going on in the art world. . . . Emily Carr has made a considerable stir in Canada and I think it is part of your job to let the people see and evaluate her achievement." Dr. Martin was apparently won over by this argument and Emily got her second solo show at the Museum. Better late than never. McCurry, too, became an enthusiastic convert to Emily's work when he saw her magnificent exhibition in Ottawa: "I have been so impressed that I think the collection should be shown to far wider audiences than it can secure in Canada. In my opinion she would certainly rate a room to herself in a new National Gallery building, if a sufficient number of her outstanding works can be secured for the nation."

However, these changes of attitude came too late to appease Emily. In 1944 she was still nursing her 1939 grudge when writing to Ira Dilworth about a talk she had had with Dr. Stern: "I told him *I hated Montreal* and wanted nothing to do with that outfit. He said he knew they had treated me badly but he had nothing to do with the Gallery himself."

The *Montreal Star* wrote on January 29, 1946: "Many aspects of the art of the British Columbia painter, the late Emily Carr, are shown by the exhibition, an unusually large one for a single painter. . . . Two of the largest galleries are filled with oil pictures, most of them characteristic forest pictures, and two other galleries contain water colors and drawings in black and white. The oil pictures support each other well and are much better seen together than mixed with works of other painters. The forest pictures are all seen and painted in Miss Carr's quite personal way; they are not so much pictures of woodland scenery as expressions of the aloofness and mystery of the forests of the Pacific coast."

Victoria **Provincial Library** **February**

Emily Carr

The Victoria Section of the B.C. Historical Society paid tribute to Emily in the B.C. Provincial Library on February 25 when seven pictures, purchased shortly after her death, were put on display for the first time. The five women members of the Legislature who shamed the Government into acquiring the paintings were specially invited guests as were all members of the Legislature and the trustees of Emily's estate. The newly-purchased pictures were: *Tanu; Skidegate; Yan Bear Totem;* two forest scenes and *Totem in Green Trees. Kispiox Village,* a large canvas painted in 1912 and the only Carr picture in possession of the Government when Emily died (presented in 1933 with funds I collected from friends and organizations) was also on display along with originals from the collections of Major Cuthbert Holmes and Alan Morkell.

Vancouver **Vancouver Art Gallery** **May 1-16**

Emily Carr: Her paintings and Sketches (Memorial show)

Vancouver was the fourth and final scheduled stop for this large and important exhibition. After a successful run, it was fragmented—some pictures being returned East or to private collections, others being stored at VAG or sent on tour. It was a big event for the city since the homecoming of Emily's Trust pictures in this Memorial show was timed to coincide with their presentation by the trustees to VAG. The composition of the show was again different in Vancouver. VAG borrowed to fill in the blanks and Lawren Harris made up a revised list. Emily was, of course, welcomed home with enthusiasm and a new wing for the Gallery was soon being planned to house her great collection. (See chapter: "The Emily Carr Trust.")

Victoria **Little Centre, 965 Yates Street*** **June**

Emily Carr Memorial Exhibition

Selected exhibits from the Emily Carr Memorial Exhibition in Vancouver were sent to the new art gallery in Victoria, which was sponsored by the Vancouver Island Region of the Federation of Canadian Artists, and opened with this special display of Emily's works on June 1st. The arrangements were made with VAG by Lawren Harris who also suggested that the Federation approach NGC for the loan of *Blunden Harbour* and *Heina,* then on

** The Little Centre on Yates Street had a long, hard struggle before developing into today's fine and beautiful gallery—the Art Gallery of Greater Victoria. The Yates Street location was only temporary and new quarters were found about three years later at 823 Broughton Street where it functioned under a new name, the Arts Centre of Greater Victoria. On November 21, 1951, the Centre moved again to a permanent home in the old Spencer house at 1040 Moss Street, which was the nucleus of the greatly expanded present gallery. It also simultaneously assumed a new title, the one it still bears today.*

view in Vancouver. Permission was granted by NGC on learning that the new gallery had been certified fireproof by the Victoria Fire Marshall. The Victoria *Times* reported on June 3rd: "It is uniquely appropriate that Victoria's first step toward a permanent art gallery should be marked by a rare and representative exhibition of paintings by the late Emily Carr, richly-endowed native daughter, who lived a greater part of her life in this city and here produced much of her finest work. National, Provincial and private collections have supplied the exhibition and Lawren Harris has selected paintings from NGC that will not be shown in the West for several years. The Little Centre . . . was opened to the public on Sunday at 965 Yates Street, once an automobile showroom."

Lawren Harris, who worked hard to promote these Memorial exhibitions, took great pride and pleasure in their enthusiastic acceptance. After the formal opening at VAG on May 1, which was "quite an event," he wrote to Willie Newcombe in Victoria: "The Emily Carr Memorial Exhibition is a great success—it looks wonderful on the gallery walls with all the pictures in their new frames." The frames were provided by the Emily Carr Trust.

Edmonton **Museum of Arts** **September**

Emily Carr

In 1946, Carr shows were also held in other western cities. The Edmonton *Journal* wrote on September 19: "Paintings by Emily Carr being shown at the Museum of Arts are assembled and circulated by a Memorial Trust formed to deal with those works which were left when the artist died. Twenty pictures comprise the exhibition, representative of several phases of her outlook. The paintings are unique, original and unlike any known school of painting, although some influence of the former Group of Seven is noticeable."

Calgary **Coste House** **October**

Emily Carr

The Calgary *Herald* wrote on October 19: "An exhibition of paintings of the late Emily Carr, one of Western Canada's most outstanding painters, who devoted the major years of her life to portraying the British Columbia Indians and their lands, will be opened Sunday at the Coste House. . . . Thursday evening J.W.G. Macdonald, B.A. (Edin.), Head of the Fine Arts Branch of the Institute of Technology and Art, will give a lecture on Miss Carr and her work at Coste House. Mr. Macdonald was a close [sic] friend of Emily Carr and visited her in the Northern British Columbia country which was the scene of many of her paintings." (Note: This statement is open to question.)

Winnipeg **Winnipeg Art Gallery** **December 1-28**

Emily Carr

The Winnipeg *Free Press* wrote on December 5: "All in oil, the pictures deal almost exclusively with three of Miss Carr's favorite subjects—forests, individual trees, and totem poles. With a unique feeling for the life and movement in patterns of pines, spruces and poplars, Miss Carr succeeded in conveying a spirit as well as a landscape. The show, arranged under the auspices of VAG, opened on the first of December at the Winnipeg Art Gallery in the Civic Auditorium."

The Gallery knew nothing about this exhibition when I wrote asking for information and was glad to have it on file. As a matter of fact, this gallery was very late in recognizing Emily's work. They did, however, put on a number of exhibitions containing her paintings in the fifties—three in 1953; two in 1955; one in 1957 and one in 1960.

1947

Victoria **Crystal Ballroom, Empress Hotel** **April 17**

A collection of Emily's paintings was exhibited for one evening on the occasion of the premiere showing of the documentary *Klee Wyck* produced by the National Film Board. The event was sponsored by Victoria's art gallery, the Little Centre. Ira Dilworth gave the opening address before a distinguished gathering of more than 300 guests, among them the Lieutenant Governor of B.C. and the Mayor of Victoria. Also present were Emily's sister Alice and George C. Clutesi, the Indian artist who appeared in the film and to whom Emily had left her painting materials. Typical of such Victoria gestures to honor Emily, the social aspect was stressed. Ira's remarks were quoted at length, but not one single comment was made in the press about the paintings.

1948

Vancouver **Vancouver Art Gallery** **June**

Emily Carr

The Vancouver *Daily Province*, June 18, 1948, states: "A special Emily Carr Exhibition will continue this weekend at VAG."

1949
Victoria **Arts Centre of Greater Victoria** **May 1-15**
823 Broughton St.

Emily Carr

This exhibition, which ran for two weeks, was opened by Alice Carr. The pictures shown made up the personal collection of Major Cuthbert Holmes, prominent Victoria business man. Included in the thirty works were beach scenes done in Victoria, Indian subjects and several forest paintings. Of special interest was the portrait of Alice done in 1909.

1949-1950
Seattle **Henry Gallery, University of Washington** **December 1 -January 2**

Emily Carr Memorial Exhibition

Twenty-five of the largest canvasses from VAG's collection of Emily Carr paintings were shown, filling two large rooms. According to VAG files, they later traveled to several centers in the United States, among them San Francisco, where they were exhibited at the Legion of Honor Museum. This was the first time that a special solo exhibition of Trust pictures had left Canada.

After a short biography, one reads high praise of Emily's work in the introduction to the exhibition catalogue: "Emily Carr was one of the first artists to discover the plastic amplitude, design and pattern that exists in Pacific Coast forms for modern expression in paint. Her understanding of the outlook and native culture of the Indians she knew so well, gave her paintings of totems, Indian villages and the forest a quality and power which no artist had achieved before. In her early paintings she worked for history and cold fact—descriptive, rather than the more incisive spirit of the British Columbia woods, trees and totems which came later. The canvasses of her later period were seen, painted and felt in terms of life, mood and spirit."

A critic wrote about this Seattle show in the Vancouver *Daily Province*, December 8, 1949: "There's keen interest in these typically British Columbia pictures, which have been hung with heads, masks and motifs of Indian art. There's interest, too, in the three Canadian films being shown—*Emily and Her Work, Totem Art* and the beautiful and artistic *The Loon's Necklace*."

1951
Winnipeg **Winnipeg Art Gallery** **April**

Emily Carr

Winnipeg *Free Press*, April 24, 1951: "Down at the art gallery

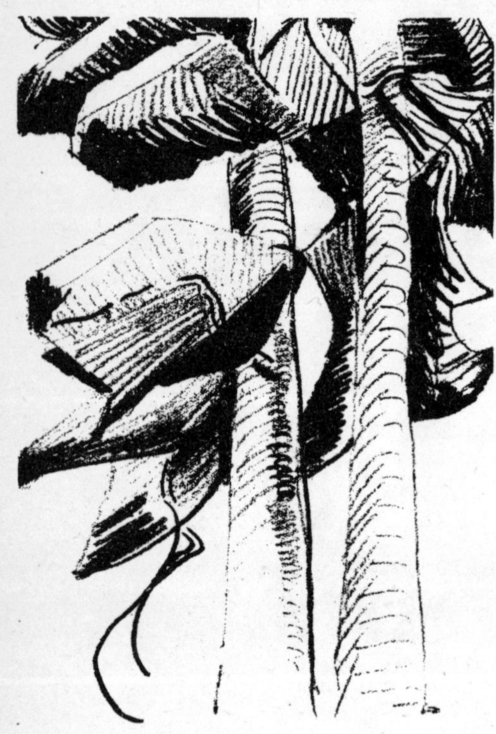

are nineteen paintings . . . you will find there at least three totem poles, weird records of history . . . but it is in the depths of the mighty forest that Emily Carr's brush wrests itself from her small hands and seizes upon the paint and the canvas as one who would wrestle till the dawn breaks."

1952
University of Toronto **Alumni Hall, Victoria College** **October 23 -November 21**

Emily Carr

The Varsity, November 4, 1952: "A representative group of paintings by a woman who is possibly the greatest painter Canada has yet produced."

1954
Victoria **Art Gallery of Greater Victoria** **July**

Emily Carr

This exhibition was held in conjunction with a display of work by S. Deane Drummond, the Province's first professional artist. Both shows opened July 6. Both artists were women.

Ottawa **National Gallery of Canada** **November**

Emily Carr

Time magazine, Art Section, November 22, 1954: "This week in Ottawa, NGC opened a small show of Emily Carr's oils and water colors."

1957
London, Ontario **Public Art Museum** **May**

Emily Carr

The London *Evening Free Press*, May 25, 1957: "The old main gallery of the London Public Art Museum glows and glooms these days because fifty canvasses and sketches by Emily Carr are on view . . ."

1958
Windsor, Ontario **Willistead Art Gallery** **January 8-29**

Emily Carr

Windsor *Daily Star*, January 4, 1958: "*Kitseukla 1912* by Emily Carr is among the major canvasses lent by VAG for the first major Emily Carr exhibition in the Windsor area." Forty-seven works.

Saskatoon **Saskatoon Art Centre** **February**

Emily Carr

Saskatoon *Star Phoenix,* February 22, 1958: "Ten paintings from the Mendel collection are now on view. . . . The exhibition opened Friday with some remarks about Emily Carr by Mrs. Murray Adaskin who at one time visited the artist." (The author drove Mr. and Mrs. Adaskin to Metchosin to meet Emily in 1935.)

Sarnia **Public Library and Art Gallery** **February**

Emily Carr

The Sarnia *Observer* reporter wrote on January 30 that "The Chief Librarian says he may have to strip the walls of the library to hang the collection of paintings scheduled for February. All of the pictures haven't arrived yet but he had four boxes of Emily Carr canvasses just arrived from Scotland and valued at $60,000. He said about eight more boxes will be arriving before the end of this month."

This reporter had discovered something new: "Emily Carr's paintings . . . reveal an oversize inferiority complex. Acquaintances say she loved the deep silent woods. Her canvasses say she worshipped the strength and stalwart beauty of British Columbia's great trees. With sweeping strokes she transmits the life force that she felt around her in the woods into the trees. They are alive . . ."

The Curator informed me that there had only been two exhibitions of Emily's work in their gallery. This first one was held in the old building and consisted "mainly of paintings of tree stumps."

Hamilton, Ontario **Art Gallery of Hamilton** **March-April**

Emily Carr

Forty-three paintings and drawings. The Hamilton *Spectator,* March 21, 1958, stated that: "The work of one of the greatest artists Canada has produced is now on display . . . in her brooding, nearly mystic canvasses, she conveys some of the tense drama of life."

Victoria **Art Gallery of Greater Victoria** **September 30 -October 19**

Oil Paintings from the Emily Carr Trust

The exhibition catalogue, with its preface by Curator Colin Graham and an introduction by Lawren Harris, lists thirty-six paintings and the Victoria *Times,* September 29, 1958, reported that, "An exhibition of many of Emily Carr's greatest paintings will go on view in the art gallery Tuesday. They have been chosen from the 150 [sic] works which Emily Carr bequeathed as a Trust collection to the Province and which, since her death, have been held at the Vancouver Art Gallery [sic]. This collection has been restricted to Vancouver in the absence of a fireproof gallery in Victoria. The new centennial gallery has removed this restriction and, as a result of its opening, the trustees . . . have agreed to make the whole collection available to Victoria on a loan basis. The exhibition will consist of a large group of big canvasses of forest and totem scenes as well as of oil sketches which the artist made on the spot." This was the first exhibition of Trust pictures in Emily's native city since 1946 when a small group of these paintings was shown.

1959

Calgary — **Provincial Institute of Technology and Art (now the Alberta College of Art)** — **January**

Emily Carr

This was an exhibition of original Carr paintings and West Coast Indian and African art. The Carr paintings and Indian work were loaned by the Glenbow-Alberta Institute and the African exhibit was from a New York collection loaned through the auspices of NGC.

Montreal — **Montreal Museum of Fine Arts** — **May 12-June 2**

Emily Carr—Canada's Greatest?

The Montreal *Gazette* of May 9, 1959, wrote that, "the second exhibition of the Junior Association of MMFA will be on view at the Stable Gallery. It was opened by Dr. Arthur Lismer. The exhibition catalogue listed thirty-four paintings, oils and water colors, said to be valued at $125,000."

1960

Stratford, Ontario — **Festival Arena** — **July**

Color on Canvas—Emily Carr

The London *Free Press* of July 16 wrote: "[Emily Carr's] transference of Indian lore and Canadian scenery, and also of her own feelings about them, to canvas can be seen in an exhibition at the Stratford Shakespearian Festival this summer. A section of the Festival Arena is a veritable tribute to Emily Carr with its seventeen oils from various periods in her career."

1962

Victoria	**Hudson's Bay Company Store**	**July 13-August 4**
Vancouver	**Hudson's Bay Company Store**	**August 8-17**

The World of Emily Carr

A new exhibition of about 150 paintings from the Newcombe Collection acquired a short time before the show by the Provincial Government. Sponsored by the Hudson's Bay Company and shown in their stores. A lavishly illustrated catalogue with excellent biography of Emily and description of the Newcombe collection by Flora Hamilton Burns. Any errors in the text are understandable considering the date and lack of research material.

1963

University of Toronto	**Hart House**	**September 16 -October 13**

Our Most Powerful Artist—A Woman

The Toronto *Telegram* of October 12 wrote a particularly interesting review: "The mass entry of women into professional art is a very recent phenomenon. During the Victorian era, every young lady pretending to good breeding took drawing and painting lessons as part of her preparation for life. But art as a career was unthinkable. The number of Canadian women artists prior to the past twenty-five years was very small. . . . Charlotte Schreiber, Florence Carlyle, Laura Muntz, Prudence Heward, Hortense Gordon were a few. Looming above them all was the singular figure of Emily Carr. Emily Carr is perhaps the most powerfully original Canadian painter, regardless of sex. It is fitting that a major exhibition of her work should head up several shows by women painters currently on view in local galleries. The Emily Carr exhibition at the University of Toronto's Hart House Gallery reveals what can be achieved by a woman of genius who is prepared to devote her entire life to creative painting . . . only a woman willing to exist in solitude, her movements governed by her career, could have created such a compelling body of work. Her success is reflected in the twenty-six works in the Hart House show."

1966

Vancouver	**Bayshore Inn**	**October 19**
Victoria	**Empress Hotel**	**October 24**

Hundreds and Thousands

To mark the occasion of the publication of Emily's long-awaited journals, Clarke, Irwin arranged their first two receptions in Vancouver and Victoria on the above-noted dates. The original hand-written journals were displayed at both receptions against a background of original paintings from the book and from other collections. The Victoria event, held during Emily Carr Week, was at first scheduled to take place at the Art Gallery of Greater Victoria, but the Gallery had to bow out due to limited space and other complications. A few of Emily's friends, including myself, declined, for personal reasons, to stand in the reception line. Willard Ireland, Provincial Legislative Librarian, spoke on Emily's painting and writing.

1967
Waterloo, Ontario University of Waterloo October 15 -November 12
Emily Carr

The Centennial Presentation of the Gallery of the Theatre of the Arts.

1968
Vancouver Vancouver Art Gallery
Carrs on Wheels—Emily Carr 1871-1945 (traveling)

Twenty-seven paintings and drawings. This was the first touring show of Carr works organized by the Extension Service of VAG. There were three circuits of the same exhibit which took the show to the Okanagan, the Kootenays and Northern B.C. At the end of the tour, Nanaimo was host to the show for a three weeks stay, opening on October 21.

1969
Sarnia Public Library and Art Gallery January 4-31
Emily Carr Paintings

The second of only two Emily Carr exhibitions to be held at this Gallery. On display were: eight oils on canvas; two oils on board; nine oils on paper; five water colors; one charcoal.

1971
Vancouver Vancouver Art Gallery May 18-August 29
Emily Carr: A Centennial Exhibition

Organized by VAG to celebrate the one-hundredth anniversary of Emily's birth. Traveled to:
MMFA September 24-November 14

The Royal Ontario Museum
Toronto, February 15-March 15, 1972

Following the gala opening of this exhibition, crowds from Vancouver to Montreal flocked to see the 120 works on display and to pay tribute to Emily. I contributed just a jot to the success of the exhibition by providing a taping of my reminiscences and my famous photograph of Emily standing in the door of her caravan. Blown up to life size, it filled a whole end wall in the historical room at the Gallery (less the presence of my sister Ruth who had been chopped off) and the impact was tremendous. Emily seemed to be right there with us, and I had to suppress an impulse to greet her. How youthful, almost pretty, she still looked at age sixty-five despite her round body and ungainly stance. The camera was much kinder to her than she was to herself in the self-portrait on the cover of the exhibition catalogue.

The taped reminiscences were intended to run continuously in the historical room as background commentary; but the day I visited the Gallery, my voice was stilled owing to mechanical failure. Just as well—quiet was needed to enjoy the old, sometimes faded photographs, many of which I had not seen before. Nor had I seen some of the paintings, because Emily had not wished to show her friends many of the early ones. The collection of Trust pictures, seen *en masse*, was impressive—almost overpowering—and left me floundering in my own emotions. I was torn between joy because Emily was at last harvesting her due measure of admiration and success, and sorrow because she had not lived to savor much of it. The show was superb. In my opinion, it lacked but one thing—imagination in hanging. Montreal, as we know, had always lagged behind the other large Canadian cities in recognition of Emily's work. But now, when the Centennial Exhibition reached MMFA in September, it made amends for any past neglect. The Montreal *Star* wrote on September 25, 1971: "The large Emily Carr retrospective that opened at the MMFA yesterday brings a timely and long warranted exhibition of her work to Montreal. Timely because 1971 is the centenary year of her birth—an occasion for the re-inspection of an artist's work; long warranted because in the history of Canadian art Emily Carr has no feminine peer and a show of such scope has never been mounted here."

The next stop-over on Emily's centennial exhibition circuit was at the Royal Ontario Museum, Toronto, held there because of AGT's inability to book the show owing to expansion plans.

An excerpt from *Books in Canada*, February 1972, gives Toronto's view of Emily and her work at this time: "She was, simply, one of Canada's few authentic home-grown geniuses. Probably because she was a woman, there has long been a tendency to play down this fact. She is also, more narrowly, one of the few creative people to survive the power and tyranny of the West Coast landscape. She was not submerged by it, although she stood in awe of it and realized its power. The exhibition mounted at the Royal Ontario Museum mixes memorabilia with canvasses, souvenirs with sketches and draws for us the portrait of a singular Canadian. . . . Through her paintings one can trace her artistic and spiritual development and her gradual realization of the oneness of all life."

Victoria　　Art Gallery of Greater Victoria　　December 14 -mid-February 1972

Emily Carr: A Centennial Exhibition

The final Carr centennial exhibition in Canada took place in Victoria and Emily thus rounded out her 100 year cycle where she began. I believe she would have liked it that way for, despite her ranting against Victorians, Victoria was the one place she truly and steadfastly loved. She had the same love-hate relationship with her town that she had with her family; but the old ties and old affections always prevailed.

On first consideration of the late December date of this exhibition, it might seem that AGGV was as tardy in its acclaim of Emily's work as the city and its inhabitants had once been. But design, not neglect, determined the date. Director Colin Graham wanted the opening to mark the centenary of Emily's birth (December 13) and came within a hair's breadth of making it fit. He also had a financial problem of no mean proportion since the Gallery was not yet plump from ingested government grants, and insurance on Emily's works had reached dizzying heights. He therefore had to choose between mounting a big show for a couple of weeks or a small show for a couple of months, and opted for the latter. Big or small, it was a disappointing show—not as good as some of the more or less regular Emily Carr exhibitions held in the summer. Perhaps due to the unusual drain on the Trust collection during the centennial year, VAG simply ran out of good pictures. In any case, there were three oil on paper sketches on the walls of the Gallery that should have been sent to hospital rather than on tour. (See chapter: "EHS versus VAG.") Adding considerable interest to the opening of this exhibition was an hour-long performance of a dramatization entitled *Emily Carr: A Centennial Portrait.* The script was by Bill Thomas, whose selections from Emily's prose writings were linked by narrative, and effectively staged. I spoke briefly after the play about my friendship with Emily, and a group of my paintings of her, done from life sketches or my own photographs, was on display for the first time.

1972

Paris — Centre culturel canadien, rue de Constantine — May 4, June 11

Emily Carr—Exposition du Centenaire

A l'occasion du centième anniversaire de la naissance d'Emily Carr, le Centre culturel canadien présente une rétrospective de l'oeuvre de ce peintre qui fut toujours profondément marqué par les images grandioses offertes par la nature de son pays. On évoque l'influence des expressionnistes allemands . . . à contempler ces arbres géants dans la nuit profonde des forêts canadiennes, ces silencieux totems indiens, l'espace tourbillonnant d'éléments dans le ciel. Loin de nous ici toute référence à une peinture féminine. (*Le Figaro,* Mai '72.)

They told me at the Centre that 4,365 Parisian visitors viewed this exhibition.

, England — Commonwealth Institute, Kensington — August

Emily Carr (The Laughing One on the West Coast)

In its review of August 19, 1972, the *Daily Telegraph* expresses the opinion that "Special relevance for our particular moment attaches to the Emily Carr exhibition which has just opened at the Commonwealth Institute. This is because a balanced appreciation of it can advance the understanding, now being pursued with more seriousness than for several decades, of two problems crucial to art. These are what can art hope to achieve, and how can its ends be realized? . . . Emily Carr's art appears simple. It is far removed from the theorising about art, tinged, or rather too often saturated with the esoteric, that has become fashionable. She was unconcerned with the movements and 'isms' of art. Rather Emily Carr was a woman who lived her life in obscurity in British Columbia, at a time when the westernmost part of Canada was unconcerned with international intellectual movements. She loved the Indians, and her art was devoted to them and their world. . . . There could be nothing further removed from the Canadian Pavilion at the present

Venice Biennale, so consciously acceptable to the *avant garde*, or from the painting of men like Riopelle and Borduas who have drawn Canadian art into the mainstream of international *avant garde* art."

II Canadian Societies Exhibitions 1906-1945

Exhibitions in which she participated during her lifetime, with a few added for special reasons—up to 1960.

For Evelyn McMann, in appreciation.

The Vancouver Studio Club and School of Art, the first organized art society to which Emily belonged, gave her her first opportunity to exhibit regularly with a group. The VSC was formed about two years before she went to Vancouver to reside and teach.* A studio was acquired in the Haddon Building, 633 Hastings Street, and arrangements made for classes in life, still-life and outdoor sketching. A sketch club was associated with the VSC and Emily took part in their regular sketch competitions and teas. She also contributed to all the Club's exhibitions until she left for France in 1910, and again in 1912 after her return. The Club has been ridiculed by Emily for the social aspect of its activities, but it did much for the advancement of art and artists in the city of Vancouver, and even in other parts of the Province. By late 1908 it had more than 100 members.

* *The VSC was formed at a meeting of a few amateur artists at the old Hotel Vancouver, February 23, 1904.* Vancouver News Advertiser, *March 13, 1904.*

Arriving in Vancouver from Victoria in late December 1905 or, more probably, early January 1906, Emily taught for a time at the VSC—disguised as the Vancouver Ladies' Art Club in her writings. It is obvious from a search of contemporary press items that no organization with that name ever existed. It is also clear that Emily was referring to the VSC when she wrote in her autobiography: "The Vancouver Ladies' Art Club was succeeded by the Fine Arts Society. . . ."* She means, of course, the British Columbia Society of Fine Arts, which did indeed succeed the VSC. Since Emily was so active in the VSC and profited so enormously from the opportunity it gave her to bring her work before the public, it is hard to understand (unless one recognizes the pattern of such recriminations in her artistic life) why she claimed in her autobiography that she was too young, serious and "modern" to suit the "cluster of society women" who ran the Ladies' Art Club, and that she "was dismissed after a month."* But the fact remains that she was engaged to direct a sketch club

* Growing Pains *pp. 306-307.*

* *Ibid p. 275.*

for field work the following summer under the auspices of the VSC,* which suggests that there had not been any dissatisfaction with her teaching, let alone any dismissal.

* *Vancouver* Daily Province, *January 25, 1906.*

The VSC first came to the attention of the public in November 1904 when it arranged a loan exhibition. In April 1906* they held a showing of old china and lace, and later that year, wishing to broaden its scope, the Club invited professional artists of the Province to participate in a first annual exhibition. A number of well-known painters, including Emily, responded to this invitation.

* *Date taken from a short history of the VSC in the Vancouver* Daily Province *of November 7, 1908. But W.W. Thom, in his unpublished manuscript "Fine Art in Vancouver 1886-1930," gives the date as* May *1906. He is usually right.*

1906
Vancouver Haddon Building, 633 Hastings St. November 20-21
Vancouver Studio Club and School of Art

First Annual Exhibition

A most encouraging beginning. About sixty pictures were hung and a number found purchasers. Three were acquired by the Club through their system of votes plus a draw, but Emily's work was not chosen.

1907
Vancouver Haddon Building November 22-23
Vancouver Studio Club and School of Art

Second Annual Exhibition

In the advance press notice for this exhibition, only three names were mentioned as "drawing cards," and Emily's was one. The *Daily Province* of November 7, 1908, in a short history of the Club, said this *Second Annual Exhibition* was "a distinct advance upon the First, not only in the number of exhibitors, but in the quality of the work." Four paintings were purchased by the Club, and this year one of them was Emily's. The choice of her work surely belies her contention that the members despised her paintings. She was also extremely popular as a teacher at this time and held regular and successful exhibitions of her pupils' work in her studio. Her name was probably mentioned in the contemporary press more frequently than any other artist of the day.

1908
Vancouver Haddon Building May 18-20
Vancouver Studio Club and School of Art

Beginning in 1908, the Club exhibitions became semi-annual events and all artists, professional and amateur, were invited to submit work. According to the *Daily Province* of May 20, in this spring show Emily entered "a characteristic study of a Chinese boy, a picture that holds the attention, as well as Hindu and Japanese figure studies. Her studio is also represented by several bold mountain views." Another review said that she also showed two genre paintings.

Vancouver — Haddon Building — November 13-16
Vancouver Studio Club and School of Art

The *Daily Province* of October 31 reported that the November exhibition promised to excel that held the previous spring in which so great an interest was taken by the artists and the public. Emily was listed among the painters who had already applied for space. On November 14, the same newspaper wrote: "The exhibition of pictures at the Studio Club is an interesting milestone on the path of art in Vancouver and in the history of an association that has kept steadily on with its work in a cause that merits the interest of all good citizens. For art is a flower of civilization that is a necessary accompaniment of progress. . . ."

In existence until about 1913, VSC played an active role in the development of art in Vancouver. The members may have been tea drinkers, as Emily described them, but they were not, as she claimed, just an amateur group of dabblers. Some of the best local artists of the day were both members and exhibitors. In late 1908, however, a founding group of twenty professional and semi-professional painters, including Emily, banded together to organize a new and more progressive society along the lines of the Ontario Society of Artists. Their plans culminated in a meeting at 651 Hastings Street on November 13, at which final arrangements were made.* The new Society was incorporated February 23, 1909, as the British Columbia Society of Fine Arts.** One of the principal aims of both these groups (VSC and BCSFA), and later the B.C. Art League,*** was to establish an art gallery in Vancouver.

1909
Vancouver — Dominion Hall — April 20-28
British Columbia Society of Fine Arts

First Annual Exhibition of the newly-incorporated Society

This was probably the first juried show in the city's art history. The judges selected 179 works and their decision was final. A prolific worker, then as later, Emily was nearly always represented by the maximum number of entries allowed, in this case, ten water colors of widely diversified subject matter, all

* *Vancouver* Daily Province, *November 14, 1908.*

** *Tom Fripp was its first president. In 1949 the Society's name was changed to the B.C. Society of Artists when a new charter was granted on December 7. As well as holding annual exhibitions, this Society pioneered traveling art exhibitions in British Columbia. In 1967 it was decided to terminate the charter and disband, and to donate the balance of the funds to the Community Arts Council.*

*** *Incorporated under the Benevolent Societies Act on December 18, 1920. The League was committed to the encouragement of art in Vancouver and to the acquisition of an art school and an art gallery for the city. In* "broadly painted and well handled."

Vancouver Haddon Building June 19-July 17
Vancouver Studio Club and School of Art

Emily exhibited eight paintings at prices ranging from $5.00 to $50.00. "Felix Penne," reviewer for the *B.C. Saturday Sunset* wrote on July 3: "It is pleasant to find that although Vancouver has reached the era of 'skyscrapers' and utilitarianism is very pronounced, the aesthetic sentiment finds earnest, nay poetic expression. The small, but certainly admirable exhibition of pictures opened the other day under the auspices of 'The Vancouver Studio Club' is a promise of the future. . . . M.E. Carr (and others) have clearly proved that round Vancouver is a real 'artists' country.' " The *Daily Province* critic, who mentioned only five painters in his review of June 26, praised Emily as "an artist of strong personality, which finds expression in vigorous work, the quality [of which] improves steadily. Her subjects have a distinctiveness which makes them easily recognized by one familiar with her style. There is a strength and genuineness about her pictures, a concern for the character of the subject, and a persuasiveness of color that draws the attention away from the technique, which, nevertheless is as admirable and brilliant as the most critical could ask. Her paintings are not only strong in color, but show delight in effects of sunshine and atmosphere as well as a bold, free touch and the use of a large opulent line."

Vancouver Haddon Building October 28-November 6
The Vancouver Studio Club and School of Art

"Felix Penne" of the *B.C. Saturday Sunset* wrote on October 30: "I have not known the work of M.E. Carr long enough to speak positively of what this artist has done in the past yet I will venture the opinion that in breadth of treatment, boldness and 'grip' the artist shows much improvement. *Cliffs by Beacon Hill* has the breadth and 'go' of a scenic artist. I use that comparison in its best sense. Other pictures of the same artist deserve equally favorable mention."

Vancouver Mercantile Building November
British Columbia Society of Fine Arts

Second Annual Exhibition

135 paintings. Emily exhibited her usual ten.

September 1921 arrangements were made with the B.C. Manufacturers Association to stage exhibitions and house collections which would form the nucleus of a permanent art gallery in rooms at 309 Cordova Street. In June 1922 activities moved to 929 Granville Street. In January 1930 membership was 300 and headquarters were at 649 Seymour Street. In November 1923 the Commercial Arts and Crafts School had been opened at the School Board offices on Hamilton Street, and in October 1931 the Vancouver Art Gallery opened on Georgia Street.

1910
Vancouver **Pender Hall** **May**
British Columbia Society of Fine Arts

Third Annual Exhibition

Eighty-five paintings. Emily exhibited six—among them her engaging and well-known water color of Indian children: *Indian School at Lytton.* The *Daily Province* critic stated on May 14 that, "There have been many visitors this week to the exhibition of pictures which is being held in the smaller Pender Hall by the BCSFA. While the collection is not as extensive, either in number or variety, as the last placed on view by the Society, the quality of the work in the present show is unquestionably advanced. . . . Owing to her unfortunate illness, Miss Carr is not as well represented as usual . . . [she] has been seriously ill for the past few weeks and has gone to Victoria for a change of air." Another notice in the same paper reported in the social column on June 10 that Emily had recovered from her illness and would be leaving for Paris in a few weeks. But in Paris she suffered a serious relapse which greatly interfered with her studies. (See Chronology.)

In "Felix Penne's" review in the *B.C. Saturday Sunset* of May 14, he gives us some idea of the difficulties encountered by the Society in their search for suitable exhibition space. Their first exhibition, he said, was held in very cramped quarters, and the second "was in a stone cellar at the top of a skyscraper (if a cellar can be at the top of a building). But this, the third exhibition, is in an annex of Pender Hall. The room is lofty, well-lit with northern light and admirably adapted for an exhibition. There are nearly 200 exhibits . . . the entire exhibition is excellent, encouraging and most creditable to Vancouver. . . . Emily Carr [has] some figures and still life, and landscape at which she is much better."

1911
Victoria **Alexandra Club** **October 5-7**
Island Arts and Crafts Club

Second Annual Exhibition

Emily exhibited four water colors.

Established in 1909, the name of the Club was changed to the more familiar Island Arts and Crafts *Society* only in 1922. This Club deserves credit for keeping the flame of art alive in Victoria and for providing local artists with their one opportunity to exhibit annually, even though they showed a marked resistance to anything new or experimental. Even Emily, whose diatribes against this worthy society are well-known, admitted that it was "better than nothing" and contributed to their exhibitions quite regularly between 1911 and 1937. The *Daily Colonist* of October 6 set a record for the length of their review and the amount of fuzzy bombast packed into it. Emily did not stand a chance with a critic who could write: "The ordinary exhibition of amateur—and for that matter of professional—pictures induces in the art lover a sinking feeling of ennui. The exhibits as a rule are about one percent inspiration and ninety-nine percent of sheer labor. But this year's exhibition . . . is wholly artistic and pleasing to the most diletante [sic] of tastes." After extravagantly praising an unknown newcomer "whose work would win honors in the best salons of Italy, Germany and France," the reviewer pointed out, in a descending scale, the merits of the other exhibitors. Emily's name is listed, but bare of comment. Near the end of the write-up, however, in a picture by picture criticism, she is finally handed a few scant words of appreciation: "Miss M. Carr's wood scene is a strong composition of one who knows the value of color and is not afraid to use it."

Since this exhibition took place more than a month before the accepted date of Emily's return from France (November 11),* it is impossible to say whether the return date is in question, or whether Emily's family entered the work for her. She did not, in any case, exhibit pictures done in France. I searched both the Victoria *Times* and the *Daily Colonist* for the months of September, October, November and December 1911, but found no mention of Emily's return home.

* *See:* Emily Carr: Her Paintings and Sketches, *p. 13 and* Emily Carr: A Centennial Exhibition *(1971 and 1975 editions), p. 89.*

1912
Vancouver — Haddon Building — March
Vancouver Studio Club and School of Art

Not only the members of this Club exhibited, but also a few from the BCSFA. The *Daily Province* wrote on March 21 that, "Miss Carr is back from abroad and exhibits four strikingly rich decorative subjects." According to an earlier item in the same paper (February 3), Emily must have left Victoria to resume her teaching and exhibiting activities in Vancouver in January, as she was already occupying her new studio at 1465 West Broadway by the beginning of February. This VSC show was her first opportunity to display her work done in France.

Vancouver **Haddon Building** **October**
Vancouver Studio Club and School of Art

For her work in this, her last exhibition with VSC, Emily received warm words of praise in press notices, though no one commented about her French entries. In the *Sun* review of October 10, her Indian paintings were said to be "perhaps the most striking series in the hall . . . and are most weird and wonderful creations of Kispioux and Ktsukit villages." Two days later, the *Daily Province* critic wrote that her Indian villages and totem poles were "so vigorous and accurately descriptive that they might well find a place in a public gallery, though they scarcely come into the category of ordinary pictures."

Apparently, Emily did not exhibit with the BCSFA in 1912 since no Carr paintings are listed in the catalogue for their exhibition of November 25-30. Is it possible that the Society disapproved of the "new art" she learned in France and refused to hang her modern work? Or, because of friction with some of the members, did she herself withhold it? She certainly gives some inkling of discord with the Society: "My pictures were hung either on the ceiling or on the floor and were jeered at, insulted. Members of the 'Fine Arts' joked at my work, laughing with reporters. Press notices were humiliating."*

* Growing Pains, *p. 307.*

I found no humiliating press notices for 1912, but something went drastically wrong with Emily's life in Vancouver about this time. Because her classes fell off and there was little understanding for her work (or so she claimed), she decided to move back to Victoria the following year. She did not exhibit with the BCSFA again until 1929, but from then on until her death she was an occasional contributor.

1913
Victoria **Alexandra Club** **October 16-18**
Island Arts and Crafts Club

Fourth Annual Exhibition

Emily exhibited seventeen pictures—eight oils, nine water colors.* Nine were Indian paintings, eight were done in France, mostly in Brittany. This exhibition drew both favorable and unfavorable comment from the Victoria press. The *Times* praised her work, noting that her Indian totem pictures were "highly decorative" and her Brittany paintings "excellent in composition, showing post-impressionism in its least aggressive form." But the *Daily Colonist* took exception to the vivid colors of Emily's "new art," though her drawing was judged "impeccable." "But

* *One, cat. no. 222,* Queen Charlotte Island Totem Poles, *is listed without the artist's name; but title, price and grouping leave little doubt that the painting was Emily's.*

the coloring is not the higher key that is vouchsafed of ordinary mortals to perceive . . . her blues and yellows and reds are just as blinding as her greens."

1916
Victoria **October 24-28**
Island Arts and Crafts Club

Seventh Annual Exhibition
Four rugs, no paintings.

1924
Victoria **Belmont Building** **October 20-25**

Island Arts and Crafts *Society*
Emily exhibited four oils, four water colors.

1925
Victoria **Art Gallery, Crystal Garden** **October 20-31**
Island Arts and Crafts Society

Sixteenth Annual Exhibition
Emily exhibited three oils, two water colors, and a collection of handmade pottery made from B.C. clay.

1926
Victoria **Art Gallery, Crystal Garden** **October 19-30**
Island Arts and Crafts Society

Seventeenth Annual Exhibition
A very large exhibition—121 water colors, fifty-five oils. Emily exhibited four oils and a collection of pottery.

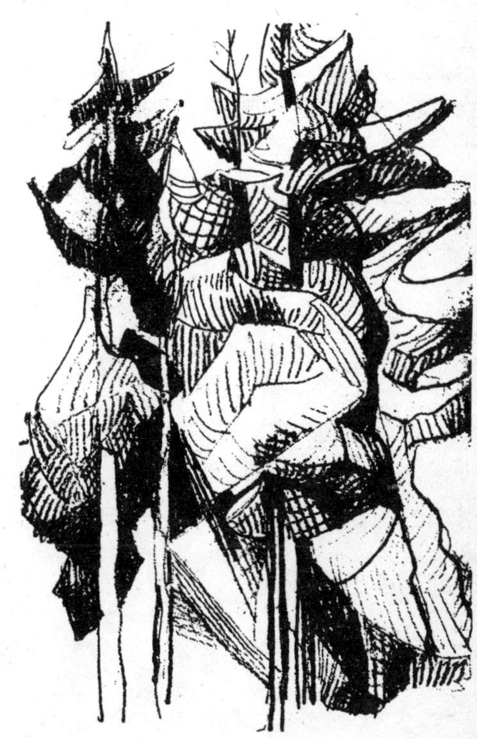

1928
Vancouver **B.C. Art Gallery, 929 Granville St.** **February 18**
Palette and Chisel Club **-March 3**

Second Annual Exhibition
The history of this Club is very elusive and, despite frustrating efforts to trace its activities, many gaps still remain. VAG has no knowledge of the Club's exhibitions until 1935, though several may have taken place there between 1931 and that date. The Vancouver Public Library has only scattered references to the Club and the few surviving ex-members have not replied to letters of enquiry. No catalogues or lists have been

located. However, Ms. Bea Lennie, well-known in the Vancouver art world in the early days, has recalled that the Palette and Chisel Club was formed about 1924 by the prominent sculptor Charles Marega who was its first (and only) president. The club was essentially a small protest or splinter group of the BCSFA, though some of the dissidents retained their society membership after joining the smaller group which had not more than a dozen members. The minutes of the B.C. Art League, on file at the Vancouver City Archives, record that the Palette and Chisel Club held its first exhibition at the Art League gallery (the B.C. Art Gallery) at 929 Granville Street in 1926. Enthusiastic reviews appeared in the Vancouver press (*Daily Province, Sun* and *Western Tribune*) but Emily was not mentioned in any.

Evidently the P&CC did not hold an exhibition in 1927 as none is reported in the Minutes of the B.C. Art League, nor in the *Province* or the *Sun,* the reason no doubt why the *Province* art critic, "Diogenes," in his review of February 18, 1928, refers to the 1928 show as the Club's second exhibition. It has therefore been listed here as the *Second Annual.*

"Diogenes" wrote that the Club members, though trained in academic methods of art, had for some time longed to kick over the traces and show what they could do if they forgot the ways of the painters of the past. He found their exhibition "full of brightness, color, and intriguing quality," despite the deplored modernistic trend, and managed to write a column more than fifteen inches long without once referring to Emily. This is proof that Emily could have participated in other P&CC exhibitions without our knowledge, since "Diogenes" found her work "repellent"* and simply ignored her. Fortunately, we know from her correspondence with the director of NGC that her paintings were hung in this show. In his letter of March 19, 1928, he agreed with Emily that the critics had treated her shabbily: "The kind of criticism from Vancouver of your work in a recent Palette and Chisel exhibition is pathetic and I am not surprised you don't show much of your work there."

* *"Diogenes" uses this word in a long review, "A Modernistic Painter" in which he describes Emily, her work and her exhibitions (Vancouver* Daily Province, *March 10, 1930).*

Victoria — Belmont Building — October 23-31
Island Arts and Crafts Society

*Nineteenth Annual Exhibition**

Emily exhibited six oils, three water colors, a hooked rug (Indian design) and handmade pottery. She used three different signatures on nine paintings: M.E. Carr; M. Emily Carr and E. Carr.

* *According to the revised VAG catalogue* Emily Carr: A Centennial Exhibition, *Emily was also represented in the 1927 IA&CS exhibition (October 25-31). But her name is not listed in their 1927 exhibition catalogue, even in the crafts section; nor is she mentioned in the* Daily Colonist *review of this show (October 25, 1927).*

1929

Toronto — Art Gallery of Toronto — March
Ontario Society of Artists

Annual Exhibition

Emily's first participation with this group. She exhibited *Skidegate* and *Totems, Kitwancool.*

Victoria — Belmont Building — October 22-31
Island Arts and Crafts Society

Twentieth Annual Exhibition

Emily exhibited four oils, four water colors and a collection of handmade pottery.

Vancouver — B.C. Art Gallery, 929 Granville St. — November 16-30
British Columbia Society of Fine Arts

Winter Exhibition

Eighty-nine works shown. Emily exhibited four.

1930

Vancouver — B.C. Art Gallery, 649 Seymour St. — February 15 -March 15
Palette and Chisel Club

Fourth Annual Exhibition

Emily was probably so annoyed with the critics for slighting her work in 1928 that she did not enter any paintings in the 1929 P&CC exhibition. At least none is mentioned in either the *Province* or *Sun* reviews. But her itch to exhibit took over again in 1930 and she tried once more. The *Sun* of February 17 reported that the opening of this show was a gala affair attended by an enthusiastic gathering of about 100 spectators, which augured well for the success of the exhibition. A great variety of subjects was presented in the works of, among others, Statira Frame, Ernva Code, M. Emily Carr, Grace Melvin and M.O. Verral. No criticism of the paintings was given.

Toronto — Art Gallery of Toronto — March
Ontario Society of Artists

Annual Exhibition

Emily exhibited *British Columbia Forest* and *Gitwangak Totem Poles.*

Lawren Harris greatly encouraged Emily when he wrote: "Your canvasses hang in the OSA show. The consensus of opinion, best opinion, is that they are a very great advance on your previous work. It is as if your ideas, vision, feelings, were coming to precise expression; yet nowhere is the work mechanical, laboured or obvious. . . . Keep on . . ."*

* Growing Pains, *p. 348. Although this quotation is not dated, it is clear from the number of pictures shown and their titles that it refers to the 1930 exhibition.*

Toronto Art Gallery of Toronto April
Exhibition by the Group of Seven (and invited contributors)

Emily exhibited: *Nirvana; Forest; Kispiox, Indian Village; Western Canadian Forest; June 9th 1928.* A great event for Emily. She was thrilled to be invited to exhibit with the Group for the first time and went East to see for herself how her pictures stood up alongside those of her idols. She was disappointed on the whole as she felt that her work looked "mean and small" hanging in such illustrious company. She was therefore almost unbelieving when some of the Group expressed amazement at the improvement and greater freedom of her painting.

Same exhibition traveled to:
Art Association of Montreal May 3-18

Victoria Board of Trade Building October 28-November 8
Island Arts and Crafts Society

Twenty-first Annual Exhibition

On November 11, Emily wrote to Nan Cheney about this show:

The Arts and Crafts exhibition has been on. It was just awful. Made me *sick.* I was not for sending in but one of the old tabs persuaded me, and Miss Hembroff would not send unless I did. So I swung in 6. Of course they loathed them. Two oils and 4 water colours.* Instead of yowling about them, they tried just ignoring them and me. This time they just did not exist, nobody made one remark or one mention of them (the oils were two of my largest) and they were filthily sarcastic the one day I went, saying: "Oh, how gracious of you to deign to come to the show, etc." They made me feel just sore and whipped really. I don't think I'll send again. What's the use? Somehow I feel they just degrade art, make it mean and little and I feel it hurts one's work and outlook. It would be best to stay apart. One hates their ideals bemuddied and really Victoria's idea of art is degrading. Miss Hembroff . . . she's been studying in Paris . . . sent in a pencil sketch of a nude. One of the filthy old men said the most revolting things to her face about it, talking of it in the lowest terms of 'nakedness.' They refused to hang it . . .*

* *Only five are listed in the catalogue—five oils, no water colors.*

* *But under pressure from Emily, they did accept two others: one,* Quatre Nus, *shocked the group on two scores: It had not one nude, but four! And they were cubistic! The story of Emily's stormy defense of this "indecent" painting is told in* M.E.—A Portrayal of Emily Carr, *p. 37.*

1931

Toronto **Art Gallery of Toronto** **March**
Ontario Society of Artists

Annual Exhibition

Emily's third and final exhibition with this Society. Only one painting shown: *Totem and Forest.*

Vancouver **Vancouver Art Gallery** **October**
Palette and Chisel Club

First Annual Exhibition at VAG?

This exhibition is included with reservations. Although listed in VAG's 1975 revised *Emily Carr: A Centennial Exhibition,* it has been impossible to trace, and VAG's listing may possibly be in error. The Minutes of the B.C. Art League note that this Club's exhibition was expected to take place in February as usual, but no confirmation of the date followed in later Minutes, nor in local newspapers. If the Club show was really held in October (which does not follow its pattern of spring exhibitions), it could only have been at VAG, yet this institution has no record of it today. Nor did the *Daily Province* or the *Sun* review a P&CC exhibition during October 1931, when the new Vancouver Art Gallery was opened. One thing only speaks in favor of such an exhibition: a P&CC show held at VAG in 1933 was called their *Third Annual.*

Toronto **Art Gallery of Toronto** **December 31**
Exhibition by the Group of Seven (and invited contributors)

Although the Group dominated an exhibition of contemporary Canadian paintings in New York the following year, this 1931 show was, strictly speaking, their last. It was held only in Toronto—no traveling. Emily was represented by: *Indian Cemetery; Thunder Bird; Trees; Red Cedar; Little Pine.* She wrote to Nan Cheney on December 14, full of problems:"I sent to the Group and the express was $18.75 *one way.* I've had to lower rents and things are very tight. . . . Besides, I do feel while McCurry is in power I won't get any show and it's dreadful getting anything home again ever. They've never bothered to buy anything except those two or three old, original water colours which they show as samples of my work and make me sick. Lawren Harris tells me the Group show is very good this year."

1932
Victoria **Belmont Building** **October 11-22**
Island Arts and Crafts Society

Twenty-third Annual Exhibition

Emily exhibited: *Indian Village, B.C.; Tree; Thunder Bird; Red Cedar.*

The young moderns in Victoria finally rebelled!

When Max Maynard was asked to assume the vice-presidency of the Society early in 1932, he demurred but finally agreed on condition that they allow him a separate room at their next exhibition in which to hang the works of the few modern painters in Victoria. This was the one and only time that the Society officially recognized the modern artists by giving them this space to themselves. Emily naturally headed the list, which included—besides Max and the author—Jack Shadbolt, Ina D.D. Uhthoff and a young pupil of Max's, Ronald Bladen, who traded eggs from his father's farm for his art lessons. With youthful zeal and Emily's blessing, Max determined to enlighten "the old fogeys" of the Arts and Crafts and wrote an excellent leaflet, *The Modern Point of View,* which I have always referred to as "Max's Manifesto." A pile of these manifestoes was placed on the table in our "Modern Room" for distribution; but one day, when Max was unwary enough to leave the exhibition unattended, they all mysteriously disappeared. Unfortunately, not a single copy seems to have survived.

Emily was mollified by the attempt of the Arts and Crafts to appease her, and her comments to Nan Cheney on October 22 were strangely subdued: "It's over [the Arts and Crafts show]. They gave us a more modern room (a small poor one) to ourselves this year. That was a step. . . . The good crits are almost worse than the bad. Most times they credit you with something you never thought of for a moment."

Besides Emily's four paintings, the "Modern Room" was hung with seven by Jack Shadbolt; five by Max Maynard; four by the author and one each by Ina D.D. Uhthoff and Ronald Bladen.

The *Times* of October 12 had this to say: "Though the orthodox exhibits outnumbered the 'modern' considerably, it is perhaps significant that at last the exponents of the latter have secured a room to themselves—in fact two small rooms—and here the casual spectator succeeds in having his attention arrested. Miss Emily Carr's four ample canvasses stand out in this section for their boldness, their heavy touch and the sweep of their conception. Her *Thunderbird* . . . has been shown in the Paris Salon and it is undoubtedly worthy of this distinction."

One wonders where the reporter got such erroneous information since the two paintings accepted for the 1911 Salon were of French origin.

1933
Toronto — Art Gallery of Toronto — April
Canadian Society of Painters in Water Color (traveling)

Sixth Annual Exhibition

The annual exhibitions of this Society were regularly held at AGT (the first in 1926)* but Emily was represented in only this one show. It comprised 158 works, though only fifty-four were circulated. Two Carr paintings were accepted: *An Indian House, Koskima Village, B.C.* and *Zuuoqua* [sic].

* *The numbering is off because no annual exhibitions took place in 1928 and 1932.*

The NGC sponsored a series of traveling exhibitions, based on the annual CSPWC shows in Toronto from 1933 to 1944, but no catalogue was published for the first exhibition in 1933. It is assumed, however, that at least one of Emily's paintings traveled with the 1933 exhibition, since it went to VAG in September of that year. Emily never became a member of the CSPWC.

After being displayed for a month at the NGC (no catalogue), a selection of works made by a Committee of the Trustees of the NGC in cooperation with CSPWC was sent to Edinburgh to be shown, by invitation of the Royal Scottish Society of Painters in Water Color, at their Fifty-third Annual Exhibition at the Royal Scottish Academy Gallery from January 27 to March 4, 1933. The exhibition was then sent on an English tour starting March 18 in Stockport and traveling to Blackpool, Eastbourne, Bury, Northampton, and Burton-on-Trent before ending at Leamington Spa on August 25, 1934.

All reviews of the Canadian exhibition were favorable, indeed enthusiastic. The Glasgow *Times* of January 30, 1933, for instance, reported: "It is high time that we saw what artists in other parts of the Empire are doing, if they are painting with the same imagination, and have developed as vigorous a technique, as these Canadians have done . . ."

Emily's water colors chosen by the Committee were: *Grave Pole, Alert Bay* and *Kispiox Village.* She mentions the exhibition herself in the November 16, 1932, entry in her journals: "A wire from Brown asking three water colors for the Royal Scottish Water Color Society. I am glad because maybe it shows that Brown feels kindlier towards me and also sees he cannot get me through Vancouver. My water colors are not so good. I have none spot fresh and somehow I cannot feel things done two years ago are yourself today."*

* Hundreds and Thousands, *p. 31.*

Vancouver **Vancouver Art Gallery** **May 20-31**
Palette and Chisel Club

Third Annual Exhibition

This exhibition was held in the Lecture Room; about a dozen artists were represented.

The *Daily Province* of May 22 reports: "Emily Carr, Victoria artist who has gained a great deal of attention in Eastern Canada and the U.S., shows two large canvasses, *Vanquished,* a macabre landscape of desolate country, and *Kispiox Village,* a well-designed composition with her usual totem motif."

Atlantic City **Heinz Ocean Pier, Heinz Art Salon** **Summer**

Annual Art Exhibition

Canadian Group of Painters (first exhibition of the new Society)

Early in 1933, the Group of Seven, founded in 1920, and the storm center of Canadian art for more than a decade, ceased to exist as such and was absorbed into a larger society, the Canadian Group of Painters. Emily was one of the founding members as were all of the Group of Seven painters. Their first exhibition was held in Atlantic City and most of the members were represented by three or four works. Among Emily's entries were her two widely-known masterpieces: *Indian Church* and *Wood Interior.*

Toronto **Art Gallery of Toronto** **November**
Canadian Group of Painters (traveling)

First exhibition of the new Society held in Canada.

Paintings by twenty-five invited contributors supplemented the work of the twenty-eight members. (The next exhibition was not held until 1936.) Emily was in the East (her third and last trip) while this show was in progress and she wrote me a few words about it: "The Group of 28 show was interesting [but] it did not come up to the Group of Seven shows by a long way. Lacked their dignity and unity. But there was interesting stuff there all the same. I shall have to get busy when I get back. . . . I am returning very keen to renew the struggle in spite of the fact my things looked awful there."

Emily was unhappy about her two contributions to the show: *In a Wood, B.C.* and *The Mountain.* "My own two pictures (they did not hang the third) were very unconvincing hanging there. To a few people they spoke, saying nothing but hinting at a struggle for something. My frames were shocking . . . But no frame, however rich, could have helped. An empty cup is an empty cup, though it may have a fine gold rim. Yet strangely I am not cast down. I can rise above the humility of my failure with an intense desire to search deeper . . ."*

* Hundreds and Thousands, *p. 78.*

1934
Montreal Art Association of Montreal
Canadian Group of Painters

Selections from the Toronto exhibition of November, 1933.

Emily's same two paintings were on view in Montreal. Later, after they had been returned to Victoria, she expressed some dissatisfaction with the eastern exhibition: "My canvasses came from Toronto yesterday. Took $7.40 to pay express, which leaves me $1.40 to live on for one week and buy dog food as well. What's the good of sending to exhibitions? First I sent to get the crits of the men in the East, which were helpful. Now they don't give me any. Why? I got *nothing* this time. Two people, neither of them artists, caught the meaning. One of the mountain and one of the trees. Just two people. Is that all I gave? It's rather disheartening, this painting. Is it useless and selfish? . . . The pictures look so much better in their own studio! Now, at home, they seem to mean a little. In Toronto they looked poor, mean and awful."* Emily seems a little hard on her artist friends in the East. After all, she had heard many appreciative comments on her work while visiting in Toronto.

* Hundreds and Thousands, *p. 98.*

She continued her plaint four months later: "No word from the East. What's the matter with those people? . . . Their crits don't help any more. They're drifting in art and not pushing on. . . . The Group's collapsed and the new group hasn't taken hold. Maybe it's up to us Westerners to wriggle up a bit. No mistake, the times *are* depressing. People simply can't afford the price of transportation to shows. I can't, and I work with no idea of exhibiting but just to squeak ahead a little."*

* *Ibid, p. 135.*

Victoria Belmont Building October 22-27
Island Arts and Crafts Society

Twenty-fifth Annual Exhibition

Emily exhibited: *Indian Village, Lillooet; Cordova Bay; In a Wood.* As usual, she blasted the long-suffering Society: "There was a tea party today at the Arts and Crafts exhibition. I was invited among some ten artists and club members. The whole affair ached with horridness. The show had just opened and a straggle of the type that always go on opening days were there, faded people who have time to kill, people with no particular job and of no particular age, belonging to no particular 'set.' . . . There wasn't *one* of us young or vital, no spirit, no poetry, no youth, just prosy flesh picking with tired hands from meagre plates of sparsely buttered bread and dice of uninteresting cake. Oh, the pity! We represented (more or less) Victoria art! Oh, that is not art! I do not think there can be any such thing as *societies* for art. Those are 'snarling' societies (I myself no better than the rest). The fellowship of art is out among the angels in wide space and high skies, things one cannot word and can only feel dimly."*

Hundreds and Thousands, *p. 153.*

1935
Victoria — Belmont Building — November 4-9
Island Arts and Crafts Society

Twenty-Sixth Annual Exhibition

185 works. Emily exhibited two oils.

On November 5, after devoting much of his article to the Club's plans for financing a permanent gallery, the *Daily Colonist's* critic praised the quality of the exhibition (125 water colors, 40 oils, 20 pastels), then listed eighteen names of "senior" exhibitors before casually mentioning Emily, "whose pictures are so well known in the East."

1936
Toronto — Art Gallery of Toronto — January
Canadian Group of Painters (traveling)

Third Exhibition (second in Canada)

Emily exhibited: *Wood Interior; The Forest; B.C. Landscape*

She barely made this show because of severe financial problems, which she had explained to Nan Cheney the previous October: "I am trying my best to get rid of the house (of All Sorts). It is just killing. Rents so low and so hard to get tenants at all. The place needs modernizing and doing up and I have not a bean. Nothing *sells* these days but I am trying to swap it for a hut. . . . I saw a notice that there is to be a Group Show in January. Shan't be able to send. Costs too much." However, by the end of 1935 Emily's financial worries had eased a little. Negotiations for the disposal of her apartment house were promising, and she somehow found the means to enter the exhibition.

Ottawa **National Gallery of Canada** **February**
Canadian Group of Painters (traveling)

Selections from the Toronto exhibition of January, 1936.

Only *The Forest* and *Wood Interior* were shown in Ottawa. Both these paintings were later sold (1938) at $40 each—one to Miss Kathleen Fenwick* and one to Donald Buchanan.* There were two catalogues for this traveling exhibition. One group, with thirty-eight works, traveled from May to September. The other, with thirty-six works, to October 1937.

* *Miss Kathleen Fenwick (1901-1973) was Curator of Prints and Drawings at NGC.*

* *Donald Buchanan (1908-1966) was Supervisor for Talks for CBC (1937-1940); Supervisor of Displays, National Film Board (1944-1945); Supervisor of Special Graphic Projects, National Film Board (1946); Editor of* Canadian Art; *Director of the National Design Council (1948-1955); and Associate Director of the National Gallery of Canada (1955-1960). Wrote many articles.*

Vancouver **Vancouver Art Gallery** **October 13-25**
Canadian Group of Painters

Selections from the Toronto and Ottawa exhibitions

Thirty-six works.

I invited Emily to visit Vancouver to see this show, and she replied: "[It is] always my luck to be too late for exes. You see, I did not realize it was the Canadian Group showing. I thought it was just one of their National Gallery traveling exhibits wherein they usually display all Canada's third-rate pictures. . . . Well, it is better for my pocket not to go. . . . I do understand what you say about the Eastern group being posterish and a bit bizarre. The new group have tried to follow the old group. The old group were to start commercial artists who burst forth and followed a real idea with an ideal ahead and they accomplished something—and something big. The new group were *admirers* of the old group and wanted to copy them but they had not the ideal within themselves. They paint to the old group's formula, whereas the old group utilized their commercial designing. The new group sort of took that as their finish . . . whether it was the praise and glory that turned the heads of the group, I don't know, but it seems to me they have all fallen down or stopped. They have lost something but perhaps this is just natural. They did their job and are now past. We all have to face that. We can't go on forever and must sit back and fold up and leave it to others to do the going on. . . . I would like to have seen A.Y. Jackson's stuff. . . . Did my papers not look tuppency among all the canvasses? It was A.Y. Jackson who framed them I believe. You said awfully nice things but I'd like to have seen for myself how papery they looked beside the canvasses."

Vancouver Vancouver Art Gallery June 26-July 12
British Columbia Society of Fine Arts

Twenty-sixth Annual Exhibition

Eighty-six works. Emily exhibited: *Reforestation* and *Shoreline, Victoria.* A sale was still a big event in Emily's life in mid-1936, and she was excited about making several early this year. In her journal entry of July 8, she bubbles over with amazement: "I'm just whizzy. Sold four pictures! One from the Vancouver Gallery, *Shoreline;* one paper sketch; one French cottage; one Victoria. What a help to finances!" Then, two weeks later, she mentions the sales again: "Received $120 for picture *Shoreline.* Gallery took $30 commission from $150 sale price to Mrs. de Pencier. Also got $75 for [the other] three sketches from Miss de Pencier."* The *Daily Province* reviewed this exhibition on June 27: "Emily Carr, whose work has been lauded by eastern critics as exemplifying the mood of the coast, shows two canvasses, both rhythmic in treatment . . ."

* Hundreds and Thousands, *pp. 248-249.*

1937

Vancouver Vancouver Art Gallery April 16-May 2
British Columbia Society of Fine Arts

Twenty-seventh Annual Exhibition

Eighty-four works.

Emily said she sent four pictures to Vancouver: *Masset Bears; Metchosin; Alive;* and *Woods Without Men;* but, curiously, *Masset Bears* is not listed in the catalogue. Did she make a mistake, or was it turned down by the jury?

The *Daily Province* reviewer wrote: "The whirling rhythm of the pine trees have caught the imagination of Miss Emily Carr in her three landscapes. . . . It will be remembered that Mme. Leopold Stokowski, wife of the celebrated composer and conductor, who was greatly impressed with this artist's work during her short stay in Victoria, is buying one of her pictures, *Up the Nass River,* and suggesting arrangements for a possible exhibition in New York."

Victoria Belmont Building October 20-27
Island Arts and Crafts Society

Twenty-eighth Annual Exhibition

This was the last IA&CS exhibition to which Emily herself contributed. Her paintings were shown again in 1940 and 1941, but on loan. In the 1937 show Emily exhibited: *In the Forest* and *Masset Bears.* In this final exhibition with the "millstone round the neck of art," as Emily once described the Society,* she is at last accorded full recognition by at least one of the two press critics. In fact, she is the only painter specifically named in the half-column review in the *Times* of October 21: "The pictorial section ... ranges from the internationally-known oils of Emily Carr through a well-selected collection of portraits in oils, water colors and black and white. . . . In all there are ninety-nine water colors, twenty-three oils and nineteen pastel and black and white subjects." However, the *Daily Colonist* review of the same date mentions only the names of conveners and overlooks Emily's work completely. Nor were there any follow-up reports to rectify this omission. Later coverage, always in the social column, was confined to daily lists of the tea hostesses.

* *NGC. Emily to Eric Brown, March 26, 1939: "I am ashamed often that I have not done my bit better in Victoria, but really the Arts and Crafts Society are like a millstone round the neck of art."*

In all, Emily entered seventy-one titles in twelve IA&CS exhibitions from 1911 to 1937, excluding 1916 when only rugs were shown.

Toronto Art Gallery of Toronto November-December
Canadian Group of Painters (traveling)

Fourth Exhibition (Third in Canada)

Emily exhibited: *Swirl; Lillooet Indian Village; Little Pine;* and *Old and New Forest.* In a November letter to me, Emily wrote: "I am not sending over for the 'Canadian Group' but using some of the stuff I have over there (the three Mr. Band took back):* *Lillooet Indian Village; Goldstream Park* and *Swirl* . . . those three have not been shown in the East before." For some unknown reason, *Goldstream Park* was not hung, but two other paintings, *Little Pine* and *Old and New Forest* were entered for her. By the time the show reached NGC in 1938, only two of these paintings were still listed: *Swirl* and *Old and New Forest.*

* *C.S. Band, former Director of the Art Gallery of Toronto and one of the first well-known collectors to purchase Emily's work.*

In December, 1937, Emily again wrote to me with added comment on this exhibition: "I got a catalogue of the Canadian Group show. There was an abstract by Lawren Harris. I was much disappointed. Just like all the rest of the abstracts. Might be the inside of a machine or carpenter's shop—hard, unrelated lines. Perhaps it may be lovely in color. I don't know. It certainly did not impress me."

1938
Montreal Art Association of Montreal

Traveling exhibition, selections from the 1937 AGT show.

1938
Ottawa **National Gallery of Canada**
Canadian Group of Painters (traveling)

Fourth exhibition (third in Canada with new catalogue)

Emily exhibited: *Swirl* and *Old and New Forest.*

Even before this exhibition opened in Toronto in November 1937, Emily had told me something of the events leading up to it: "I had a note about the Canadian Group show from A.Y. Jackson. They still send me addressed to 646 Simcoe Street—makes me tired. They're such a bunch of slackers. I am not going to send over special as there are lots of my things kicking around the East now. Possibly they will rake one up. What's got into us all? We're a nasty outfit—artists." Among the four paintings in the Toronto exhibition that A.Y. Jackson, or others, "raked up" was *Swirl* which Emily sent East regretfully. She once told me: "One I did like. It was not very big and I called it 'Swirl.' Mr. Band fell for it at once and I rather hated to part with it. Usually I don't care."

Vancouver **Vancouver Art Gallery** **April 29-May 15**
British Columbia Society of Fine Arts

Twenty-eighth Annual Exhibition

Seventy-eight works. Emily exhibited: *My Forest; Swirl; Old and New Forest.*

On April 25 Emily wrote to Ruth Humphrey: "... got three canvasses off to Vancouver to the B.C. Fine Arts today. They have made me an honorary member—equivalent to the Arts and Crafts in Victoria—well no, it is better than that (nothing could be worse than an Art Society). Oh Art, Art, what a filthy thing they've turned the *name* into—all the piffle and muck they write—everybody and anybody who can gain money and 'talk reputation' thereby, all posing as lecturers, critics, and Radio talkers on!!!!!Art!!!!! Just now I feel fed up . . . probably comes from being completely dissatisfied with my own work at present."

1939
New York World's Fair **June 10-July 31**
Canadian Society of Painters in Water Color

Eighty-one works. Emily exhibited: *Totem.*

New York World's Fair **August 1-September 15**
Canadian Group of Painters

Sixty-four works. Emily exhibited: *Something Unknown; A Rushing Sea of Undergrowth.*

In 1938 the Canadian Government requested NGC to accept the responsibility for the Canadian Section of Fine Arts at the New York World's Fair, enough space being allotted for seventy-five pictures. It was decided to confine the exhibition to work of contemporary painters, and in order that a comprehensive view of Canadian art might be presented, to hold a series of exhibitions, each lasting six weeks. NGC's invitation to five chartered art societies to arrange these shows resulted in a series of four very successful exhibitions—the two concerning Emily being listed above.

One of the two paintings shown with the Canadian Group of Painters exhibition at the New York World's Fair, *A Rushing Sea of Undergrowth,* was one of Emily's favorites, and apparently a favorite with the public too, since it has been widely circulated. It was exhibited in four important shows in the thirties, in four more in the forties, and several times in each succeeding decade. It was also the subject of one of the crank letters Emily occasionally received about both her paintings and her animals. In a 1942 letter to Ira Dilworth, she tells us of the reaction of one such crank to *A Rushing Sea:* "I got a filthy letter today—you know Delisle Parker did a full-page write-up on my work in the Vancouver *Province* with three reproductions. Today an anonymous came—a scrawled half-sheet: 'From Vancouver *Province: The Lady Artist from Victoria.* Her picture of *A Rushing Sea of Undergrowth.* Probably 99 people out of 100 would think as I do. This is just about the *rottenest looking daub that anyone could imagine.* Looks like the nightmare of a dope fiend. T'isnt even funny.' "

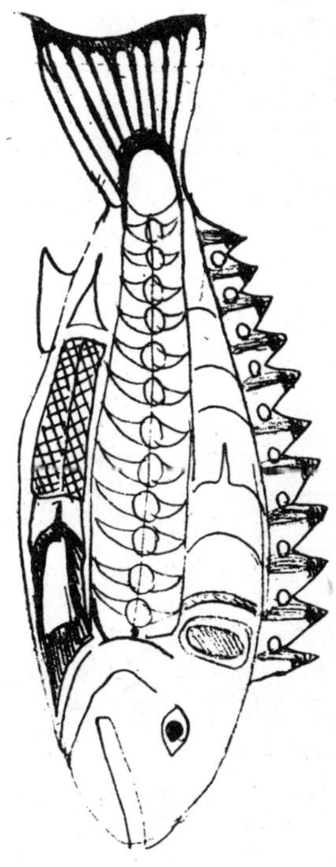

Ottawa National Gallery of Canada August-September
Canadian Society of Painters in Water Color
(traveling 1939-1940)

Eighty-one works—New York World's Fair exhibition.

Later shown in galleries in London, Winnipeg, Regina and Edmonton.

Nova Scotia Provincial Exhibition
Canadian Group of Painters

of National Gallery origin

Toronto Art Gallery of Toronto October-November
Canadian Group of Painters
Also Art Association of Montreal

Emily exhibited: *Old Tree at Dusk; A Rushing Sea of Undergrowth; Something Unknown;* and *Trees in the Sky.*

She again mentioned the Canadian Group of Painters in her letter to Eric Brown of March 26, 1939: "I'm sure the National Gallery has done much throughout Canada to further art and is gaining a fine collection. There is good stuff in our country, both material and young people—if they were only a bit more serious and had more stick-to-it. They want to be full-fledged, money-making artists straight off. I do feel too that the Canadian Group should contrive an exhibition at *least* every *second* year. Do they do *anything* to further art except collect the annual fee? Which, by the way, is *never* acknowledged. There are many younger artists who ought to be filling the ranks."

1940

Victoria **April 8-13**

Island Arts and Crafts Society

Thirty-first Annual Exhibition

Emily did not enter any paintings this year. Those on view were loaned by Mrs. Maltwood.

Vancouver **Vancouver Art Gallery** **May 17-June 2**

British Columbia Society of Fine Arts

Thirtieth Annual Exhibition

Sixty-six works. Emily exhibited *Spring; A Cedar; Vancouver Island.* What with the move to St. Andrews St. in February and then a bout of 'flu, Emily found it difficult to prepare paintings for this show, but told Nan Cheney on May 1, that she was "hoping to have two pictures (not very big) for the B.C. Artists [sic] in May." She somehow managed three. She shipped them to Vancouver just before leaving for her last sketching trip to Metchosin, and suffered a stroke three days after the exhibition closed. Very ill all summer, she was barely able to prepare her May-June sketches for her solo exhibition at VAG in November.

1941

Victoria **April 28-May 3**

Island Arts and Crafts Society

Thirty-second Annual Exhibition

Emily did not enter paintings in this exhibition. Those on view were loaned by Mrs. Maltwood.

Vancouver **Vancouver Art Gallery** **May 16-June 1**

British Columbia Society of Fine Arts

Thirty-first Annual Exhibition

Seventy-five works. Emily exhibited: *Bent Tree; A Tawny Knoll; Sombreness Sunlit; The Mountain.*

1942

Toronto **Art Gallery of Toronto** **February**

Canadian Group of Painters

Emily exhibited: *British Columbia.*

This exhibition was also shown at:

Montreal	Art Association of Montreal	
Ottawa	National Gallery of Canada	September (traveling)
Vancouver	Vancouver Art Gallery	January 15-February 4, 1943

Vancouver **Vancouver Art Gallery** **May 15-31**

British Columbia Society of Fine Arts

Thirty-Second Annual Exhibition

Emily exhibited: *Beach; Logged Lands; Typically British Columbia; Sky; Somewhere; Quiet Sunshine; Young Arbutus.* Her work won considerable praise this year. Sold four of the seven sketches on view and, for a change, got her money on the dot. Curator Grigsby's stock had always gone up and down with Emily depending on the cash returns of her exhibitions and this year he was the fair-haired boy.

1943

Vancouver **Vancouver Art Gallery** **January 15-February 4**

Canadian Group of Painters

(the 1942 Toronto exhibition circulated by the National Gallery)

Emily still represented by only one work: *British Columbia.*

The Art Gallery Bulletin, reporting on this exhibition, stated in part: "Not since 1936 has an exhibition of the work of the Canadian Group of Painters been seen in Vancouver. . . . British Columbia is represented by Bess Harris, Lawren Harris, J.W.G. Macdonald and W.P. Weston."

How could VAG exclude Emily from a review of an exhibition in such an important year as 1943? "Palette," too, in his write-up in the *Daily Province* of January 14, failed to mention the title of her painting, coupling her with J.W.G. Macdonald in summarily dismissing the "contributions from their brushes" as "typically vigorous." But he did praise the show in general as one of the most stimulating of the year. This was Emily's last appearance with the CGP. Her relations with the Group appear to have gradually deteriorated—at least it would seem so from the splutterings in her letter to Nan Cheney on June 16, 1941: "I think that art congestion in Toronto is rot. If they *worked* more and talked less [it would be] better. I'm disgusted with the Canadian Painters. They are slobs [? partly illegible]. They are little and mean. Lawren Harris is not, he's fine and generous."

But the story ends on a happier note. Three years later, when writing to Myfanwy Spencer Pavelic in June, 1944, she seemed to have forgotten her earlier resentment and even boasted a little: "I have been made an Honorary Life Member of the Canadian Group of Painters—the first one they have made. I feel very proud. It is nice of them. I always felt they had not much use for me."

Vancouver Vancouver Art Gallery May 15-June 6
British Columbia Society of Fine Arts

Thirty-third Annual Exhibition

One hundred seven works. Emily exhibited: *Old Cedar Post; Cordova Bay; At Seaton, B.C.; Alive; Old Fir Tree; Mrs. Jones's Farm.*

She seems to have lost (perhaps only temporarily) a picture from this show. It is amazing how undisturbed and mild she was in her letter of complaint to Grigsby of December 7: "Only five of the six I sent to the B.C. show [in May] came back. It may have got mislaid after the B.C. show, or it may have got stuck over in Seattle [during Emily's solo exhibition at the Art Institute of Seattle sent direct from VAG] . . . if one of the members of BCSFA *lent* it to someone. . . . I do not believe in lending on approbation . . . don't bother. If it turns up O.K. If not, O.K. too." Things had changed with advancing age and illness.

1945
Vancouver Vancouver Art Gallery May 18-June 10
British Columbia Society of Fine Arts

Thirty-fifth Annual Exhibition

Emily was listed as "the late Emily M. Carr" and all five paintings shown were NFS—loaned by friends. Three were loaned by Dr. G.G. Sedgewick, one by Cpl. Humphrey Toms and one by Mrs. Hill Cheney.

A Special Exhibition Held by the British Columbia Society of Artists
(in Emily's day, the B.C. Society of Fine Arts)

1960
Vancouver **Vancouver Art Gallery** **May 24-June 12**
British Columbia Society of Artists

Fiftieth Annual Golden Anniversary Show

Opened officially by the Governor General during his visit to Vancouver, this exhibition was said to cover an epoch in Greater Vancouver cultural history, as this senior art society in B.C., or rather its forerunner, the B.C. Society of Fine Arts, was incorporated in 1909 when the city was less than a quarter-century old. This special exhibition, in part retrospective (and which included Emily's works) was held at VAG, as were all others after 1931 when the Gallery was opened. The *Province* review of May 21, 1960, states that 1931 was also the year Emily was made a Life Member of the Society. Being suspicious of this early date, and unable to find the required information on the Society in Victoria, I wrote to Humphrey Toms, one of my long-suffering "Emily" friends in Vancouver, who obligingly examined the *Minute Book BCSFA 1917-1941*. With much embarrassment, but not a little pride, I was reminded of an Annual General Meeting of the Society (December 7, 1938) I should have remembered well without help from Humphrey or notes. The excerpt in question reads: (p. 108) "It was moved by Mrs. Brand [the author] and seconded by Mr. Hood that the appointment of Miss Emily Carr to Life Membership in the Society be confirmed. Carried."

At the earlier meeting (November 17, 1937), Emily's election to Life Membership was proposed by W.P. Weston and seconded by J.W.G. Macdonald. According to the 1939 catalogue, Emily was one of only two Life Members.

1960
Victoria **Art Gallery of Greater Victoria** **July**

The Victoria Gallery displayed a selection of twenty-nine oils from the Golden Anniversary show after it closed in Vancouver. In the *Times* of July 16, the art critic wrote that the paintings made an impressive survey ranging from a 1907 landscape to recent contemporary work and, "As Emily Carr was one of the 24 [sic] founding members of the B.C. Society of Fine Arts, you will find her water colors . . . an excellent and satisfying complementary."*

* *The text of this review is far from clear, but I could not check with AGGV as they have neither a catalogue for, or record of, this exhibition.*

III General Exhibitions 1894-1945

Exhibitions in which she participated during her lifetime, with a few added for special reasons—up to 1958.

For Charles C. Hill, in appreciation.

1894
Victoria Fair (Willows) **October 2-6**

179 entries
Assumed to be the first time Emily's work was shown in public, though the date is not firmly verified (see chapter "Emily Carr as a Painter"—The Victoria Fairs). The pen and ink sketches attributed to her placed first in this category.

1895
Victoria Fair (Willows) **September 16-21**

A fully verified date. Emily captured first prizes in pencil drawing, pen and ink sketches and "painting on china." Her friends will smile about this last honor since she rarely admitted that she had "demeaned" herself sufficiently to paint china.

1909
New Westminster Provincial Fair **October 12-16**

The art display at the Fair this year was said to be the best in its history. It included many excellent water colors and nineteen oil paintings of Canadian landscape loaned by the Canadian Government. The members of the BCSFA hung their own "very creditable" show separately, and the Vancouver *Daily Province* of October 13 reported that "Miss M. Emily Carr's strong water colors show much sympathetic appreciation of the woodland side of B.C. scenery; she has a breezy bit of Beacon Hill Park, Victoria, and several Indian subjects."

1910
Vancouver **Granville Street studio** **June 20**

A few weeks before leaving for France to study, Emily and Anne Batchelor held a joint exhibition and social evening in their studio at 1035 Granville Street. Over thirty friends and well-wishers came to view the large collection of works of both artists, and during the evening, according to the *Daily Province* of

June 21, an auction sale of a number of Emily's paintings was held. Nearly everyone present took advantage of the opportunity to secure one or more of her "clever" paintings.

1911
Paris Grand Palais des Champs Elysées October 1
Société du Salon d'Automne -November 8

Emily exhibited *La Colline* and *Le Paysage*. Her pictures were said to have been well hung among famous contemporaries such as Bonnard, Vlaminck, Rouault, Segonzac, Marquet. Emily's money ran out while sketching in Brittany late that summer and it is not yet clear whether she stayed in Paris long enough to see her paintings on display in the Salon show or not. (See the Chronology for comments on this exhibition.)

1924
Seattle Fine Arts Society 2028 Third Avenue April 4-30

Ninth Annual Exhibition of the Artists of the Pacific Northwest
Emily was awarded Second Honorary Mention in oil for one of her four entries, *Macaulay Point*.

1925
Seattle Fine Arts Society March 5-April 5

Tenth Annual Exhibition of the Artists of the Pacific Northwest

Emily exhibited four paintings. Received no awards this year.

1926
Victoria Fair (Willows) August

Emily held her own exhibition within an exhibition. She received good press reviews and high praise for her Indian pictures.

1927
Ottawa National Gallery of Canada December

Canadian West Coast Art (Native and Modern) traveling

Opened November 30 in Ottawa. Also shown in Toronto and Montreal.

In cooperation with the National Museum, Ottawa; the Royal Ontario Museum, Toronto; McGill University and the Art Association of Montreal.

The National Museum, the Royal Ontario

Museum and McGill University lent the bulk of the Indian specimens.

On the recommendation of Dr. Marius Barbeau, twenty-six of Emily's Indian paintings of the 1912 period, all oils, plus pottery and a few hooked rugs, were selected for this exhibition by Director Eric Brown of NGC when he visited Emily's studio in September 1927. Never having exhibited in the East, and almost unknown there, this event was of incalculable importance in Emily's exhibiting career. She went to Ottawa for the opening and found Barbeau and Brown full of enthusiasm and hope. Barbeau was pleased with Emily's cover design with Indian motif for the catalogue, and predicted there would be "a great jam" at the opening as "it's the best show we've had." But the great evening, Emily said, was "horrid." Few people came—apparently because of poor organization—and Emily wailed that her show was a "fizzle" and felt humiliated and defeated. However, on return from Montreal, where she had gone to see the RCA show, she found Barbeau much more optimistic; and in the end the exhibition was an overwhelming success—in all three cities.

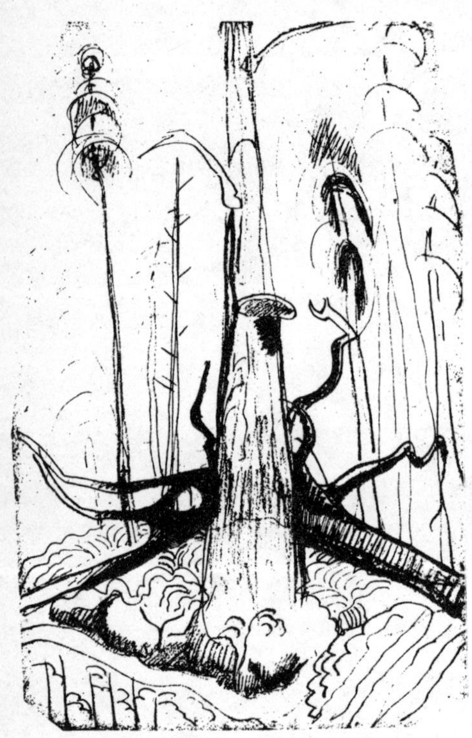

The *Toronto Star Weekly* of January 21, 1928, in a full-page, illustrated article, wrote that, "Emily Carr, whose remarkable paintings of lost Indian villages are occupying the most important space in the current exhibition of Canadian West Coast Art in the National Gallery is quite frank about her deep love for the Indians of her own province. And she cares so little for the opinions of the rest of us that she flatly refuses to have a photograph taken, in spite of the fact that she is not at all hard to look at."

In his letter of January 8, 1928, to Emily, Lawren Harris wrote: "The exhibition of West Coast Art is on at the gallery here (Toronto) and looks exceedingly well—as varied and interesting a show, I think, as we have ever had. Your work is impressive, more so than Lismer had led me to believe, and he was genuinely moved by it. . . . I really have (not) nor can have, anything to say about it in the way of frank criticism. I cannot even suggest anything. For I feel that you have found a way of your own wonderfully suited to the expression of the Indian spirit and his feeling for life and nature. Besides, the pictures are works of art in their own right, individual, finely plastic, and having creative life in them."

The Secretary of NGC, H.O. McCurry, also wrote to Emily: "The West Coast show is in Montreal at present (March 7, 1928) and seems to be very successful there too."

Marius Barbeau added his comment: "The exhibition was

opened at the Art gallery of Montreal on the 17th. I gave an address at the opening. It had been very well arranged by Holgate and Mr. Judah and will remain there until the end of March." (February 22, 1928—National Museum of Man.)

Four years later, Barbeau was still full of praise for Emily and the Canadian West Coast Art Exhibition when he wrote for publication: "And finally her painting found recognition and, indeed, proved one of the important features of the Northwest Coast [sic] Exhibition . . . of all the painters she is the one whose interpretations of the coast are, in a way, the most authentic and novel.*

* *Marius Barbeau, "The Canadian Northwest—Theme for Modern Painters,"* Magazine of Art *(American Federation of Arts, Washington) Vol XXIV No. 5 May 1932.*

The total value of all twenty-six Carr paintings was given as only $3,995.00. One, *Bear and Moon Totem,* was purchased by Barbeau. (See chapter "The Carr-Barbeau Mystery Story.")

Although other painters were invited to participate in this exhibition, Lawren Harris, Edwin Holgate, A.Y. Jackson, Langdon Kihn and F.H. Varley among them, this was really Emily's show. She was represented by far more paintings than any of the others and received the most publicity. The exhibition was a turning point in Emily's career. From then on she painted steadily, slowly won the acclaim she merited, and never felt completely isolated and abandoned again.

1928
Ottawa National Gallery of Canada January-February

Third Annual Exhibition of Canadian Art

Emily's first appearance with this annual exhibition. Brown relieved her of all responsibility by having ten of her water colors which were stored at the Gallery, framed for inclusion in this show. It was also the occasion of her first sale to the NGC as the Board of Trustees decided to purchase three of the exhibited water colors: *Tanu; Gitwangak* (Kitwanga); and *Alert Bay.**

* *On March 9, Emily wrote to Brown exultantly: "I was fearfully excited [about the sale]. There's no mistake that it will help my finances out considerably, and enable me to go north this summer."*

1929
Detroit, Michigan Convention Hall October 14-19

Women's International Exposition

Under the Auspices of
The Detroit Federation of Women's Clubs

Emily participated in this exhibition without any recorded distinctions since she won none of the four cash prizes awarded. Whether or not she was mentioned in press reviews is difficult to establish at a distance. The Detroit Institute of Arts writes that they have no reviews of the exhibition on file, and infers that the

Detroit Federation of Women's Clubs is now defunct. The very basic catalogue lists: Emily W. [sic] Carr giving her two entries, amusingly misspelled, as: *Village Street—Skidijate* and *Kispioj Indian Village.* It is perhaps worthy of mention that the Detroit Chapter Daughters of the British Empire donated $75.00 to help cover expenses incurred by the Canadian Women Painters.

Toronto **December**
Lyceum Club and Women's Art Association of Canada

The Mail and Empire of Toronto reported that an exhibition of work was held at the Women's Art Association Headquarters in which a "few bits of Emily Carr's pottery" were also shown. (No paintings.) This surely has the distinction of being the smallest Carr exhibition on record.

1930
Ottawa **National Gallery of Canada** **January-February**

Fifth Annual Exhibition of Canadian Art

Although Emily contributed to this show regularly for many years, it was not one of her favorites. She once told me that NGC used it to display all their third-rate pictures. However, others were impressed. Jehanne Bietry Salinger paid high tribute to the 1930 exhibition in the *Canadian Forum* (Vol X No. 114 Toronto March 1930): "The Fifth Annual Exhibition of Canadian Art . . . was indeed a revelation. I found (it) the answer to a question which is of uppermost interest in the mind of every Canadian: 'Has Canada already reached a point of intellectual and emotional crystallization significant enough to create a native art expression?' The answer was overflowing from the pictures I saw on the walls of NGC and it said yes on every side, a most elequent, most impressive yes. Prudence Heward of Montreal and Emily Carr of Victoria, B.C. were the two glories of the exhibition. . . . Emily Carr owes to the West Coast Indians, whom she knows so well, the source of her inspiration. . . . She represents an interesting phase of artistic evolution, and her *Indian Church,* the most daring painting of the exhibition, is a good example of it. The same tendency towards a general simplification of design and decorative values is found in this picture where she has brushed broadly a white facade of a primitive church against a background of weird tree forms done in a deep green."

It is surprising to note in this early show that more women than men were singled out for praise and comment. The reviewer for the Victoria *Daily Colonist* wrote on March 21: "*Indian Church* and the two other pictures by Emily M. Carr . . . notably her *Gitwangak Totem Poles,* as beautifully modelled as a piece of wood carving, . . . are momentous contributions to this show." The third painting was *British Columbia.* All were oils. *Indian Church,* one of Emily's best-known and popular paintings, was purchased by Lawren Harris, presumably in 1930, during or after this exhibition, since it was apparently not returned to Victoria. A few years later, he sold it to Charles S. Band on condition that he (Band) bequeath it to AGO. This he did in 1970. It is an oil on canvas (42¾ x 27⅛ in.) painted from a water color done at Friendly Cove, B.C., in 1929. Emily did at least two water colors of this church, one of which (17 x 14 in.) was sold by auction in Vancouver in March 1977 for $9,000. But the other, larger (23¾ x 18¼ in.), dated 1929 and inscribed on the face of the painting "Friendly Cove," is considered to be the original of the canvas. There is a note to this effect (though no other information) in the AGO files, and both Murray Adaskin, the first owner, and I are of the same opinion. Early 1945, Adaskin wrote a letter to Emily asking to buy a painting. She forwarded the letter to Lawren Harris who, with Ira Dilworth, arranged to let Adaskin have the Indian church water color sketch. He kept it until December 1972, then sold it, on the suggestion of A.J. Casson, through a Toronto gallery. The sketch, fortunately, is now back in B.C. and offered for sale at a Vancouver commercial gallery at $25,000—twice as much as it sold for in 1972.

The *Indian Church* oil is still assigned only a *circa* date (1930) at AGO, but I submit that the date can now be fully established as 1929 because: (1) The water color sketch was done in the summer of that year. (2) The oil on canvas was obviously completed soon after because it was exhibited for the first time October 22-31, 1929 at the Island Arts and Crafts Society exhibition in Victoria, and for the second time from November 16-30, 1929 at the British Columbia Society of Fine Arts exhibition in Vancouver. It was therefore shown for the third time at the Fifth Canadian Annual—but for the first time in the East. The price listed for this magnificent work when first shown was a paltry $175.

Washington, D.C. — Corcoran Galleries — March
American Federation of Arts — (traveling)

Contemporary Canadian Artists

This exhibition of fifty-nine works opened on March 9, 1930 in

Washington, D.C., under the auspices of the American Federation of Arts. It later traveled to Providence, R.I.; Baltimore; St. Louis and many other American cities.

The *Washington Post* critic said that, "The Canadian paintings are among the most original seen in the Corcoran Galleries in years." This was Emily's debut on the international scene in a major traveling exhibition. A report from Washington was published in the March 11, 1930 issue of the Victoria *Times*: "Emily Carr of Victoria has two remarkable studies of totem poles in barbaric colors. Her treatment of the background, in both of these pictures, is distinctly new and original and can be considered as the forerunner of a new influence on Canadian art, starting originally with the work of the British Columbia wood carvers."

Lawren Harris wrote to Emily about the selection of pictures for this exhibition: "The choice was left to (A.Y.) Jackson and me. Yours were all damned good things. I feel there is nothing being done like them in Canada . . . their spirit, feeling, design, handling, is different and tremendously expressive of the British Columbia Coast—its spirit—perhaps more than you realize. . . . Your work is a joy to us here, a real vital contribution." (*Growing Pains*, p. 347)

Seattle Art Institute of Seattle October 1-November 8

Sixteenth Annual Exhibition of Northwest Artists

With the exception of Jack Shadbolt, most of the young Vancouver and Victoria painters were represented in this show. Other contributors were Mark Tobey and Emily's University of Washington friends, Viola and Ambrose Patterson. Emily was represented by two Indian paintings at her usual inflated American price of $350 each. She would only have asked about half that much in Canada but firmly believed that all Americans were wealthy—except, of course, Mark Tobey and a few other artists. She went over to Seattle to see this exhibition which she only described as "quite interesting." On arrival home, however, she phoned me full of excitement to announce that I had won second place in oils for a nude that she herself had urged me to submit. She was equally gleeful that Max Maynard had won nothing. She was very hard on Max, partly because she was convinced that he was trying to copy her work.

1931

Baltimore Baltimore Museum of Art January 15-February 28 (traveling)

First Baltimore Pan-American Exhibition of Contemporary Paintings

According to Emily, she exhibited just one canvas in this exhibition and it was a new one—fresh off the easel. She describes it in her journals: "I was so exhausted (after her Christmas sale of pottery) I spent most of the next day in bed too tired to paint or even think, though I must hurry up with my Baltimore canvas." (*Hundreds and Thousands,* p. 23.) This work was *British Columbia Indian Village.*

Painting this canvas in December 1930 seemed to revive Emily's interest in Indian themes which had slackened somewhat after late 1928 when both Tobey and Lawren Harris had advised her to turn to new material for inspiration. In January and February 1931, she worked on *Koskimo Village. Strangled Growth* and the "*Cumshewa* big bird." This "big bird" now bears the title *Big Raven* although Emily herself always referred to it as the Thunderbird when showing it in her studio. The date assigned to it by VAG is c. 1928/29 but in my view 1931 is correct. Emily painted the *Big Raven* from a 1912 water color *Cumshewa, Queen Charlotte Islands*—a modernized but nevertheless accurate version of the early work. But she was wrong, in calling it a Thunderbird as a thunderbird is not a Haida (Q.C.I.) character.* She concentrated on Indian work long enough at this time to complete this series of paintings—and to attend a dance and potlatch at the Esquimalt Reserve—but did not often return to Indian themes again until after her illness. From May 1931 on she became completely absorbed in the woods. Emily was happy about the outcome of the Baltimore show because Lawren Harris won the $500 award. She always said he was never accorded the recognition he so richly deserved.

* *Peter Macnair, Curator of Ethnology, BCPM, suspects there are other Carr paintings in which certain totem figures are incorrectly attributed. One is* Zunoqua of the Cat Village *(see 1933 NGC* Eighth Annual Exhibition of Canadian Art*).*

Ottawa National Gallery of Canada January-February

Sixth Annual Exhibition of Canadian Art

Emily exhibited only one painting: *Indian Village, B.C.*

The Vancouver *Sunday Province* (February 1, 1931): Reta W. Myers, in her "Weekly Causerie," gives Vancouver artists (in which she includes Emily) a hearty, patriotic boost: "Probably no greater tribute could be paid to artists of Vancouver than the reception of their work in this year's exhibition of Canada's art at the National Gallery of Canada. . . . Ottawa papers have devoted more space to their work than to that of any other Canadian group." She quotes from the Ottawa *Journal:* "There are one or two points that call for special attention. One is the increasing number and power of work coming from Western Canada, another the individuality of the landscapist who strives with success to get the essential atmosphere of Canada." The Ottawa *Citizen* critic describes Emily's work as "lush and vigorous."

Toronto Canadian National Exhibition August-September Lyceum Club and Women's Art Association of Canada

The press in Toronto reported that Emily exhibited unique rugs as well as pottery with Indian totem pole design, made of red clay found at her own door. This display was held in conjunction with the Club's exhibition at the CNE.

Seattle Art Institute of Seattle September 23-November 1

Seventeenth Annual Exhibition of Northwest Artists

Emily exhibited two paintings and won the $50 first award in water color for *Zunoqua*. The Vancouver *Daily Province* (October 11, 1931): In reviewing this exhibition in her "Weekly Causerie," Reta W. Meyers amusingly underestimates Vancouver painters just as she enthusiastically overestimated them in her February review of the *Exhibition of Canadian Art*: "The fact that the exhibition went so modern is perhaps one of the reasons why so little work was shown from Vancouver. . . . only three from Vancouver (Varley—represented but did not enter anything himself—Jock Macdonald, Ernva Code, and Kate Smith). From Victoria Emily Carr and her pupil Edythe Hembroff sent two canvasses each."

People often refer to the teacher-pupil relationship between Emily and myself as they do to Varley and Vera Weatherbie. I should like to disabuse them of this idea once and for all. I was fully trained when I met Emily (four years in California and almost two in the atelier of the famous French artist and teacher André Lhote) and although I was profoundly affected by her philosophy of painting and her feeling for trees, nature, animals and religion, I did not need what a teacher normally supplies—technical training. Nor would Emily have given such assistance had I asked for it. She did not want to teach—me or anyone else. She had never wanted to go back to teaching after her disheartening experience with pupils in Vancouver on her return from France. At no time did she offer any advice or make any comment on my work while we were painting and, when we tacked our day's sketches on the wall for inspection in the evening, the discussion and criticism of them was reciprocal. There was no one-sided teacher's "crit."

1932

Ottawa — National Gallery of Canada — January-February

Seventh Annual Exhibition of Canadian Art

"The exhibition was opened by Their Excellencies, The Governor General and The Countess of Bessborough, on January 21. It was drawn, as heretofore, mainly from the current exhibitions held by the professional art societies in Canada during the previous calendar year. . . . It can be justly claimed for the 1932 exhibition that it presented a fair review of all phases of Canadian art production during 1931." (NGC Annual Reports 1931-1932.)

Emily did not herself submit anything for this show, but no doubt Eric Brown entered a picture for her—something that was being held in reserve for her in NGC. She wrote about this to Nan Cheney on December 14, 1931: "I received word from Vancouver that Mr. Brown desired me to send a canvas for the All Canadian and I have not complied. The message was indirect and I don't feel like bothering nor having the expense of shipping and crating—even to Vancouver. She wrote to Nan again two months later (February 13): "I had a letter from Mr. Barbeau. He was perplexed about what he heard of my work. Said you (Nan Cheney) told him I'd got on and A.Y.J. gave my work the black eye this year—called it monotonous, uninteresting, dull etc. . . . A.Y.J. seemed to spread slangs all over the place but I knew he *does* not care about my stuff and frankly I am not thrilled at his. So I suppose we take our work from different viewpoints. . . . Lawren Harris feels I am *going deeper* (but) haven't hit it yet and it's a case of dig. I think he's right. I imagine some of the work has gone to Ottawa so Barbeau can see for himself. *I* did not send to the Ottawa show." One oil painting, *Red Cedar,* was nevertheless hung.

New York — International Art Center of Roerich Museum — March 5 -April 5

Exhibition of Paintings By Contemporary Canadian Artists
Exhibition catalogue with introduction by Fred B. Housser.

Although this exhibition was not a true Group of Seven show, as their final one had taken place in Toronto in December 1931, the majority of the exhibitors were Group of Seven artists. But others were included, among them Emily who was represented by two paintings *Indian Church* and *Wood Interior.* It would seem at first glance that she was under-represented in this exhibition, but two entries were obviously the imposed limit on non-Group exhibitors as no other non-Group artist had more. The Group members, on the other hand, showed four, five, or even six paintings. Nine of the sixteen contributors were Group members and they entered forty of the forty-nine canvasses shown. The exhibition, like so many others, was arranged by Lawren Harris.

Ottawa National Gallery of Canada July-August

An exhibition arranged by NGC in connection with the Imperial Economic Conference.

Marius Barbeau wrote in *Saturday Night* on August 13, 1932: "A remarkable exhibition is being held at NGC during the sessions of the Imperial Conference. Many visitors in Ottawa are from countries older than Canada and are used to thinking of culture as a part of life. They know this country for its wheat and potential wealth but still have much to learn about its people and their self-expression in the aesthetic arts. This exhibition is meant to satisfy their inquisitiveness." After devoting special attention to the "gorgeous collection of paintings by J.W. Morrice and Tom Thomson," and describing and evaluating the works of "Morrice's juniors, Jackson, Gagnon and others," Barbeau praises the contributions of the "younger generation," including Emily Carr. Because Emily matured late as an artist and was fifty-six years old before her pictures were shown in the East, there was a tendency to regard her as younger than she was. Actually, she was only six years younger than Morrice.

Edmonton Museum of Arts October 22-November 6

A loan exhibition, courtesy of NGC. Emily was represented by one picture, *Alert Bay*, a water color.

San Francisco California Palace of the Legion of Honor December

Western Watercolor Painting

The Victoria *Daily Colonist* wrote on December 8 that "Miss Emily Carr, one of Victoria's most internationally known women, received honorable mention for work which she submitted for exhibition at the first annual exhibition of Western water color painting held at the California Palace of Legion of Honor in San Francisco."

Victoria **in the studio, 646 Simcoe Street** **December 14**

A four-artist show held in the two lower flats of the House of All Sorts to give publicity to Emily's proposed People's Gallery. Besides Emily, the artists were: Lee Nan—a young Chinese artist whom she befriended and promoted for a time; Mrs. Fitzherbert Bullen, and Robin Watt. Emily did not invite Jack Shadbolt, Max Maynard or me because we were too modern and she needed *popular* support for her gallery, the work of conservative painters which would appeal to the taste of still more conservative Victorians. Anything I have to add to the story of Emily's abortive plans to form a gallery—and I was intimately involved in them—is related in chapter "The People's Gallery." Other sources of information are letters to friends. For instance, on December 15 she wrote to Eric Brown that, "The exhibition I was busy with on the 14th is a scheme I have for converting the two flats below my studio into a small art gallery for the *People*. I will enclose the paper I read and I think it will convey my idea to you. I put on a show last night. There are four quite sizeable rooms, well lighted. I filled one with my Indian pictures. Mrs. Bullen I got to fill another (quite good work of a conservative type), another room a young portrait painter and the fourth a clever Chinese artist. . . . It met with *good response.* People were pleased with the rooms and the exhibition and it looks to me as if it may go through . . . a lot of people came and (for Victoria) were *quite keen.* I felt the layman's views on it were broader and finer than the artists'. Gee! I wish I had the money to put it through myself, single handed."

1933
Ottawa **National Gallery of Canada** **January - February**

Eighth Annual Exhibition of Canadian Art
288 works. Emily exhibited two pictures: *Zunoqua of the Cat Village* and *Blunden Harbour.*

She had decided not to enter more than one painting in this show and then only if she was notified by the Vancouver Committee in plenty of time to select and pack without rush. She always resented being informed about the shipping date at the last moment and expressed her annoyance this year once more in a letter to Nan Cheney of January 7: "I had not expected to send more than one East this year and that only if I got notice from Vancouver *in time,* which I did not. That's the third year (C.H.) Scott has given me one minute's notice. So I wrote and told Mr.

Brown why I was unable to send." But Brown was able to change her mind by wiring for six canvasses to be sent East express at the Gallery's expense. Greatly excited, she replied on January 3: "Thank you for your wire and letter. I've been spinning like a top ever since they came, and trying to get my canvasses in shape.... There is nothing like an exhibition to bring one on their feet up to time." But on December 23, 1932, C.H. Scott also sent a letter of complaint to Eric Brown—about Emily: "Following your second telegram asking for an increased number of exhibits—and mentioning Miss Carr—I immediately wrote to her. I enclose (her) reply . . . (which) I consider a piece of rank discourtesy, inaccurate and quite inexcusable on the ground of artistic temperament or other such refuges of the unbalanced." Emily's works in this exhibition were praised by Marius Barbeau in his review for the *Art Digest:* "Canada Holds Its Largest and Best Annual Exhibition at Ottawa: Emily Carr, Victoria, the most individual of all in self-expression (is represented) with two powerful silhouettes of totem poles and moist Pacific landscapes."* *Blunden Harbour* was shown for the first time in this exhibition. *Zunoqua Of the Cat Village* is perhaps her only work showing surrealist overtones. She has always called this particular figure the "wild woman of the woods" who is often shown with a basket on her back into which she places stolen children that she intends to eat. Curiously, her attribution of both location and figure is inaccurate as the carving depicts a male chief and stands in the village of Quattische, and not "Zunoqua" in the village of Koskimo.*

* The Art Digest, *Vol. VII, No. 12, 1933, New York.*

* *See 1931 exhibition, Baltimore, Note 1.*

Vancouver University of British Columbia Library March

Three Victoria Artists

The first showing of Emily's paintings in Vancouver (with the exception of her four entries in the BCSFA exhibition in November 1929) since her large solo exhibition in Drummond Hall in 1913. Organized by Frederick J. Brand, Assistant Professor of Mathematics at UBC, it was the first of its kind ever held at the University. Max Maynard and the author exhibited with her. This exhibition stirred up a lot of interest and controversy among students and even faculty. Letters flowed in to the correspondence column of the *Ubyssey* (the University student paper) and Frederick gave a popular lecture on Emily's work. She was enchanted and wrote to him on March 16: "I am so glad that your exhibit and speech were such a success for it meant a lot of work and worry for you and I think it was very fine and sporting of you to undertake it. Undoubtedly there is an awakening in many directions—Art among them. The crate will probably come tomorrow. Express over was 90 cts. When the man came to collect he admitted he was surprised and wondered if they'd weighed right. He and I judged it to weigh 75 lbs. or thereabouts, so I hope they keep up their mistakes on return trip." Frederick was quoted in the press as saying: "There has been a great deal of interest in modern art among the undergraduates lately, which has increased with the opportunity of seeing the creative work that is being done on this Coast. Miss Carr's canvasses, with their typical firm structural technique, and imaginative power, were felt to be particularly impressive. They included two of her earlier representative pictures of Indian villages and the later more symbolic ones, *Totem Mother, Skidegate Village, Nirvana* and *Forest Interior,* which interpret both the transcendent universal spirit of Indian totem art and the feelings evoked by the forest and land where totems were first fashioned and placed. (The *Ubyssey,* March 1933)

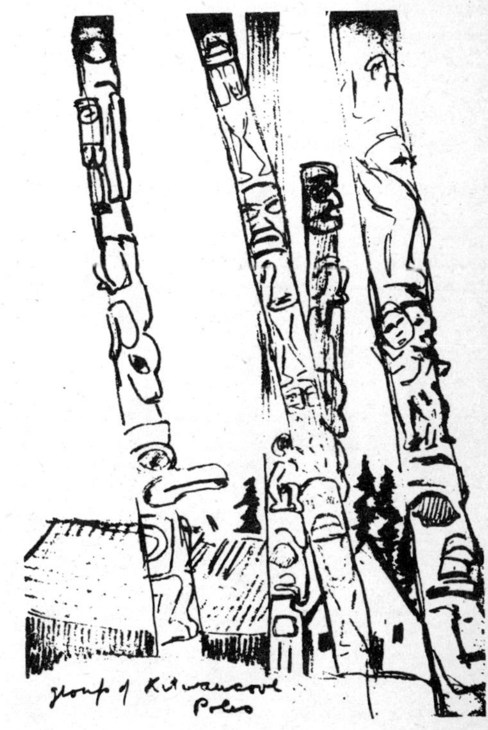

Toronto Canadian National Exhibition August 25-September 9

Emily exhibited: *Indian Village at Lillooet, B.C.* and *Victoria Shore.*

Amsterdam Stedelijk Museum September 2-October 9

International Fine Arts Exhibition

Under the auspices of the International Federation of Business and Professional Women's Clubs. This exhibition was one of their first projects.

In July a delegation of three from the Victoria Business and Professional Women's Club, including Margaret Clay, visited Emily's studio to select one of her paintings for inclusion in this exhibition since they felt that no more fitting and typical example of British Columbia art could be found than Emily's work. The canvas chosen was *Vanquished* described in the *Times* July 29 as "one of Miss Carr's finest and most recent oils . . . (which) pictures the scene of grim desolation in a deserted Indian settlement on the shores of the Queen Charlotte Islands and is full of her characteristic virility." According to the Amsterdam press, *Vanquished* received warm praise from the critics, one of whom said that it was the only picture in the show with a spiritual tendency.

Emily felt particularly flattered by this invitation to exhibit abroad, was glad it was a women's show and talked about it for days. She wrote in her journal: "The Women's Clubs are sending *Vanquished* to Amsterdam for the Convention of the Confederation of Women or Something-or-Other. Three women selected it today. Goodness, when I brought it out I felt maybe I'd gone back since I painted it three or four years ago. I believe it *is* stronger, and my heart is sick. Perhaps I'm approaching my dotage and my best is done. Oh, I must look up and pray!" (*Hundreds and Thousands,* p. 46) Emily was later made an honorary member of this Club.

Victoria Fair (Willows) **September**

For the first time, the exhibition at the Fair was put in charge of Arthur Checkley of the IA&CS. He urged Emily to cooperate and she did so by allowing him to show a "group of big oils." The Victoria *Daily Colonist* wrote September 13 1933: "Whether one likes the themes or not, Miss Carr's totem and other Coast Indian subjects have a dramatic interpretative force that arrests immediately. Nearly all (the big ones) convey a sense of the crushing, enveloping power of stupendous natural forces that swallow up and efface man's effigies as represented by totem, assembly hall or village. In this sense these paintings are powerful, and the artist handles her medium with unerring sureness." Emily's small comment to me was: "They had quite a representative show at the Willows. (I) lent 6 canvasses. From the newspaper it seemed very representative of local *masters* and *mistresses.*"

Edmonton University of Alberta, Arts Building October 16-28

An exhibition held under the auspices of the Department of Extension, it was written up in part in the *Edmonton Journal* October 17, 1933 as follows: "An exhibition of paintings and etchings of unusual interest is on display at the Arts Building . . . consisting of thirty-seven studies of Emily Carr, the well-known artist from Victoria, six pictures by Peter Whyte of Banff and a group of twelve etchings by R. Wilcox, of Toronto. . . . The drawings of Emily Carr are from Alert Bay, in Northern Vancouver Island and are characterized by bold, straight forward drawings on a large scale of rugged natural effects. The method of this artist is extremely original and forceful, values being subordinated to design. In some of the pictures, totem poles are a striking feature in the scheme. Some of the drawings are uncouth and the difficulties of treatment and rapid transcription of impressions must be taken into account in judging of their artistic worth."

While the exhibition was organized primarily to interest

the art students and assist them in their studies, "the paintings and drawings are of such outstanding character both in coloring and treatment as to be of value as an exhibition to the public. To the uninitiated some of the pictures appear like old drawings of unusual crudeness tending toward the modernistic school, but to the art student and the artist, they are of interest as demonstrating a treatment of subject and thought that is unique and original." Emily wrote to me about these two exhibitions on October 4 1933: "I have been very busy getting off my exhibition for Edmonton—25 paper sketches for a civic exhibition and the 12 canvasses for the University exhibition. The sketches I backed with mosquito netting bound with white paper and put a half-round stick top and bottom like maps and they looked fine and are strong." Putting two and two together, it is obvious that Emily either misunderstood what was wanted of her, or plans went awry in Edmonton, as all the paintings she sent (twenty-five for a "civic" exhibition and twelve canvasses for the University) were displayed together in the "Carnegie Art Exhibit" at the University. A review of the show appeared in *The Gateway*, the student newspaper, on October 27 which, Emily told me, "was without *exception* the most foolish and ignorant I have ever read." The part she complained about was the following: "She is much better known as Klee Wyck, the Indian sculptress, whose vases are in such demand at the delightful little totem poles and tourist resorts in the mountains and on the coast. Living a life of primitive simplicity, she regularly invades the wilds of B.C. to acquire the Indian viewpoint. Of her success in this there can be no doubt. Her work in both painting and pottery is done in a manner which out-Indians the Indian. No great master of technique she nevertheless uses what technique she has in a forceful impetuous way and achieves a keynote of rhythm peculiarly aboriginal. It is unfortunate, I think, that so much of her work has been sent to us. Fewer pieces, intelligently selected would have been much more impressive. . . . Whatever she lacks in technique is far overshadowed by her sincere desire to preserve and explore the art of her fellow-tribesmen, for although English born, she is indeed an Indian princess." Emily was still furious when she wrote me on December 10: ". . . (the crit) beats ours hollow. Had me a cubist, a Canadian princess and an aboriginee all in one sentence. Said unless a picture told a story or exactly represented a scene you had once witnessed it had nothing to say etc. etc." She twisted the facts a little, of course, but still it was a strange review to find in a university paper. However, Edmonton must be commended for recognizing Emily's talent in any way at such an early date—only a few months after the University of British Columbia and exactly five years before the Vancouver Art Gallery.

Edmonton **Museum of Arts** **October 19-31**

Annual Loan Exhibition

Loaned by the Canadian Society of Painters in Water Color Emily exhibited two paintings: *An Indian House* and *Zunoqua.*

1934

Victoria Fair (Willows) **September**

The art exhibition at the Fair this year was again organized by the IA&CS. Twenty-three artists exhibited, Emily being the largest individual contributor with an entire section to herself—twenty big canvasses. She mentioned this show in her journals (*Hundreds and Thousands,* p. 142): "Mr. Checkley came and saw about some sketches for the Willows Fair. I guess that's where my things belong—among the sheep and pigs at the agricultural fair. Anyhow I'd rather show among livestock than among the Arts & Crafts Society." Emily persuaded me to enter several pictures with her. One was a portrait of a little diabetic boy attending Alice Carr's school who had posed for Emily and me in her studio in 1932. It placed first in oils—which would seem incredible, considering Emily's many entries, if one did not know the mentality of the Fair judges.

Toronto **Art Gallery of Toronto** **December**

Canadian Paintings—The Collection of Hon. Vincent and Mrs. Massey.

Emily exhibited: *Totem Poles, British Columbia.*

1936

Ottawa **National Gallery of Canada** **1936-1939 traveling**

Contemporary Canadian Painting

This exhibition was arranged on behalf of the Carnegie Corporation of New York for circulation in the Southern Dominions of the British Empire. Not shown in Ottawa.

Emily submitted three pictures for this important exhibition, but only one, *Loggers' Culls* was accepted.

In 1936 this exhibition was shown in the Union of South Africa at the Palace of Fine Arts, Johannesburg, and subsequently in Capetown, Port Elizabeth, Grahamstown and

Durban. A number of the 104 works exhibited were acquired for public collections (apparently four). In 1937-1938 the exhibition (100 works) was shown in Sydney, Brisbane, Perth, Adelaide, Melbourne and Launceston. A few pictures also acquired for public collections in Australia. In February 1938 the exhibition was transferred to New Zealand and circulated to every city in that Dominion until 1939. It opened in Wellington at the National Gallery on March 11 and subsequently traveled to Wanganu, Auckland, Napier, Nelson, Christchurch and Dunedin. The reviewer for the Wanganu *Chronicle* (May 19, 1938) singled out Emily's *Loggers' Culls* for special comment: "Although the principal interest in the picture is probably the wind storm in the sky, there is a forceful reminder in the foreground of the taking away of the good trees and the leaving of the saplings that are not worth cutting down." Thus, for the first time, Emily was dubbed a protest painter and said to have deplored the ravages of industry and to have tried to put her indignation into paint. Otherwise Emily made little impression on the critics in New Zealand who gave most of their attention and praise to the former members of the Group of Seven. On its return trip, the exhibition, still containing Emily's marvellous, but unsold *Loggers' Culls* was shown in Honolulu, Hawaii in 1939.

Vancouver University of British Columbia Library February

Ten B.C. Artists

This, the second exhibition in the UBC Library organized by Frederick J. Brand, attracted wide attention in Vancouver. Invited to show with Emily were four other painters from Victoria: J. Delisle Parker, Jack Shadbolt, Max Maynard and the author; while those contributing from Vancouver were: J.W.G. Macdonald, C.H. Scott, F.H. Varley, W.P. Weston and Vera O. Weatherbie. The exhibition was opened and reviewed by Dr. G.G. Sedgewick, Head of the English Department, who commented on the trends and characteristics of modern art and then chose two paintings by Emily to illustrate the modern painter's method and viewpoint. He discussed fully *Blunden Harbour,* which he characterized as being exceptionally vigorous and well-organized, and *Scorned as Timber, Beloved of the Sky.* The latter, one of Emily's most famous paintings, was exhibited for the first time in this show and *Blunden Harbour* for the first time in the West.

Emily came to Vancouver for a week to visit Frederick and me and to see this exhibition. She describes her stay at length in her journals under entry January 28, but without specifically mentioning the exhibition. She does say, however, that she went to the "art library" where it took place. A report of the exhibition itself was given in her journals entry February 8, *1935*, a year before it was held, which is inexplicable as the publishers Clarke, Irwin, state that the journals are a continuous document from February 8 to a March date.

Vancouver **Old Hotel Vancouver** **September**

Folk Show

There appears to be no record of this show in the press. Even the hotel has disappeared. However, Emily does fortunately mention it in a letter to me: "Six of my Indian pictures are going over to Vancouver for the Folk Show at the Vancouver Hotel. The old man who borrowed them for his Indian exhibit is three-quarters crazy and the other quarter looney and does not know any more about pictures than a fat hen. *Blunden Harbour* is among them."

1936 was a big year for Emily. She gave up the House of All Sorts because of failing health, inability to maintain it and friction with tenants. She exhibited widely but inexplicably did not enter anything in the B.C. Artists Annual show at VAG that year although she hated to miss any exhibition. But if Emily's works were not on display, at least her portrait was—a portrait I did of her in her studio in December 1931. It was on view for the first time under the title *M.E.C.* The Vancouver *Daily Province* review called it "an interesting character portrait," which it was not; but it *is* one of only two portraits in existence done from life—at least in later years. Nan Cheney did the other, also in Emily's studio, in November 1937. It was sold for $250 in August 1941 and bequeathed to NGC by the late John Frederick Bligh Livesay during the year 1944-1945. The story of VAG's acquisition of my portrait is told in my first book. After an astonishing history, it was left to VAG by Lawren Harris and is now in their permanent collection.*

* M.E. A Portrayal of Emily Carr, *p. 45.*

1937

London, England **Royal Institute Galleries** **May 8-29**

Royal British Colonial Society of Artists

Exhibition of Paintings, Drawings and Sculpture by Artists of the British Empire Overseas (called the Coronation Show). Representative works by artists of Australia, Canada, India, New Zealand and South Africa.

This exhibition of contemporary works of art was organized as part of the Coronation celebrations to give visitors from overseas as well as the people in England, an opportunity of seeing for the first time a representative collection of the works of the artists of the British Empire overseas.

Despite a severe heart attack, Emily managed to get a group of fifteen paintings off to Ottawa, three of them for submission to the Coronation show. However, only one, *In a Wood,* was accepted and sent on to the Canadian Section (eighty-four works) of the exhibition in London, subsequently being shown in Liverpool (see below), Bradford, Manchester and Blackpool before returning to Canada in May 1938. A few sales were made in the East with the assistance of NGC, and the Gallery itself submitted several paintings to the trustees in the hope that a purchase might be made "because of the assistance it will afford Miss Carr at the present time." Emily was still in St. Joseph's Hospital then, worried about her skyrocketing medical costs, and was thrilled to hear about the sales made to private collectors. But she was doubtful about NGC, as we see from a letter to me written in February: "I don't understand matters yet. I can't believe the Gallery wants to buy them. I think it is just one of their borrowing spasms. . . . Don't be disappointed if it is only one of Brown's whims. I've experienced them before and shan't be disappointed if the poor old things are just off on one of their vapid little touts." Emily was still waiting to hear about a possible NGC purchase when she wrote me again on March 3: "Mr. Brown said *if* there was a surplus at the end of their fiscal year, might he put a price on two canvasses. The price was beat down but I don't know how much. . . . Brown said he *loved* my *water color* (that's a joke on him) sketch *Sky.*" (Author's note: *Sky,* an oil on paper sketch painted in a flowing water color technique, was one of the three Emily Carr works acquired by NGC early in 1937. The other two were *Heina* and *Blunden Harbour.*)

Paris Exposition Internationale (about) June-October

Emily exhibited: *Kispiox Village.* No catalogue.

This exhibition consisted predominantly of handicrafts and was arranged by Marius Barbeau for the Canadian Government Exhibition Commission. Emily also had a Klee Wyck pottery bowl of Indian design on display which was apparently damaged. In any case the Canadian Handicrafts Guild, Montreal, claimed insurance for total loss, value $10.

There is little in the way of comment to report on this

exhibition except an item in the *Royal Architectural Institute of Canada Journal* which suggests that the Canadian exhibit was awful. (Information courtesy Charles C. Hill, NGC.)

Vancouver Vancouver Art Gallery September 17-October 10

Sixth Annual British Columbia Artists Exhibition

Emily exhibited only one work: *Community House Koskimo.* As explained in a letter to me written early September, she had not at first intended to send this particular painting: "I am sending one to Vancouver . . . had planned to send a smallish one that I think the best woods I've done, but Mr. Band is due today and I want to show it to him. So I'm sending another to the Vancouver Gallery. They prefer stale things anyhow. Somehow I can't work up any enthusiasm over the Vancouver Gallery. I may be wrong. It just seems to me a place of deadness and snarls and meanness.

PS: He (Band) selected three canvasses to be sent East . . . *Lillooet Indian Village;* a woods thing, *Goldstream Park;* and a small new woods I like better than anything I've done in a woods way. [Emily had reference to *Swirl*—Always one of her favorites.]

"(Band) says he told (the Gallery) a thing or two in Vancouver about hanging foreign stuff of a mediocre quality when they ought to be trying to get a gallery of representation of their own."*

* *This is a touch of sour grapes. Emily was terribly miffed during these years because VAG steadfastly refused to give her a solo show. Her tune changed overnight a year later.*

Liverpool Walker Art Gallery October 16-January 8
(See above: The Coronation Show) 1938

Sixty-third Annual Autumn Exhibition

Ten rooms of paintings, Room VI devoted to Canadian Art. Emily was represented by *In a Wood,* an oil.

This unusually extensive exhibition was organized to celebrate the diamond jubilee of the opening of the Walker Art Gallery. It was for the most part limited to recent British works but special sections were devoted to (1) a retrospective of the work of Dame Laura Knight and (2) contemporary Canadian art. The latter formed part of an exhibition of the art of the Dominions shown in London earlier in the year.

1938

Vancouver Vancouver Art Gallery September 16-October 9

Seventh Annual British Columbia Artists Exhibition

Emily exhibited: *Arbutus Trees; Wood's Edge;* and *Overhead.* Nineteen thirty-seven and 1938 are believed to be the only two years that Emily entered paintings in this Annual, though there is a remote possibility that she could also have shown in 1935, as the catalogue for that year is still missing. The curious, and ridiculous, thing is that Emily never won the coveted Beatrice Stone medal which was awarded at various times at this show to most of her friends: 1935, P. Ustinow; 1936, Max Maynard and the author; 1941, Jack Shadbolt.

London **Tate Gallery** **October to December**
A Century of Canadian Art

Two hundred twenty-six works. The most important review of Canadian art to be shown outside the country.

The following item appears in the *NGC Annual Report 1938-1939:* "The most important special undertaking during the year was the arrangement of the 'Century of Canadian Art' exhibited at the Tate Gallery, London, which was opened on October 15, 1938 by H.R.H. the Duke of Kent. The exhibition was thoroughly successful and because of the active interest in it, the closing date was extended twice." Emily was given special mention in several of the generally favorable press reviews, among them the *Manchester Guardian* October 15, 1938: "Standing apart from this Group (the disbanded Group of Seven), which is mainly concerned with Eastern Canada, is Emily Carr, whose paintings are interpretations of the country west of the Rockies, where violence disappears and is replaced by a strange warmth and wetness, in which giant pines smother the hillsides and engulf the Indian villages of B.C. Miss Carr has found her own formula for these green, engulfing giants. Her paintings of them are half symbolic and half representational. They are utterly convincing and completely independent of any tradition, Canadian or European."

Sunday Times October 16, 1938: "Independent of the modern Canadian tradition, the powerful paintings of Emily Carr are interpretations of the scenery of the West Coast, a country of giant pines, green undergrowth and native Indian settlements with their totem poles. In her paintings there is none of the harsh and hectic quality of the Eastern Canadian artists."

The Vancouver newspapers proudly took up the chant. The *Daily Province* November 1, 1938, headlined its article: British Critics Hail Founding of Independent Painting—Work of Miss E. Carr of Victoria Given Special Notice. "There is much less direct influence from Europe than in what we have seen of contemporary painting from the U.S. The work of M. Emily Carr of Victoria, B.C., and of the late Tom Thomson of Owen Sound ... particularly attracted the U.K. critics."

Eric Brown added his praise to the others in his letter to Emily of November 30: "I have been on the point of writing you ever since I got back from London to tell you what a fine impression your work made on the critics and discerning public. It was a great pleasure to hear them expressing their appreciation of its force, originality and beauty of design and color."

Emily herself was overcome with joy at the "warm reception of my work," but at the same time a little fearful of becoming smug. She describes her reactions in her journal: "I am tired of praise. The 'goo' nauseates me. . . . I was the only one mentioned in particular in the *London Times* write-up by Eric Newton. What he wrote I think was more what he saw in my studio when he was out here than what was over there in the Tate Gallery. I have been doing portrait sketches, turning from my beloved woods for fear all this honeyed stuff, this praise, should send me to them smug." (*Hundreds and Thousands,* p. 301.)

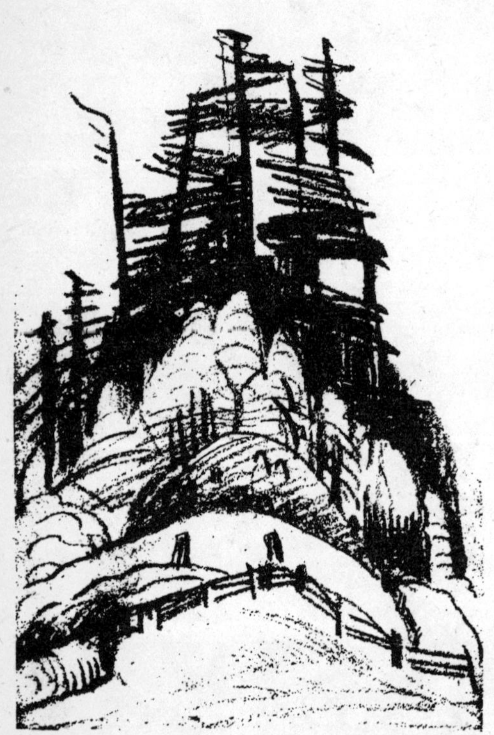

1939

Vancouver — Vancouver Art Gallery — July 4-23

Six Local Artists

Thirty exhibits—five per artist

This exhibition, arranged by J. Delisle Parker, was a repeat of the *Six Local Artists* held the previous year, but with different artists. The exhibitions were designed primarily to give tourists an idea of the work being done in B.C., a function that was taken over three years later by the annual *B.C. Artists Summer Exhibitions.* Those invited to contribute their work in 1939 were: Emily Carr; Robert Alexander; Paul Soldatkin; Elmore G. Kemp; Edythe Hembroff Brand and J. Delisle Parker. Emily is given scant mention in the Vancouver *Sun* review of July 6: "Exemplifying Emily Carr's sense of rhythm is her painting of arbutus trees." She is also listed second to last. All the other artists (with the exception of the unmentioned Kemp) received more coverage than she did. Even in 1939 she was not truly recognized.

Emily sold a painting at this exhibition which made it very worthwhile for her as she was still hard-pressed financially and sales had dropped off to zero. She wrote to give me the good news: "I sold one at 6 Artists Show (the *Arbutus*). Long, slow payments, ten months in all. Still it helps to have $5.00 per month. It's my first sale this year . . ." Nan Cheney also commented on this exhibition: "The *Six Local Artists* show is dull except for Emily's five sketches although I did like a portrait by Alexander called *Deckhand*. . . . Edythe had a well painted still life but not thrilling." She wrote again about a month later: "Emily sold one of her sketches in the *Six Local Artists* show. It was bought by a Russian girl, a pupil of (Jock) Macdonald's." (Nan to Humphrey Toms, August 6 1939.)

San Francisco **Summer**
Golden Gate International Exposition

Contemporary Art

Emily exhibited: *The Little Pine* and *Old and New Forest*

In 1937 the International Business Machines Corporation began to assemble a collection of paintings representative of the seventy-nine countries in which their company did business. Leading art authorities in the different countries were asked to select the artists and pictures which they considered typical of their countries. Two collections, each representing the seventy-nine countries, were assembled. One was shown at the New York World's Fair in 1939 and the other, the same year, in the IBM Corporation Gallery of Science and Art, Palace of Electricity and Communication, Golden Gate International Exposition, San Francisco. (The 1939 New York World's Fair show is described in the list of Canadian Societies exhibitions.)

1940

Toronto **Art Gallery of Toronto, Print Room** **March**

A four-artist exhibition

Emily Carr	12 paintings
Lawren Harris	9 paintings
Fritz Brandtner	15 paintings
Charles Comfort	9 paintings

No catalogue

Emily mentions this show in passing, more or less, in three letters to Nan Cheney: *First:* "Lawren, Comfort and I are on this month at the Grange Gallery. Rather like my broadcast—I don't know what is being used." *Second:* "Had a nice letter from A.Y. Jackson last week. (He) says Lawren, Comfort, Brandtner and me was a great success—best of three little groups they have had yet." *Third:* "Sold a picture (sketch) at the Harris, Comfort, Carr show in Toronto."

Toronto Canadian National Exhibition August 23-September 7
IBM Corporation Collection

Contemporary Art of Canada and Newfoundland

This year the IBM Corporation formed a Canada-Newfoundland (also an all-United States) Collection of Contemporary Art. An authority in each Canadian province and in Newfoundland was invited to appoint a committee to select pictures by local artists regarded as representative of the art and character of the nine provinces and Newfoundland—these ten paintings to be shown at the CNE in Toronto. A competent jury was selected and cash prizes of $200, $150 and $100 offered to the artists whose work was adjudged the best in the collection. Emily was chosen to represent British Columbia with her Indian painting *Village of Yan*. The story of the purchase of this painting is outlined as follows:

February 5, 1940: Mr. Kermode, then Director of the Provincial Museum, was asked by the IBM Corporation to assist them in choosing an appropriate picture. He consulted with W. Kaye Lamb, Provincial Librarian and Archivist, who recommended that the IBM people acquire an Emily Carr painting because he felt she was undoubtedly the best painter in the Province. A.S. Grigsby, then Curator of VAG was consulted and agreed that a Carr painting was the obvious choice. Kaye Lamb arranged a meeting with Emily and *Village of Yan*, valued at $400, was selected and recommended to IBM. But the company balked at the price which they claimed was "quite out of line with those we are paying for pictures from the other provinces of Canada and States of the American Union." Kaye Lamb flatly refused to ask Emily to reduce her price and in the end IBM capitulated. (W. Kaye Lamb to author, June 18, 1975.)

Emily seemed to think she had won a medal for *Village of Yan* when she wrote to Nan Cheney on November 18, 1940: "I got a medal last week (big as a meat plate) for my contribution to art of the world it says. Came via the big Indian I sold to the States last year." Actually every artist who exhibited in the IBM show received a specially designed medal to commemorate his or her participation. Emily did not win one of the three cash awards.

1941
Edmonton Museum of Arts April

A large exhibition of water colors from the Edmonton Group of the Alberta Society of Artists. The Edmonton *Journal* review of this show states: "Mr. J. Delisle Parker has loaned the Gallery for a period of six months a large oil painting of *Alert Bay* by Emily Carr. It is a piece of the artist's earlier work and will have more interest for many visitors than her later efforts. . . . It is not only an interesting record of an historic place, but also indicates a phase of development in the career of one of our most prominent painters."

1942
San Francisco **Museum of Art** **June 23-July 12**

Canadian Paintings

This exhibition consisted of paintings owned by people living in the San Francisco Bay area. Two paintings by Emily were included: *Kitwanga Pole* and *West Coast Eagle Totem,* both owned by Mrs. Herbert Salinger.

Calgary Exhibition and Stampede **July 6-11**

Owing to the war, work of British Columbia and Saskatchewan artists formed the only guest exhibits in fine arts at the Calgary exhibition this year, replacing shows sent out from the National Gallery before 1941. This gave Albertans a welcome opportunity to become better acquainted with creative work of contemporary western artists. Although all exhibits were of high standard, the reviewer said, on entering the British Columbia room, the strong painting, often of a somewhat experimental nature but always imaginative, was immediately apparent.

The forty-five paintings and drawings on view were selected from a successful BCSFA exhibition at VAG the previous May and were sent to Calgary by the Society. Bronco busting and a display of plastic arts are not generally associated, but this innovation in Calgary reflected an increased interest in painting in the western provinces. Emily was represented by two paintings, *Young Arbutus* and *Sky* which the reviewer felt were not among the most impressive examples of her work. (The Calgary *Herald,* July 6, 1942.) But NGC was impressed enough with *Sky* to purchase it early 1937.

Vancouver **Vancouver Art Gallery** **early July-September 2**

B.C. Artists Summer Exhibition
First Annual Exhibition
These annuals were primarily designed for the benefit of tourists but were popular with Vancouverites as well. "Palette" (J. Delisle Parker) writes in his review that the exhibition was "a major event for art lovers as never before had works by

numerous leading B.C. painters and sculptors been displayed over such a long period." "This stimulating show," he said, "suggest the main directions along which art here is traveling . . . it is difficult not to feel both pride and confidence in contemporary art in B.C. The present display contains little of the stuffy or academic." "Palette" lists a few selected works by the best-known Vancouver painters adding that they included "typical canvasses by Emily Carr." (*Daily Province*, July 9, 1942.)

Andover, Massachusetts **September 18-November 8**
Addison Gallery of American Art **(traveling)**
Phillips Academy

Contemporary Painting in Canada, also called:
Aspects of Contemporary Painting in Canada
Sixty-seven works by thirty-seven artists

Circulated in eighteen centers from coast to coast, including: The Detroit Institute of Arts, February 23-March 29 1943; The National Gallery of Canada, January 20-February 7 1944. This exhibition was organized in Andover by the Addison Gallery and opened there on September 18, 1942, not in 1943, the date given in both the NGC and VAG catalogues.

As far as Emily is concerned, this is a mystery exhibition. Her name is not listed in the exhibition catalogue, nor mentioned in two early reviews: The Boston *Christian Science Monitor* (September 21, 1942) and the New York City *The Art Digest* (October 15). In fact, she was specifically mentioned as *not* being represented in this show in the Toronto *Telegram* review (September 12, 1942) which concludes with the remark: "Too bad Emily Carr for example could not have been included. Her work would be an asset to any exhibition of this kind."

Emily's name was still not in the catalogue when the show reached Detroit or San Francisco, but her painting, *Forest Landscape*, was hung in both the Detroit Institute of Arts and the San Francisco Museum of Art.* It is not known how or when the picture was added.* The introduction to the exhibition catalogue closes thus: "The variety is understandable. It is to be expected. Canada is, with qualifications, a melting pot like the U.S. Her social ties with England and France have been more clearly retained than our European connections, perhaps, but her cultural problems are in many cases our problems too. The variety in other words, is a mark of similarity, as well as dissimilarity, between the painting of the two countries and from it the exhibition draws twofold interest. There is an opportunity here

* *The San Francisco Museum of Art to the author, April 4 1974.*

* *The Detroit Institute of Arts to the author, March 8 1977: "The painting by Miss Carr . . . was a late addition to the show as the entry was tipped in the catalogue."*

to understand ourselves as well as our neighbors by contemplating what, save for the hazards of history, might be our own image."

1943

Vancouver — Vancouver Art Gallery — February 5-25

National Gallery Loan Exhibition
Probably no catalogue

This important and interesting show was the first representative collection on a large scale sent to Vancouver from the NGC permanent collection. Such travel shows circulated by NGC, including "group" shows such as Canadian Graphics, the Canadian Society of Painters in Water Colours, the Canadian Group of Painters and the RCA, were "package" exhibitions and went from gallery to gallery as a package, with the same catalogue (if any). By decentralizing a concentration of remarkable pictures, NGC enabled communities far distant from the national capital to enjoy treasures that belong to the whole country, and to acquire a much more accurate idea of their value in the cultural life of Canada. Emily's entry, *Heina Cxoina,* a large imposing picture of an Indian village, was said to be one of her best in a field where she could speak with authority.

Vancouver — Vancouver Art Gallery — July-August

B.C. Artists Summer Exhibition
Second Annual Exhibition

In his review of this show, "Palette" writes in the *Daily Province* of July 8, that it forms an unusual assemblage of paintings selected from various exhibitions held during the previous year. He felt that visitors to the city would see a varied and fairly representative display and realize that the West was finding vigorous and individual expression. People again had the opportunity of enjoying Emily's *Cordova Bay* with its fine sweep of vibrating sky, blue water and adjacent woods as well as *Tree Trunk* and *Light Sweeping Thru'.*

1944

Ottawa — National Gallery of Canada — January 20-February 7

Contemporary Painting in Canada
(See 1942: Andover, Massachusetts, same exhibition.)

New Haven, Connecticut — Yale University Art Gallery — March 10-April 16

Canadian Art 1760-1943

Seventy-seven works. Emily exhibited: *Blunden Harbour* and *Forest Light*

The review in the New Haven *Journal-Courier* of March 11 gives so much coverage to the social aspects of the gala opening that the paintings themselves were largely overlooked. It was headlined: *Ambassadors Attend Art Gallery Exhibit* and continued: "An exhibition of the work of about sixty Canadian artists, covering the entire range of native Canadian painting, opened yesterday in the Yale Art Gallery. The exhibition, a gesture of international good will, was featured by a reception for Ray Atherton, U.S. Ambassador to Canada and Leighton McCarthy, Canadian Ambassador to the U.S. and attended by several hundred guests in the gallery." The exhibition was said to reflect the historical trends in Canada with a small representation of the earlier years and a major emphasis on the twentieth century. It was an attempt to acquaint the New Haven community with the vigor of art on the other side of the border. The critics found, in general, the designs bold and the execution forceful—the painting rugged like the country. They felt that the Canadians enjoy color—and brushwork: "The Canadians are not less modern than ourselves, but they have not foresworn vitality nor shut their eyes to light."

Emily gave her own outspoken and amusing comment on this show in an undated letter to Ira Dilworth: "I must say some of that stuff in 'Canadian Art' is repulsive—trying so hard to be outlandish (Shadboltish)." Had Emily forgotten that this was the very word so many Victorians had used to describe her work a decade before?

Vancouver Vancouver Art Gallery July 4-August 30

B.C. Artists Summer Exhibition
Third Annual Exhibition

"Palette" again reviews this popular annual in the *Daily Province* of July 7: "One is chiefly impressed by (the exhibition's) solid and significant aspect. With only a few exceptions this 1944 collection of combined talent suggests strength without violence, creative tendency and individual viewpoint with consequent variety and subject matter. It is this striving for force as opposed to prettiness and slavish imitation of nature, which seems to indicate an important trend in B.C. art." Unfortunately, Emily was represented by a poor work to illustrate force, creative tendency or individual viewpoint—namely, *Alert Bay*, an early painting in which she had long since lost interest.

Saskatoon **Art Centre** **October**

On October 4, 1944, the *Star Phoenix* reviewed an "Outline of History of Canadian Art shown in the current exhibit at the Saskatoon Art Centre . . . a display of twenty-eight pictures from the permanent collection of NGC." The Head of the University Art Department in his criticism of the paintings writes that Emily Carr's *Sky* is in a class by itself and (is done) in her "clever technique." Saskatoon is on the NGC Western Circuit and it is clear that this show also traveled to other cities. It would be difficult, and pointless, to try to trace and list them all.

1945

Toronto **Art Gallery of Toronto** **January 1945**

Development of Painting in Canada (traveling)

Two hundred thirty-nine works

Circuit:

Art Gallery of Toronto	January 1945
Art Association of Montreal	February-March 1945
Le Musée de la Province de Québec	April 1945
National Gallery of Canada	June-July 1945

Emily exhibited four paintings, including the overworked *Blunden Harbour* and *Indian Church.*

This large exhibition was the first effort to present Canadian painting as a continuous process from its beginnings in the seventeenth century to the present day. It was shown in the four cities listed above and inspired the Albany (N.Y.) Institute of History and Art to organize a smaller exhibition on the same basis. (*NGC Annual Report for 1945.)*

Emily's four works are listed under Section VI-4 of the exhibition catalogue which is preceded by the comment: "Other trends, some of which are international, now broaden the scope of Canadian painting. These trends range from regionalism, where emphasis is laid on the inherent picturesqueness of certain localities and types of people, to expressionism or the distortion of form and color of natural objects to achieve an emotional and aesthetic effect, and to abstract or purely subjective painting in which no attempt is made to represent objects in the outside world. To illustrate the increasing variety of handling and diversity of viewpoint, the paintings in this group are arranged according to subject matter."

New York **National Arts Club** **March**

(N.Y. March 9) The Montreal *Gazette* of March 10, 1945, under the heading "Canadian Paintings Showing in New York," writes that " Highlight of a quiet week in Manhattan was the opening in the National Arts Club of an exhibition of British and Canadian paintings. Among those represented were Pegi Nicol and B. Cogill Haworth. . . . Transportation difficulties had delayed arrival of some canvasses . . . notably a west coast Indian scene by the late Emily Carr of Vancouver (sic)."

This exhibition was also written up in the Ottawa *Citizen* March 8, 1945: "Among the speakers at the opening ceremonies were Gregory Evans, British Consul-General in New York, and Theodore Newton, Canadian representative on the United Nations Information Board. Mr. Newton paid tribute to the work of Emily Carr, noted Canadian artist and writer who died recently in Victoria, B.C.: 'She was a woman of charm and great talent,' he said. He emphasized the role of international art exhibits in strengthening international amity." This show was mentioned again months later in the Windsor (Ontario) *Daily Star* of July 28, 1945: "New York had two exhibitions of Canadian painting this past spring, both of which were well received. One collection was shown by the National Gallery and the Wartime Information Board and remained for seven weeks in the National Arts Club, one of the oldest established art centers in New York. Artists represented included Emily Carr, Arthur Lismer, Goodrich Roberts, Carl Schaefer, Edwin Holgate and about a dozen others."

Vancouver **Vancouver Art Gallery** **July 3-August 26**

B.C. Artists Summer Exhibition
Fourth Annual
Although all the pictures in this Fourth Annual had previously been displayed at the Gallery, it was said to be a fresh and lively group of paintings by leading contemporary B.C. Artists—including Emily Carr. Her one work on view, *Loggers' Culls,* was not given any special write-up, or even identified, in the Vancouver *Sun* review of July 9 1945. Nor was it mentioned that Emily had died just four months before the show opened or that B.C. had lost its finest and most renowned artist.

Toronto **Art Gallery of Toronto** **September 21**

Members Loan Exhibition
Emily's works exhibited:

Mount Douglas Park
Midsummer Night
Fishing Stages
Seascape
Trees, Goldstream Flats

1946

Albany (N.Y.) **Institute of History and Art** **January 10 -March 10**

Painting in Canada—A Selective Historical Survey

Sixty-nine or seventy-one works (both numbers given).

Not sponsored by NGC, but many works were lent by the gallery.

Extract from the exhibition catalogue: "The study of Canadian art being still in its infancy, the present show makes no claim as a definite survey . . . it was intended to be a good-will exhibition seeking to further an understanding between Canada and the U.S. by bringing the best of creative work done in Canada to this country. . . . Painters in our country have been far more numerous, probably because of the larger number of inhabitants . . . however in the proportion of artists to the population, Canada might be found to lead. Certainly the quality of the work produced, as shown by this exhibition, merits Canadian artists more consideration and study by the people of the U.S. than they have received in the past. Without this great pioneer showing of Canadian paintings (*The Development of Painting in Canada* [1945] see above), the present selective exhibit would not have been possible. Thirty-seven examples from there were chosen . . . to form the nucleus of the Albany show, roughly one-third of the early section of this exhibit and two-thirds of the late section." Emily is not mentioned in the short history given, but comes first under the heading: "Modern Notes." She is represented by *Blunden Harbour* with attached biographical sketch.

Paris **Musée d'Art moderne**

Emily Carr: "Elle avait beaucoup peint, s'attachant surtout aux paysages de la Colombie britannique. Cette fondatrice de l'école canadienne moderne était représentée en 1946 a l'exposition ouverte à Paris, au Musée d' art moderne, par l'Organization des Nations Unies. Elle avait exposé au Salon d'Automne de 1911." (Dictionnaire des Peintres, Sculpteurs, Dessinateurs et Graveurs, E. Benezit, Librairie Gründ 1949.)

1947

New York **Riverside Museum** **April 27-May 18**

Canadian Women Artists

Sponsored by the National Council of Women of Canada and the National Council of Women of the U.S.

Emily's works exhibited: *In the Woods; Trees* and *Guyasdoms D'Sonoqua*

The foreword to the catalogue explains: "The present exhibition is a small one—consisting of only seventy-four canvasses and papers. The collection was selected from 536 submissions . . . in its modest numbers, we have included works by some of our finest women painters—not because they happen to be women painters, but because they are artists first. Most of the artists represented here are young. But not all of them: Emily Carr, for instance. . . . Some of her best and *youngest* paintings were made in her last years, years in which she also wrote four distinguished autobiographical books which were 'best sellers' and medal winners in Canada. Her paintings are so respected and beloved in Canada that the Vancouver Art Gallery is building a special wing to house them permanently."

Emily was the only artist selected for special comment—a signal honor. She was also the only one represented by more than one painting.

Toronto Fine Arts Galleries, Eaton's College Street
September 2-19

Canadian Women Artists
First showing in Canada of the same exhibition presented in New York City in April-May (see above).

The purpose was to exhibit in New York a representative showing of paintings by Canadian women artists from coast to coast. The project obtained the support of the Canadian Arts Council and the Canadian Government (Department of External Affairs) and the exhibition was well received in New York by the press and public alike. To quote the words of Pegi Nicol MacLeod, Canadian painter resident in New York, "a warm wind blew from the north this spring in New York freshening the air and thawing the coldest art critics."

Emily was not an active feminist. She did, however, champion women *artists* staunchly, sometimes fiercely, if she felt they were the butt of male discrimination. But her reactions were always personal. Nothing irked her more than a man who unthinkingly and patronizingly said (and a few of them did) "You paint very well indeed—for a woman." She also resented anyone saying that her work was "strong and *masculine*" (and many did). She has written herself, more than once, that she disliked A.Y. Jackson—and his work—because she felt he was prejudiced against women artists; but on the whole, she gave little thought to this subject as she was too engrossed with more pressing and personal problems. Occasionally, however, some event or remark would stir her dormant indignation and she would place herself squarely on the side of some woman, or the cause of women, as she did in her journals in April 1937: "I have been thinking that I am a shirker. I have dodged publicity, hated write-ups and all that splutter. Well, that's all selfish conceit that embarrassed me. I have been forgetting Canada and forgetting women painters. It's them I ought to be upholding, nothing to do with puny me at all. (*Hundreds and Thousands*, p. 287.)

Toronto **Art Gallery of Toronto** **October-November**

Selected Canadian Paintings from the Private Collections of C.S. Band, R.S. McLaughlin, and J.S. McLean
Emily's works exhibited:

Grey
Indian Church
Inside a Forest
Potlatch Welcome
Nirvana
(all from the C.S. Band collection)
Upward Trend
(from the J.S. McLean collection)
Guyasdoms D'Sonoqua
(from the AGT collection)

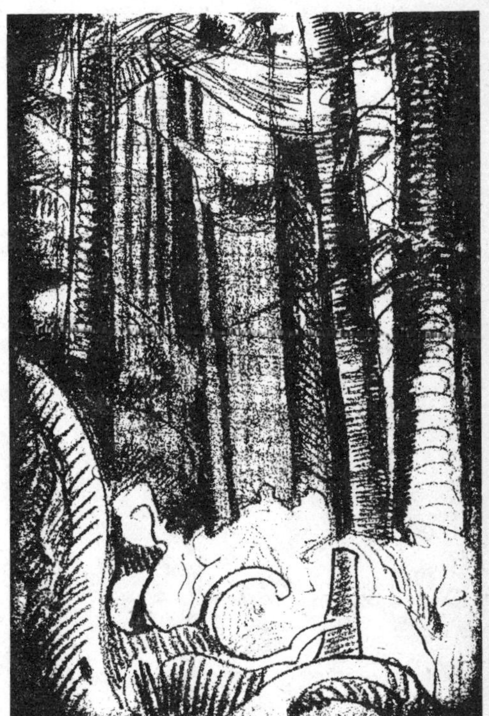

1948
Toronto **Art Gallery of Toronto** **January**
The Toledo Museum of Art **-April**

Two Cities Collection
Emily exhibited: *Western Forest* (reproduced) purchased by AGT in 1937

From the catalogue: "The exhibition ranges from the fifteenth century to the present day and in consequence embraces the wide variations in viewpoint and technique which have occurred in these five centuries. . . . Quotations from (the painters') own writings and those of contemporaries have been added to indicate further the aims of individuals and groups." A long quotation from Emily's writing is used as a caption under the illustration of her painting: "Woods you are very sly, picking those moments when you are quiet and off guard to reveal yourselves to us, folding us in your calm, accepting us to the sway, the rhythm of your spaces, space interwoven with the calm that rests forever in you. For all that you stand so firmly rooted, so still, you quiver, there is movement in every leaf. Woods you are not only a group of trees. Rather you are low space intertwined with growth."

West Palm Beach, Florida **April-May**
Norton Gallery and School of Art

Six Canadian Painters

The six painters were: Emily Carr; David B. Milne; Fritz Brandtner; Goodrich Roberts; Henri Masson; Stanley Cosgrove.

Exhibited: Seven of Emily's oils.

She is described as "a painter who had the courage to break away from a style which had brought her local acclaim and to begin late in life a phase of experiment and innovation which brought her to the front rank among creative artists. She was sixty before she was discovered nationally and seventy before her late works began to appear in collections."

Toronto **Canadian National Exhibition** **August 27 -September 11**

Canadian Painting and Sculpture Owned by Canadians

Victoria **Art Gallery and Studio** **October 1-15**
1121½ Douglas Street

The Victoria *Daily Colonist* reported on October 10, 1948: "Included in the fifty-one exhibits are three paintings by Emily Carr. Among her earlier works, they are said by some experts to have been from the time when she was doing her best work."

1949

Toronto **Fine Arts Galleries** **April**
Eaton's College Street

Emily's *Untitled (Forest Landscape),* in the collection of University College, University of Toronto, and which hangs in the Women's Union on St. George Street, was purchased from the Fine Arts Galleries on April 22, 1949, by Marion Ferguson, the Dean of Women, University College. A Carmichael painting was purchased at the same time, thus obviating the possibility that Eaton's was holding a solo Carr show, although it is not known today whether the pictures were purchased from an exhibition or from stock.

This oil on paper sketch was probably painted at Albert Head in 1935. One of Emily's more famous canvasses, *A Rushing Sea of Undergrowth,* was later painted from it.

1950

Vancouver **Vancouver Art Gallery** **January 3-22**

Eighteen Canadian Paintings

Sponsored by the Dominion Gallery, Montreal
Emily exhibited: *Fir Tree; Woods; Mountain Peak Cheekeye*

Montreal **Dominion Gallery** **September-October**

Artists of Fame and Promise
Exhibition of painting and sculpture of Canadian artists
Emily's works exhibited: *Loggers' Cabin*

1951
Winnipeg **Art Gallery** **July**

Forgotten Greats

The Winnipeg *Tribune* of July 4, 1951 explains the origin of this exhibition: "For years a valuable collection of Canadian paintings has been piled in a dark vault in the School of Art, Kennedy Street, apparently half forgotten. Then last spring, the Director of the Art Gallery was seeking work for a Canadian exhibition. In the course of scouting around he heard there were some paintings stored in the school. 'I found more than 100,' he said. Today the collection is on view in the Art Gallery. It includes water colors, pencil sketches and prints by Lismer, Jackson, Emily Carr and Lawren Harris. . . . Among others an Emily Carr whose tree swirls in characteristic fashion . . ."

Vancouver **Vancouver Art Gallery** **September 26**

Exhibitions Opening the New Vancouver Art Gallery

With its increased and improved facilities and the two new Emily Carr Memorial Galleries, the new Gallery was said to be the finest and most modern in Canada. Various exhibits were on view, among them Pre-Columbian Gold, sixteen drawings by Alistair Bell (former Carr trustee) and the Founders' Collection. But Emily's show in her new Memorial Galleries was the outstanding feature of this important event. Twenty-two oils were exhibited, twenty-one drawings and even a case of her pottery was on display in the smaller gallery.

1952
Venice Biennale

In Canada's first appearance at the Venice Biennale this year, chosen to represent current Canadian art were: Emily Carr, David Milne, Goodridge Roberts and Alfred Pellan.

1957
Edinburgh, Scotland **December**

Royal Scottish Academy Galleries
Scottish Society of Women Artists
Annual Exhibition

In response to my enquiry, the President of this Society, Euphen Alexander, wrote on May 20, 1974 that Emily had been invited to participate in their annual exhibition in 1957. She had forgotten, of course, that Emily was no longer alive then and that they had probably acquired her paintings through VAG. They displayed twenty-eight of her works.

The *Scotsman* critic wrote: "The main loan work is a large collection of the work of the Canadian painter Emily Carr (1871-1945). The effect of these paintings is at first sight at once formidable and monotonous, but as one looks at them further, one becomes fascinated by the strange luminous landscape of trees and totem poles and one sees that this is the work of a sincere and gifted artist whose chosen range was narrow but whose thought and feeling were deep."

1958
Vancouver **Vancouver Art Gallery** **June 10-August 31**

100 Years of British Columbia Art

A massive survey of art in British Columbia during the first hundred years of its history as a province. The exhibition was divided into six sections. Three galleries displayed the art of the Pacific Coast Indians. Another gallery featured painting and sculpture; the Emily Carr gallery displayed her major works. The large catalogue accompanying this exhibition lists nineteen Carr paintings, nine of which were reproduced. The introduction, written by Lawren Harris, describes the birth of the Emily Carr Collection and the planning and building of the new Vancouver Art Gallery which was to house it. The same introduction was used in the catalogue for the exhibition *Oil Paintings from the Emily Carr Trust Collection* held at the Art Gallery of Greater Victoria from September 30 to October 19 the same year.

IV A Guide To Studio Exhibitions

For more details, see Part I, Solo Exhibitions except for 1910 and 1932 which are listed in Part III, General Exhibitions.

For Humphrey Toms, in appreciation

Vancouver

1910
Just before leaving Vancouver to study in France, Emily and Miss Anne Batchelor held a reception and exhibition at Emily's Granville Street studio.

1912
First studio show after returning to Vancouver from France. Held at 1465 West Broadway.

1912
On Friday evening, April 12, and on subsequent Fridays during the month, Emily's pictures on view at her West Broadway studio.

Victoria

1913
After moving into the House of All Sorts, 646 Simcoe Street, in June, Emily held an "at home" and exhibition the same month.

1928
A show in the studio, 646 Simcoe Street, to display the Indian work Emily had done that summer in the North.

1930
A studio exhibition combined with Emily's last annual Christmas sale of pottery.

1931
A public exhibition in the studio to show work being shipped East for exhibitions.

1932
A four-artist show held in the two lower flats of the House of All Sorts, 646 Simcoe Street, to give publicity to Emily's proposed People's Gallery.

1934
Exhibition and party for twenty-five invited guests.

1935
A series of exhibitions in a downstairs flat of the House of All Sorts.

1935
A two-day exhibition in the lower east flat by request of Provincial Normal (Summer) School.

1936
A public viewing of Emily's work in her cottage at 316 Beckley Avenue.

Bibliography

I have confined myself primarily to original sources in researching this work, except for Emily's own books and the numerous articles mentioned in the text. I have also read or occasionally quoted from the following publications.

F.B. Housser, *A Canadian Art Movement* (The Macmillan Company of Canada Limited, Toronto, 1926).

Marius Barbeau, *The Downfall of Temlaham* (The Macmillan Company of Canada Limited, Toronto, 1928—first edition. Hurtig Publishers, Edmonton, 1973—new edition).

Marius Barbeau, *Totem Poles,* Vols. I and II. (Department of Resources and Development, National Museum of Canada, Anthropological Series No. 30, King's Printer, Ottawa, 1950 and 1951).

William C. Seitz, *Mark Tobey* (Museum of Modern Art, New York, 1962).

F. Maud Brown, *Breaking Barriers* (The Society for Art Publications, 1964).

A.Y. Jackson, *A Painter's Country* (Clarke, Irwin and Company Limited, Toronto, 1964).

Flora Hamilton Burns, "Emily Carr," *The Clear Spirit,* Twenty Canadian Women and their Times, edited by Mary Quayle, (University of Toronto Press, Toronto, 1967, for the Canadian Federation of University Women).

William Wylie Thom, *The Fine Arts in Vancouver 1886-1930: An Historical Survey* (unpublished Master's thesis, Department of Fine Arts, University of British Columbia, 1969).

Paul Duval. *Four Decades* (Clarke, Irwin and Company Limited, Toronto, 1972).

William Withrow, *Contemporary Canadian Painting* (McClelland and Stewart Limited, Toronto, 1972).

Barry Lord, *The History of Painting in Canada: Towards a People's Art* (NC Press, 1974).

Charles C. Hill, *Canadian Painting in the Thirties* (The National Gallery of Canada, for the Corporation of the National Museums of Canada, Ottawa, 1975).

Index

Printed in Canada